IRISH UNIONISM

1885–1923

NORTHERN IRELAND PUBLIC RECORD OFFICE

IRISH UNIONISM
1885-1923

A documentary history
edited by

PATRICK BUCKLAND

Lecturer in Modern History
University of Liverpool

BELFAST
HER MAJESTY'S STATIONERY OFFICE
1973

Printed in Northern Ireland for Her Majesty's Stationery Office
by Nelson & Knox (N.I.) Ltd., Belfast.

Table of contents

List of illustrations

1. A poem, 'We meet: a voice from the Ulster convention', by J. S. Drennan, celebrating the convention of Ulster unionists held in the Ulster Hall, Belfast, 17 June 1892, to protest against home rule **(3)**.

2. Deposition of J. Dunne, Coolcran, Co. Fermanagh, crown witness, giving evidence against S. Clarke for his part in the Tempo incident, 1896 **(37)**.

3. A song entitled 'For Union and for King', part of an official programme for a demonstration of southern unionists, organised by the I.U.A. in the Rotunda rink, Dublin, 10 October 1911 **84(b)**.

4. Copy of Ulster's solemn league and covenant signed by Sir Edward Carson **(119)**.

5. Handbill announcing a meeting organised by the U.A.I. in conjunction with the York Conservative Association, 4 December 1908 **(164)**.

6. Leaflet describing the City of Cork Volunteer Training Corps **(185)**.

Preface

This present volume of documents is intended to show how materials deposited in the Northern Ireland Public Record Office can assist in a study of Irish unionism in the period 1885–1923 and is one of a series of volumes indicating the nature and range of historical material available there. It is neither a history of Irish unionism, nor, since it has been drawn from one depository, is it a definitive collection of documents in the manner of *English historical documents*. The object is to draw attention to the nature and extent of the documentary evidence in the N.I.P.R.O. relating to Irish unionism.

A minimum of annotation has been used, though brief commentaries have been included to enable the reader to put the documents into their proper context. The original spelling and punctuation have been preserved and, where possible, documents have been given in full. For ease of reading the documents and commentaries have been arranged according to topics within each chapter. In this way it is hoped that the volume will be of interest to the general reader of Irish history and of use to students in sixth forms and colleges engaged in project work.

The term 'unionist' has been used to describe opponents of home rule, whether liberal or conservative; and the term 'home rule' has been used loosely to describe any movement for the re-establishment of an Irish parliament.

Acknowledgements

This book has been made possible by the cooperation of the donors of the various collections used and listed below.

I should like to thank the Deputy Keeper of the Records, N.I.P.R.O., and members of his staff for their help in the preparation of this book and advice regarding the presentation and transcription of the documents.

I also wish to express my appreciation to my colleagues in the School of History in the University of Liverpool for their tolerant attitude in this summer term of 1970, when the book was largely compiled.

Patrick Buckland
University of Liverpool

Abbreviations

A.P.L.	(Unionist) Anti-Partition League
I.L.P.U.	Irish Loyal and Patriotic Union
I.U.A.	Irish Unionist Alliance
N.I.P.R.O.	Northern Ireland Public Record Office
R.I.C.	Royal Irish Constabulary
S.U.C.	Southern Unionist Committee
U.A.I.	Unionist Associations of Ireland
U.C.C.	Unionist Clubs Council
U.U.C.	Ulster Unionist Council
U.V.F.	Ulster Volunteer Force
*	Denotes a copy of a letter made and retained by the writer

Introduction

After 1885 Ireland was divided into two clearly defined political camps. On the one hand, there was the majority, the nationalist, movement. Nationalists tended to be celtic and catholic, and the movement drew its strength from the southern Irish democracy. Dating from 1870 as an effective movement, it demanded the restoration of the Irish parliament abolished by the act of union of 1800. By the twentieth century the Irish parliamentary party's demand for a limited form of home rule within the empire had been replaced by Sinn Fein's demand for an independent Irish republic. On the other hand, there was the minority, the unionist, movement. As an organised and distinctive movement it dated from 1885. It was a reaction against the development of the nationalist movement on class and sectarian lines and a response to the extension of the Irish franchise in 1884. It drew its strength from the protestant Anglo- and Scotch- Irish, the product of successive plantations, and enabled former liberals and conservatives to cooperate in attempting to maintain minority, ascendancy interests and influence. Unionists opposed the demand for an Irish parliament and argued that Ireland's interests could be best served by preserving the legislative union between Great Britain and Ireland. Despite an impressive record of endeavour, unionism remained a minority movement. Whereas nationalists were able for many years to return over 80 M.P.s to Westminster, unionists could only hope to return at most 26 (in 1918).

The unionist movement was itself divided into two groups. There were the unionists in the historic nine-county province of Ulster, who were strongest in the six north-eastern counties, and there were the unionists of the three southern provinces. In Ulster, unionists represented an almost self-contained society, ranging from landowners and businessmen to tenant farmers and industrial and agricultural labourers. Among this community there developed a fierce and aggressive unionism, often unfairly equated with orangeism. The attitude of these Ulster unionists, prepared if necessary to resist Dublin rule by armed force, contrasted markedly with that of their fellow unionists in the southern provinces who were fewer and less self-contained. For instance, in Ulster, in 1911, there were 890,880 protestants out of a population of 1,581,969 and Ulster unionists could usually count on winning half of the parliamentary representation of that province. In the three southern provinces, however, where there were only some 256,699 protestants scattered among a Roman Catholic population of 2,551,854, unionists could barely rely upon returning three members to parliament.

These census and electoral figures are important. They indicate not only the relative strength but also the different social and political situations of unionists in Ulster and in the south of Ireland. Whereas the Ulstermen represented a social pyramid, the southern unionists formed the tip of the social pyramid in the south of Ireland. They tended to be not only protestant and anglicised but also aristocratic and landed, with a leaven of Roman Catholic landowners, intellectuals from Trinity College, Dublin, and eminent businessmen. Moreover, they were scattered throughout the three southern provinces in isolated groups and could never contemplate unconstitutional action.

These differences overrode what may be called a common protestant ethic and determined the fact that Ulster and southern unionism should exist as separate, sometimes competing, movements. Occasionally, they cooperated, as in the joint committee of the Unionist Associations of Ireland (1907–15) for propaganda work in Great Britain, but otherwise they maintained separate organisations. The southern unionists were organised into the Irish Loyal and Patriotic Union (1885–after 1891 it was known as the Irish Unionist Alliance), and the Unionist Anti-Partition League (1919). The first central Ulster unionist organisation was the Ulster Loyalist Anti-Repeal Union founded in 1886 and dissolved in 1911: it was not until 1904–5 that the present Ulster Unionist Council was formed to mobilise effectively unionist energies in Ulster.

Broadly speaking, the history of southern and Ulster unionism falls into two parts. Up until the outbreak of the first world war, 4 August 1914, Irish unionists were determined to defeat home rule absolutely. They not only organised in Ireland but also carried on in British politics an almost continuous campaign against home rule. Many detailed objections were advanced against the various home rule bills, but it was the principle of home rule that Irish unionists objected to. Their determination to prevent the re-establishment of a Dublin parliament was clearly demonstrated in the prolonged crisis over the third home rule bill.

After the second general election of 1910 the continuance in office of H. H. Asquith's liberal government depended once again upon the goodwill of the Irish parliamentary party who held the balance between the parties in the house of commons. Having modified the powers of the house of lords with the parliament act of August 1911, the liberals introduced the third home rule bill into the house of commons on 11 April 1912. The bill offered Ireland only a narrow measure of autonomy in that it proposed to establish a Dublin parliament of two chambers but reserved to the imperial parliament wide powers and retained Irish representation at Westminster. Nevertheless, it was fiercely denounced by Irish unionists and their unionist allies in Great Britain. It was not just that the bill contained inadequate safeguards for minorities (for instance, the second chamber was to be an elective one which, it was argued, would only reproduce the nationalist majority in the lower house). It was the whole concept of home rule that they opposed.

Unlike the home rule crises of 1886 and 1893, the fight against the 1912 bill was a prolonged one. The parliament act of 1911 had deprived the house of lords of the power of killing measures sent up from the house of commons; but the lords were left a suspensory veto which enabled them to hold up measures for two years. The unionist majority in the lords took full advantage of this power. They forced the liberal government to pass the third home rule bill through the house of commons three times, so that it was not until 25 May 1914 that the bill completed its parliamentary circuit. In the meantime, the opponents of home rule organised: in Ireland, the Ulster unionists planned resistance to the Dublin parliament, and in Great Britain Ulster and southern unionists combined to try and force a referendum on the home rule issue.

The outbreak of war ushered in the second phase of Irish unionism. Outright opposition to any form of home rule became impossible. The third home rule bill was put on the statute book on 18 September 1914, and the British public and politicians, absorbed in the war effort and then in the problems of post-war reconstruction, had little patience with Irish unionist objections to home rule. Because of these altered conditions, Irish unionists were forced to compromise. Ulster unionists had to accept a form of home rule for the six counties of Antrim, Armagh, Down, Fermanagh, Londonderry, and Tyrone. The present government of Northern Ireland was established under the government of Ireland act (1920) and achieved stability by 1923. Southern unionists also had gradually to abandon all opposition to home rule. Some moved more quickly than others. A section led by Lord Midleton, chairman of the I.U.A. and afterwards president of the A.P.L., tried to shape a settlement of the Irish question on terms favourable to themselves, and did, in fact, play a part in the settlement of 1921–2. Others, reinforced by the unionists of the three Ulster counties, opposed any form of compromise but eventually found the old unionist position untenable. By 1922, with the establishment of the Irish Free State in the twenty-six counties under the Anglo-Irish treaty of December 1921, the unionist movement had petered out in the south.

It is difficult to exaggerate the significance of Irish unionism for British and Irish history in the late nineteenth and early twentieth centuries. Firstly, the Irish unionists' opposition to home rule and their agitation in British politics delayed a settlement of the Irish question. This delay not only embittered British political life but also, by undermining the authority of the moderate Irish parliamentary party, assisted the ascendancy of extreme nationalism. The role of Ulster unionism in delaying a settlement has long been recognised but the importance of southern unionism is often overlooked. One of the biggest obstacles to home rule, especially in 1912–14, was the opposition of the unionist party of Great Britain with its majority in the house of lords. And it could be argued that the reason for this unionist intransigence was concern for the southern unionist minority, whose political activities deterred opposition leaders from working for a compromise settlement on the basis of the exclusion of Ulster. Secondly, Irish unionists influenced the eventual settlement of the Irish question. Southern unionist willingness to accept home rule and to mediate between the British government and Sinn Fein paved the way for the treaty negotiations of 1921. Ulster unionist determination not to submit to Dublin rule frustrated the nationalist desire for a united Ireland and resulted in partition.

There are four broad questions to be asked about Irish unionism. Who were the Irish unionists? Why did they oppose home rule? How did they oppose it? How effective was their opposition? These questions give rise to a number of subsidiary ones such as: when did the unionist movement emerge; what difficulties did the movement face; and how did Irish unionists respond to the inevitability of home rule after 1914?

The wide range of material available in the N.I.P.R.O. helps to answer some of these questions. Firstly, there is a large collection of printed material, including press cuttings and items produced by Irish unionists for propaganda purposes. The latter comprise maps, posters, leaflets and pamphlets, often bound in annual volumes, and copies of *Notes from Ireland*. *Notes* was a regular bulletin of Irish affairs: a useful source for the study of Irish history in the home rule period, it first appeared on 25 September 1886 as a 'record of the sayings and doings of the Parnellite party in furtherance of the "separatist policy" for Ireland; and of facts connected with the country, for the information of the imperial parliament, the press, and the public generally.' Secondly, there are minute books relating to various committees set up by such Irish unionist organisations as the I.L.P.U., I.U.A., U.U.C. and

Unionist Clubs Council. Thirdly, some of the correspondence conducted by and with the various unionist organisations has been preserved—particularly for the I.U.A. in 1892–3 and the U.U.C. in 1912–14. Fourthly, there are several collections of the private correspondence and papers of individual Irish unionists. (Particularly useful are the papers of a Tyrone unionist, H. de F. Montgomery, a landed gentleman closely involved with unionism in the south as well as in the north; and the papers of Sir Edward, later Lord, Carson, the Ulster unionist leader between 1910 and 1921.) A fifth source is the various diaries, such as Lady Craigavon's and Major 'Fred' Crawford's, that have been deposited in the office. Sixthly, there are several large collections of solicitors' papers. Occasionally there is some useful evidence relating to Irish unionism in these collections, especially when one of the partners in the firm was an active unionist. Often overlooked are barristers' briefs relating to election petitions, the registration of voters and trials following sectarian riots. A seventh source is a wide range of material relating to the administration of landed estates. Lastly, there are reminiscences of Irish unionists or their sympathisers. Some of these take the form of reports on interviews between members of staff of the N.I.P.R.O. and surviving unionists prominent in the period under review.

Such material does not answer all the questions relating to Irish unionism. Students interested in the more progressive southern unionists, in Irish unionist activity at a high, cabinet, level, and in the impact of Irish unionist agitation upon politicians and public opinion in Britain, should look at British newspapers, *Hansard,* parliamentary papers, and the papers of British and Irish politicians deposited elsewhere. The collections represented by this volume should prove useful in identifying Irish unionists, in highlighting their problems, in explaining some of their objections to home rule, and in studying their organisation in Ireland and their campaign in the British constituencies.

Chapter I

The opponents of home rule: the general case stated

The opponents of home rule in Ireland tended to be protestant and of English or Scottish descent, the Anglo-Irish or the Scotch-Irish. In the south unionists also tended to be propertied and aristocratic; in Ulster, unionists represented a wider section of society, though the leadership was largely in the hands of the landed classes and businessmen. They were all, in fact, supporters of the protestant ascendancy, and opposed the home rule movement in the late nineteenth century because it aimed at the establishment of a parliament in Dublin which would be dominated by catholics. They objected to the establishment of such an Irish parliament on two broad grounds. On the one hand, they were quite satisfied with the *status quo,* holding that Ireland had prospered under the union and that the union could and should be usefully maintained for Ireland's continued benefit. On the other hand, they thought that Ireland's future and the prospects of the protestant minority would be poor under a Dublin parliament.

The object of this and the next two chapters is to show how the material in the N.I.P.R.O., particularly a large pamphlet collection in the archives of the I.L.P.U., can be used to build up a picture of the opponents of home rule and of their objections to home rule.

II

The two broad grounds upon which Irish unionists opposed home rule are given in the various resolutions passed by and the pamphlets issued by Irish unionists or their organisations. In the first place, they believed that the union system of government was beneficial to Ireland and to the Irish. Denying the nationalist argument that the union was ruining Ireland economically and socially, they held that in the nineteenth

1

century the British connection had assisted the economic and social development of all classes and creeds, particularly by way of legislation on behalf of Roman Catholics, by land acts and later by what may be conveniently described as social security measures. Indeed, there was evolved an Irish unionist interpretation of Irish economic and social history, most forcefully expressed in a statement submitted by the I.L.P.U. to the prime minister in 1886. Issued as a pamphlet and sub-titled *The union vindicated*, the statement used an impressive range of statistical material to prove the case that prior to the union Ireland's prosperity was declining, but that since the union Ireland had prospered. Moreover, Irish unionists thought that the union could be usefully maintained, holding that, if shown just cause, the British people and the British parliament would be willing to maintain the union to foster economic and social development and to regulate social and political tension in Ireland. They had many contacts in British politics and society which they could exploit.

1 Extracts from a 67–page pamphlet, *Statement submitted to the prime minister by the I.L.P.U.: part III. The union vindicated. Ireland's progress 1782–1800–1886,* published by the I.L.P.U. in 1886 (D 989C/3/5):

PERHAPS no great question was ever submitted to the consideration of Parliament respecting which there is less knowledge or more misrepresentation than that now about to engage the attention of the Legislature; and certainly there is no branch of that question which has been more persistently misrepresented, and which is less understood, than the relative condition of Ireland before and after the Union.

By dint of confident assertion, again and again repeated, a sort of vague impression has been left upon the public mind that the state of Ireland before the Union was one of general happiness and progress, due mainly, if not wholly, to the fostering care of a native Parliament; that the Union gave the first check to this growing prosperity; and that the country has been going from bad to worse ever since.

If this were so—if during the period from 1782 to 1800, the only time when Ireland had even the semblance of an independent Parliament, the country had made giant strides in prosperity, as is popularly supposed; if that prosperity had been suddenly arrested by the Union, or had even gradually declined during subsequent years, the demand for Home Rule, as a panacea for all the ills of Ireland, would not be so wholly illogical as it is.

But the fact is not so; nay, the very opposite is the fact. Far from advancing in prosperity, Ireland actually retrograded during the period referred to; and not only did the Union not check an advance, wholly imaginary, but it arrested the well-developed downward tendency, and infused new life into the languishing prosperity of the country. . . .

(p. 7)

The legislative record of the Irish Parliament, during its brief period of 'glorious independence,' is not a particularly brilliant one: the time of its members was almost entirely taken up with fierce party conflicts, enlivened by personal attacks and recriminations, from which they were sometimes diverted by the irruption of armed mobs into the chamber, and, on one memorable occasion, by the malicious burning of the Senate house over their heads. . . .

(p. 24)

We now proceed to compare, or rather to contrast, the state of Ireland during the eighteen years preceding the Union, with its condition immediately after and ever since.

In dealing with this portion of our subject we propose to consider separately the period between the Union and the Famine—from 1800 to 1845—and that which has elapsed since. We shall adopt this course for two reasons— first, because the statistics are, in many cases, differently made up in each period, rendering it very difficult to compare them with sufficient exactness; but chiefly because owing to the social changes consequent on the famine, to the establishment of free trade, the extension of the railway system, the development of the cross-channel traffic, and other causes, the conditions of the Irish problem have been radically changed. In seeking to show that Ireland has benefited by the Legislative and Commercial Union with Great Britain, it would scarcely be fair to claim for that measure the growth of prosperity which is more directly due to the causes we have enumerated. We do claim for the Union that it has enabled Ireland to avail herself more readily and more advantageously of the benefits of the enlightened principles of legislation and of the marvellous results of scientific research, which have placed the latter half of the nineteenth century so far in advance of any previous epoch. But we do not claim for the Union that it has produced all the good results which have succeeded it, any more than we admit that it has caused the evils ascribed to it by the agitators.

Hence, we prefer to rest our case upon the advantages which Ireland derived from the Union during the period subsequent to that measure down to 1845, while the conditions under which it operated were in many respects the same as during the preceding period, and when its effects were more directly felt. If we can show, by trustworthy evidence, that the state of Ireland from 1800 to 1845 was one of recuperative energy and progress, we shall not hesitate to claim for the Act of Union that it largely contributed to, if it did not cause, that progress; especially as we have already shown that Ireland immediately before the Union had been in a condition of decay.

3

Starting then, as before, with the tonnage of ships owned and registered at Irish ports, and comparing periods of three years each, prior and subsequent to the Union, we find these remarkable results:—

TABLE IV.

Years.	Tons.	Increase per cent. over First Period.
1797, '98, and '99,	112,333	——
1824, '25, and '26,	225,766	101·0
1833, '34, and '35,	337,772	200·7
1843, '44, and '45,	631,981	462·6

This Table affords evidence complete and conclusive of the rapid and steady growth of Irish trade between the Union and 1845. During the three years ending with 1826 the tonnage exceeded by over 100 per cent. the tonnage for the triennial period ending with 1799; during the three years ending with 1835, another 100 per cent. was added to the increase; and in the three years ending with 1845 the increase was no less than 463 per cent. as compared with the three years immediately preceding the Union. Let us state this more plainly. In 1825 the tonnage of ships registered at Irish ports was *double* what it had been at the Union; ten years later, in 1835, it had increased to *treble* the amount; and ten years later it had risen to more than *five and a-half times* the tonnage registered at the time of the Union. We have already shown that for some years previous to the Union this tonnage had been steadily falling. Can we hesitate to attribute the remarkable increase immediately after the Union to the direct influence of that measure, which opened all the avenues of British commerce to Irish enterprise? Can there be a more conclusive proof that the Union of the two countries, so far from extinguishing the trade of Ireland, not only arrested its decay, but stimulated it to renewed vitality, than the fact that within forty-five years the registered tonnage at Irish ports had increased over five-and-a-half fold? This increase will appear even more remarkable, if we recall the history of the time. . . .

(p. 37)

We do not forget that at intervals, during this latter period, there was sharp distress in different parts of the country, and that, at its close, the shadow of a great impending calamity was already projected over the land; but both the occasional distress and the final calamity were produced by causes wholly local; and would have been infinitely worse were it not for the more intimate connexion with England which had been established by the Union.

4

It is not our intention to dwell upon the period of famine, which began with the failure of the potato crop in 1846, and which continued, in greater or less intensity, down to 1851; though there is no period, since the Union, at which the English connexion proved of greater advantage to Ireland. Who, that remembers that awful time, can doubt that but for the active sympathy and assistance, both public and private, afforded by the English people, the sufferings of the poor in Ireland would have been immeasurably greater than they were? Speaking from personal knowledge, we can assert that for a great portion of the time during which the famine lasted multitudes of persons, over large areas of the country, were indebted for their daily bread to the funds supplied from England, over and above the enormous grants by Parliament for their relief. What they might have expected, had they been unhappily living under Home Rule, may be gathered from the experience of a similar calamity in 1740–1, the *'bliadhain an air'*, or year of slaughter, 'when the ordinary churchyards were not large enough to contain those who died by the roadside, or who were taken from the deserted cabins'; and when no measures were adopted either by the Legislature or the Executive to relieve the distress.

We shall not, however, dwell upon this; we but refer to it as dividing the time that has elapsed since the Union into two well-defined periods, during the former of which Ireland advanced rapidly on the path of national progress; and during the latter of which she has enjoyed a measure of prosperity far surpassing anything known in her history, and seldom paralleled in the history of any other country.

It is like attempting to prove an axiom to seek to establish by evidence that the condition of Ireland now is immeasurably superior to anything that existed at the beginning of the present century. We do not speak of the advance in the arts of civilization which has taken place in all countries during the last sixty or seventy years, and in which Ireland has participated to the fullest extent: we refer to the growth of material prosperity, to the increase of wealth, and consequently of comfort, among all classes of the people.

We but repeat, what is well known to every one who has bestowed attention on the subject, that, in every detail which goes to make up the sum of civilized life, the Irish people are at this moment very far in advance of the condition of their ancestors at the time of the Union. They are better housed, better clad, better fed; they receive better prices for the produce of their farms, and higher wages for their labour; they have greater liberty and better protection in health, abundant provision for sickness, and facilities for the education and advancement in life of their children, such as were undreamt of eighty years ago. No measure has been passed, since the Union, for the benefit of the English or Scotch people, in which they have not shared; and many Acts have been passed specially for their benefit which have not been extended to Scotland or England. These are facts which cannot be controverted, and which no one, except hireling agitators, would attempt to deny or distort.

5

None know better than the agitators themselves that the state of Ireland from 1852 to 1879 was one of scarcely interrupted progress and prosperity; hence they usually omit these twenty-eight years from their harangues, and profess to find in the condition of the country, since 1879, evidence of that decadence which they know they must establish before they can hope that their demand for Home Rule, as a necessary remedy, would be listened to.

But they cannot be permitted to fix the terms of the discussion in their own fashion. Even granting, for argument's sake, that the twenty-eight years of prosperity, from 1852 to 1879, have been followed by seven years of depression, it does not follow either that the depression will be permanent, or that the condition of the country has been brought so low as that an organic change in the British Constitution is required to save it from ruin; least of all, does it follow that such organic change would restore the exceptional prosperity which Ireland so long enjoyed; on the contrary, the sad experience of the ante-Union period points to a very different result.

The truth is, that the more thoroughly we examine the condition of Ireland at the present time, and the more closely we compare it with the condition of the country during the thirty-three years that have elapsed since the famine, the more evidence do we find that, notwithstanding the long-continued stagnation of trade, and the present depression in the prices of agricultural produce, there is nothing exceptional or alarming in our position, so far as the elements of material prosperity are concerned; and were it not for the dangerous agitation which for party purposes has been allowed to develop itself in our midst, we have no hesitation in saying that the state of Ireland to-day would compare not unfavourably with that of any other portion of the United Kingdom. The depression in the prices of agricultural produce, and the stagnation of trade, are quite as keenly felt in England and Scotland as in Ireland—possibly more so—but we hear of no proposal to pull the Constitution to pieces as the only remedy for the distress. English and Scotch people know that there must be periods of stagnation and depression as well as periods of prosperity; and they know that they must wait patiently for the return of good times. They do not believe that the foundations of national prosperity will be laid anew by the repudiation of contracts, or by driving the wealthy and cultured classes out of the country. Orators preaching communistic doctrines may spout at debating clubs or hole-and-corner meetings; but they are not listened to by the mass of the English or Scotch people; they are not applauded in their National Press; they are not encouraged by their National Churches. It is only in Ireland that such doctrines find favour; it is only in Ireland that half-educated men, whose only qualification consists in fluency of speech, are accepted as economists and statesmen, whose utterances are to be received *ex cathedra* without question or proof. . . .

(p. 42)

Let us first test the development of Irish commerce, from 1852 onwards, by the amount of shipping frequenting Irish ports during the period.

The following Table will enable us to do this at a glance:—

TABLE X.

Year.	Tonnage inwards.	Tonnage outwards.
1852, ...	3,047,941	2,238,171
1884, ...	6,723,269	6,578,578
Increase in 1885 over 1852, . . . }	3,675,328	4,340,307
Increase per cent., . . .	120·6	193·9

We see here that in 32 years, from 1852 to 1884, inclusive, the tonnage entering the Irish ports was considerably more than doubled; and that the tonnage cleared outwards was all but trebled within the same period. For every 100 tons of shipping entered in 1852 there were 220 tons entered in 1885; and for every 100 tons cleared in the former year, there were no less than 294 tons cleared in the latter.

If we combine the tonnage inwards and outwards, we find an aggregate increase of 151.6 per cent.; in other words, the commerce of Ireland in 1884 was two and a-half times as great as it was in 1852. We have not yet complete returns for 1885.

We may also measure the advance in prosperity made by Ireland since 1852 by the increase in the revenue of the country. In 1852, the gross revenue of Ireland was £4,414,413, and in 1885 the amount was £7,770,626—being an increase of 76 per cent., or, more popularly expressed, for every £100 of revenue raised in Ireland in 1852, the amount raised in 1883 was £176. There can be no more conclusive evidence of the prosperity of a country than the elasticity of its revenue, especially when it is raised by indirect taxation, and the people have practically the power to tax themselves. It is simply impossible to reconcile the increase of the revenue raised in Ireland during the last thirty-three years—the lifetime of a single generation—with any other hypothesis than the obvious one that the condition of the country has improved at least in the same ratio.

It may be a surprise to many to learn that, during the same period the revenue of Ireland increased in a greater ratio than that of the other portions of the United Kingdom; nevertheless, such is the fact. The gross public revenue of Great Britain in 1852, was £47,818,593, and the gross revenue of Ireland in the same year, was £4,414,433. As we have already seen, the gross revenue of Ireland in 1885 was £7,770,626—showing an increase of 76 per cent. over the revenue raised in 1852. If the revenue of Great Britain had increased in the same ratio during the same period, the gross amount in 1885 would have been £84,160,724, whereas the actual amount was only £82,566,095, thus exhibiting a deficiency of £1,594,629, or very nearly 2 per cent. How can this extraordinary fact be explained, except on the assumption that Ireland has been the most prosperous portion of the United Kingdom during the last thirty-three years? . . .

(p. 48)

But it will be said that Ireland is not a commercial country; that Ireland is an agricultural country,; and that her progress must be measured, not by her advance in commerce, not by the increase in revenue, not by the accumulation of available capital, or by the development of her railway system, but by the growth of her agriculture in all its forms, and by the prosperity of her farming class. To this objection there is the obvious answer, that if Ireland be, as in fact she is, an agricultural country, the increase in her commerce, and the other evidences of progress which we have adduced, must depend directly on her agricultural prosperity. If the people of a country be poor, and if the staple industry of a country be in a state of decay, commerce must diminish; there will be less to export, and less demand for imported goods; there will be less consumption of duty-paying articles, whether of necessity or of luxury; there will be less accumulation of capital, and less ability or desire to sink money in investments. Hence the prosperity of the agricultural classes in [I]reland may be directly and confidently inferred from her increased commercial activity. Even in manufacturing countries, the land is recognized as the ultimate source of wealth: when the farming classes are prosperous, all share in the prosperity; and *vice versâ*, if the farming class be not thriving, the commercial classes soon feel the effects of the agricultural depression. We might, therefore, rest our case on the proofs of progress we have already given, and leave the issue with confidence to the verdict of the public. But we shall not content ourselves with an inductive argument, however convincing, when we are in a position to bring forward direct evidence.

As these pages are written chiefly for English and Scotch readers, we must begin by begging of them to put out of their minds the too prevalent idea that the agricultural prosperity of Ireland depends, even in the remotest degree, on the price of wheat. The climate of Ireland is not suited to the growth of this crop, and it could not be grown profitably, unless it commanded a price much higher than any which could be obtained for it in recent years. Hence, wheat has practically gone out of cultivation in Ireland, and the price of wheat no longer affects the prosperity of the Irish farmer. This fact is placed beyond controversy by the agricultural statistics collected annually with great care by the local Constabulary, and published, with commendable promptitude, by the Registrar-General of Ireland. From the last returns we find that, of five million acres under crops in Ireland in 1885, only seventy-one thousand acres, or 1.4 per cent. of the whole, were under wheat; in other words, for every acre of wheat grown in Ireland in 1885, there were seventy acres under other crops. It is most important to bear this fact in mind; for the people of England, who are themselves suffering from the fall in the price

8

of wheat, are likely to fall into the error of supposing that the same cause is producing the same effect in Ireland.

But, in reality, no comparison, based on the price of wheat, can be instituted between the two countries, and no inference can be drawn from the effects of the fall in price of wheat in England as to the probable or actual effects of that fall in Ireland; for while only 71,000 acres of wheat are now grown in Ireland, there are still 2,350,000 acres under wheat in England; in other words, while 1 acre in every 5½ of tillage land in England is sown with wheat, the corresponding acreage in Ireland is only 1 in 70.

Barley is another crop which, though more grown in Ireland than wheat, falls very far short in extent of that grown in England. In 1885 the acreage of barley and bere in Ireland was only 188,000 acres, against 1,884,000, or more than ten times the area in England. In other words, while 1 acre in every 6½ under tillage in England is sown with barley or bere, the corresponding area in Ireland is 1 acre in every 26.

It is therefore plain that no deduction, drawn from the price of wheat or barley, is of the slightest use in comparing the agricultural position and prospects of agriculture in Ireland with those in England, and that the fall in the prices of those cereals must be entirely excluded from consideration.

The staple cereal of Ireland is oats, and it alone admits of comparison with Great Britain. In 1885, the area in Ireland under oats, was 1,328,000 acres; the area in England was 1,647,000 acres; and in Scotland and Wales, 1,293,000 acres. It is plain, therefore, that any alteration in the price of oats will affect all parts of the United Kingdom alike. Let us now see how it affects Ireland.

In 1852 the area of land under crops in Ireland was 5,740,000 acres, of which 2,283,000 acres, or 1 acre in every 2½, were under oats. In 1885, of 5,000,000 acres in tillage, 1,328,000 acres, or 1 acre in 3¾, were under oats. This shows a falling off of 955,000 acres, or 41.8 per cent. in the period of 33 years; and if the growth of oats has become, as is alleged, a losing concern, the farmers of Ireland are rather to be congratulated on having escaped loss over more than a fourth of the country. But, judged by the relative prices, the cultivation of oats is more profitable now than it was in 1852, in the ratio of 5 to 4, on the lowest present market rates, and considerably more on the highest; while the value of the straw has increased to an enormous extent— more than sufficient to cover the increased cost of production. The diminution in the area of oats grown in Ireland, therefore, is not to be explained by any reduction in the profits to be made by its cultivation. It has taken place because Irish farmers have found out that they can employ their capital more profitably in other directions, and that a less amount of labour will enable them to secure an equal or greater amount of money. No man will, of his own choice, continue to pursue a laborious calling if he can earn as much, or more, by a less toilsome one; and Irish farmers are wonderfully like other people in this respect.

For the last thirty years the breeding and rearing of young stock have yielded, acre for acre, far larger profits, and at infinitely less labour, than the growth of grain; and hence a great deal of land has been laid down to grass; but the growth of oats is more profitable now than it was in 1852, and the farmers who adhere to its cultivation are gainers to the extent of the extra profit; and as those who have discontinued the growth of oats are presumably making a larger profit in some other branch of agriculture, the country is the gainer; and is, by so much, more prosperous now than in 1852. For the reasons already stated, it would be waste of time to estimate the effect of the fall of prices of the other cereals, on the prosperity of the country. The smallness of the area over which they are cultivated renders any change in their price practically inappreciable. . . .

(p. 56)

These increases of 37 per cent. in number of black cattle, 33 per cent. in the number of sheep, and 18 per cent. in the number of pigs in Ireland, are of themselves sufficiently strong evidence of agricultural prosperity; but it is only by combining the increase in the numbers with the advance in prices, that the full extent of the improved position of the Irish farmers can be measured.

The following Table will make this plain:—

TABLE XIV.

Description.	Value in 1852.	Value in 1885.	Increase in Value.	Increase per cent.
	£	£	£	
Cattle, . . .	24,760,000	50,745,000	25,985,000	105·0
Sheep, . . .	3,529,000	6,086,000	2,557,000	72·5
Pigs, . . .	2,091,000	3,173,000	1,083,000	151·8
Totals, . . .	30,380,000	60,004,000	29,624,000	97·5

In arriving at the values given in this Table, we estimate the average prices as follows:—Black cattle at £8 a-piece in 1852, and at £12 in 1885; sheep at £1 7*s.* in 1852, and at £1 15*s.* in 1885; and pigs at £1 19*s.* in 1852, and at £2 10*s.* in 1885. These prices are the result of a wide and careful induction; and are, we believe, as near the truth as it is possible to make such estimates. If we have erred the error is against ourselves, for our prices are higher for 1852 than those adopted by the Census Commissioners as the basis of their calculations in the preceding year; while those which we have adopted for 1885 are lower than the prices published last year in *Thom's Almanac,* as the result of careful investigations specially made for the Proprietor of that invaluable statistical summary. It may be well to mention that the total value of the cattle, sheep, and pigs in Ireland, in 1885, as given in *Thom's Almanac,* was £63,512,277.

10

From this Table we see that, valuing the cattle, sheep, and pigs owned by Irish farmers in 1852 at the average prices then current, and similarly estimating the value in 1885, there has been an increase in value of over £29,000,000, amounting to 97.5 per cent.—or, in other words, the farmers of Ireland last year possessed £197 10s. worth of live stock for every £100 worth owned by them in 1852.

We do not think it necessary to adduce further statistical proof that the agricultural wealth of Ireland has increased enormously since the famine. What is true of oats live stock cattle is true of every other farm product, except potatoes and wool. These two articles alone are cheaper now than they were in 1852. Few in Ireland will regret the cheapness of potatoes, on which so many in the poorer parts of the country depend for food; and we believe that the decrease in the value of the wool crop is more than compensated for by the increased value of eggs and poultry, the exportation of which has become a profitable branch of trade in every part of the country. . . .

(p. 59)

Our second proof of the increased prosperity of the people is drawn from the improvement in their dwellings. On this head we have no returns later than 1881, the year of the last census; but we shall compare the condition of the people in that year, in respect of dwellings, with the state of things in 1851.

TABLE XV.

Class of House Accommodation.	Number of Families.		Increase + or Decrease —
	1851.	1881.	
First Class, . . .	39,370	96,568	+ 57,198
Second Class, . . .	292,280	467,387	+175,107
Third Class, . . .	588,440	390,094	− 198,346
Fourth Class, . . .	284,229	41,025	− 243,204
Totals, ...	1,204,319	995,074	− 209,246

(p. 61)

. . . . If we add together the families living in first and second-class houses and also those living in houses of third and fourth-class, we find that while in 1851 there were in round numbers 873,000 families living in the poorer classes of house, or 72.3 per cent. of the whole, and only 27.7 per cent. occupying the two better classes of house; there were in 1881, only 43.3 per cent. living

11

in the poorer classes of house, and 56.7 per cent. living in the better class; only 4.1 per cent. of the whole being housed in mud cabins. If this be not evidence of marvellous progress in domestic comfort, in the short space of 33 years, we know not what evidence means. . . .

(p. 64)

When Ireland entered on her career of prosperity in 1852, she had not a third of the resources at her command that she has now; and we confess ourselves utterly unable to comprehend by what process of perverse reasoning the conclusion has been arrived at that she is on the brink of ruin, and must inevitably sink into the abyss, unless the Constitution under which she has so abundantly prospered be abrogated, and that under which she went to decay, from 1782 to 1800, established in its stead. To our mind, the progress of Ireland since the Union, and especially since the famine, affords the strongest presumptive proof that her future should be even more prosperous than her past. When she rose from her ashes, in 1852, there might have been reason to look doubtfully towards the future; and yet we see how she has progressed since. Why should we fear the future now, when we are so much better prepared to meet it? . . .

2 Extract from a 29-page pamphlet, *Union or separation,* published in 1886 by the I.L.P.U., arguing among other things that Roman Catholics as such had no grievance against the union (D. 989C/3/5):

. . . Is there a country in the whole world where the Roman Catholic Church has such complete immunity from State interference, such perfect liberty, as in Ireland under the British Crown? From the day that Catholic Emancipation was granted by the Protestant Parliament of England, the history of Irish legislation has been a history of redress of grievances and concessions to Roman Catholics. For them the system of National Education, to which Catholic Ireland owes so much, was established, and in their interests it has been mainly administered. For them a comprehensive scheme of Intermediate Education was subsequently introduced. For them the Queen's Colleges and the Queen's University were originally founded; and when they failed to please, the Royal University was established in their stead. For them the clergy of the Established Church were stripped of a fourth of their incomes, and payment of the remaining three-fourths transferred from the Catholic tenants to the Protestant Landlord. For them various disabilities—some serious, others trifling but galling in their nature—have been from time to time removed from the Statute Book, until not a trace of religious ascendancy remains. For them, finally, the Established Church of Ireland, whose status and property had been doubly guaranteed by the Act of Union, and by the Emancipation Act, was disestablished and disendowed. Why should not the candid, the thoughtful, the liberal Roman Catholics of Ireland be loyal to the connection under which they have reaped such a harvest of benefit? It is an insult to the intelligence and to the honesty of such men to class them among the enemies of England. We are aware that those in favour of separation are almost exclusively Roman Catholics; but we deny that they are so because they are Roman Catholics. They are hostile to the British connection because they want the ownership of the land without paying for it, and Parliament has not yet sunk so low as to buy off their hostility by such a degrading ransom.

No doubt there are in the lowest stratum of the Irish Roman Catholics many ignorant and fanatical bigots who hate England because she is a representative Protestant power; but until the contrary is proved beyond the possibility of doubt, or proclaimed by themselves, we refuse to believe that enlightened Irish Roman Catholics approve of the revolutionary projects of Mr. Parnell and his associates. If such be among the ranks of the Parnellites, it is not necessarily because they are Roman Catholics; their Catholicism is a concurrent circumstance, not a cause, scarcely even a factor, of their political opinions. . . .

III

Confidence in the British willingness to maintain the union was an essential part of the southern unionist case against home rule, but Ulster unionism was more self-reliant. Ulstermen were conscious of an almost separate sense of identity, which was evident at the time of the fenian outbreaks in the late 1860s, when some landlords armed their 'sound' tenants with rifles. Although they preferred English militia to armed tenants, they were sure that the 'black north will take care of itself and let the government send troops to the south and west where there may be a rising if the Yankees are such fools to attempt invasion'. This confident self-sufficiency recurred in the home rule debate. Ulstermen argued that under the union economic prosperity and social and religious harmony had been established there. What sectarian bitterness did exist they attributed to the Ancient Order of Hibernians and to the aggressive attitude of Roman Catholic clergymen, particularly in respect of mixed marriages in 1910–11 (see pp 72-3).

3 A poem, 'We meet: a voice from the Ulster convention', by J. S. Drennan, celebrating the convention of Ulster unionists held in the Ulster Hall, Belfast, 17 June 1892, to protest against home rule (Mic 127/30):

WE MEET!

(A VOICE FROM THE ULSTER CONVENTION.)

WE meet ; we Ulstermen have hied
    From vale and mountain, garth and town :
    From Antrim's glens and hills of Down ;
From Derry, with her " Gates " of pride ;
  Dungannon, with her camp of fame :
The barrier cliffs of Donegal,
Where the fierce western billows fall ;
  From grey Armagh of sainted name ;
  From fair Fermanagh's lough and street ;
From Cavan and from Monaghan—
With march and mind as of one man
    In Ulster's capital we meet.

We meet that Ulster's voice be heard
  Beyond the blare of fife and drum,
  From cot and castle, plough and loom,
To utter one determined word.
  We speak not here in accents low ;
We whisper not our thought to-day.
Traitors would have us own their sway
    Let England hear our answer—No !

We will not bend to men arrayed
  To break the law and rend the State ;
  We will not "league" with fraud and hate
To blight our country and degrade.
  Let shifting statesmen smile or frown,
Let knaves and minions clash or cling,
No upstart whipped shall be our King !
    No mitre shall o'ertop our Crown.

Let cruel cowards prowl and lurk,
  We will not join their furtive bands ;
  We will not clasp their reeking hands,
Nor fear to ban their bloody work.
  We read not freedom's license thus,
Not thus religion's mandates trace —
To maim old men, young girls deface
    Are deeds for dastards—not for us.

Nor will we upright hearts constrain
  To mate with crime and sanction wrong,
  Or be by priest's tyrannic tongue
Inhibited from mart and fame.

Such deeds, such creeds, we scorn and shun ;
And by our hearths and fathers' graves,
No day shall see us willing slaves
  Of men who such have held and done.

Wake, Erin ! wake to thy disgrace !
  'Tis as thy children thus we ask ;
  Fling off, tear up, the hideous mask
That thus conceals our mother's face.
  Despise, denounce, the sordid art
That bribes to guilt by lure of gain,
With falsehood wraps the simple brain,
  With falsehood steels the tender heart.

Be honest and humane again !
  Take counsel of the wise and good,
  And make thy sons one brotherhood
Of patriotic Irishmen !
  Then the white hand of peace shall bring
To guard thy breast from guile and grief
A shamrock of quadruple leaf,
  A harp fresh tuned in every string !

And England, sovereign of the sea,
  Despite the severing streak of brine,
  With laws and liberty like thine,
We'll still our Union hold with thee ;
  And deem the intervening flood
Bearing rich freights from quay to quay
Is but an artery to convey
  And intermingle nutrient blood.

To share and swell thy empire's store,
  Thy friends to aid, thy foes defy,
  Is better than apart to lie
A beggar realm at Europe's door.
  By freedom linked, with hearts allied,
Albion and Erin ever stand—
In peace like sisters hand in hand,
  Against opponents side by side.

Thus Ulster's message to repeat,
  Sternly to speak her steadfast mind,
  Many—and with a host behind—
We meet—as yet unarmed we meet.

Belfast, June 17th, 1892.
                A DELEGATE.

W. & G. Baird, Printers Belfast.—8599.

John Swanwick Drennan

14

4 Extracts from a special report adopted by the U.U.C. at its annual meeting, 30 January 1911, denying a nationalist assertion (6 January) that there was 'no Ulster question' (D 972/17/1912):

... Very persistent efforts are being made in the English Press to belittle the strength of the Ulster position. Ulster Unionists rest their case upon what they believe to be the impregnable foundation of the right to have their equal citizenship in the United Kingdom maintained unimpaired. They have built up their industries and brought Ulster to its present prosperous condition under the protection of the Imperial Parliament and relying on that protection being continued. Any policy which deprives them of this safeguard they would regard as a criminal betrayal of their birthright. This position they are prepared to maintain at all hazard. Among recent attacks upon the Ulster position one is contained in a manifesto intended for perusal in England and Scotland, issued by the Nationalist Leader, Mr. John Redmond, and in this document he declares that "There is no Ulster question." In support of this strange doctrine he lays stress on the admitted fact that the Protestant— which, with very few exceptions, means the Unionist—population of Ulster is only 55.9 per cent. of the whole. Ulster Unionists have never put forward the absurd contention that their province as a whole is overwhelmingly Protestant. But they do claim that in the six Ulster counties in which, or in large sections of which, there are to be found loyalty to the Throne, industrial enterprise, commercial prosperity, independent religious and political opinion, enthusiasm for social reform, and contribution of the best talent within their borders to the various public services of the United Kingdom and of the Empire—in these counties the proportion of Unionists to Nationalists in the population is within a small fraction of as two is to one. Again, if we take the Rateable Valuation of these six counties as compared with that of the other three, which are preponderatingly Nationalist, the ratio is practically as five and one-half is to one—a condition which illustrates the important fact that where there is prosperity in Ulster it is associated with Unionist life and work. Mr. Redmond indeed attempts to belittle the resources of Ulster by making a comparison of the rateable value per head of the people of Ulster in relation to that of the population of Leinster and Munster. Remember that the agricultural valuation on which he relies is Griffiths', taken 60 years ago, and which is of course immensely higher than would be a valuation taken to-day of the same land, the second term rents of which have been reduced by 40 per cent. On the other hand, in order to allow for depreciation, wear and tear, repairs, &c., it is the official practice to value industrial and commercial buildings and plant on a lower amount than cost or than their value as going concerns. These considerations at once put out of court Mr. Redmond's conclusions based upon comparisons on his "per head" principle of the relative wealth of Ulster with its abounding manufacturing establishments and the agricultural southern provinces. But apart from this, it must be remembered that Ulster is by nature the poorest province in Ireland; that its farms are small compared with the immense grazing and dairying farms in Leinster and Munster; that its population (as by census of 1901) of 1,582,826, as compared with 1,152,829 in Leinster and 1,076,188 in

Munster, is greatly swollen by the attraction of large bodies of artisans and their families to Belfast, Londonderry, Ballymena, Portadown, and all the other busy centres of manufacturing industry in the province, who naturally live in houses of modest valuation. The real matter of congratulation is that this large population in Ulster is united in building up the great industries and commercial activity, which are an example to the rest of Ireland, and that its Protestant members, down to the humblest of them (and not a few Roman Catholics) are determinedly loyal to the Imperial Constitution under which their prosperous position has been made possible. . . .

Mr. Redmond devotes considerable attention to the charge of Religious Intolerance so freely made against Ulster Unionists. Everyone who knows Ulster is aware that in recent years, owing largely to the unifying effects of Unionist remedial policy in Ireland, the kindly feeling of Protestants towards Roman Catholics has been steadily growing, and it was accordingly all the greater shock that, owing to the relentless attitude taken up by the Romanist Authorities in the recent Mixed Marriage Scandal in Belfast—an action which Mr. Redmond, though challenged to do so, has failed to repudiate— the growing friendliness between the denominations has received a check. It may be remarked, however, that the charge of bigotry against Ulster does not come very consistently from a political leader whose most powerful hench-man, Mr. Joseph Devlin (the man who, according to a recent statement by Mr. Redmond, is the actual governor of Ireland), operates his policy through the secret and exclusive society called the Ancient Order of Hibernians. The British democracy ought to know that this Society is exclusively, rigidly sectarian, that it strictly debars Protestants from its ranks, and that now the ban of the Roman Catholic Hierarchy has been removed from it, many priests are to be found in its membership. The Society claims descent from a seventeenth century Irish combination against the progress of British autho-rity in Ireland, and especially against the Protestant plantation of Ulster. Its characteristics are its exclusive Roman Catholicism, its deadly hostility to England, and its determination to work for the complete national independ-ence of Ireland.

. . . Belfast Unionists are twitted with the comparative liberality of Dublin Nationalists in regard to electing political opponents to the Office of Lord Mayor. In Belfast the office of Lord Mayor does not carry a salary; its tenure involves large expenditure, which, it appears, only representatives of the prosperous Unionist section of the community are disposed to undertake. Two or three years ago the so-called bigoted Belfast Corporation appointed a prominent Roman Catholic to the office of High Sheriff. In Dublin the Lord Mayorality carries with it a handsome salary, and for the last twenty-nine years no Unionist has enjoyed either the Lord Mayorality of Dublin or its salary. It is interesting to know that in the County Council of Londonderry, consisting of 19 Unionists and 6 Nationalist members, during the last nine years at each election of a Vice-Chairman a Nationalist has been elected. This Council, again, is entitled to send two members to the Agricultural Council of the Department of Agriculture, and one of these is a Nationalist. . . .

There is only space further to remark that Mr. Redmond has entirely omitted to thank the British democracy, on behalf of their Irish brethren, for the special favours, in the way of generous remedial legislation, over and above those granted to themselves, which Ireland as an integral but poorly endowed constituent of the United Kingdom enjoys. He has also omitted to specify a single grievance under which Ireland labours and which could not be more effectively dealt with by an Imperial than by a local Parliament. He has also failed to point out that, by the Local Government Act, Irishmen have now practically the same control over their local affairs which the British democracy possesses, while they have far more than their legitimate proportion of representation in Imperial Parliament. He has not mentioned a single particular in which Ireland would be better off under Home Rule than she is under the Legislative Union. Will Mr. Redmond put to the test his professions of affection for the British democracy by submitting, through a Referendum, the question of Home Rule for Ireland as a single issue to the decision of the people of the United Kingdom?

The truth is that the occupation of Mr. Redmond and his colleagues is simply Agitation and nothing more. . . .

It is because this remedial policy is anathema to the official Irish Nationalist Party that Ulster and the loyal minority in Ireland are determined that no local majority in Ireland shall bear rule over them. At the same time they will continue their efforts to promote the good of Ulster and of all Ireland, relying on the continued protection and equal justice of Imperial Parliament, through whose wise and beneficial legislation, under Unionist Governments, Ulster and the whole country have recently attained to a record degree of prosperity. Until Mr. Redmond and his colleagues turn the other provinces of Ireland into "Ulsters," the Ulster question will, with ever increasing force, continue to confront them. But should they decide to conform Leinster, Munster, and Connaught to the Ulster ideal of industry and self-help, the Irish Question will be at an end, and Irishmen, North and South, will be found permanently united in their loyalty to the principle of ONE FLAG, ONE CROWN, ONE PARLIAMENT.

IV

The second broad ground of objection to home rule, as it had developed by the 1880s, was fear of the consequences of the establishment of a Dublin parliament. The changing composition of the home rule party and the identification of the home rule movement with the question of sectarian education and with the land struggle, especially with the class antagonism of the Land League, convinced many Irishmen that an Irish parliament would be dominated by lower class Roman Catholics with no respect for persons or property.

There were really two fears. On the one hand, Irish unionists found the very idea of catholic democratic rule unattractive, since they had been accustomed to centuries of protestant dominance in public life. They might have been able to stomach a restored Irish parliament dominated by a Roman Catholic gentry, but not, as the historian Lecky put it, one dominated by the national league, priests and fenians and professional agitators 'supported by the votes of the peasantry . . . and subsidised from America by avowed enemies of the British empire'. On the other hand, they did not trust an Irish parliament so constituted to deal with them or with Ireland's interests fairly and believed that home rule, the modification of the union, would result in the abrogation of civil and religious liberty and in economic and social chaos (see also **27, 28, 85**). All Irish unionists were distrustful of Irish nationalism, but, as a comparison between the tone of the Ulster covenant and that of resolutions passed by southern unionists in 1911 **(84, 119)** shows, Ulster unionists felt their suspicions more deeply and expressed them more vehemently.

5 Extracts from a 31-page pamphlet, *A guide to the 'eighty-six',* published in 1886 by the I.L.P.U., attributing to the eighty-six home rule M.P.s elected in 1885 dishonourable and treasonable actions (D 989C/3/5):

. . . Mr. BIGGAR, a member of Parliament, a colleague of Mr. PARNELL and a member of the National League, has given it as his opinion that it is the duty of Irishmen who are members of the League "to use their exertions to get everything in favour of the person who is charged with such a crime as shooting a landlord." It is our ambition, and, on the whole, we believe it to be a more laudable one, to get a fair and honest hearing for those who are accused of no crime other than that of trusting the good faith of England, and of striving to obey the law of the land.

(p.10)

. . . There is hardly a member of the Eighty-six whose record would not be of interest; but space does not permit of a complete history. There is one prominent member of the party, however, whom it would be a pity to pass over altogether.

Next time Mr. MATTHEW HARRIS, M.P., rises in the House of Commons it will be an advantage if honourable members have the advantage of being acquainted with the following episodes in his history:—In 1886 Mr. MATTHEW HARRIS is a member of the Imperial Parliament and an *employé* of Mr.

PARNELL. In 1882—the year of the Phoenix Park murders—Mr. HARRIS was also an *employé* of Mr. PARNELL and a member of the Land League. It appears that in that year Mr. MICHAEL DAVITT and Mr. HARRIS fell out. Mr. HARRIS had committed himself to the statement that landlords should be shot down "like partridges in September." Mr. DAVITT, who, to his credit, has frequently objected to the baser forms of Parnellite crime, reprimanded Mr. HARRIS, and appears to have done so with considerable energy: indeed, if Mr. HARRIS is to be believed, he described that gentleman as "a snake, a traitor, a slanderer, a coward, a hireling of the enemy, a felon-setter, and a monster to be avoided as a leper." It is not for us to dispute Mr. DAVITT's judgment; he knew his man better than we pretend to; but the old Land Leaguer and present Member of Parliament appears to have been somewhat stung by his colleague's strictures. He wrote a long letter to Mr. O'BRIEN's paper, in which he certainly did his best to match Mr. DAVITT's epithets. Mr. MATTHEW HARRIS's (M.P.) Billingsgate is neither interesting nor important; but, in view of his present position, the following passage from his letter—a passage deliberately circulated among tens of thousands of Irish people—is important. This is what he says:—

"I tell that gentleman (Mr. Davitt), that though I do not go about from platform to platform canting about cruelty to animals, or caterwauling about the death of Lord Cavendish, I have as great, and I believe a greater abhorrence to the taking of human life than he has."

Those who have studied Mr. MATTHEW HARRIS' career may doubt the second part of his proposition. No one will do him the injustice of doubting the first. . . .

(p.30)

From the time when the member for Cork [Parnell] took up the business of "directing public opinion," down to the time when his chief director succeeded in eluding the police, and terminated his connexion with the Ladies' Land League, no less than 10,000 crimes were committed in Ireland, which crimes, in the opinion of nearly every member of Her Majesty's Government, of most of the Irish judges, and of a good many other people besides, were the direct handiwork of the society over which the member for Cork and Mr. P. J. Sheridan presided. . . .

(p.31)

This is not all, or nearly all, that could be said with regard to the Parnellites, their methods, and their aims. It can be indefinitely supplemented; but enough has been said to show that whoever hands over the lives and fortunes of his countrymen to the control of the men who lead the Irish National Land League will commit a crime. Of course it must not be forgotten that a National League Government means a return of all Mr. Parnell's old friends who ran away when the criminal law was strengthened. This is a responsibility which everyone who supports a Parnellite administration must be prepared to face. Some harsh judgments have been expressed in these pages with regard to the Parnellites; if the phrases appear inadequate, and the condemnation

19

too weak, we would refer our readers to the speeches of the Prime Minister of England, of Sir WILLIAM HARCOURT, of Lord SPENCER, of Mr. CHAMBER-LAIN, Mr. TREVELYAN, Mr. SHAW LEFEVRE, most of the Irish Law Officers of the Crown during the last five years, and the majority of the Irish judges.

6 Extracts from a 29-page pamphlet, *Union or separation,* published in 1886 by the I.L.P.U., noting among other things the 'lower class' nature of the home rule movement (D 989C/3/5):

(p. 11)

... Between those Roman Catholic laymen who have the courage to avow their sentiments of loyalty, and the fanatical rabble who rave against England— it is no longer against the 'Saxon'—there is a large mass of opinion, much of which is in favour of the Union, and much, no doubt, hostile to it; but, owing to the terrorism that prevails, it is impossible to say with certainty what proportion is on either side. Of one thing, however, we may be absolutely certain, that all the Roman Catholics of wealth and position, all the men of intelligence and culture, all who give strength and dignity to a cause, are on the side of loyalty and order. Of this we fortunately have evidence that cannot be controverted; we have but to summon Mr. Parnell's Parliamentary phalanx into court, and our case is proved. If the educated intellect, if the business energy, if the wealth of Catholic Ireland are on the side of revolution, why are they not to be found among the members sent to represent that cause in Parliament? No one knows better than Mr. Parnell how important it would be for his cause that he should be able to point to such men among his Parliamentary followers. No one will believe that he would not have been eager to secure their services if he could have done so. Why are they not there? We mention no names; but we challenge Mr. Parnell to show us among his eighty-five followers five such men. We go further: we challenge him to produce from among the whole number one man who is recognised in Ireland as a leader of Catholic opinion in any shape or form. There are plenty of such men in Ireland—men known and trusted by their co-religion-ists; men who have won for Irish Catholics many of the rights and privileges they possess, and who have never wavered in support of their cause. Why are these men not to be found among the representatives of Ireland in the new Parliament? The answer is, because they are unanimously opposed to the revolutionary designs of Mr. Parnell and his followers; because they are loyal to the English connection, from which they and their Church have derived so many benefits; because they foresee the condition of chaos and ruin to which their unhappy country would be reduced if it were handed over to be gov-erned by Mr. Parnell and his communistic crew. With what audacity can Mr. Parnell and his advocates in the Press assert that he represents the opinions or the aspirations of the Catholics of Ireland, if he cannot produce from among his eighty-five followers one single representative Catholic—one man recognized as a leader or exponent of Catholic opinion, or authorized to speak on behalf of the Catholics of Ireland?

Those politicians in England who think that they are bound to entertain Mr. Parnell's demands, because he makes them in the name of the 'Irish people,' should ponder well on these facts. If Mr. Parnell does not speak with the authority of the Protestants of Ireland, who form one-fourth of the population; if he does not speak in the name of the respectable and intelligent Catholics of Ireland, who certainly form at least another fourth of the population, in whose name and by what authority does he speak?

Let us grant for a moment, what we by no means admit, that Mr. Parnell represents the sentiments of the remaining half of the people of Ireland—let us see of what that half is composed. We say with perfect knowledge that it consists of the lowest half of the population; of tenant-farmers on a small scale, who aim at acquiring the ownership of the land they till without the usual preliminary operation of paying for it; of labourers who covet the land occupied by the farmers, and who see no adequate reason why they should not get their share of the plunder; but chiefly of the disaffected masses who have been taught for the past forty years by the seditious newspapers that find their way into every Irish peasant's house, to hate everything English, and to believe that separation from England would restore an era of national greatness and prosperity, such as is popularly believed to have existed in Ireland sometime before the birth of Christ. . . .

(p. 27)

Let there be no mistake in this matter. An Irish Parliament will be composed of the same elements as are found among the Irish Members now gathered under the banner unfurled by Mr. Parnell; only its members will be more numerous, more hostile to the friends of England, more unscrupulous— if that be possible—and more rapacious, less restrained by decency or prudence than they are now. And there is this further consideration, that then they will have full power to give effect to their hostility. If some eighty or ninety of the six hundred and seventy Members of the United Parliament can set the authority of the rest at defiance, how will they be controlled in an assembly of their own, where they will be in a majority of four to one? . . .

Chapter II

The opponents of home rule: the Irish landlords

Statements such as those quoted in chapter I represent in a generalised form the objections to home rule of a wide range of social and economic groups. While united in opposition to home rule and able to appreciate the objections of other individuals and groups, each individual and group had their own particular fear of home rule. The object of this and the next chapter is to describe the attitudes of some of these groups in more depth. General statements often obscured the deeper feelings of various groups, and it could be said that the various anti-home rule resolutions (**4,84,119**) represent almost the lowest common denominator between the various interest groups supporting the union. For instance, the difference between the tone of Ulster unionism and that of southern unionism can be largely explained by the fact that Ulster unionism represented many often conflicting interests, whereas southern unionism was more socially homogeneous; and by the fact that sectarian feelings ran higher in Ulster than in the southern provinces.

The materials in the N.I.P.R.O. tell us little of the groups at the lower end of the social scale; but they do help to explain or to describe in more depth the position and attitudes of several groups opposed to home rule: the businessmen; the protestant churches; those interested in higher education; and particularly the landed classes.

II

The earliest and most active Irish opponents of home rule were members of the old protestant landed ascendancy in the north and in the south. They were landlords who for years had occupied a dominant and, they thought, responsible role in Irish society. They have had their critics who have condemned them as exploiters of their tenantry, neglectful of the duties of property and sheltering behind agents.

The most famous absentee landlord of his generation was the 2nd marquis of Clanricarde (1832–1916), who owned some

57,000 acres in Galway and who used to insist upon rents or eviction. The result was that the 'plan of campaign' was implemented on his estate in the late 1880s with much publicity. Landlords, however, refused to accept Clanricarde as typical. They were, so they said, well aware that they had duties as well as rights and were quick to defend themselves against criticisms that were made in the 1880s. On the one hand, they acknowledged the duties of property; and, on the other, they tried to counter anti-landlord propaganda. They published lengthy and well-argued pamphlets, playing down the number of actual evictions, and denied that eviction necessarily involved cruelty and hardship to thousands of families. As they pointed out, on occasion eviction involved eviction from an oyster bed!

7 Extract from a 35-page pamphlet issued in 1889 by the I.L.P.U., entitled *The plan of campaign illustrated. Extra No. IV. Correspondence on the Clanricarde estate addressed to the editor of the 'Times':* **(a)** letter from T. W. Russell, 20 January 1889, criticising Clanricarde's neglect of his duties as a landlord; and **(b)** letter from the 4th earl of Erne, Crom Castle, Co. Fermanagh, 27 January, protesting against Russell's interference and blaming land agitation and land legislation for the apparent neglect of landlordly duties (D 989C/3/15A):

(p. 21)

(a)

. . . I now come to Lord Clanricarde himself, and, as I said at the beginning of this letter, his is a case for very plain speaking. On the morning of Thursday last I drove through the Portumna demesne. It covers 1,400 acres. Towards the right stand the ruins of the old castle, burnt some thirty years ago. They constitute a most picturesque object. Further on there is another castle going to ruin in a different way. After the fire which destroyed the ancestral mansion the late Marquis set to work and built a noble edifice entirely worthy of the demesne. There it stands, roofed and glazed, with the carpenter-work inside unfinished, and the outer doors unhung—never touched since the late Lord Clanricarde's death, in 1874. Of course, it is rapidly going to destruction. From this spot the prospect is a most lovely one. The Shannon flows within a few hundred yards of the house. In the distance the Galtees and the Devil's Bit are visible. As I stood and wondered at all around, I could not help exclaiming that this was a heritage it were well worth while to hold in fee. Near the stables, which open off a splendid courtyard, and which are now converted into a dwelling-house for Mr. Tener, there is a fine old Abbey, built, I believe, by the Dominicans in the 13th century. It might almost be made into a second Fountains. But it is going to wreck and ruin. One has to wade through muck and dirt to inspect it. Here in a hole in the wall lie the remains of the late Marquis and Marchioness. Close by are visible the excavations for, and the foundations of, a vault, designed by the late Marquis. But the work has been left where he left it. I was told that the remains of the late Lord Dunkellin, the brilliant leader of the Adullamites, lie in a neglected portion of the graveyard at Athenry. I asked Mr. Tener and others what Lord Clanricarde, with his vast rent-roll, contributed to the schools and charities on the estate. I found annual benefactions amounting to £10, and no more. At Loughrea the Resident magistrate, Mr. Hickson, deemed it necessary to apologize for his quarters, and declared he could not bring his family to live there. I asked why it was so. He could not get Lord Clanricarde to put a house in repair. This was his reply. I found the District Inspector much in the same plight. And the authorities told me they could not get even the police barrack repaired. Lord Clanricarde may say that he is a mere rent-charger; that he is not now the owner of the land. He could not plead this prior to 1881. He has never been near the place since 1872.* Few on the estate would know him were he now to visit it. I say that this man has abdicated his position. He has neglected every duty devolving on the owner of land. He has rights, and is not slow to demand the support of the Crown in enforcing them. It is time to tell his Lordship that he has also duties, and that by the systematic neglect of these in every particular he has become a public danger to the State. I do not know what Mr. Balfour will do. But I should fancy that at this moment Lord Clanricarde is to him the greatest Irish difficulty. His Lordship takes it easily enough in the Albany. Nothing that happens is at all likely to impair his digestion. Mr. Tener, acting for him, considers himself the man in the breach, the real defender at once of the British Empire and the Moral Law. Surrounded by an armed guard, the like of which is not to be seen on this side of Texas, he sallies forth to execute Lord Clanricarde's orders. He has done and will do his duty faithfully. Were there no other interests involved I should be glad to see the battle fought out between the League and Lord Clanricarde. They are entirely worthy of each other. But there are other interests at stake. And on the ground that Lord Clanricarde has so completely abdicated his functions as to imperil the interests of the State itself, I, for one, should heartily support a special Bill to relieve the County of Galway of his influence. I may be told that this is an extreme proposal. Of course it is. But I see no wrong to Lord Clanricarde in it. Let the Land Commission value his land. Let him be paid for it. Let him have his ducats. Thank God there is but one Lord Clanricarde. If it were otherwise the country would be in worse plight than it is.—I am, yours truly,

    T. W. RUSSELL.

---

* This is an error. He was at his father's funeral in 1874.

(b)

    SIR,—As the result of a somewhat inquisitorial research into Lord Clanricarde's private affairs, Mr. T. W. Russell has communicated the following facts to the public through the medium of your columns:—

    1. That the amount of Lord Clanricarde's subscriptions to schools and charities does not exceed £10.

2. That he has not completed the family mansion commenced by his father, the late Marquis.

3. That he is allowing an old abbey in the grounds attached to his residence to tumble down.

4. That he has not built a vault for the reception of the remains of his father and mother; and

5. That he will not keep in proper repair houses for the resident magistrate, district inspector, and constabulary.

The remedy suggested by Mr. Russell for the above state of things is apparently the compulsory expropriation of Lord Clanricarde by special Act of Parliament. It is not clear whether such expropriation is to include lands in his own hands as well as those let to tenants. If it is, I fear that a rather inconvenient precedent will be set, and that there may be an ugly rush to get rid of expensive and unprofitable mansions and demesnes, possibly through the employment of the same tactics as have proved so successful in Lord Clanricarde's case.

But, if the compulsory sale of their farms to the occupying tenants is alone contemplated, is it likely that the future proprietors will subscribe much more liberally than Lord Clanricarde to schools and charities; that they will finish the building of the castle of Portumna; prevent the abbey from falling further into decay; build a vault for the reception of the remains of the late Marquis and his wife; and provide the resident magistrate, district inspector, and constabulary with suitable residences? If they will not, and I do not think it will be for one moment contended that they will, I fail to see how the condition of the district will be bettered by a change of proprietorship.

Has it never occurred to Mr. Russell that the state of things which he has described, and which, unfortunately, is only a specimen of what is occurring elsewhere, is the inevitable outcome of a course of legislation which, besides curtailing seriously the incomes of the landlords, has deprived them of all interest in the country and has taken away from them every inducement to reside on and improve their estates? Your obedient servant,

ERNE.

8 23-page pamphlet, *A year's evictions in Ireland: January to December, 1886: statement and returns,* issued in 1887 by the I.L.P.U., price one penny, denying exaggerated reports of wholesale and cruel evictions —the appendices and footnotes have been omitted: (D 989C/3/6A):

IN Parliament, in the Press, and on Home Rule platforms, throughout the length and breadth of England, the changes have been rung upon the atrocities committed by Irish landlords in connexion with Irish land. Irish evictions are made the subject of regular quarterly parliamentary returns, and the sum total of those events have been summarized since the time of the Famine: and not merely so, but Mr. Michael Mulhall, aided by a vivid imagination and the multiplication table, has made every **person** evicted into a **family,** and with a generosity that puts the Census Commissioners to shame, counting **seven** individuals to every family, establishes, apparently to the satisfaction of Mr. Gladstone, the astounding proposition that since 1849 no fewer than **3,668,000** individuals have been evicted in Ireland!

And not only have the figures, both real and fictitious, been published, but the public are given to understand that every one of these cases is attended with circumstances of unheard-of cruelty. Mr. Gladstone has described them as "sentences of death," while less eminent authorities describe the tenants against whom these decrees have been executed as being "houseless and homeless," as "thrown on the roadside," or, according to the picturesque description of an English newspaper, "wandering aimlessly over the storm-swept hills."

With a view of correcting the erroneous impression created by these repeated and gross misstatements, the Irish Loyal and Patriotic Union determined, if possible, to ascertain the essential particulars in connexion with the evictions which took place in Ireland during the year 1886.

The first proceeding was to obtain from the Sheriff of each county an authoritative List of the Ejectment Decrees executed by him during the year, and the Committee of the Irish Loyal and Patriotic Union have gratefully to acknowledge the promptitude and readiness with which most of these officials placed the information at their disposal. The number of evictions stated in the Parliamentary papers to have taken place in Ireland during 1886 is **3781**. In a few instances the Committee, owing to changes in the shrievalty, and other causes, were unable to obtain the necessary information; but the lists received from these officials, numbering altogether **3533** cases, practically covers the whole ground.

Upon the receipt of the Sheriff's return, a form was immediately despatched to the plaintiff in each case, asking for an accurate statement of every particular that would be likely to throw light upon the circumstances attending the eviction.

In one or two counties—Kerry and Armagh more particularly—the Sheriffs had not kept a record of the addresses of the plaintiffs, and consequently it was found impossible to despatch the necessary forms to them, except where public lists or private local inquiries enabled the Committee to ascertain the addresses. However, in spite of these and other manifest disadvantages, the Committee think they may claim to have succeeded fairly well in their undertaking, when it is remembered that they have ascertained the particulars in no fewer than 3024 cases out of the total of **3533**, and that in 16 counties the information is available in almost **every case** returned by the Sheriff.

The first thing that will strike the reader who is unacquainted with the facts is, that **over 14 per cent. of the evictions accounted for are not from agricultural holdings at all,** or even from holdings with which land has anything whatever to do, but are evictions from **dwelling-houses** mainly situated in cities and towns. The number of these evictions is **434** out of the total of **3024.**

Besides these there were **67** evictions, if they can be so called, from **"townparks,"** and other non-agricultural holdings, such as osier-beds. (In one case there was an "eviction" from an oyster-bed.) Townparks, it may be stated, are fields or small portions of land adjacent to a town, and are held by persons living in that town for their accommodation; they are not "agricultural holdings," and are specially excluded from the provisions of the Land Act of 1881.

Proceeding still further, we find that the Sheriff executed decrees in **305 cases** where **the defendant did not reside on the holding,** but resided upon an adjacent farm, or had left the place derelict. It is evident that the scenes so often pictured in connexion with Irish evictions could not have taken place in this class of case. In fact, in these **305** cases there was no actual eviction at all.

There remain, therefore, to be dealt with **2218** cases of eviction from agricultural holdings on which the tenants resided at the time of the eviction.

An analysis of these cases shows that in 198 of them the cause of action was "On Title"—that is, the tenants had no legal right whatever to the holding. In some cases they were trespassers, in others they were wrongfully in possession under disputed wills and settlements, and in many of them the eviction was brought about by the tenant being indebted to the local shopkeeper or money lender, who sold the interest to satisfy his demand.

The elimination of the cases of title leaves 2020 cases of eviction from agricultural holdings with residences for non-payment of rent to be dealt with. These are really the cases which demand serious investigation.

Proceeding to examine the nature of the tenancy in each of these **2020** cases, we find that in **113** cases the farms were held under **lease,** in **668** the rents had been **judicially fixed** by the Land Court, and in **348** they were either non-judicial yearly tenancies, or cases in which no information was obtainable upon this point.

But the crucial question comes, were these **2020** families thrown from their homes on the roadside? Despite Nationalist oratory, a dispassionate investigation shows that in no fewer than **518** of the cases the defendants have been actually reinstated as **tenants,** and in **916** cases as **caretakers,** pending redemption. And what will appear still stranger is the fact that in **41** cases (**23** of them being in Ulster) the tenant, **even after eviction,** sold his right of redemption. To the ordinary English mind it is, no doubt, a cherished article of faith that once a man is evicted his interest is gone for ever. So far is this from being true, the tenant not only has six months after the eviction to redeem his holding, but, as these figures go to show, can even during that period sell his equity of redemption, free himself from all arrears with his landlord, and in many instances put a considerable sum in his pocket. For instance, in one case, in the county Kilkenny, a tenant was evicted from 3 holdings for non-payment of 2½ years' rent, amounting to £150. The interest was sold (in this case *after* the period for redemption had expired), and after paying the amount of rent due, the tenant received £300. In another case in the same county a tenant owed £30, the amount of 3 years' rent. His equity of redemption was subsequently sold for a sum equal to 15 years' rent, viz. £150. Again, in Fermanagh, a tenant evicted for non-payment of 2 years' rent, amounting to £8 7s., sold his interest to a neighbouring farmer for £100, while another tenant in the same county, also evicted for non-payment of 2 years' rent, amounting to £12 11s. 4d., sold his interest for £45.

It will be noticed that this privilege is more largely availed of in Ulster than in the other provinces.

The sum total of the eviction record is, that **out of 2020 cases there were 545, or about 27 per cent., in which tenants were evicted from agricultural holdings, on which there were residences, for non-payment of rent, and were not re-admitted in any form by the landlord.**

An inquiry into the legal status of these 545 evicted tenants shows (*a*) that they have a period of six months' grace after the date of eviction, during which they can redeem their holdings or (*b*) sell their equity of redemption (*c*). During that period the landlord will have to account to them for any profit he could have made out of their farms And, further, (*d*) during these six months the tenant, in case he does not wish to redeem, can obtain from his landlord payment for all improvements which he may have made, namely, permanent buildings, reclamation of waste lands, or unexhausted manures; and (*e*) in case the rent does not exceed £15, in addition to the value of the improvement, a sum which may equal 7 years' rent, where the court declares the rent to have been an exorbitant one. (See an "Irish Tenant's Privileges," Appendix A, p. 473).

It only remains to add, that before proceeding to evict a tenant a landlord is bound, under a penalty of £20, to give 48 hours' notice to the Relieving Officer of the Poor Law Union, so that shelter and food may be provided for the evicted family.

Another point, which is a fair subject for inquiry, is the amount of rent generally owing by a tenant before extreme proceedings are taken against him. It will be apparent that much need for enlightenment exists with regard to this feature of the Land Question, when it is mentioned that one speaker in England—a man of considerable local influence—recently gave a circumstantial account, to a large meeting in the place in which he resides, of a family he had interviewed when in Ireland, that had been evicted from an agricultural holding in the South for non-payment of a quarter's rent! Of course no one possessing even the most elementary acquaintance with the law would have been guilty of making such an absurd statement: the fact being that **a tenant cannot be evicted for non-payment unless there is at least one year's rent due.** But, as a matter of fact, Irish landlords do not, in the vast majority of cases, avail themselves of this right. Indeed, in only 12 per cent. of the cases have proceedings been taken for non-payment of merely one year's rent, and in 52 per cent., or over half the total number, the amount of rent due was two and a-half years' and over, while **the average amount of rent due in the 760 cases dealt with in the return under consideration was two and a-half years' at the time of obtaining the decree.** Without the slightest exaggeration, it may safely be said that **the average amount of rent due at the time of eviction in these cases was three and a-half years,** because a considerable time often elapses after the decree is pronounced before it is put into force.

TABLE I.—*Analysis of Eviction Returns,*

NAME OF COUNTY.	No. of Cases returned by Sheriff.	Cases in which detailed Information has been received.	NATURE OF HOLDING.			
			Houses only.	Town Parks, or other Non-agricultural Holding.	Agricultural Holdings without Residence.	Agricultural Holdings with Residence.
	1	2	3	4	5	6
Donegal, ...	330	329	31	8	40	250
Monaghan, . . .	150	150	7	4	18	121
Cavan, . . .	146	145	5	4	9	127
Tyrone, . . .	136	136	10	3	9	114
Down, . . .	88	75	25	5	11	34
Londonderry, . . .	56	54	8	2	1	43
Fermanagh, . . .	56	52	—	1	5	46
Armagh, . . .	76	15	2	—	5	8
Antrim, . . .	49	48	7	3	5	33
Total of ULSTER, .	1087	1004	95	30	103	776
King's County, . . .	62	62	21	1	4	36
Queen's County, . .	63	63	21	1	5	36
Carlow, . . .	31	31	13	—	8	10
Wicklow, . . .	35	32	14	1	3	14
Longford, . . .	68	63	4	—	8	51
Louth, . . .	27	27	16	—	2	9
Meath, . . .	47	36	9	7	2	18
Westmeath, . .	62	50	10	1	4	35
Kildare, . . .	27	22	10	—	6	6
Dublin, . . .	40	26	24	—	1	1
Kilkenny, . . .	51	46	7	4	7	28
Wexford, . . .	111	92	18	2	12	60
Total of LEINSTER, . .	624	550	167	17	62	304
Clare, ...	75	75	20	4	8	43
Cork, ...	84	84	3	—	3	78
Tipperary, . . .	57	46	2	2	8	34
Waterford, . . .	58	52	10	—	3	39
Kerry, . . .	448	189	31	—	9	149
Limerick, . . .	61	61	8	2	12	39
Total of MUNSTER, . .	783	507	74	8	43	382
Galway, . . .	229	224	28	—	22	174
Mayo, . . .	372	316	33	8	35	240
Roscommon, . . .	192	187	7	4	14	162
Sligo, . . .	75	67	16	—	6	45
Leitrim, . . .	171	169	14	—	20	135
Total of CONNAUGHT, .	1039	963	98	12	97	756
TOTAL, . . .	**3533**	**3024**	**434**	**67**	**305**	**2218**

AGRICULTURAL HOLDINGS WITH RESIDENCES. ☞ (SEE COL. 6.)

PROCEEDINGS INSTITUTED.		EVICTIONS FOR NON-PAYMENT OF RENT. ☞ (SEE COL. 8.)						
		NATURE OF TENANCY.						
On Title. 7	For Non-payment of Rent. 8	Leasehold. 9	Judicial Tenancies. 10	Non-Judicial Yearly Tenancies. 11	Reinstated as Tenant. 12	Right of Redemption sold by Tenant after Eviction. 13	Reinstated as Caretaker. 14	Not readmitted. 15
20	230	6	123	101	45	5	139	41
10	111	2	42	67	18	2	79	12
10	117	5	27	85	36	5	63	13
—	114	3	50	61	34	3	74	3
6	28	3	7	18	9	1	11	7
19	24	—	8	16	6	2	8	8
—	46	—	21	25	7	3	18	18
—	8	3	3	2	6	—	—	2
—	33	4	10	19	19	2	5	7
65	711	26	291	394	180	23	397	111
4	32	—	5	27	7	—	10	15
6	30	1	11	18	4	—	18	8
2	8	2	—	6	2	—	4	2
4	10	—	3	7	1	—	8	1
3	48	—	10	38	7	—	24	17
4	5	—	1	4	—	—	3	2
5	13	—	3	10	2	—	7	4
6	29	2	6	21	4	—	15	10
1	5	3	1	1	1	—	3	1
—	1	—	—	1	1	—	—	—
2	26	—	6	20	11	2	8	5
16	44	7	4	33	5	—	21	18
53	251	15	50	186	45	2	121	83
11	32	—	5	27	5	—	6	21
2	76	44	9	23	8	—	45	23
3	31	2	9	20	9	—	15	7
7	32	3	15	14	4	1	8	19
2	147	12	38	97	32	2	49	64
5	34	—	2	32	4	2	16	12
30	352	61	78	213	62	5	139	146
11	163	1	24	138	43	—	48	72
21	219	3	113	103	96	6	80	37
9	153	2	61	90	60	1	62	30
6	39	—	13	26	9	1	24	5
3	132	5	38	89	23	3	45	61
50	706	11	249	446	231	11	259	205
198	**2020**	**113**	**668**	**1239**	**518**	**41**	**916**	**545**

TABLE II.

Amount of Rent due (in years) at time of Eviction.

NAME OF COUNTY.	Total.	1	1½	2	2½	3	3½	4	4½	5	5½	6	6½ and over	Average.
Donegal,	230	10	20	40	25	64	21	18	2	7	2	13	8	2½
Monaghan,	111	2	21	20	14	24	10	13	4	1	—	—	2	3
Cavan,	117	12	24	28	14	13	7	10	2	2	1	1	3	2
Tyrone,*.	113	12	11	31	15	13	8	12	4	3	—	2	2	3
Down,	28	5	1	8	6	6	—	1	—	—	1	—	—	2
Londonderry,	24	4	1	4	2	3	1	5	1	—	—	1	2	3
Fermanagh,	46	5	9	12	9	4	4	1	1	1	—	—	—	2
Armagh,.	8	1	—	2	2	2	—	—	—	—	—	—	1	3
Antrim,	33	3	1	10	6	7	3	2	1	—	—	—	—	2½
Total of ULSTER,	710	54	88	155	93	136	54	62	15	14	4	17	18	2½
King's Co.,	32	4	3	4	3	3	—	1	2	2	1	3	6	3
Queen's Co.,*	29	—	—	4	5	3	5	5	3	—	3	1	—	3½
Carlow,	8	—	1	6	—	—	—	—	—	1	—	—	—	2
Wicklow,	10	—	2	1	3	1	3	—	—	—	—	—	—	2½
Longford,	48	13	9	9	8	4	2	3	—	—	—	—	—	2
Louth,	5	1	1	1	—	1	—	1	—	—	—	—	—	2
Meath,	13	7	1	1	3	—	—	1	—	—	—	—	—	1
Westmeath,	29	12	5	4	2	1	1	1	—	1	1	—	1	2½
Kildare,.	5	—	1	2	1	—	—	—	1	—	—	—	—	2½
Dublin,	1	—	1	—	—	—	—	—	—	—	—	—	—	1½
Kilkenny,	26	1	8	3	4	4	2	3	—	—	—	—	—	2
Wexford,	44	2	12	5	7	2	4	7	—	—	—	2	3	3
Total of LEINSTER,	250	40	44	40	36	19	17	22	7	4	5	6	10	2½
Clare,	32	1	4	4	7	9	—	1	—	1	—	3	2	3
Cork,	76	19	14	24	5	7	1	4	—	2	—	—	—	2
Tipperary,	31	5	10	5	2	5	3	1	—	—	—	—	—	2
Waterford,	32	6	8	8	2	2	3	1	2	—	—	—	—	2
Kerry,	147	26	34	39	17	17	4	3	2	3	—	1	1	2
Limerick,	34	11	9	9	4	1	—	—	—	—	—	—	—	1½
Total of MUNSTER.	352	68	79	89	37	41	11	10	4	6	—	4	3	2
Galway,	163	12	49	22	26	15	10	6	—	4	5	7	7	2½
Mayo,	219	29	38	42	35	26	16	11	7	6	4	1	4	2¼
Roscommon,	153	29	26	31	27	7	13	6	2	1	5	4	2	2
Sligo,	39	6	7	8	7	3	2	2	—	—	—	1	3	2
Leitrim,	132	—	22	31	20	27	11	12	2	1	1	2	3	2½
Total of CONNAUGHT,	706	76	142	134	115	78	52	37	11	12	15	15	19	2¼
TOTAL,.	2018	238	353	418	281	274	134	131	37	36	24	42	50	2½

*NOTE.—In one case in Tyrone, and one in Queen's County, no information is given.

The following statement analyses in detail **2018** cases of eviction for non-payment from agricultural holdings with residences, calculating in each case only the amount of rent due when proceedings were first commenced for recovery of possession. Two cases in which no information is given accounts for the total of **2020** given above. (See Table II.)

238 cases, or 11.8 per cent., in which 1 year's rent was due.

353	,,	17.05	,,	,,	$1\frac{1}{2}$	,,
418	,,	20.17	,,	,,	2	,,
281	,,	13.9	,,	,,	$2\frac{1}{2}$	,,
274	,,	13.6	,,	,,	3	,,
134	,,	6.7	,,	,,	$3\frac{1}{2}$	,,
131	,,	6.5	,,	,,	4	,,
37	,,	1.8	,,	,,	$4\frac{1}{2}$	,,
36	,,	1.7	,,	,,	5	,,
24	,,	1.1	,,	,,	$5\frac{1}{2}$	,,
42	,,	2.1	,,	,,	6	,,
50	,,	2.6	,,	over	$6\frac{1}{2}$	,,

III

Among the various collections in the N.I.P.R.O. relating to landlords and landed estates, there is a very good illustration of a landlord executing his duties to the best of his abilities—in the Montgomery papers. The Montgomery family had come to Ireland at the beginning of the seventeenth century from Ayrshire, Scotland. Hugh de Fellenberg Montgomery of Blessingbourne, Fivemiletown, Co. Tyrone, was born in 1844 and died in 1924. Educated at Christ Church College, Oxford, and a captain of the Fermanagh militia, he succeeded to the family estates in 1868. They were extensive, 7,996 acres in Co. Fermanagh, 4,552 in Co. Tyrone. In 1878 the gross annual valuation of these 12,448 acres was £4,925. This substantial valuation did not mean that Montgomery was without financial difficulties, as he had a family to raise, suffered from ill-health requiring costly medical treatment and sojourns abroad, and was the victim of credit squeezes caused by periods of economic stress in Ireland which reduced rents and made credit difficult. Moreover he felt a victim of Gladstone's second land act of 1881.

Under the terms of this act, land courts had been set up to fix a 'judicial rent', on application from either landlord or tenant. The courts could determine a rent or, alternatively, a landlord and tenant could come to an agreement and have this agreed rent registered as a judicial rent. Rents so fixed were originally to stand for fifteen years; but this provision was modified by the land act of 1887 which permitted these first term rents to be altered in accordance with falling agricultural prices. Since the procedures of the courts were slow and the principles upon which they operated not always evident, and since rents were almost invariably lowered, the courts became a source of grievance among landlords. On the first term rents, they suffered a reduction of 20.7%, or an annual loss of £1,551,339; on the second term rents the reduction was 19.5%, involving an annual loss of £491,591. Altogether between 1881 and 1903 landlords lost some £30 million through the operation of judicial rents, with little hope of interrupting the downward trend. They could appeal but the expense of appeal was high, on the average £10, and out of all proportion to the results obtained. Up to 1894 appeals had cost £105 for each £1 added to the rent. Not unnaturally, therefore, Montgomery was one of the fiercest critics of the 1881 act.

9 Letter from H. de F. Montgomery to his solicitor, G. Ford, Lincoln's Inn Fields, London, 28 June 1872, seeking advice on raising money towards the building of a new house at Blessingbourne (D 627/235):

Dear Mr. Ford—I find myself—with my growing family—under the necessity of building myself a house at Blessingbourne, but find that, at present prices, I cannot get one built that would suit me for less than about £7000, while all the ready money I have at present at command is about £3500. I write to ask you, therefore, what powers I have under my settlements to raise a couple of thousand for such a purpose and to ask your advice generally on the matter. I should also be obliged if you would look at the builder's contract for me before I sign it and see that it is all square and safe. I have asked Mr Cockerell the architect to have it sent to you for that purpose as soon as it is ready.

Till July 8th my address is the Barracks. Enniskillen. where I am doing all the drill the rain allows of with our militia—After that I shall be at Blessingbourne. believe me Yrs very truly

Hugh de F Montgomery

10 Letter from Montgomery, Cannes, to Ford, 18 February 1881, explaining his financial difficulties (D 627/308):

Dear Mr. Ford—My uncle, Mr. Charles Müller, has ascertained for me, from his legal adviser that property in Switzerland owned by foreigners is not subject to the lex loci as regards inheritance and testamentary powers but to

the law of the owners country. Does the English law treat "foreign posses-
sions" in land as realty or personalty? If the former it will hardly be worth
my while making a codicil for this matter as it will go, as I wish, to my eldest
son without it. If, however, it would, for any reason be wiser for me to leave
it in black and white, will you kindly prepare a codicil for me, simply leaving
all property I may be possessed of in Switzerland—or my share of the Hofwyl
estate—or however it should be expressed—to my eldest son.

I also want your help in another matter. I outran the constable considerably in building and furnishing my new house at Blessingbourne—altogether
to the tune of some £8000. About £5000 of this I raised on promissary [*sic*]
notes in the country; the rest I got leave to overdraw at the Northern Banking
Co.'s (Ireland) Bank, expecting to be able to pay it off very soon—at the rate
of from £500 to £1000 a year, at least. I have, however, had a run of bad luck
since. An abortive railway scheme. Expensive journeys in search of health.
Dr's bills, abatements of rent grants; in aid of distress in 1879 &c&c and I
find that at the end of six years the paying off has not yet begun. The promissary [*sic*] notes are still out and the over draught at the bank having been at
one time reduced to £800 is now up to £3000 again. It is not unlikely that
rents may be rather ill paid for some time to come and one does not know
what may turn up and I have come to the conclusion that it would be more
comfortable for me to get a permanent loan of £3000 (at 4 or 4½ per cent) for
6 or 8 or 10 years and do away with this overdraught (of which they may any
day run up the interest to 7 or 8 per cent—though hitherto it has only varied
between 5 & 6—) and set to work to pay off the promissary [*sic*] notes steadily
during that period if circumstances allow it. Do you think you could get this
for me on the securities in your hands? There is no absolute hurry for a few
weeks or months. The Bank people are not objecting and I shall shortly get
some rents, wherewith to reduce the figure a little.

Let me have your opinion at your leisure and believe me Yrs very truly

Hugh de F Montgomery.

11 Letter from Montgomery, writing from Bailey's Hotel, Gloucester
Road, London, to Ford, 22 May 1881, on the difficulty of obtaining
a mortgage on the security of Irish property (D 627/322):

Dear Mr. Ford—It is a bore about this money but, as you say, it cannot
be helped.

The only thing that occurs to me is to ask you to tell me candidly whether
you think the distrust of Irish landed security is so strong and widespread as
to make the chance of my getting the £3000 here within, say, two months at
a reasonable rate, really a bad one, as in that case I had better try to get it in
Ireland from one of the Banks there, which are full of money, but wont lend
at less than 5 per cent usually.

Ceteris paribus, I would rather get it here as the securities are with you.

Do you think that it is necessary or desirable for me to make any addition
to my will with regard to my Swis [*sic*] property, which, as at present advised
I wish to leave to my eldest son, or may I leave the law to give it to him?
Yrs very truly

Hugh de F. Montgomery

12 Letter from Montgomery to Ford, 5 November 1882, expressing dissatisfaction with the new land courts which reduced rents too much for landlords and insufficiently for tenants (D 627/331):

Dear Mr. Ford—Thanks for your note and for having carried through the sale of 15 Norfolk Crescent for me, and lodged the money.

I shall not clear as much as I at one time hoped to get for the house & contents, but I am very glad to have the whole thing, with the various worries &c. connected with it off my mind—as it no longer suits me or is likely to suit me to live in that quarter. The general state of this country is on the mend, but we are in a most uncomfortable position with regard to our rents, the mode in which the Land Act has been administered and the preaching of demagogues having persuaded every tenant in the country that his rent should be substantially reduced—however moderate it may have been.

The working of the Land Commission Courts is so slow & the costs of having cases heard in them so considerable that most of us are trying (like the snakes in the legend of St Patrick who "committed suicide to save themselves from slaughter") to come to some settlement by giving reductions in all directions, whether really called for or not—but this too is a very difficult process, as the amount of reduction a tenant is disposed to accept to agree to a judicial rent depends usually entirely on the man's character and the special irrational crotchet on the subject of rent he has taught himself out of the popular press and not at all on the merits, or even the relative merits of the case.

Sweeping as the reductions of rent in the Land Commission Courts seem to us, there is now an almost universal outcry among the tenants here in Ulster (hitherto the contented province) that they are far too small and altogether inadequate. The season has turned out so badly in some respects that I live in dread of this outcry developing into a new and very serious agitation.

I am often inclined to despair of any end to it all short of ruin to landlords and confusion for everyone else—but I think the sounder view is that if we get a steady government and a couple of good harvests sooner or later farmers will get tired of agitating & forget some of their wild notions Yrs very truly

Hugh de F Montgomery

13 Letter from Montgomery to Ford, 7 October 1887, describing his continuing financial difficulties and his attempts to overcome them (D 627/345):

Dear Mr. Ford—My agent, Mr. Pomeroy, has written, he tells me, for some documents from you for my use, in my absence, but is not sure whether he directed his letter right, so, in case of accidents, I also write to ask you to let him have a copy of the £18000 old mortgage and also of the £3000 mortgage to Mr. McG. Bond. I suppose you hold copies of these documents.

I am negociating [*sic*] for a loan of a larger sum with which to pay off Mr. Bond as well as a number of promissory notes on which I have borrowed considerable sums from time to time expecting to be able to pay them off out of income which the continual slicing down of rents & the expense of educating six boys—4 at school—has made hopeless for the present.

It is also important that these debts should be brought into such a shape that, in case I am to be "bought out" as a landlord I can, as a limited owner, apply the proceeds to clear them off.

Things do not look very bright—but if the government is firm I believe the worst is over. Yrs very truly

Hugh de F Montgomery

IV

These personal financial difficulties did not prevent Montgomery from carrying out his duties as a landlord. He was almost a model landlord, protestant and unionist. He was an active unionist who maintained close contact with unionists in the three southern provinces, an active member of the synod of the Church of Ireland, and an untiring champion of landlord rights. Nevertheless, contrary to the popular view of men of his ilk, he took his duties as a landlord seriously. Like many, if not most, men in his position in localised, paternalist Irish society, he saw himself as and acted, perhaps more than most, as half magistrate and landlord, half friend and counsellor, anxious to act in the best interests of his tenants and locality. Although tending towards atheism, he attended church regularly to set a good example and took an interest in developing the locality, helping to establish among other things a local railway.

He was a very humane man. He took an interest in the specific problems of his servants (such as his former butler, whom he went to great trouble to save from the evils of drink), tenants or groups in the locality. He helped the shop assistants at Fivemiletown to win a half day holiday per week, and although at times in conflict with the local Roman Catholic priest—as distinct from the laity—he was solicitous of the welfare of his catholic tenantry. Most importantly, he was ready to help his tenants in time of distress by granting reductions in rent and by contributing to relief committees, particularly in the early 1880s. Although criticised for not making larger reductions, he had to pay attention to the

37

opinion of neighbouring landlords and the advice of his agent, John Pomeroy, who pointed out that conditions varied from estate to estate and that reductions made upon one sorely distressed estate need not apply to another less severely hit.

14 Letter from Montgomery, writing from Aix-les-Bains, to Ford, 3 October 1877, expressing concern over the future of his former butler who was in danger of drinking himself to death—the name of the butler has been left blank (D 627/244):

Dear Mr. Ford—The ailment that I think I mentioned last time I had occasion to write to you has now driven me abroad for the winter, at any rate, & possibly for longer, in hopes that a drier climate may effect what doctors and rest have failed to do.

I now want you to help me to try and make an arrangement to prevent our mutual friend [—] from going to the bad in my absence—I am afraid not a hopeful job. His character—though, I believe, incorruptible as to honesty to his employers, is otherwise very weak, almost childish & since the death of his wife who kept him in great order, he has been getting into the way of drinking occasionally, I believe simply from want of power of saying no to certain friends or acquaintances. As long as he was with me he was, of course, under a certain restraint, but now that is removed I am afraid that, unless he can be induced to enter into some stringent arrangement, he will go to the devil post haste. He has been so faithful a servant for so long that I would do a good deal to prevent this if possible. Under the circumstances I did not think him fit to bring out with me—much less to leave in charge of my house in Ireland & I thought it would be mistaken kindness to leave him independent in London (when my house is let) on good wages. I therefore gave him a months warning and he ceased to be my servant on the 27th. ult. I told him at the time my reasons & also that, if he would agree to it, I should shortly propose to him some arrangement by which he might keep up his connexion with me while seeking some regular employment elsewhere for 6 months or more & by which, if on my return he could bring me a trustworthy character or testimonial of perfect sobriety, he should get good wages & some honorable & easy employment from me again. He has, however, some £500 or more in the funds besides £50 he lent me some time ago & which for the present I hold on to (giving him 4% for it), and being such a fool as he now is it would be necessary to induce him to hand over this money to someone in trust for him or his heirs if we are to have any hope of reformation by putting him on short commons for a time. This is one reason why I have recourse to you in the matter as, of course, this, if practicable, must be arranged by a lawyer. The other reason is that I was so much bothered with preparations before leaving London that I found no time to think about the details of any plan for his restraint. May I ask you to send for him at your convenience and propose to him on my behalf (1) that he should put his savings out of his power to touch, except by your or my consent. (2) that he should seek regular work—if possible at his old trade of plasterer—with a thoroughly respectable employer whose word as to his sobriety we can take (3) that while looking for such employment or if thrown out of it not by his own fault, or if bona fide ill (as he sometimes is) he will get a small allowance from me sufficient to pay his rent & get him food but no drink. (4) that if after 8 or 9 months he brings me a perfectly satisfactory character from his employer I will take him into my service again at £30 or £40 a year & his board—not as butler, but as confidential servant—clerk of works over buildings in Ireland &c&c & to make himself generally useful as hitherto in Ireland or in London as may be required (I will not put him again over servants who have never transgressed in that way).

Of course I shall be obliged for any suggestions from you in the way of improvements on this plan—or any substitute for it. My only hope of his agreeing to it lies in the fact that when spoken seriously to on the subject he admits that he will ruin himself body and soul with drink if he goes on as he has been doing. On the other hand, however, I am sorry to say he seems very soon to get over the effects of a lecture and during the last few months he has once or twice attempted to deny the offence or make excuses, which up to this summer he never attempted to do. This is a very bad sign. He also on my visitation & after some days deliberation (insisted on by me) signed a promise in the summer of last year to drink, while in my service, no intoxicating liquor except the beer he got with his meals—His having broken this is another bad feature, so you see it is a forlorn hope after all—but I shall be much obliged, if you will do what you can to make it succeed, as it will be most painful to see a man who served my aunt for so many years—to say nothing of myself—drink himself to death—as I'm sure he will if he is left alone—I sometimes think the company etc. he got into in his connexion with the W. divorce may have had something to do with his falling into bad habits. I know his wife before her death used to think his good manners were being corrupted by the evil communications of that time. We shall be here for another ten days and after that

care of W. Congreve Esq.

H.BM's.V. Consul

San Remo. Italy

will find me. [—]'s lodgings are 133 Marylebone Road, W. I shall hope to hear from you when you have leisure to attend to this matter. There is no great hurry, as [—] will have money in hand when I have paid him the balance of his wages &c which I shall do in a few days when I get his account which is now on its way. Yrs very faithfully

Hugh de F. Montgomery

15 Letter from Sir Victor Brooke, Colebrook, Co. Fermanagh, to Montgomery, 6 September 1879, arguing that they have less need to grant abatements than some of their neighbours (D 627/307B):

Wrench has received a letter fr. Pomeroy relative to the reduction of rent, or rather abatement to meet present circumstances. My own idea is that you and I are v. differently situated to Ld. Erne, Archdale & John Porter &c who have granted abatements. None of our property is subject to the flooding wh. has rendered a large part of properties near L[ough]. Erne absolutely unproductive this villainous season; nor ar[e] we shaking in our shoes at the prospect of future elections. Times are bad even for our men, but I think that the badness hits individuals & not the mass. As individual cases occur I shall abate where I see that it is absolutely called for, but the better-to-do lot must take the bitter with the sweet, & weather the storm as I must do myself. Nearly all my property is let under the Govt. valuation & the tenants have had their land on v. easy terms except in a few cases in the mountain districts. I believe you are made in the same box, however. Let me know what y[our]. opinion is in the matter.

We were very glad to see Mrs. Montgomery. vy truly

Victor Brooke

16 Letter from J. Pomeroy, Killeter, to Montgomery, 1 December 1879, playing down the extent of distress in Fivemiletown in the harsh winter of 1879, but suggesting various ways of providing employment there through the winter (D 627/286A):

Dear Montgomery—There is not anything like the distress you seem to think at Fivemiletown: for the last 2 years there has always been a want of work and more or less a want of firing in the winter there & the people who were in the habit of stealing turf are now obliged to steal sticks from their neighbors [*sic*] fences. There are always people who would wish you to give & spend money to no end, it adds to their honor & glory & costs them nothing but knowing how ill you can afford it I am very unwilling to let you spend money which partly encourages idleness & improvidence

I think if possible I will make thinnings which can well be spared do quite well unless there comes another of these hard frosts everybody else is just doing the same as far as possible & if I am obliged to use coal I can take from the store at the house and re-place it later coal not seeming to be inclined to rise. When I go to Blessingbourne next I will set Casey to the clearing of the place next the avenue & if I find it absolutely necessary will set some other work going

I have the spot for the new school and Masters house to drain, fence and plant and the Alderwood [?] forge at present school also to fence, open drain and plant. £3 a week would employ 8 or 10 men for 8 weeks till the 1st of March when there will be spring work and only cost £24.

I think £4 or £5 sent to Rev. Woods to provide clothing where necessary for some of the children & old people in Muluavale [Mullavale] would probably be the best thing there but the people there are really none of them badly off they took in grazing cattle and the people who had to pay them were the real people to be pitied. I got an answer from the Board to say the school business was now in the hands of the Board of Works for report. I have now written to the Board of Works

I find there is a determination here not to pay any rent as they are getting no abatement the owners holding that when the tenant right is as high as from 20 to 30 years purchase they have no real reason to give an abatement— The men here who are giving trouble are all of the class that the Lendrums & Browes are with you: of course there are some miserable people up in the mountains but I could manage to nurse them through—When writing last I forgot to tell you that Alexander had never furnished his account I think he is just as careless as ever & am caused constant anxiety by him. I have got the £618 for the purchase of Troray [Trory] Glebe at which I am pleased. We are going to send Arthur to Uppingham at Easter. Yours sincerely

John A. Pomeroy.

17 Printed circular sent by Montgomery to his tenants, 10 February 1881, announcing rent abatements of 20% for tenants paying £10 and under and 10% for tenants paying over £10 (D 627/307A):

Having been informed that, notwithstanding the good harvest of last year, many tenant farmers have not yet recovered from the effects of the preceding bad times, I have decided to offer 20 per cent. on the half-year's rent now due to all tenants from year to year on my BLESSINGBOURNE ESTATE, whose holdings are rented at £10 per annum and under, and 10 per cent. to those whose holdings are rented at over £10 per annum, who pay on or before the 30th April next.

Tenants of holdings rented at £10 or under will also receive the same abatement on all arrears due from the year 1879, paid on or before the date above mentioned.

I hope we may now look forward to some good seasons, and that no further abatements of this kind will be required for a long time.

Some of my tenants have suggested that their rents ought to be permanently reduced. As soon as the new Land Act has been made law, and the present excitement and agitation has subsided, I shall be prepared to inquire into all such cases, and refer any in which my decision does not satisfy the tenant to some impartial tribunal for settlement, or to have the whole property re-valued under the direction of such a tribunal and the rents readjusted with due regard to tenants' interests in the value of their improvements. Where rents were raised to the full value in prosperous times during the last 10 or 20 years they ought, most likely, to be now reduced.

As few, if any, of my agricultural rents have been so raised. I do not believe that much permanent reduction can be needful on my property.

It is much to be deplored that thoughtless persons should have prepared disappointment for many tenant farmers, by leading them to expect reductions of rent, such as neither landlords nor legislation can possibly give them.

HUGH De F. MONTGOMERY.

18 Letter from J. Pomeroy to Montgomery, Cannes, 17 April 1881, discussing the nature and extent of distress in the Fivemiletown area and how Montgomery could best assist the distressed (D 627/297A):

Dear Montgomery—Did I send you a list of the abatements for flood that I proposed making in Ardelea? If I did & you have it would you kindly send me a note of them for I have mislaid my own notes.

I was in Fivemiletown yesterday. There are no less than 55 families or individuals being relieved by the Committee in 5miletown & the neighborhood [*sic*] on your property at a weekly expense of about £4.10.0. Out of those there are only 7 cases where there is a working man in the family & they have work at 1/3 & 1/11 a day but have large families the rest are old men & women & cripples.

The shopkeepers & relief committee say that these people are all absolutely in want & must get the relief but a great many other people say that they are in much the same state as usual except that they cannot live as they used to do on what they get now their habits having changed during the good times & that they are therefore badly off in spite of food being so cheap—I dont know what to think but I can see no reason why those who are getting relief now should not get it to the end of the chapter, except where there is a laboring man & if this turns out a good year no doubt some time or other the farmers will be able to give more wages & probably some employment even to the cripples &c in the way of light work. You had heard that the Committee decided on applying again got £20 (I think it was) from the "Herald" fund, none of the proprietors in the district had contributed a halfpenny. there are about an equal number receiving relief on the Aughentain[e] estate as on the Blessingbourne. I really dont know what you can do better than subscribing to the relief fund because if you are disposed to think that there is really distress your taking the thing on your own shoulders would lead to a permanent charge of £4.10 a week till nobody knows when. I cannot help thinking that the £12 a week divided among the shopkeepers of ready money has something to say to it. At any rate you know now all that I know or think.

The foundations of the school are opened & stones raised &c I wish you had been here to fix the exact site. However I think it is all right. I lodged £90 to your C[redi]t yesterday & I should think it probable that I shall get £200 on the fair day but can'nt [*sic*] tell for money is doubtless scarce & the abatements make a great hole in each rent as one gets it. I remain yours sincerely

J. A. Pomeroy

V

It is quite understandable that because of their dominant position in Irish society, landlords should oppose the home rule movement which by the 1880s had developed on class and sectarian lines. Perhaps the most important factor in determining the landlord attitudes to the home rule movement was its identification with the class hatred and disorder of the Land League and subsequent agitations. There were many indications of landlord reaction to agrarian disorder, but one of the more lasting was the Cork Defence Union. It was founded in 1885 in order to protect landlords and tenants from the consequences of censure by the National League.

19

Extracts from a 24-page pamphlet issued by the Cork Defence Union, March 1886, describing its aims and achievements, and including **(a)** the objects of the Union; **(b)** the executive committee and officers; **(c)** letter from the Union to Mr Gladstone describing its work; and **(d)** some case studies in boycotting (T 2759/2):

(a)

1. This Union to be non-sectarian and non-political.

2. To unite together all friends of law and order of all classes in this county in a body, for their mutual defence and protection.

3. To resist the tyranny now exercised over many persons in this country by a body calling themselves "The Irish National League."

4. To assist and support as far as possible all persons—landowners, merchants, farmers, shopkeepers, artisans, or labourers—who, for asserting their just and lawful rights, have incurred the censure of, and been boycotted or otherwise interfered with by, the National League.

5. To assist any boycotted persons—farmers, shopkeepers, or others—who may require aid in selling their farm produce or goods; to furnish them with supplies, where necessary; and establish agencies requisite for those purposes.

6. By co-operation among the members, to enable them to carry on their respective occupations and trades; being all pledged to afford mutual assistance and protection to one another.

7. Where desirable, to work in concert with other associations in other parts of Ireland having the same objects in view.

(b)

THE EARL OF BANDON, *President*	VISCOUNT DONERAILE, *Vice-President*
A H. SMITH BARRY, Esq., *Chairman*	SIR A. WARREN, Bart., *Vice-Chairman*
LT.-COL. JOHNSON, *Hon. Sec.*	T. F. CARROLL, Esq., *Hon. Treasurer*
WM. GUEST LANE, Esq., *Solicitor*	CAPT. BAINBRIDGE, R.N.
WM. H. BEAMISH, Esq.	SIR GEO. COLTHURST, Bart.
C. PURDON COOTE, Esq.	J. PENROSE FITZGERALD, ESQ.
S. FRENCH, ESQ.	R. D. HARE, Esq.
J. HEGARTY, Esq.	R. E. LONGFIELD, Esq.
J. PIKE, Esq.	R. M. SANDERS, Esq.
CAPT. D. R. P. SARSFIELD	H. L. TIVY, Esq.

M. BEATTIE, *Secretary*.

Offices—69, SOUTH MALL, CORK.

(c)

Sir—As you have invited information from Ireland concerning the condition of the country, we beg, on behalf of the Cork Defence Union, to forward a report relating to the system of boycotting that has been prevalent in that county.

The Cork Defence Union was founded in the early part of October last, for the purpose of assisting boycotted persons, and ensuring the liberty of those suffering from the tyranny of the National League.

The report appended contains a summary of some cases that have been brought under the notice of the Cork Defence Union since the date of its formation. This report does not profess to be, by any means, an account of all cases of persons who have been intimidated by the National League, for the great majority of the victims have, we have every reason to believe, considered it advisable silently to acquiesce; deeming that the power of the League was greater than that of any private organization, or even than of Her Majesty's Government. This report is simply a short statement of a few representative cases. The system of boycotting, which commenced in 1880, continued in full force until the end of 1882; it then seems to have been in some degree relaxed, until in the end of the summer of 1885, it again appeared in renewed vigour.

It will be observed, from a study of this report, that the pressure exercised by the National League affects landowners and farmers of the larger class far less than it does small farmers, labourers, or small tradesmen; these latter being unable, from want of capital, to sustain a prolonged attack upon their means or business.

We would, further, draw your attention to the fact, that in the more severe cases of boycotting, and when the victim has shown a determination to resist, shots have been fired into his house, or violence of some kind has been attempted; proving that boycotting is not a substitute for, but simply a preliminary to, outrage.

It should not be considered, that because so large a number of cases of boycotting are reported from the County of Cork, the influence of the League is stronger there than it is in other parts of the south of Ireland. The fact is, that from the knowledge of an organization such as the Cork Defence Union being in existence, people considered "obnoxious" to the League are encouraged to resist its tyrannical decrees, and to maintain positions which the law says they are justified in holding; whereas, in other parts of the country, where no protection is forthcoming, they succumb beneath the dictates of the League, join that body, and their cases are never heard of at all. This is especially the case with regard to tradesmen, whose business it is extremely easy to injure, and whom it is excessively hard for any organization, public or private, to support.

The only remedy in such cases would seem to be the re-establishment throughout the country of the authority of Her Majesty the Queen.

The Cork Defence Union having nothing to do with the question of the collection of rents, and information concerning crime and outrage being more easily procurable through the medium of the police, this report professes to deal only with cases affecting the interference with personal liberty.

We have the honor to remain, Sir,

Your obedient Servants,

SIGNED ON BEHALF OF THE COMMITTEE,

A. H. SMITH-BARRY,

CHAIRMAN.

(d)

No.	Name and Address	Occupation	HOW INTERFERED WITH	SUPPOSED CAUSE	REMARKS
1	Michael Hegarty, Dunmanus, Schull	Farmer and Blacksmith	No one will employ or work for him—refused necessary supplies by all local traders—unable to sell his farm produce—always under police protection, even when attending Mass.	Providing police with cars in September, 1885.	Boycotting still continued—cannot attend fair or market without police protection.
2	Mrs. Hurley, Durrus, Bantry	(Widow) Farmer	Sister to above—dairyman ordered not to rent her dairy—servants deterred from working for her—all supplies refused by local traders.	Her children assisted their uncle, Michael Hegarty, mentioned above.	Boycotting still continued, and recently (Feb. 18, 1886) several fences on her farm have been thrown down and destroyed.
3	J. Beamish, Maylane House, Dunmanway	Farmer	Unable to get corn threshed, cattle sold, or horses shod.	Declined to join the National League.	Has been boycotted for three years, and is so still.
4	S. F. Beamish, Glounda House	Farmer	Same as above.	Similar offence.	Has been boycotted for three years, same as above.
5	—	Landowner	Labourers compelled to leave at harvest time (1885).	Declined to obey the local branch of the League as to extent of rent reductions.	

(d) *continued*

No.	Name and Address	Occupation	HOW INTERFERED WITH	SUPPOSED CAUSE	REMARKS
6	Mrs. Begley, Bennett's Grove, Clonakilty	Farmer	Servants and labourers compelled to leave—cannot get her horses shod, or farm produce sold.	Renting a vacant farm.	Boycotting continues, but some of her labourers have returned to their work.
7	Isaac Notter, Crookhaven	Farmer, Ship Chandler, and Contractor	Men refused to work his schooner attending Fastnet Lighthouse with supplies—gunboat sent round to relieve lightkeepers (Dec., 1885); and ultimately the Irish Lights Commissioners had to provide men for schooner—domestic and farm servants also compelled to leave his employment.	Declined to obey the dictates of the local League, to grant reduction of 25 per cent. of judicial rents on the property of his wife.	A rival contractor is secretary to the local branch of the National League. This man (Isaac Notter) has since submitted, and the boycotting ceased. He has had to pay the reduction demanded, as well as all law costs incurred.
8	Mrs. Holmes, Ballymacshaneboy	Landowner	Labourers refused to work for her—unable to sell farm produce or cattle in local markets.	Evicted a tenant four years ago for non-payment of 2 years' rent.	
9	—	Shopkeeper	No person allowed to purchase goods at his shop.	Sheriff's Officer.	
10	Daniel Rourke, Dunmanway	Blacksmith	No one permitted to employ him.	Disobeyed the orders of the league in working for boycotted farmers.	Still under ban of boycotting.....

46

VI

Irish unionist landlord suspicions about the malevolent exclusiveness of the home rule movement thus arose in the early 1880s. The question is why did attitudes formed in the 1880s persist down to and beyond the first world war.

Two points are worth noticing at this stage. On the one hand, the dominant position of landlords in Irish society was not wholly undermined by changes that occurred in the late nineteenth century. Despite the establishment of judicial rents and despite Wyndham's land act in 1903, traditions died hard. It could even be argued that the dissatisfaction of landlords and their organisation, the Irish Landowners' Convention, with the judicial rent procedure and the slow working out of land purchase, gave landlords a heightened sense of identity. For long ascendancy attitudes remained.

On the other hand, the ascendancy's suspicions of the home rule movement seemed confirmed or justified by two factors. First, the result of the introduction in 1898 of democratic local government and the supersession of the old grand juries worried them. In the south at least few opponents of home rule sat on the new county councils, and this fact confirmed unionist fears that they would have no say in the running of a self-governing Ireland. Secondly, landlords denied the validity of the then current concept of Irish nationalism. They persuaded themselves that no real nationalist movement existed, arguing that Ireland had never been a separate and historic nation. Moreover, they were for long able to convince themselves that the various demands for home rule or independence did not represent the wishes of the mass of the nation and that the losers would be the mass of ordinary men and women, deprived of the support and protection of the benevolent landed classes. This conviction enabled men such as James Mackay Wilson of Currygrane, Co. Longford (eldest brother of the famous, assassinated field-marshal, Henry Wilson), to justify their opposition to a movement that dominated elections in Ireland for over forty years. For instance Wilson, in good unionist tradition, refused to see the return of seventy-three Sinn

Feiners in the general election of 1918 as a vote in favour of self-government. Instead, he tried to explain away the result: the threat of conscription made in April 1918 rather than nationalism largely explained the support accorded to Sinn Fein—support which he argued was more apparent than real.

20 Letter from the 1st marquis of Dufferin and Ava, a former governor-general of Canada and viceroy of India, to E. Carson, 24 April 1897, expressing his solidarity with his fellow landlords and his willingness to attend a demonstration organised by the Irish Landowners' Convention to demand a revision of the judicial rent procedure (D 1507/1/ 1897/1):

Private

My dear Mr. Carson—I am very much obliged to you for your letter, and it only makes me regret all the more that I could not manage to catch you when you were in this neighbourhood. I would willingly have gone over to Mount Stewart to see you on Wednesday, had there been any chance of my catching the train which Lord Londonderry indicated; but, being Chairman of a meeting in Belfast, this it was impossible for me to do.

It is with much hesitation that I have decided to take part in the proceedings of the [Landowners'] Convention, for I feel that I have but a very imperfect notion of the elements of the problem which confronts us, and it is some consolation to me to find that some misgivings which I expressed the other day to Lord Lansdowne in regard to the result of an enquiry by English and Scotch experts, are shared by yourself. Last week I wrote to Lord Lansdowne in the following terms:—"I am not at all sure that a Commission of English and Scotch experts and land agents, with their large ideas and their conception of the status of British tenant farmers, may not follow the example of Balaam in deciding between the claims of the Irish peasantry and their landlords." The fact is the whole thing is in such a mess, and every principle not only of justice but of practical good-sense, has been so thwarted by Mr. Gladstone's blundering legislation, that the situation is irremediable. An enquiry into the proceedings of the Irish Land Courts might result in showing the blind, capricious and inconsistent way in which they work, and even, perhaps, that their general scale of reductions has been excessive; but I should fear that the ultimate upshot of this would not very much improve our position.

Again, with regard to a demand for compensation. We have undoubtedly been unjustifiably deprived of our estates, and the rights inherent in the landlord have been manifestly transferred to the tenant, in addition to any claims which may be advanced on his behalf under the plea of tenant-right and improvements. But it seems to me quite hopeless to expect that the English taxpayer will put his hand into his pocket to remedy the injustice which has been done us. Perhaps some ingenious suggestion may be made for the alleviation of our lot, though I myself have no very clear conception of the way in which such a desirable result could be reached.

But to tell the truth I have been so hustled and so busy ever since my return home, that I have not had any opportunity of discussing and threshing out such proposals as may be in the air. It is for this very reason that I should have preferred to stand aside for the present. On the other hand I cannot help feeling that one is bound to stand by one's fellow landlords in whatever effort they may engage.

There are two benefits, however, which may result from our proceedings. On the one hand they may make the Sub-Commissioners a little more careful in future; and, on the other, if we can succeed in persuading the English public that we have been badly treated, there may be less danger of fresh legislation to our further detriment. Yours Sincerely

Dufferin and Ava

21 'Reflections', written by J. M. Wilson, c.1915–16, emphasising the importance to Ireland of the landed gentry (D 989A/11/9):

No greater disaster could, in my opinion, overtake a country such as Ireland than the total elimination of its resident gentry—a process which alas, is already far advanced.

As one travels through the country one is astonished to see so many derelict houses, & neglected demesnes, the houses formerly in many cases of an independent & virile section of the body politic, not free from faults indeed—as what section is?—but, taken as a whole, forming I venture to assert oases of culture, of uprightness and of fair dealing, in what will otherwise be a desert of dead uniformity where the poor will have no one to appeal to except the Priest or the local Shopkeeper (rapidly becoming a local magnate)—whence the rich will fly, & where lofty ideals, whether of social or imperial interest will be smothered in an atmosphere of superstition, greed, & Chicanery. As in local, so in Nat[ional] administration there can be no mo[re] hope for a country from which the cultured element has been divorced, & the helpful friend of the poor & the protector of the weak driven to seek new surroundings & new occupations. It is surely the duty wherever possible, of the so called English garrison in Ireland to retain its hold, to leaven society with its hopes and aspirations that their common country may never become the plaything of a base political clique, whose ambition would be— in spite of all their protests—to see an Ireland in the grip of a Tamany [*sic*] Hall administration, where mendacity wd. flourish, corruption would be rampant & industry wd decay—I believe in my heart that even in these days of dreadful crisis with the enemy at our very gates if a perfectly secret plebiscite could be taken, a large majority would be cast in favour of retaining those members of the L.lord class in Ireland, a class whose blood is so freely shed for the Empire who for year[s] have done their best to discharge their onerous & often thankless duties by their humble neighbours all over Ireland.

22 Table of political representation on Irish county councils, February 1911, compiled by the Unionist Associations of Ireland, published in *Notes from Ireland,* March 1911, and showing the virtual exclusion of unionists from the southern county councils (D 989C/3/44A):

Counties	Unionist	Nation-alist	Indefinite	Radical	Total Members
ULSTER.					
Antrim . . .	20	1	—	4	25
Armagh . . .	21	8	1	—	30
Cavan . . .	—	25	—	—	25
Donegal . . .	5	26	—	1	32
Down . . .	17	9	—	4	30
Fermanagh . . .	15	12	—	—	27
Londonderry . .	18	6	—	—	24
Monaghan . . .	3	23	1	—	27
Tyrone . . .	16	12	—	1	29
Total . . .	**115**	**122**	**2**	**10**	**249**

MUNSTER.	Unionist	Nationalist	Indefinite	Total Members
Clare	—	29	—	29
Cork	—	54	—	54
Kerry	—	28	—	28
Limerick . . .	1	29	—	30
Tipperary (North Riding) .	—	27	—	27
Tipperary (South Riding) .	—	32	—	32
Waterford . . .	1	26	—	27
Total . . .	2	225	—	227
LEINSTER.				
Carlow . . .	—	25		25
Dublin . . .	4	21	1	26
Kildare . . .	1	26	1	28
Kilkenny . . .	1	28	—	29
King's County . .	1	26	—	27
Longford . . .	—	23	1	24
Louth	1	31	—	32
Meath . . .	2	27	—	29
Queen's County . .	—	29	—	29
Westmeath . . .	1	30	—	31
Wexford . . .	1	24	1	26
Wicklow . . .	—	27	—	27
Total . . .	12	317	4	333
CONNAUGHT.				
Galway . . .	1	31	—	32
Leitrim . . .	—	23	—	23
Mayo . . .	—	33	—	33
Roscommon . . .	—	29	—	29
Sligo	—	26	—	26
Total . . .	1	142	—	143

ANALYSIS.

Province	Unionist	Nation-alist	Indefinite	Radical	Total
ULSTER . . .	115	122	2	10	249
MUNSTER . .	2	225	—	—	227
LEINSTER . .	12	317	4	—	333
CONNAUGHT . .	1	142	—	—	143
Total . . .	130	806	6	10	952

23 *Letter from H. de F. Montgomery to Miss M. ffolliott of Holly-brook, Co. Sligo, 28 August 1918, dismissing as unimportant a 'catechism' of Irish nationalism by Darrell Figgis, and denying the validity of Ireland's claim to be a nation (D 627/432):

Dear Miss ffolliott—I sent the "catechism" to James Stronge for his opinion, he says, "I do not know how such a document should be treated. Of course to go to the root of the matter the answer is, that Ireland never was a nation in any reasonable sense of the expression, and moreover England came to Ireland by Irish invitation and the British Government never had any chance of gaining much from Ireland and might have left Ireland to stew in her own juice but for her dangerous proximity to England;" to which may be added that in that case, Ireland would, in the opinion of Edmund Burke, have been "the most wretched the most distracted and the most desolate part of the habitable globe".

Burke used to be considered a very illustrious and patriotic Irishman, but our latter-day patriots have transferred their allegiance to a Spanish half-cast [*sic*].

Taking this catechism section by section (I) An Irishman may give his "true and best service" to Ireland in many ways, but Ireland not being a nation in the sense in which England, Scotland, France Spain &c, are nations this talk of "loyalty" to Ireland is essentially nonsense.

Still more obviously nonsense is the statement that a man belonging to one country cannot be loyal to another country. A citizen of any country can be loyal to any other country to whom he is bound by honour or by interest to be loyal.

At the present time every Englishman is bound to be loyal to France, Italy, America, Belgium, Servia &c, and every Frenchman is bound to be loyal to England, Italy, America &c, and so forth. Irishmen are not asked to be loyal to *England*; they are required to be loyal to the United Kingdom of Great Britain and Ireland, of which they are *de facto* and *de jure* citizens and subjects. It would however be perfectly reasonable to ask any Irishman to be loyal to England, because it is his interest to be loyal to England, England being his best and chief customer for everything he produces, and to quote Burke again "Little do many people in Ireland consider how much of its

51

prosperity has been owing to and still depends upon its intimate connection with this Kingdom." (II) In this the catechist contradicts himself flatly where he says that he is loyal to an Ireland free and independent, and then states that Ireland is not free and independent. The catechist says truly, that Irishmen fought for centuries, but most of this fighting was done not against England but against each other. The English first came to Ireland on the invitation of Irishmen. A certain number of Englishmen and Scotchmen grew rich on what they took in Ireland, but it is absurd to say that England has grown fat and great on the spoils of Ireland.

The distinction attempted to be drawn between being "overcome" and being "conquered" is fanciful.

The fact that certain Irishmen are found who desire to rebel, with the object of breaking up the Union between the three Kingdoms, does not contradict the fact that Ireland was conquered and partly settled by the conquerors, so that a very large proportion of the present inhabitants of Ireland are descendants of English & Scotch settlers, who had just as much right, and just as little right to possess themselves of the land of those who were conquered and extruded as the so-called Celts or Gaels, who were so extruded had a few centuries previously to possess themselves of the land occupied by its previous possessors, who were conquered and extruded by the Gaels.

The Irishman who is loyal to the Crown and Constitution of the United Kingdom is no more open to the reproach of being a slave than a Scotchman or a Welshman who is loyal to that Crown and Constitution, or than a Breton or a Provencal or a Burgundian who is loyal to France, or a French Canadian who is loyal to the Dominion.

To go through every section of this document would be to do too much honour to such nonsense. It may, however, be worth pointing out that the suggestion that Ireland was once free and independent and renowned through-out the world for her learning and her dignity, and that Ireland in those days brought civilization to England has no historical basis.

English civilization was derived from Rome, Northern Germany and Normandy. Ireland was a welter of warring tribes in the midst of which there was a very remarkable development of a form of monastic christianity, which undoubtedly sent out Missionaries to various parts of Europe, and to parts of Scotland and England. This form of christianity was, however, superseded by the form adopted by the Saxon Rulers of the Southern part of England from Rome, that form being more positive and better organized.

There are certain remains of Bardic poetry and Brehon law which show that the warring tribes in Ireland had some sort of civilization, which, had the geographical position of Ireland been quite different, might have de-veloped on lines of its own, but, for all practical purposes, civilization as we know it, was introduced into and imposed upon Ireland by England.

England ruled Ireland, till the Union, with the help of a Parliament consisting almost exclusively of the representatives of protestant English and Scotch settlers. The act of Union, supplemented by Catholic emancipation

52

and subsequent reform acts elevated Ireland from being an anomalous and ill-governed dependency to the advantageous position of an integral part of the constitutional United Kingdom of Great Britain and Ireland; and conferred on it all the advantages of sharing in the control of the British Empire. Those who have appreciated this position, and made the best of it bacame [*sic*] prosperous and happy and loyal; those who have not, are neither one nor the other, nor ever will be.

The Irish language was never the language of a free united and independent Ireland; various dialects of this language were at one time spoken in different parts of Ireland, but, a very large proportion of the present inhabitants of this island are not descended from persons who spoke this language, but from persons who spoke English. For many generations Ireland has been for all practical purposes an English-speaking country. English is the leading literary and business language of the world, and to try at this time of day to make Ireland an Irish-speaking country is a perverse and retrograde proceeding.

To rake up and summarise the sufferings of the ancient Irish people at the hands partly of English armies and rulers, but more often of other sections of native Irishmen, can serve no useful purpose at this time of day. The methods of waging war, and putting down and keeping down opposition in Ireland were not more atrocious, (if as much so) than the similar methods adopted in other countries at the same period: for instance: the much decried penal laws, which the catechist refers to in the misleading phrase: "she tried to forbid religion to Irishmen", were a mild and gentle code compared to the measures taken in France against protestants after the revocation of the edict of Nantes.

If you still hanker after an exposure of the fallacies in the "catechism", perhaps the above rather hasty criticisms may be of some use to you; anything like an exhaustive dealing with them would, it seem to me, give the document an importance which it certainly does not deserve, and probably does not possess. Yours very truly,

H de F Montgomery

24 Extracts from a piece entitled 'Self-determination', by J. M. Wilson, c. December 1921, attempting to refute the argument that the 1918 general election in Ireland was a vote in favour of Sinn Fein and separation from the British empire (D 989A/8/10):

The theory on which the Government have based their proposal to cut Ireland adrift from the Empire has been the passing popularity of the phrase "self-determination". It has been pleaded that for the last forty years Ireland has returned a majority of members in favour of self-government. That majority never appeared to tell [until?] the group that favoured this political change tacked on to their suggested Revolution the proposal to create a peasant proprietary out of the tenant farmers. Instantly this vague movement of vague discontent, which has hitherto only attracted a few intellectuals, and the inevitable section of mankind that thinks a change of some kind spells better things, was reinforced by 400,000 tenant farmers, all voters, and the labourers that they controlled, numbering another 350,000.

Whatever the Irish [Parliamentary] Party of the day may have preached in England, they spoke of nothing but land in Ireland. The movement was purely agrarian. . . .Immediately that the agrarian revolution was accomplished the farmers deposed Mr. Parnell, broke up his organisation, and gave the movement no further real support. An Irish Party, wracked with dissensions, financed, as regards three fourths of its funds, by the English Liberals and the Irish Americans, still existed. It was only retained to finish off the transfer of land from the landlord to the tenant, and, provided it fulfilled this function, and did not interfere with the farmers it was tolerated. In 1910 this caucus showed signs of inducing the Liberals to pass a Home Rule Bill. Instantly the rural districts became restive. . . . From 1912 to 1915 the Irish Party only held their own by lavish subsidies from the Liberal Party, and unsparing use of the patronage of the Executive. The mere mention of the practicability of a change caused everyone with something to lose, from a farm to a business, from a post in a business to work in a factory, to stampede out of the movement, hitherto supported as a vague expression of general discontent, a formula to bind together farmers who sought their landlord's lands, labourers who sought the farmers' lands, and placehunters who sought for places at the expense of both. Outside these elements, no one had supported the movement. Manufacturers, merchants, and professional men regarded it with contempt. The artisans held aloof. Over a million Protestants regarded it only as a policy of exploiting them under the guise of religion.

The Election of 1918

This election was held at the close of the war. It was held at a time when the Government was thoroughly unpopular. High taxes and state control had made large numbers of subjects anxious to express their discontent by voting for whosoever gave the Government the greatest annoyance. The post-war discontent which caused riots in Glawgow [sic], Liverpool, and London, and led to great unrest in Labour circles, took the form in Ireland of a vague Revolutionary Republican movement, which attracted everyone who was discontented, from Government officials whose posts were on the verge of abolition through economy, to unemployed labourers bewildered by economic conditions.

The Irish Party was now thoroughly hated. To please the Radicals and to further their political ideal of maintaining the land question as a grievance to exploit, they had repealed Land Purchase. Thousands of unpurchased farmers regarded them as traitors or bunglers. They were held to blame for all the taxes that had been created by the Liberals in 1911. The graziers had never forgiven their support of three cattle embargoes. Thousands of householders had not forgotten their ostentatious advocacy of the Insurance Act. More than that, when they had weilded [sic] the patronage of the Government, for every place-hunter they rewarded, they made emenies [sic] of a hundred they did not reward. The thousands of idle young men, whose one aim and object in life was to secure some post in a Government office, attributed their failure to the callousness of the local M.P., who had promoted his relatives and not them. Lastly, they were held to blame for all the administrative acts the Government had been compelled to adopt during the war. In fact, no one could give any valid reason why these members should be returned to enjoy £400 a year.

The question of Conscription was what brought the Revolutionary Party into power. No one likes to be conscribed. It is only nations like the French that can, at a general election, ratify conscription, and extend the period of service by a year. Even Mr. Lloyd George had, at the election of 1918, to promise to conscribe no more men to take the place of those already in the Army, to release from service all soldiers garrisoned in England, and to pass an Act extending for a further period the engagements of those soldiers who were abroad, and could not influence the electors. All during the war, in England extreme radicals and socialists maintained a guerrilla warfare with the recruiting authorities, conscientious objectors gave the greatest trouble, and the tribunals were working at full pressure to cope with the claims for exemption.

When it was proposed to conscribe Ireland, the Revolutionary Party made this the chief plank in their platform. They were instantly supported by the Roman Catholic Church, which in Ireland, as in Melbourne and Ottawa, had adopted a very hostile attitude towards the Allies. All that vast multitude which desired to profit out of the war and not to fight in it, became very friendly to their saviours. Men with small businesses, farmers with one sone [sic] or one labourer, clerks in snug positions, timid young men with pacifist views in time of war and bloody aims in time of peace, turned with relief to this doctring [sic] that Ireland was "an independent nation whom aliens had no moral right to conscribe."

Vain was it for the Irish Party to protest that they were quite as zealous in the matter. Their opponents retorted that their zeal was of no account. They were but a minority of the House of Commons. The new apostles preached the defeat of conscription by the threat of rebellion. They openly advocated armed force, and Mr. Griffith declared "we will seek help from Germany or any other nation". An embarrassed Government shrank from the challenge. Conscription was withdrawn. In the high places of Downing Street it was declared that Imperial statesmen paid more heed to violence than to votes or arguments. It spelt the doom of a constitutional movement. It was the supreme justification of violence for political ends, be they exemption from conscription, or unpopular taxes, or confiscation of the goods of a minority with no guns. A new era of ways and means opened for every discontented sect, and the general election was fought on this policy for remedy of grievances versus the old method of votes, speeches, discussion and divisions. The election was fought on the cry of "Vote for those who saved you from conscription", and it was fought in the absence of every loyalist of military age, such persons being abroad in the services.

The Result

At first sight the result seemed an overwhelming victory for secession from the Empire. Excluding the four University representatives, the result was 22 loyalists, 7 Nationalists desiring a change in the constitution, and 72 Republicans and secessionists. What made it more marked was that in 22 constituencies the rebels were unopposed, and in only two constituencies did a loyalist get a walk over.

The figures, however, require careful scrutiny. Apart from the important point as to how many voters voted for the Republican through dislike of the Nationalists or mere irritation at things as they were, by no strain of the imagination can one regard the Nationalists as sympathetic with this extreme programme. No Nationalist member of [*sic*] ex-member has given the "Treaty" his benediction. Their old supporters have suffered exceedingly from the outrages of the Republicans. Some of the Nationalist members fought in the late war. Many had sons in the Army. The majority were strong supporters of instant enlistment.

The principal [*sic*] of self-determination involves a clear cut issue on the question of secession or adhesion to an Empire. This is the only election we have on which to judge the question. It is first clear that a large number of extraneous issues were intorduced [*sic*] to confuse the issue, and those issues were of considerable advantage to the Republican Party. Secondly a vote of the whole electorate should be taken to justify anyone in assuming that Ireland desires to secede. Not 55% of the electorate voted. In default of a full vote, we must examine the election returns before we dare assums [*sic*] an expression of Irish opinion in favour of a "sovereign state". We must to prove that assumption have a large, clear, and obvious majority before we dare assume a popular desire for a great and far-reaching constitutional change, which alters the basis of the whole Empire and which, if once adopted, cannot be repealed save by a revolution or a miracle.

The Unionist vote cast at the last election was 336,550. In constituencies where the Republicans polled only a handful, they put forward candidates. We may therefore safely assume that 70% of the two constituencies they did not contest were loyalist. This brings the total up to 363,150.

We now turn to the unopposed returns. A Protestant Republican is almost unknown. In Ireland it is doubtful if a dozen such could be found. Propaganda has essayed to obscure this fact by parading a few English Radicals, resident in Dublin, or Scotch Socialists resident in Belfast, who because they are not Irish Roman Catholics are introduced as members of the Church of Ireland, or Irish Presbyterians. On examination they are usually found to be "alien" agnostics. We may, therefore, regard as a salient political fact in Ireland that every member of the Church of Ireland, every Irish Presbyterian, and every Irish Methodist is a loyalist. Not one of these would any more dream of voting for or sympathising with the rebel Republicans than a Frenchman would vote for German control of Alsace-Lorraine, or a Pole for the domination of Russian Bolshevists.

The Irish census shows that 60% of the population are over the age of 20. If we take 60% of the Protestant population in the counties where there was no contest, the strong Loyalist vote that will not tamper with the Union increases remarkably. The figures are as follows:—

Recorded Vote	363,150
Munster	35,400
Leinster	132,000
Connaught	13,440
Cavan	9,960
Donegal	20,880
Total	574,830
Less Unionist Vote recorded in South and in one Donegal seat	25,844
	548,986

In addition to this there is another consideration. There is a very large number of loyalist Roman Catholics. There are, for instance 9,000 Roman Catholic members of the R.I.C., who do not appear on the Register, and did not vote at the Elections. Between soldiers and sailore [sic], the Comrades of the Great War total 220,000. Not one of these would touch this movement with a forty foot pole, save about half a dozen black sheep. They have been attacked, hounded out of employment, denied employment on public works, and generally regarded as pariahs by "the friends of liberty". If we take two-thirds of these as Roman Catholics and add the 9,000 Constabulary, we get a solid male vote of 155,600. This brings our loyalist total up to 704,550. These are the active and enthusiastic loyalists. These are those marked out for destruction. These are those who see in a change what English people would see in German ironclads sailing up the Thames.

We now turn to the Constitutional Nationalist, to the man who voted against Mr. Griffith, and Mr. de Valera, to the man who was in favour of Ireland remaining in the Empire, but who had a vague idea of Irish self-government "subject to the supremacy of the Imperial Parliament", with Irish members sitting at Westminster as of yore. Even in that election, with all the dice loaded against him, his recorded vote was 240,800. This nondescript vote, certainly not pro-German or pro-Russian, certainly not Republican, certainly not revolutionary, and certainly not in favour of "the Sovereign assembly" of the "Free State", if added to the loyalist gives us more than half the Register of Voters. Outside lies [sic] all the peasant proprietors, who dread a democratic assembly sitting in Dublin, the elder priests, two of whose bishops are avowed Unionists, the Roman Catholic shopkeeper. blackmailed by the gunmen and forbidden to sell English goods, and that class known as the Roman Catholic loyalist of the middle classes, whom old election agents put at over 100,000.

The majority vanishes on a little proving. The election of 1918, the most favourable ever fought for the cause of sedition is but a broken rood [sic] for the exponents of self-determination to utilise. . . .

Chapter III

The opponents of home rule: the businessmen and the protestant churches

The landed classes were not immediately supported by businessmen in the north and south. The continued violence of the land movement after the 1881 act may have helped to break down class barriers and create sympathy among businessmen for landlords, as fellow property owners; but businessmen in the main were always reluctant to support unionism too openly. In the south especially, they felt in a difficult position owing to their dependence upon nationalists in the country towns; and in April 1892, when the I.U.A. was arranging a monster demonstration in Dublin against home rule, the committee had difficulty in persuading businessmen to take part. Only by toning down one anti-home rule resolution could they persuade Thomas Pim junior, director of one of the largest commercial concerns in Ireland, Pim and Sons, to take part.

Eventually, however, businessmen took an active and increasing interest in opposition to home rule. Detailed statements of businessmen's objections to home rule were issued and they took an active part in unionist organisation, especially in the north. During the crisis over the third home rule bill, 1911–14, Ulster businessmen formed themselves into a committee of the Ulster Unionist Council to assist in financing opposition to the bill (see chapter VII). The anti-imperialism of home rule and the association of that movement with disorder led businessmen, who depended upon stable conditions and imperial connections for profits and capital, to consider positively the merits of maintaining the union. An imperial subsidy helped to provide a wide range of services that a separate Ireland could hardly finance, and there was considerable evidence of the possible adverse effects that home rule would have upon the Irish economic and financial world. A favourite argument was 'the commercial earthquake that took place when the home rule bill was brought in' in 1886. Moreover, in view of the involvement of Ulster protestant workingmen in the unionist movement, it could be argued that businessmen (such as J. Milne Barbour of the Linen Thread Company, a future minister of finance for Northern Ireland, and Sir George Clark of Workman, Clark, & Co., shipbuilders, chairman of the businessmen's committee) had an interest in helping to direct that movement in Ulster.

25 Letter from R. MacGeagh of MacGeagh and MacLaine, flax, tow and linen yarn spinners, Shrigley Mills, Killyleagh, Co. Down, writing from Belfast, to H. de F. Montgomery, 23 January 1889, expressing sympathy with the landlords (D 627/428/79):

Dear Mr. Montgomery—Your letter is so interesting, and goes so fully and comprehensively into the whole question of the complex judicial machinery at present in operation to determine the meum and tuum of landlord and tenant, that I regret it cannot have a wider circulation than what I presume I am at liberty to give to it, or to the views it expresses, in my own private circle; and, indeed, I almost regret that I have put you to some [sic] much trouble replying to my very loose remarks on the subject. I do not profess to be an expert on the Land question. I followed it with deep interest many years ago, when the tenant farmers were struggling against a despotic and practically irresponsible landocracy, without representation, or the protection of the ballot; but since the passing of the Ballot Act, and, especially the successive Land Acts, my sympathies have completely changed sides, as I never had any class prejudice in the matter, but went in solely for equal justice and fair play. Now I think the landlords, generally, are the victims of the tenants' greed and dishonesty, which both parties in the state have contributed to stimulate, by reluctant concessions. Therefore, I have ceased to give an ear to tenant appeals on almost any question at issue between them and the landlords lest a revulsion of feeling should land me on the unpopular side. But I should be very glad to see the whole question settled, for the peace and prosperity of the country, and I very much concur with your idea of the only possible mode of an ultimate and permanent settlement.

Of course, you are quite at liberty to keep the cuttings I sent you, and I shall be glad if an effective reply can be given to either of the letters—I am sorry you mentioned my name to the I.L.P.U. as the critic of those great Protestant guns, I referred to, as I have no great wish to bring their thunder on my head.

If you would not make use of my name in connection with this suggestion, I would privately hint to yourself that, in the organisation you propose for Belfast with Sir John Preston and T. Sinclair as Presidents, a much better than the former might be selected (and a much worse could not be) I don't think any Liberals would work with him, and I believe all Conservatives would prefer working without him. Sir W. Ewart, or his son Quartus, would be much more popular and less objectionable. But this, entre nous Very sincerely yours

R MacGeagh

26 Letter from T. Pim junior of Pim and Sons, Dublin, to the secretary of the I.U.A., 27 April 1892, explaining that businessmen in Dublin had to be wary of opposing the nationalist movement (D989A/8/2):

Dear Sir—I am very glad you have altered the Resolution in the way proposed You should recollect that we Business Men in Dublin live by the Nationalists in the Country Towns and there is no use in abusing them. Very few Business Men will take any part & where I am willing to fight I dont think your association should ask me to move a Resolution which would be brought up against me in every town in Southern Ireland.

However as you have altered it I have nothing more to say except that I had expected this evening a copy of the proposed proceedings & Resolution as amended.

Please let me know to 22 Wm. Street tomorrow if Ladies are open to go to this meeting. My Daughters want to go but they are not sure if either on platform or elsewhere it is open to Ladies. Are there any Ladies Tickets. I am Yours truly

Thos Pim Jr

27 Southern businessmen's protest against and criticism of the financial proposals contained in the third home rule bill, bearing '151 signatures of leading men engaged in trade and commerce south of Ulster', and reprinted in *Notes from Ireland*, December 1913 (D 989C/3/66):

WE, the undersigned, being actively engaged in the trade and commerce of the three Southern Provinces of Ireland, and being seriously concerned at the effect on those interests of the financial proposals in the present Home Rule Bill, desire to make known the following facts:—

(1) Home Rule is frequently pressed on British electors as a scheme to enable them to "cut their loss." This is not the case presented in Ireland, where it would be too obvious that cutting the loss to Great Britain could only mean "cutting the gain" to Ireland. This country is now in the extremely favourable position of profiting from the large and beneficent schemes of material development and social reform such as Land Purchase, the creation of the Department of Agriculture and Technical Instruction, the Congested Districts Board and Old Age Pensions which have been granted under the Imperial Parliament. If Home Rule had been conceded in earlier years it is now certain that the British Parliament would not, and the Irish Parliament could not, have extended such reforms to Ireland. This would have meant that, in respect of old age pensions alone, Ireland would have been deprived of nearly £3,000,000 a year of Imperial expenditure.

(2) The tendencies of modern legislation and the declarations of statesmen all point to the conclusion that wide and costly schemes of social betterment will continue to be inaugurated, whatever party may be in power. We fear that the financial inability of any Irish Parliament in the near future to extend to the Irish people the great boons of the social reforms which they

would have enjoyed under the Union will cause discontent among the Irish democracy. If the Irish Parliament, desiring to allay such discontent, should attempt to emulate the measures of their wealthier neighbours across the Channel, the Irish Chancellor of the Exchequer will be compelled to resort to special forms of taxation, within the very rigid and restricted limits permitted by the Home Rule Bill, but this must inevitably involve financial sacrifices which will heavily handicap our industries. On the one hand, therefore, we foresee that the people will be discontented if the reforms enacted in Great Britain are not also adopted in Ireland; on the other hand, we are confident that if we are compelled to live up to a standard set by Great Britain, our prosperity will be endangered by disproportionately heavy burdens on Irish industry.

(3) Taking a wider and more general view we ask, as business men, whether and how far the financial prospects of Ireland are likely to be favoured or prejudiced by Home Rule. Ireland is a comparatively poor country. For her development it is essential she should retain all the capital that is already here and attract other capital from without. It appears to us that the prospects of inevitable extra taxation will drive fluid Irish capital away; and that the uncertainties of the course which Irish methods of taxation will assume will cause new British and foreign capital to be inordinately shy of investment in this country. The scarcity of capital and of cash which will result will also react on the trading credit on which business is based. The present course of business will be disturbed and future development checked by the onerous rates on which alone, owing to the above causes, credit will be granted.

(4) Moreover we realise that the rates at which it will be possible to float an Irish Government loan will be much higher than would have to be paid at present. Lord MacDonnell, at a time when money was much cheaper than at present, publicly admitted that an Irish Government might have to pay 5 per cent. for its money, or what is the same thing, could not issue a 3 per cent. loan at a price higher than 60. On such terms even the most productive of Irish undertakings could not be profitably financed, and it is more than likely that no Irish Government will have the courage to attempt any loan on these terms.

(5) We do not overlook the fact that the Home Rule Bill appears to provide lenders with ample security for any loan. The Irish Government will have the power (by Clause 23) if it so chooses, and the Irish Parliament approves, to offer the Transferred Sum as security for loans. In that event it will be the statutory duty of the Joint Exchequer Board to deduct from the sum which reaches them from the Imperial Treasury the interest and sinking fund payments on account of the lenders. The value of this security from the point of view of the lender is bound to be prejudicially affected by a number of considerations, the most important being that the Imperial Treasury will have a first charge on it. The sum which reaches the Joint Exchequer Board may be very seriously reduced by the deductions which the British Treasury are empowered to make. Among these are the deductions on account of any

arrears in the payment of annuities under the Land Purchase Acts, a deduction which might become serious in the event of agricultural depression arising, it may be, from a succession of bad harvests. Those people in Great Britain who may undertake to finance an Irish loan might not be favourably disposed to assume for granted the continual prompt payment of the annuities. Any failure in this direction will depreciate the value of the security offered; and this is a business risk they will not ignore when fixing the price of the loan. Further, it would be well within the power of an Irish Parliament to transfer certain services from the taxes to the rates, making good the new burden on the rates by a compensating reduction in taxes. This operation would reduce the Transferred Sum and again depreciate the security offered for the loan.

(6) The Bill provides that loans in Ireland shall cease to be advanced either by the Public Works Loans Commissioners or out of the Local Loans Fund. This will seriously retard the industrial and social development of the country. Farmers in Ireland—and in an exceptional degree those in the provinces of Leinster, Munster and Connaught—have been in the habit of borrowing extensively and upon easy terms from the Board of Works for the purpose of permanent improvements. The withdrawal of these facilities will compel those of the agricultural classes who desire to make such capital expenditure to borrow upon much more onerous conditions, and will tend to throw many of them into the hands of the money-lenders. Again, the vast majority of the loans obtained by Urban and County Authorities for Public Works and schemes of social development and sanitation have been financed through the Local Loans Fund. In future such loans will have to be raised through the Banks, and the probable effect will be that Irish Local Bodies having to carry out such improvements will have to pay a distinctly higher rate of interest than they have done in the past, and that the charges upon the ratepayers will be much increased.

(7) One of the leading objections to the financial scheme of the Home Rule Bill is that it offers no conceivable prospect of reduced taxation. Assuming a prosperous Ireland, the growing tax-revenue, which is one of the natural results of such prosperity, should be available, as in every independent country, to finance new services or additional expenditure on old services, or to reduce taxation. By the scheme of the Bill, any such additional revenue would not reach the Irish Exchequer at all. It would remain with the Imperial Exchequer as a set-off against the so-called deficit. It would be available to reduce British taxation, but not the Irish burden. The Irish Government can benefit only from any economies they might effect in the cost of running the Transferred Services. The closest scrutiny of the details of the present expenditure leaves not the smallest hope that—except the most trifling sums—any economies are possible in this direction. It follows, therefore, that practically the whole of any increased cost of old services and the entire cost of new services must be financed by the Irish Government. For this it will be necessary either to impose new taxes or borrow. The latter expedient may be at once dismissed. However advantageous borrowing may be, either to an individual or a Government, in meeting a temporary financial difficulty, it is a wholly unsuitable means of meeting a permanent deficit.

(8) Taxation will, therefore, have to be resorted to, and the question arises what tax-resources are available to an Irish Government? We examine these in detail—

(a) *Customs and Excise on Beer and Spirits.*—Under the Bill these duties can be raised in Ireland to any extent. From the point of view of revenue, however, it is generally admitted that they are now taxed as high as possible. Additional taxation—by its effect in reducing consumption—is likely to produce less rather than more revenue.

(b) *Income Tax.*—The Bill deprives the Irish Parliament of the power to vary the rate from that in force at the time under the authority of the Imperial Parliament. They could, however, vary the existing exemptions and abatements—lowering the exemption limit from the present figure of £160 and reducing the abatements on incomes under £700— to produce an additional revenue from income tax of not more than 10 per cent. The maximum yield of such a change in the levying of income tax in Ireland might be as much as £150,000, or less than $1\frac{1}{2}$ per cent. of the total cost of all Irish services. We think, however, that even if this operation could be carried through, there are grave objections to its employment. A reduction in the exemption limit would bring into the income tax net a large number of persons who have hitherto escaped and would not fall uniformly on all parts of Ireland. It would fall entirely on the less remunerated members of the professional classes, on the shopkeeping classes in the country and the towns, on a large number of farmers, and probably most heavily on many of those belonging to the artisan classes in the North and some few industries in the South, where wages are comparatively high and approximate to the level of wages in Great Britain. However unintentional the effect, such an incidence would be inevitably regarded as discriminating taxation.

(c) *Other Customs Duties.*—These are now levied on articles like tea, sugar, coffee, cocoa, and dried fruits and tobacco. Together these yield nearly £3,000,000, the revenue from tea being £600,000 and from tobacco £1,800,000. The maximum yield of a 10 per cent. surtax on all these Customs duties would, therefore, be less than £300,000, and to the extent which tea or tobacco is exempted from additional taxation even this sum would be correspondingly reduced. On account of the odium which, we believe, would be incurred by any Irish Government who increased the duties on tea, sugar and tobacco, we think that no attempt to raise these duties is probable, and therefore they cannot be regarded as a fruitful source of revenue.

(d) *The Death Duties.*—At best an additional 10 per cent, might produce about £90,000. This additional duty,—which under the conditions brought about by Land Purchase would fall very largely on the farmer, —would be very difficult to collect and, in our opinion, would not readily be resorted to.

(9) Summarising what has gone before, it appears clear that the power of securing further revenue by operating on the existing Imperial taxes within

the limits rigidly set by the Bill could produce no substantial amounts, and that even such amounts as could be thus raised, might have disastrous economic or political consequences which the Government would certainly desire to avoid. Unless, therefore, the course recommended by the Committee on Irish Finance appointed by the present Liberal Government in October, 1911, to consider the financial relations between Ireland and the other component parts of the United Kingdom is adopted and the scale of old age pensions is reduced it will be necessary to exhaust every possibility of new taxation, or resort to borrowing. What new taxes are possible under the Bill?

(e) *Taxation of Land.*—The Bill gives to the Irish Parliament unlimited powers to devise new taxes not substantially the same as any existing Imperial tax levied in Ireland. It is thought in some quarters that some new tax on land might be devised which would be permitted by the Bill. This would be difficult in view of the considerable variety of land taxes which the present Government has already imposed and to which further additions may be made in the near future. But assuming that such a tax could be devised by the Irish Parliament, it is notorious that in its effects it must fall with peculiar severity on the three Southern Provinces. At the back and at the base of all industrial activities in Ireland is the farming industry which, in turn, rests on the land. County rates, which already fall entirely on the land, will have to be heavily increased under Home Rule, because the Imperial Exchequer contribution, on account of Local Rates, will be stereotyped in amount and will not increase with the needs of the expenditure of the local authorities on whose behalf they are paid. To add novel Irish land taxes to those already existing would certainly injure agricultural development and react on every class of traders in the country. Such taxes are to us inconceivable.

(f) *Graduated Income Tax.*—Any variation of rates is ruled out by the Bill. All that could be done has been already described above.

(g) *Special Tax on Certain Industries.*—Though such a scheme of taxation is possible, the Government would probably hesitate to adopt it because of its tendency to drive the affected industry from Ireland. Whatever the cause may be some of the leading manufacturers in Ireland have made arrangements already for the transfer of a large part of their works to England and elsewhere. This alteration of the locality where wages will be paid will react seriously on the revenue upon which the Irish Chancellor will be entitled to draw. Special taxation of industries would certainly accelerate this movement.

(10) We must at this point observe that whatever the taxes or the system of taxation imposed or employed in the New Ireland it is morally certain that the total burden of taxation and its incidence on the members of the different economic classes will be always heavier than among the corresponding classes in the United Kingdom. This arises in the first place from the provision that the growing yield of existing taxes will not be available for Irish purposes but will flow into the Imperial Exchequer and thus reduce the taxation which

would have been otherwise levied in Great Britain. In the second place the field of taxes which an independent Irish Parliament might have imposed on Irish taxpayers is considerably curtailed by the 10 per cent. limitation; this limitation is avowedly imposed in British interests, and has the effect of restricting the activities of an Irish Parliament to less desirable, less defensible and less economic forms of taxation. In the third place the course of expenditure under an Irish Government, at least during the early years of its existence, when the expenses of new Irish offices will be added to other increases, will certainly tend more rapidly upwards than if the Union were maintained. This is an inevitable result of the direct and implied promises and pledges of the present Home Rule Party. Finally, we have been assured by the official spokesmen of the present Government—the Chancellor of the Exchequer and the Attorney-General—that in any new expenditure incurred by the Imperial Parliament on behalf of the common services of the United Kingdom or the Empire, a contribution will be demanded from Ireland. Those services are rapidly increasing in cost, and even contribution on the most moderate basis which the curtailed representation of 42 members from Ireland will be able to secure, will certainly bear heavily on the Irish taxpayer.

(11) We are also convinced that the new Customs and Postal arrangements under the Bill will affect commerce very injuriously.

(12) On all these grounds, then, the financial prospect of the Ireland of the future under the present Home Rule Bill is exceedingly gloomy. Faced on the one hand by large increases of expenditure, and on the other hand by growing demands on the Irish taxpayer by the Imperial Parliament, how can the annual accounts be balanced? When every available resource of taxation has been employed, and every interest and industry in Ireland has been harassed and made discontented, a gap will still remain to be filled. Only by means of loans will a Chancellor of the Irish Exchequer be able to escape his immediate difficulties. But, as has been already pointed out, this resource cannot be resorted to, except on onerous terms, and then only as a temporary expedient. It will only postpone an aggravated problem for solution by some later Government.

(13) Recapitulating all that has gone before it appears to us as business men that the Home Rule scheme in the present Bill must be debited with the following:—The progress of Social Reforms will be checked; capital will be deflected from Ireland; business credit will be granted only on more onerous terms; Irish Government loans will be impossible except at high rates; the local authorities will be compelled, in general, to obtain any cash needed for capital expenditure from the banks or other lenders who will be obliged to charge higher rates of interest than at present; local rates are likely to rise; the natural increments of revenue from Imperial taxes will not belong to the Irish Government; expenditure must rise and new taxes will have to be imposed; the field of taxation is so limited by the provisions of the Bill that any appreciable sum can be raised only by uneconomic, untried, harassing and discriminating methods, or by reducing the scale of old age pensions; and a flight of manufacturing industries to other countries must be anticipated. Against these there can only be set to the credit of the proposal the

satisfaction of national sentiment, with all that this phrase may connote in the minds of different individuals.

(14) In our opinion, therefore, it is not in the interests of Ireland that this Bill should pass.

28 Leaflets issued in 1893 by the I.U.A.: **(a)** 'Home rule and Irish securities'; and **(b)** 'Home rule and Irish stocks'; both being reprints of contributions to *The Economist,* 18 May 1889, and *The Times,* 7 and 28 May 1892, pointing out that the Irish stocks fell during the home rule episode of 1886 and subsequently recovered under unionist government (D 989C/3/23A):

(a)

THE past half-year has witnessed a further enhancement of the market value of bank shares. . . . The paid-up capital of the joint-stock banks of the United Kingdom, valued at market prices, is now worth fully $4\frac{3}{4}$ millions more than in October last, and nearly $7\frac{3}{4}$ millions more than it was twelve months ago.

With but trifling increase in the amount of paid-up capital of the English banks its aggregate value has increased since May, 1885, by nearly £17,500,000. In the same interval the Scotch banks, with more than a sixth of the capital of English institutions, have realized a gain of only £170,000, while in the case of the Irish banks, an amount of paid-up capital only about £200,000 less than that invested four years ago is now valued at £2,300,000 less than it then was. For the fall in the value of the Irish bank shares the Gladstonian Home Rule agitation is in the main responsible. The introduction of Mr. Gladstone's Home Rule Bill was followed by a heavy fall in all Irish securities. In October, 1885, the market value of the £6,719,000 which constituted the paid-up capital of the Irish banks was £18,207,000, and in May, after Mr. Gladstone's scheme had been submitted to Parliament, the market value of the same amount of paid-up capital had fallen to £14,934,000 —a drop of nearly $3\frac{1}{2}$ millions. Since the advent of the Unionist Government, however, there has been a gradual recovery, and a considerable portion of what was lost has been regained. The shares of the Scotch banks have been free from the ups and downs to which those of the Irish institutions have been subjected. They have, in fact, remained practically stationary. . . . We estimate that the total deposits of the English banks amounted, on the 31st of December last, to £363,000,000, as compared with £359,000,000 on the 30th June previous. The deposits of the metropolitan banks show very little, if any, increase. The Scotch and Irish banks also show increased deposits. Scotland £85,000,000 as against £83,000,000, and Ireland £36,500,000 as against £34,500,000.—*Economist,* 18th May, 1889.

A CASE IN POINT.

COLONEL SAUNDERSON, M.P., contributes the following letter to the *Times:*—

It is difficult to follow the line of reasoning adopted by Mr. Morley in his speech at the Liberal Club yesterday (4th May).

Mr. Morley tried to convict Lord Londonderry of talking nonsense when he said in his speech the other day in Dublin that an Irish Government would have to pay 30 or 40 per cent. if they wished to borrow money. This, Mr. Morley says, is an absurd statement, and points triumphantly by way of proof to the fact that the Dublin Corporation succeeded recently in borrowing 1¼ million at 3¾ per cent. This fact, according to Mr. Morley, utterly pulverizes poor Lord Londonderry.

What on earth, I should like to know, has the undoubtedly satisfactory condition of Irish securities of a public character got to do with the condition of Irish securities if a Home Rule Government should be established in Ireland? I utterly fail to understand. The easy terms on which the Corporation of Dublin secured their money is a proof that under the Unionist Government public security has been restored in Ireland.

Mr. Morley ought not to forget the commercial earthquake that took place, when the Home Rule Bill was brought in, in securities of all kinds, and the immediate recovery in the value of all kinds of shares and stocks which occurred when the Home Rule Bill was defeated in 1886.

A circumstance happened which ought to have brought these facts before Mr. Morley's mind, of which I should wish to remind him.

The Cavan and Leitrim Steam Tramway had succeeded in passing through all the parliamentary stages, and all that remained to be done was to raise the necessary capital. No difficulty was anticipated in the operation, as the security of the county rates was looked on as first-rate security.

The money was promised by London banks, and the solicitor of the company, with two other gentlemen connected with the undertaking, went over to London to complete the final arrangements. *To their dismay the bankers told them that the Home Rule Bill had entirely changed the aspect of affairs, and that no money would be advanced under these changed conditions on Irish securities on any terms.*

It occurred to these gentlemen, under these changed and unfortunate circumstances, that the best thing they could do would be to pay a visit to Mr. Morley, then Chief Secretary for Ireland.

These gentlemen gave me an account of the interview, and authorised me to make use of their names and information as I might see fit.

They informed Mr. Morley of the plight in which they found themselves, and of the blighting effect the Home Rule Bill had exerted on the financial operation in which they were engaged, and also pointed out to him what a strong argument against Home Rule would be supplied to his Unionist opponents should they learn of their failure and its cause.

Something apparently operated on Mr. Morley's mind, for soon after the interview Mr. Morley brought an amending Bill into the House of Commons and passed it without debate through all its stages, which enabled the Treasury to lend money on the security of tramway shares. So the Cavan line got the money, and has, I am glad to say, succeeded. These things must have faded from Mr. Morley's memory, or he would not have ventured to ridicule Lord Londonderry.—*Times,* 7th May, 1892.

(b)

MR. WILFRED BECKER, of Manchester, writing to the *Times* on the 28th May, 1892, says:—

In a letter which appeared in your columns on the 7th inst., Colonel Saunderson referred to the commercial earthquake that took place when the Home Rule Bill was brought in, and to the subsequent recovery in the value of securities of all kinds.

Will you allow me, in corroboration of this remark, to place before your readers the following table, which deals with the Stocks of the Bank of Ireland and of the three great Irish Railways; the table gives the highest and lowest prices touched by these Stocks in the ten years ending December 31st last, and shows the extent of the fluctuations in each year. [*See overleaf.*]

In order to make more apparent the nature of the movements which took place, a chart is appended of the highest and lowest prices of Bank of Ireland stock in each year of the period under consideration. The chart simply shows the *maxima* and *minima* without indicating the order in which they occurred, the *maximum* for every year being given first.

FLUCTUATIONS IN THE PRICE OF BANK OF IRELAND STOCK.

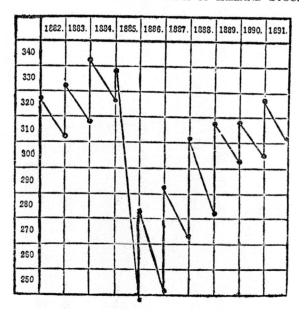

Dealing with the diagram, it is obvious that the exceptional causes at work in the years 1885 and 1886 were of a most powerful and depressing nature. When we come to examine the course of prices during these years, the close connection between the fall in values and the growth of the Home Rule Scheme becomes apparent. During the early part of 1885 there was nothing unusual in the fluctuations. It is true that the Bank of Munster

Table showing the Fluctuations in the Price of Bank of Ireland Stock and of the Ordinary Stocks of the Three Principal Irish Railways from 1882 to 1891.

NAME.	1882. H.	1882. L.	1883. H.	1883. L.	1884. H.	1884. L.	1885. H.	1885. L.	1886. H.	1886. L.	1887. H.	1887. L.	1888. H.	1888. L.	1889. H.	1889. L.	1890. H.	1890. L.	1891. H.	1891. L.
Bank of Ireland	327	311	331	316	340½	325½	338	249	264	250	291	273	310	280	317	302	319	304½	327	331
Extent of fluctuations	16		15		15		89		34		18		30		15		14½		16	
Gt. Southern & Western Railway	117	106¾	124	116¼	121	113⅜	117¼	97¾	103	90	106½	98	113	100½	126¾	112¾	120⅞	110	121	114½
Extent of fluctuations	10¼		7¾		7⅝		19½		13		8½		12½		14		10⅞		6½	
Great Northern Railway (Ireland)	120½	116½	123	116	117¼	113	117	101	104¾	94½	101¼	94	123¾	104¼	130¾	120½	127¼	118⅝	132½	125¼
Extent of fluctuations	4		7		4¼		16		10¼		7¼		19½		10¼		8⅝		7¼	
Midland Great Western Railway	90	79¼	92	82⅜	85⅞	78	78¾	63	82	60½	83½	74	97¾	74½	110	95¾	109¼	99½	109½	103⅜
Extent of fluctuations	10¾		9⅝		7⅞		15¾		21½		9½		23¼		14¼		9¾		6⅛	

stopped payment on July 14, but the price of the stock was then 331. The following are the quotations as the year went on:—September 1, 329; October 1, 317; November 3, 310; December 1, 305; December 17, 300; December 19, 275, 273, 274 ex div.; December 28, 249. It was on December 18 that the National Press Agency stated that "Mr. Gladstone has definitely adopted the policy of Home Rule for Ireland," and your own leading article on that day speaks of the profound impression which had thus been produced.

It will be seen that immediately after this announcement the price of Bank of Ireland Stock fell to a point very much below the *minimum* of previous years, though the absolutely lowest figure was not touched till a few days later. It may be of interest to state that Mr. Gladstone's Bill was introduced on April 8th, 1886, the price of Bank stock on the 9th was 258; on June 9, when the Bill had just been thrown out, it was 263, and it rose during the latter part of the year to 284. It would occupy too much of your space to enter with equal detail into the changes in the price of the great railways, but an examination of the table will show that in every case the years 1885 and 1886 are remarkable for extremely low *minima* and very great fluctuations. It was not until the third quarter of 1885 that the Home Rule doctrine was seriously put forward, and the proposals were happily rejected by the House of Commons before the end of the second quarter in 1886. The wide fluctuations of 1885 were caused by the fall from the prices ruling under normal conditions in the early part of the year to those following on the panic which Mr. Gladstone's proposals produced among Irish investors, and those of 1886 are due to the recovery which set in when these proposals were rejected.

Hardly less exceptional than the fluctuations of 1885 and 1886 are those observable in 1888. Mr. Balfour had then been at the helm for some considerable time, during which firm and steady government (or brutal coercion, as our Gladstonian friends prefer to call it) had produced its natural results. Confidence had returned, dividends were increasing, prices advanced by "leaps and bounds." During the last three years of the decade this process went on more gradually, so that in 1891 we see a still higher range of values established for all the three great Irish railways; while, curiously enough, for Bank of Ireland stock the *maxima* and *minima* are exactly the same in 1891 as in 1882, though the dividend was 11½ per cent. against 12 per cent.

29 Letter from J. M. Barbour, writing from the Glasgow office of the Linen Thread Company, to G. Clark, 26 March 1914, apologising for his inability to attend a meeting of the businessmen's committee of the U.U.C., and expressing concern at the effects of the mobilisation of the Ulster Volunteer Force (D 1327/4/2B):

Dear George—I am over here attending a Directors' Meeting and shall be detained over to-morrow and so am very sorry I shall be unable to attend the Conference of Business Men's Committee to-morrow afternoon.

I have been maing [*sic*] enquiries and find that in the Works of The Linen Thread Company it so happens that a good many of the volunteers are in groups in different departments, and in some small departments of great importance, such as the Boiler House and Engine Drivers, possibly the whole staff are in the volunteers, so any extensive scheme of mobilisation would have a very disturbing effect, and I think it is a very important matter just now that workpeople should be kept employed as much as possible. This is just as important from a political standpoint as for any commercial reason.

It is with the greatest regret that I have heard of the death of the Lord Mayor. It would be regrettable under any circumstances, but still more so at our present juncture. Yours faithfully

J. Milne Barbour

II

Unionism in Ireland can almost be equated with protestantism, much to the disgust of such comparatively rare protestant home rulers as Alexander Duncan, Methodist and former chairman of the Athy, Co. Kildare, town commissioners, and Jeremiah Jordan, successively nationalist M.P. for West Clare, South Meath and South Fermanagh. Protestantism, or rather apprehension of Roman Catholicism, was one of the bonds that bound together groups whose interests otherwise did not always coincide. The protestant churches were in the main active opponents of home rule, which some protestants regarded as implying Rome rule and necessarily involving the persecution of protestants. Not all unionists would have accepted such an extreme view, sometimes obscenely expressed, but they were mistrustful of the Roman Catholic church, which they regarded as spiritually and politically over-ambitious.

These fears were occasionally underlined by the acts of individual priests, the hierarchy or the pope. The intervention of the Roman Catholic clergy in the general election of 1892, following the O'Shea divorce and the split in the home rule party, was duly noted; and the decree *Ne temere* promulgated by the pope in 1908 alarmed protestants especially in Ulster. It declared that marriages between Roman Catholics and protestants not solemnised according to the rites of the Roman Catholic church were null and void; and in 1910 much controversy was aroused by the application of the decree in a case in Belfast. Alexander McCann, instigated it was alleged by his priest, left his protestant wife and took away the children.

Moreover, although it did not apply to Ireland, protestants objected to the *Motu proprio* (papal letter), '*Quantavis diligentia*', issued in 1911 and condemning those who took priests into civil courts. Most protestants, therefore, did think that there would at least be discrimination against them and against protestant institutions in a home rule Ireland, in view of the large Roman Catholic majority.

30 Letter from A. Duncan, Athy, Co. Kildare, to J. Jordan, 4 May 1886, deploring the unthinking attitude of protestants in his district towards home rule (D 2073/2/1) :

My dear Sir—Your favour to hand. In these parts the Protestants all are about 1 in 10, composed of Irish Church, Presbyterians, Methodists, Brethren and an odd antique of a quaker. The Church folk, all afraid of the loss of the Landlords who are the chief payers of the voluntary portion req[uire]d to support their agents—now only clerics. Few of them able to see over their Church spectacles and all who read fed with the pabulum of "Daily Express". The Presbyterians as a rule too busy in their farms to weigh well such a weighty question as the "Rule" one, but all ready to reap any advantage accruing from the Land bill. They however need to be broadened to confidence in the independent & nonclerical Irish Legislation of the future.

The majority of Methodists are willing to see the whole only from a sectarian standpoint, rather than the higher and nobler one of our countrys need & independence, somewhat influenced by that daft section of the Advocate—the political. A few get the M[ethodist] Times (which is very useful) but the "Dailies" are either "Express" or "Irish Times". Only in an odd case is the Freeman taken in—a real loss to themselves.

However, the no. of enquirers—ready to learn—is increasing &, notwithstanding the "Prim" type and the tory Popes of our conference, I expect that the touchstone of the Com[mittee of] Privlege [*sic*] action—on which I am prepared to hit hard, if health permits—will shew a large minority at least. A few of our ministers on the District—possibly a fifth of them, see the reasonableness of Home Rule, but most of them see the matter from the point & in the light of Arthurs pamphlet.

The old fashioned ascendancy notion & distrust & the creation of the local & past prejudices still hold our laity, e.g. at a service I took for text, "How beautiful are the feet &c"—using the whole verse to shew how the beautiful & the good—in nature, in society, in National relations, as in the spiritual life, comes from "Gods reign" stating that the text was suggested by its happy use, in part, by an MP in Parliament. Well, that gave offence, & some old & mulish folk who could think of Wesly [*sic*] only as a "Rebel" wont soon forgive me. Such is humanity! But, withall [*sic*], I feel that the weakness & superficiality of the arguments against are being seen in the light of such utterances as Spensers [*sic*], Chief Sec, Dalhousie Gladstone &c, & that time will quickly dissipate—each one in their own locality considerately [*sic*] helping—the clouds overhead. Just now, perhaps, a twentieth of the elderly ones of our Sect can swallow the whole, & not more than about the 5th of our Juniors, but their eyes will gradually open.

What a splendid manifesto of Gladstones yesterday! He is a giant! I wrote a reply to John Bonds fierce letter in M[ethodist] Times, but they feared re-opening the controversy. . . .

P.S. 'I should say that of all sects outside the E[stablished] C[hurch]'s there prevails an <u>uncertainty</u> & to some extent <u>indifference</u>, & not much <u>dread</u>[?] of their <u>liberties</u>. I am my dear Sir truly yrs

A Duncan

31 Letter from H. Stubbs, Danby, Ballyshannon, Co. Donegal, unionist candidate for South Donegal in the 1892 general election, to the secretary of the I.U.A., 4 August 1892, describing among other things the intervention of certain Roman Catholic priests on behalf of his anti-Parnellite opponent, J. G. Swift McNeill, who was returned by 3,930 votes to 1,400 (D 989A/8/2):

My dear Sir—Since the receipt of yr. Circular asking particulars respecting the interference of R.C. Priests at the late Elections, I have been engaged prosecuting enquiries so as to have as accurate information as possible on the subject.

On the whole I am of opinion that the Priests <u>designedly</u> abstained as much as possible from obtrusive interference at the recent Election in this Division (South Donegal), and with the exception of Ardara, regarding which station I have not as yet heard, owing to the absence of the Sol[icito]r. who had charge for me there, they did not, that I am aware of, act as persona-tion agents.

However, I saw two or three of them outside the Booths in Ballyshannon, evidently assisting, & giving their countenance & support to the Nationalist Voters—The Rev. Mons. McFadden, of Donegal took a prominent part on behalf of my opponent, Mr. Swift McNeill, being his principal Nominator, and, although Mr. McNeill was present on the Nomination Day himself, it was Mons. McFadden, who had charge of, and paid down, as I myself saw, the £200 to the Sheriff's Representative. Further, after the Declaration of the Poll, Mons. McFadden acted as Mr. McNeill's representative in his absence, & proposed for him the usual vote of thanks to the Sheriff.

Rev. Canon McKenna of Bundoran also took a rather prominent part in support of Mr. McNeill, & attended on the Platform at a public Meeting in Ballyshannon, & made a speech on the same occasion; I have also been told that in the Bundoran Chapel he told his Congregation they must no matter at what inconvenience go in on the Polling Day and record their votes.

Rev. J. Dorrian C.C. of Ballyshannon took the Chair at the public meeting here, above alluded to, and I send you a copy of the "Donegal Independent" with a report of their speeches; it also contains particulars of Mr. McNeill's Nomination Papers, as well as other information regarding the late contest in this Division, which may be of use to you. And any further information in my power I shall be happy to give, on hearing from you.

I think I have reason to be very well satisfied with the result of the Election in this Division, as I succeeded in reducing the Nationalist Majority by nearly a thousand votes, having polled the highest Unionist vote; while on the other hand the Nationalists never scored so low before. I certainly worked hard, & my brother did the same; while the Unionists I may say almost to a man backed me well up. And the result wld. have been even more satisfactory but for the wretched state of the Register. My brother (Mr. Alfred Stubbs, Ll.B., Solr.) has now taken this matter up, & since the Election has been very busy sending in Unionist Claims, numbering nearly 150; he is now preparing for the more difficult work of serving objections on the many Voters on the other side, who have no right to be on the Register.

This of course will involve much labour & considerable expense. But although we have at present no funds for this purpose, we determined not to allow the opportunity to pass, but to tackle the work & trust for proper support and the necessary funds, to the future. Had we permitted the Coming Revision to pass without an effort to improve the Unionist position in this Division, the present Register with its many bogus voters wld. have been fixed upon us for another year.

I thought it well to write to you thus fully on the general situation in this Constituency, knowing the interest your Society, as well as yourself, takes in the Unionist Cause in Ireland. I am, Dear Sir, yrs. very faithfully

H. Stubbs

32 Extracts from a 24-page pamphlet, *Why are the methodists of Ireland opposed to home rule,* written by the Rev. W. Nicholas and published in 1893 by the I.U.A., stating among other things the argument against home rule on religious gounds (D 989C/3/23A):

(p.18)   HOME RULE OPPOSED TO LIBERTY.

The Methodists of Ireland are opposed to Home Rule *because they are sincere lovers of civil and religious liberty.*

In every struggle of the past they have been on the side of liberty, they are so still, and in the name of liberty they object to Home Rule. It has often been said Home Rule means Rome Rule. There are three million and a half of Roman Catholics to one million and a quarter of Protestants. It is evident that Roman Catholic influence must be predominant in an Irish Parliament. Will the Romish Church control that influence, or will any large section of the Roman Catholic laity act independently of their clergy? That the dispute in the Nationalist ranks over Mr. Parnell has caused a certain cleavage between the priests and people must be admitted. It must at the same time be admitted that hitherto the priests have proved themselves to be masters of the situation; their power has not gone; it is not even shaken. We do not prophesy. When the power of the priesthood is broken we shall have other considerations to urge. Meanwhile, dealing with things as they are, the dominant power in the Nationalist ranks is the power of the Church of Rome. Frequently persons who claim to be superior in judgment, insight, and information tell us that Rome is not a factor to be taken into account in dealing with Irish politics, that it is antiquated to dread her power, and that in the nineteenth century men may be trusted to think and to act for themselves. These people are doctrinaires; they have a great faculty for ignoring facts. Drawing inferences from facts is quite beneath their dignity.

ROMISH CLAIMS.

Now Rome claims this control over political matters Of the multitude of proofs that might be given let us take an extract from a recent letter written by the Roman Catholic Bishop of Down and Connor. In a circular letter to his priests he says: "I request you to explain at the masses on Sunday that the question wherein action is morally right or morally wrong is essentially a question of morals, and as such is necessarily subject to the judgment of ecclesiastical authority, and every such question must be dealt with by the authority which is alone competent to deal with it on moral grounds, namely, by the pastors of the Church who have received the divine commandment to teach and direct the faith and morals of the people to whom the holy Gospel was committed to their charge. . . . Dissuade them from listening to the advice of those who at present teach disobedience to the pastors when the inspired apostles command to obey thus: 'Obey your prelates, and be subject to them, for they being to watch over you to render an account of your souls.' " But not only is this claim made, but by the overwhelming majority of Roman Catholics in Ireland it is admitted, and admitted *con amore*. An ungrudging and willing obedience is rendered by an affectionate and superstitious people.

The majority of the Nationalists are completely under the control of the Romish Church.

ROMISH INTOLERANCE.

When has Rome declared in favour of religious liberty? When has Rome given religious liberty where she had sufficient power to withhold it? We need not look at Roman Catholic States, but look at lower Canada, under the British crown. A recent traveller, whose sympathies are with Rome, tells us that the day-schools there are but extensions of the confessional, and that a man afflicted with rheumatism was recently fined eight dols. because at some Romish service he only kneeled on one knee instead of kneeling on both! Is it not highly probable that an Irish Parliament would endow the Roman Catholic Church, would endow Roman Catholic educational institutions, and would put down any effort to gain religious liberty on the part of any section of the Roman Catholic people, and interfere in every way in which an executive government could interfere with the exercise of liberty on the part of the Protestants, especially on the small Protestant populations of the south and west?

DR. DOLLINGER.

Mr. Matthews, the Home Secretary, a Roman Catholic, said a few days ago that the Protestants of Ireland "would have reason to fear for their property, their liberties, and their faith if the power of government and legislation were handed over to those who were their hereditary enemies."

The eminent Old Catholic, Dr. Dollinger, one of the greatest authorities on historical questions, "used to laugh at Cardinal Manning's heroic audacity in asserting that Roman Catholics have never persecuted Protestants in the past, and are never likely to do so in the future. One of the first things that an Irish Parliament would do would be to take possession of Trinity College and turn it into a Roman Catholic university."

OPINIONS OF THE PRESBYTERIANS.

The Presbyterians have just issued a manifesto in which they say:—"We accordingly feel that the proposal to give Ireland Home Rule most seriously threatens our religious liberties, which would in numberless ways be imperilled under an Irish National Parliament, the majority in which would be elected on the nomination of the Roman Catholic priests. Judging from the past, such a Parliament would claim and exercise the right to tax Protestants for the maintenance of educational institutions in the direct interests of Roman Catholicism, would legalise the desecration of the Lord's Day, and would ultimately establish and endow the Roman Catholic Religion in Ireland. From these and many other evils we are preserved by the Imperial Parliament."

HOME RULE AND EDUCATION.

Archbishop Walsh has condemned time after time the "mixed" school and "mixed" college, *i.e.,* the school and college in which Protestants and Roman Catholics are taught together. Every Roman Catholic bishop and priest agrees with him. By their action they have almost destroyed the model schools and have kept numbers of Roman Catholic students from Trinity College (which is free to them) and from the Royal University. They want schools and colleges in which can be exhibited the emblems of their faith, manned by Roman Catholics, and completely under the control of the Roman Catholic Church. This would seriously injure the quality of the education given in those institutions, would intensify the religious bigotry and animosity at present existing. In all those districts, and they are numerous, in which there are not sufficient Protestant children to maintain a Protestant school they would be compelled to attend a school in which were images of the Virgin Mary and Crucifixes and Roman Catholic teaching. It is almost inconceivable that Methodists and Nonconformists would try to force such an intolerable state of things upon Methodists and Nonconformists in Ireland. Yet when they aid Home Rule politicians they are doing it. Some may be so carried away by political zeal and party spirit as to be utterly recreant to their own principles; it is probable that some are so and that their opinions not being formed by reason, cannot be overturned by reason. But of the majority we are persuaded better things, and hope that when the case is fairly put before them they will not be led astray by the glamour of a great name but will uphold in Ireland the principles dear to every true Protestant and will give their valuable aid to strengthen the imperilled position of their brethren in a land in which they are in a minority and have a hard struggle in their conflict with a wily and unscrupulous opposition.

Because, then, of their love of civil and religious liberty, and to secure as large a measure of it as possible for Protestants and Romanists alike, the Methodists of Ireland object to Home Rule. . . .

77

33 Extracts from the *Annual report* of the U.U.C. for 1912, reporting the protests of the Presbyterian and Methodist Churches against the liberal government's intention to introduce a third home rule bill in 1912, and the resolutions passed by the general synod of the Church of Ireland expressing attachment to the legislative union, after the introduction of that bill in April 1912 (D 972/17/1912):

PRESBYTERIAN CONVENTION.

This Convention was non-political in character, and was entirely organised by the members of the Presbyterian Church. It was held in Belfast on 1st February, and was one of the most remarkable demonstrations ever held in the Province. No less than eleven meetings were required to accommodate those who desired to be present. The result showed the unchangeable opposition of the Presbyterian Church in Ireland to the Home Rule proposals. The following resolution was unanimously adopted at all the meetings:—

"That we, the members of this great Convention, representing the overwhelming majority of Irish Presbyterians, assembled irrespective of the diverse opinions which we individually hold upon the political questions of the day, having in view the early introduction by his Majesty's Government in the coming Session of a Bill to establish a Parliament in Dublin with an Executive responsible to it, hereby record our unalterable opposition to all such proposals. Under Home Rule as foreshadowed, the Parliament and the Executive alike are certain to be controlled by a majority subject to the direction of the authors of the Ne Temere and Motu Proprio Decrees, against whose domination all safeguards designed for the protection of the Protestant minority, embracing almost one-third of the total population of Ireland, would be wholly valueless.

We are confident that, among other disastrous results, under Home Rule,

(a) Our religious and civil liberties would be greatly imperilled;

(b) Our industrial and agricultural interests would be seriously crippled, with calamitous results to all dependent on them, to whatever religious creed they might belong;

(c) The many philanthropic and missionary enterprises of our Church at home and abroad would in consequence be greatly curtailed;

(d) Presbyterian minorities in all parts of Ireland (many of them consisting of settlers from Scotland) would in most cases, through the unavoidable shutting down of small and struggling congregations, lose the religious ministrations which they now enjoy; and

(e) In view of the long-continued action of the Roman Catholic hierarchy in the direction of denominationalising education in Ireland, the children of such minorities would be deprived in all the provinces of Ireland of places of instruction which they might frequent, as they do now, without danger to their faith.

We call upon the Government, with whose policy, apart from the question of Home Rule, so many of us are in general sympathy, to save us from the disaster which Home Rule would render inevitable. And should the Government fail us, we would earnestly appeal to our co-religionists of all shades of political opinion in Great Britain to save us while there is yet time from such overwhelming calamity. Seeing that so-called safeguards cannot avail, surely there rests an obligation upon our fellow-citizens of the same faith to stand by us in securing the rejection of a policy so dangerous to our highest interests. We appeal to them to remember that we Presbyterians are now in Ireland because three centuries ago our forefathers were 'planted' in Ulster by the English Government in order that, by their loyalty and industry they might secure the peace and prosperity of our province and promote the mutual welfare of both countries. Our fathers and ourselves having done our best to fulfil the trust committed to us, we feel that it would be an unworthy requital should we now, notwithstanding our solemn protest, be deprived of the heritage we enjoy as fellow-citizens in the United Kingdom of equal status with our English and Scotch co-religionists.

In our opposition to Home Rule we are actuated by no spirit of sectarian exclusiveness, and we seek for no ascendancy, religious or otherwise. Many of us were active sharers in the struggle which, over forty years ago, secured religious equality and initiated land reform in Ireland; and, if permitted, we are all of us ready to co-operate with Irishmen of every creed in the advancement of the social, moral, and material prosperity of our common country. Our demand is, as a matter of elementary right and justice, the undisturbed continuance of our present place in the Constitution under which our Church and our country have so signally prospered.

Our Scottish forefathers, in their struggles for religious freedom and civil rights, cast their burden on the Lord Omnipotent, who gave them signal victory. Facing as we now do dangers similar to theirs, we shall follow in their footsteps and emulate their faith. In the profound belief that God reigns, we commit our cause in all confidence to Him." . . .

METHODIST CONVENTION.

Following the example of the Presbyterian Church, the Methodists of Ireland recorded their emphatic protest against the Home Rule proposals of the Government. On March 14th they held five meetings, which were crowded to overflowing. The following resolutions were passed unanimously at all the meetings:—

"Whereas a Home Rule Bill for Ireland is again to be pressed upon the acceptance of Parliament, notwithstanding the earnest protests that were uttered in past years against the establishment of a separate Legislature in Ireland, this meeting of Methodists from every part of Ireland, and representing the vast majority of Irish Methodists, affirms that it abides by the declarations heretofore made by the Conferences of 1886 and 1893, and resolves—

1. That our attachment to the Legislative Union between great Britain and Ireland is absolutely unchanged.

2. That in our deliberate and solemn conviction there is nothing in the history or necessities of this country which requires such far-reaching national changes; but we believe as firmly as ever that the maintenance of the Union, unimpaired and inviolate, is still essential both to the moral and material well being of this portion of the United Kingdom, and that to tamper with it, as now proposed, would be to inflict a grievous wrong upon Ireland itself, especially upon the loyal, law-abiding, and prosperous portion of the community, and would, moreover, open and prepare the way for further changes in the Constitution of very wide and far-reaching evil consequences, especially imperilling the best interests of education, temperance, and Sabbath observance.

3. That our conviction and alarm have been greatly intensified during the last few years by the encroachments of the Papal power in the United Kingdom, as specially illustrated by the promulgation of the Ne Temere and Motu Proprio Decrees, the latter interfering with the rights and privileges of the subject and the former with the civil law in regard to marriage, and threatening the peace and purity and safety of the home.

4. That we still disavow, as utterly alien to the spirit which we have inherited from the fathers and founders of the Methodist Church, all feelings of enmity or ill-will to any class in the community, and all desire for or sympathy with the idea of domination or ascendancy by any class on the ground of religious faith; but, inasmuch as we highly prize the religious equality and freedom which now prevail, we cannot be indifferent to the peril which would threaten that equality and freedom under the rule of such a Legislative Assembly and Executive Government as is proposed to be established.

5. That, holding such views, we believe we should be recreant to our duty as loyal subjects of the King if we failed to give expression to them, or if we refused to co-operate in the earnest efforts being made to expose the mistaken policy which is fraught with such mischief.

That this meeting requests the Executive Committee to continue to watch our interests, and pledges itself to provide the necessary funds for the diffusion of such literature as the Committee may deem to be advisable." ...

THE CHURCH OF IRELAND AND HOME RULE.

A Special Meeting of the General Synod of the Church of Ireland was held on April 16th, when the following resolutions were passed:—

"That we, the Bishops, Clergy, and Laity of the Church of Ireland, solemnly assembled in General Synod, and invoking the guidance and protection of Almighty God, hereby reaffirm our constant allegiance to the Throne, and our unswerving attachment to the Legislative Union now subsisting between Great Britain and Ireland. And we make this declaration at the present crisis not as adherents of a party nor on behalf of a class, but as a body of Irishmen, representing more than half a million of Irish people, holding various political opinions, and following different callings, but sharing at the same time a common desire for the honour and welfare of our native land."

"That thankfully recognising the increase of prosperity and industry in Ireland during recent years, and considering this improvement to be largely due to the beneficial legislation of the Imperial Parliament, which has put the farmers of a large portion of the country into an independent and secure position, we protest against the passing of any measure which would arrest our advance, place the progressive elements of the community at the mercy of the unprogressive, strengthen those forces of disorder still existing among us, and render life and property insecure. We cannot accept any assurances that either the property of our Church or our civil and religious liberty may safely be entrusted to a Parliament in which we should be outnumbered by men who are dominated by traditions and aspirations wholly different from our own."

"That, as Irishmen who love their country and earnestly desire its welfare, we hereby record our devotion to the great Empire of which the United Kingdom is the centre and head. We recognise the advantage and honour we derive from our present Imperial position, and the conspicuous place which Irishmen have long held among those to whom the Empire owes its prosperity and its fame. We, therefore, protest, in the interests both of our country and of the Empire, against any measure that could endanger the Legislative Union between Great Britain and Ireland. We appeal to our co-religionists in Great Britain not to desert their brethren in Ireland, nor to suffer them to be thrust out from their inheritance and citizenship."

These pronouncements, taken in conjunction with the resolutions passed at the great Presbyterian and Methodist Meetings, show how widespread is the hostility of the Protestant Churches in Ireland to any measure tending to weaken the Legislative Union.

III

Such fears of catholic domination were shared by many academics from the protestant foundation of Trinity College, Dublin. These were men such as Provost Jellett, Professor Edward Dowden, some of whose views on the union are to be found in his published letters, and Dr Thomas Maguire, professor of moral philosophy, fellow and tutor of Trinity College, and member of the university council. He was also a member of the senate of the Royal University of Ireland and examiner in classics to the board of intermediate education of Ireland; and as a 'loyal Roman Catholic' he was particularly concerned with the possible harmful effects of home rule and clerical domination upon higher education. His views are well expressed in an article published in 1886, largely in reply to articles which had appeared in the *Dublin Review,* volumes xx and xxvii (second series).

34 Extracts from an 11-page pamphlet, *The effects of home rule on the higher education,* written in 1886 by T. Maguire, arguing that clerical control of higher education would leave Ireland 'as intellectual as Ashantee'—the footnotes have been omitted (D989C/3/5):

(p.4)

... But granting that 'Roman Catholic Education' means anything, it means placing education in the hands of the Bishops, and of the Bishops exclusively; for it is mere thimble-rig to put a few laymen on a Board who may be always relied on to vote square with the Bishops. I can understand and respect the *non-possumus* of the Churchman, but I will not submit to the *non-possumus* of a Chief-Baron or a Deputy-Lieutenant. But if you give the control to the Bishops, I see no reason why the distribution of educational *materiel* should not be according to arithmetic. The Catholics are three to one, therefore give one-fourth of everything to the Protestants, and three-fourths to the Roman Catholics. Why not? asks the Briton—English, Scotch, or Welsh. I will tell them.

It is certain that a large and logical section of the Roman Catholic Church is conscientiously opposed to the spread of education. This is proved beyond doubt by the following extract from the *Dublin Review*—a Review with whose teaching in philosophy, and the border-land between science and philosophy, I am entirely in harmony.

For the information of Protestants, I may add that each article in the *Dublin Review* was, before publication, submitted to the Three Censors appointed to examine its bearings on 'Faith, Morals, and Ecclesiastical Prudence.' It is therefore authoritative as an exponent of opinion. It is as follows:—

'Now, it is a plain fact that by giving Catholic youth a higher education you open a new and very large avenue, by which the godless spirit of the times may gain admittance. And unless they be furnished with fully sufficient moral and intellectual protection, you expose them to imminent danger, not merely of holding the Faith with less simplicity and heartiness (though this would be bad enough), but of wilfully admitting a fully deliberate doubt as to its truth—or, in other words, of actual apostasy. It is this which makes the whole subject so anxious, and which makes one a little impatient with commonplaces about marching with the times, and aiming at progress, and growing in largeness of thought. We are very far from meaning that ignorance is the Catholic youth's *best* preservative against intellectual danger, but it is a very powerful one, nevertheless, and those who deny this are but inventing a theory in the very teeth of manifest facts. A Catholic destitute of intellectual tastes, whether in a higher or a lower rank, may, probably enough, be tempted to idleness, frivolity, gambling, sensuality; but in none but the very rarest cases will he be tempted to that which (in the Catholic view) is an immeasurably greater calamity than any of these, or all put together, viz. deliberate doubt on the truth of his religion. It is simply undeniable, we say, that the absence of higher education is a powerful preservative against apostasy, and those who watch over souls will reasonably refuse to bear part in withdrawing that preservative, until they are satisfied that some other very sufficient substitute is provided. It is the work of higher education, as such, to cultivate and enlarge the mind; but it is the work of *Catholic* higher education, as such, so to cultivate and enlarge the mind as to guard against the danger that such cultivation do immeasurably more harm than good. Now, the Church's interest is not in higher education, as such, but in *Catholic* higher education.'

Now, all that I know of the matter confirms this. When in Galway College I heard the following story of the present Archbishop of Tuam. If it is untrue, I never heard it contradicted, and it is certainly *ben trovato:*—The Bishop closed a school, and when one of the villagers asked how he was to send his children to school, the Bishop replied, 'What do *they* want with school? Let them learn their Catechism.' And it must be allowed, that if salvation and enlightenment are incompatible, the Ultramontane logic is triumphant. Porson's pause will not outweigh an eternity of weal or woe.

Now let us apply this to Ireland. At present the teaching of the Roman Catholic laity in Ireland is not conducted by Irish-reared Roman Catholic priests. It is conducted by converts from the English Universities, foreign priests of distinction, and principally by members of Trinity College, and of the late Queen's University—many of them Protestants. I see no provision made for raising up a school of native clerical teachers. This is not for want of numbers; for the Irish priesthood are infinitely more numerous now than they were when the population of Ireland had passed its eight million. Ireland, besides supplying her own Church, largely recruits the Catholic clergy in England, the rest of the Empire, and America. It is possible, then, for the Bishops to dismiss all the non-Maynooth auxiliaries, and practically crush all the higher education. What is the value of the present system of coaching for the Intermediate Examinations, and for those of the Royal University? The success of the Roman Catholic Schools and Colleges at these Examinations is constantly appealed to as a reason why educational funds should be divided *per capita.* Now I happen to be able to say something on this point. The Examination Papers of the Royal University were for years systematically tapped. As a Senator of the Royal University and a Member of the Convocation, I am about to bring the matter before the Senate and Convocation. As to the Intermediate, the Courses are so miserably short, and the time for preparation is so long, as to necessitate cramming. In regard to marking, I have been obliged, under the Intermediate system, to give marks, when in Trinity College or the Queen's University I should have given none; and my experience as a classical examiner is borne out by the experience of the mathematical examiners. When I examined in Greek the composition was vile; but I was surprised to see how well was done a passage in Thucydides supposed to be unprepared. I *now* believe the paper was tapped. Papers have to be reset at the eleventh hour in both institutions—the Intermediate and the Royal. Would English University men believe that the printed Examination Papers before issue were left under a hearthrug in a room of the Royal University? It is a fact.

What would be the fate of an Irishman who differed from the Bishops? The Ultramontanes have always advocated the punishment of *opinion*, so far as public sentiment would sanction such infliction. The point I wish to impress on Protestants is, that the language of the Ultramontanes is calculated to deceive. The Church, they say, never persecutes and has never persecuted; that is, they will not force a man to profess what he does not seriously believe, but they will punish him for believing that which he does seriously believe. The Ultramontanes will not force a man to profess Catholicity if he seriously rejects it, but they will burn him, if public opinion allows them, because he is a non-Catholic.

If anyone deny that the advocacy of persecution is seriously advanced, he can read the questions discussed in the *Dublin Review,* in an article on Dr. Mivart. Dr. Mivart upholds the rights of conscience in matters outside of dogma, just as here in Ireland the Bull of Adrian is rejected by Gallicans, like Father Behan—a pillar of private judgment. His words best illustrate what I mean: 'Cardinal Newman and several other eminent authorities believe that the Bull of Pope Adrian was a genuine Bull; but that made no matter whatever, for the subject of the Bull was outside infallible Pontifical competence.'

My argument briefly is this:—Catholic education is education under Bishops: if under Bishops, it is but the creature of a day. Home Rule would place education in the hands of the Bishops, with whom it would be as an infant in the tender mercies of the baby-farmer. If not under the Bishops, it must be free. There is no alternative.

The immediate result of Home Rule would be to place education in the hands of the Bishops, certainly for a time. But this means crushing it for at least three generations, and perhaps for ever. The present generation would submit. Their children would be taught to submit; and the third might produce an Irish Voltaire of coarse grain. But, on the other hand, it might not; and Ireland would become as intellectual as Ashantee. I for one should prefer the men who swear by Sir Charles M'Carthy's coat to those who swear by Justin M'Carthy's Histories.

IV

In respect of religious antagonism, there is an interesting difference between unionism in the north and that in the south. In the south, where protestants belonged mainly to the Church of Ireland, a greater degree of religious toleration prevailed and supporters of the union included 'Catholics of substance and repute' **(85)**. In the north, however, where there was a strong Presbyterian element and the social composition of protestantism was different, sectarian feelings ran deeper. Country towns and Belfast were often clearly divided into protestant and Roman Catholic areas.

Such rivalries often revealed themselves, sometimes unexpectedly, in riots and affrays in places such as Tempo in Co. Fermanagh and Portadown in Co. Armagh. There had been party fights in Tempo in 1885, 1886 and 1895, and on 28 August 1896 protestants and Roman Catholics again clashed on fair day. The upshot of the stone-throwing and window-smashing was the prosecution, among others, of one Samuel Clarke for taking part in the affray. Clarke, a protestant solicitor and son of the well-respected dispensary doctor, had, on his own private admission, taken part in the stone-throwing, but was acquitted at the Ulster winter assize of 1896. A well organised defence ensured that the charges of assault and affray would not hold. Doubt was cast on the character of the crown's civilian witnesses, while their evidence of identification was also disputed—the defence held that Clarke had been wearing a low black cap and not a grey cap as crown witnesses alleged. The briefs relating to his defence thus make interesting reading and help to build up a picture of how easily this and similar sectarian affrays could develop, starting with a pub brawl and the ringing of church bells, and drawing in all classes.

The Portadown affray, which suprised the Irish chief secretary, Augustine Birrell, was a more one-sided affair. It involved on 31 March 1916 the destruction of a brick wall by an armed party and was one incident in a series of attempts by orangemen and unionists to prevent the building of a hall for the Ancient Order of Hibernians in a largely protestant area. The fact that the building was being erected under police protection did not deter men with a 'siege of Derry' mentality.

35 Statement by S. Clarke, containing a brief history of affrays in Tempo and of his share in that of 1896, as part of the 'Case for defence' in 'The Queen v. Clarke and others' (D 1096/9/2):

The defendant is prosecuted along with four other Protestants and five Roman Catholics for taking part in a Riot in Tempo on the night of Friday the 28th August 96. Tempo is a village with about 450 Inhabitants in the County of Fermanagh about 7 miles from Enniskillen. There were two small party fights there during the Elections of '85 & '86 but matters had quieted down again until the Election in 1892. In the Election of 1892 the protestants assembled in Tempo to celebrate the return of Mr. Dane M.P. and [the] Rev. Mr. Gaughran P.P. then in Tempo gathered in a rival mob ringing the Chapel Bell to do so. However a riot was averted on that date. On the 28th Decr. 1895 The Roman Catholic band came with a mob of men playing up into the Protestant end of the Town cheering & calling party cries when a free fight ensued between the two parties & the Nationalists smashed in with stones and sticks windows in the houses of Alexander Scholes Mr. T. D. Clements: Rev. Mr. Clements of the Manse Presbyterian clergyman: Mr. Thos. Gibson; Mr. Robert Porter & one of Dr. Clarkes windows who are all inoffensive Protestants. The Sergeant of the R.I.C. issued no summonses or proceedings for this smashing.

Tempo consists of one long street & is divided into two halves a Protestant half & a Roman Catholic half. There is no Protestant living in the Roman Catholic end except Thomas Wilson publican but a good number (upwards of 15 or 20) of Roman Catholics live in the Protestant end of the Town. The country districts surrounding the Roman Catholic end are mostly populated with Roman Catholics. & vice versa round the Protestant end. On the night of the 28th August 1896 I was sitting writing in my fathers (Dr. Clarke) house in Tempo. My father is the Dispensary Doctor in Tempo. About 9 o/c p.m. Sergeant Malone R.I.C. came to my father to ask him to try & quell the row then going on & my father went away with Sergt. I went out down the street also to where the Protestants my father & the Sergt. were standing & stones were coming very quickly from the R.C. crowd & some of the Protestants were returning them. There was a slight lull then & the Sergt. (Malone) asked Mr. Watson (a Protestant) if he (Mr. Watson) would bring the Protestants back as far as Jollys hotel & he (Sergeant) would induce the R.Cs. to go back to the Chapel so as to further separate them. The Protestant party were then at Mr. Watsons shop & Mr. Watson to show both sides he had confidence in this peacefull [*sic*] arrangement & that nothing would be touched took both his shop assistants out of the shop and after almost half an hour was spent in pulling and persuading the Protestants the whole crowd was got back as far as Jollys hotel & then we could distinctly hear the stones hammering off the back of Mr. Watsons house & about 18 or 20 R.Cs. were hammering at it as far as we could judge. & at the same time the Catholic crowd advanced instead of retiring & number of them got into two entries or laneways that are almost opposite Mr. Watsons house on the other side of the Street & from these they (the R.Cs.) threw stones through Mr. Watsons front shop windows. Mr. Watson then said out loudly "That he had come back here (to Jollys) & left his house & place unguarded but had been tricked" (or words to that effect) & as every law was violated then he went back to defend his own house & place & he asked any person there who professed to be a friend of his to help him.

Then the Protestant party went with Mr. Watson to his house & I (S.C. Clarke) went with them. I had neither stick nor stone in my hand as I had brought no stick from the house with me When we got back to Mr. Watsons facing a shower of stones from the Catholic party I stumbled over an oak staff which I kept with me during the remainder of the night. The Protestant crowd then never let the Catholic party past Mr. Watsons during the remainder of the night. When we were at Mr. Watsons the Catholic party were yelling "We took the Town on the 28th December and we are coming up to do the same again" & calling "Orange whelps" &c. & keeping the shower of stones going which the Protestant party returned. Some time after our return

86

to Mr. Watsons a number of our Protestant men went up by the back of Mr. Watsons house to chase the Nationalists who had gone round behind & who were hammering the stones off the back of Mr. Watsons house & I went with them & we (protestants) chased the Nationalists from there. At the back of Mr Watsons house there is an old lane which runs paralell [*sic*] to the main Street & comes out on the Commons or Fair Green Hill. Both the main Street on the one side & this old lane come out at different corners of the Commons. One side of the Street and the office houses at the back run along between them as far as the Commons. The office houses & yards on this side of the street are caved away into the side of the hill & the old laneway is a great deal higher than the main Street: in fact it is even higher than the houses on the main Street. The Nationalists ran back as far as the Commons to get stones & as our side were unable to get any stones there as the stones at the back of Mr. Watsons house had been cleared away by the R.Cs. then we (protestants) went down into the Main Street through Mr. Watsons laneway again. When standing in Mr. Watsons laneway I remember seeing two or three Nationalist fellows in Bernard Breens entry (which is only one house down the street from Watsons on the opposite side) firing across the street at Watsons entry, where several of us were standing in taking shelter from the shower of stones coming up the Street. As soon as these Nationalist fellows got to Breens entry corner they commenced pegging away with stones both at us in the Entry and at Mr. Watsons house & running out on the sidepath and firing at us & then stepping quickly back & escaping the stones which the Protestants & Catholics were sending at one another. So the parties in Watsons entry fired at these fellows in Breens entry as quick as the [*sic*] could show [throw] in order to make it too hot for them to stand their [*sic*] firing at their leisure & certainly I pegged away at the R.Cs. as well as the rest. However the Nationalists at Breens corner left it in about 5 minutes or so & I do not believe I fired any after that. These Nationalists however were 30 yards or so away & any of the Protestants who were in the Entry with me are not important witnesses and wont be called. There is a man named Michael McManus (a nationalist) who lives beside Mr. Watson who I believe alleges he saw me throw stones but he could not have seen me as I was in the Entry which is built over. After these Nationalists left Breens entry we were safe enough in Watsons entry until a number of them got into Ellidges entry which is exactly opposite Watsons entry. They were firing across & I went over to the far side of the street & suddenly put the staff in my hand round the corner. I found then I fortunately had it over about one foot of the head of a Nationalist fellow who had a stone ready to fire in his right hand I asked the fellow what was he doing there He said he was not doing anything only what any one else was doing. & I then said you are throwing stones at Mr. Watsons house & the Protestants who are in his entry and begone out of this & if you attempt to throw that stone I'll hit you over the head with this stick. There were at least two other fellows there also but they all went off down the lane. I returned to the other side of the street again at Mr. Watsons entry & I believe they stopped when down the lane and had an interchange of stones with a couple of Protestants who were standing on the street but I fired none down the lane. About 12 o/c p.m. or so the Protestants were all declaring that they would go down with sticks & clear the town of the opposing party and have done with the matter & some one suggested that some part should go up the back lane that runs up at the back of my fathers (Dr. Clarkes) house & round to near the Commons & meet the crowd of Nationalists who would be sure to run up the Commons to get firing stones in safety on the heads of the protestants below. A number of Protestant men went up this lane which is called (Preaching house Lane) & I went with them. When going around the lane turns & to get into the top of the Commons it is necessary to cross a field & some of the Protestants did not know the way but several including myself did know & we went on round to the Commons & certainly met the Nationalists coming running along in a stream round the end of Patrick Owens house & up the Commons all firing stones as they went along down at the Protestants who were chasing them along the Street. The Protestants on the Commons then fought with & chased the Nationalists off the Commons & this old back lane & we all then went right up the Town to Mr. Watsons again & on our way back up the Town stones were thrown at the Protestant party out of the windows in the Nationalist houses and the Protestant party retaliated by throwing stones at the Nationalists in the Nationalists windows. When coming back through the Nationalist end of the Town a Nationalist named Connolly apparently drunk ran out & commenced striking all around him at the Protestants & was being speedily overpowered when my father & myself caught him & saved him and pulled [him] away down half way through the R.C. end again & left him safely out of danger. There was also another R.C. named Flanagan at the time Connolly was there who my father & I told to go home & he ran off to his own end.

After the police came I was chatting at Mr. Gibsons door with Mr. Gibson when Father Gallagher the P.P. of Tempo came up and said He had heard on reliable authority I was the ringleader of the mob to break his windows I replied that was not true I could assure him as [sic] once that a stone had broken a window I shouted to take care of Father Gallaghers windows. Father Gallagher said he had not seen me do it but he couldnt but believe his authority for stating that I had led the Protestants to smash his window. I replied he might disbelieve me if he liked but to tell his reliable authority with my compliments that he was a liar.

36 Deposition of J. Donnelly, Edenmore, Co. Fermanagh, crown witness, accusing S. Clarke of assaulting him during the Tempo incident, 1896 (D 1096/9/2):

I live about ½ a mile from Tempo. I was employed as yardman by Mr Porter in Tempo on 28th August 1896 being fair day at Tempo Mr Porter lives in the E[nnis]killen end of the town. In consequence of a row going on about 9 pm I went down the town as far as Mr Watson's. There was a crowd at Mr Watsons. I turned back to the diamond again & went straight round to Barney Breen's yard. When I went to the yard the stones were coming so quick from the street that I returned and went through Barney Breen's garden & up the mill-race & well lane on to the road at the fair green. I was about Father Gallagher's house & the fair green for a couple of hours & when at the top of the fair green I saw a crowd of about 20 coming across Mrs Maguire's field. I thought it was between 11 & 12 o'clock then I had no watch. The crowd came out on the fair green [including] Mr Samuel Clarke the defendant now present and Robert Haren to the best cf my opinion. When Mr Clarke came forward to the paling at the side of the gate I first knew it was he. To the best of my opinion he came over the paling he pushed it down anyway. I was about 2 yards from the gate at the time. I turned to go back to the street at Father Gallagher's when I was struck from behind by Samuel Clarke there was no other person near me. I was struck between the 2 shoulders & knocked down After I was knocked down I heard S C Clarke say "Scatter boys & do your work" Mr Clarke & the crowd then went down the commons towards Father Gallagher's. When I was knocked down I shouted I was murdered by Sam Clarke. Pat Slavin was near me. As the crowd was going towards Father Gallaghers and Thomas Maguire's they were throwing stones. I do not know who threw the stones but I heard glass breaking in Father Gallagher's house. The crowd went down the street in the direction of Mr Watson's. I heard nothing the whole time but the smash of glass The glass in Father Gallaghers windows was all broken & the woodwork of most of the windows also was broken

Cross-examined by Mr Falls solicitor—

At the present time I earn nothing & do nothing I live with my father and do odd jobs about Tempo. I was at one time a letter carrier & was convicted of stealing money out of a letter & got 3 months imprisonment for the offence at Fermanagh assizes I think at the summer assizes of 1887. I was since convicted of trespass in persuit [*sic*] of game & fined 10/– I was once convicted of drunkenness about 5 years ago On the night of the 28th August 1896 I left Mr Porter's about 9 pm and got to the commons about 9.30 pm I threw no stones that night. Mr Clarke was about 3 yds in advance of the crowd Bob Haren was beside Mr Clarke. I am not positive it was Haren. I knew Haren before this. Mr Clarke had a grey cap on his head. I did not see Mr Clarke assault anyone else that night or do anything.

37

Deposition of J. Dunne, Coolcran, Co. Fermanagh, crown witness, giving evidence against S. Clarke for his part in the Tempo incident, 1896 (D 1096/9/2)

The Deposition of James Dunne of Coolcran

I live about 1½ miles from Tempo I went in there about 10pm on the night of the 28th August 1896 Some time after I went in I went to the fair-green I saw a crowd there of about 30 persons the crowd were throwing stones down the Commons in the direction of the priests house In the stonethrowing crowd I knew Mr Sam Clarke the Defendant now present. He was throwing stones in the direction of the Priests house. A stone struck me on the right elbow I do not know who threw it. The crowd remained after I was struck about 5 minutes and then went down the town. As they went down the town I heard the glass falling I do not know if Defendant was in that crowd

Cross-examined by Mr Falls Solicitor

I came into Tempo when I heard the bells ringing to see what it was about. I came about 10pm and left for home when I heard the strange police coming I decline to answer whether I was throwing stones I was with a crowd near the priests house The crowd were about the middle of the fair-green opposite to the priests house a little nearer the top than to the middle I went up to see who were in the crowd I got within a yard of Mr Clarke before I knew him. He wore a cap. I was a member of the Tempo Temperance catholic band which played last December when Mr. Clements window was broken.

38

Deposition of Sergeant T. Malone, Tempo R.I.C., relating to the Tempo incident, 1896 (D 1096/9/2):

... I am Sergt in charge of Tempo sub-district and was in charge of the police there on the night of the 28th. August 1896 the fair day there. Something after 8 pm that night there was a quarrel opposite Wilsons public house and a crowd collected there. There was a scuffle going on & very loud talk Constable Prior and myself went up to the crowd & were joined there by Constable Colahan we separated the crowd into 2 parts. As they were separating there were stones thrown. One of these parts consisted of Catholics and the other of protestants. The protestants went to Watson's and the Catholic's [*sic*] to Murphy's corner. I went to the Catholic crowd and stood speaking to them whilst speaking to the Catholic crowd I saw 3 or 4 persons come out of Wilsons public house who fired stones towards the Catholic crowd where I was standing The Catholic crowd threw stones at them I cautioned the Catholic crowd not to throw stones and went over to Wilsons. The 3 or 4 men went into wilsons before I arrived there. I remained a few minutes in Wilsons and then went to the Protestant crowd which was at Watsons when I got to the crowd I spoke to them there were stones being thrown by both crowds at this time The stone throwing continued at intervals during the night and party expressions were used I had to take refuge in a house part of the time owing to the stonethrowing. Several windows were smashed & house wrecked. The Church & Chapel bells both were rung and people came in afterwards. This state of things continued up to about 1 am next morning extra police began to arrive at 1 a.m. and continued to arrive till 1.30 a.m The streets were cleared about 2 a.m. I was at the fair green about 11 p.m. and was not there again till after the extra police arrived. I saw the defendant now present at James Kerr's door about 9.30 p.m. There was a stonethrowing mob there at the time I saw him take no part in the riot then or any other time that night. I saw him again in a crowd on the street nearly opposite Kerr's about 10:30 p.m. I spoke to him on the first occasion & asked him to use his influence with the protestant party to get them back off the town and he told me he had no influence with them. That was all the conversation I had with him that night.

Cross-examined by Mr Falls Solicitor:—

The defendant is a gentleman of the highest character as far as I know and his family are people of position in Tempo. When the riot commenced I went at once to his father's house for assistance. At my request his father used his influence to quell the disturbance as well as he could and was wounded I believe in doing so at least I saw him a few days after with a cut on his forehead and a black eye when I asked Mr Clarke the defendant to assist in pulling back the protestants Mr Kerr was present.

39

Counsel's advice as to how S. Clarke's defence should be conducted, 26 November 1896 (D 1096/9/2):

I think that in the interests of Mr. Clarke who alone, so far as I can follow the depositions, has more than a chance of escape from the grave charge formulated against him his case should be represented by separate & independent Counsel. The positive evidence of the Police as to the assistance rendered to the peace of the town by Mr. Clarkes father and the remarkable fact that the evidence of the three Constables who were in charge of the town & about the streets all night is silent as to any complicity of Mr. Clarke in any part of the disturbance lead me to anticipate that it will not be possible to get a jury to convict Mr. Clarke of any misconduct on that night. But undoubtedly there is substantive evidence against him: and it is unfortunate that no part of the evidence brings any one of the three constables on to the fair green at or about the time when Mr. Clarke is alleged to have been most active according to the evidence of the civilian witnesses for the crown: Every effort must therefore be directed to discrediting these crown witnesses: and if their previous character leaves them open to damaging cross-examination materials for this purpose, clear and cogent should be placed at Counsels disposal. Thus the effect of their testimony will be weakened—and when to the natural uncertainty thus created is added the facts about Mr. Clarke's cap and his clothing I think we need have little doubt that a conviction cannot be obtained against Mr. Clarke.

The two Beatty witnesses should attend: also Mr. Kerr: Mrs. Clarke to give evidence as to Mr. Clarkes clothing & cap and Miss Clarke who I understand can strongly supplement her mothers evidence on this point, and, if possible, some independent person who can stand cross-examination as to his conduct that night and who will swear that Mr. Clarke wore a low black hat in [?] the streets. It will be unnecessary to produce any witnesses as to character: Mrs. Clarke & Miss Clarke must be prepared to explain clearly to the jury why they noticed Mr. Clarke's hat and clothing so particularly on that occasion & to say that he bore no marks either on clothing or person of having taken part that night in any scenes of violence. It would be useful to have another respectable witness—who will stand the fire of cross-examination—not likely, by the way, to be very deadly, to depose to Mr. Clarkes conduct that night at difficult times & places throughout the night: but the witness must be carefully selected and should be put through a course of examination before being presented to the jury. Anything which shows by respectable witnesses Mr Clarkes conduct to have been utterly at variance with that described by the Civilian witnesses at difficult periods of the night will weigh most powerfully with the Jury. Nothing further occurs to me except to direct that the clothing Mr. Clarke wore that night and the hat should be forthcoming at the trial.

40 Letter from the Irish chief secretary, A. Birrell, to Sir Edward Carson, 31 March 1916, enclosing **(b)** a copy of a telegraphed police report of an affray at Portadown (D 1507/1/1916/6):

(a)

My dear Sir Edward—I enclose a telegram just arrived which relates to a curious proceeding near Portadown. It is rather a novelty, & though beyond the demolition of a building & a great deal of gunpowder nothing of great consequence has as yet happened I thought you should be told about it—as so far we have had next to no trouble in the North

I was very glad to see you in & about the House again, though it is no pleasure to be there. Yours v sincerely

Augustine Birrell

(b)

Copy wire received in Irish office 3.24 p.m. 31.3.16.
Under Secretary to Chief Secretary.

Following telegram received from Dist. Inspector Portadown (begins)

Yesterday between 2.30 & 3 p.m. while men were engaged in building a new A[ncient]. O[rder of] H[ibernian] Hall in Breagh S[ub?]. D[ivision?]. Birches, shots were fired from a distance, but no one was injured. At 4.50 a.m. today about 200 men arrived with rifles, revolvers, & swords & bayonets, marched in fours to the site of the hall & after firing about 200 shots demolished the brick wall built yesterday, and smashed all the bricks. These men who are all believed to be neighbouring Orangemen & Unionists were all disguised & none of them were identified by the police patrol which was present. The patrol attempted to follow them when leaving & about 20 rifles were turned on them & ball cartridges fired in their direction without hitting them—in all about 600 or 700 shots were fired. During the demolition of the material about 20 men were posted at a distance round the building with orders to shoot at any person approaching. ends.

41 Letter from W. Moore, Moore Lodge, Kilrea, Belfast, unionist M.P. for North Armagh and an official of the Orange Order, to Carson, 4 April 1916, explaining the origin of the Portadown affray (D 1507/1/6/34):

My dear Carson—I had a deputation of 3 men from Clonmakate yesterday.

You must understand that in that country there are clear demarcations of Protestant and Roman Catholic territory, and processions are not allowed to pass through opposing districts as a well recognised police rule there.

Maghery is the Nationalist head quarters 3 miles away. This townland (of Breagh) contains 12 Protestant families & 4 R.C. 2 of whom and the P.P. are opposed to the erection of this Hall. The site chosen is close to an Orange Hall, a Masonic Hall two churches (C of Ireland & Presbyterian) & in the centre of a triangle with 3 Protestant schools. It is looked upon by the Protestants as a mere act of aggression and boasted of as such by the Nationalists. They began it three years ago & it was levelled. They began it again about 18 months ago & it was again levelled. Nothing more happened until this time they were afforded police protection. Police protection should not be afforded for an act of aggression.

If the police are now withdrawn the Nationalists will never attempt to go on with it & nothing more will be heard of it. James Campbell might speak to Birrell about it. No one was assaulted or hurt & there can hardly be a prosecution. If the police protection is continued & the Nationalists build under it possibly lives will be lost. Our people asked me if they would be given police protection to build an Orange Hall in Maghery? This is not in Portadown District but in Loughgall where the D[istrict] M[aster] has not the same influence. I can do nothing with them. They look on themselves as bound to stop this just as if they were in Derry during the siege. Yours ever

W. Moore

Chapter IV

The emergence of the unionist movement in Ireland 1885-6

Prior to 1885–6 the opponents of the nationalist movement in Ireland had shown little energy in combating home rule and had been divided politically, into liberals and conservatives. In these years, however, efforts were made by the opponents of home rule to mobilise their resources and to sink old party differences, particularly to fight the Parnellites in the general election of November–December 1885. This was the first election following what some contemporaries regarded as 'almost the final reform act', and Parnell's opponents, especially in the south, were hoping to disprove his boast that his party would sweep the board with the enlarged electorate. Liberal and conservative opponents of home rule in the three southern provinces combined more readily than those of Ulster, but by the middle of 1886 old party designations had been abandoned in Ulster as well.

The object of this chapter is to show how the documents in the N.I.P.R.O. can be used to build up a picture of unionist efforts to organise for the first time in 1885–6 and the difficulties unionists encountered.

II

In the three southern provinces the opponents of home rule began to organise energetically by 1885. How closely their opposition was related to the land question may be seen in the emergence of local organisations, such as the Cork Defence Union **(19)**, designed to protect individuals and estates from the consequences of agrarian agitation. Founder members of such organisations were also behind the re-alignment of parties precipitated by the extension of the franchise in 1884. The franchise act of 1884 extended the household franchise to the counties and boroughs in Ireland. It was accompanied in 1885 by a redistribution act abolishing or reducing the representation of certain boroughs. Leaving the number of

Irish members unchanged, the act deprived most of the smaller Irish boroughs of their separate representation, merging them into (revised) county divisions.

Although the significance of the third reform act for Parnell's sweeping success in the general election of 1885 has been exaggerated, the extension of the franchise against a background of what may be described as class warfare encouraged liberal and conservative opponents of home rule to sink their differences and cooperate against the common enemy. On the one hand, some hoped that with a wider and untried electorate the Parnellite movement might be checked at the next general election, if all loyalists sank their differences and cooperated in contesting the elections. On the other hand, others, less optimistic of electoral success, wanted loyalists to organise in order to show British politicians that loyalism was not dead in Ireland and that the traditional classes were still a significant force in politics. The Anglo-Irish had been not a little piqued that the British parties had allowed the extension of the Irish franchise, which, they thought, was tantamount to handing Ireland over to the nationalists. Since Parnellites were boasting that they would sweep the electoral board at the next election, it was felt necessary to organise to prove that the demand for home rule was not unanimous. It was thus a combination of apprehension, pique and determination that led in 1885 to new political groupings.

In parliament Irish opponents of home rule did not form a distinctive organisation until January 1886, but outside of parliament they were quicker to organise. Thus on 1 May 1885 was founded the I.L.P.U., though for reasons of security it did not announce its existence publicly until 16 October. It hoped to fight Parnellites in the three southern provinces in the forthcoming general election; and adopted a simple programme, the maintenance of the union. Thus seeking to cut across old party lines by providing a platform wide enough for the 'enlightened men' of any party, the I.L.P.U. met a widely felt need for loyalist combination in the south and was soon supported by local branches.

In the event 54 of the southern seats had anti-home rule candidates, and in some respects the results were not encouraging. Only two unionists were returned in the south—for the unopposed seats of ,Dublin University; the average unionist poll was only ten per cent, though in Dublin and Cork respectable minority votes were recorded; and there were complaints of lack of energy on the part of many unionist candidates.

Nevertheless, the effort was not entirely wasted, for the basis had been laid for a new movement which was to abandon political activity only in 1922. On the one hand, the I.L.P.U. had been active in the elections and could find some satisfaction in looking at the election figures for all Ireland. Of an electorate of 741,984, some 59% or 438,001 had voted in the 78 contested elections; 292,895 votes had been cast for nationalists and 145,106 for liberal and conservative candidates; thus, of the total electorate 39.5% had voted nationalist, 19.5% for the opponents of home rule, and of those who voted about 66.8% did so for nationalists and 33.2% for their opponents. Therefore, it was argued that had there been representation proportionate to votes given, the ratio of 1 : 2 would have given 34 unionists and 69 nationalists, instead of the 18 unionists and 85 nationalists actually returned. On the other hand, liberals and conservatives had found it possible to combine, despite divergent views on other issues, on 'one single plank—maintenance of the union'. All but eight of the anti-home rule candidates were conservatives, but the conservative candidates had not tried to fight on a narrow party platform. Unfortunately, apart from a press report of the first annual general meeting of the I.L.P.U., 8 January 1886, there is little material in the N.I.P.R.O. relating to the early months of the southern unionist organisation.

42 Extracts from a report in the *Irish Times,* 9 January 1886, of the first annual general meeting of the I.L.P.U., 8 January, containing **(a)** a report by the executive committee of the work done in the 1885 general election; and **(b)** a speech by Viscount de Vesci, one of the originators of the association, reviewing and justifying such action (T 2759/1):

(a)

The Union published and circulated 286,000 leaflets and pamphlets during the elections irrespective of those put in circulation by the candidates themselves.

Special attention is directed to the Irish election returns, with details of voting in the contested elections, which were issued by the union at the close of the elections.

The following facts have been brought out by the action of the I.L.P.U.:—

Taking together all the contested elections in Ireland, the number of votes cast for Separation barely exceeded one-half of the electors; one quarter, roughly speaking, voted against Separation, and the remaining quarter abstained from voting.

If the representation of all Ireland were at all in proportion to the number of votes given, the Unionists would have 34 representatives, the Separatists 69.

As is already known, the operations of the Irish Loyal and Patriotic Union were confined to the three Southern provinces of Munster, Leinster, and Connaught.

For these three provinces 52 contests in all took place, and there were 18 uncontested elections.

The I.L.P.U. contributed to the expenses of the Unionist candidates in accordance with the circular issued to its supporters, subsidising candidates to an extent not less than the sheriff's nomination fees.

For the purpose of the association a considerable sum was subscribed, each subscriber receiving a formal receipt, with the undertaking that neither the name nor amount of his subscription should be made public without the sanction of such.

For this reason no list of subscribers is published.

(b)

... We have been much criticised in our work—for working, as it has been said, in secret, and in not divulging names. But I think you will acknowledge that there has been one name in regard to which there has been no secret, and that is the name of Mr. Houston. (Hear, hear.) Every member of the I.L.P.U. has seen the name of Mr Houston in some form or another, whether at the foot of circulars or letters, and I don't think I exaggerate when I say that the services rendered by him and his assistants have been characterised by the greatest zeal, ability, and tact. (Hear, hear.) I don't think that zeal is too strong a word to use, when we bear in mind the fact that not only are the duties since the commencement of the Union very arduous, but for six weeks prior to the election the office hours, as a rule, commenced at 10 o'clock in the morning and were rarely over until 12 o'clock at night, and sometimes it was 1 or 2 o'clock in the morning. ... The association has circulated 14,000 pamphlets speaking roughly, and 270,000 leaflets. The leaflets were in any form as opportunity occurred of calling attention to the devices and tactics of the Parnellite party. ... [We] brought them and their operations to the bar of public opinion, and in no way that I have seen, through their Press, or otherwise have they attempted to defend themselves, or to rebut the accusations that we have brought against them. ... [Judging by] the voting in the contested constituencies it would appear that one half of the registered electorate voted for Separation, and the remainder over the other quarter who voted against it we claim on your behalf, in accordance with our distinct challenge, to claim the whole of those who abstained from voting for obvious and various reasons. We have been much criticised for having promoted electoral contests. A great many people have said that we ought to have allowed the whole of the elections to go by default. I would answer, first, that the election which is just over was one of the most important ever known, being the first after what we may look upon almost as the final reform bill; and, secondly, that if such contests had not taken place the demand for Home Rule, coming as it would have as the unanimous desire of Ireland, must have been conceded by England.

III

In Ulster the opponents of home rule were slower to organise, largely because there were so many obstacles to overcome. Such difficulties not only inhibited cooperation among protestants and between liberals and conservatives, but also prevented energetic action on the part of either party in face of the challenge posed by electoral reform.

First, there was apathy and parochialism, especially among conservatives. Except in Belfast, conservative organisation was rudimentary. Constituency organisation had been slow to develop. Candidates were usually selected by the local county families and then approved at public meetings. The candidates were responsible for their own expenses and hired a lawyer to look after the register and to organise the campaign. This loose organisation encouraged both parochialism and passivity.

Secondly, there was a strong liberal tradition in Ulster.

Thirdly, orangeism was a divisive force. Prior to the 1880s the institution had been in decline, but in the early 1880s it revived. The nationalist victory in a by-election in Monaghan in July 1883 and nationalist threats to stage meetings throughout Ulster gave orangemen an opportunity to organise violent counter-demonstrations. Some members of the gentry and aristocracy, such as Edward Saunderson, a Cavan landowner and formerly whig member for that county, quickly took over the leadership of the revived movement, but others, liberals and conservatives alike, disapproved of the institution. They were suspicious of its largely working class character and its exuberant sectarianism, particularly when its energy was directed as much against fellow conservatives as against nationalists and liberals.

Fourthly, the land question was a divisive factor. Gladstone's land act of 1881 had not solved the question of the relations between tenants and landlords. Both were dissatisfied with the system of dual ownership established by the act, the gravest defect of which was the absence of any definition of fair rent and of any provision laying down a method for its determination. Protestant tenant farmers in Ulster thought that an insufficient allowance was being made for improvements carried out by them, while their landlords reckoned that judicial rents were far too low.

In 1885 there were attempts to overcome some of these problems, but in the main the general election of that year in Ulster saw the opponents of home rule unprepared. Ulster, which had hitherto been almost untouched by the nationalist challenge, conceded 17 of its 33 seats to a well-organised nationalist party. The remaining 16 went to conservatives.

This experience awoke some conservative and liberal opponents of home rule to the dangers of allowing old rivalries to hinder resistance to a common enemy. It led to serious attempts in 1886 to sink party differences in an effort to mobilise loyalist forces and defeat the home rule movement in future elections. Local organisation got under way with the appearance of registration societies such as the North West Loyalist Registration and Electoral Association, a comprehensive association formed to organise unionist electoral resources in constituencies like South Derry, where old party rivalries had permitted the return of that liveliest of nationalists, Tim Healy. Great efforts were made to see that both liberals and conservatives got fair treatment in any association.

Despite the obvious incentive to organise on an inter-party basis, attempts to organise centrally and in Belfast were fraught with difficulties. Some eminent Ulstermen looked to the Irish Loyal and Patriotic Union to coordinate unionist energies in Ireland, and they repudiated as 'dead and useless' the Irish Loyal Union which had been formed in Belfast in August 1885;

but other protestants in Ulster apparently thought that Ulster unionists had their own special interests at stake and preferred to organise on a provincial basis. Thus on 8 January 1886 was founded the Ulster Loyalist Anti-Repeal Union, which with several changes in name and in constitution remained in existence as the central core of the unionist party in Ulster. However, it was largely conservative in inspiration, and it was greeted with suspicion by the liberal press in Ulster. There was a strong liberal tradition in Ulster and a strong attachment to Gladstone, which liberals were reluctant to abandon, particularly as the scope of the home rule proposals was not then known. Thus in the first quarter of 1886 liberals went through a period of uncertainty leavened by a little hope, and sent a deputation (which included Adam Duffin, a Belfast linen merchant) at the end of March to seek reassurance and guidance from such liberal leaders as John Bright, Lords Spencer and Hartington, and Joseph Chamberlain. They found them equally uncertain as to their leader's real intentions; but the situation was clarified by the introduction of the first home rule bill on 8 April.

The bill was deemed contrary to liberal principles, and in face of this definite threat to establish a parliament in Dublin with (what were considered to be) only illusory guarantees for minorities, old party antagonisms paled into insignificance. The actual proposal to hand Ulster loyalists 'over to their inveterate nationalist foes' overcame sectional differences and led liberals to consider a realignment of parties in Ulster, as in Great Britain. On 14 April 1886 a mass meeting of conservatives and liberals was held in the Ulster Hall, Belfast, to protest against home rule; and on 30 April a meeting of liberals, protesting against home rule, formalised the developing split in the party by setting up a committee to publicise their objections to home rule. On 4 June this committee decided to call itself the Ulster Liberal Unionist Committee.

While the press is an indispensable source for the realignment of parties in Ulster in 1885-6, the materials available in the N.I.P.R.O. do illustrate many of the difficulties that the emergent unionist movement had to face.

43 Copy of an undated (but c.1873?) memorandum by H. de F. Montgomery criticising the Orange Order for its harmful and divisive effect on Irish protestantism and society (T 1089/412):

It is impossible that a country can be truly free and prosperous unless its inhabitants live and work together as one people and cease to be divided into two tribes by barriers of race or creed. There are two influences at work to keep Irishmen so divided, the one popish bigotry represented by the ultra-montane priesthood and the other protestant bigotry as represented by the Orange Institution. It is the interest of the Romish Church to keep her followers as much as possible a people apart as the intellectual contact with protestants in this age of enlightenment would tend to shake their allegiance and destroy the power and influence of that church—this was most clearly illustrated in the opposition they offered this spring to Mr. Gladstone's University bill otherwise so favourably constituted for them. It should manifestly be the policy of protestants, patriots and foes of priestcraft to encourage as much as possible free and equal intercourse between their fellow countrymen of different persuasions and obliterate in all matters unconnected with special religious dogmas and forms of worship all the lines of demarcation between them. In the matter of primary education most protestants appear to perceive this and support the national system of mixed education. The priesthood perceive it too and are now opposing that system. But those protestants who uphold Orangeism appear not to perceive that the very existence of their institution and still more the days they choose for their public, conspicuous and noisy (by which I do not mean disorderly, but refer only to the drumming) gatherings perpetuate the most rigid and bitter line of demarcation possible by recalling the time when the different races and creeds who inhabited and still inhabit Ireland fought against each other in a fierce and bloody civil war. What can be better calculated to keep the descendants of the vanquished party—forming a large numerical majority of the inhabitants of the country—disloyal and disinclined to change or modify their religious and political opinions than to keep them constantly reminded of their defeat and with it of the oppression they subsequently endured and which they are told about in heightened colours by those whose interest it is that they should be more loyal to Rome than to Britain and Ireland's true interests—I maintain then that Orangeism and especially the July celebrations play directly into the hands of the most dangerous and bigoted portion of the priesthood and they are opposed to the true interests of protestantism and patriotism.

In every civilized country heathen or Christian it has been the rule—a rule dictated as much by policy as by Christianity and indeed the simplest morality—not to celebrate the triumphs of civil war. And in no country does the application of this rule seem more called for than in Ireland—for in many countries civil wars have been waged between different portions of the same state—the belligerents have been locally divided—as in America, Switzerland and Germany so that local celebrations of victory might be held without immediate offence to the vanquished—but here there is hardly a townland where men of different creeds—descendants of the victors and the vanquished are not found living side by side and yet in Ireland alone are the events of past civil wars publicly commemorated.

Waterloo was perhaps the hardest fought battle ever won by British valour and for many years it was the custom to celebrate the anniversary thereof by military reviews and public dinners and festivities. When an alliance was arranged between England and France these celebrations were discontinued with the approval of all good and reasonable men but in Ireland we still celebrate the anniversary of the Boyne though the vanquished are now not merely allies but fellow citizens fellow countrymen and in every sense neighbours, whom to love as ourselves Christ asserted to be as great a commandment as to love our God!

The existence of the orange institution is in my opinion mischievous and opposed to the true interests of protestantism—understood as the religion founded on the right of private judgement—and of our country— but the institution in theory is far superior to its practice—which is growing inconsistent with its rules. The Orangeman according to the rules is to take the scripture for his rule of faith and practice and generally cultivate righteousness. If there is one principle fundamental to Christianity and to all morality it is the "golden rule" "Do unto others as ye would that they should do unto you". Suppose now that King William had happened to be cowardly and faithless as James was and that James had happened to be brave and faithful as William was and that as an inevitable consequence the Catholic party finally had won the fight and ruled the protestants for many years with a rod of iron, would the protestants have liked the anniversaries of their defeats and subjections loudly celebrated before their faces year by year. There can be but one answer. One of the first rules of the Society is then constantly violated by their most regular, characteristic and conspicuous practice, of celebrating conspicuously with flags and drums the anniversaries of the Boyne and Aughrim. Another ordnance is that an orangeman must be courteous and that he should abstain from all uncharitable words actions or sentiments towards his Roman Catholic brethren. It would be hard to conceive a greater breach of courtesy and every rule of ordinary good taste and Christian charity than to be constantly reminding your neighbour that you once beat him and subjected him—or that your forefather did so to his forefather—or keep the anniversary of the event in a manner sufficiently noisy to preclude all possibility of his not observing it—and if of at all susceptible character of being annoyed by it.

Some of the rules which follow appear to be inconsistent with the stated basis and general qualification. We are told in the first paragraph in this little book that the association will not admit into its brotherhood any whom an intolerant spirit leads to persecute injure or upbraid any man on account of his religious opinions. But it is surely an intolerant spirit that lead the framers of the rule to lay down (p.12) that "any member dishonouring the Institution by marrying a Roman Catholic shall be expelled" and it seems to me a case of both injury and upbraiding on account of religious opinions if not of persecuting to lay it down that an association would be dishonoured by the union of a member with a virtuous woman of a respectable family because she is a Roman Catholic. With regard to the rule as to anniversaries (XXVII) I will only observe that as the 5th of November is to be observed "in compliance with an act of parliament requiring an annual thanksgiving" somewhat inconsistently on the same day for the preservation of one James Stuart and the deposition of another—that act of parliament having been repealed in compliance with the good sense and good taste of British public opinion, the Orangemen's celebration of that day should in consistency also be dropped. My objection to the celebration of the 12th July in general I have already stated but I must here say that if it was celebrated according to the letter of this rule it would be comparatively unobjectionable viz., in the same manner as that prescribed for the celebration of the 5th November, i.e., by attending divine worship or otherwise meeting together in grateful observance of that anniversary: but carefully abstaining from anything in word or behaviour which might unnecessarily give offence. The natural reading of which would be to abstain from processions, banners, drumming, playing tunes of songs jeering at or triumphing over the papist party—and to meet quietly in some private place and give thanks for God's mercies in times past or, may be, drink in an orderly quiet and decorous fashion to the glorious memory of William—indisputably one of England's greatest kings. Of extra public celebrations of other anniversaries of civil strife on July 1st, August 12th, etc., no mention is made in the rules so I must regard them as unnecessary and irregular even from an Orange point of view.

Having spoken thus strongly against the principles and practice of Orangemen in general I wish to express as strongly my respect and regard for the large majority of Orangemen as individuals, a more trustworthy well intentioned and gallant body of men are I believe not often to be met with and little or no blame can attach to them individually for observing practises[*sic*] which they have been brought up to consider not only blameless but meritorious. This is a time of rapid enlightenment and growth and change in public opinion and I confidently hope to live to see the time when the heartiness and energy of this fine race may be turned into channels more calculated to benefit our country. True, noblemen, gentry and clergy have to some number lately joined the institution whose education according to my account ought to have taught them better but I believe that of these some have joined because they were brought up to it and have given as little thought to the matter as the most ignorant farmer, some from the desire of exercising power and influence over so fine a body of men (these forget that the ambition of power and influence is only justifiable when it is desired for the sake of doing good to one's country and mankind), some with the honest belief that by gaining power and influence over Orangemen they could direct their energies into better courses than they would take if left to themselves; these do not consider that they may be doing more harm by the means by which they acquire power and influence than they will be able to do good with this power and influence when acquired and that in these democratic days it is at least as likely that the stream will carry them off their legs as that they will direct the stream. Others again join and encourage Orangeism because they think that by keeping the protestant minority apart from the bulk of their fellow countrymen and giving them their support and countenance and fostering their dread of their Catholic fellow countrymen they will procure support for their class privileges which are threatened by the advance of representative institutions. These men are short sighted themselves—they can only postpone the change for a short time and make it more violent and worse for themselves when it comes—and they seek to degrade protestantism by making it a bulwark of political stagnation and obstructiveness instead of what it naturally is—or should be—a religion of progress, and they enable the Roman clergy to represent themselves as apostles of freedom, and protestantism as a tyrannous and slavish system.

Others less selfish but equally mistaken believe Orangeism to be a bulwark against the agitation for repeal or Home Rule. The more loudly Orange meetings when celebrating extinct civil war and obsolete party spirit pronounce against Home Rule the more inclined will the majority of Irishmen who are taught by the keeping up of these anniversaries to regard themselves as the hereditary enemies of protestantism, be inclined to fall into the arms of the agitators, and even if the minority proves strong enough to hold its own the country must remain in an unsatisfactory and disaffected condition as long as it is ruled in a manner different from what the majority desire. Let those who oppose Home Rule borrow some wisdom and prudence from the Home Rulers themselves and try to obliterate religious barriers, and a strong party of adherents of all creeds, who have a stake in the country and are growing in prosperity under the present system and know not how it might be under Home Rule, could be formed in defence of the union.

To sum up these observations. While I like and honour the great majority of Orangemen I cannot approve or countenance the institution and celebrations because I consider them opposed to the true interests of Ireland, of protestantism and of civil and religious liberty and to the principles of Christianity, morality, good taste and good policy inasmuch as they tend to divide Irishmen into hostile sects, play into the hands of the bigoted ultramontane party and the Home Rule agitators, violate the golden rule and postpone the development of Ireland's prosperity and freedom civil and religious.

44 Letter from A. Duffin, writing from 29 University Square, London, to his wife, Maria, 27 March 1886, describing the activities of a delegation of Ulster liberals visiting London to discuss the prospects of the forthcoming home rule bill with liberal leaders other than Gladstone (Mic 127/2):

Dearest—I sent you a wire this morning which I fear will disappoint you, but I can't get away—probably not until Tuesday afternoon. I have just come away after a long interview with John Bright which has had a rather depressing effect on me. He is a splendid old fellow & fully appreciates our position, loathes the 86 Parnellites even more than we do, but is quite hopeless or very nearly so. He says they must get rid of these scoundrels in the House & what then is the alternative to Home Rule. Only coercion more stringent than ever and the expulsion of the Irish members & the general feeling here is that party government will not allow such a course to be taken or pursued with success. It is sickening. Lord Spencer says just the same. He is going in for Home Rule as the only alternative to faltering coercion.

The probability is that Mr Gladstone's prestige & wonderful power of persuading himself & other people will carry his scheme through the house of Commons. I only hope he will make it thorough. If we are to have it at all, it is the only thing that is of any use & besides there is more chance of his being beaten on it

There seems to be just a chance of Hartington & Goschen forming a Govt. with Conservative support.

I saw Mr. Hibbert & had a long talk with him yesterday & am to see him again on Monday. He was very kind & glad to hear all I had to say—but says he knows just nothing of Gladstones scheme.

I am going to dine with the Garretts tomorrow & will go out early to have a walk.

I have got rather a bad headache which comes of two nights of heavy dinners at the Reform Club followed by animated political discussion. I hope poor old John Bright is not as tired as I am—we had two long hours of it with him. The perfect candour of all these great men is wonderful. There is just one point on which they all agree—an abiding hatred and contempt of the Irish Parliamentary party. Good bye Ever Yours

A. D.

IV

These and other obstacles to the successful organisation in Ulster of opposition to home rule can be seen at work in the general election of 1885 in North Fermanagh and North Armagh. North Fermanagh illustrates the problems of apathy, the land question and of defective organisation on the part of the conservatives. The conservative candidate was a landlord, Captain John Caldwell Bloomfield of Castle Caldwell, Co. Fermanagh, not an ideal candidate but a man with an appreciation of the needs of agricultural Ireland. His energetic agent was an Enniskillen solicitor, J. Whiteside Dane. Dane tried to inject life into Bloomfield's meetings and to present Bloomfield as a man who cared as much for tenant farmer as for landlord interests. He went out of his way to find farmers to speak at Bloomfield's meetings, and arranged transport to bring them from outlying districts to the polling stations.

However, neither Dane's energy nor Bloomfield's confidence in the wide appeal of his views could overcome tenant farmer hostility and local apathy. The election register was

106

faulty, because the Constitutional Club had not had enough funds to supervise it; and funds were not readily forthcoming for the election campaign. Some landlords were slow to subscribe, while traders in the towns did not think that the election was their responsibility. The nationalists, on the other hand, were lively and active—particularly at polling stations— and took up the land question. Thus, though the conservatives were supposed to have a majority in the constituency, they lost the election. The nationalist, 'Willie' Redmond, brother of the future leader of the Irish parliamentary party, was returned with a majority of 433 (3,255 votes to 2,822 on a register of 6,687). Since Fermanagh had been hitherto safely conservative, the result was a bitter blow to the conservatives, one of whom blamed it on 'the abstention of many rotten renegade protestants from voting'.

45 *Extracts from J. W. Dane's letter-book, 24 October–9 November 1885, showing the care he took to ensure a good turn-out of farmers and cheer-leaders at Bloomfield's election meetings on 26 October and 10 November: **(a)** to Capt. C. Barton, The Waterfoot, Pettigoe, Co. Fermanagh, 24 October 1885; **(b)** to the Rev. Mr Chapind, Ashfield, Lisbellaw, Co. Fermanagh, 24 October 1885; and **(c)** to S. McCreery, Lisbellaw, 9 November 1885 (Cal. D 1390/26/7):

(a)

Can you arrange to bring a farme[r] up from your district to support Bloomfield on the platform on Monday 1.30

The less landlords we have the better but we must have some farmers are the correct cards if we can get them.

F. Brooke will stand for South [Fermanagh], Porter having decided not to stand.   Yours sincerely.

(b)

Please come in on Monday and be prepared to speak as a farmer in support of Bloomfield whom every loyal man irrespective of creed or politics should now rally round as a protest against the seditious preaching of the Nationalists etc. [?] who are going in for separation.

You can make a first class address and I am sure you will do so to oblige.   Yours very truly.

(c)

If you could manage to have a "few boys" in at Bloomfield's meeting here to-morrow 2 o'clock to lead the applause from different parts of the house it would be a good thing [?]—there is no enthusiasm at all—our last meeting was too dead and not at all alive.   Yours very truly.

46 *Letter from Dane to Col. J. M. Richardson of Rossfad, Ballina-mallard, Co. Fermanagh, 12 November 1885, taken from Dane's letter-book, commenting on criticisms of the inactivity of the Constitutional Club (Cal. D 1390/26/7):

I received your letter of 11th instant covering cheque value £1 for 2 years subscription to [the] Constitutional Club. I enclose you herein [a] receipt for the amounts.

As regards Mr Bloomfield's expenses all subscriptions must be sent to me as election agent, and I am the person responsible for its expenditure.

It is very easy for you and others to abuse the Constitutional Club, but it is not [fair] to blame us in the first place owing to the great apathy of the Constitutional Party; there are only about 90 members, above fifty paying 2s. 6d. per year and forty paying 10s. 0d. so that our income is under £30, which will not pay working expenses. Early in the year about May or June we made a very strong appeal for funds to all the leading men in the county, you included, to enable us to do some work, but the only response was £2. 2s. 0d sent by Dr. Robert Collum of London.

I think these facts will perhaps justify the inactivity of the C[onstitutional] C[lub]. Besides the conduct [?] of the members [?] for the county [?] prevented others from interfering. But next year I believe that the people will work [?] the Register. Yours very truly.

47 Letter from J. Baxter, Tempo, Co. Fermanagh, to Dane, 27 November 1885, suggesting the provision of transport to the polls and drawing his attention to nationalist allegations about Bloomfield as a landlord (D 1390/26/2/23):

Dear Sir—I am sure you are interested in the return of Mr Bloomfield for our division of the Cy. I hence thought of making the following suggestions to you as his agent.

There are as you know a great many small farmers and labourers who have now votes: but some of them might not be disposed to walk a distance of 7 or 8 miles to the place of polling and would not like to pay a car As an example—I was speaking to a tenant of poor Mr Johnstons on the day of his funeral. He told me plainly that he would not walk a foot except provided with some mode of Transfer [*sic*].

You and Mr. Bloomfield will be in Tempo fair tomorrow and you can speak to Dr. Clarke (who is a good man and true to the cause) he will talk to men of [who?] have cars & horses and allow [*sic*] them to bring their neighbours who have no mode of conveyance with them by this means no voter will be left at home that wishes to go to the place of polling.

Again it is circulated through this vicinity that Mr. Bloomfield is a bad landlord. I heard one of the Nat[ional] League Party myself telling that when the Barrister asked him to give his tenants time to pay their rents he refused to do so. To circulate as widely as possible the address of the R[oman]-Catholics of the parish of Belleek and Father McKennas letter to Mr. Bloomfield would contradict this lying report.

I will see you on tomorrow in the mean time I will do all I possibly can to further our cause. Yours respectfully

J Baxter

48 *Letter from Dane to the 3rd earl of Enniskillen, Florence Court, Enniskillen, Co. Fermanagh, 17 November 1885, taken from Dane's letter-book, appealing for an early subscription towards Bloomfield's election expenses (Cal. D 1390/26/7):

My Lord—I am in receipt of your letter of this day's date and in reply beg to say that inclusive of what we have been promised by Mr. William Archdale M.P. D'Arcy Irvine and Captain Archdale we have so far only £580 while our estimated expenses will be £800 at lowest.

I am informed that in South Fermanagh six hundred pounds has been subscribed by five gentlemen [alo]ne.

I am aware that many people here are awaiting the announcement of the amount of your subscription as Lord of the Soil as well as that of Lord Cole, before subscribing themselves.

So far I have only received in round numbers £80 and expenses must be met if we are to go to the Poll. Yours very truly.

49 Letter from E. M. Archdale, Crock na Crieve, Ballinamallard, Co. Fermanagh, to Dane, 6 December 1885, enclosing a subscription towards Bloomfield's election expenses and urging the need for registration work in the future (D 1390/26/1/2):

My dear Dane—I enclose cheque for 10.0.0. for the elections. Will we have enough funds. I would like to start a fund for the Registry next year & if my 10.0.0. is enough for the elections would be glad to give another 5.0.0. towards it. There were a terrible lot of bad Protestant votes on Lord Enniskillens estate this side of Enniskillen the damned ruffians should be choked—Hope you are none the worse for your exertions Very truly yours

E. M. Archdale

Lord Ely won't subscribe I saw his letters—

50 Note from C. M. Stewart, Enniskillen, to Dane, 19 December 1885, declining to contribute to Bloomfield's election expenses (D 1390/26/1/2):

re—"Election Expenses"

Dear Sir—As the Gentry of the South division of this County dont go outside themselves for above I have thought our gentry here should be as large hearted as they and I am truly yours

C. M. Stewart

51

Memorandum on nationalist activity at polling booths in the North Fermanagh election, 1885 (D 1390/26/2/22):

Booth number Two. Hoey Presiding officer—This Booth was in the Dispensary at Archway under Booth number one which was in Court House upstairs such was the crowd in this archway that it was almost impossible to effect an entry. Up till four oclock the door of this Booth was never shut while Illiterates were voting and a police-man remained present in the Booth all the Time & one at the Door. Most of the Time a priest stood in the archway within Hearing with two of Redmonds agents at the open door within earshot & asking Every man his name—. On Capt. Bloomfields remonstrating at 4.15 pm. about this the presiding officer stated he had no instructions that the door should be kept closed or constabulary [removed ?]. Philip Timoney an agent there all day (having made a declaration) said this had occurred in Mr. Danes presence Earlier in the day & that he Mr. Dane had taken no exception to same Mr. Dane replied he had no recollection of the fact but that in any case it was not his business to teach the presiding officer his duty.

V

The North Armagh constituency was the creation of the 1885 redistribution act, and in 1885 it illustrates liberal-conservative rivalry, local jealousies and the disruptive influence of the Orange Order.

Any speedy breakdown of traditional party barriers in face of the home rule threat was unlikely, since party divisions ran deep in the area, breaking out, for instance, in rioting in Portadown in October 1884. In opposition to conservative expressions of approval, on 17 October, of the action of the house of lords in holding up the third reform bill, the liberals of Portadown held a meeting in the town hall on 22 October in support of the franchise bill. As the leading speaker, Thomas Dickson, liberal M.P. for Co. Tyrone, and his friends were leaving the hall, stones were thrown and a riot ensued. Dickson was badly hurt and the government proceeded against 82 people under the 1882 crimes act. Conservatives attributed the violence to mill girls and boys and to the passivity of liberal J.P.s. The liberals, on the other hand, blamed the conservatives; and when on 29 October they held another meeting, addressed among others by Thomas Shillington (secundus), extra forces were drafted into the area to maintain the peace—much to the disgust of conservatives who objected to the expense. Such rivalries meant that in the general election of 1885 there was a liberal candidate, Thomas Shillington (secundus), as well as a conservative.

The conservative vote had been progressively organised throughout 1885, though these efforts had encountered the problem of local jealousies. For instance, the Portadown conservative association recognised the need to coordinate conservative energies in the new division, but, 'being the strongest' and not wishing 'to play second fiddle', rejected the idea of one constitutional association with a branch in each polling district.

Whatever benefits may have been gained from such efforts to organise were almost jeopardised by a dispute between non-orange conservatives and orangemen. The orange pace-setter was the Rev. Thomas Ellis, the grand chaplain of the grand orange lodge of Co. Armagh, who thought conservative and constitutional associations almost superfluous and who regarded the Orange Order as the best means of coordinating protestant and loyalist energies. Conservatives in various polling districts had chosen as the North Armagh candidate John Monroe, the solicitor-general for Ireland in Salisbury's first ministry (1885); but on 6 July the Armagh orangemen resolved that Major Edward Saunderson, the whig recently converted to orangeism and conservatism, should contest North Armagh and that Monroe should contest Mid-Armagh. Saunderson's name had not previously been mentioned in connection with Armagh, and for the next few months there was a running battle in North Armagh between Monroe's supporters and the orangemen, who refused to back down or submit to a test poll. Eventually, Monroe, impressed by the orangemen's determination and concerned about the effects of a possible defeat upon his reputation, withdrew his candidature at the beginning of October.

Nevertheless, the danger of a split conservative vote remained. The orangemen's action had aroused much resentment, and Monroe and the president of the Portadown Constitutional Association, J. Buckby Atkinson, a solicitor, thought about finding another conservative candidate who could defeat Saunderson and the orangemen. Atkinson even advocated dissolving the constitutional association. Such plans did not come to fruition owing to a widespread fear that two conservative candidates would allow a liberal or a nationalist to slip in, and Saunderson was enabled to win the seat by 4,192 votes to 2,375. (He retained it until his death in October 1906.)

52 Draft petition to Rt. Hon. E. Gibson, M.P. for Dublin University, 2 November 1884, giving the conservative version of the Portadown riots of 22 October 1884 (D 1252/42/3/6):

We think it is our Duty as Loyal people residing in Portadown to send to you as the champion of Irish Conservatives the History of a riot that took place here on Wednesday the 22nd Ultimo.

Portadown and neighbourhood is almost altogether Protestant for instance the Population of Portadown is upwards of 8,000 of which about 1,600 are Roman Catholics. The Protestant Population of Portadown is with a few exception [*sic*] purely Conservative; and these few have been for years working to break up the Conservative Party

There being such an agitation throughout the Country against the House of Lords over the Franchise bill. The Conservatives of Portadown had a meeting in its support. It is alleged by the Liberals such a Meeting was not contemplated until the Liberals said they would have a Meeting this is untrue in fact and cannot be substantiated (The Liberal Meeting was not announced till two days after the placards were posted for this Conservative Meeting.) The Conservative Meeting was a great source of annoyance to the Liberals and they convened a Meeting to be held on the 22nd Ultimo when Thomas A. Dickson the shining light of the Liberals in Ulster was to address them denouncing the House of Lords. The Meeting was a miserable failure unfortunately a crowd of boys and girls mill workers averaging from 10 to 16 gathered at the Assembly Room where the Meeting was held, hooted, sang songs, and eventually threw stones. These rowdies are mostly employes [*sic*] of the Liberals. The D[istrict] M[aster] & D[eputy] D[istrict] M[aster] of the Orange Socty had given strict orders that no drum should be beaten & no interference to be made with the liberal Meeting & this order was strictly obeyed & several leading Conservatives who are not Orangemen had used their influence in the same direction—believed that everything would pass off quietly.

No one in the Town ever for a moment thought that were [there?] would be any disturbance and as soon as the respectable Inhabitants of the Town heard of a likelihood of such a thing they turned out and did all in their power to assist the Constabulary and Thomas Shillington Esqr. J.P. There was a Mr. Joseph Acheson, J.P. who is a Liberal and a Justice of the Peace and altho' he was on the Street all the time (from before the Stone throwing commenced until it ceased) he never assisted in any way to keep the Peace nor did he give any suggestions how it should be done.

Some of The Liberals no doubt were badly hurt. Now they say that the Conservatives of this Town organised this mob. that statement is untrue and without the slightest foundation. This is the thanks the Conservatives get for protecting the Liberals.

The Liberals also attack the Resident Magistrate and Constabulary This is unwarrantable no one ever thought a mob of rowdies would collect and throw stones. Since Captain Whelan came here the Town has been quiet and well conducted and he is a favorite with all persons no matter what is their religious persuasion The Constabulary always do their duty. The fact is the Liberals do not know how to have revenge against the Conservatives Upon last Wednesday [29 October] there was an Indignation Meeting held and there was drafted into Portadown between 600 & 700 men including cavalry, Infantry and Police it was a farce. The Meeting was held & at it there were under 200 composed of liberals and some Conservatives who went through curiosity. The General Public are very much annoyed at such expense being put on the Town and neighbourhood 50 men would have been sufficient to preserve the peace of the Town. We send you the Speeches delivered at the Indignation Meeting. With a few exceptions there is not a true statement in one of them We send you also [a] copy of the Resolutions to be passed by the Town Commisioners [*sic*] here on Monday the 3rd Instant

We wish you and Colonel King Harman to know these facts as Thomas A. Dickson will be airing himself in The House early next week and we are anxious not to be misrepresented.

It should be made very plain that Thos Shillington JP. is not the Thos S[hillington] Secundus & that Thos. S. Secundus is not a J.P. at all—but that his name is frequently in the liberal newspapers without Secundus attached to it—manifestly for the purpose of conveying the impression that it is T.S. primus—who is a staunch conservative

So far from the presence of Conservatives on the Street being a dis-advantage to the liberals—had it not been for their efforts the consequences would have been more serious—out of six JP's. 4 are liberals—and they did nothing whatever to provide protection. The only one who did anything was T[homas]. S[hillington]. JP. D[istrict]. I[nspector]. Smith didhis best also to preserve the peace.

53 Draft resolutions of the Portadown Constitutional Association, May 1885, inviting the cooperation of all loyalist associations in North Armagh (D 1250/42/3/49):

I   That this Association cordially invite the Co-operation and fraternity of all Conservative and Constitutional Associations and Institution[s] of Loyalists within the Northern Division of County Armagh,

For the more complete and thorough organization of the Division

For the selection of a vigorous able and eloquent Parliamentary Representative, and

For unity of action and purpose

II That this Association cannot and will not recognise the right of any Association Institution or Individual outside the Northern Division to interfere in the selection of a Parliamentary Representative,

III That a copy of these Resolutions be forwarded to the Lurgan Loughgall and Charlemont Associations requesting them to adopt the foregoing or similar Resolutions.

54 Draft letter from J. B. Atkinson, chairman of the Portadown Constitutional Association, to J. Atkinson, of Loughgall, honorary secretary of the Co. Armagh Constitutional Association, 21 May 1885, explaining the attitude of Portadown conservatives towards organisation in North Armagh (D 1252/42/3/23):

My dear Atkinson—Your letter not being marked private I considered I would have been acting ultra vires for me to reply to your letter without bringing it before our association I have laid your letter of yesterday before our association this evening. They are pleased that you are connected with the North Division and know you will be one of the most active members in the division for furthering the Conservative Cause: I know and our association acknowledges with gratitude your services for the last five years and hope you will not now retire from working: I was anxious and so were the members of our association most anxious to have one Constitutional Association for this division with branch associations in each Polling District, but upon due consideration we abandoned this idea. The first thing struck me 'Where are the Head Quarters of this Association to be?' I thought Lurgan might not be satisfied that Portadown should be the Head Quarters and Portadown would not consent that Lurgan or Amagh should be Head Quarters because this is the centre of the District and it would be unreasonable and unfair to bring voters from Portadown Clonmacate and Loughgall Districts to Lurgan or to Armagh, Portadown being the most convenient for the majority of voters, the only place there would be the slightest inconvenience to is Charlemont District, a great many of the Loughgall Farmers would like to join Portadown Several have called on me and said so. I would suggest the advisability of Loughgall and Charlemont joining Portadown Association and then Lurgan might do likewise and in this way your idea would be worked out, having one Association with its branches under the one set of Rules making Portadown its Head Quarters, it having the largest Voting Power in the Conservative interests.

I would have been only too glad to have had a conference of the whole district but I was afraid and thought better to go on our own hook which we did and then Lurgan followed. Our people thought that the Armagh people wished to get us under their control and that is why the words "that to be under the control of any association outside the North Division" were used.

Let me know if you are satisfied that Loughgall & Charlemont should be brought into our association Our Rules if objectionable in any way can be remodelled.

Our Association do not for one moment think you wished to dictate to them in any way. they thought others did.
P.S. We think there should be an association formed in Loughgall & Charlemont—and we will be only too happy to assist you. Will you have a talk.

55 Extracts from a pamphlet, entitled *The action of the grand orange lodge of the county of Armagh (and the reasons thereof) on the 6th July 1885,* by the Rev. T. Ellis, grand chaplain, published in October 1885, explaining the importance of the Orange Order and why the Armagh orangemen insisted on Major Saunderson's candidature for North Armagh (D 1252/42/3/47):

. . . I never have approved of Orangemen joining the Conservative Association of this county, for the simple reason that . . . they are already organized under the most perfect system that exists in Ireland; . . . Months before any candidate's name had been mentioned for either North or Mid-Armagh, the County Grand Lodge declared as its opinion, that since North Armagh was the most Orange District in Ireland, and since it had been the cradle of Orangeism, every effort should be made to return, for that District, a man who was not ashamed to wear the Orange Colours across his heart, and who, from love of the order and from knowledge of its principles, could defend the organization against all attacks in the House of Commons; and therefore it unanimously passed a resolution that it could not, and would not, give its support to any Candidate for North Armagh who was not an Orangeman. . . . They [the orangemen] decided to run MAJOR SAUNDERSON for North, and Mr. MONROE for Mid-Armagh, and the reasons which led them to this conclusion were as follows:—

1. They were bound by a resolution that declared that they could not support any Candidate who was not an Orangeman for North Armagh, therefore MAJOR SAUNDERSON being an Orangeman and Mr. MONROE not, the former was qualified and the other was not, for North Armagh.

2. The Manufacturing influence being greater in the North and the Agricultural interest greater in Mid-Armagh, it was deemed prudent, as MAJOR SAUNDERSON was a Landlord and Mr. MONROE not, to run the Landlord for North and the SOLICITOR-GENERAL for Mid-Armagh.

3. As attacks were more frequently made by the National Party on the Orangemen of Portadown and Lurgan than on those in Mid-Armagh, it was considered that MAJOR SAUNDERSON rather than the SOLICITOR-GENERAL, should represent North Armagh, inasmuch as the one would be able to defend the Orangemen on the floor of the House of Commons, when the other might be called upon, in his official capacity, to prosecute them in a Court of Justice.

And I have no hesitation in asserting that the Grand Lodge were as anxious to secure the return of Mr. MONROE for Mid-Armagh as they were that of MAJOR SAUNDERSON for North Armagh, for both resolutions where [*sic*] passed unanimously and with acclamation, and with my own lips I proposed Mr. MONROE. . . .

Mr. MONROE, I believe, thinks that I have treated him badly, and asserts that I have spoken unkindly of him: to both of these propositions I give the most emphatic denial. . . .

I cannot conclude these observations better than by quoting the words of one (the late lamented STEWART BLACKER) whose memory will ever be immortal in the neighbourhood of Portadown.

"The advantage of the Orange Society is, that on its platform all shades of evangelical Protestantism can meet with fraternal regard and joint reciprocity. It has also shown itself the only lasting method of action; all the various attempts which exigencies from time to time have called forth, have soon faded away, but the Orange organization is ever fresh and vigorous, and in spite of the slurs and calumnies cast against it by foes and pretended friends, it is ever ready and willing to uphold the cause of truth and loyalty.

Now that the Body is fully united, and that we know the value of our strength and position, such a continued action must be taken, as will in future ensure our friends and upholders being respected. The press, the pulpit, and the platform, must be made to give us fair play, or we, abhorring all shams, no matter with what plausible titles adorned, of Conservatives or Constitutionalists, will know the reason why. Let us stand by our colours 'The Orange and the Blue,' with the good old Union Jack, and let us drive Popery and Radicalism before us, as we have done many a time before, and hope to do many a time again.

'For happy homes, for altars free, we draw the ready sword;
For freedom, truth, and for our God's unmutilated Word;
These, these, the war-cry of our march; our hope the Lord on high;
Then put your trust in God my boys, and keep your powder dry.' "

56 Letter from W. J. Locke, Woodhouse Street, Portadown, deputy district grand master, to J. B. Atkinson, 15 September 1885, reporting the views of local orangemen on the question of a test vote (D 1252/42/3/33):

Sir—I wish to inform you that a meeting composed of ab[ou]t 600 electors of this District was held in the Orange Hall for the purpose of taking into consideration the advisability of taking a test vote of the Division in order to effect a Settlement. The unanimous feeling of the meeting was that no such test vote is required, as they believe it is quite evident to any person who has the majority and they utterly refuse to Submit to any such test vote. I am, Sir, Yours respectfully

W. J. Locke

57 Extracts from a severely critical draft reply to the Rev. T. Ellis's pamphlet **(55)**, written but not published by J. B. Atkinson, October 1885 (D 1252/42/3/47):

The Rev. Thomas Ellis A.M.G.C. Armagh, who finishes up all his speeches by saying he is not such a fool as he looks, has taken upon himself to write a Pamphlet (if it may be so called) upon the action of the Grand Orange Lodge of the County of Armagh; and I think that I, as a Conservative and not an Orangeman or member of any Secret Society, should not, for the sake of Conservatism, allow such a document to go unchallenged, as it tends to mislead the Public and gain for an Institution which, in my opinion, is unorganised and without honesty of purpose, a position that it does not, nor ever did deserve. Mr. Monroe was badly treated and by Mr. Ellis in particular; and I, being anxious to let the Public draw their own conclusions as to who is to blame, make this statement, in the hope not only of preventing the Reverend Gentleman or his County Grand Lodge, as he is pleased to call it, ever again interfering in attempting to destroy Conservatism but of giving a death-blow to Orangeism. . . .

I quite agree with the Rev. Gentleman that Orangemen of a certain class should not be allowed to join any Conservative Association for the simple reason that they are not men of honor and organisation is impossible until they become honorable and not "brute force" men. . . . three of the Constitutional Associations of North Armagh before the 6th July last convened meetings At Lurgan, the largest Polling District in North Armagh. Mr. Monroe was unanimously selected as the Candidate. The name of Major Saunderson never was mentioned. At Portadown the three Candidates mentioned were Mr. Monroe, Mr. W. Ellison Macartney and Mr. T. G. Peel. The two former were duly proposed and seconded. Mr. T. G. Peel was duly proposed by Mr. George A. Locke who did so at the request and by the directions of the Rev. T. Ellis. Upon a vote being taken, Mr. Monroe had the majority. At Clonmacate—Mr. Monroe was unanimously selected as the Candidate. Lurgan Polling District has a Constituency of 3,200; Portadown, 2,747; Clonmacate 1,200 and Loughgall 847. Mr. W. Ellison Macartney was told that the Conservatives of North Armagh wished to run Mr. Monroe and he like a gentleman retired saying "he would be no party to a split"; at least these are the words he made use of to me. Now the question comes who brought forward Major Saunderson; and who caused the split and put North Armagh into this awkward position?—It was the Rev. Thomas Ellis.

Mr. Ellis met me at Killylea Station before the Meeting of the different Associations. He then asked me if I knew Major Saunderson. I said I had met him once. He informed me that "he was a great friend of his, had an income of £12,000 a year and that he would like him to be put up for North Armagh. His Orange brethren at Portadown were for Mr W. Ellison Macartney; but he would soon end that."—I replied: "The man I wish should be the Candidate is John Monroe. He contested Monaghan; he is known to the people; was born near Lurgan; and is, in my opinion, the man to pull together the Conservatives of North Armagh."—Now, the Rev Mr. Ellis's mind being as stated, why did he send one Lester of Killylea to George

A. Locke to propose Mr. Peel?—Why did he allow Mr. Wm. John Locke to propose Mr. W. Ellison Macartney?—I can tell.—Some of the Portadown Orangemen are dupes.

He said to himself:—"I do not care how I act towards the Conservatives or my brother Orangemen. I have got a converted Whig with £12,000 a year ready for the affray,—a good man for the Orangemen to pluck. I will fix the Conservatives by forcing Saunderson on; The Government will compel Monroe to withdraw and I can then master the situation." . . .

Now it would be well to let the Public know the strength of Orangeism in North Armagh. This is the fallacy.—There are only, out of a Constituency of 7,943, 1,000 Orangemen sitting and non-sitting members. There are 5,000 Protestants and about 2,000 Roman Catholics. Why should the Orangemen claim the right of selecting a Candidate? They cannot return a man without the Constitutionalists; and if we, as Constitutionalists, do not now vote for Major Saunderson and he is opposed by a Liberal or Nationalist, the Orangemen cannot return him.—No attacks were ever made by the National Party on the Orangemen of Portadown and Lurgan except when they deserved it and could not be defended by any man with sincerity.

I have given this matter of the conduct of the Grand Lodge Some Consideration and there is only one way of ending such unseemly conduct on the part of the Grand Lodge and that is for the present Constitutional Associations to be broken up. Let us have a Constitutional Association composed of Conservatives, non-Orangemen; and only admit those Orangemen into it who will sign a paper to be bound by the Rules of the Association; or let the Constitutional Association be composed exclusively of non-Orangemen. There is no use in the Rev. T. Ellis appealing to a body of Electors to co-operate in the common cause. That is impossible when he heads a democracy of a few hundreds against thousands. . . . All I can tell him is this,—if he wants to find out his voting strength, I am prepared to give him a trial at the coming Election. . . .

58 Letter from J. Monroe, writing from the Law Room, Dublin Castle, to J. B. Atkinson, 26 September 1885, expressing concern at the dispute in North Armagh and doubts about his chances of success there (D 1252/42/3/39):

My dear Atkinson—I have received your letter & Enclosure. The latter I send on to Hillsborough. While I was away the Attorney Genl. had interviews with J. Orr Q.C. & with little Augustus Johnston. Orr is of opinion that the Orangemen in the Division are strong & that they are against us. Johnston says that in Loughgall the people though they believe that Saunderson acted badly, will vote for him as they do not wish to alienate the orange vote Saunderson from his letter is manifestly impressed with the idea that he has a large majority. When in Loughgall Mr Orr told me our opponents had canvassed & we had not and he was afraid if a test ballot had been accepted our friends wouldnt have taken the trouble to come in It is very difficult for me to know how far we are correct in our surmises. I know all the power of

the lodges in certain districts will be worked against us & I will be blamed for not being able to make things square. I dont see what is to come out of the proposed meeting or how the weight of opinion is to be ascertained. I fear if the parties met unless there was Somebody to determine the weight of opinion, the meeting wd. be worse than useless. Could a requisition not be obtained signed by Masters & officers of lodges in my favour. This wd. be something practical to go on. At present we have no evidence of opinion at all reliable. If I fought this battle & was beaten either by Saunderson or a liberal it wd. do me no end of harm with my party: but at the same time I am anxious for a solution which will leave our people their own self respect. Truly Yours
                    J. L. Monroe

59 Letter from J. Monroe to Atkinson, 3 October 1885, suggesting means by which he could retire from the contest without conceding the seat to 'the Saunderson clique' (D 1252/42/3/43):

Strictly Private for your own eyes only & then burn

My dear Atkinson—Our party leaders are still very averse to the appearance of a fight between the Govt. and one of their nominal supporters. They cant enter into the feelings of a particular constituency. Now you know what my feelings on the subject are. You know what I gave up to fight the constituency & you know what chagrin it gives me to make way for those who have played so scurvy a trick. Now if I could retire & any scheme could be devised to win the constituency from the Saunderson clique I think our people ought to be satisfied. The plan remember is one of your own & must not come from me. I dont think Sir Wm. Verner would be a good man to start now. You must have a man who can rouse the people & speak to & carry the working classes. I dont think there is any man in the constituency who would care to come forward under the circumstances. The only possible men are yourself & Malcolm & you both seem averse to it. The man I would suggest wd. be Mr Kane who fought Monaghan with me. He is a capital platform speaker. He isnt an orangeman: but he has the full confidence of the orange democracy & wd. denounce Saunderson as an orange upstart who was destroying the institution to advance himself. He could speak to the working men, particularly the weavers in a way that no law officer could. He would being a Presbyterian, get the Presbyterian interest & I think he might receive even the Parnellite vote. I am rather afraid of the Parnellites owing to my being counsel so often against them & having refused to defend Parnell. But Mr Kane would be preferred either to Saunderson or a liberal. I think Mr Kane could win against all comers and drive Saunderson out of the field. He will not spare him. I think this would satisfy our friends. Lord A[rthur Hill] is coming up again on Monday Could you informally take the views of our friends & come up with Lord A. Dont mention this Suggestion as coming from me. I would rather it came from the people themselves. I will not make any suggestion to Lord A. myself. You can speak to him on the subject as you please.—Ever Yours Sincerely
                    J. L. M.

60 Letter from J. Crossle, Dungannon, to Atkinson, 17 October 1885, urging that no conservative should stand against Saunderson in Monroe's place (D 1252/42/3/45):

My dear Atkinson—I wrote to you today but I did not then understand the position of affairs in North Armagh. As Major Saunderson is still in the field it would be impossible for Sir William Verner to come forward as a Candidate as since the retirement of Mr Monroe, he was induced to join with his own lodge in promising to support the Candidature of Major Saunderson & he cannot now possibly go back of [*sic*] his promise. Of course he will be both pleased & flattered by the kindness of his friends. I am a great friend of Mr Monroe and I feel that he has been very badly treated but may I take the liberty of saying I fear it is wrong now to put up a Candidate for N. Armagh because Saundersons party have acted badly & I think foolishly for the sake of the County—it will I fear injure the Protestant Cause & Mr Monroes Govt. by permitting a Nationalist to be returned, and I feel certain that Mr Monroe himself would strongly disapprove of it. There are very few places in Ireland where a Conservative can be returned. I believe N. Armagh is one of them, and surely the best men in it are not going to destroy their cause by useless Division. Pardon me but I cannot help writing this.—Ever faithfully yrs

James Crossle

Chapter V

Southern unionist organisation
1886-1914

Their success in establishing themselves in 1885 encouraged southern unionists to further action in 1886. They tried to extend their activities and to work on two fronts. On the one hand, they tried to secure the cooperation of Ulster unionists and to organise unionist energies in the four provinces. On the other, they tried to extend their activities to Great Britain, carrying on an anti-home rule propaganda throughout British politics. This ambitious scheme was designed to satisfy those afraid that British opinion might endorse home rule and those who thought that the battle of the union could only be won in Ireland. This was always a problem for southern unionists. Should they concentrate their energies in Ireland, endeavouring to create a party on a scale to rival that of the Parnellites? Or, should they accept the fact that the nationalists had a hold, legitimate or otherwise, over the majority of the Irish electors, and thus concentrate their resources and activity in British politics, ensuring that a British parliament would resist the nationalist demand, and maintaining a sufficient organisation in Ireland for that purpose? For a long time they tried to fight on both fronts at the same time.

The object of this chapter is to show how material in the N.I.P.R.O. can be used to document the progress and scope of southern unionist organisation in Ireland between 1886 and 1914.

61 Extracts from a report in the *Irish Times,* 9 January 1886, of the first annual general meeting of the I.L.P.U., 8 January, containing **(a)** the resolutions extending the scope of the association, and **(b)** part of a speech by the Rev. J. H. Jellett, provost of Trinity College, Dublin, urging electoral and registration work by unionists in the south of Ireland (T 2759/1):

(a)

To form one United Association for all Ireland for the purpose of maintaining the Union existing between Great Britain and Ireland, and upholding the rights and liberties to which every Irishman is entitled under the laws and constitution of the United Kingdom. . . .

To use every Constitutional means to carry out the objects for which the I.L.P.U. was formed, on the same lines on which the I.L.P.U. has been hitherto conducted, and invite all Unionists, especially those who have capital invested in commercial undertakings, or who are otherwise interested in Irish industrial enterprises, irrespective of creed or party, to join. . . .

To organise local branches for the purpose of carrying out the objects of the association.

To make proper arrangements for the supplying of accurate information on Irish affairs to Members of Parliament, and others interested, and for this purpose to utilise the different local branches in connection with offices established in Dublin and London.

To take into consideration any measure affecting Ireland which may be submitted to the Imperial Parliament, and to take such action in regard thereto as circumstances may dictate.

To endeavour to form a sound public opinion by the spread of literature bearing upon the disastrous effect produced by the so-called Nationalist agitation upon all trade and commerce in the country.

To make and assist all such efforts as may be considered necessary or advisable to secure a proper representation of the Unionist strength.

To organise public meetings throughout the United Kingdom, at which members of the association and others could attend, and properly represent the condition of Ireland and the true character of the so-called Nationalist movement.

That the work of the society be confined to operations of a political nature.

(b)

. . . Now, what are we to do?—because that is one great question, and I think it can be very briefly, answered. . . . what you have to do is this—to let the voice of Loyal Ireland be heard. (Hear, and applause.) Let it not be supposed that Loyalists don't exist here at all, or that they are in such very small numbers that their voice may safely be disregarded. (Hear, hear.) That is what you must try to do, and there are several ways of doing it. You must do it by attending to the registries, and you must do it by fighting any elections. I make this reservation—you must fight every election where you can hope to poll a considerable number of votes—that constituency ought to be fought. (Hear, hear.) Let me give you an example. I have myself a vote in the County of Cork. Well I went down to Cork this time to give my vote— (applause)—knowing perfectly well that I should be in a hopeless minority, but knowing also that it was important we should poll there as many votes as possible, and having a good expectation that we should poll a fair number. We did pol [*sic*] something between 1,400 and 1,500, and it is most desirable, especially now that the papers have adopted the plan of adding up the votes given in every constituency, and, comparing them in the aggregate, it is most important that in every place where a respectable number of votes can be polled that those votes should be recorded. (Hear.) One word more. You must absolutely for the present sink all minor differences. (Hear.) I know that we are divided on many points, and I don't deny their importance; but, in the face of the danger with which we are now threatened, you must allow those points to sink into oblivion, and I ask of you all to do so. (Hear.) I ask of you all to forget whether you are Whigs or Tories, Protestants or Roman Catholics, and only think of yourselves as the citizens of a country which is assailed by the greatest danger that has ever threatened its existence, and from which danger it is your duty to save it, and a duty in which I firmly believe, if firmly, courageously carried out, you must be successful. (Loud applause.)

62 Resolutions passed by the executive council of the I.L.P.U., 14, 20 May, 23 July 1886, 1 April and 10 June 1887, relating to the question of whether work in Ireland or work in Great Britain should receive priority (D 989A/1/3):

(a)

Proposed by Mr. Wilson Seconded by Mr. Hogg:—

That the Council confirm the following resolution passed by the Organisation Committee:—

That having heard the resolution of the London Sub-Committee regarding Registration of voters in various places in Ireland, this Committee is of opinion that in the present condition of the finances of the I.L.P.U., the matter cannot be undertaken.

(b)

Proposed by Profr. Mahaffy Seconded by Dr. Maguire

That the Council of the I.L.P.U. recommends that every seat held by a Parnellite in Ireland should be contested; if any exceptions be found advisable preference should be given to those seats which polled the strongest loyal minority at the last election

Amendment proposed by Mr. Ross Seconded by Mr. Patton

That it is advisable that the Union contest or assist in contesting those seats where a substantial number of votes can be polled

This amendment, on being put, was declared lost.

Further amendment proposed by Mr. J. Malcolm Inglis Seconded by Mr. R. Bagwell

That all the words after "that" be left [out] and instead thereof the following be inserted—The organising Committee to bring up from time to time a list of the seats which they consider ought to be contested with the view of giving early intimation to the I.L.P.U. local branches in which such seats are situated.

This amendment was carried.

It was also put as Substantive Resolution and carried.

(c)

Proposed by R. de la Poer. Seconded by J. E. Ryan & Resolved

That the Organising Committee be authorised to consider all applications for funds for Registration purposes and to make grants in all cases they think good.

Proposed by H. de F. Montgomery Seconded by R. de la Poer & Resolved

That the I.L.P.U. now renew and concentrate its efforts in Great Britain in forming public opinion in those districts in which Gladstonians have been returned to Parliament beginning with Leith where an important election will shortly take place.

(d)

Moved by Mr. H. de F. Montgomery seconded by Mr. W. R. F. Godley and Resolved

That the attention of the Committee of the Liberal Unionist Association and the Conservative Central Office be drawn to the immediate urgency of selecting Unionist candidates whether Liberal or Conservative acceptible [sic] to and ready to contest every constituency that may become vacant either at Bye Elections or at a General Election having regard to the enormous influence that the result of every election has upon the general public opinion upon the vital question of the maintenance of the Legislative Union of Gt Britain and Ireland.

(e)

Proposed by Mr. P. La Touche Seconded by Mr. G. R. F. Goodbody.

That the attention of the Executive and the London Committee be called to the half yearly statement of accounts, by which it appears that the cost of meetings had been nearly three times the estimate, while publications have exceeded the estimate by over £200. In the opinion of the Council it is advisable that the expenditure on these items should be reduced, as claims have been put forward for assistance by certain local registration societies which the Council consider it would be greatly to the benefit of the Unionist cause for this association to accede to.

II

In the early years it seemed possible to sustain a complicated party organisation in Ireland. The Parnellite split prompted a re-organisation of the Irish Loyal and Patriotic Union, which in 1891 became the Irish Unionist Alliance, adopting an ambitious programme. As in 1886 a special worker was employed on a short-term basis to stimulate unionist organisation in various parliamentary constituencies. Unfortunately few of the reports of this organiser, Lionel Pleignier, organising secretary of the East Perthshire Conservative and Liberal Unionist Association, seem to have survived, but there is evidence that prospects at this stage looked bright.

On the one hand, there was potential support, and some branches in the southern provinces were active in the normal manner of constituency parties. In Dublin and parts of Cork unionist organisations, such as the Bray branch of the I.L.P.U. and the Cork Hundred, arranged a variety of activities to keep up the interest of their members, and elsewhere unionists were active at least in superintending the electoral register. For instance, the unionists of Queen's Co. were active at the revision of the parliamentary register in 1892, demanding that some nationalists be struck off and other unionists put on the voters' list. They were pleased to be able to report a net increase in the number of unionists on the register. In the Leix division they made a net gain of forty voters and the nationalists lost 420; and though in the Ossory division the unionists lost on balance 5 votes [159–(115 + 39)], the nationalists lost 827 [1,311–(477 + 7)].

On the other hand, some Ulster unionists seemed to identify their interests with those of their fellow unionists in the south and looked to Dublin rather than to Belfast for aid. For instance, the Ulster unionist registration societies for long received subsidies from the I.U.A. and were represented on its general council.

63 Extracts from the new constitution of the I.L.P.U., which now extended its scope and changed its name to the I.U.A., 8 April 1891 (D 989A/1/4):

PREAMBLE.
In order

(1) to continue, extend and render more efficient the work initiated and carried on since May, 1885, by the Irish Loyal and Patriotic Union,

(2) to further consolidate the several Unionist Associations existing in Ireland, and

(3) to establish cordial relations with the Unionist Associations that have since been formed in England and Scotland,

It is desirable to alter the name, and in some respects the Constitution of the Irish Loyal and Patriotic Union.

NAME.

1.—The Association shall in future be known as the Irish Unionist Alliance.

FUNDAMENTAL PRINCIPLE.

2.—The Fundamental Principle of the Irish Unionist Alliance shall be—
The maintenance of the Legislative Union now existing between Great Britain
and Ireland.

3.—The Irish Unionist Alliance shall be composed of—

(i.). A Divisional Association in each Constituency.

(ii.)—A General Council of—

(*a*) Representatives from each of the Divisional Associations.

(*c*) [*sic*] Representatives of various other Unionist organizations.

(*b*) Selected members chosen from present Council of the Irish Loyal
and Patriotic Union.

MEMBERSHIP.

4—(i.)—The Members and Associates of the Irish Unionist Alliance shall
be those who assent to the fundamental principle upon which it is established,
and who are—

(*a*) Subscribers to its general funds.

(*b*) Members of Unionist Associations referred to in par 11 (iii.)

(*c*) Those who are admitted to Membership of Divisional Associations
in accordance with the provisions hereinafter contained.

(ii.)—The amount of the Annual Subscription should not be less than
One Shilling.

(iii.)—The financial year of the Irish Unionist Alliance shall end on the
31st December in each year.

DIVISIONAL ASSOCIATIONS.

5.—A Divisional Association of the Irish Unionist Alliance shall be
primarily considered to have it sphere of operations confined to the particular
constituency in which it is situated.

6.—Divisional Associations of the Irish Unionist Alliance shall exist for
all of any of the following objects:—

(i.) The consolidation of the Unionist strength of the locality and
(where practicable) the organization of Branches under their control in the
various Polling Districts.

(ii.)—The promotion of efficiency in the Unionist interests of Parliamentary Registration.

(iii.)—The promotion of efficiency of Municipal and Poor Law
Registers.

(iv.)—The promotion of public meetings.

(v.)—To act as an Intelligence Department in keeping the Central
Executive informed of matters occurring in the District affecting the general
interests of Irish Unionists.

(vi.) The distribution of Unionist literature in the District.

Divisional Council.

7.—The Divisional Association shall be governed by a Divisional Council, which shall consist of Representatives from each Polling District Branch under the jurisdiction of the Divisional Association.

8.—The Divisional Council shall have the right to determine the number of Representatives to be apportioned to each Polling District, provided that no Polling District shall have a right to elect more than six members. Until the formation of a Divisional Council, the Central Executive Committee shall exercise such power of determination. . . .

GENERAL COUNCIL.

11.—The General Council of the Irish Unionist Alliance shall consist of three Sections.

(i.)—The first section shall consist of,

(*a*) Presidents,

(*b*) Vice-Presidents.
The present Presidents, and Vice-Presidents of the Irish Loyal and Patriotic Union shall continue in office.

(*c*) Members selected by the present Council form its body. The number comprising this section (*c*) of the General Council shall not exceed 20.

(ii.)—The second section shall consist of,

(*a*) Two representatives from each Divisional Association of the Irish Unionist Alliance.

(*b*) In Constituencies where no Divisional Association of the Irish Unionist Alliance exists at present, two members of the late General Council of the Irish Loyal and Patriotic Union residing or having property in the Division, may be nominated a Provisional Committee for the purpose of establishing Polling District Branches. Members of the Provisional Committee for any Constituency shall be deemed to represent their respective Divisions, and to be Members of the General Council of the Irish Unionist Alliance until a Divisional Council is formed, when their term of office shall be considered to have expired.

(iii.)—The third section shall consist of

Representatives chosen by the various Unionist organizations (other than Divisional Associations) at present existing in Ireland, who agree to affiliate with the Irish Unionist Alliance. The number of representatives, which each of such organizations shall be empowered to return shall be fixed by the General Council, and may be altered from time to time.

12. The three sections of which the General Council is composed shall form one body, and vote and act together.

13. The functions, powers, and duties of the General Council shall be:—

(*a*) The supervision and control within the powers delegated to it of existing Divisional Associations.

(*b*) The formation of Divisional Associations in constituencies where they do not at present exist.

(*c*) The preparation, publication, and circulation of Unionist literature, and the maintenance of a staff of speakers to address meetings from time to time throughout the United Kingdom.

(*d*) The maintenance of an Intelligence Department.

(*e*) That with a view to the prosecution of any of the duties mentioned above (*a*, *b*, *c* and *d*), the General Council shall, in addition to the funds provided by Divisional Associations, maintain a general fund, which shall be under the control of the Central Executive Committee, and to which they shall invite subscriptions. . . .

The General Executive Committee.

15. The Central Executive of the Irish Unionist Alliance shall consist of:—

    (i.)—The Presidents.

    (ii.)—The Vice-Presidents.

    (iii.)—40 Members elected annually by the General Council, of which at least five shall be chosen from each province.

16.—The Executive Committee shall be the administrative body of the Irish Unionist Alliance, and shall meet at such times as it may arrange. It shall have the power to appoint and dismiss all Officers, to regulate the rate of their remuneration and conditions of service, and generally to control the finances of the Union, subject to the direction of the General Council. . . .

64 The annual report of the Bray branch of the I.L.P.U., printed as an appendix to the I.L.P.U.'s *Annual report* for 1890, describing the varied activities of the branch over the previous year (D 989A/7/1):

During the past twelve months the important work of the Branch in connection with Registration has been actively carried out by the Registration Sub-Committee, assisted by the able services of the Inspectors, Messrs. Keating and Hewitt.

The Parliamentary Register for Bray and Enniskerry Polling Districts is now almost completely purged of unqualified separatist voters. To maintain this state of things unceasing vigilance will be required and employed.

At the Rathdown Union the lodgment of new Unionist claims, and the removal of time-expired proxies, have been attended to.

At the Bray Township Municipal Election three vacancies in the East Ward were contested by Unionist Candidates of whom two were successful.

The third seat was obtained by a civil engineer of reputation, whose service will, no doubt, be valuable to the ratepayers of Bray in connection with the new harbour.

The Council of the I.L.P.U. having issued last July a revised Constitution, with a view to a thorough and effective organization of the Irish constituencies, the Bray Branch elected, at a General Meeting, held on 21st August, 1890, the members of the Standing Committees to fill the various offices created for the Polling Districts of Bray, Enniskerry, and Cabinteely.

Thus the Bray Branch was the first to take up its due position under the new system, while maintaining its original organization unchanged.

During the past year three evening meetings and concerts have been held, to which members were admitted free, and the public on payment.

The Reading Room has been open daily for the use of the member and visitors.

It is hoped that members will, if possible, increase their subscriptions this January, as it is desired that the Committee should send a larger sum than usual to the Central Office of the I.L.P.U., in view of coming election contests.

At the present remarkable juncture in political affairs, the leaders of the so-called Irish Nationalist Party have undertaken the work, previously the province of the I.L.P.U., of showing to the public the real character and objects of the agitation. They have done this with a completeness that leaves but little to be desired, and have thereby, every one of them, lost the confidence of large masses of their former supporters in Ireland, as well as presumably the bulk of those in England, from whose eyes the veil has at last been lifted.

The combined attempt of Mr. Gladstone and Mr. Parnell to deceive the Irish people having been laid bare, the forces of obstruction are now shattered; consequently the Unionist Government has for the first time a fair field for the development of its wise and generous Irish policy, from which a great and speedily visible improvement in the state of the country is to be confidently expected.

Loyal and Patriotic Irishmen will therefore do well to give the strongest possible support, both moral and material, to the Government through the coming campaign in all parts of the United Kingdom.

65 Letter from L. Pleignier, writing from Skibbereen, Co. Cork, to the secretary of the I.U.A., 27 August 1891, enclosing confidential reports of his preliminary visits to Cos Louth and Cavan earlier in the month 'in connection with promoting the branch organisation of the I.U.A'. (D 989A/8/2):

Dear Mr. Cox—I have made arrangements by which the whole of the five weeks that I shall have worked under the auspices of the I.U.A. will have been fully occupied.

Enclosed is a report of my preliminary visits to Co. Louth and Co. Cavan.

Here (Co. Cork) all my efforts are being concentrated upon seeing our friends all about the Div[isio]n. and thus taking the first steps in connection with future efforts.

129

I am glad to say that my own private friends about here are supporting and helping me very much in my efforts.

The confidential report of all my work down here will be sent you later on.

I leave here at the beginning of next week for Co. Louth, taking a meeting in Co. Carlow on my way.

Further, in order to avoid expense and trouble to the alliance, I have made arrangements to stay with friends, in the various parts, up to the end of the five weeks.

The various branches of the Becher [Beecher] family with whom I have long been intimately acquainted are a great power in these parts and are helping me much.

I am writing Mr. Day concerning certain details regarding posters, letters etc:

At the end of the campaign I will draw up for your perusal a résumé regarding "general conclusions" and "suggestions".

The good work continues to proceed at least as successfully as I expected.
Yours very Truly,

Lionel Pleignier

Report on Preliminary Visit to Co. Louth.

With a view to making arrangements for a week's active campaign later on, I paid a preliminary visit to Co. Louth, arriving there on Thurs. Aug. 13th.

I first went to see Gen. Stubbs, Dromiskin: chairman for the N. Louth Divn., him I found possessed of full information regarding the division, very anxious to give me every help, and evidently very pleased at the idea of some active measures being taken to promote our cause in the Divn.

In company with him I called upon several people in Castlebellingham (S. Louth) in connection with a future public meeting and in connection with party organization.

The schoolmaster, Mr. Stephen Kelleher is likely subrosa [sic] to help us a good deal, but his position naturally precludes him from taking an open and active part in the propagation.

Some such position as Hon. Treas. would best suit him when the district branch is formed.

Mr. McKee, at the Brewery, we also saw, he is likely to prove a useful man, and his position would give him considerable influence in helping us: fortunately he is a man of independent spirit, and in course of time would not mind, probably, actively forwarding the unionist propaganda in this district.

The others we saw were Gen. Woolsey, Milestown: Mr. Wm. Doran, Ardee; Mr. Wm. Ruxton; Ardee House: Mr. Arthur McCann Ardee House: the Hon. C. B. Bellew etc: to all of these the general and myself explained the necessity of organizing and combining in view of the coming Local Govt. act, and also in view of the fact that the unionist strength underneath the surface, which is afraid to put itself forward unless backed up by an organization of some sort is undoubtedly greater than is generally supposed.

I regard the general as a most useful man for the position he holds, his energy and his "never say die" nature, being just the very thing wanted in N. Louth; and if these qualities can only, in course of time, be communicated to some of the gentlemen I met while in the Divn. much might be done.

While in N. Louth I may say I took the opportunity of bicycling over a large portion of the country in order to get thoroughly acquainted therewith.

On Friday evening I went over to Dundalk: and called upon Mr. Dempster, bookseller etc, after a short conversation I came to the conclusion that although Mr. Dempster was probably a sound Unionist he looked at the matter very much from a business point of view, and in expectation of getting orders from the party in the event of an election.

Still in the formation of a district branch it would be advisable to give him some such post as a Vice-chairmanship, or if he would take it, the Hon, Treasurership.

On Mr. Finch, the Educational Institute I also called, he is the man for the Hon. Sec.ship of the Dundalk distr[ict]. branch, if he can only be got. and I think he can, for he is as keen as needles on the cause, this will be seen to on the occasion of my coming visit.

Mr. Strong, agent to Lord Roden, was not at his office; but Mr. Turner, who was there told me that Lord Roden had intimated to Mr. Strong that he was not to take any active part in politics. I represented the inadvisability of this course in view of the coming Local Govt. act, and I hope to see Mr. Strong on the occasion of my next visit.

I further secured that the Dundalk Herald (unionist) would do its very best to back up any propaganda in the Divn.

I am glad to say that the result of my preliminary visit has been the arrangement of a vigorous campaign, both in connection with organization and public meetings, for my coming visit: at the public meetings I propose principally to lecture on my "recent experiences round about Ireland", introducing in a careful way Unionist doctrines.

The following meetings have already been arranged for me:—

Carlingford:	3p.m: Sept. 3rd.
Dundalk:	8 p.m: sept. 3rd
Louth polling distr:	sept 4th. (aft.)
Dromiskin:	sept. 4th. (evg.)
Castlebellingham:	sept 5th.
Ardee (I expect.)	Sept. 9th.

regarding which a report will be presented later on.

Report on preliminary Visit to Co. Cavan.

Having some old friends at Shercock, Co. Cavan, among whom was Mr. C. Adams, Sec. to the district branch, I went over there for three days.

With pleasure I have to say that Mr. Adams is working up his district most energetically. Though his father Capt. Adams of Shinan, displays some lack of energy in forwarding the unionist cause: this, I suppose, as in other cases in connection with Irish landlords is due to the series of blows they have received, although the severity of these has apparently been somewhat due to want of timeous combination among that class.

Mr Adams has arranged a meeting for me to take place on Mon. Sept. 7th. and he has also done his best to get the secs. and others in the surrounding districts to take an interest in my mission.

A report of the future work in connection with this Div'n will be duly forwarded.

66 Letter from J. H. Scott, Park View, Cork, to the secretary of the I.U.A., 24 February 1893, describing unionist organisation in Cork city (D 989A/8/2):

Dear Sir—Replying to circular recd. yesterday (unsigned) I quite approve of the steps suggested to be taken.

We have here in this District the Unionist Hundred (of which I am Chairman) it was elected by the ratepayers of each Ward in the City—(11 representatives sit for each of the 8 Wards and 12 are elected for the Liberties which adjoin the City each Ward has its Committee & the organization is in active work & doing good service to the cause of the Union.

The following are the principal officers

President	Henry L. Young JP. Leemount
Vice Presidents	Sir Geo Colthurst DL Blarney Castle Edwin Hale JP. Pinehurst Joseph Pike DL. Dunsland
Secretary	Graham A. Goold Solicitor Grand Parade [?]

If you communicate with these gentlemen we will all help I am sure

The Primrose League also works well. The President is R. E. Longfield D.L. Longueville Mallow and the Hon Secretaries are
Mrs. T. I. Babington Mt. Verden Terrace and Miss Verling Gregg, Marlborough House.

We have been trying to arrange for a large public meeting here soon. I am calling a meeting of the "Hundred" for next week to work it up We are very anxious to get a big speaker down Is there any chance of our being able to get Col. Saunderson or Mr. Carson? Yours faithfully

John Harley Scott

67

A report on unionist activity at the Queen's Co. parliamentary revision of 1892, showing the reduction of nationalist and the increase of unionist voters in the 1893 register (D 989A/8/2):

POLLING DISTRICT.	NUMBER OF VOTERS STRUCK OFF ORIGINAL REGISTER.		NUMBER OF VOTERS PUT ON SUPPLEMENTAL LISTS for '93		NUMBER OF CLAIMANTS PUT ON.	
	UNIONISTS.	NATIONALISTS.	UNIONISTS.	NATIONALISTS.	UNIONISTS.	NATIONALISTS.
LEIX						
Abbeyleix .	22	138	25	78	14	—
Ballybrittas .	16	60	9	31	5	—
Ballylinan .	8	98	11	57	5	2
Ballickmoyler	9	75	7	56	2	3
Clonbrock .	8	39	5	40	8	2
Maryborough	30	134	21	103	17	18
Portarlington	23	61	18	41	—	5
Stradbally .	14	177	11	40	3	3
Timahoe .	5	70	10	33	4	—
TOTAL .	135	852	117	479	58	33
OSSORY						
Ballacolla .	8	150	8	25	4	—
Borris-in-Ossory .	13	67	3	28	2	—
Clonaslie .	6	62	6	35	—	—
Coolrain .	18	213	11	27	7	4
Durrow .	24	172	7	34	11	—
Errill . .	4	9	2	9	2	—
Mountmellick	34	153	42	103	2	—
Mountrath .	27	249	23	135	6	—
Rathdowney .	25	236	13	51	5	3
TOTAL .	159	1311	115	447	39	7

68 Extract from the minute book of the executive council of the I.U.A., 5 December 1893, giving the schedule of representation of other organisations, including Ulster unionist registration associations, on the general council (D 989A/1/4):

The following schedule of representation of Organizations upon the new Council was adopted:—

Mid Armagh.			1.
Londonderry City Registration Association.			1.
East Donegal	,,	,,	1.
North Tyrone	,,	,,	1.
South ,,	,,	,,	1.
East ,,	,,	,,	1.
North Fermanagh	,,	,,	1.
South ,,	,,	,,	1.
North Monaghan	,,	,,	1.
East Cavan	,,	,,	1.
West ,,	,,	,,	1.
Orange Body.			9.
Primrose League.			5.
Liberal Union of Ireland.			3.
Unionist Clubs' Council.			3.
Constitutional Club.			3.
City & County Conservative Club.			2.
			36.

It was also resolved that the Unionist Registration Associations in Ulster, not included in the above list, should be invited to send representatives to the Council.

III

In time, however, southern unionist hopes were belied, and the impossibility of establishing one mass party organisation for all Irish unionists became evident. In the first place, Ulster unionists were gradually drawn into a separate organisation, and by the time of the third home rule bill they often saw southern unionists' interests as competing with their own. This was particularly true over the question of the exclusion of Ulster. Southern unionists felt unable to support fully Ulster's armed preparations for resisting the third home rule bill, complaining of 'Carsonism' and Sir Edward Carson's 'silly proposals to march to Cork etc.'; and many disagreed with Ulster unionists over the principle of exclusion. The Ulster unionists thought that in the event of home rule being forced on Ireland they had a right to opt out if they could, whereas southern unionists thought that their own and Ireland's best interests would be served by a united Ireland containing the substantial Ulster minority. They supported the Ulster case against the third home rule bill largely for tactical reasons, believing that home rule without Ulster would be unworkable and unacceptable to nationalists.

This latent disagreement came to the surface in the Irish convention, 1917–18, when, much to Ulstermen's disgust, the southern unionist delegates unsuccessfully tried to force an all-Ireland parliament on them and opposed exclusion. There was also disagreement over the question of proportional representation, which in 1919 southern unionists managed to have introduced into local elections in Ireland. Southern unionists hoped that this provision would enable them to take again an active part in Irish political life, while Ulster unionists regarded such endeavours to secure minority representation as not only futile but also likely to jeopardise precarious unionist majorities in certain Ulster counties.

69 Draft letter from H. de F. Montgomery to the 11th Baron Farnham, of Farnham, Co. Cavan, chairman of the I.U.A., 25 March 1919, arguing against proportional representation in Irish local elections (D 627/437):

My Dear Farnham—I did not feel disposed to spoil the pleasure of your visit yesterday by entering upon an argument. Moreover, I was still too much under the influence of the dregs of flu, to feel fit for a disputation. I am, however, (having slept upon it) so clearly convinced that the handing over of the Tyrone County Council and District Councils to Sinn Feiners, will do the Unionist Cause more harm than the opening of Southern Councils to Unionist minorities will do it good, and I am so anxious to avoid more trouble between Northern and Southern Unionists now that the great trouble maker, Midleton has been extruded, that I am inflicting upon you a letter. Apart from the very strong local Tyrone view, and what I may call the six county view, it appears to me that the Unionist Cause will be seriously weakened by the curtailing of such a large area as Tyrone, of the already too small section of Ireland where Unionists and Protestants have any chance of obtaining appointments as Dispensary doctors, County Officials, Clerks of Unionis [*sic*] etc. etc. It seems to me from the widest point of view, that the conversion of a Unionist majority into a separatist majority or vice versa is more important than the setting up a score of counties of minority representation which will be in a minority. I quite admit that it will be for the public advantage that (say) you and Fane Vernon should have seats on the Cavan County Council, but after all it is the majority that rules, and it is the majority that makes all appointments. You may influence the Council in a few matters where politics can be kept out, but I venture to think that the amount of good you can do will be very small compared to what the majority can do in its own way.

I think all the members of the present I.U. Alliance have more or less admitted the correctness of my contention that the necessity of excluding six counties from any scheme of Home Rule, is in the present state of public opinion in Great Britain and Ireland, by far the most effective barrier against any sort of Home Rule. When, at the time of the Buckingham Palace Conference just before the war, the bone of contention was whether two or four counties should be excluded, the fact that in County Tyrone the Unionists were able to hold the County Council and five of the District Councils was taken together with the evidence that the Protestants in Tyrone paid more than two-thirds of the rates, a strong argument in favour of including Tyrone in the Ulster Pale. The Unionists lost control of the Fermanagh County Council by mismanagement. If the Tyrone County Council and most of the District Councils go, the case for the inclusion of Fermanagh and Tyrone inside the pale will be much weakened, there being an R.C. majority, that is, presumably, a Home Rule majority, according to the census on both these counties. If the area which is bound to get separate treatment is reduced from six counties to four, it appears to me that the Ulster barrier that now exists against Home Rule for any part of Ireland is substantially weakened, and that no amount of minority representation that you can possibly get under P.R. in Cavan or anywhere else, will make up to you for this weakening of your great bulwark. I hope therefore, that you will prevent the I.U.A. taking up a strong line in favour of P.R. Up to the present those who are actively promoting P.R. seem to be Midletonites or rather shaky Farnhamites. The private memorandum that has been issued to all the members in favour of P.R. bears the names of Maurice Dockrell, Walter Guinness, Prettyman [*sic*] Newman, Sydney Robinson and Edward Woods. There are, I believe other names which have not been mentioned to me. When you go over, I think you ought to see Coote as well as Carson and Archdale and other Ulster members. Coote is not altogether an admirable person, and I find one cannot talk perfectly freely to him, as he is capable of repeating things you say to him in private conversation, when he thinks they will serve his purpose at a pinch, and repeating them not altogether correctly. He was, however, nominated as a candidate here by a large majority of delegates; he thoroughly understands the operation of L[ocal]. G[overnment]. in Tyrone, and represents the Unionist and Orange democracy here, and he knows what their feelings will be if they think they are being sacrificed as regards local government for the sake of giving advantages to Southern Unionists which they are unable to regard being of a very practical turn of mind, as of anything like the value to them (the Southern Unionists) that their present majority on the County and District Councils here are [*sic*] to them (the Tyrone Unionists). We

136

have, by the shedding of Midleton & Co. avoided the risk that was imminent from the day the Convention broke up till the day of Midleton's resignation, of a serious estrangement between Northern and Southern Unionists, and it would be a thousand pities and a great injury to the Cause, if a fresh split occurred over the head of P.R. As far as I understand the situation you cannot avoid such a split by persuading Ulster Unionist members to accept P.R., involving as it does the loss of Tyrone.

You won't, I think, take it amiss, if I point out that while your desire for minority representation on local councils, is a good many degrees less foolish than the Midletonite acceptance of Bishop O'Donnells so called "safe guards", the feeling at the bottom of your action in favouring P.R. at the expense of the solidity of Unionist Ulster, is not entirely without resemblance to their action in jumping at provisions which would enable them, as they thought, for a few years to play a part in a Dublin Parliament.

We are having a meeting to-morrow after the County Council meeting at Omagh, at which we shall have some expert opinion as to the possibility of holding the Tyrone Councils under P.R, We may possibly arrive at some conclusions which will somewhat modify the intense hostility we now feel to P.R. I will write you further after this meeting, but think it better to send off this statement of my present views without losing a post. . . .

70 *Letter from C. C. Craig, M.P. for South Antrim, to Lord Farnham, 12 May 1919, declining on behalf of the U.U.C. a southern unionist proposal to revive the joint committee of the U.A.I. (D 989A/8/23):

Dear Lord Farnham—We had a meeting yesterday with reference to 25 Victoria St. and to the question of Propaganda and of the Work to be done in London, in connection therewith. We decided to re-organise our establishment in London, and to make it a branch of the Ulster Unionist Council. It was felt that for these purposes separate offices would be required, and that we would have more than enough work to occupy a whole-time Secretary and Staff.

It seemed to us that the premises at present occupied by the Union Defence League at 25 Victoria Street could probably be redistributed amongst us in such a way that each of the Associations might, if they wanted them, have separate and distinct offices, each with their own staff.

With regard to the question of a Joint Committee, we felt that while desiring to work with you to the utmost of our ability in the common cause, it would not be possible to have any formal and permanent Committee for this purpose. We feel we must have a free hand, and although we realise that our aims are the same as those of the Irish Unionist Alliance, we feel that there are occasions on which the attainment of those aims will be sought along different lines.

As an instance of this, I might point out to you the divergence of views existing between us in the North and many members of your Alliance on the subject of the Proportional Representation Bill, and I think you will see that matters of grave importance such as that could not possibly be dealt with by a Joint Committee.

This applies to questions of policy, but the same difficulties arise even in the question of propaganda, as we have found in the past, and I might mention, as an instance of this, the difficulty with regard to Pamphlets sent out from the Ulster point of view, which sometimes offend the susceptibilities of people coming from the South.

Under these circumstances we came to the conclusion that while willing to give you every assistance in our power, it was not desirable to have anything in the nature of a Standing Joint Committee either for policy or for propaganda which might in any degree interfere with the liberty of action of either of us: but I need hardly tell you that we are most anxious to work in the closest accord with you for the common aim we both have before us.

If in spite of the decision to which we have come, you care to meet us we could arrange a meeting as suggested by you for some time in the week beginning the nineteenth inst. Yours very truly

(Signed) Charles C. Craig

IV

Not only was it impossible for the I.U.A. to represent the views of Ulster unionists, it also proved impossible to establish a conventional mass party even in the three southern provinces. This failure was due in part to the limited social basis of southern unionism, and in part to political apathy on the part of the Anglo-Irish. In some respects political apathy was a function of the limited social basis, for the scattered Anglo-Irish were reluctant to take any action that might antagonise the nationalist majority among whom they had to live. Except, therefore, in certain areas, where the Anglo-Irish were strongest, branches of the I.U.A. tended to be weak and dependent upon the energy and initiative of a single individual. An energetically promoted re-organisation in 1893 **(74)** did not remedy this situation and by 1906 the I.U.A. recognised its limitations. In that year it abandoned ambitious schemes of constituency branches and sub-branches and contented itself with the formation of county committees. The intention was merely to maintain sufficient organisation in Ireland to sustain a campaign in British politics against home rule.

71 Letter from Miss A. M. Rowan, Princes Quay, Tralee, Co. Kerry, to the secretary of the I.U.A., 15 October 1892, explaining the difficulties of maintaining elaborate unionist organisation in Co. Kerry (D 989A/8/2):

Dear Mr. Cox—In reply to yours of 13th., I have talked to Col Rowan about it & he thinks with me that it will be almost impossible to get a conference (a) together. Moreover that those who would attend a conference or [are] not persons who will be inclined to work, rather those who come, because others come, so they are ashamed to remain at home. (b) Except I.U.A. & P[rimrose] L[eague] there are not any associations in Kerry likely to assist. (c) is therefore impracticable. (d) Individual action in isolated places is all we can count upon. This I think could be set in motion in both N. & W. Kerry, but E. & S. are quite terra incognita politically to me. 3. & 4. might be undertaken by individuals—if you prepare forms to be filled in. But the preparing these masses of information takes more time & thought than any body here who is competent to undertake the work, has to spare. "A." such particulars are not always accessible. "B" photos impossible for want of a cheap photographer. "C" newspapers are an item of expense which all do not indulge in—(I know I cannot see national papers I want to read, because I cannot afford to spend pennies freely.) Therefore sending newspapers is not a thing easily done. (iii) Some actions of Boards are curious. Here is a speci-men—Tralee union had now two paid Guardians. Seed [?] rate is not being paid up. One of these Guardians has ordered the collector to call upon the tenants security for the money. My brother is security for some tenants of his. He has been applied to by the collector to pay up for these men. Rents are not paid—So—a paternal Gov. adds insult to injury—claiming the tenants debt from the landlord who is himself an unpaid creditor of the tenants!

In Kerry there are so few who will take any trouble, or do anything unless they are paid for working.

I quite see your plan is admirable the difficulty will be to have it carried out properly. I know few who will do anything, though many will approve of the suggestion & some promise to assist. Day by day I get less & less help. and yet now opportunity to work offers in a way that shows much good could be done if only there were workers—Irish people are too pleasure loving & indolent. I think individual action is all you can count upon in Kerry for this work. In N[orth]. K[erry]. Major Rice will no doubt act as a "head", and perhaps get help from friends. At Abbeyfeale B. O Connor of Kilmainham would give some help. Dr. Busteed—Castlegregory would I feel sure also assist. Mr. John McCarthy Church St. in Listowel, gives me a little help, but his handwriting is difficult to decipher, & I think he is rather lethargic. Mr. Hussey is the most capable also the most active man here, but he is always very occupied & as I have before remarked this work takes a great deal of time.

Personally I will do all I can to help—But I am terribly overworked. L.s.d. are not coming in as they ought & I am struggling to earn by my pen. I am at the present moment getting to the end of a job which may come in useful. I have made a sketch in six parts of law made by Irish Parliaments from 1300 to 1800. They are a curious revelation—showing racial hate is a modern invention & that religious hate is also a new invention of the evil one. Penal

laws were revivals of old laws of Hen[ry]. and Rich[ard].III, & used alternately by Mary & Eliz[abeth], etc, to coerce those they disliked. These will
make a pamphlet. I am anxious to dispose of the M.SS. but as yet cannot
get any publisher to take up my idea, which is, that this book will be a handy
one when Mr. Gladstones Home Rule is being discussed—on each of the six
sections I make a few brief comments.

I heard from Mr. Hussey-Walsh today from Cirencester—He wanted [a]
list of outrages, etc, under [the] Gladstonian reign. I sent off a budget.

I herewith enclose some more cuttings.

I have been touring to the wild west of Kerry. Farmers in these wilds are
more comfortable than in more civilised parts—they appear well off. yet no
rent is the "word" going round, though some are turning a deaf ear to the
hint, & are in mortal terror for fear of Home Rule & increased taxation
therefrom. No more at present from yrs. truly

A. M. Rowan

72 Address of Sir Augustus Warren of Warren's Court, Co. Cork, to a
meeting of the Unionist Clubs Council held in the Central Hall,
Belfast, 2 May 1893, explaining the difficulties of organising clubs
in the southern counties (D 1327/1/1):

My lords and gentlemen, I have much pleasure in attending this large
representative meeting of the Presidents of Unionist clubs from all parts of
Ireland, and I wish to point out that it is extremely important that a very
strong letter or circular should be sent to the unionist clubs in the southern
counties of Ireland. Really, all they want is to have properly explained and
pointed out to them the very great danger they incur by not joining and
combining together, and forming clubs under the present organisation.
(Applause.) I called a meeting for the purpose of forming a club, and got
together a good many after a time, but numbers do not understand the
movement. They are simply like a flock of sheep without a shepherd to lead
them. There is one thing which I notice in meetings in the South, the men are
afraid of the results if it goes out among their neighbours and they are afraid
they will be punished, as they were under the Land League, and I speak
particularly of a good many Roman Catholic farmers in the South. They are
all hesitating, and the difficulty is to get at them. I am sorry to say there are
a good many Protestants [who] will not come in and join. They do not like
to sign the pledge. I think if a strong circular were drawn up and letters also,
and sent to some of the influential men in the different counties, it would
have a good effect in this direction. Many people do not understand the
position. Several Unionists are asking for what purpose are they to enrol—
are they eventually to fight, &c., and who is to lead them. They have started
four or five clubs, but people hesitate to enrol. Meetings are called, there is
a great deal of talk, and soforth. Lord Londonderry came to Cork and spoke
to the point. They have done nothing since. They don't organise, and they
do not know how, and there is no one to do so and explain matters clearly·

I am afraid ladies cannot be organised in our clubs. They must organise themselves, and they can help us in a variety of ways. What we want is men who are able to do something at present and will be able to do something in the future. We can do nothing against Home Rule without men thoroughly organised on the club system. (Applause.) I therefore beg to propose a resolution:—"That this council invite all Unionists in Ireland either to join existing Unionist clubs or to form themselves into Unionist clubs where no such organisation already exists." And I venture to add that a strong circular should be sent from the Unionist Clubs Council to the Southern counties in Ireland, explaining the organisation and constitution of the clubs, and I may assure you that it will be of very great advantage to the Unionist cause.

73 Leading article from *Notes from Ireland,* June 1906, commenting on the recent reorganisation of the I.U.A. prompted by the 'devolution crisis' of 1904–5 and the return of the liberals to office (T 2759/3):

On the next page will be found the text of the Revised Constitution of the Irish Unionist Alliance, recently adopted by the General Council.

A comparison of the new with the former rules and regulations of the Alliance, which have been in operation since the year 1893, will show that the object of the revision has been to simplify the conduct or procedure of the Alliance, and to render more than ever efficient the working powers of the organisation—to make the governing Council solidly representative of the Unionism of all the Irish Counties, by the formation in every County of a County Committee, whose members, by virtue of their membership, shall become elected to and form the dominant body of the General Council.

It is hardly necessary to state that the motive object of the Alliance remains as it has been since the organisation was established more than twenty years ago, viz:—"The maintenance of the Legislative Union between Great Britain and Ireland." Perhaps at no time since the Irish Unionist Alliance first took its place as a Unionist defensive force in Irish politics has there been as much need of such a force as at present. In former years of struggle and stress the issue was comparatively a simple and straightforward one. Now, to the once clearly defined array of avowed enemies of the Union, who were then the only foes to be reckoned with, are allied misguided persons, who while ostensibly attached to the Union are doing all in their power to promote measures which cannot but in their results be highly detrimental to the Union, and jeopardise even the Imperial connection between Great Britain and Ireland. There are also new Irish disloyal movements in the field which while proclaiming themselves to be non-sectarian and non-political are, on their own free confession, making straight for a separate and an independent Ireland. To add to the political dangers of the time, there is a Ministry in power whose declared Irish policy is one of granting in piecemeal fashion the full demands of the Irish parties who aspire to break up the connection between England and Ireland.

The time is surely one for Unionists to be up and doing. Providence, it is said, helps those who help themselves, and than that there could be no better motto for Irish Unionists at the present critical juncture. Should a feeling of apathy, of which there is happily no symptom as yet (as was proved by the extensive work which the Alliance was enabled to accomplish during the late General Election), obtain a hold upon Irish Unionists, it will not unnaturally be regarded both in Ireland and Great Britain as a surrender of their long-cherished principles. A solid organisation which will embrace every county in the four provinces, such as is now designed by the Irish Unionist Alliance, and which has already made most encouraging progress, will strengthen and unify Unionist feeling and action in Ireland, and those leading members of the Alliance who are now promoting the work sincerely trust that every County that has not yet selected its County Committee of Unionists will promptly rise to the necessity of doing so. It is not intended by the Alliance to trouble County Committees to hold local meetings at present, or to embarrass them with unnecessary work, but the Alliance is most anxious to have a body of Unionists in every County on whose support and assistance it can rely in time of emergency.

In this matter the Alliance cordially invites the co-operation—so often and so helpfully given before—of the Irish Unionist Press, metropolitan and provincial, as well as the fraternal support of leading Unionists in the Counties which have not yet become organised in the manner above indicated.

V

Taking advantage of their strengths—social solidarity, wealth and connections in British politics—southern unionists maintained a limited but lively organisation capable of mobilising what unionist energies did exist in the south. Four points are worth noticing about the organisation. Firstly, a feature of the ideal and actual schemes of organisation was strong organisation at the centre, with offices first in Dawson Street and then at 109 Grafton Street, Dublin. Although the general council was the supreme governing body, the affairs of the I.U.A. were run by an executive committee, which in times of home rule crises often worked through sub-committees, by the chief officers (notably the chairman, vice-chairmen and honorary secretaries) and by a paid secretary. Secondly, there were among the Anglo-Irish active individuals ready to exploit social contacts to mobilise unionist energies, particularly in times of crisis. Thirdly, the I.U.A., by providing for the representation of other unionist bodies, such as local con-servative clubs, the Primrose League and the Orange Order, on the general council, was able to coordinate the activities of such organisations. Fourthly, though the link between the protestant churches and unionism in the south was not as close as in the north, the I.U.A. did on occasion like to prod the churches into action and to seek their cooperation, e.g. in the organisation of petitions.

74 Extracts from a 12-page pamphlet entitled *The Irish Unionist Alliance. An account of its work and organisation,* issued in 1893 by the I.U.A., describing the state of the organisation at the time of the second home rule bill (D 989C/3/25):

(p.6)

It may be of interest to our readers to describe briefly the method in which the Alliance has carried on its work. By doing so we shall best be able to give some idea of the magnitude of its task, and the completeness of the machinery which its leaders have constructed to enable it efficiently to perform its work.

THE COUNCIL AND EXECUTIVE COMMITTEE.

The supreme governing body of the Alliance is the Council, which only meets twice or three times a year, and is composed of the foremost men in the ranks of the Unionists of Ireland. But the body upon the members of which the duty of carrying on the actual work of the Association devolves is the Executive Committee, upon which serve men the most influential and respected leaders in the mercantile and commercial ranks of the country, men occupying high positions in the great banking establishments and in the industrial life of Ireland. This influential and representative body meets twice each week, and they decide questions of policy and finance referred to them by the various sub-committees immediately engaged in the work of the Alliance, which is divided between six departmental committees. The work of the latter is reported weekly to the Executive Body. The departmental committees are admirably constructed, and they have each a secretary who is constantly engaged, under their direction, in the management of his department.

THE PRESS COMMITTEE.

The Press Committee, composed of men of acknowledged literary abilities, has entrusted to it the preparation and circulation of literature bearing on the Home Rule question. Some slight idea of the magnitude of the operations of this single committee of some nine gentlemen may be gained from the fact that since March last three millions of leaflets dealing with various phases of the question have been scattered broadcast by them throughout England, Ireland, Scotland and Wales. At present the committee is engaged distributing 250,000 pamphlets in advocacy of the Union through the various polling districts of Lancashire. The constituencies in which bye-elections took place

143

were especially attended to by the Press Committee, and every individual voter received leaflets by post from the offices of the Alliance. As questions arise in the discussions on the Home Rule Bill, such as the proposals affecting the Constabulary or the Civil Service, new pamphlets or leaflets dealing tersely and trenchantly with the subject are produced, and are widely distributed. Posters are also made use of extensively, and with much effect. Some of the leaflets have been translated into the Welsh language, and been distributed in the Welsh-speaking districts of the Principality. The Press Committee has also under consideration the issuing by post of a million and a quarter leaflets, a project which in postage stamps alone would involve an expenditure of £2,500. NOTES FROM IRELAND, a weekly publication which has done good service in the past, has been recently enlarged and improved. It gives as heretofore numerous extracts from Irish newspapers (chiefly Nationalist) illustrative of the working of the principles of the Nationalist party, and it leaves these extracts to speak for themselves, which they usually do with striking effect. A new feature of this publication is headed "A Diurnal," which gives a brief record, under each day, of "Events Relating to Ireland."

THE SPEAKERS' COMMITTEE.

Another Committee is the Speakers' Committee, and as an illustration of the work of the gentlemen who compose this department of the Alliance— gentlemen whose voices have during the last two years been heard in every part of the United Kingdom—we may give an epitome of their operations during June. In that month a staff of fifteen speakers addressed ninety meetings in different parts of England; meetings of business men were held in a number of important mercantile centres in England, and were addressed by deputations of Irish merchants. The meetings were held, amongst other places, at Stafford, Walsall, Wednesbury, Huddersfield, Carlisle, Whitehaven, Barrow, Wolverhampton, &c. Special attention was devoted to the election contests in Linlithgowshire, where the Unionists gained such an important victory, and at Pontefract, where the Gladstonians so narrowly escaped defeat. The strongest testimony to the value of the services rendered by the Alliance speakers in West-Lothian, in securing the return of Captain Hope, has been given by the *Scotsman* and other leading journals in Scotland. In addition to this army of speakers there are also now employed a number of men who may be described as colporteurs, and who go from house to house distributing Unionist literature. In conjunction with the Ladies' Liberal Unionist Association of England and the Central Conservative Association, the Alliance has a number of ladies at work "spreading the light." At present the Executive have under consideration the advisability of putting one or two Anti-Home Rule vans on the road. Each of these will have attached to it a gentleman qualified to speak on the question, and a man to distribute literature, and, of course, a driver. The expense of this undertaking is estimated at £500 per annum for each van.

THE BILL COMMITTEE.

The Bill Committee, on which the law is well represented, has charge of all the Parliamentary work. This Committee is in constant communication with the members of the Irish Unionist Parliamentary Party, who, it may be stated, hold meetings twice a week at the London Offices of the Alliance, and who are in this way furnished with information upon all the numerous questions which crop up at intervals in the discussions upon the Bill.

THE ORGANISATION COMMITTEE.

The Organisation Committee is, perhaps, the most important of the departmental committees, and its work is more difficult and extensive than that of any of the other sub-committees. The very important work of the registration of the Unionists of Ireland is the principal work at present engaging the attention of this committee. For this purpose a branch association is formed in each constituency or county, and each of these areas is split up into suitable divisions. Sometimes the parish, sometimes the polling district is selected as the most convenient area. In each of these divisions a district branch is formed, the Unionists of the district register themselves in their district branch, and it is forthwith affiliated to the Central Association. Every Unionist over sixteen years of age will be registered, and it is intended also to keep a register of lady associates over sixteen years of age. The Council of Organisation will be formed of delegates from the various branches, and each branch will be represented on the Council in proportion to the strength of its membership. The Governing Body will, therefore, be a thoroughly representative one. An excellent idea is to be carried out in connection with this organisation, namely, the formation of a number of auxiliary branches throughout Great Britain. With this object a strong provisional Committee is being formed in London, with the sanction of the Unionist members of both Houses of Parliament, for the purpose of dividing London into suitable districts, and organising auxiliary branches. It is in contemplation to extend this movement to the whole of Great Britain. When these Auxiliary Branches are formed, it is intended to link them with the Irish organisation in the following manner:—A particular branch in England will be made the partner, as it were, of a particular branch in Ireland. They will mutually aid each other, and a concentration of energy will thus be secured, which will prove most advantageous, and which could not be obtained were the two organisations to be joined only in a general way. Each Branch in England will be brought into intimate connection with an Irish district, and it will be possible, without much difficulty, to receive and distribute information both in the sister country and at home. Some idea of the extent of the organisation as it already exists throughout Ireland will be gathered from the statistics given below, it being premised, however, that the work of forming branches is still going on vigorously. In the County of Carlow, in addition to the county branch, there are seventeen district branches, all in active working order. Clare has, so far, only one branch, with its headquarters at Ennis. The work of organising the County of Cork is progressing, and it is hoped that in a very short time there will be as many as twenty branches within the county. In East Galway division there are several branches, in Central Galway nine, and in West Galway four. In the County Kerry there is as yet but one branch —that of Tralee. Kildare has eleven district branches, and Kilkenny has twelve. King's County has been for a long time well organised in both .

divisions, and good work has been done. In North Leitrim there is the branch at work, and in South Leitrim there are ten district branches. County Louth has nine district branches, County Longford eleven, County Mayo two, Leix division of Queen's County has six district branches, and Ossory division about an equal number. In North Roscommon there is a branch at Boyle, and a number of district branches are in course of formation. In South Roscommon division a branch has been formed at Roscommon, and district branches are being formed. Sligo has seventeen district branches, North Tipperary has eight, and there are also branches in South-East Tipperary and Mid-Tipperary. Westmeath has seventeen district branches, North Wexford nine, West Wicklow eleven, and East Wicklow eight, and there are also branches in East and West Waterford. A very full enrolment of members is expected to be effected by the end of the present month, and it is intended shortly to publish a full list of the branches and of their officers.

THE FINANCE COMMITTEE.

The Finance Committee is made up of men quite capable of managing this all-important department, and in their hands the finance of the Alliance is as safe as its most zealous supporters could wish. . . .

THE LADIES' COMMITTEE.

The Ladies' Committee has been decidedly active, and has done much valuable work. Their chief task has been that of promoting the Women's Memorial to the Queen. This memorial will shortly be ready for presentation. The number of signatures already received in the office is over 70,000, and returns have still to be received from a number of counties. The Ladies, too, have special charge of the distribution of newspapers in Great Britain, special attention being paid to constituencies in which at the General Election the majorities for Mr. Gladstone were small. Local committees of ladies were formed throughout Ireland. To each of these committees a constituency was assigned—the selection of the constituency being made by the local committees themselves if they so desired. Addresses are furnished to them, and to these addresses the committees post newspapers and send packages of various kinds of literature. Some members of the committee also write letters to local papers in the different constituencies, explaining and advocating Unionist views. The number of papers despatched each week by the Ladies' Committee from the central offices is about 12,000. Many of these are sent in small parcels to friends who have undertaken to distribute them in their several districts; others are addressed to reading-rooms, to hotels, to workingmen's clubs, or to individuals. The ladies also supply selected addresses to such members of the general public as undertake to post their own newspapers, a record being kept of the addresses so supplied. It is calculated that the total number of Irish Unionist newspapers thus circulated each week amounts to 20,000. One lady residing in England, who has taken an active part in the distribution of newspapers, writes:—"The papers are most thankfully received, and are doing a great deal of good. They have created a great sensation, and are passed from one to another until they are worn out."

This, in short, is the work of the Irish Unionist Alliance—a work in the highest degree important. The Unionists of Ireland have given the Alliance a duty to perform, and its most strenuous opponents could not but say that that duty is being performed as thoroughly as possible. It is an expensive work too, but all work of the kind is necessarily expensive, and the Unionists of Ireland have not grumbled at the expense. They have generously and liberally contributed to the funds of the Alliance, and they had—from the fact that men like Lord Iveagh and Lord Ardilaun were willing, nay anxious, to guarantee large sums when the Guarantee Fund was first opened— sufficient assurance that the money would be spent in the way most likely to achieve the best results.

75 Letter from J. Penrose, Estate Office, Athboy, Co. Meath, 24 February 1893, urging upon the I.U.A. a more active propaganda in Great Britain, and offering to collect funds locally (D 989A/8/2):

Dear Sir—You have of course seen Mr. Culverwell's letter in Thursdays papers

I quite agree with him in thinking that THE thing for us to do at once is to send more speakers to England & Scotland to try to get at the Voters in the Gladstonian & doubtful constituencies.

May I ask you whether it is the intention of your Committee to act on this suggestion, & whether if you had more funds at your disposal you would send more speakers to England?

If your answer is Yes I should like to take the opportunity offered by the presence of many County Gentlemen at Trim on Monday at the Grand Jury to make an effort to start collections in each parish in the County Meath at the same time that the proposed petitions are being signed.

I shall be at the Grand Jury at Trim on Monday so if you are unable to reply to this on Saturday may I ask you to telegraph to me to Grand Jury Room Trim before 2 o'c on that day. If you choose to telegraph the word "Yes" I shall understand it in the sense suggested above

I shall propose that one man be appointed in each parish of the County (not Diocese as the latter includes part of Westmeath & Kings Co) as a collector & I suppose if you are sent their names & addresses you could send them circulars to send out stating what it is you propose to do if you can get sufficient means.

I enclose a letter I have written to the papers & if you think well of them [*sic*] may I trouble you to post them after you have altered them in any way you think advisable.

If you think well of the suggestion contained in them but think that it would be better that it should come from your self or your Committee put my letters in the fire

I think it most important, that in this Crisis the Grand Juries should not confine their energies to passing resolutions. Yrs. faithfully

J. Penrose

76 Letter from R. Philpot, Woodmount, Arklow, Co. Wicklow, 2 March 1893, offering to collect signatures for a petition against the second home rule bill, and urging the I.U.A. to use the Methodist and other protestant churches as a medium for getting up petitions (D 989A/8/2):

Dear Sir—Being desirous of securing signatures of the Congregation attending the Methodist Church at Arklow to the petition against Mr. Gladstone's Home Rule proposals, now before Parliament, I beg to ask if you will kindly send me in course of post one form of petition with written heading and about three with printed heading which I shall endeavour to make immediate use of.

I hope to be excused for remarking that The Committee of the Irish Unionist Alliance must be aware that the Methodists of Ireland, almost to an individual, are ardently attached to the legislative union of Great Britain & Ireland and that they would gladly exert any reasonable effort to strengthen Unionist principles. Such being the case it does not seem too much to expect that each Methodist Clergyman in Ireland (whose name & address appears in the Minutes of Conference) with a few exceptions (those who decline entering the political arena under any circumstances, who I repeat are very few, and could be pointed out by Dr. Evans of Abbey St Methodist church, and in such exceptional cases a staunch Unionist member of the congregation to which such neutral minister is attached should be immediately supplied with forms of petition & circulars accompanying soliciting their prompt action & instructing them how to proceed. I greatly fear that many who would act willingly & efficiently are not aware of your arrangements and may not feel called on to apply to you if you do not make the advance to them. While attending to the Methodist church in Ireland I do not think it applies less to any other Protestant denomination and sincerely hope that all shall be supplied with the petitions. I am Sir faithfully yours

Robert Philpot

77 Extracts from the minute book of the executive committee of the I.U.A., 24 November, 8 and 15 December 1893, relating to a proposal by the Liberal Union of Ireland to invite Joseph Chamberlain to address a meeting of unionists in Dublin (D 989A/1/5):

(a)

The following resolution passed at a meeting of the Liberal Union held on Nov 22nd., was read.
Resolved: That the Executive Committee of the Liberal Union of Ireland regard it as most important, in the interest of the Unionist cause, that the Right Hon. Joseph Chamberlain M.P., the Liberal Unionist leader in the House of Commons, be invited to address a Meeting in Dublin in the early part of next year, and they suggest that the Irish Unionist Alliance as representing all sections of Unionists in the Southern Provinces, at once take into consideration the subject of such a visit, and give this Committee an expression of their views.

The following resolution was then passed:—

That this Committee cordially approve of the suggestion of the Liberal Union, that the Rt Hon Joseph Chamberlain M.P. should be invited to address a public meeting of Unionists in Dublin in the early part of next year, and the I.U.A. will be glad to join in the invitation and to organise and pay the expenses of such meeting. And that the resolution of the Liberal Union, with this resolution be forwarded to the Primrose League., Orange Body., Constitutional Club., City & Co Conservative Club., & the Conservative Workingmen's Club and that they be asked to co-operate in the invitation.

(b)

Resolutions were read from the following bodies, endorsing the invitation to Mr Chamberlain to visit Dublin early next year:- Co Dublin Grand Orange Lodge., City of Dublin, North Co Dublin, and South Co Dublin Unionist Registration Associations., Beaconsfield Habitation of the Primrose League., City & Co Conservative Club., and the Constitutional Club.

It was resolved that Mr Wm Kenny, M.P., be requested to make suitable arrangements for presenting these resolutions to Mr Chamberlain.

(c)

A resolution from the City of Dublin Grand Orange Lodge, endorsing the invitation to Mr Chamberlain, was received.

VI

The work done by the I.L.P.U. and the I.U.A. in Ireland was in the main limited to the maintenance of the union and was strictly constitutional and legal. This did not please everybody.

In the first place, some enthusiastic and indiscreet unionists were closely involved in the purchase of the ill-famed Pigott letters, which appeared to implicate Parnell in the Phoenix Park murders; and the only suspicion of underhand dealing occurred at the time of the special commission, 1889. The energetic secretary of the I.L.P.U., Houston, had procured the letters, and there was some suggestion that they had been purchased out of the I.L.P.U.'s funds. Parnell asserted that behind Pigott there was a conspiracy to effect his ruin, and he demanded that the Union's books be submitted for examination by the commission. The I.L.P.U. agreed to submit its books to the judges or an independent observer but objected to opening its books to its political opponents. In the event, the judges decided that the books were not relevant to the issues before the commission. It seems that Houston was acting on his own initiative, and though he was supported by four prominent unionists, there is no evidence to suggest that they were acting on behalf of the I.L.P.U. Members of the I.L.P.U. protested that they had no responsibility for Houston's action, and their own auditors, in a special report, confirmed that none of the I.L.P.U.'s funds had gone towards the purchase of the Pigott letters. In a sense, however, the judges' decision was unfortunate, because the I.L.P.U.'s political opponents felt able to continue to make unjustifiable allegations.

In the second place, if the southern unionists in the main acted legally and honourably, they also acted constitutionally. This is not to say that all unionists in the south were satisfied with constitutional activity only. In 1912–14 a few unionists, some of whom were based upon the Kingstown and District Unionist Club, emulated Ulster, practised drilling and formed a volunteer group; but these were exceptional and found it difficult to make headway. There was no widespread attempt or general determination on the part of southern unionists to resist home rule by armed force.

78 Circular issued by the I.L.P.U. to 'members and friends', 30 August 1889, refuting allegations that the I.L.P.U.'s funds had been used in the purchase of the Pigott letters (D 989A/1/4):

Portions of the evidence given on behalf of the *Times* at the Special Commission sitting in London have given occasion for the most unwarrantable and unscrupulous assertions by the political opponents of the Union, with respect to the application of the funds of this Association. It has been alleged in the most reckless manner by the Parnellite Members of Parliament and their Counsel, that moneys under the control of this Association were applied in the purchase or procurement of the letters known as the Pigott letters, and it has been suggested that these moneys, if not directly given, were indirectly employed for that purpose through the medium of the Secretary, Mr. Houston, or the late Dr. Maguire, or through some other source.

So far was the pretended belief in these allegations carried that the Secretary of the Association was summoned to attend before the Special Commission with the books of the Association, whereupon the Executive Committee gave immediate directions for their production. In accordance with those directions every book of the Irish Loyal and Patriotic Union was in Court in charge of the Secretary and Assistant-Secretary on the 12th of July last, when Mr. Houston, as Secretary, having been examined as to the willingness of the Association to allow the books to be inspected, stated that every book was at the disposal of their Lordships for inspection, but that the Committee objected to allow an examination of them by political opponents. The Judges were then pressed by Counsel to direct that the books should be open for general inspection, but their Lordships refused to make any such order, on the ground that their production had no bearing on any issue before the Commission.

An extract from the official shorthand writer's report, giving a full statement of the proposals made by Mr. Houston and the Attorney-General on behalf of the Association, together with the Judges' ruling, is subjoined hereto.

It will thus be seen that this Council, **while willing to allow the Judges, their secretary, or any independent gentleman, to inspect the books from cover to cover,** object to the declared enemies of the Association being permitted to make themselves acquainted with the affairs of the Union, or the sources or extent of its funds.

The ruling of the Judges against the inspection of the books has enabled our enemies to continue their reckless assertions of improper use of moneys of the Association. Your Council therefore think it desirable, although they cannot stop these calumnies, **to absolutely assure their members and friends— (1) That the books of the Association are all in existence. (2) That the Accounts have been regularly audited from time to time. (3) That no portion of the funds has been applied, directly or indirectly, by payment or loan, to or through the late Dr. Maguire, Mr. Houston, or any other person, or in any other way, for the purchase or procurement of the Pigott letters.** (See also Auditor's Special Report, p. 4.)

In conclusion, the Council desire to further assure the Members of the Association that, recalling the important and universally acknowledged services rendered by the Irish Loyal and Patriotic Union, they will relax none of their efforts in carrying out the objects for which the Association was established, namely, the Maintenance of the Legislative Union between Great Britain and Ireland.

APPENDIX A.

REPORT LAID BEFORE THE COUNCIL BY THE ASSISTANT-SECRETARY (MR. COX)

OF

PROCEEDINGS BEFORE THE ROYAL COMMISSION.

In accordance with the order of the Executive Committee, I proceeded to London on the 2nd July with the books and documents asked for in the Secretary's (Mr. Houston's) subpoena. While there I was also served with a subpoena by Messrs. Lewis & Lewis to produce the books at the Special Commission. In obedience to this subpoena I brought the books, &c., to the Royal Courts of Justice. I was present during the examination of the Secretary on the 12th day of July, and submit the following report of what took place:—

SIR CHARLES RUSSELL (addressing Mr. Houston) asked—

'Have you any objection to the books being examined by their Lordships or by me?' Mr. Houston replied: 'Well, I am instructed by the Committee to state **that every book that we have is at the disposal of their Lordships for inspection,** but they have an objection to allow the books to be inspected by political opponents, for them to investigate every item.'

After some further discussion THE PRESIDENT said:—

'We are of opinion that the production of the books of the Loyal and Patriotic Union has not any bearing upon any issue before us.'

In the course of further argument the ATTORNEY-GENERAL said:—

'I have no actual right to intervene in this matter, but I should like your Lordships to understand simply the position my learned friends and I myself take up in regard to this matter. My Lords, I understand the objection taken by Mr. Houston not in any shape or form to be an objection to full and proper disclosure being given in order that your Lordships may ascertain if there is any truth in the suggestion that the Loyal and Patriotic Union were the persons who repaid Dr. Maguire, or that that money was in fact an advance from the Loyal and Patriotic Union through Dr. Maguire, and as to that, Mr. Houston having pledged his oath that there was nothing of the kind, that he always believed it was a private advance, and that, to his own knowledge the money never was repaid, as it goes to the credit of Mr. Houston, who has, to a certain extent, had to give evidence in this case, I should desire the fullest investigation. But the objection taken by Mr. Houston, if I may be allowed to refer to it, was not an unnatural one. He said, "I am certain of the fact, and I am willing that the Commission shall satisfy itself of that fact, or any other fact." But, my Lords, his objection was that there was no ground for giving political opponents a free range of inquiry upon other matters which are in no shape or form germane to any issue. And taking the ground which Mr. Asquith has last urged, we desire to say, my Lords, that in so far as it is for us **we would suggest that the books should be examined by Mr. Cunynghame or any independent person they choose to appoint, with a view to test the credibility and the truth of Mr. Houston's statement, with reference to the sum received from Dr. Maguire or any other matter relevant to this inquiry.** But the objection which was—fairly, as I humbly submit—taken by Mr. Houston, was that they should not be handed over for a general inquiry by political opponents into entries made which have no reference to it at all.'

After further discussion, THE PRESIDENT (after consultation with his learned colleagues) said:—

'We are all clearly of opinion, that the inspection insisted upon as a matter of right ought not to be granted.'

APPENDIX B.

SPECIAL REPORT BY AUDITOR.

In addition to the regular periodical Certificates of the Auditor, he has furnished the Council with the following Special Report:—

"I certify that I have Audited the Accounts of the Irish Loyal and Patriotic Union from its commencement in the year 1885, and that no part of the Funds of the Union were disbursed directly or indirectly for the purchase or procurement of the Pigott letters.

"J. STEWART KINCAID,

"29th August, 1889.   *"Auditor."*

79 Extracts from the minute book of the Kingstown and District Unionist Club, 6, 27 June, 4 July, 1 August, 12 September 1912, relating to proposals to form drilling and rifle sections (D 950/1/147):

(a)

The members of the deputation to Mr. Stewart, agent to Lord Longford, gave an account of their interview with him. The Hon Secretary described the nature & tenor of the conversation on the subject of a place to drill in & Mr. Dormer the same as regards employment, & Mr. Foote as regards registration. The interview was described by all three as well as by the President as a most satisfactory one & Mr. Stewart's determination to consider the whole matter & let them know further was noted.

(b)

It was proposed by Mr. Exshaw seconded by Mr. Dormer & passed unanimously that the Hon Sec should write to Mr. Lauder to see if it could be arranged that the K & Ds U Club can hold physical culture classes in the Hall at 42 York road.

Proposed by Mr. Anderson seconded by Mr. Foote that the Hon Sec write to the Hon Sec Erin Rifle Clubs 10 Rutland Square Dublin & ask him if the K & Ds U club can form a rifle club to be afiliated [*sic*] with them. Agreed to unanimously.

Proposed by Mr. Anderson & seconded by Mr. Exshaw that the Hon Sec see Mr. Devlin, Principal of the Grammar School in York Road, Kingstown, & ask him to allow the K & Ds U. C. to use the principal room in the school for purposes of physical culture. Agreed to unanimously.

(c)

Major Forth then announced his success[ful] negotiations with Mr. Bently, the Principal of Monkstown Park School for the use of their grounds for the purpose of physical culture & that Mr. Bently had very kindly & obligingly placed Monkstown Park at the disposal of the Club when not in use by the School at certain hours of the day up to the 31st July & at any hour during the succeeding six weeks from the 1st August. It was then agreed to that the first physical culture exercises should be carried out at 8 p.m., on Tuesday the 9th July 1912.

(d)

The Vice President opened the meeting by a brief account of the steps that had been taken towards the drilling of such members of the club who presented themselves at the Monkstown Park School, pointing out that they would practically get the advantages of drill & physical culture without any expense, the importance attached to drilling by the clubs in the North of Ireland & after exhorting them to attend with regularity read from a cutting from the Irish Times the account of an interesting parade by the Londonderry City Unionist Club.

(e)

The Vice President informed them he had received a letter from Mr. Lauder, Sec Joint Building Committee of the Hall 42 York Road saying his Committee placed the Hall at the disposal of the club for the purposes of physical culture for the moderate charge of 2/6 a night every Saturday night from 8 to 10. It was unanimously agreed to that these terms should be agreed to & that the first drill in the Hall should be held on Saturday 24th Sept. at 8 p.m. . . .

Mr. Trings spoke on the subject of obtaining a hall other than the Orange Hall as it prevented many Roman Catholics from coming & suggested that a house should be got from Lords Longford & de Vesci.

Mr Ladd pointed out the almost certain refusal of the Lords of the Soil.

Mr Foote [said] that a deputation had been to Mr. Stewart.

Mr Beegan [said] that the Lords of the Soil should be informed we were fighting in their interests.

The Vice President pointed out that Lords Longford & de Vesci had been approached both direct on the subject of Corrig school as a club House & through Mr. Stewart their agent for permission to use Corrig school grounds or house for physical culture & that they had met with a refusal on both occasions. . . .

The Vice President informed the meeting that the Daily Mirror's Staff Photographer had offered to have a photo inserted in the Mirror of a drill or route march of the club if one was sent him, but that the difficulty lay in it being impossible to have a photo taken at 8 p.m or of getting up a drill in the day [-time] owing to so few being able to attend.

On the strong representation of Mr. Ladd that it would be inimical to the interests of many of the members to appear in a photo in a public paper as part of a drill class the Vice President put the matter to the vote & declared that the noes were in the majority against it. The project of having a photo taken therefore fell to the ground. . . . . The Vice President informed the club that before the next step could be taken towards the formation of a rifle club that a list of thirty members & their addresses would have to be sent to Colonel Winter in London accompanied by ten shillings. He called for more names as only about eighteen had sent in their names. The exact number could not at the moment be ascertained as Mr. B. N. Blood had left the list at home. . . . The meeting was then brought to a close by the singing of the National Anthem which was led by Mr. Good.

VII

The I.U.A., besides being criticised by those southern unionists who preferred more underhand or more militant forms of activity, also came in for criticism from a third angle. This third, and more serious, criticism was that it concentrated upon a limited aim—the maintenance of the union—and at least until 1918 tended to ignore social and economic problems. In the eyes of critics like the Anglo-Irish novelist, James Owen Hannay (who wrote under the pseudonym of George A. Birmingham), the Irish gentry—the backbone of the I.U.A.— forgot their duties to Ireland in their absorption in imperial and United Kingdom concerns.

When the I.U.A. did take up a stand on matters not directly related to the union, it did so in a most conservative way, as the unionist government of Lord Salisbury, 1895–1903, discovered to its embarrassment. For instance, when in 1898 the government democratised local government in Ireland, substituting elective county councils for the old grand juries, the I.U.A. attempted to limit the effects of the measure. In order to retain power in the hands of the landed gentry, a sub-committee set up by the I.U.A. recommended that four amendments should be aimed at: dual membership for electoral divisions (to allow for the election of former *ex-officio* grand jurors alongside the men normally elected to the boards of guardians); disability of illiterates to vote; substantial rating qualification; and maintenance of the right of traverse before a judge (an appeal against decisions by the county council). Such amendments, which would have destroyed the democratic purpose of the bill, were not accepted by the government. Since the government had a tendency to ignore Anglo-Irish views in other measures, it is not surprising that some southern unionists became extremely critical of the reformist policy, especially when the policy operated at a time of renewed land agitation aiming at the compulsory expropriation of landlords.

This dissatisfaction showed itself in the *Annual reports* of the I.U.A., and, more dramatically, in the general election of 1900. Horace Plunkett was the first vice-president of the newly established department of agriculture and technical instruction. He seemed to epitomise all that was misguided in government policy, because he had appointed as secretary to the department T. P. Gill, a nationalist, who though no longer active in politics had been associated with the 'plan of campaign'. Thus in the general election of 1900 a perfervid unionist, F. Elrington Ball, the historian and honorary secretary of the I.U.A., contested Plunkett's seat in Dublin Co. South. The unionist vote was split, the Guinness brothers, for instance, supporting opposing candidates; and the nationalist candidate slipped in. (In 1895 the voting had been: Plunkett 4,901; Haviland Burke (Parnellite) 2,962. In 1900 the voting was: J. J. Mooney (Nationalist) 3,410; Plunkett 2,906; Ball 1,539.)

This negative class attitude on the part of prominent unionists such as Ball perturbed the historian W. E. H. Lecky, who sat for Dublin University from 1896 to 1903. As well as losing southern unionists a valuable seat, this attitude threatened to lose them British sympathy. Yet it could also be said that the split in 1900 justified the limited plank adopted by the southern unionist association since its inception. There were many issues which concerned southern unionists, but they did not necessarily agree on how to solve them, and in any case they did not consider equitable solutions likely unless these issues were discussed within the framework of the act of union. The important thing was to maintain the union. It was this which justified the single, simple principle adopted by the I.L.P.U. and the I.U.A.

80 Extracts from the *Annual report* of the I.U.A. for 1899: **(a)** complaints about the nature of recent official appointments in Ireland; and **(b)** the leading article in the *Dublin Daily Express,* 31 May 1900, endorsing the I.U.A.'s complaints about the neglect of loyalists by Lord Salisbury's government (D 989A/7/2):

(a)

The Alliance have received numerous communications complaining of the manner in which the bestowal of office by the Government has been exercised in Ireland.

The writers say that these appointments almost invariably show the tendency of the Government to attend to the recommendations of the disloyal, rather than to the recommendations of those who made every exertion to support the Crown and Constitutional Government.

In no case has the policy of the administration been more strikingly exemplified than in the recent appointments to high official positions in the new Agricultural Department. Special attention is drawn to the appointment of Mr. T. P. Gill to the Secretaryship of the Agricultural Board. When the Bill was passing through the House of Commons Mr. Gerald Balfour distinctly stated that the officials of the new Department would be selected from those having special or expert knowledge of the subject of Agriculture, and that such knowledge would be considered as the principal, if not the sole recommendation to the post. Such a promise seemed almost superfluous.

The Alliance submits that the appointment of Mr. Gill was a direct contravention of these explicit pledges, Mr. Gill neither has, nor professed to have, nor can profess to have, a practical knowledge of the subject. His profession was that of a Journalist. He was a member of the Editorial staff of *United Ireland* when that Journal was edited by Mr. W. O'Brien during the stormy years of the early eighties. He took an active part, when an M.P., in the organisation of the "Plan of Campaign," in association with Messrs. Dillon and O'Brien, a conspiracy which the Judges of the Supreme Court of Ireland declared to be criminal, and which was stated by a Rescript of the Pope to be immoral. During Mr. A. J. Balfour's term of Chief Secretary in Ireland, it was found necessary to issue a warrant against him for participation in the Plan of Campaign. More recently he became chief of staff of the *Daily Express*, a paper hitherto known for its uncompromising support of the Constitutional party. While he was connected with that paper it quickly lost hold of the public. In a short time the Court took possession, and Mr. Gill's connection then ceased.

Other appointments calculated to please the disloyal might be quoted, the recipients of which have not shown any special technical knowledge or any extraordinary business capacity in the duties they were appointed to discharge.

In view of these facts, and others of a similar tendency, it is not surprising that loyalist sympathy is alienated throughout the country. Unionists (and even those of the highest experience and ability) find themselves systematically ignored under the present administration and almost every path of public usefulness closed to them.

The permitted revival of the old methods of local tyranny, the indifference of the administration to the wrongs suffered by law-abiding subjects of the Queen, the bestowal of office upon a person disqualified for trust by participation in a criminal conspiracy, have produced a feeling of indignation among Irish loyalists, the strength and volume of which the Alliance can testify to, and which, whether it be viewed as just or unjust, must be reckoned with as a force. The body of facts already stated, together with the action of the Government in other matters, such as that connected with the Dublin Boundaries Bill, Erasmus Smith Schools, &c., have resulted in such a want of confidence and a sense of alienation that if a General Election were now imminent it would be impossible for the Alliance to rally Unionists, as in 1895, to support the present administration. Nor in the event of the introduction of another Home Rule Bill could the Executive of the Alliance act on behalf of their convictions with an expectation of that full and energetic support which led to such important results on previous occasions.

(b)

The full report of the annual meeting of the Council of the Irish Unionist Alliance, which we publish this morning, will provide gloomy reading for the loyalists of Ireland, despite the fact that during the past year there has been little occasion or opportunity for active operations on the part of the Alliance. Yesterday's proceedings were an emphatic expression of the feelings of the Constitutional party in Ireland at the treatment which they have received at the hands of "the strongest Government of the century." In the year 1895, as Mr. James Wilson reminded the meeting, Lord Salisbury and the Duke of Devonshire publicly thanked the Alliance for its services in helping to return that Government to power. In the year 1900 the representative of the Queen in Ireland refuses to receive a deputation of the Alliance, which sought to lay before him, in the name of the Irish Unionists, certain instances of the Government's honesty and gratitude. Mr. Wilson could not understand the reasons of this startling change of front. The reasons, however, were made sufficiently plain at yesterday's meeting. One is that the Government conceives itself to have no further use for those Irish Unionists whose efforts turned the scale in its favour in 1895. Another reason is that, with an insight which does credit to its cunning but infinite discredit to its honour, the Government sacrifices the Irish loyalist on the altar of his own loyalty, and forbids him to resist injustice on the plea that resistance will endanger the Act of Parliament by which justice was promised to him. A third reason is that the Government finds it necessary to propitiate the party in Ireland which has no loyal scruples, and that the Irish Unionists form the readiest and cheapest sop to Cerberus. The statement which Lord Cadogan has refused to receive at the hands of the Alliance is a striking exposition of the rewards which await Irish loyalty under a Conservative Administration, and an astonishing proof of the extremes to which the Government will go in pursuit of its policy of killing Home Rule by kindness. We hope that the statement will be circulated broadcast among those English electors to whom the Government will presently point out that Ireland is "one of the most peaceful provinces in Her Majesty's Empire." The English electors ought to be told that the criminal negligence of the Government has encouraged the resuscitation of the Land League, that this old organisation under the new name which Mr. O'Brien has given to it dominates whole counties in the West and South of Ireland, and is daily extending the sphere of the old, but effective, methods of terrorism and boycotting. They ought to be told that the same Government has, at one blow, deprived the educated classes throughout Ireland of a share in the administration of their local affairs. It will, we hope, be made clear to them that, as Sir Thomas Butler said, "the name of a loyalist or of a Unionist is a bar to any office or preferment in this country." The Unionist Alliance, it is true, is not composed of office-seekers. Its members do not complain because they themselves have been deprived of office, but because office has been given to persons whose only qualification was rank disloyalty to the constitution which now turns to them the other cheek. The Alliance represents no special class, and no particular interest. It consists of Irish Unionists drawn together by the bond of their common devotion to a great cause. There was not a word of personal or class complaint in their statement to Lord Cadogan, and not a hint of selfish ambition. They object to the appointment of disloyalists to office, because that office is too often the mere reward of disloyalty, and not the recognition of any claim of service or fitness. The Alliance have referred at length to the "locus classicus" in this ignoble chapter of killing Home Rule by kindness—the appointment of Mr. T. P. Gill to the post of Secretary of the new Department. It is an instance, and only one of many instances, of the insult which is consistently offered to the intelligence and loyalty of Irish Unionists. Is it any wonder that this policy has "resulted in such a want of confidence and sense of alienation that, if a General Election were now imminent"—and it is now imminent—"it would be impossible for the Alliance to rally Unionists, as in 1895, to support the present Administration?" Under circumstances so eminently discouraging as these, it reflects the utmost credit on the Irish Unionist Alliance that it continues to carry on its work with unfaltering courage and conviction, and with the assurance that, the more formidable the enemy, the greater the need of active and fearless resistance. The Report, which we publish this morning, is an excellent record of unobtrusive work, and Irish unionists owe a deep debt of gratitude to Sir Thomas Butler, the Honorary Secretaries of the Alliance, Mr. W. Farquharson, and those other gentlemen who have done so much hard work in the Unionist cause. The retirement of Sir Thomas Butler from the position of Chairman is a distinct loss to the Alliance. We cannot do better than conclude with the warning words which the Alliance now addresses to the Unionists of Ireland:—"A time may soon arrive when the organisation that has borne so conspicuous a part in securing Unionist government may be required once more to fight a constitutional battle against the forces of disloyalty and disunion." When that time comes the Alliance will be ready to prove that it is no mere personal discontent or chagrin which inspires its hostility to the conduct of the present Government, but that a deep and steadfast loyalty to the great principle of the Union compels its resistance to a policy by which that principle is gradually but surely undermined.

81 Letter from W. E. H. Lecky at the Athenaeum, Pall Mall, London, to H. de F. Montgomery, 26 November 1900, deploring the attitude of officials of the I.U.A., such as F. E. Ball (T 1089/297):

Dear Mr Montgomery—I have been out of town w[hic]h must be my apology for not having before answered your interesting letter. I have certainly no wish to make a split in the Unionist party & am quite willing, as you suggest,—if others do not move in the matter to w[hic]h you refer—to do nothing at present. At the same time it appears to be obvious that as long as Mr Ball remains first honorary Sec. of the Alliance it will be inevitable that that body should be associated with the movement of w[hic]h he was the head & front—the avowed & conspicuous leader. I think that this shd be the case in the body w[hic]h ought to represent the whole force of Irish Unionism is deplorable & I think it still more deplorable that Irish landlordism shd (however unjustly) be identified with the spirit & policy which prevailed at the last election in Dublin. Irish landlordism has not too many friends (even on the Conservatist [*sic*] benches) in England & apart from the fact that the 2 most important Unionist seats out of Ulster have been lost, & that in the eyes of the ministers their obligations to the party have been cancelled & that we have no longer a right to approach them as their supporters, An amount of discredit has been thrown upon our party w[hic]h I think those Gentlemen in Dublin who are so satisfied with their recent achievements hardly realize. They are probably misled by the fact that there are 2 or 3 Irish sympathisers— only one I think of much importance—in the English press. It is a great good fortune that so many members of our party are in the Government & I hope their influence may be for good—but outside the Government it is totally evident that Ulster Unionism is the only form of Irish Unionism w[hic]h is likely for some time to come to count as a serious political force. It wd be difficult indeed to concieve [*sic*] a party more impotent that that w[hic]h is now represented by the majority of your Committee. However as I have said I have not the smallest wish to do any thing to aggravate the situation. The Compulsory Sale Movement must break down from the impossibility of getting parliament to advance the money & for my own part if I speak on the subject I mean to do so as little as possible from the point of view of class interest—as much as possible from the point of view of those who regard it as certain to drain Ireland of a vast portion of her wealth & to set up a state of things that wd be utterly ruinous to the poorer tenants. I am afraid the cry will injure the working of Voluntary sales & I shall be very glad if we can get the Government to do anything w[hic]h will in any degree accellerate [*sic*] them. Believe [me] dear Mr Montgomery Yours sincerely [?]

W E H Lecky

82 Letter from J. O. Hannay, The Rectory, Westport, Co. Mayo, to Montgomery, 29 May 1907, regretting that the Irish gentry have neglected their duties to Ireland through being 'dazzled' by the British and imperial connection (T 1089/324):

My dear Mr. Montgomery—I must thank you very much for your most interesting letter which I shall digest slowly as you advise, I am sure, with great benefit to myself.

I do not in the least mind confessing to you that I am not so hopeful about the Gaelic League as I was two years ago. I thought then that it was setting the people in this part of Ireland & other similar parts free from the twin tyrannies which are crushing our lives out—the tyranny of the preist [*sic*] & the tyranny of the political boss. I still believe that it has done this to some extent & is doing it by awakening the intellect of the people & setting them thinking. In my own personal experience I have come across so many instances of independent thought & courage created by the League's teaching that I shall always, I hope, remain a member of the League & support its work. But I find of late that some of the leaders of the movement are becoming cowardly & are truckling to priests & politicians. I therefore intend, though this is private as yet, to withdraw next August from my position as one of the executive committee.

I am not myself either worried or frightened by what is called sedition & disloyalty. I only recognise one loyalty as binding as a duty on me, loyalty to Ireland & to Edward VII as de facto & I believe de jure king of Ireland. I do not admit that I have any duty of loyalty to England or the empire. It is arguable that our connection with England & the very close union which exists between the two kingdoms is to our advantage & I am not at all sure that I would not have it continue for a time, at all counts [events?], on the supposition that it is to our advantage as things are at present in Ireland. But I cannot help recognising that the Union of 1800 has brought in its train a series of most intolerable evils for Ireland. The power of the Protestant gentry has been broken during the last hundred years & their leadership is almost entirely gone. I regard this as a misfortune for Ireland so great, that even an immense increase of material wealth, if such had come to us, would be no compensation. Our gentry are by far the best class in the country, the best class of men, I believe, in any country. But their eyes were dazzled with England's greatness & the prospect of imperial power. As a result of the union they have served England & the empire instead of serving Ireland—I speak of the class generally: There are of course shining exceptions —therefore they have lost their position in Ireland.—Instead of our gentry we now have as leaders priests & demagogues. I attribute the rise of these two classes directly to the union with England. It has of late years been the consistent & almost openly declared policy of English statesmen to govern Ireland along the lines of least resistance. They have so shaped their course as to throw the wealth & power of the country into the hands of papist ecclesiastics & their obedient servants the political charlatans. Nothing worse in the way of government is discoverable in the pages of history. The naked tyranny of a dictator or frank anarchy would in my opinion be preferable to the present system under which men's property is insecure, their characters degraded, their minds starved & their souls enslaved. And for this condition of our country the union with England & the spread of the imperial idea is directly responsible.

I hold that the people of Ireland are beginning to find this condition intolerable. There are signs on all sides of intellectual & moral awakening & several forces are at work promoting this awakening. The Gaelic League, in spite of the cowardice of its leaders, is one. The propaganda of the Sinn Fein

161

party is another. The literary, dramatic & artistic revival is a third, working indirectly but really. A fourth, perhaps the greatest of all, is Horace Plunkett's work. In a few years I hope that our people will be sufficiently educated & awake to make a dissolution of the present union with England safe & highly advantageous to us. If the knot is cut as I hope it will be cut decisively at one blow I feel absolutely certain that our gentry will regain their ancient position of rulers in Ireland. They are the best men in Ireland & it will not take them long to chase the priests & demagogues back into the holes from which they have emerged of late. Then we shall have an Ireland united, as I hope and believe, to England by the link of the crown & made genuinly [*sic*] friendly to England by community of national interests. At present, as it seems to me, the gentry & the best classes of people in Ireland can effect nothing because of their loyalty to England. They are in the ridiculous position of men trying to fight for their lives with one hand tied behind their backs. The English for whom they are sacrificing everything simply laugh at them & take every opportunity of betraying & insulting them. Why, under the circumstances they go on being loyal to England, I cannot understand. It isn't as if our gentry were cowards. They are not. It isn't as if they were fools. Many of them may be, but they have men of brains enough to lead them out of the slough.

Now I feel sure that you will disagree with three fourths of what I have written, but you wrote to me with such delightful frankness that I should be paying you a poor compliment by writing back in any other way. I may be all wrong. I have lived the best years of my life in a corner of Mayo. I've met few men, until the last couple of years, who thought about anything. I have had to work out my political ideas such as they are all by myself. I haven't anything to say for myself except that I have never consciously thought or spoken dishonestly. I feel pretty sure therefore that you won't be actually angry with my letter.

I had intended writing something about your pamphlets which I have read with great interest. But this letter is already a pamphlet in itself. I am very sincerely yours

James O. Hannay

P.S. I wish I could act on your more than kind suggestion & pay you a visit. But I cannot get away this Summer except for ten days & then I am going to my native Bushmills to pay a long promised visit to the MacNaghtens.

VIII

Notwithstanding the criticisms of their organisation and methods, the southern unionists had an impressive record of endeavour in Ireland. Apart from subsidising Ulster unionism, and apart from contesting a handful of seats in the south of Ireland, the energies of the I.U.A. were directed to holding excellently managed meetings, getting up manifestoes and petitions, and organising tours of Ireland for British electors.

The meetings were of two kinds. There were spectacular demonstrations held in Dublin to enable leading British unionists to meet Irish unionists. They were superbly stage-managed and the atmosphere both impressed and pleased politicians such as Austen Chamberlain, who in December 1906 had addressed the meeting described below. Chamberlain had not wanted to cross the Irish sea and was unhappy with his speech, but he was pleased that its 'reception was all that I could desire'. As he told his stepmother, 'as a unionist demonstration it was a great success. The Rotunda was crowded. So was the overflow, and many were turned away, unable to get admission to either. It has given the unionists over there the tonic they needed and I hear they are all very happy and pleased'. In addition to the Dublin demonstrations there were local, county meetings. In 1885 the I.L.P.U. had financed 48 election contests, but the number of contests rapidly declined so that by the early twentieth century contests involving unionists normally took place only in Dublin city and county. Unable to point to electoral returns to prove the existence of unionist sentiment in the south, southern unionists used their local, county meetings as proof of the existence of opposition to home rule in the south of Ireland. Such meetings were all the more necessary at the time of the third home rule bill (1912–14), when Ulster was in danger of overshadowing southern unionism: accordingly, after the introduction of the third home rule bill a series of county demonstrations was held in 1912, sometimes in the face of strong nationalist opposition, as at Limerick on 10 October.

Similar care was taken over the organisation of manifestoes and petitions, to make sure that they were adequately supported, as indicated above (74, 76). All such activity was designed to support the anti-home rule campaign in Britain so that the intensity of southern unionist activity depended on the state of home rule politics. Thus, for instance, by the time the third home rule bill was coming up for its third reading in the house of lords—in 1914, one or two deputations of between ten and fifteen electors were arriving from Britain weekly to inspect certain areas illustrating (alleged) nationalist incompetence and terrorism. After visiting the south, these visitors then travelled north where they were shown monuments to unionist energy and enterprise.

83 Part of a report in the *Dublin Daily Express,* 8 December 1906, describing the atmosphere prevailing at the meeting of Dublin unionists held in the Rotunda, Dublin, 7 December, and addressed by Austen Chamberlain (T 2759/4):

One has to go back a considerable time to recall a similar scene of earnestness and enthusiasm to that which was witnessed at the Rotunda last night, when the Unionists of Dublin assembled in their thousands to give unequivocal proof once again of their fealty to the Unionist cause and their unswerving resistance to Home Rule in any shape or form. In numbers and determination and in the spirit of vigorous unanimity which dominated the vast gathering of people the meeting far surpassed the most sanguine expectations of its organisers. The Round Room, it was known beforehand, could not possibly contain all who were anxious to take part in the proceedings, and arrangements were consequently made for an overflow meeting in the large Concert Room, so that the greatest possible number should have an opportunity of hearing the distinguished speakers of the evening. Even this proved entirely inadequate to meet the great rush for accommodation within the building, and admission had reluctantly to be refused to many hundreds for whom there was no room. Ticketholders began to assemble at the doors long before the time fixed for their opening, and fully an hour before the time appointed for the chair to be taken the Round Room was filled to its fullest capacity, and the public entrance doors had to be closed. The balcony was specially reserved for ladies, who equally with the sterner sex showed their anxiety to obtain places. An adequate staff of stewards superintended the seating arrangements, and the huge audience found their places with a minimum of crush and inconvenience. The historic chamber looked its brightest and best under a very elaborate and well-chosen scheme of decoration. The front of the balcony and the windows overlooking it were tastefully draped and festooned in red, white and blue. Across the platform ran a dainty border of flowering plants and exotics, while at the back was an elaborate and artistic arrangement of flags and banners, surmounted by the motto, "One United Empire," and at either side further devices, bearing the words "No Home Rule" and "No Devolution." A band, which was stationed in the balcony, discoursed a number of stirring patriotic airs while the audience waited, and as such patriotic airs as "Rule Britannia" and "Hearts of Oak" were played the enthusiasm rose by leaps and bounds. In the intervals between the instrumental selections this found additional expression vocally, when "The National Anthem," "Soldiers of Our Queen," and other airs which appealed to the general sentiment were sung by hundreds of voices. At frequent intervals also loud cheers were given to herald the arrival on the platform of well-known citizens or prominent local leaders in politics. In this way the period of waiting had no moments of dulness, and it was before an inspiriting audience such as this, whose feelings had been roused to the keenest pitch of expectation, that the Right Hon. Austen Chamberlain, M.P., Sir Edward Carson, K.C., M.P., Mr. Long, M.P., and the other distinguished speakers of the evening appeared, when they were conducted to their places on the platform by Professor Dowden, whose genial presence in the chair has always such an encouraging influence at the great mass meetings of Dublin Unionists held from time to time. Mr. Chamberlain, who was accompanied by Mrs. Chamberlain, was given a reception generous in its warmth and enthusiasm, and the ringing cheers in his honour, which were renewed again and again as the audience stood up in their places, must have shown him how gratefully his presence on such an important occasion was regarded. . . .

84 Official programme for a demonstration of southern unionists, organised by the I.U.A. in the Rotunda rink, Dublin, 10 October 1911, at 7.30 p.m., including **(b)** a song entitled 'For union and for king' (D 989C/4/1):

DEMONSTRATION OF UNIONISTS

Representative of the Provinces of

LEINSTER, MUNSTER, CONNAUGHT,

WILL BE HELD IN

THE ROTUNDA RINK,

RUTLAND SQUARE, DUBLIN,

TUESDAY, 10th OCTOBER, 1911.

At 7.30 p.m.

THE RIGHT HONOURABLE LORD ARDILAUN IN THE CHAIR.

---

1. Proposed by Sir William Goff, Bart.;
   Seconded by Mr. Marcus Goodbody.
   "That The Right Hon. Lord Ardilaun do take the Chair.
2. Letters of Apology.   To be read.
3. Chairman's Address.
4. Mr. G. F. Stewart, D.L., will read the Protest and Declaration to be adopted by the Meeting.

PROTEST AND DECLARATION.

We, Irishmen, belonging to the three Southern Provinces, being of all creeds and classes, representing many separate interests, and sharing a common desire for the honour and welfare of our country, hereby declare our unalterable determination to uphold the Legislative Union between Great Britain and Ireland.

We protest against the creation of a separate Parliament for Ireland, whether independent or subordinate.

We protest against the creation of an Executive, dependent for its existence upon the pleasure of such a Parliament.

We do so upon the following grounds:—

Because any measure for the creation of a separate Irish Parliament, and a separate Irish Executive, would produce most dangerous social confusion, involving a disastrous conflict of interests and classes, and a serious risk of civil war.

Because such a measure would endanger the commercial relations between Ireland and Great Britain, and would cause in Ireland widespread financial distrust, followed by a complete paralysis of enterprise.

Because such a measure would imperil personal liberty, freedom of opinion, and the spirit of tolerance in Ireland.

Because such a measure, instead of effecting a settlement, would inevitably pave the way for further efforts towards the complete separation of Ireland from Great Britain.

Because no statutory limitations restricting the authority of an Irish Legislative Assembly, or the power of an Irish Executive, could protect the freedom and the rights of minorities in this country.

Because such a measure would hand over Ireland to the Government of a party which, notwithstanding professions, the political purpose of which is obvious, has proved itself during its long course of action unworthy of the exercise of power by its repeated defiance of the law, and disregard of the elementary principles of honesty, liberty and justice.

Because the great measures enacted in recent years by the Imperial Parliament have resulted in such industrial, agricultural, social and educational progress that our country has been steadily advancing in prosperity, and we view with the gravest alarm an experiment which must in large measure destroy the good work already done, and hinder the progress now in operation.

Finally, regarding the question from a wider point of view than that which concerns alone the internal government of Ireland, highly prizing as we do the advantages we derive from our present Imperial position, and being justly proud of the place which Irishmen have long held amongst those to whom the Empire owes its prosperity and fame, having been always faithful in our allegiance to our Sovereigns, and upholders of the Constitution, we protest against any change that will deprive us of our birthright, by which we stand on equal ground with our fellow-countrymen of Great Britain, as subjects of our King and as citizens of the British Empire.

5. Proposed by SIR HENRY BLAKE, G.C.M.G.;
    Seconded by MR. GERALD GUINNESS, D.L.
    "That this Convention hereby adopts the Declaration now read, and

earnestly appeals to the Electors of the United Kingdom to give effect to its objects and policy by supporting the maintenance of the Legislative Union in its integrity, and the preservation to the people of Ireland of equality of rights and privileges with the people of Great Britain as fellow-citizens of the United Kingdom."

6. SONG—"For Union and for King."

7. Proposed by SIR MAURICE DOCKRELL;
   Seconded by MR. J. B. POWELL, K.C.

"That the Unionists of the three Southern Provinces, represented in this meeting, heartily join with their Ulster brethren in acclaiming Sir Edward Carson as leader of the Irish Unionist Party, and desire to give expression to their stern and unalterable determination to stand by him to the uttermost in resisting the disruption of the Legislative Union, and the menace to civil and religious liberty in Ireland involved in the establishment of a separate Parliament in Dublin."

8. Reply by THE RIGHT HONOURABLE SIR EDWARD CARSON, K.C., M.P.

9. Proposed by MAJOR O'CONNOR;
   Seconded by CAPTAIN BRYAN COOPER.

"That the best thanks of the meeting be tendered to Lord Ardilaun for his kindness in presiding."

GOD SAVE THE KING.

84(b)

For Union and for King.

Words by LIEUT.-COLONEL DUDLEY SAMPSON.

Music by LADY ARTHUR HILL.

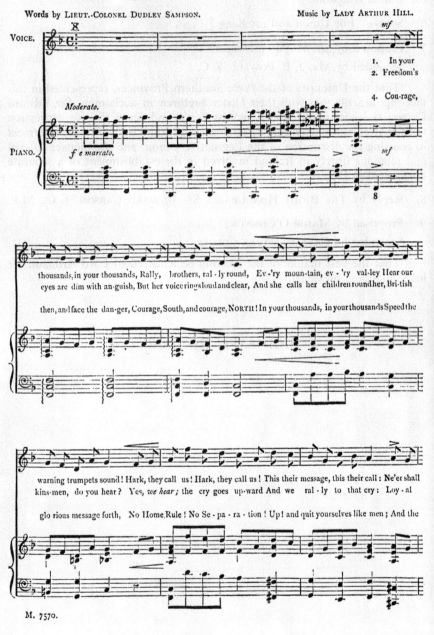

M. 7570.

85 Extracts from *Notes from Ireland,* November 1912: **(a)** reporting the last in a series of county meetings of southern unionists protesting against the third home rule bill; and **(b)** reprinting a letter from Lord Midleton to *The Times* (21 October 1912) which adduced such meetings as evidence of the existence of a widespread unionist opinion in the south as well as in the north of Ireland (D 989C/3/44A):

(a)

The series of County Meetings in the Provinces south of Ulster, organised by the Irish Unionist Alliance, which have been held during the summer and autumn of 1912 for the purpose of protesting against Home Rule, were concluded in the Town Hall, Carlow (for the County of Carlow), on the 16th October, 1912.

The following are brief summaries of the County Meetings held during the month of October, which have been fully reported in the daily Press:—

COUNTY OF LIMERICK.—On the afternoon of 10th October the Right Hon. George Wyndham, M.P., was the principal speaker at a crowded meeting of Unionists, held in the Theatre Royal, Limerick. The meeting was organised by the Limerick Branch of the Irish Unionist Alliance, and was representative of the Unionists of the county. A hostile crowd of Nationalists assembled in the street opposite the entrance to the theatre, and jeered at the ticket-holders as they entered the building. The presence of a force of police had a restraining influence on the crowd, who offered no violence towards those who differed from them in their political opinions. During the progress of the meeting the cheers of the Nationalist crowd outside could be heard. Some ill-advised Nationalists obtained admission to the theatre, and attempted to interrupt the speakers, but they were assisted out of the building by the stewards. The organised ruffianism that occurred after the meeting, and on succeeding nights in the streets of Limerick, is dealt with in another place, and in the leaflet that is enclosed with the present number of NOTES FROM IRELAND.

On the motion of Mr. J. Ellis Goodbody, seconded by Mr. William Waller, D.L., the chair was taken by Lord Massy.

Letters of apology were read from Lord Monteagle, Lord Barrymore, Mr. J. Greene Barry, D.L.; Major-General Lloyd, Lord Inchiquin, Mr. T. J. Franks, D.L.; Lord Clarina, Lord Muskerry, etc., etc.

Speeches were delivered by Lord Massy, Mr. Wyndham, Sir Charles Barrington, D.L.; Mr. F. E. Kearney, LL.D., and others. The meeting concluded with the singing of the National Anthem.

COUNTY OF KILKENNY.—One of the largest meetings of the anti-Home Rule series in the South and West was held in the historic home of the Butlers, Kilkenny Castle. The gathering was not confined to residents of the county, as many Unionists came from neighbouring counties, anxious to prove their devotion to the cause of the Union. The meeting was held in the famous Picture Gallery. A platform draped with Union Jacks was erected at the end of the Gallery, and seating accommodation was provided for over a thousand persons. There was hardly a vacant chair. The speeches were followed with keen attention, and the proceedings throughout were marked by enthusiasm. The Marquis of Ormonde presided, and other speakers included Mr. T. Ponsonby, Mr. H. C. Gregory, Lord Midleton, Mr. R. Bagwell, Lord Annaly, Lord Kenmare, and Lord Desart.

The Marquis of Ormonde in his opening remarks said that the meeting was called together to protest against the measure at present before Parliament, because if it became law they believed it would be detrimental to the people of Ireland from a material point of view. He thought that they all knew that neither he nor those beside him on the platform would be there if that meeting were in the slightest degree of a sectarian character. (Hear, hear.) The best relations always existed between people of every creed and class in Kilkenny, and he trusted that those relations would ever continue. (Hear, hear.) He did not think that those who differed from them now would desire to restrain their freedom or to prevent them from voicing their opinions, or to allow their present differences to interfere with their good relations. (Applause.)

Mr. E. K. B. Tighe read letters of apology from Lord Bessborough, Lord Duncannon, Colonel Villiers Stuart, Mr. Bruen, and others, expressing cordial sympathy with the objects of the meeting.

Colonel Wyndham Quin read the terms of the resolution that has been adopted at all similar meetings in the South and West.

The proceedings concluded with the singing of the National Anthem.

The *Freeman's Journal* (14th October), in a depreciatory report of the meeting, has the following paragraph:—

"In connection with the arrangements for the meeting an interesting incident occurred. A local firm had lent some barrels for the construction of the platform, but when the matter came officially before the directors of the firm they at once issued an order requiring the barrels to be returned, with the result that the platform had to be dismantled, and erected on another foundation."

COUNTY OF CARLOW.—On the 16th October, 1912, under the auspices of the Carlow Branch of the Irish Unionist Alliance a meeting of the Unionists of Co. Carlow was held in the Town Hall, Carlow, to protest against Home Rule for Ireland. Unionists assembled in large numbers to take part in the proceedings, which were most enthusiastic throughout. Amongst the audience were a number of farmers, who, recognising the seriousness of the present situation, were determined to contribute their quota to any movement for the defeat of the Home Rule Bill. The spacious hall was severely taxed to find accommodation for those desiring to be present. Many had to be satisfied with standing room. Lord Rathdonnell presided.

Letters were received from the leaders of the Unionists in both Houses of Parliament.

Lord Lansdowne wrote:—

I am glad to hear that you are to have a Unionist meeting at Carlow, and I hope it will be well attended and enthusiastic. It is important to bring home to the minds of the people here that it is not in Ulster only that Home Rule is regarded with abhorrence and apprehension. Throughout the other provinces there are scattered thousands of loyal subjects who are not less opposed to the breaking up of the Union, and not less convinced that the paper safeguards embodied in the Government Bill are no more value than the profuse assurances of the Nationalist leaders. The resolute attitude of Ulster has produced a remarkable effect upon the public opinion in this country, and no effort should be spared to prove that all Irish Unionists are one in regard to this vital issue.

Mr. Bonar Law wrote:—

I am very pleased to hear of the meeting which is to be held at Carlow on the 16th inst. to protest against Home Rule. I believe that under the present circumstances it is simply impossible that this Bill can ever be carried into law; but nothing can be more important than to show how strong is the opposition to it in all parts of Ireland.

The speakers included the Chairman, Mr. Henry Bruen, D.L.; Mr. A. W. Samuels, K.C.; Sir Richard Butler, Bart.; Mr. Edward Wilson, J.P.; Sir Henry Blake, G.C.M.G.; Mr. R. D. Pack Beresford, D.L., and Mr. B. F. Bagenal, D.L. A hearty vote of thanks was passed to the speakers.

The Co. Carlow meeting brought to a successful close this year's series of County Meetings of Unionists in the provinces of Leinster, Munster, and Connaught.

(b)

Sir—In more than one speech since the introduction of the Home Rule Bill the Prime Minister, admitting the animus against the Bill in Ulster, has assumed that the Unionist population in the other three provinces views the Bill with composure. The author of "Obiter Dicta" made an effective comment on this belief when he blurted out his epigram that "land purchase was more important than Home Rule." Mr. Birrell, without any undue strain on himself of residence in Ireland, has realised the most striking factor at this moment of tension in that so-called Home Rulers care more about the advantages they can obtain from the British connection than about obsolete political grievances.

This is not a stirring look-out for the Liberal Party. To pass a first-class measure through Parliament requires the driving-power of enthusiasm: the evidence of this in Ireland is all on the other side. Ulster holds the field, but Unionists outside Ulster have rallied as they have never done before, and at all their meetings Catholics of substance and repute have risked obloquy and ignored threats to show their alarm at the prospect of being governed by Nationalists, even though they be co-religionists.

In the last six months large meetings have taken place in such centres as Cork, Waterford, Tralee, Sligo, Limerick, Kilkenny, etc., and resolutions of vehement protest have been adopted against the Bill. One notable effect has been produced by these meetings. Originally ignored by the local Leaguers as of little account, the breach developed by them in the Nationalist ranks caused the speakers to be mobbed at Limerick a fortnight ago, while the Catholics who intended to speak at Kilkenny were marked down and threatened.

These facts should be made known to British electors, some of whom realise that Irishmen who have bought their land through British credit and wish to enjoy it, or who have profited by the gain of £27,000,000 in trade since 1904 under British laws, are not eager to cheer "last link" speeches.

But most Liberal politicians would be staggered if they knew how many of Mr. Redmond's reputed sympathizers in the South and West of Ireland are supporting by letter the Unionist meetings which they dare not openly attend.

I trust Mr. Birrell will continue to enlighten Mr. Asquith on this matter. Yours, etc.,

MIDLETON

86 *Letter from R. J. Shaw, the secretary of the I.U.A., to P. Wicks, Sir Edward Carson's secretary, 15 June 1914, drawing attention to the role of local unionists in the tours of Ireland organised jointly by the I.U.A. and U.U.C. for British electors (D 989A/8/4):

Dear Wicks—I do not see any reason why Sir Edward should do anything for Mr. Campbell, whose letters I now return to you. Some little time ago I made a reduction in the canvassing staff of the Group in which he was employed, and asked our agent to choose out the two least satisfactory canvassers and dismiss them. Campbell was one of them, and at the time of his dismissal he stated that he was perfectly satisfied with the treatment he had received from us.

I wonder whether the following matter would be a nuisance to Sir Edward, if not, would you ask him about it: As you know, we have had a very large number of tours, consisting largely of Radicals from a great many different constituencies both in England and Scotland who have been going round Ireland and studying Irish conditions. The results have been extremely good.

The success of these tours is very largely due to the enthusiasm and self-sacrifice of local Unionists in small towns in Ireland, who have given a great deal of time and trouble to them, and who have both themselves interviewed the visitors, and got other Unionists to do so. I need hardly say that this action of [sic] their part does not make their lives any the easier. I think that if Sir Edward would write a letter of appreciation to the following people whose names I give you it would be an enormous gratification and encouragement to them.

The first person I suggest is Mr. Michael McCann, Lismoy House, Newtown Forbes, Co. Longford. He is a Roman Catholic, and a big farmer, and as I daresay you know has been severely boycotted. He has entertained a very great number of these tourists at his house, frequently feeding them, and he and his wife have done as much as anybody in Ireland to convert the Radical visitors.

The second person who might be written to is H. V. Macnamara, Esq., D.L., Ennistymon House, Co. Clare, who has made admirable arrangements for the reception of tours in Ennis, and who has done splendid work in Co. Clare during the last year. He lives in one of the worst districts in Ireland, and has shown the very greatest pluck.

I have no doubt that both these men will go on working for the tours as long as they are asked to do so, but they have earned so well of the Unionist party, and have put up such a tough fight, that I feel that they would enormously appreciate a letter from Sir Edward. Yours sincerely,

[*unsigned*]

87 Report by a deputation of workingmen from the Loughborough division of Leicestershire following their visit to Ireland organised by the Unionist Associations of Ireland, June 1914 (D 989C/1/20):

The **UNANIMOUS REPORT** of a Deputation comprising **EIGHT LIBERAL and SIX UNIONIST WORKING MEN,** from the Mid or Loughborough Division of Leicestershire, appointed to investigate the Irish question on the spot, **and from a strictly non-political point of view,** from Monday, June the 1st to Saturday, June 6th inclusive returning to Leicester at mid-day on Sunday, June the 7th, 1914.

The tour included visits to Dublin, Sligo, Enniskillen and Belfast, and, throughout, every facility was afforded the members of the Deputation to interview all classes, and to obtain every information on the principal points at issue.

1. The condition of the Rates in the South and West of Ireland, particularly in Dublin and Sligo, and of Local Government generally, was in a very *un*satisfactory condition, and compared most unfavourably with the state of things in Belfast and Enniskillen. The Municipal administration in the Nationalist districts visited by the deputation being very loose, whereas the management of the local affairs in Ulster was in much better state of efficiency with a much lower rate.

2. From personal observation, from the inspection of various works, and from the information obtained, the deputation found it impossible to compare the state of Ulster with other parts of Ireland regarding industry, cleanliness and prosperity.

3. In the City of Belfast great prosperity and commercial enterprise were found, whereas in Dublin the slums were simply appalling some of the worst houses belonging to members of the Dublin Corporation. The Rates of the latter City were 11s. 5½d. in the £, in Belfast 7s. 5d. The Municipal Buildings and Technical Institute were the finest we have seen.

4. The deputation are convinced that this plan of sending deputations of working men to Ireland, comprising all shades of political opinion, is a thoroughly sound one, and calculated to remove many erroneous impressions with regard to the Irish question. The fullest investigation is invited, and every member of the deputation is at liberty to pursue his enquiries in whatever direction he thinks fit.

5. The Deputation have been much impressed by the evident sincerity and earnestness of the people of Ulster, and their determination to resist the domination of an Irish Parliament; and they are of opinion that the subject of Home Rule is of great national importance, and if enforced in its present form would be a grave injustice to Ulster.

Signed:—

GEORGE CARRINGTON (*Hathern*).

A. CAURAH (*Thringstone*).

WM. DAWS (48, *Wharncliffe Road, Loughborough*).

AMOS DEXTER, JUN. (*Shepshed*).

HARRY GARDNER (*Groby*).

ALLEN GRAIN, SEN. (*Shepshed*).

D. S. HACK (*Quorn*).

JOHN HANDFORD (*Mountsorrel*).

D. HARRISON (*Ratby*).

JOHN KIRCHIN, JUN. (*Mountsorrel*).

F. S. MELLERS (*Loughborough*).

WM. NEWTON (*Shaw Lane*).

GEORGE WHITE (*Quorn*).

THOS. WOOD (65, *Morley Street, Loughborough*).

Chapter VI

Ulster unionist organisation 1886-1911

Although by 1886 a recognisable unionist movement had emerged in Ulster, it was in its early years a mere shadow of the monolithic organisation usually associated with Ulster unionism. Unlike unionism in the south, Ulster unionism was a potential mass movement, based on the large protestant population of that province; but it, too, had problems to overcome in order to make possible effective resistance to the demand for home rule.

First, there was the difficulty of providing an organisational framework in which otherwise diverse elements could cooperate to maintain the union. Differences in outlook, between orangemen and others, had still to be overcome; and the land question long remained to weaken unionist organisation, central and local. Secondly, there was the problem of directing and sustaining unionist energies in a useful defence of the union. There was always the problem of the depth of sectarian feeling; there was the danger that such feelings would erupt at critical moments into riots and violence on a larger scale than, say, that of the 'Tempo affair'. Lastly, there was the problem of convincing the British electorate and parliament of the unwisdom of trying to foist home rule upon Ulster.

The object of this and the following chapter is to show how documents in the N.I.P.R.O. can be used to study some of the problems facing Ulster unionism after 1886 and the way in which they were solved; particularly at the time of the third home rule bill, 1912-14, when Ulster unionist organisation achieved its peak of efficiency.

II

Slowly, in the late 1880s and in the 1890s, unionist energies became more united and organised. On the one hand, in face of the home rule issue some differences of opinion were overcome, as former liberals, like H. de F. Montgomery, concealed their distaste for orangeism. In 1893, Montgomery allowed the local orangemen, deprived of an excursion to Derry, to celebrate the Twelfth of July in a field opposite Blessingbourne House, and even agreed to address the assembly. On the other hand, local loyalist registration societies tried to mobilise unionist forces in their constituencies, with the encouragement of the I.L.P.U. and the Irish registration department of the (British) Unionist Joint Committee and its leading organiser, John Boraston. The North Fermanagh Loyalist Registration Association, for instance, actively supervised the electoral register in that constituency, sometimes regardless of cost. In the court of the revising barrister the association's agents challenged the right of nationalists to be on the register, and resisted attempts by nationalists to strike off unionist voters.

The work of the North Fermanagh association can be seen in the number of barristers' briefs relating to appeals against decisions made by the revising barrister. These briefs contain a statement (including the objection raised to a voter and the reasons for the judgement) of the case drawn up by the revising barrister for the decision of the court of appeal; and they also contain the comments of the local unionist solicitor, who in the 1890s was Charles F. Falls of Dublin and Enniskillen, secretary of the association. Of the briefs given below, the first relates to an appeal by a unionist voter, John Brown, against the revising barrister's decision to strike him off the register. Since Brown's father had died without leaving a will, it was argued that he shared the tenancy of his late father's farm with his mother, and was thus not qualified to vote. The second brief relates to an optimistic appeal against the dismissal of an objection to a nationalist voter, Patrick Morris, who had not, it was alleged, completed the residential period necessary to qualify for the vote.

88 Letter from J. W. Ellison-Macartney, Clogher Park, Clogher, Co. Tyrone, M.P. for Co. Tyrone and a leading orangeman, to H. de F. Montgomery, 15 June 1893, thanking him for offering to lend a field for a Twelfth of July demonstration (D 627/428/216):

My dear Montgomery—Thanks many for yours of Monday relative to the 12th July meeting. We could not have anything better than the field facing Blessingbourne House and I am sure that the Lodges will appreciate your kindness in letting us have the use of it for that occasion. Your suggestion about asking the Red House people to supply temperance refreshments is an excellent one & I shall interview them on Friday next on the subject —So far as the Orangemen of the District are concerned I shall do all in my power to prevent any abuse of your permission taking place—But there are dealers in lemonade & soda water etc who will expect permission from you to enter the grounds & dispose of their wares. They are I believe, denizens of Fivemiletown Yours very truly

J. W. Ellison Macartney

89 Letter from Ellison-Macartney to Montgomery, 11 July 1893, enclosing a copy of the resolutions to be moved at the next day's orange demonstration (D 627/428/217):

Dear Montgomery—I enclose resolutions the first to be moved and seconded by Orangemen

The second also but spoken to by Non Orangemen

The third D[itt]o.—I leave it to you to choose whether you will speak to the 2d. or 3d—I believe the entrance to the field is nearly opposite to the Roman Catholic Chapel? At all events there will be a flag or something, to mark the entrance—

We from this end will alight at Ballyvadden [Ballyvaddan] & march through Fivemiletown & march back from the Fair Green to the field. I hope we shall be favoured by dry weather & every effort will be made to maintain sobriety—

The bulk of our members will return by the 3.39 train from Fivemiletown.

Yours very truly

J W Ellison Macartney

Resolution 1. We the Orangemen of the L[oyal] O[range] District of Fivemiletown in the Co of Tyrone assembled to celebrate the 203 anniversary of the memorable Victory gained at the Boyne by King William the third of glorious memory hereby declare our stedfast [*sic*] adherence to the principles of civil & religious liberty thereby established in these realms, and our firm determination to lay down our lives in their defence rather than allow them to be wrested from us.

Resolution 2. In common with our loyalist fellow subjects in England & Scotland as well as in Ireland we deprecate the insidious & profligate & unpatriotic attempt now being made by a self seeking & reckless old politician abetted by a motley and heterogeneous rabble of professional agitators to smuggle through the House of Commons, with[out] the necessary full debate of its provisions a measure calculated to uproot the Constitution under which we live and to imperil our lives, our liberties & our worldly substance.

Resolution 3 Lastly we would record our undying allegiance to the Gracious Monarch who has so long and so wisely wielded the sceptre over the Mighty Empire of which Ireland forms an integral part, our ardent attachment to the Constitution of the United Kingdom, and our fixed resolve never to submit to laws enacted by an Irish Parliament of which the members would be the nominees & puppets of the Roman Priesthood—

90 Letter from J. Boraston of the Unionist Joint Committee, writing from the Imperial Hotel, Belfast, to Montgomery, 12 May 1889, thanking him for his assistance in contacting local unionist officials and registration societies (D 627/428/101):

My dear Montgomery—I can hardly thank you enough for the immense help you have given me. Owing to that I have broken the back of the work in 5 constituencies in less than half the time I expected to have to devote to them.

After we parted on Friday I saw Irvine. Lord Arthur Hills letter produced an excellent effect on him & he at once made me free of his books and records. I believe he has done good work in one way. The register had been reduced from 7065 in /87 to 5942 now, & if this is not explainable by a reduction in population, which Irvine denies, it goes some way to support his contention that the hostile majority has been reduced on paper to 382. Financially however things are in a mess. Irvine claims to be £395. 16. 4 out of pocket (exclusive of fees) He professes not to care very much about this, but there is a worse feature in the non payment of witnesses. He tells me that there is great dissatisfaction so much indeed that he dare not call his Committees together unless something is done to wipe off the witnesses claims. The situation is aggravated by the Treasurer having in some cases paid part of the witnesses in a polling district by which the unpaid ones are naturally annoyed, feeling a sense of injustice in addition to the money loss. It would take (so he says) £80 to £100 to clear off these liabilities if this were found he could then run the coming revision.

I write in confidence he complains of his Treasurer "Jack Porter" Says he wont close his a/cs & that he cant get information from him. It is clear that I must see Porter. Irvine says a popular Treasr. Montgomery of Fivemiletown for choice, would be the making of his Assn. What do you say to that?

Of course I shall go to Enniskillen again & Irvine offers to get a few of his people together to meet me.

Omagh—Thompson is in town & I was unable to see any of the men whose names you gave me, owing to the funeral of a Mrs Thacke [?]. I however interviewed N Carson & C. J. Barr of the "Constitution" James Elliott JP (L[iberal] U[nionist]) Jas Kirkpatrick JP (LU) James Bell & Robert Bell (LUs) & Charles Mullin (Con) Solr. to the N Tyrone Assn. an active politician in Mid [-Tyrone]. Mullin has agreed to get me a meeting at some later day.

Obtained inspection of all books &c for East [Tyrone] at Dungannon

Wish you a pleasant visit to town & with many thanks Believe me Yours v truly

    John Boraston

91 Extracts from a brief relating to the appeal by J. Brown, a unionist voter, against a decision at the 1893 North Fermanagh revision to strike him off the electoral register: **(a)** the decision of the revising barrister, 26 December 1893, against which Brown appealed—the underlinings were made by Brown's solicitor, C. F. Falls; and **(b)** notes on the case by Falls for use in the appeal (D 1390/26/5/1):

(a)

At a Court held at Enniskillen, on the 26th of September, 1893, for the Revision of the Lists of Parliamentary Voters for the Polling District of Enniskillen, in the Division of North Fermanagh,

The name of JOHN BROWN appeared at No. 126 on the Register of Voters as the Rated Occupier of a farm situate at Whitehill, in the said Polling District, and he was objected to on the grounds that he did not occupy same as sole tenant or owner thereof.

The following are the material facts which have been established by the evidence:—

ROBERT BROWN, the father of the Voter, was the prior owner and tenant of the house and farm, which constitute the qualifying premises. Prior to his death, which occurred in December, 1881, he had served a notice upon his landlord to have a fair rent fixed. He died intestate, leaving his widow and the Voter, his son, his only next-of-kin him surviving, and in occupation of the qualifying premises On the 9th of August 1882, the Voter, with, as he stated, the consent of his mother, settled *the fair rent case with* the landlord, and the Voter and landlord thereupon entered into and signed an agreement under the Land Act, 1881, fixing the fair rent. In this agreement the Voter was treated as the tenant of the farm, and he has since been tenant to the landlord, and has paid all rent and obtained receipts therefor in his own name, with as the Voter stated, the knowledge and consent of his mother. It was not proved that the Voter's mother had gone to the landlord at the time of the Voter's making the agreement with him, or of the putting his name in the rent receipts, or that her alleged consent to these transactions had been communicated to the landlord. The mother lives and has all along lived on the farm, helping to work it, and is maintained by the produce of the farm, and in no respect was there any change in her position in the household, or in her mode of support from the time when her husband was living. The Voter's mother was not produced before me, nor any evidence given on behalf of the Voter to show that the Voter's mother had released or surrendered her rights under her husband's intestacy, while on the other hand no evidence was produced on behalf of the Objector to show that the Voter's mother made any claim upon the farm beyond the evidence hereinbefore detailed, and the nature of it.

Under the above circumstances I came to the conclusion in fact that the Voter's mother had never relinquished or released in any way her claim upon the qualifying premises, or consented that the Voter should hold the tenancy discharged from her claim, but that there was in fact throughout a joint beneficial occupation of the qualifying premises by the Voter and his mother, and I, therefore, struck out the Voter's name. If I was wrong in so doing his name should be re-instated on the Register.

Dated 26th day of September, 1893.

MILES KEHOE,

Assistant Revising Barrister for the North
Fermanagh Division of the County of Fermanagh.

(b)

The following are the reported cases

1st. Carruther's Case. Fowler v Hanrahan No 28 of 1888 page 10 Lawson 1888–89 which is precisely on all fours with this one. see the dictum of Morris CJ.

2" Kirkpatrick v Murphy. page 13 Lawson's 1890–91 is in our favour

The authority upon which the Revising Barrister ruled against us was 3rd. Simpson v Hanrahan Page 8. Lawson 1892–93, which appears to be a case in point

In the present case however no opportunity was given to the voter, who has been registered for the last 9 years, to produce his mother, as he was peremptorily ruled off on the very last day of the Revision Sessions. If he had got an opportunity of producing his mother she would have shown that a settlement was arrived at between her and the voter as regards the distribution of the assets of deceased, and that the mother accepted a sum of money (which was in fact bequeathed to her by her husband's unproved will) which was paid to her by the voter and is at present in her own possession lodged in Bank

This is a dreadfully hard case and if we do not succeed on the appeal we are bound to lose a large number of votes next year

Of course, the success of this case involves the over ruling of Simpson's case, but in this one the voter was on the Register for years, Whereas in Simpson's he was only claiming to get on for the first time

92 Extracts from a brief relating to the appeal by J. H. Charlton on behalf of the North Fermanagh Loyalist Registration Association against a decision at the 1894 North Fermanagh revision to dismiss an objection lodged against Patrick Morris, a nationalist voter: **(a)** the statement drawn up by the revising barrister—the underlining was made by the unionist solicitor; and **(b)** the unionist solicitor's marginal comment on the underlined passage (D 1390/26/5/1):

(a)

At an Adjourned Court held by me at Irvinestown, in the County of Fermanagh, on Thursday, the 11th day of October, 1894, for the Revision of the Lists of Parliamentary Voters for the Polling District of Irvinestown, in the North Fermanagh Division of the County of Fermanagh,

The name of Patrick Morris appeared at No. 36 on the Clerk of the Union's Supplemental List of Inhabitant Occupiers (No. 12) as the Inhabitant Occupier of a house at Forthill, and he was objected to on the grounds that he had not inhabited said house during the whole of the qualifying period.

The right of the said Patrick Morris to be registered was admitted by the Objector save for the following question of law:—

The said Patrick Morris was, during the qualifying period, arrested by the police on a criminal charge, and on the day of his arrest was brought before a magistrate who remanded him, upon warrant, to gaol for a week without bail. During this week Morris was confined in Sligo Gaol, and on its expiration he was brought up at Petty Sessions, and the charge having been investigated, informations were taken, and he was returned for trial at the Quarter Sessions and allowed out on bail pending trial which has not yet taken place.

Under these circumstances it was contended on behalf of the Objector that the said Patrick Morris was disqualified by reason of his having been compulsorily absent from his said house during the week above-mentioned.

On behalf of the said Patrick Morris it was contended that as his trial had not yet taken place, I was bound to assume him innocent of the charge, and that, therefore, his confinement in gaol was his misfortune, not his fault.

I yielded to this latter contention, and following, as I thought, the case of Connolly v. Riddall, placed Morris' name upon the Register. If I was wrong in so doing his name should be expunged.

Notice of appeal having been given from this decision, I nominate the Objector, James H. Charlton, of Enniskillen, in the County of Fermanagh, to be the Appellant, and the said Patrick Morris, of Forthill, and James W. Hanrahan, of Enniskillen, Clerk of the Crown and Peace for the County of Fermanagh, both in the County of Fermanagh, to be the Respondents in this appeal.

Dated 11th day of October, 1894.

DENIS B. SULLIVAN,
Assistant Revising Barrister for the County
of Fermanagh.

(b)

He will be tried before this appeal is heard, and is sure to be convicted. Will send Certificate. Query can the Court look at it?

III

Unionism in Ulster received a fillip from the democratisation of local government, on English lines, in 1898. The county council and urban elections became a battle ground for party politics. The N.I.P.R.O. has a variety of material illustrating the party spirit operating in local politics, for example the papers of Colonel R. H. Wallace, a unionist and protestant candidate, who was defeated by jubilant and abusive nationalists in the county council elections for Down in 1899.

As interesting as personal correspondence are legal papers, such as those relating to the disputed elections to the Fermanagh county council in the period 1899–1902. These legal papers contain a variety of material including copies of the minutes of some of the annual meetings of the council. It is an interesting council, divided almost equally between nationalists and unionists in respect of elected members. After the first elections, in 1899, the unionists had increased a small, and disputed, majority by coopting additional members; but in 1902 the position was reversed. The return, in dubious circumstances, of one Thomas Gavin for the Lisnaskea electoral division gave nationalists a majority of the elected members on the county council. Despite the protests of, among others, the defeated unionist candidate for Lisnaskea, George Arnold, the nationalists promptly enlarged this majority by coopting two nationalists as additional members; and then replaced the previous (unionist) chairman, Lord Erne, with the nationalist Jeremiah Jordan. Meantime, in an effort to restore the unionist position and prestige, Arnold petitioned against Gavin's return. On the one hand, he argued that Gavin had not obtained a legal majority, because some of his supporters had already voted in another electoral division. On the other hand, he argued that since Gavin was surety for current council contracts he was disqualified from offering himself for election and that some voters, including Gavin himself, were aware of this at the time. The result was that Gavin was unseated and Arnold given the seat.

So elated were some unionists by this victory that, despite legal advice and the reservations of the earl of Erne, they began to make what could have proved a costly attempt to remove from the council those members coopted with the help of Gavin's vote, and thus restore a unionist majority and chairman. Eventually saner views prevailed, but the incident does illustrate the fillip given to unionist organisation and sentiment by the reform of local government.

Urban elections in Fermanagh were also infected by the party spirit. In 1905 the unionists were worried by the nationalists' boast that they would be able to unseat with ease four of the unionist candidates if they were returned at the Enniskillen urban council elections of that year.

93 Letter from F. MacLaughlin, dispensary doctor of Strangford, Co. Down, to Col. R. H. Wallace of Myra Castle, Co. Down, 8 April 1899, describing nationalist reactions to Wallace's defeat in the county council election, and **(b)** enclosing the speech made by the successful nationalist candidate (D 2223/21/14/13):

(a)

Dear Colonel Wallace—You made a grand fight, and I am sorry we were unable to put you at the head of the Poll. I am afraid in this district the majority of votes against you were polled, tho' every Unionist even a blind bedridden man turned out to vote for you—To give you a specimen of what we might expect from McGrath and his party. A howling mob paraded the streets here last night, insulting the Protestants with vile language and cursing the surrounding gentry, whose bread they eat, and who keep them here. Finally they came in front of my house and Magrath delivered the enclosed speech; the reason of their animosity was, I had stopped several cases of personation on the part of his supporters. I am glad to see we have a majority on the Bench [?] and the Protestant interests I feel confident will not be neglected. I am yrs fait[hful]ly

F MacLaughlin

(b)

"As to this Strangford Dispensary Dr who took a part against us—I am returned in spite of their efforts, and now we will retaliate on these people (pointing to my house) they have no right of inheritance in this country no more than the meanest beggars who crawl in the streets of Strangford. This is our land and we will have none here, but those professing the ancient religion of the country."

Bad language of every description, and cursing of all Protestants followed

94 Certified copy of the minutes of the annual meeting of the Fermanagh county council on 16 June 1902, recording the voting in the cooption of additional members and in the election of officers, and being part of the petitioner's (G. Arnold's) case in the Lisnaskea election petition (D 1390/26/5/2):

FERMANAGH COUNTY COUNCIL.

MINUTES OF ANNUAL MEETING.

16th. June 1902.

The Annual Meeting of the County Council after the triennial Election was held on above date at 2P.M. The Earl of Erne K.P. Chairman Presiding.

Also present:— Sir Arthur Douglas Brooke Vice Chairman, Viscount Corry D.L., Wm. D'Arcy Irvine D.L., James O'Donnell, John Maguire, John Duffy, John M'Hugh, John Lendrum, Patrick Blake, James Tierney J.P., Owen M'Barron, William Teelle [Teele], J.P., John Carroll, Terence Ferguson Capt. C. C. D'Arcy Irvine, J.P. E. M. Archdale, D.L.,M.P., Robert Phillips, Christopher Wilson, Wm.Hurst J.P., Thomas Gavin, Patrick Owens, Thomas Plunkett, Jeremiah Jordan J.P.,M.P., Luke Cassidy — 25

Each Councillor before taking his seat handed to the Secretary his Declaration of Acceptance of Office.

Mr. George Arnold of Lisnaskea came before the Council and protested and objected to Mr. Thomas Gavin sitting, acting, or voting as County Councillor for the County Electoral Division of Lisnaskea, and claiming that he Mr. Arnold had been elected to that office by a majority of lawful votes. Mr. Arnold handed in a written statement to this effect which was received by the Chairman.

Proposed by Mr. M'Barron

Seconded by Lord Corry

Resolved:— "That two additional members be co-opted"—Passed unanimously.

Proposed by John M'Hugh

Seconded by Patrick Owens

"That Mr. Hugh Robert Lindsay of Enniskillen be chosen an additional member of the Council."

Proposed by E. M. Archdale

Seconded by Wm.D'Arcy Irvine

"That Col J. Douglas Johnstone of Snowhill be co-opted an additional member of the Council".

On a division there voted for Mr. Lindsay:—
James O'Donnell, John Maguire, John Duffy, John M'Hugh Patrick Blake, James Tierney, Owen M'Barron, John Carroll, Terence Ferguson, Thomas Gavin, Patrick Owens, Jeremiah Jordan, & Luke Cassidy. — 13

There voted for Col Johnstone:— The Earl of Erne, Sir A. D. Brooke, Viscount Corry, Wm. D'Arcy Irvine, John Lendrum, Wm. Teele, Capt. C. C. D'Arcy Irvine, E. M. Archdale, Robert Phillips, Christopher Wilson, Wm. Hurst, & Thomas Plunkett — 12

Col J. Douglas Johnstone protested against and objected to the vote given by Mr. Thomas Gavin in favour of Mr. Hugh R. Lindsay for co-option as an additional Councillor on the grounds that the said Thomas Gavin had not been legally elected to the office of County Councillor, and he handed in a written statement to this effect which was received by the Chairman.

The Chairman declared Mr. Hugh R. Lindsay elected by a majority of one and he then took his seat on the Council.

Proposed by Owen M'Barron,

Seconded by John Carroll

"That Mr. Patrick Crumley of Enniskillen be co-opted an additional member of this Council".

Proposed by Viscount Corry,

Seconded by William Teele

"That Mr. R. W. Strathearn J.P. be co-opted an additional member of this Council."

There voted for Mr. Crumley:—James O'Donnell, John Maguire John Duffy, Hugh R. Lindsay, John M'Hugh, Patrick Blake, James Tierney, Owen M'Barron, John Carroll, Terence Ferguson, Thomas Gavin, Patrick Owens, Jeremiah Jordan, Luke Cassidy — 14

For Mr. Strathearn:— The Earl of Erne, Sir A. D. Brooke, Viscount Corry, Wm. D'Arcy Irvine, John Lendrum, Wm. Teele, Capt. C. C. D'Arcy Irvine, E. M. Archdale, Robert Phillips, Christopher Wilson, Wm. Hurst, Thomas Plunkett — 12.

Mr. Strathearn came before the Council and protested against and objected to the votes recorded by Mr. Thomas Gavin, and Mr. Hugh R. Lindsay in favour of Mr. Crumley the said Thomas Gavin not having been legally elected to the office of County Councillor, and the said Hugh R. Lindsay having been co-opted by the illegal vote of the said Thomas Gavin and handed in a statement to that effect which was received by the Chairman.

The Chairman declared Mr. Crumley elected by a majority of 2 and he thereupon took his seat at the Council.

Lord Erne vacated the Chair and Sir A. D. Brooke, Vice Chairman presided for the purpose of electing a Chairman for the ensuing year.

Proposed by C. C. D'Arcy Irvine

Seconded by Christopher Wilson

"That the Right Honble. The Earl of Erne be elected Chairman of this Council for the ensuing year."

Proposed by John M'Hugh

Seconded by James Tierney

"That Mr. Jeremiah Jordan M.P. be Chairman"

There voted for Lord Erne:—

Sir A. D. Brooke, The Earl of Erne, Viscount Corry, Wm. D'Arcy Irvine, John Lendrum, Wm. Teele, Capt. C. C. D'Arcy Irvine, Edward M. Archdale, Robert Phillips, Christopher Wilson, Wm. Hurst, Thomas Plunkett — 12

There voted for Mr. Jordan:—

Janes [*sic*] O'Donnell, John Maguire, John Duffy, Patrick Crumley, Hugh R. Lindsay, John M'Hugh Patrick Blake James Tierney, Owen M'Barron John Carroll, Terence Ferguson Thomas Gavin, Patrick Owens, Jeremiah Jordan, Luke Cassidy — 15

Lord Erne protested against and objected to the votes just recorded by Mr. Thomas Gavin, Mr. Patrick Crumley and Mr. Hugh R. Lindsay, in favour of Mr. Jeremiah Jordan for the office of Chairman the said Thomas not having legally been elected to the office of County Councillor and the said Hugh R. Lindsay having been co-opted by the illegal vote of the said Thomas Gavin, and the said Patrick Crumley having been co-opted by the illegal votes of the said Thomas Gavin and Hugh R. Lindsay, and handed in a wr[i]tten statement to this effect which was received by the Chairman.

The Chairman declared Mr. Jeremiah Jordan elected Chairman for the coming year by a majority [*sic*] of 3 subject to the protest handed in by Lord Erne.

Mr. Jordan thereupon took the Chair.

Viscount Corry Proposed

Mr. Plunkett Seconded

> "That a Vice-Chairman be appointed"

Passed unanimously.

Proposed by Terence Ferguson

Seconded by John Carroll

> "That Mr Crumley be Vice-Chairman".

Proposed by Thomas Plunkett

Seconded by Robert Phillips

> "That Sir A. D. Brooke be Vice-Chairman".

On a division there voted for Mr. Crumley:— James O'Donnell John Maguire, John Duffy, Patrick Crumley, Hugh R. Lindsay John M'Hugh, Patrick Blake, James Tierney, Owen M'Barron, John Carroll, Terence Ferguson, Thomas Gavin, Patrick Owens, Jeremiah Jordan, Luke Cassidy— 15

There voted for Sir. A. D. Brooke:— The Earl of Erne, Sir A. D. Brooke, Viscount Corry, Wm. D'Arcy Irvine, John Lendrum, Wm. Teele, Capt C. C. D'Arcy Irvine, E. M. Archdale, Robert Phillips, Christopher Wilson Wm. Hurst, Thomas Plunkett. 12

Sir A. D. Brooke protested and objected to the votes given by Mr. Thomas Gavin, Mr. Hugh R. Lindsay, and Mr. Patrick Crumley, in favour of Mr. Crumley for the office of Vice-Chairman the said Thomas Gavin having been illegally elected to the office of County Councillor, and the said Hugh R. Lindsay having been co-opted by the illegal vote of the said Thomas Gavin, and the said Patrick Crumley, having been co-opted by the votes of the said Thomas Gavin and Hugh R. Lindsay.

The Chairman declared Mr. Patrick Crumley elected by a majority of 3 votes.

The following Committees were unanimously appointed:—

The County's proportion of the Joint Committee of Management of the Omagh District Lunatic Asylum—

Patrick Crumley J.P., Jeremiah Jordan, M.P., Rt. Rev. Monsignor Smollen P.P., Viscount Corry D.L., and Thomas Plunkett

EMERGENCY COMMITTEE:—

Patrick Crumley, William Teele, and Hugh R. Lindsay.

FINANCE COMMITTEE:—

The Earl of Erne K.P., E. M. Archdale, M.P., Viscount Corry D.L., Hugh R. Lindsay, J.P., Patrick Crumley, J.P., William Teele J.P., John Carroll, John M'Hugh, Thomas Plunkett, James O'Donnell and Luke Cassidy.

COUNTY INFIRMARY COMMITTEE:—

John M'Hugh, Patrick Blake, Thomas Plunkett, Thomas Gavin, Patrick M'Mahon, Rev. Peter Farnan P.P., Peter Heslin, Richard Herbert, James M'Govern, Sir A. D. Brooke, Wm. Teele, J. Arthur Irwin.

AGRICULTURE AND TECHNICAL INSTRUCTION:—

Proposed by E. M. Archdale,

Seconded by Patrick Crumley

Resolved:— "That we hereby appoint the following to be the Committee of Agriculture and Technical Instruction in this County for the ensuing 3 years with full powers to administer the Agriculture and Technical Instruction Acts and Acts relating thereto:—

The Earl of Erne K.P., Hugh R. Lindsay J.P., Viscount Corry D.L., E. M. Archdale M.P., Jeremiah Jordan M.P., Sir A. D. Brooke Rev. John Hall, Rt. Rev Monsignor Smollen, P.P. Hon Cecil Corry Patrick Crumley J.P., Edward Mitchell, William Ritchie, James Eadie, Thomas Morrow, W. R. Whyte, Dr. Humphreys J.P., Thomas W West, Thomas Crudden, Edward Archdale D.L., James Tierney J.P., John M'Hugh, George Arnold J.P., Rev J E M'Kenna, C.C., Revd. Canon Ovenden D.D., John Maguire, William Teele J.P., A. P. T. Collum, D.L. Rev Thomas Gallagher C.C., Rev Joseph O'Connor C.C., Rev Thomas Maguire C.C.,

Proposed by Viscount Corry

Seconded by Christopher Wilson

Resolved:— "That we hereby delegate and appoint the County Committee of Agriculture and Technical Instruction to be our Executive Committee under the Diseases of Animals Act 1894 and Acts incorporated therewith". Passed unanimously.

> Jeremiah Jordan
> E. M. Archdale
> Wm. D'Arcy Irvine.

95 Extract from a statement of the petitioner's (G. Arnold's) case in the Lisnaskea election petition, 1902, drawn up 'for counsel to advise' (D 1390/26/5/2):

For the three years prior to June 1902 the Petitioner was the elected county councillor for the Lisnaskea County Electoral Division and at the election in June last he was opposed by Mr. Thomas Gavin of Lisnaskea the Respondent who contested the Division in the Nationlist [*sic*] interest. Both

Candidates were properly nominated, the Election was held on 4th June, and the votes were counted in Enniskillen Courthouse on the 5th June, and re-counted on the application of Petitioner.

The Poll was declared as follows:—

Respondent	263
Petitioner	262

Majority for Gavin   1

The Returning Officer thereupon declared the seat to be Respondents.

On the day of the declaration of the Poll Petitioner was informed that a man named John Dunne, who is registered as an elector in the County Electoral Division of Maguiresbridge (Brookeborough Unit No. 52 on Register) and also in the Lisnaskea County Electoral Division (Deer Park unit No. 684 on Local Government Supplement) voted first on the day of the Election at Brookeboro in the County Electoral Division of Maguire's Bridge for one of the Candidates for County Councillor there; and subsequently voted in Deerpark in the County Electoral Division of Lisnaskea for the Respondent.

By Article 18 (1) of the County and Rural District Councillors Election Order of 16th February 1889 (Vanston page 418) a voter is prohibited from voting for a County Councillor in more than one County Electoral Division in the County. It is therefore contended by Petitioner that the first vote given by Dunne (namely that in the Maguiresbridge County Electoral Division in which he resides) is the valid vote not only because it was the first but because it was given in the Division in which Dunne resides (Rogers on Elections Vol. 2. page 134 St. Andrews Election 4 O M and H page 32). If this is so and Dunne's vote in the Lisnaskea Division is rejected it would leave each of the Candidates having 262 votes and by Article 21 of the beforementioned Election Order it is provided that where an equality of votes exists there is to be a lot drawn by the Returning Officer to decide which Candidate is to have the seat. However this provision as to drawing lots would not appear to apply to an equality of votes after a scrutiny (2 Rogers 259) but that in such case the Election is void and a casual vacancy would appear then to occur (Rogers Vol 2 p 99).

On the question of proof as to whether Dunne voted in both Divisions for County Councillor it should perhaps be stated that in the Brookeboro District Electoral Division there was no contest for District Councillors so that each voter who voted in Brookeboro must have voted for a County Councillor and we have definite evidence that Dunne took the voting paperes [*sic*] for both the County and District Councillors when he subsequently voted in Deerpark in the Lisnaskea Division and he also admitted to two persons that he had voted for County Councillor at both places.

It was with knowledge of the foregoing facts that the first Petition dated the 12th June was presented but directly after that Petition was presented it came to the Petitioner's knowledge that Respondent was a surety upon two contracts made with the County Council and neither of which are contracts which had been entered into with the Grand Jury and continued under the County Council.

The first contract is one entered into by a man named William Hunter of Lislea and is "to repair 478 perches of the old road from Congo to Drumroo in the townlands of Congo, Corrard, Clay, Curryann, Drumbaghlin and Drumroo" and the sureties upon the contract are the said Thomas Gavin of Lisnaskea the Respondent and one Andrew Mair of Ballyreagh. The Bond, a copy of which is briefed is dated the 3" day of July (should be August) 1901 and is in the sum of £130. 19. 0. This Contract should have been completed on the 1" day of June 1902 but at the date of the Election (4th June) it had not been completed nor paid for. It was however in full existence on the day of the "Nomination" which is included in the word "Election".

The second Contract is one entered into by a man named Michael Mc.Donald of Killycrutteen and is "to keep in repair for five years from 1" January 1900 188 perches of the road from Newtown Butler to Swanlinbar between Keady Bridge and the Barony Boundary" and the Sureties upon the Contract are said Thomas Gavin of Lisnaskea the Respondent and one Francis Hughes of Derrycorban. The Bond is dated the 18th day of November 1899 and is in the sum of £10. 15. 5. copy is briefed herewith.

On becoming aware of the above facts and acting under the advice of Junior Counsel the Petitioner presented the second Petition alleging that the Respondent was such surety and that by reason thereof he was disqualified for being elected as a County Counciller [*sic*] and further alleging that certain Electors voted for the Respondent with a knowledge of his disqualification and the grounds thereof and praying that the Respondent might be declared disqualified and his Election declared void and further that all votes given for the Respondent with a knowledge of his disqualification might upon a scrutiny be rejected and claiming the seat for the Petitioner. The Petition also alleges that aliens voted and that their votes might on scrutiny be rejected.

The Petitioner contends that the Respondent is disqualified owing to his being "concerned" in a Contract entered into with the Council within the meaning of Article 12 (4) of the Application of Enactments Order (Vanston p 179) and he does not come within the exemption contained in Article 14 of the Local Government Order of 22" December 1898 (Vanston p 164) which is given to persons who are sureties upon Contracts originally entered into with the Grand Jury and transferred to the County Council by virtue of the Act.

The inference to be drawn from the last named Article would appear to be strongly in favour of the Petitioners contention that a surety is sufficiently concerned in the contract to disqualify him unless he can show that he is specially exempted as in the case of sureties upon transferred Contracts.

Upon the question of Voters voting with a knowledge of the Respondents disqualification the Petitioner has met with considerable difficulty in connecting any voter in the Lisnaskea Division except the Respondent himself, sufficiently with the transaction to raise a strong presumption that he was aware of the facts out of which the disqualification arose.

However the Respondent himself is a voter in the Lisnaskea Division and of course voted for himself and he must have been aware of the facts upon which his disqualification was grounded even if he did not know that these facts did disqualify him and it is contended that mere knowledge of the facts grounding the disqualification is sufficient to cause the vote to be rejected as all are presumed to know the law. . .

96 Printed circular, issued October 1902 (after the successful outcome of the Lisnaskea election petition) by W. Teele of Enniskillen on behalf of the unionist county councillors, appealing for funds to defray the cost of proceedings against other nationalist members of the county council (D 1390/26/4/4):

Dear Sir or Madam—At a meeting of the Unionist County Councillors held on the 24th inst., it was decided that having regard to the satisfactory result of the Lisnaskea Election Petition, proceedings should at once be instituted for the purpose of unseating the Nationalist Councillors and the Chairman and Vice-Chairman who were co-opted by means of Mr Gavin's illegal vote.

It is expected that we will thus be able to restore the Unionist Majority upon the County Council, which would never have been lost if the Lisnaskea Election had not resulted in Mr. Gavin being wrongfully declared entitled to the seat.

For the purpose of defraying the expense of the necessary proceedings it was decided at the meeting to open a Subscription List, to which all Loyalists may contribute.

I confidently appeal to you for your support in a matter of such importance to the Unionist cause in this County, and I enclose a stamped envelope for your reply. Sincerely yours,

WILLIAM TEELE
Treasurer appointed at said meeting.

97 Letter from W. G. Chartres, Drumcramph, Co. Fermanagh, to J. H. Charlton of Enniskillen, solicitor and official of the North Fermanagh Loyalist Registration Association, 8 November 1902, urging energetic action in the collection of funds to reconstruct the county council in foot of the Lisnaskea election petition (D 1390/26/5/2):

Dear Charleton [*sic*]—As I see by "Times" the initial steps have been taken to reconstruct our Co. Council, and as it is a procedure which is certain to incur a large amount of expenses, with no great certainty of success, The general collection should proceed at once with the least possible delay, and as you are aware it is one of the most difficult tasks to get anything deacent [*sic*] from our party. I still think the very best plan is a "parochial collection" I mean to send the cards say four to each Irish Church Minister & Senior Mithodist [*sic*] Minister also with a strong worded appeal in printed form and signed by [the] Petitioners, or committee, & would also suggest that the cards be divided between male and female collectors as the latter can always do best, even where others fail, I have left this matter before the District Lodge of Maguiresbridge last night and my suggestion is fully approved of. I am sure Rev A. Davis would assist in this matter, as he is aware of all the parishes in the confines of the Co. I am certain the Clergy would all take it up heartily and know the best <u>Collectors</u>. hoping I am not unduly trespassing on you. As you are aware I am most desirous of the success of this matter, and the Country folk are quite ignorant of its importance, and far reaching consequences. I hope to see you Fair Day. Wishing you, God speed I remain faithfully Yours

Wm. G Chartres

98 *Letter from J. H. Charlton to G. Fetherstonhaugh, prospective unionist candidate and later M.P. for North Fermanagh, 2 January 1905, asking his advice on nationalist views on the ease with which they might be able to unseat the unionist town councillors in Enniskillen after the 1905 elections (D 1390/26/6, pp. 63–4):

Dear Mr. Fetherstonhaugh—Please note that you will be required to leave Amiens Street by the 9 a.m. train on Friday for the Pettigoe Meeting as you probably would not arrive there until 9. p.m. by the train leaving at 2.45, as it runs "anyhow" on the Bundoran line. Mr. Falls will join you here, passing through at 12.40.

The Nominations for our Urban Elections here will be on Thursday next. We have selected Candidates for each Ward, but I understand the Nationalists are chuckling at the prospect of being able to unseat four of them on Petition on the following grounds:—

Mr. Falls	That he participates in the profit of work done under the County Council as their Solicitor, and that the "bargain" between him and the County Council is a bargain with the Urban District Council. See Application of Enactments Order 1898. Article 12 (4) (e), Vanston. P. 179.
Mr Dundas.	That he is paid collector for the Enniskillen Gas Co. who have a Contract for the Public Lighting of the Town with the Urban Council, and that he participates in the profit of such Contract by receiving a Commission from the Gas Co. on the amounts collected by him. He does not now collect the amounts of the Contracts with the Urban Council or any other public bodies, but simply the private consumer's accounts. Note that by (5) (c) of above Article his employers, the shareholders of the Gas Co., are exempted from disqualification.
Mr. Ritchie and Mr. Trimble	That both have Printing Contracts with the Co. Council and that such Contracts are equivalent to Contracts with the Urban Council under article 12(4) (e). The Urban Council is independent of, and not in any way subordinate

193

to the Co. Council, but the Urban Council contribute to the amount of those Printing Contracts per their valuation, pro rata with the remainder of the County. I think the "Council of a District" referred to in the sub-article is a "rural" District which is subordinate to the Co. Council, and not an Urban Council which is a wholly independent body.

Would you mind taking a rough look at Vanston Page 179, and let me know what you think of above contentions. The time between now and the Nomination is so short, that I cannot make enquiries for authorities. Yours truly,

J. H. Charlton.

IV

These developments at a local level were matched by attempts to organise centrally. In 1892 there was formed the Ulster Convention League which among other things arranged the massive unionist demonstration in Belfast on 17 June 1892; and 1893 saw the foundation of the Ulster Defence Union and the Unionist clubs movement, a largely Ulster movement with a central council meeting in Belfast. Nevertheless, the land question continued to prove an obstacle to reliable unionist organisation in Ulster.

Despite some modifications to the 1881 act, tenants still thought that insufficient allowance was being made for improvements carried out by them, and, led by T. W. Russell, the liberally minded opponent of home rule and M.P. for South Tyrone (1886-1910) and then North Tyrone (1910-18), came increasingly to demand compulsory purchase. For their part, landlords, such as H. de F. Montgomery, continued to believe that reductions were too high; and, while not opposed to the establishment of peasant proprietorships, opposed compulsory purchase as unjust, impracticable, calculated to undermine the union, and inimical to the interests of protestant farmers. Montgomery disliked Russell's views, especially following the Morley committee. This committee, set up in 1894, criticised the lack of uniform procedure in the operation of the land acts, particularly as it left the tenant interest undefined and unprotected. The liberal government's bill based on the report was not carried, but in the general election of 1895 several unionist candidates in Ulster took up some of the committee's ideas. Much to Montgomery's disgust, Russell offered further safeguards for tenants, and even Gerald Balfour, the new unionist chief secretary, took up the tenants' case. Though some landlords, such as Montgomery at the North Fermanagh election of 1892, did vote for unionist candidates who took up the tenants' case, mutual suspicion in general inhibited wholehearted cooperation at provincial and constituency levels between landlords and protestant tenant farmers. This suspicion may have helped to make the unionists of South Tyrone—including even Montgomery—reluctant to join in with the Ulster Convention League; and it led to the defeat of James Craig, the nominee of the North Fermanagh Loyalist Registration Association (and the future prime minister of Northern Ireland), in a parliamentary by-election in North Fermanagh in March 1903.

North Fermanagh had been won for the unionists in 1892 by Richard Dane, who had taken as one of his planks 'compulsory sale and purchase upon such terms as shall be fair and just'. He died in 1898 and the seat was retained for unionists by a local landlord, E. M. Archdale of Ballinamallard. He resigned in 1903, and the subsequent by-election took place just before the terms of Wyndham's land bill were announced in the house of commons. Despite the forecast of the unionist agent, Charles Falls, the official unionists and Craig lost the seat to Edward Mitchell, a farmer with 200 acres. Contesting the seat as a Russellite and an independent unionist, Mitchell justified his opposition to the official unionist on the ground that the local loyalist association was a corrupt body that had neglected the interests of the people, the tenant farmers. Seeing the issue in terms of the 'people's cause' against the 'landlord wolves', he took as his plank compulsory purchase, and was returned with a majority of 152. (In 1906, however, the local unionist association regained by 88 votes the seat, which thereafter remained unionist.)

99 Letter from A. Duffin, writing from Donaghadee, Co. Down, to H. de F. Montgomery, 27 August 1892, regretting the decision of the South Tyrone Loyalist Registration Association not to join in with the Ulster Convention League (D 627/428/193):

My dear Montgomery—I am rather sorry that the S. Tyrone Assn. will have nothing to do with the Convention League You would not have had to dread any officious interference and we might have been of service. I quite understand your position in affiliation with the Irish Unionist Alliance and the danger of multiplying channels for collecting and distributing funds. At the same time the League will be of use especially in keeping various Unionist elements in Ulster in harmony & so far as I can see there is no fear of the work getting left without proper control in <u>dangerous</u> hands.

I hope you will get a good fighting man to conduct the business in the Revision Courts. If I, or the Ctee. of the League can be of any use in this respect, whether your Assn. falls in with us or not, we shall be glad to aid. It is hard to find & to spare a good man, unless one of the three we have had in West Belfast could be set free & I think that might be done. They are all good, Wylie, W. Young, and Lewis, the last a capital court man.

I think there is no fear of the Convention League out-stepping the lines of its proper work now. Finnegan will be an active & useful worker, but not <u>primum mobile</u>, & so far as possible kept in the back-ground.

Is Mulholland to vacate N. Derry and if so for <u>whom</u>? Yours faithfully

Adam Duffin

100 Letter from R. M. Dane, unionist M.P. for North Fermanagh (1892–8), writing from 'Dane's committee rooms', Old White Hart Hotel, Enniskillen, to Montgomery, 11 June 1892, thanking him for his 'patriotic and unselfish' support in the North Fermanagh election 'just won' (D 627/428/182):

Private

My dear Montgomery—I wish to place upon record my appreciation of the Patriotic & unselfish stand you made in support of the Unionist cause at the election just won. The course adopted by yourself, Porter-Porter, D'Arcy Irvine & other Landowners in this Division having regard to my pledges in support of compulsory sale & purchase considerably minimized the great Difficulties I had to contend with.

I have written The Duke of Abercorn & Lord Erne pointing out (as I did some months ago to Mr Balfour) that his question must be tackled in Ulster & that all fair mided Landowners should meet & confer as to some Liberal & Fair course of united action—If something is not done the Judicial Rents will not be paid and we shall have an agitation amongst the best & most Honest Farmers in Ulster—I am sure you will accept my word for it that I voice the views of the best of the Farmers in this matter who feel that they have not so far touched any of the benefits of Land Purchase.

I would like to see this question settled & that by the Unionist Party. Sincerely yours

Richard M. Dane

101 *Letter from Montgomery to Dane, Enniskillen, 12 July 1892, explaining why he supported Dane (D 627/428/189):

My dear Dane—I had no hesitation or difficulty in giving you, as the Unionist candidate any little help & support I could, though I disapproved of your advocacy of compulsory purchase. On former occasions, when a candidate whom many tenants regarded as a "landlords man" was up we exhorted them to put aside selfish class views and vote for him, for the sake of the Union and our common rights & liberties, civil and religious. We were bound, when the Unionist candidate was a "tenants man", to practice [sic] what we preached, & we have done so.

As to the question of "Land purchase", I have been an advocate of a large extenstion [sic] of occupying ownership for many years, and am prepared to renew the efforts I made, in conjunction with the Irish Landowners committee, when Mr. Balfours measures were under discussion, to mould the law so as to make it easier for landlords to sell at a price that will bring relief to tenants and for tenants to offer a price that will be fair to landlords; but to compulsory sale or purchase I remain uncompromisingly opposed, holding that it is, in principle grossly unjust to landlords; that, in practice, [it is] totally impossible to carry out, no land commission being capable of fixing a fair price; that it is part of the propaganda of the land league conspiracy for undermining British rule, by ruining & expelling the gentry & that protestant tenants in adopting the demand, are cutting a rod for their own backs, as—the principle once admitted—there is nothing to prevent a Radical government applying it to any body of Protestant occupiers that a Popish or Fenian majority wish removed out of any part of Ireland to make room for "men of their own". Yrs very truly

H de F Montgomery.

102 Draft letter from Montgomery to J. Chamberlain, 31 July 1895, complaining of the attitude of Russell and other members of the unionist party on the land question (D 627/428/273):

Dear Mr. Chamberlain—Owing, on the one hand, to the solid support of the landlords and the good organization of our party, and, on the other, to the phenomenal feebleness of the opposition candidate Russell was returned by a bigger majority than I anticipated. The peculiarity of the election, as far as it came under my eye, was the heavy poll combined with a total absence of enthusiasm or even interest in the result. The voters on both sides all came in to vote as they were bid, but seemed for the most part to regard the candidates as a brace of humbugs between whom there was very little to choose.

With a view to the settlement of the country, it is most unfortunate that it should have been thought necessary to give "assurances" about a Land Bill which Russell and several other Unionist candidates have been bragging about in a way to lead electors to think they mean a great deal more than perhaps they do. It is equally unfortunate that Gerald Balfour was authorized to mention so many points in his Leeds speech. These promises were quite needless & useless. They did not enable Unionists to hold North Tyrone nor to win East Tyrone or any other seat. Nor have they gained us 50 votes in any of the constituencies we have held by substantial majorities.

The language held here about the alleged "assurances" and "written pledges" and about Gerald Balfours speech has placed fresh obstacles in the way of the operation of the purchase acts and of all sorts of amicable arrangements between landlords and tenants. Since Russell began his antics about the select committee and Morley's bill tenants have been holding back from all arrangements, for purchase or otherwise—waiting to see what the new land act would do for them. But for these so-called assurances, as expounded by Russell and other Unionist candidates taking their cue from him, the result of the general election would have ended the deadlock and with it the agrarian agitation in Ulster which, except as regards a handful of fanatics, is purely the creation of competitive politicians. A great opportunity has been thrown away. Tenants will now all hold back to see what Balfour's new land bill will be like, and will form extravagant expectations about it.

The passage about tenants improvements in GB's speech I regard as very ill-advised, as it implies an admission by the government that such improvements are not already sufficiently protected—in opposition to the opinion formed by W. Kenny & other competent students of the evidence before Morley's select committee.

This passage, as interpreted must obstruct the attainment of the two sound points in G.B's statement, the simplification and cheapening of procedure in the fair rent courts, and the more rapid & effective working of the purchase acts. Neither are [sic] possible except on the basis of the acceptance of existing judicial rents as having been approximately fair when fixed & the pocketing of their respective grievances regarding them by both landlord & tenant.

Read (as it will be) in the light of Russells preposterous proposals & promises on the subject, the passage about exclusions—especially town-parks —must also have bad effects.

If the purchase acts are ultimately to be of general operation, you must look to vesting lands about small towns in your future Parish Councils for alotments [sic] &c, and (apart from the immediate injustice to the owner) you cannot do a worse thing than to set up a highly competitive statutory tenants interest in such land, on the top of the landlords interest that will have to be bought out.

Russell opened his election campaign in S. Tyrone with a statement that you had told him that your views on the Irish Land Question were practically the same as his. If there was any chance of this being taken in connexion

198

with his speech on the 2d reading it might not be very misleading or mischievous—but it will be taken in connexion, not with that speech, but with his subsequent exposition of his views at Belfast on May 31st. last—when he proved to the satisfaction not only of the "Ballymoney Land League" but of every landlord who read his speech that he was a thorough supporter of Morley's land bill, was opposed to all amendments to it, except his own, and that his own amendments were all either (A) calculated to make the proposed confiscation of landlords property more complete or (B) mere whitewash to conceal iniquities from British eyes without modifying their real effect.

Sir Thomas Lea is reported as saying that the Government is pledged to bring in a bill "on the lines of the Report of the select Committee" and I hear that in some of his unreported speeches in S. Tyrone Russell was more explicit and used words that conveyed to his hearers the idea that he had a promise from Lord Salisbury "in black and white" to pass an act embodying all the most iniquitous provisions of Morley's bill.

All this will create needless difficulties for the government as well as keep the minds of the tenants unsettled and hamper all efforts at local improvements by landowners which the general result of the election would encourage them to undertake.

Excuse the length of this letter and believe me sincerely yrs

H de F Montgomery.

103 Letter from W. Irvine and H. H. Aiken, two unionist workers, to C. F. Falls, secretary to the North Fermanagh Loyalist Registration Association, 6 April 1893, complaining of the behaviour of a local landlord, C. R. Barton of The Waterfoot, Pettigoe, Co. Fermanagh, which they claim is damaging the unionist cause in the area (D1390/26/4/15):

Dear Mr. Falls—Mr. Charles R. Barton is engaged in enrolling Clonelly and Brookhill districts and as he has taken the matter [into] his own hands and has spread abroad reports to the effect that we have obtained considerable sums of money from the Registration Association from time to time to his knowledge, he being a member of the Finance Committee, we regret that, unless a stop be put to his conduct, we cannot continue to act as District Secretaries, or to be the victims of his petty persecution.

We consider that the Loyalist cause in this district is seriously threatened by his public speeches, private slanders, and unwarranted interference, and that a considerable number of Mr. Dane's supporters who hold strong views on the Land question will be alienated from the Unionist party by Mr. Bartons action, as the interests of the landlords are generally believed by the farming class to be the sum and substance of Mr. Barton's political faith We are of opinion that many of his statements—such as that Balfour's Local Government is as bad as Gladstone's Home Rule—are most injudicious and contrary to the views of the Unionists of this district

We wish to direct your attention to the fact that the meeting called by us on your instructions to protest against Home Rule was disturbed and practically rendered abortive by Mr. Barton indulging in a disorderly and insulting attack on the Chairman (Revd. M. R. Davies) and on us, that he objected to the signing of petitions, that we protested against the introduction of matters foreign to the object of the meeting, that the Chairman ruled in our favour, and that notwithstanding that the Methodist and Presbyterian ministers who were present upheld the ruling of the Chairman, Mr Barton has since declined to attend the services in the Parish Church and has stated that he will not in future subscribe to its funds.

We are anxious that the charges of corrupt and dishonourable conduct and motives which we have reason to believe have been privately circulated should be stated publicly so as to give us an opportunity of defending ourselves and we decline to allow our church, its clergy, or ourselves to be scurrilously attacked in Unionist meetings

Under the circumstances we do not consider that we could be responsible for carrying on the work in this district

We desire to acknowledge the kindness and consideration with which we have been at all times treated by you and Mr. Charlton, and to express our regret that by the tyrannical and insulting conduct of one individual we will be prohibited from taking a part, as we have hitherto done to the best of our ability in furtherance of the Unionist cause at elections and at revision courts Yours faithfully

William Irvine

H. H. Aiken

104 *Letter from C. F. Falls to E. M. Archdale, unionist M.P. for North Fermanagh since 1898, 9 February 1903, urging him either to postpone or to bring forward his resignation from parliament in view of the impending land bill (D 1390/26/6, pp 3–4):

Dear Archdale—I cannot possibly see how the introduction of the Land Act could assist us in North Fermanagh, but on the other hand I can see how it will ruin us.

No matter how liberal the terms of the Bill may be, it will still be open to Russell to say, they are not liberal enough and that if the tenants will stick to him he will get them better terms. This [much] he will do as of course he does not intend to be extinguished and the tenants will follow him [for] the chance of getting more than the Government [is] willing to give. At the present moment Russell is no stronger than any other land reformer as they are all willing to go as far as the Convention, and no one knows what is before them. But once give Russell the handle to criticise the Bill, more especially if you support it, and we are placed in a very different position. I believe we can win the seat now, but if you remain on until the Bill is introduced, I firmly believe we will lose it. There is also another question for consideration. Unless you consent to remain on until the end of this Parliament, where are we going to

get a man who will be prepared to spend £600 on a contest and £400 on pay[ing] our debt, if he is only to have one [single?] Parliament with a prospect of Redistribution of seats? I believe no one will do it. I certainly think it is [high?] time [an? effort?] was made about this debt which [should? be?] extinguished if the seat is lost. Teele tells me that you will not remain after Easter. If that is so, it is merely a matter of tactics and I certainly think the entire question should be laid before the Whips and Captn. Middleton.
Yours Sincerely
Charles F. Falls.

V

The virtual solution of the land question with Wyndham's land act of 1903 removed one of the biggest obstacles to the effective coordination of unionist energies in Ulster. The opportunity for such a coordination came in 1904, with the 'MacDonnell mystery' or 'devolution crisis'.

On 26 September 1904 a scheme of devolution, by which a central Irish council was to exercise (within the framework of the union) a measure of local authority, was suggested by a non-party body of Irishmen led by Lord Dunraven and organised as the Irish Reform Association. Since Sir Antony MacDonnell, the unconventional and Roman Catholic undersecretary at Dublin Castle, had been cooperating (though without the chief secretary's knowledge) with the association, the unionist government was suspected of conniving at the scheme, which Irish unionists roundly condemned. Since Ulster unionists were already critical of what they regarded as the government's over–conciliatory policy towards Irish nationalists, they vigorously attacked the government in and out of parliament, forced the resignation of the chief secretary, George Wyndham, and the Ulster unionist M.P.s took the opportunity 'to revive on a war footing for active work the various Ulster defence associations'.

Thus a central unionist association was formed at a meeting of Ulster unionists in the Y.M.C.A. Minor Hall, Belfast, on 2 December; and in March 1905 it publicly assumed the name of the Ulster Unionist Council. The U.U.C. comprised Ulster unionist M.P.s and peers and all local unionist associations, unionist clubs and orange lodges in Ulster; its delegates were appointed by every polling district and drawn from all classes and creeds and were thus representative of the Ulster (protestant) people; and the democratic method of election provided a permanent electoral machinery in the constituencies. At meetings of the U.U.C. all manner of issues were soon under discussion, including proposals for a redistribution of seats which would have the effect of reducing Irish representation at Westminster. But the great potential of the organisation was not realised until the crisis over the third home rule bill, 1912–14. Until then the organisation of the U.U.C. tended to be slack and its finances weak.

105 *Letter from F. H. Crawford, unionist gun-runner, Wilson Street Works, Belfast, to the 5th earl of Ranfurly of the Ulster Loyalist Union, 14 December 1906, describing among other things Belfast unionists' disillusionment with A. J. Balfour, the leader of the British unionist party (D 1700/10):

Dear Lord Ranfurly—There is nothing I would like better than to buckle on the old armour & place myself in the foremost fighting line for the Union under your leadership as I used to be. But unfortunately my father is past all business & the whole responsibility is now on my shoulders. Under these circumstances I am afraid I will not be able to do the sort of work I used to. However there are other ways I shall be able to help you, perhaps quite as much as going over to speak and debate viz. try and get others to go in my place. If I can help you in this way let me know and I shall send forward some names that I have a list of.

I had intended to write to you on a matter that is most important but will take delicate handling. Viz There is a rumour or was a rumour that Mr. A. J. Balfour wd. be asked during the spring or early summer, to come over here to a monster demonstration to be held as a protest against Home Rule. I can't find out who is at the bottom of this movement or if it is really a fact that such an idea is on the tapis. I write to let you know the felling [sic] in the North of Ireland towards Mr. Balfour so that before he is asked you might put the facts before the leaders of Unionist party. At one time all unionists in North of Ireland trusted Mr. Balfour completely. When he allowed out the Dynamitards, the orange working man was suspicious, when he started his Catholic University Campaign, all the Unionists here distrusted him & when he was a party to the appointment of Sir Anthony McDonnell [sic] every true Unionist here thought him a traitor and what is more they still think worse of him than they did of Gladstone. If he came over here he would be hooted off the platform. If this happened it would be nothing short of a disaster to the cause by making an enemy of him. The last Ulster Hall demonstration under the Duke of Abercorn ought to make our leaders very careful of what they do in the future.

Since the McDonnell incident we have lost a lot of staunch Unionist workmen in Belfast. They consider themselves betrayed by their leader Mr. Balfour & have gone in for the labour & socialist programme. This is what we have to combat locally. The old unionist enthusiasm is dead among the masses here. These are facts and all in touch with the working man, like myself, knows [*sic*] it. If I can help you in any other way I am at your service In Summer I am not quite so busy & might spare a week or two but not in Winter Yours very Sinc[ere]ly

Fred. H. Crawford

106 Printed letter sent out by the Ulster unionist parliamentary party, 17 November 1904, inviting orangemen to attend a meeting on 2 December to consider the formation of a central unionist organisation (D 1327/7/6A):

DEAR SIR—I am directed by the Ulster Unionist Parliamentary Party to invite your attendance at a Meeting to be held in Belfast on Friday, December 2nd, to consider the formation of a Central Unionist Organization.

The object of the Meeting is to get together leading representative Unionists in Ulster, and it was considered impossible at the preliminary meeting to adhere too closely to the precise representation of each Constituency. You will, however, note that the Draft Scheme, five copies of which I enclose, under which the business of the Council, when formed, will be conducted, does provide for proportional representation of each Constituency. The Ulster Parliamentary Party were aware of the difficulty, owing to the regulations of the Orange Institution as to half-yearly and other meetings, of securing an elected representation for the preliminary meeting, and considered that the best way of meeting this difficulty was to request the respective Grand Masters to invite four members from each County Grand Lodge. I am, therefore, directed to express the hope that you will invite four members of your County Grand Lodge to be present with you at the PRELIMINARY MEETING, TO BE HELD IN THE Y.M.C.A. MINOR HALL, ON FRIDAY, DECEMBER 2nd, at TWO O'CLOCK.

I further enclose you five copies of the letter about to be sent to each gentleman who will attend, from which you will see that the scheme is purely tentative, and the fullest discussion and amendments are invited. I am asked to point out that in the opinion of the Ulster Members it would be premature to invite any Association to join the Ulster Union until they are in a position to judge of the scheme as finally settled, and as this cannot be until after the Meeting of December 2nd, you will understand that your attendance will not bind the County Grand Lodge as to their final action in respect of the scheme. Yours faithfully,

T. H. GIBSON,
Secretary (*pro tem*),
Ulster Union of Constitutional Associations.

107 Extract from the agenda of the meeting of Ulster unionists in the Minor Hall, Belfast, 2 December 1904, giving the resolution establishing the U.U.C. (D 1327/7/6A):

That an Ulster Council be formed, and that its objects shall be to form an Ulster Union for bringing into line all Local Unionist Associations in the Province of Ulster, with a view to consistent and continuous political action; to act as a further connecting link between Ulster Unionists and their Parliamentary representatives; to settle in consultation with them the Parliamentary Policy, and to be the medium of expressing Ulster Unionist opinion, as current events may from time to time require, and generally to advance and defend the interests of Ulster Unionism in the Unionist Party.

108 Extracts from the agenda of the first meeting of the U.U.C. in the Ulster Minor Hall, 3 March 1905, giving notices of motion: **(a)** sent in by the delegates from the Ulster Liberal Unionist Association; **(b)** proposed by W. W. Barnhill, B.L., seconded by W. T. Millar, J.P.; and **(c)** proposed by Dr W. Gibson, J.P., seconded by E. Leathem (D 1327/7/6A):

(a)

That we have observed with deep disappointment the action of the Government (as disclosed in the correspondence of the Chief Secretary during September, 1902, and in recent Ministerial admissions in Parliament), by which in defiance of well-established constitutional usage, and without the knowledge of Parliament or of the country, they endowed an official of the permanent Civil Service in Ireland with powers of influencing the policy and acts of the Irish Administration, which should be entrusted only to a Minister personally responsible to Parliament.

That we cordially recognise the valuable services rendered by the Ulster Unionist members in bringing to light the circumstances in which this extraordinary unconstitutional blunder was made, and urges [sic] upon them that while continuing to maintain their vigilant watch on the administrative action of the Irish Government, they should, in the interests of the maintenance of the Legislative Union and of the unimpared [sic] efficiency of Imperial Parliament, press upon the Cabinet the supreme importance of effectively settling the all-important question of Redistribution during the present session.

That we have read with great satisfaction the letter of the Prime Minister of the 27th February, 1905, addressed to the Solicitor-General for Scotland emphasing [sic] the danger that the policy of Home Rule only awaits the advent of the Opposition to power again to become active, militant, and perilous and that, therefore, it rests with the Unionist party in the future, as in the past, to defend the Constitution of the country.

That we confidently call upon the Prime Minister so to adjust the policy of the Government in Ireland as to enable Irish Unionists to close their ranks, and in co-operation with the rest of the Unionist Party to present an unbroken front against the common enemy.

(b)

That the Ulster Unionist Members have the sanction of this Council in not supporting the Government until the Lord Lieutenant, Chief Secretary, and Under-Secretary be removed from Office.

(c)

That this meeting of the Council of Constitutional Associations in Ulster desires to place on record its cordial appreciation of the services rendered by the Ulster Unionist Members, in unmasking the unconstitutional plot by which a civil servant was invested with powers that should only be delegated to a responsible minister of the Crown; and approves of a continuation of their present attitude toward the Government until the present anomalies in the Government of Ireland have been remedied.

That in view of the admission by the Government in the King's Speech, and considering the great injustice of holding a General Election on the present divisions, this meeting is strongly of opinion that a Bill for the Redistribution of Parliamentary Seats should be passed during the existence of the present Parliament.

That the Unionists of Ireland are hereby called upon to close up their ranks, subordinating all minor differences to the all-important question of the maintenance of the Union; and this Council emphatically declares the determination of Irish Unionists to oppose any scheme, no matter by what name designated, that would place the loyal minority at the mercy of the disloyal majority.

109 Extracts, relating to the efficiency of the U.U.C., taken from the report of an interview between Sir Wilson Hungerford, U.U.C. official and later chief unionist agent in Northern Ireland, and members of staff of the N.I.P.R.O., November 1965 (PRB 987):

Sir Wilson Hungerford was brought into the Ulster Unionist Council Office at the suggestion of Stewart Blacker Quin in 1912. The finances of the organisation were in something of a mess at this time and his first job was to create an orderly financial system. At this time Sir Dawson Bates was still only part-time secretary of the organisation and he had little or no clerical staff to assist him. The administrative machinery had not been developed to cope with the ramifications of the Anti-Home Rule Campaign. . . .

When Sir Wilson first came to the office . . . he found the administrative machinery quite inadequate to cope with the scale of the Anti-Home Rule Campaign which was being waged. He gave two illustrations of the amateurish methods which he found. His earliest memory of arrival in the office was seeing a large pile of angry letters from every newspaper office in Ireland protesting at the receipt of a mere 5/– postal order to pay for the insertion of a large advertisement; this ad. . . . had been sent out to every Irish newspaper which appeared in the Press Guide, along with a 5/– postal order. Another example of casual improvisation was the printing of red, white and blue badges on paper, when the supply of metal badges ran out; these paper badges were rather hideous, "more like a rosette to be tied on a prize bull at an Agricultural Show than something to be worn".

Chapter VII

Ulster unionist organisation at the time of the third home rule bill

The full potential of the U.U.C. was realised at the time of the third home rule bill introduced in April 1912. Then Ulster unionists roundly declared that they would resist the bill, and threatened not only to refuse to pay taxes but also to establish their own government defended by an armed force of volunteers. On 25 September 1911, 400 delegates to the U.U.C. unanimously agreed upon a policy to resist the establishment of a home rule parliament, and appointed a committee to submit a constitution for a provisional government to operate when the third home rule bill passed through parliament under the parliament act. Such a scheme was approved on 24 September 1913 by the 500 delegates to a reformed and enlarged U.U.C., and on 10 July 1914 this provisional government met for the first time as such. The provisional government was, if necessary, to be defended by an armed Ulster Volunteer Force, which was backed by an indemnity fund of over one million pounds sterling in aid of the prospective disabled, widowed and orphaned. By July 1914 the volunteers were allowed by their headquarters to carry arms openly 'whether they have or have not gun licences'; and there were elaborate plans to evacuate women and children in the event of civil war breaking out.

II

Such determination and such schemes were made possible by solid and resourceful organisation in depth. The headquarters of Ulster unionism was moved to the Old Town Hall, Belfast; and apart from the introduction of such capable administrators as Sir Wilson Hungerford, two points are worth noticing in respect of organisation.

In the first place, though Ulster unionism is usually identified with orangeism, in the years 1911–14 it was the unionist clubs movement rather than the orange lodges that provided the basis for 'grass roots' organisation. The unionist clubs movement, in abeyance since 1895, was revived in 1911 at the suggestion of the U.U.C., and it grew steadily. By February 1914, 371 clubs had been formed, and they engaged in a wide range of activities, conventional and otherwise.

Secondly, steps were taken to strengthen the central organisation by closely associating Ulster businessmen with the work of the U.U.C. On the one hand, the U.U.C. formed a committee of businessmen, the secretary of which was G. R. Reid, a Belfast solicitor, to advise on the commercial problems involved in resistance to home rule, particularly in respect of the non-payment of taxes. On the other hand, the businessmen and a benevolent Belfast Banking Co. put the finances of the U.U.C. on a firmer footing by assuming, among other things, the management of the Sir Edward Carson Unionist Defence Fund, originally promulgated in January 1912 to finance antihome rule propaganda in Great Britain.

110 Report of the work done by the unionist clubs in 1911, submitted to the executive committee by the secretary to the U.C.C., 4 December 1911 (D 1327/1/2):

Number of Clubs actually formed   171
    „   „   „   to be formed during the current month   10
Number of Clubs linked   47

CRAIGAVON DEMONSTRATION: The arrangements for the representation of the Clubs at the Demonstration [23 September 1911] were in the hands of the Sub-Committee appointed by the Executive Committee at their meeting on August 30th. This Sub-Committee still meets the representatives of the Ulster Unionist Council and Orange Body in connection with the forthcoming Demonstration on April 9th, 1912.
                                              The number of clubs represented at Craigavon was 140.
                                              Number of Club members who actually attended (including those who, being Orangemen, marched with their Lodges) = 13000 [out of the 50,000 demonstrators].

DEPUTATIONS.   A Deputation of nine Representatives from Wales attended the Craigavon Demonstration, and were entertained during their stay in Belfast by the Windsor and Malone Club.
                                              A party of 17 Liberal Unionist workers visiting Ireland were received by representatives of several Clubs, and during their stay in Belfast were entertained by members of the City Clubs.

ORGANISATION. The Scheme of organisation proposed some months ago was re-circulated last month and has now been taken up by many Clubs. The system of District Centres controlling groups of small Clubs is proving most satisfactory where adopted ie., in Mid-Tyrone—Dungannon—Cookstown—and South Armagh.

LINKING. A copy of the report on the work done by Randalstown has been circulated to all Clubs—several Clubs are already sending members over to their "linked" Associations [in Great Britain].

NEWS BUREAU. At present 19 Nationalist papers and 42 English Radical papers are being taken regularly in the Clubs office—

Fourteen members of City Clubs have kindly volunteered to write letters in reply to Radical Home Rule speeches etc.

The Nationalist news-papers are sent to selected individuals in England and Scotland who have undertaken to see that they are used by speakers, and otherwise brought to notice.

LETTER WRITING TO DOUBTFUL VOTERS. In view of increased work in the Clubs Office and the fact that many Clubs are already "linked" these are now being dealt with by the Womens' Unionist Associations, but any Clubs not linked can still be supplied with addresses of doubtful voters.

111

Extracts from the minute book of the businessmen's executive committee, recording the proceedings at meetings held in the Old Town Hall, Belfast, on 19, 27 August and 2 September 1913, to discuss the feasibility of withholding taxes as a protest against home rule (D 1327/3/7):

(a)

It was decided that the secretary should report on the effect of refusal on the part of public bodies to pay taxes or repay Government loans. . . . Mr. Garrett Campbell brought forward a number of queries as to the effect on individuals in event of their refusing to pay taxes, and one of the members undertook to have them answered.

(b)

The Secretary reported that he had received Returns from the County Councils of Antrim, Down, Derry, and Tyrone, also from the City of Belfast, showing what annual Grants were received by them from the Government and what sums were paid to the Government. These Returns showed that a much larger sum was received from the Government, and, under these circumstances, the Committee decided that any proposal to withhold payments to the Government by these public bodies would not be workable.

The question of refusal to pay Income-Tax was then discussed at considerable length. Several points as to the method of carrying out this refusal were considered, and the Committee finally decided that they should proceed on the basis of recommending that all payers of Income-Tax should abstain from paying as from 1st January, 1914. The Secretary was instructed to draw up a draft scheme setting out the views of the Committee, and to bring it before the committee on their next meeting on Tuesday, 2nd September.

(c)

The Secretary, as instructed at the previous meeting, read a draft scheme dealing with the question of payment of Income Tax, which was discussed at some length, and Mr. R. A. Mitchell read a report from the members of the Wholesale Whiskey and Tobacco Trades, pointing out the difficulty which these Trades had in refusing to pay Customs or Excise duty, and it was decided by the Committee that to refuse such payments was not practicable without destroying such business in Belfast. It was decided that the first paragraph in the draft scheme (regarding Income-Tax) should be adopted as a Resolution to be submitted to a Meeting of Business men from the whole of Ulster, to be held in the Ulster Hall at 12 o'clock on Friday, 31st October.

112 Letter from R. M. Liddell, managing director of William Liddell and Co. Ltd., linen manufacturers of Belfast and Lurgan, honorary secretary and treasurer of the Sir Edward Carson Unionist Defence Fund committee, to Carson, 17 January 1912, reporting optimistically on the first meeting of the committee (D 1507/1/1912/1):

Dear Sir Edward—We held our first Committee Meeting of The Sir Edward Carson Unionist Defence Fund yesterday, and after transacting various business in connection with organisation for collection of funds, etc., we passed the papers round to those present, and [I] am pleased to say that altogether, with a few subscriptions promised by some friends outside the Committee, the total promised amounted to £10,200.

It was decided at the Meeting not to ask for subscriptions for 1913 just yet; but to get in all we possibly can now for 1912, and on Friday next our Executive and Organising Committees meet, and we then get down to solid work for tapping the various trades etc., in Ulster.

I saw James Craig after our Meeting was over, and as there was a question cropped up in reference to conflicting with the General Fund, I asked him to write you about it, so that you could send us a letter which would be placed before our Executive Sub-Committee if possible on Friday, and clear the air over the question which arose.

You will see from enclosed that cheques are to be made payable either to you or Lord Dunleath, and I would feel obliged if you would kindly ask your Secretary to send me particulars of any cheques which may go direct to you, so that we can strike those names off our list, and not canvass them further.

I believe you told me you had received a cheque from Mr. Robert Thompson, M.P. He was not present at our Meeting yesterday, but if he has sent you a subscription it will be necessary for me to have a note of it, so that our canvassers may not get after him again; and as everybody who is subscribing to this Fund is receiving an official receipt, I presume it will be necessary to send him one also.

It was decided at our Meeting yesterday that no list of the names of the subscribers should be published, and as this turns out to be a most important point bearing on the success of our appeal, it is absolutely essential that all names should be kept secret and not made public.

There are several men, representing large industries like Whiskey, etc., who fear their trade would suffer if their names were made public, and we will do much better by not publishing their names, and must accede to their request.

The money has started to come in to-day, and by the end of the week, and certainly not later than Tuesday next, Lord Dunleath will be able to send you a substantial remittance.

The enclosed form is a copy of what we are using at present, and the wording of this might be slightly altered at Friday's Meeting; but if not, a duplicate of it will be enclosed with our printed appeal, which is being drafted for approval on Friday.

I will endeavour to keep you as well posted as possible, and let you know from time to time how we are getting along; but I know only too well how busy you are, and do not want you to bother replying to or answering any of my letters except I should ask you particularly to let me have an answer to some question of importance.

The only query to be answered in this letter is I think the one in reference to subscriptions paid, or perhaps promised to you direct from Ulster. If promised and not paid, our Organisation will get after them and do our best to collect.

Would you kindly have any replies addressed to this Office, as I am here every day, and will attend to all communications sent to me by you or your Secretary.

> Yours faithfully,
> R. M. Liddell

113 Letter from the 2nd Baron Dunleath, Ballywalter Park, Co. Down, chairman of the Carson Defence Fund committee, to Sir Edward Carson, 19 January 1912, making arrangements for the transfer to Carson of the first sum collected by the committee (D 1507/1/1912/3):

My dear Sir Edward—I understand that you have already been informed that over £10,000 will be subscribed by the Committee and their friends to your Union[ist] Defence Fund. There is a general impression that a much larger sum will be raised than the £24,000 which you mentioned as the amount required to carry on the educational campaign in England & Scotland, on the same scale on which it has recently been conducted. I have instructed the Manager of the Belfast Banking Co. to send to your Bankers £4900 as soon as this sum has been lodged.

Will you kindly write to the Manager giving him the name & address of your Bank. We have made £4900 the amount of first remittance to you, because our Hon Secretary Mr Liddell informed us that £100 had already been sent direct to you.

We intend to commence collecting in Belfast, and the principal commercial towns near Belfast. We cannot tell, yet, whether we can extend our efforts as far as Londonderry & other towns at some distance from Belfast. If County Committees are formed, we shall have to keep in touch with them to prevent over lapping.

I believe that the people connected with the Ulster Industries will supply any money you may require in the course of the next two years. Believe me Yours sincerely

Dunleath

114 Extract, relating to the U.U.C.'s finances, taken from the report of the interview between Sir Wilson Hungerford and members of staff of the N.I.P.R.O., November 1965 (PRB 987):

... During the period 1911–1914 the Liberal Government had the Inland Revenue Department pressing the Ulster Unionist Council for information about its finances. An audited annual balance sheet showing an income and expenditure of about £1,000 was produced by the Ulster Unionist Council to meet the requirements of the Inland Revenue and the real finances were, however, to be found in the Carson Defence Fund which was under the control of Sir James Craig; Sir Wilson had an audited account of the Carson Defence Fund given him by Craig c. 1920. This gave detailed information about contributions and expenditure. Included in this account were contributions from Walter Long for £54,000 (possibly £45,000) which were almost certainly from the Union Defence League in London; there were also substantial contributions from the Banks and leading landowners and industrialists. Over £100,000 was raised, more than half of which was spent on the purchase of 2 ships and guns for the Larne Gun Running. Payments were made through the Belfast Bank and there was never any query about the account being overdrawn; Sir Wilson remembered writing a cheque for £16,000, knowing full well that there was nothing in the Bank Account to cover it. At one stage there was such apprehension about the intentions of the Liberal Government that the funds were placed in a French Bank for safety. Sir James Craig handed over, c. 1922, a cache of money, remaining in his hands from the Carson Defence Fund, to be used as Unionist Party Funds and administered by Andrew Sharman Crawford, W. R. Young and "Johnnie" Andrews. ...

III

The effectiveness of the U.U.C. proved the key to the solving of the two other problems facing Ulster unionism— sustaining a disciplined interest in unionism in Ulster, and convincing the British people of the determination of Ulster unionists not to have home rule. In fact these two problems were interconnected. Ever since the riots in Belfast and other parts of Ulster in the summer of 1886, Ulster unionist leaders had recognised the danger of feelings erupting into senseless violence and discrediting Ulster unionism in the eyes of the British public.

These problems had exercised the Unionist Clubs Council in 1893, when the second home rule bill was about to complete its passage through the house of commons; and had even worried the fiery Major Frederick H. Crawford, the Belfast businessman and gun-runner, in the summer of 1907, when riots, the gravest since 1886, were indirectly sparked off by a dock strike for which James Larkin, the labour leader, was largely responsible. Disaffection among the police at the time of this strike caused the government to draft some 6,000 troops into Belfast for the protection of life and property. This move antagonised the nationalists. On Sunday, 11 August, the military and police were assaulted by a mob in the Cullingtree and Falls Road area—in former years a centre of nationalist disturbance —and the streets had to be cleared by cavalry charges. Although on this occasion protestants were not, as Crawford noted with relief, involved in the rioting, the episode still demonstrated the violence of sectarian feeling in Ulster. To unionist leaders it underlined the need to maintain political discipline, a need which they were acutely aware of at the time of the third home rule bill, 1912–14. For instance, the revived Unionist Clubs Council, which received many suggestions from the various local clubs, spent a good deal of time sifting and discussing them, and tried to dissuade the clubs from taking any action that might provoke sectarian disturbances.

115 Extracts from the minute book of the executive committee of the U.C.C., 25 April, 27 July, 8 and 18 (two meetings) August 1893, expressing the committee's concern for the maintenance of law and order in Belfast, and discussing the clubs' contribution thereto, as the second home rule bill completed its passage through the house of commons (D 1327/1/2):

(a)

The meeting was convened to consider the action, if any, of the U. Clubs with regard to disturbances at Queen's Island.

The following resolution proposed by Rev. R. R. Kane, S.L.P., & seconded by Robt. Tennent Esqr. J.P., was carried unanimously.

"That we are much gratified to receive the most reassuring reports of the state of feeling in our City, and we implore our friends everywhere to use their best efforts to restore our perfect tranquillity, and we hereby express our cordial readiness to assist in every way in our power in the maintenance of peace and order, which we believe to be of vital consequence to our Unionist Cause."

(b)

On the motion of Mr. Bristow seconded by Major Price the following resolution was passed unanimously:—

"That the Committees of Unionist Clubs be requested to meet (where considered necessary) to consult as to the best measures to be taken to preserve the peace after the third reading of the Home Rule Bill; also to consider the advisability of organising within each Club (where deemed expedient) a number of members who would endeavour to maintain the peace, as far as possible, within the Club's district."

(c)

At the previous meeting it was resolved not to draw public attention to the possibility of disturbance on the occasion of the Bill passing the third reading stage, but to communicate with the various clubs privately on the subject.

(d)

It was decided that the Clubs should hold meetings and impress upon members that firstly they should keep themselves in check, and then be ready to assist in any way in keeping the peace.

After considerable discussion, on the motion of the President, seconded by Captain Ritchie, J.P., the following resolution was carried unanimously:—

"That this meeting of the Representatives of the Belfast Unionist Clubs resolves to use all the influence of the Belfast Clubs on the side of law and order, and will do everything in their power at all times to maintain the peace of the City."

(e)

The minutes of the previous meeting were read and confirmed, after which the President reported he had had a private interview with Commissioner Singleton and understood from him that the police authorities did not wish the Unionist Clubs as such to assist in quelling any possible disturbance. It would be far more to the purpose to so organise and discipline the Clubs that their members would be prevented from going out into the streets, or hostile territory, where they might become exasperated by the jubilation or taunts of the opposite party. The police would be glad to know of some officers of Clubs to whom they might look for assistance in case of need, and it was stated by the Secretary of one of the Clubs that his assistance had actually been asked by them. But it was felt that it would be a great mistake to wear any kind of distinctive badge. The President urged the thorough organisation of each Club, by subdividing responsibility, and the necessity of influencing members to stay at home.

Several gentlemen addressed the meeting, and discussed the matter at length; finally, on the motion of Mr. Montgomery, seconded by Mr. Ross Bell the following resolution was adopted unanimously:— "That this meeting of representatives of the Belfast Unionist Clubs confirms the resolution passed at its last meeting, and decides to give every assistance to the Constabulary in preserving the peace of the City in whatever way may be found most desirable."

116 *Letter from F. H. Crawford, Wilson Street Works, Belfast, to Major R. W. Doyne of Ashton, Gorey, Co. Wexford, 20 August 1907, discussing the implications of the Belfast strike (D 1700/10):

My dear Major Doyne—I was very pleased to get a letter from you & see by it you are so well.

I am thankful to say our strike troubles are over for the present.

It was simply a political move on the part of a section of the Nationalists to discredit Belfast, connived at by Birrell, to try and shift the searchlight of inquiry from the County Mayo & the South & West. It would have done very well for Birrell if the police had not mutinied, when they did they upset his apple cart & made him change his tune, He was very glad to have the whole affair patched up as quickly as possible.

If it had not been for this the strike would not have been settled yet.

What a blessing all the rioting took place in the Catholic Quarter of the City. This branded the whole thing as a Nationalist movement. Larkin the leader is the grandson of Larkin the Manchester Martyr(?).

I was threatened, not because the strikers had any quarrell [sic] with me, but because of the political work I had done in West Belfast

The whole strike was a big political plot to ruin Belfast trade. The Nationalists are sick of people pointing out to them the Prosperity of Belfast & protestant Ulster, they want to ruin us & this is one move in that direction. The serious part of the business is that they have duped a lot of protestants, who call themselves Independent orangemen, & a few demagogues who love to hear their own voice.

With kindest regards to Mrs. Doyne & yourself from both of us Your sincere friend

Fred. H. Crawford.

117 Extracts from the minute book of the executive committee of the U.C.C., 19 June 1912, 19 February and 23 April 1913, which show how the central committee was guided in its reaction to suggestions from local clubs by its overriding concern to avoid sectarian disturbances (D 1327/1/2):

(a)

The Secretary reported that the following resolution had been received from the Windsor & Stranmillis Club.

Resolution passed at General Committee Meeting, May 13th:—

"That this Meeting of General Committee of the Windsor and Stranmillis Unionist Club considers it advisable in view of the approaching tourist season, with its influx of English and Scottish tourists, that members of all Unionist Clubs in Ireland should wear on all possible occasions their button hole badge, to prove to these visitors the extent of the movement and Ulster's opposition to Home Rule; that copies be sent to Secretary Unionist Clubs of Ireland and to the Clubs in the Central Division of Belfast."

The Secretary was directed to circulate copies of the resolution to Clubs in localities frequented by visitors during the Summer months.

(b)

The following letter received from Cliftonville Unionist Club was read:—

"At a meeting of above Club held on the 14th inst., the following resolution was passed "That it be an instruction to the delegates of this Club on the Ulster Unionist Clubs' Council that at the next meeting of said body they move a resolution calling upon said Council to use its influence with all Protestant employers of labour in Ulster, to get them to dismiss as occasion offers their Home Rule employees"

Mr Swanston (President) and Mr H. T. Whitaker (Secretary) attended the meeting on behalf of the Cliftonville Unionist Club.

Mr Whitaker having placed before the meeting the views of the Club in forwarding the above Resolution, the matter was discussed and it was proposed by Mr G. S. Clark, seconded by Mr W. H. Webb that the Cliftonville Club be asked to withdraw their notice of motion for the annual meeting of the Clubs Council, and that their Secretary be asked to explain to the Club the reasons given by the Executive Committee for not bringing forward the Resolution.

Passed unanimously.

(c)

A circular letter from Mr R. J. Hyndman, assistant secretary of Londonderry Unionist Club, addressed to the Belfast and other Ulster Clubs, on the subject of a proposed rally of the Drilled Sections of Ulster Unionist Clubs to be held in Derry, on a Saturday in the month of June, was read, together with other correspondence on the subject which had passed between Mr Hyndman and the Clubs office.

Mr D. J. Thompson attended, representing Londonderry Unionist Club, and explained that the original idea of his Club was to have a Demonstration of the drilled sections of the North West Clubs in the district from Coleraine to Omagh, but that invitations had been sent to Belfast and other Ulster Clubs to take part.

After a discussion in which Colonel Sharman Crawford, Major F. H. Crawford, Mr Smythe-Edwards and Mr Montgomery took part,

it was proposed by Major F. H. Crawford,

Seconded by Rev David McLaughlin and passed unanimously:—

that a letter be sent to Mr Hyndman, assistant Secretary of Londonderry

Unionist Club, stating it to be the opinion of this Committee that the proposed Demonstration in Derry should be confined to Clubs in a district comprising Derry City, and extending say from Derry to Omagh and Coleraine as at first arranged for: that it should not be confined to drilled sections, and that no rifles or arms should be carried.

That Mr Hyndman should be requested to issue a circular letter to all the Clubs outside the above District which had received his previous circular, withdrawing the invitation to them to attend, and that the Chairman, Colonel Sharman Crawford and Mr B. W. D. Montgomery should prepare a draft circular accordingly.

It was proposed by Mr W. H. Webb.

Seconded by Colonel Sharman Crawford and unanimously

Resolved that a circular be sent to all Clubs directing that in future no step should be taken without previously advising Headquarters.

IV

The problem of directing and sustaining unionist energies was overcome in two ways. In the first place, there were elaborately staged demonstrations.

One such demonstration, which stopped Belfast's tram service for nine and a half hours, was held at the North-East Agricultural Society's show grounds at Balmoral, a suburb of Belfast, on Easter Tuesday, 9 April 1912. It was addressed by Andrew Bonar Law, leader of the unionist party in the house of commons, who urged Ulster to resist home rule and to burst the boom erected by the parliament act; 100,000 men marched past the several platforms; and the solemn proceedings were opened with prayers by the primate of all Ireland and the moderator of the Presbyterian church and the opening of the 90th psalm. 'The spectacular aspect of the meeting had been planned with great care. On entering the grounds the main column divided into two streams passing on either side of the saluting base, and in the centre of the enclosure there was a tower with a 90-foot high flagstaff, on which was broken, at the instant of passing the resolution against home rule, a giant union jack measuring 48 feet by 25 feet, said to be the largest ever woven.' The drama was the result of careful and increasingly efficient planning over a long period by a demonstration sub-committee chaired by Sir James Henderson, proprietor of the *Belfast News-Letter*, and consisting of representatives from the U.U.C., the U.C.C., and the Orange Order. This sub-committee also negotiated the transfer of the Ulster unionists' headquarters to the Old Town Hall, Belfast.

Even more solemn, though less well-minuted, was the signing of Ulster's solemn league and covenant. 28 September 1912 was declared a public holiday by the U.U.C., and the covenant was signed in ceremonies throughout the province. In Belfast it was signed by more than 200,000 men, Carson leading the way in the ceremony. An impressive demonstration, serving as a safety-valve for popular emotion and at the same time to convince the world of the 'solidarity, determination, and self-discipline' of the Ulster protestants, it was conducted in an atmosphere of religious devotion. However it did not necessarily bind the signatories (the lists of whose names are in the N.I.P.R.O.) to eternal opposition to home rule: their obligation was confined to the present crisis, or so at least it was argued both at the time of signing and during the subsequent crises of 1916 and 1920.

118 Extracts from the minute book of the demonstration joint sub-committee, 27 October, 8, 15, 22 December 1911, 12 January, 19, 26 February, 4 March 1912, relating to arrangements for the Easter Tuesday demonstration, 9 April 1912; and the negotiations for the renting of the Old Town Hall, Belfast, as the Ulster unionist head-quarters (D 1327/3/1):

(a) 27 October 1911

Possible sites for the Demonstration on Easter Tuesday, 9 April, were then considered, and Sir James Henderson kindly undertook to interview some of the members of the Corporation with a view of ascertaining the possibility of obtaining the Ormeau Park, and it was decided that the Committee should attend as a Deputation before the Corporation, if Sir James Henderson deemed it necessary. It was left in Sir James Henderson's hands as to when the next meeting of the Committee should be held to receive his report.

Sir James Henderson reported the progress he had made in regard to obtaining the use of the Old Town Hall, and Sir James very kindly promised to make further enquiries with a view of ascertaining what rates were payable on the Hall, and if a letting could be made of a portion of the Building.

(b) 8 December 1911

The Chairman reported as to the negotiations he had with the Town

Clerk and read a letter from him, regarding the taking of the tenancy of the Old Town Hall, and ultimately the following resolution was passed:—

"That we submit an offer to the Belfast Corporation to take a letting of the Old Town Hall for two years, from the 1st. February, 1912, at the yearly rent of £400, free of all rates and taxes, with the option of renewing the tenancy for a third year.

The Corporation to put the Hall in habitable repair and condition, and to put in the necessary plumbing fittings, including those for electric light and gas.

That the following be appointed a deputation to attend the meeting of the Improvement Committee on Tuesday next, and submit such offer:— Sir James Henderson, D.L.; Mr. Lloyd Campbell; Mr. B. W. D. Montgomery; Colonel Sharman-Crawford, D.L.; and Mr. W. R. Young."

The Chairman also reported as to the possibility of obtaining the Ormeau Park for Easter Tuesday, and the matter was held over; Captain Hall kindly undertaking to make further enquiries in regard to the suitability of the North-East Show Grounds.

(c) 15 December 1911

Sir James Henderson reported that a Deputation had attended at the City Hall on the Improvement Committee on Tuesday last, and made an offer to that Committee of £400 a year, free of taxes, for the Town Hall. The Chairman also read a letter from the Town Clerk declining the offer, and after consideration the following resolution was passed; on the motion of Mr. Sclater, seconded by Captain Craig:—

"That we renew our offer to the Belfast Corporation, but increasing the amount of rent offered to £550, including all rates and taxes, and that the former deputation be asked to again see the Improvement Committee and submit this offer".

Sir James Henderson very kindly undertook to make the necessary arrangements for the reception, by the Improvement Committee, of the Deputation.

Captain Hall reported as to the interview he had had with the Secretary of the North-East Agricultural Association with the view of getting that ground for Easter Tuesday, and after discussion it was decided to Ask Colonel Crawford to negotiate with the Association, with a view of ascertaining what terms the Association would let grounds for easter Tuesday.

It was arranged that Mr. Bates should submit a plan to an Engineer with a view of ascertaining as to the accommodation which the grounds afforded?

(d) 22 December 1911

Sir James Henderson reported that the Deputation had attended at the City Hall on the Improvement Committee, on Tuesday last, and made an offer to that Committee of £550 a year, free of taxes, for the Old Town Hall, and that this offer was accepted.

The Secretary read a report from Mr. Calwell dealing with the suitability of the North-East Show Grounds, and reported that he had written to the Secretary of the North-East Agricultural Association asking on what terms that Association would be prepared to hire the grounds to the Committee on Easter Tuesday? It was decided to appoint the following as a Committee to attend at the Meeting of the Association when this matter would be brought up:— Sir James Henderson, D.L.; Colonel Wallace, D.L.; Messrs W. H. H. Lyons, D.L.; B. W. D. Montgomery, W. R. Young, and Lloyd Campbell. Mr. Bates was requested to communicate with Colonel Crawford with a view of endeavouring to hold a meeting of the Associations, if possible, at an early date.

(e) 12 January 1912

Sir James Henderson reported that the recommendation of the Improvement Committee had been confirmed by the Corporation at their last meeting.

Colonel Crawford announced that he had arranged with the North-East Agricultural Association for the use of their grounds for Easter Tuesday for £75 and an indemnity against all damage.

The following were appointed as a Sub-Committee to take charge of the management of the Old Town Hall, including the purchase of furniture and the appointment of a suitable caretaker:—Sir James Henderson, Mr. Lloyd Campbell, Colonel Wallace, Mr. Bates, Captain Hall, and Major McCammon.

(f) 19 February 1912

Captain Hall explained what had been done with regard to the Railway arrangements, and also as regards the Show Grounds at Balmoral, and these were approved of.

It was unanimously decided to have a badge, practically identical with the one used at the Ulster Unionist Convention in 1892.

It was unanimously decided to send an advertisement of the Demonstration to all Unionist papers in Ireland. Sir Jas. Henderson advised the Committee that a sum of six shillings should cover the prepayment of such advertisement.

(g) 26 February 1912

It was decided to accept Messrs McCaw, Stevenson & Orr's Badge, and it was left in the hands of Sir James Henderson and Mr. Bates to order one thousand at the best terms possible. It was also decided to allow Messrs McCaw, Stevenson & Orr to sell it to the outside public, should it be so desired.

Mr. Bates read the correspondence he had with Sir John B. Lonsdale and Mr. Craig, regarding visiting Members of Parliament, and Mr. Clark kindly consented to see some of the English Unionist Members on Monday.

The Map of the route was submitted, and it was arranged that the matter should be left in Major McCammon and Captain Hall's hands.

Captain Hall reported, regarding the replies of some of the Newspapers as to the price paid for the recent advertisement, and it was decided not to take any further action for the present.

The Secretaries were instructed to form and summon a Stewards & Traffic Committee.

(h) 4 March 1912

Resolved:— That the following arrangements—as submitted to the Committee be approved and confirmed:—

1. PLATFORMS

That Mr. R. I. Calwell be requested to proceed with specifications for platforms in the Show Ground as under:—

(A) A covered platform in the judging rings (marked A) triangular in plan, capable of seating 300 persons. Accomodation [*sic*] to be provided under this platform for a carriage.

(B) In front of centre of Grand Stand:— A covered platform (marked B) extending across the existing pathway—semi-circular fronted, with press table and seats out-rigged on Canti levers [*sic*].

A thoroughfare with 7'0" head room to be provided under this platform.

(C) In rear of Deramore Hall (marked C):— An observation platform height sufficient to allow a clear view of the judging rings and jumping enclosure. Top of platform to accommodate 100 persons. To be provided with two flights of steps.

2. SPEECHES

That speeches shall be delivered from platforms A and B only.

3. MARCH PAST

That the troops shall march past the leaders on platform A, in four columns of 4's. The outer Columns shall, after passing the saluting point, wheel outwards and disperse over the judging rings. That the outer columns of 4's shall continue in formation and march between the Deramore and Harberton Halls to the Jumping Enclosure by gate narked [*sic*] X, and there disperse—

Gates Y and Z to be left for the general public.

4. ROADWAY AND RAILS

That "corduroy" roads, constructed of old sleepers, be laid across the grass in the judging rings for the marching columns, and that rails be erected to prevent the crowd pressing upon the columns. That the rails surrounding the track in the jumping enclosure be removed where necessary.

5. ENTRANCES

That the public be admitted only by gates marked A and E. That the marching columns enter by gates B–C– and D. That the Central gate (C) be enlarged to admit two columns of 4's That the turnstiles be removed:

6. ROUTE OF PROCESSION

That arrangements be made with the G.N.R. to detrain all parties arriving by their line at Dunmurry —(? or at Derriaghy or Lambeg) that the troops march in two columns of 4's from the city and also from Dunmurry—one column on each side of the road—via Lisburn Road—the centre of the roadway to be kept clear for ordinary traffic—footpassengers to keep to the footpaths. The head of all four columns (No. 1 District Belfast Grand Lodge leading the right hand, and Templepatrick (Premier) Unionist Club the left hand column coming from City direction) to be in position 10 yards from their respective gates of the Show Ground, ready to advance at 11.a.m. sharp.

That the Police and tramway authorities be approached with a view to securing that the general public shall proceed to the Show Grounds via Malone Rd and Balmoral Avenue: that the tram service in Lisburn Rd be suspended from 8.30 am. till 2pm, and that notices be posted in LISBURN, and also at the junction of Lisburn and Malone roads (with direction posts where necessary) asking ordinary traffic to take the Old Lisburn Road via HILLHALL—

7. CATERING

That no intoxicants be sold on the grounds. That the Caterers be allotted: —the Londonderry Hall—the wooden sheds in judging rings—cart shed—and Grand Stand bars.

That luncheon be provided by the Committee for Press and distinguished visitors in the Dining Rooms (? and in one section of Grand Stand Bars.).

8. DECORATIONS

That the only decorations required in or about the Show Grounds shall be Union Jacks hoisted on the centre and corners of Grand Stands, and at each entrance gate—small trophies and canopies on stands A and B.

That a large flagstaff be erected at Stand C, and the largest possible Union Jack be provided for same.

9. CARRIAGE ENCLOSURE AND ENTRANCE FOR TICKET HOLDERS

That the building site outside the Show Grounds be used as a carriage enclosure—charge for standing private carriages and motors to be 5/– each.

That a footpath be provided outside the Show Grounds enclosure from Gate A to a small entrance to be constructed at point marked F.

That Stand tickets 250 at 5/– each be handed to the Ulster Womens Unionist Council for the use of their members.

10. INSTRUCTION TO SECRETARIES

That the Secretaries be instructed to proceed with the following works:—
1. Erection of Stands.
2. Hire of sleepers.

3. Erection of rails.

4. Erection of flagstaff at Stand C. and provision of large size Union Jack.

5. Decorations.

6. Footpath to Stand Entrance.

Arising out of the above, it be now resolved:—

1. That a "Traffic and Stewards Committee" be formed, representative of all bodies taking part in the procession.

That this Committee be instructed to make all arrangements with regard to providing and instructing Stewards for the Show Grounds, carriage enclosure, gates, streets, and all stations: also to detailing the streets to be used and positions to be taken up by the various bodies joining the procession.

2. That a Catering Committee be formed, with full powers to deal with the contractors and settle all matters connected with Catering.

3. That a Hospitality Committee be appointed to deal with accomodation [*sic*] of M.P's and distinguished visitors.

With reference to para 1 of above:—Mr Geo. S. Clark said that it was the opinion of those M.P.s and others whom he had had the opportunity of consulting in London that it would be advisable that speeches be delivered from at least 4 platforms.

It was resolved to utilise the "Observation Platform" as well as the "Grand Stand" and "March Past" Platforms for speakers, and also to erect an additional platform where recommended by the Secretaries in consultation with Mr Calwell.

Mr Macmillan (Ulster Menu Company) was in attendance, and the subject of Catering was discussed.

It was resolved to appoint the following Sub-Committees, with powers in each case to add to their numbers:—

CATERING COMMITTEE   Mr W. H. H. Lyons—Major F. Crawford.

HOSPITALITY COMMITTEE Col Sharman Crawford—Mr Sclater
Mr G. S. Clark. Mr. W. R. Young.

SPEAKERS COMMITTEE Sir J. Henderson Rt Hon Thos Sinclair
Mr J. R. Fisher Mr G. S. Clark

PRESS COMMITTEE Mr G. R. Reid

119

Copy of Ulster's solemn league and covenant signed by Sir Edward Carson. (D 1496/3):

Ulster's
Solemn League and Covenant.

Being convinced in our consciences that Home Rule would be disastrous to the material well-being of Ulster as well as of the whole of Ireland, subversive of our civil and religious freedom, destructive of our citizenship and perilous to the unity of the Empire, we, whose names are underwritten, men of Ulster, loyal subjects of His Gracious Majesty King George V., humbly relying on the God whom our fathers in days of stress and trial confidently trusted, do hereby pledge ourselves in solemn Covenant throughout this our time of threatened calamity to stand by one another in defending for ourselves and our children our cherished position of equal citizenship in the United Kingdom and in using all means which may be found necessary to defeat the present conspiracy to set up a Home Rule Parliament in Ireland. ¶ And in the event of such a Parliament being forced upon us we further solemnly and mutually pledge ourselves to refuse to recognise its authority. ¶ In sure confidence that God will defend the right we hereto subscribe our names. ¶ And further, we individually declare that we have not already signed this Covenant.

The above was signed by me at _Belfast_.
"Ulster Day," Saturday, 28th September, 1912.

Edward Carson

——— God Save the King. ———

120 *Letter from A. Duffin to the joint secretaries of the Ulster day (the demonstration joint) sub-committee, 8 October 1912, insisting that the pledge of the covenant applied only to 'the present situation' (Mic 127/14):

Dear Sir—I wish to put on record for myself and others taking the same view that, in signing the Ulster covenant, we read it as a pledge applying only to the present situation, which is not quite clearly expressed in its terms.

I agree entirely as to the present bill and unconstitutional procedure which is attempted to pass it, but in the event of some measure of home rule becoming law after having been fairly submitted to the constituencies of the United Kingdom I hold myself free to exercise my own judgment as to what course I pursue. Yours faithfully,

ADAM DUFFIN

V

The second way in which energies were sustained and disciplined was through the Ulster Volunteer Force. In January 1912 some Ulster unionists had begun openly to raise and drill a military force, keeping within the letter of the law by applying for and obtaining the sanction of the local magistrates. (Any two justices of the peace could authorise drilling and other military operations within the area of their jurisdiction provided that the object was to render citizens more efficient for the purpose of maintaining the constitution of the United Kingdom as established.)

Towards the end of 1912, the standing committee of the U.U.C. decided that these volunteers should be united into a single body known as the Ulster Volunteer Force. This decision was announced at the annual meeting of the council in January 1913, and recruitment was limited to 100,000 men who had signed the covenant and were between the ages of 17 and 65. In July 1913 Lt-colonel Sir George Richardson was appointed commander of the force. Directed by a strong headquarters staff which issued frequent and detailed orders, the force was, as described below, organised into county divisions, which were supervised by county committees (complete with secretary), and further divided into regiments and battalions. In addition, there were a number of supporting corps: the medical corps, motor car corps, nursing corps, Ulster signalling and despatch rider corps, and the Ballymena and Enniskillen horse. Altogether the U.V.F. enrolled about 90,000 men, who drilled with or without arms in orange halls or, weather permitting, in the parks and demesnes of sympathetic landowners. It was an economical organisation (gunrunning apart), whose finances were arranged by a military finance committee. Perhaps the most striking quality of the U.V.F. was its thoroughness, as the work of its intelligence service in Co. Antrim shows.

In the N.I.P.R.O. there is a wide range of material dealing with the volunteers (extensively used by Dr. A. T. Q. Stewart in his stimulating book, *The Ulster crisis* [1967]); but the growth and problems of the organisation can be seen in material relating to the force in Co. Down and to the second battalion of the South Down regiment. The decision to organise the volunteers in Co. Down was made on 20 December 1912 by a small group of prominent landowners, professional men and businessmen. By 7 October 1913, 6,058 men had enrolled in the four Down regiments, and eventually the figure reached 11,000. One of the members of the county committee was Captain Roger Hall, J.P., D.L., of Narrow Water, Warrenpoint. Formerly a captain in the Royal Irish Fusiliers, he commanded the second battalion of the South Down regiment of the U.V.F., and some of his papers are deposited in the N.I.P.R.O. They illustrate a number of points: the growth and popularity of the force, yet the way control was kept in the hands of the 'upper classes'; the importance of the unionist clubs as a basis for the local organisation of the force; the rigorous selection procedures, the drilling in and out of doors, and the discipline of the force; the personal rivalries that complicated the running of the force; and the way in which headquarters's orders were translated into practice, resulting by the summer of 1914 in the open carrying of arms.

121 Printed leaflet describing the organisation of the U.V.F., issued sometime in 1913 (D 1327/4/9):

The Ulster Volunteers will be organised by Counties into County

Divisions. Each Division will consist of a variable number of Regiments, according to the strength of the Volunteers, and each Regiment will comprise, for the same reason, a variable number of Battalions.

The Regiment will thus take the place of the Brigade, and will be commanded by a Colonel with an Adjutant as Staff Officer.

Each Battalion of the Regiment will be commanded by a Major, or Lieut.-Colonel, with an Adjutant, and, if it can be arranged, 3 Battalions will constitute the Regiment.

The Companies to form these Battalions will vary numerically, according to the method adopted for linking the various localities together, to form, in the first instance, the Company, and afterwards the Battalion.

EXAMPLE OF ORGANIZATION OF A BATTALION:

2nd Battalion..Regiment.

District.	Locality.	No. Enr.	No. on Parade.		
A.	1	123	80	4 Sects.	A. Co.
B.	1	98	70	4 Sects.	B. Co.
C.	1	56	40	2 Sects.	} C. Co.
	2	66	50	3 Sects.	
D.	1	76	40	2 Sects.	} D. Co.
	2	50	50	3 Sects.	
	1	37	30	1 Sect.	
E.	2	35	35	2 Sects.(?) } E. Co.	
	3	39	35	1 Sect.	
	1	54	42	2 Sects.	
F.	2	36	30	1 Sect. } F. Co.	
	3	70	25	1 Sect.	
G.	1	132	50	3 Sects.	} G. Co.
	2	46	36	2 Sects.	
H.	1	83	60	3 Sects.	H. Co.
		1,001	663 [*sic*]		

This is the actual organization of a certain County Battalion, the Districts instead of being named are lettered, and the Localities instead of being named are numbered.

NOTES.

1. Ascertain the proposed names of the Officers to Command the Companies, also ascertain if Section and Squad Leaders have been appointed.

2. Note how it is proposed that Localities should be linked together to form Companies, and Districts to form Battalions.

3. In order to distinguish the different Regiments, it has practically been decided to have an armlet with the name of the Regiment and Battalion, thus:— $\frac{\text{U.V.F.}}{\text{CAVAN}}$ 2 —means 2nd Battalion, Cavan Regiment. The armlets will be khaki canvas, with strap attachment, printing in black, and it is proposed that one thin black line through the armlet will denote a Squad Leader, two thin black lines a Section Commander, and three thin black lines Serjeant-Majors and others. Officers' Arm Badges to be Red Canvas.

4. What Musketry arrangements, if any, are made in the County? Any open Ranges or 30 yards Ranges available for practice with Service Rifle?

5. Is there anyone in the County who would be able to undertake Local Army Service Corps duties, etc.?

122 Statement for the military finance committee of the amounts provisionally sanctioned by J. Craig for the U.V.F. for the year beginning 1 August 1913 (D 1327/4/23):

ULSTER SIGNALLING & DESPATCH RIDING CORPS

Estimated expenses for year	350	0	0		
Pay. per annum.	200	0	0	550 0 0

U.V.F. HEADQUARTERS.

Pay per annum	400	0	0		
Provision of quarters for G.O.C. and C.S.O. and Staff, per annum.	540	0	0		
Travelling Expenses.	200	0	0	1140 0 0

COUNTIES.

Pay of County Instructors—					
14 Counties @ £52 per annum	728	0	0		
Travelling Expenses Co. Instructors.—					
9 Counties @ £26 per annum	234	0	0		
5 „ @ £6 „ „	30	0	0		
Remuneration of County Secretaries— @ rate of £15 first 2000 enrolled, and £4 per additional thousand.					
Estimated amount say	350	0	0	1342 0 0

HEADQUARTERS OFFICE EXPENSES.

Salaries, say	90	0	0

Ulster unionist organisation at the time of the third home rule bill

Office Expenses, say	100 0 0	
Office Furniture, say	100 0 0	
Rent	50 0 0	
Lighting	10 0 0	
Printing and Stationery, say	100 0 0	
Postages, say	25 0 0	
Sundries, say	100 0 0	575 0 0

Total. £3607 0 0

U. V. F.
AUTHORIZED EXPENDITURE.

County.	County Secretary's remuneration.	Pay of County Instructor.	Travelling Expenses of Instructor.	Total.
	£ s. d.	£ s. d.	£ s. d.	£ s. d.
ANTRIM . . .	35 0 0	52 0 0	26 0 0	113 0 0
ARMAGH. . .	24 0 0	52 0 0	26 0 0	102 0 0
BELFAST N. . .	35 0 0	52 0 0	6 10 0	93 10 0
„ S. . .	31 0 0	52 0 0	6 10 0	89 10 0
„ E. . .	31 0 0	52 0 0	6 10 0	89 10 0
„ W. . .	19 0 0	52 0 0	6 10 0	77 10 0
CAVAN . . .	15 0 0	52 0 0	26 0 0	93 0 0
DERRY CITY . .	19 0 0	52 0 0	6 10 0	77 10 0
DOWN . . .	31 0 0	52 0 0	26 0 0	109 0 0
DONEGAL . .	15 0 0	52 0 0	26 0 0	93 0 0
FERMANAGH . .	19 0 0	52 0 0	26 0 0	97 0 0
LONDONDERRY CO.	23 0 0	52 0 0	26 0 0	101 0 0
MONAGHAN . .	15 0 0	52 0 0	26 0 0	93 0 0
TYRONE . . .	27 0 0	52 0 0	26 0 0	105 0 0
TOTAL . . .	339 0 0	728 0 0	266 10 0	1333 10 0

123

Extract from the minute book of the Co. Down committee of the U.V.F., recording the first meeting of that committee at the Old Town Hall, Belfast, 20 December 1912 (D 1327/4/1):

Present:

Lord Dunleath, Dr Knight & Rev Mr Wright representing North Down

Capt Holt Waring D.L. Messrs John Graham & Jas McIlroy,, West ,,

Viscount Bangor & Mr S. H. Hall-Thompson ,, East ,,

Capt Roger Hall D.L. Messrs A. Morrow & C. H. Murland ,, South ,,

A letter of apology was received from Jas Cleland J.P.

Lord Dunleath was unanimously appointed Chairman.

Proposed by Capt Waring & seconded by Mr Hall Thompson and passed that Chas. H. Murland undertake the duties of Hon[orary] Sec[retary] of Co. Committee as a temporary measure pending the appointment of a permanent secretary

Mr Hall Thompson asked to be informed as to the qualifications of the members of the Force & as to whether they were to be picked men, Dr. Knight & C. H. Murland also pressed the question & Mr Edward Sclater having entered the meeting said that his impression was that all within the age limits who had signed the Covenant, should be enrolled and out of these should be picked those who were able-bodied & willing to bear arms. The general feeling of the meeting was that only those who had drilled or were willing to drill & to bear arms should be enrolled & a resolution to that effect was carried unanimously.

It was resolved that discretionary powers should be given to Divisional Representatives to increase their numbers from three to four if desirable. Five County Representatives [on the central committee in Belfast] were then elected viz:—Viscount Bangor, Lord Dunleath, Capt Waring D.L. Rev Dr Wright & C. H. Murland

Colonel Wallace & Col Sharman-Crawford entered the meeting & C. H. Murland asked for a ruling as to the qualification of members of the Force & they gave an authoritative reply that only those men were to be enrolled who, in addition to being within the age limits & having signed the Covenant were also willing to drill (or have drilled) & to bear arms.

Lord Bangor asked Col. Wallace were arms to be issued to the members of the force & when? Col. Wallace replied that [if] any member of the U.V.F. asked this question, he should be told that arms would be issued from Headquarters when considered necessary Col. Sharman-Crawford added that arms would not necessarily be issued to every member of the U.V.F.

Enrolment forms O. Form C1 & O Form C2 were issued to the Divisional Representatives with a view to starting the enrolment at once & the proceedings terminated.

124

'O Form. H.1.', being a return of the members of the Co. Down committee of the U.V.F., 23 December 1912 (D 1327/4/18):

NAME	OCCUPATION	ADDRESS
COUNTY REPRESENTATIVES		
Lord Dunleath Chairman	Gentleman	Ballywalter Park, Ballywalter N[orth]
Lord Bangor	do	Castleward, Downpatrick E[ast]
Holt Waring D.L.	do	Waringstown W[est]
Rev Dr Wright	Presbyterian minister	Newtownards N[orth]
Chas. H. Murland	Flax Spinner	Annsborough S[outh]
DIVISIONAL REPRESENTATIVES		
Captain Roger Hall	Gentleman	Narrow Water Warrenpoint S[outh]
S. H. Hall-Thompson	Manufacturer	Drum House, Dunmurry E[ast]
James McIlroy	Baker	Rathfriland Street, Banbridge W[est]
John Graham	Contractor	Dromore W[est]
Andrew Morrow	Gentleman	Windsor Hill, Rathfriland S[outh]
Dr Knight	Medical Practitioner	Donaghadee N[orth]
James Cleland	Gentleman	Tobar Mhuire, Crossgar E[ast]

COUNTY SECRETARY (pro. tem)

Chas. H. Murland

125

Letter from J. A. Orr, 11 Merchants Quay, Newry, Newry district representative for the 2nd battalion South Down regiment of the U.V.F., to R. Hall, 20 January 1913, describing the progress of enrolment in the district (D 1540/3/5):

Dear Sir—Just a line to report progress in connection with Ulster Volunteer Force. I got your letter brought before the Newry District L[oyal]. O[range]. L[odge] and they appointed the W[orshipful]. M[aster]. of each Lodge as a committee to confer with your humble [servant], we had a meeting and divided the District into 6 Localities viz Tinkerhill, Creeve Newry 1st. & 2nd. Altnaveigh and Mullaghglass the two last named are in Co Armagh but belong to the Newry District I appointed Leaders in 5 of the divisions and left the other Leadership open for the present as I think it would be better to go out and make arrangements in the division. I attended Altnaveigh on last Friday night for the first meeting and got 25 volunteers but there is [sic] about 15 more who could not attend that night I was

231

thinking of enrolling all good men I could get in each Locality about 150 in all and when they are drilled if there was [sic] too many I could pick whatever number was required. please say if this will meet with your approval. I am arranging for each Locality being drilled weekly and once a month having one combined drill in Newry if I can get a suitable place. You might send me on some more forms both of declaration and enrolment and when completed I will return them to you. Yours faithfully

Joseph A. Orr.

P.S I think all will be in working order before end of week

J. A. Orr.

126 Letter from Orr to Hall, 1 October 1913, complaining about the attitude of the Newry Unionist Club towards the control of the U.V.F. there (D 1540/3/12):

Dear Sir—There was a Committee meeting of the Unionist Club held here last night, and they decided to take over control of the Newry Volunteer Force, they also decided that there was no call to appoint leaders of localities, as that arrangement was done away with when each Squad elected there [sic] leader, I could not follow them in that argument, would you kindly let me know if it is so and what position I now stand in as I took it I was appointed District Representative of Newry under your Supervision if the Unionist Club is to be in charge would it not be better for me to hand them over all declarations &c. this I will be pleased to do on hearing from you.

There are 268 volunteers signed on in Newry up to date and I am getting them filled in on enrollment [sic] form[s] and [will] have them ready for you in a day or two.

Mr. Moorhead had a meeting in Sheepbridge Orange Hall to raise a Force there was [sic] 45 attended and he asked me to go out on Friday night to enroll them, (this is a place I went to twice but could not get a meeting) as he consented to act as leader of locality I told him I would be pleased to do so.

I herewith enclose you Mr. Maitland's receipt for the parcel you sent up, which I hope will meet with your approval Yours truly

Joseph A. Orr

127 Letter from J. M. Boyle, solicitor of 38 Newry Hill Street, Newry, a U.V.F. company commander, to Hall, 9 October 1913, explaining the attitude and importance of the Newry Unionist Club to the U.V.F. (D 1540/3/16A):

Dear Capt. Hall—I have your letter and appreciate the honour of your selecting me as a Company Commander, and will do my best to fill the position satisfactorily.

I have a copy of the little book and note as to organization which should be done at once, though there will be difficulty in allocating the fresh recruits coming in.

I may say that no person wishes to interfere with Mr. Orr's working in the slightest, but only to assist him, and anything else is purely imagination on his part.

The U.V.F. merely existed in name here until Sir Edward Carson's letter to Unionist Clubs was received when the Newry Club called a general meeting to enrol Volunteers and get to work immediately, at which Meeting 98 members enrolled. It is solely due to the Officials of the Newry Club that the movement here has been such a success as it is, and it is the Club who has organised the drilling and other matters. One of our Drill Instructors was giving trouble, and the Committee wished to deal with him under our Rules (copy of which I enclose) when Mr Orr raised the question that the U.V.F. was separate and dintinct [*sic*] from the Club and had nothing whatever to do with same.

Of course we contested this view but were quite satisfied if some person in authority would undertake to deal with any breaches of discipline.

Since then the graver matter of the band and the same drill instructor's conduct on that occasion has arisen which Mr Nesbitt has written you about.

Mr Orr and I went to Benagh last night and signed on 28 there which will very soon treble itself.

We had a great turn out of nearly 200 at Carnmeen. Yours sincerely,

J. Moore Boyle.

128 Letter from R. Nesbitt, adjutant to the 2nd battalion South Down regiment, to Hall, 8 October 1913, reporting an incident involving indiscipline on the part of an instructor in the Newry volunteers (D 1540/3/14):

Sir—An unfortunate incident occurred last Friday night during a route march of the Newry Volunteers to Bessbrook.

The Local Band came with us & I instructed them as to the road to take & I was surprised when I found that they passed by the turning arranged—when I went up to the Leader of the Band he informed me they would go on to the "Pump" a little further on & as we were entering the Village of Bessbrook I consented—A policeman (Bessbrook) appeared on the scene shortly afterwards & informed me he had been requested by the principal Unionist Leaders in the Village viz:—Mr Smith, Secty. Unionist Club & Mr McKnight District Grand Master, Orangemen & others to ask me not to march the Volunteers to this "Pump" as it was "out of bounds" neither parties Unionist or Nationalist being allowed there so I went up to the Band Leader & asked him to halt the band but they would not do so and said they would go to the "Pump" & very threatening language was used to me & I was told I had no control over the Band (which I admit) & consigned to "Hades" etc etc.

I immediately wheeled the Volunteers to the left down a side road & halted them, the Band going straight ahead—There was some grumbling in the ranks about the Band & I got the opinion of three Committee Members viz. Messrs Agnew, Ferris & Mullan as to the course to be taken—they unanimously decided not to wait for the band coming back but to march back without it (I might mention that a few men of the front section went on with the Band)—I turned the Battn. about, right-wheel & marched back accordingly

Instructor Morrow called on the men to fall out & follow the Band inciting them to disobey orders (really mutiny) but I am proud to say when I called the Vols. to stand steady & obey my orders not a single Volunteer fell out showing splendid discipline of which any Line Regt. might feel proud— It appears to have been a pre-arranged affair by the Band & we would be well rid of them & also any others refusing to obey orders.

I am very sorry to have to bring this to your notice & for troubling you with such a long letter but I think it is necessary so that you may decide the matter—

The Volunteers are marching to Carnmeen tonight on the kind invitation of Mr. Moorhead—

We will have three Armagh Pipers with us. Yours obediently

Robt. Nesbitt

129 Letter from Nesbitt to Hall, 29 October 1913, reporting on the progress of drilling and other exercises (D 1540/3/21):

Sir—I have come to the conclusion that Mr. David McCrum would make the most suitable Sergt Major for the Newry Battn. and respectfully suggest that you should appoint him.

The B.S.A's are in great demand at present Monday & Thursday nights and Wednesday afternoons—

If you could let me have say a dozen more service rifles in addition to the five we already have they would prove useful as only four men can be instructed at one time in the rifle exercises at present & it is very slow work.

The squad organisation is nearly completed.

I am drilling a new detachment at Creeve Orange Hall on Wednesday nights which Mr Mullan has raised, last Wednesday was the first night & we had 47 men present & enrolled all new members I expect a full company will be formed soon.

Another recruit to the Newry Volunteers today (Mr. Robert Sands) I heard that he was only waiting to be asked to join & informed Mr. Mullan who interviewed & enlisted him accordingly. I shall be glad to hear from you if you approve of McCrum as S.M. We are working away at rifle exercises, skirmishing signals etc the only drawback is want of space, the drill hall is not even high enough, but everything is working nicely. Yours obediently

Robert Nesbitt

P.S. The Drill Hall is open every night except Saturday & Sunday

130 A corrected version of 'O Form. H. 2.' for Co. Down, being a return by division, locality and district, of the numbers enrolled in the U.V.F. in the county, 7 October 1913 (D 1327/4/19):

DIVISION: NORTH   NO. ENROLLED: 1621

LOCALITY	NO. ENR.	DISTRICT	NO. ENR.
Donaghdee [sic] Town	72	Donaghadee 1 Coy	94
Ballyhay	22		
Holywood Town	205	Holywood 2 Coys	325
Knocknagoney	21		
Craigavad	35		
Cultra	39		
Ballykeel	25		
Princetown	119	Bangor 5 Coys	550
Helen's Bay	42		
Bangor Town	172		
Conlig	34		
Ballyholme	127		
Cotton	56		
Newtownards Town	322	Newtownards 3 Coys	322
Comber Town	177	Comber 2 Coys	177
Ballywalter	85	Upper Ards 1 Coy	103
Kirkistown	18		
Portaferry Town	50	Portaferry	50
			1621

DIVISION: SOUTH   NO. ENROLLED: 1336

LOCALITY	NO. ENR.	DISTRICT	NO. ENR.
Creeve	14	Newry	39
Altnaveigh	25		
Warrenpoint	36	Warrenpoint	103
Narrow Water	20		
Rostrevor	47		
Kilkeel Town	132	Kilkeel	352
Ballinran	79		
Derryoge	21		
Brackney	20		
Cranfield	25		
Maghereagh	25		
Ballymagough	25		
Glenloughan	25		
Ballymartin	100	Newcastle	413
Annalong	105		
Newcastle Town	66		
Bryansford	67		
Castlewellan	40		
Ballywillwill	20		
Aghlisnafin	15		
Rathfriland	289	Rathfriland	360
Ballybrick	48		
Annahunshigo	23		
Katesbridge	—		
Corbet	—		
Ballyroney	—		
Benraw	—		
Tyrella	69		1267

235

DIVISION: EAST   NO. ENROLLED: 1106

LOCALITY	NO. ENR.	DISTRICT	NO. ENR.
Seaforde	15		
Clough	12		
Drumaroad	7		
Drumcaw	24	Seaforde	73
Tullymurry	8		
Castlenavan	7		
Dundrum Town	50	Kilmegan	50
Downpatrick Town	63		
Hollymount	32	Downpatrick	132
Woodgrange	37		
Ardglass	23		
Killough	25	Ardglass	69
Ballyclander	21		
Ballyculter	27		
Strangford	16	Ballyculter	62
Castleward	19		
Crossgar	121	Crossgar	121
		Listooder	50?
Ballynahinch Town	197		
Drumaness	75	Ballynahinch	272
Drumbeg	29		
Drumbo	22		
Ballyskeagh	36	Drumbo	200
Edenderry	22		
Purdysburn	19		
Tullynacross	72		
Duneight	8	Deneight	8
Killyleagh	69	Killyleagh	69?
			1037

DIVISION: WEST   NO. ENROLLED: 1995

LOCALITY	NO. ENR.	DISTRICT	NO. ENR.
Magherana	41		
Tullyherron	59		
Kinghill	23	Waringstown	263
Donaghcloney	140		
Dunbarton	97		
Gilford Town	35		
The Park	18	Gilford	207
Tullylish	32		
Ballymacanallen	25		
Banbridge	700	Banbridge	700
Glasker	25		
Caskinn	21		
Creevy	6		
Legananny	12	Loughbrickland	190
Derrydrummuck	8		
Loughbrickland	118		
		Dromore	252?
		Hillsborough	232?
Springhill	15		
Magheralin	36		
Kilmore	8	Magheralin	81
Ballynagarrick	22		
Moira	70	Moira	70
			1995

131

Justices' certificate, 16 December 1913, granting an application by R. Hall, on behalf of the 2nd battalion South Down regiment, for permission to drill etc. (D 1540/3/27D):

I, Roger Hall being the Commander of the 2nd Battalion, SOUTH DOWN Regiment of the ULSTER VOLUNTEER FORCE, am authorized on behalf of the members thereof to apply to you for lawful authority to them to hold meetings for the purpose of training and drilling themselves, and of being trained and drilled to the use of arms for the purpose of practising Military exercises, movements, and evolutions.

And I am authorized on their behalf to give the assurance that they desire this authority as faithful Subjects of His Majesty the King, and their undertaking that such authority is sought and will be used by them only to make them more efficient Citizens for the purpose of maintaining the Constitution of the United Kingdom as now established and protecting their rights and liberties thereunder.

We, being two Justices of the Peace in and for Co. Down hereby give to the members of the above 2nd. Battn. S Down Regt. the Authority for which application is above made, and authorize them to act accordingly thereunder.

16th day of December 1913   E. Pedlow J.P.

J. E. Connor J.P.

132

Report by R. Nesbitt on a 'mobilisation parade state' held by the 2nd battalion South Down regiment, 24 April 1914 (D 1540/3/37C):

"A"	Coy (Newry)	(1.55 a.m 25th.)	all ranks		79
"B"	„ „	„ „ „	„ „		94
"C"	„ „	„ „ „	„ „		83
"D"	„ (Altnaveigh)	„ „ „	„ „		39
"E"	„ (Creeve)	10.15 p.m	„ „		72
"F"	„ (Sheepbridge)	11.25 „	„ „		35
„	„ (Band Hut)	11.40 „	„ „		17
"G"	„ (Mayobridge)	11 p.m.	„ „		64
"H"	„ (Warrenpoint)	2.50 a.m 25th	„ „		75
"K"	„ (Rostrevor)	3.12 „ „	„ „		31
"L.M.N & O"	„ (Kilkeel & Mourne Park)	4.10 a.m 25th.	„ „		233
					⎯⎯
					822
	2nd. in Command, Adjutant & Medical Officer				3
					⎯⎯
				Total	825

133

Order issued, 14 July 1914, by B. J. Glenny, the company commander, notifying the Warrenpoint company of the U.V.F. of a special parade to be held on 17 July 1914 (D 1540/3/82B):

There will be a special Parade of the Company on Friday evening 17th inst. at 8 P.M.

Full equipment to be worn by every man on parade, including bandolier, belt, haversack, and putties.

Captain Hall will command and will march the Company to Arnos Vale, where the Rostrevor Company will be met and skirmishing take place.

Every man on Parade will be supplied with a Rifle which will be carried with a fixed bayonet on this occasion.

Commencing Saturday next at 6 P.M. every man is to attend Narrow Water shooting range and fire five rounds with the new Mauser Rifle. Records will be kept so that incompetent men and those who do not attend will be noted. Practice will continue all next week excepting Wednesday.

B. J. Glenny

VI

In many respects the Ulstermen's image as stern fighters was marred in 1912 and 1913 by the fact that they were not fully armed. Though they had been smuggling rifles and ammunition for years, the quantities imported were small. Most volunteers had to parade with wooden rifles, some of which were enterprisingly provided in pitch pine or spruce by a Belfast firm. This lack not only enabled some English radicals to ridicule the volunteers and Ulster unionism; it also created discontent among volunteers at a headquarters and at a local level.

This discontent was sharpened on 4 December 1913 when one of Carson's parliamentary colleagues, J. H. Campbell, unionist M.P. for Dublin University, said in a speech at Manchester that a ban on the importation of arms would be proclaimed 'within a day or two'. The ban was announced on 5 December, and members of the U.V.F. at all levels felt piqued that news about it had not been passed on confidentially by their political leaders four days earlier: earlier and confidential intelligence would have given individuals time to bring in more arms before the ban was imposed. The headquarters staff felt ignored and inadequately prepared for any confrontation with government forces, and on 17 December 1913 at a meeting in London asked their political leaders a number of reproachful questions, including questions about arms. At a local level there was competition for and dissatisfaction with the limited number of arms and ammunition available, and the disgruntled committee of the Co. Antrim volunteers sent a deputation to Carson and Craig on 20 January 1914 to express their dissatisfaction.

To remedy this situation Ulster's political leaders decided in January 1914 to ignore the ban on the importation of arms and to ask 'Fred' Crawford, experienced in arms smuggling, to organise further smuggling. On 17 January Colonel G. Hacket Pain, the chief staff officer of the U.V.F., had written to Crawford asking for a statement of arms already imported by him and their present and intended distribution; he also asked whether Crawford would be willing to undertake further gun-running if authorised by Carson, and would draw up an estimate of the time, funds and help required for the purchase, landing and distribution of the arms and ammunition. Crawford said he would undertake further arms smuggling on certain conditions which were acceded to. The arms were bought in Germany, the whole operation was surrounded in secrecy, and there were occasional scares and alarums and disagreements, as over the question of where the arms should be landed. Of the dozen or so who knew of the plans, some, believing that a clash with the authorities was inevitable, favoured a provocative landing in Belfast and distributing the arms by train. The more cautious element, including Captain Frank Hall, a Unionist clubs' representative and military secretary of the U.V.F., favoured a landing at Larne, about which William Chaine, the chairman of the harbour board and enthusiastic commander of the 2nd battalion, Central Antrim regiment of the U.V.F., was able to supply adequate intelligence.

After considerable discussion the cautious view prevailed. On the night of 24–25 April 1914, under the cover of a test mobilisation and while a diversion was staged in Belfast, the 'Clydevalley' landed 35,000 rifles and 5 million rounds of ammunition at Larne. General Sir William Adair, commander of the Antrim U.V.F., was in charge at Larne and with him was Captain (later Sir) Wilfrid Spender, the assistant quartermaster general of the U.V.F., who had been closely involved in the plans, especially when at the beginning of April it was feared that the original arms-ship, the 'Fanny', had been captured with her cargo. The cargo was packed in bundles of five rifles, each rifle with 100 rounds of ammunition, and was speedily and efficiently distributed throughout the province by the motor car corps. This corps had been formed in the previous December and, on 20 April 1914, had been issued especially detailed instructions. As Dr Stewart has remarked: 'For the first time ever, careful and far-seeing plans were made for the assembly of several hundred motor cars at a given time and place for a military purpose, and for their subsequent dispersal. This was a brilliant piece of staff work, in which nothing was left to chance'. Ulster unionists were jubilant. Nevertheless, it had been a tense episode, and Spender was glad to return to the Antrim coast to relax with his wife, Lilian, an enthusiastic member of the nursing corps.

134 Report by J. Craig (?) of a meeting in London, 17 December 1913, between Ulster unionist political leaders and the staff of U.V.F. about military preparedness (D 1327/4/21):

The Military authorities recognise that the Military plans must be secondary to, and must depend on the political policy settled by the leaders. They therefore desire that the political leaders will give information on the following Military matters:—

(1) What early developments should the Military leaders be prepared to meet, especially in regard to the following contingencies:—

(a) Seizure of arms on a large scale.

(a) Resistance. Organised if possible. No shooting.

(b) Seizure of arms from individuals on a small scale, and with no provocation on the part of the individuals.

(b) See (a).

(c) If action is taken against the Leaders in England.

(c) Not probable. Bonar Law come to Ulster.

(d) If action is taken against the Leaders in Ulster.

(d) Leader (Carson) come to Ulster at once.

(e) If the Belfast population show grave signs of getting restive and riots appear likely.

(e) Every effort should be used to stop.

(f) If the Imperial Government begin to draft into Ulster (or the borders of Ulster) large numbers of extra troops or police.

(f) Must hear of beforehand. Action then considered.

NOTE.   It is suggested that Sir Edward Carson might think it advisable to issue confidentially to certain residents in Ulster, a circular which could be read out, if he were himself arrested, or advising patience till his return to Belfast in the case of an emergency happening whilst he is away from Ulster.

(2) In regard to arms.

(a) Is it intended that no steps shall be taken at present in regard to continuing the importation of arms into Ulster?	(a) Officially. Yes.
(b) If importation is to be discontinued, should plans be made for their future importation on a large scale in view of possible emergencies?	(b) Yes.
(c) Should it be found that one month is required to put any plans for the importation of arms into effect, will the Political Leaders assume full responsibility for giving the notice required. (It is pointed out however that the importation of arms later is likely to be very much harder, as the crisis approaches).	

(3) Special Service Force.

In regard to the Special Service Force being raised by enrolling 3,000 men from Belfast Battalions,

(a) do the Leaders approve of any publicity being given?	(a) As little as possible.
(b) Do they agree that the time has come for their equipment, taking into account that it will take 2 months to equip them?	(b) Yes.
(c) If the political leaders think that this should be proceeded with at once will they allot the necessary funds. (Probably £10,000 will supply most of the articles, bandoliers, boots, greatcoats, etc.)	(c) If possible

(d) If the time has not yet come, will the Political leaders assume full responsibility for giving the necessary notice?

(4) <u>Information.</u>

Certain information regarding the proclamation against the importation of arms was first given out by Mr. Campbell, K.C., M.P., in a Speech. This information, if it had been given to the Military authorities confidentially 4 days earlier would have enabled a large extra number of arms to have been imported.

Much dissatisfaction has been expressed among the rank and file that this notice was not given them by Headquarters of the U.V.F., and serious monetary loss has been entailed in consequence by private people. It is hoped that the Political Leaders will take account of the grave Military disadvantages which are entailed by making public announcements of this kind, and that these disadvantages will be weighed carefully against the Political advantages which may accrue from any such public announcement.

It is suggested that some person in the confidence of the leaders may be given complete information, whether verified or not. He should be instructed to give to the Military authorities such information as is likely to be useful from a Military point of view.

It was understood that Mr. Lloyd Campbell had been selected for this post, but it is believed that he was not kept informed of the rumours regarding the arms' proclamation. It is essential that the gentleman selected should be in intimate touch with the political and Military affairs of the moment.

4. Explained by Jas. Campbell & 'Leader'.

I emphasised the fact that merest rumour may prove of utmost importance by fitting in with other movements.

135 Statement on the arms question laid before Sir Edward Carson and James Craig, 20 January 1914, by a deputation of Co. Antrim volunteers, consisting of General Sir William Adair, the commander, and three regimental commanders (D 1238/108):

At [a] Meeting of [the] Co. Antrim U.V.F. Committee on 6th January 1914 very great dissatisfaction was expressed at the inadequate supply of arms—even for instructional purposes; only 150. ·303 Rifles and carbines and 50 Vetterlis had been issued for a force of 10,700 men, no ammunition being allowed for the latter rifle.

It was decided to request that a deputation should be granted an interview with Capt. Craig to express the Committee's feelings. Since then about 150 more Vetterlis have been assigned and certain rifles privately obtained have been taken on charge bringing the number of weapons up to 377, i.e.:—1 to every 28–29 men but there is only ammunition for about 180 of these rifles, i.e:—one for every 59 men.

Battalion Commanders all report that the men are manifesting considerable disappointment at the present condition of affairs and are tiring of elementary drill.

Four Regimental and Battalion Commanders belong to the Houses of Parliament and will have to leave Antrim to attend to their Parliamentary duties without having been able to bring their men up to any degree of efficiency in the use of arms. No prospect is seen of being able to replace these Commanders, and the report as to failure of a due supply of ex-officers coming from England is not encouraging.

It is believed that other Counties have been given a larger proportion of arms for which ammunition is forthcoming; the Co. Antrim Committee would be glad to receive some information on this point, and if the report is true, some explanation seems due.

Other Counties withheld some part of their collected money from the Carson Fund for the purpose of buying arms and are thus better situated than Antrim. The County therefore asks for a grant of money with which to arm itself, if more rifles and ammunition are not forthcoming,

There may be political or military reasons for differential treatment but neither the Civil or Military portion of the Committee have been granted any information on the subject. Some slight degree of confidence on the part of the Executive would enable the Military leaders to use their energies in the best possible direction. At present they are absolutely without any lead in the matter.

136 Letter from F. H. Crawford to Col. G. Hacket Pain, chief staff officer, U.V.F. headquarters, 19 January 1914, laying down the conditions on which he would be prepared to undertake a large scale gun-running; and **(b)** detailing the whereabouts of the arms and ammunition so far purchased for the U.V.F. (D 1327/4/21):

Dear Colonel Hacket-Pain—Yours of 17th. inst. to hand and in answer to questions 1, 2, & 3, contained therein, I herewith attach detailed statement giving all the information you require.

In answer to question 3a.

I much prefer having nothing to do with further importation of arms &

ammunition for business and family reasons.

If however I do undertake this work, it would be on the following conditions.

1. That at least 20,000, (say twenty thousand) rifles & bayonets with 2,000,000 (say two million) rounds of ammunition (viz 200 rounds per rifle) be brought in at one time.

2. That the whole of the funds to purchase these be forthcoming before I make a definate [*sic*] move.

3. That my instructions are given to me in writing The person with authority to vary any of the conditions be appointed at the same time. No one else to have power to interfere with the arrangements come to either financial or otherwise.

4. I herewith attach also an estimate of cost of carrying out above programme and landing the rifles and ammunition in Ulster, & time it would take from date of order till they were here.

5. My duty would be to get all alongside quay, but some one must be nominated to work with me responsible for their distribution. I have a plan but think better not to put it in on paper.

6. The attached estimate is necessarily very vague & rough, prices vary from week to week. A war breaking out may double the price of some or increase it by 20% in other sorts. This actually took place when the Tripoli war broke out. I shall give to the person named as the authority, notice of any great variation in my estimates, and if a large increase in cost is required, his sanction must be obtained before contracts are signed.

7. No one else shall (with the sanction of H.Qrs.) compete with me in buying arms & amtin. [*sic*] in the country or source from which I shall obtain them.

8. H.Qrs. will deprecate any attempts to run in guns on a small scale till after this venture has been put thro', as it would probably draw down on our coasts a patrol of torpedo or other war craft & frustrate our more important work

9. I recommend the arms & ammunition now in B'ham for which we are responsible, to be handed over to the British League for the support of Ulster and the Union at cost price, failing to come to this arrangement, that they be asked to help us to lift these & place them at convenient places on the coasts of England, Scotland & Wales. These movements would mislead the authorities as to our real plans

In answer to 6B. As already stated I attach estimate giving full details.

I believe this to be quite feasible & can be carried out. Of course any plan is liable to failure, but with the men I have worked with so far, and the care that would be taken in choosing others which would be necessary to carry out this work, the chance of discovery, till the ship was actually alongside at her destination, would to my mind be comparitively [*sic*] small.

To speak more definately [*sic*] I should require to study charts etc showing home & neutral waters etc Yours faithfully

Fred. H. Crawford

P.S. I shall do all in my power to assist any one appointed by H.Qrs. to carry out this scheme to a successful issue

Pattern	Article	No proposed	Cost	Time	Remarks
ITALIAN	Rifle & bayonet	20000	13000 0 0	6 weeks or 4 months	The time depends on whether the Italian Govt. is selling ammunition or not, & estimate varies accordingly between 6 weeks & 4 months.
	Ammunition	2 Milln	11000 0 0	6 weeks or 4 months	advantages
					Cheapness Same calibre etc as those we have.
	Incidental		2000 0 0	Time Required to be landed in Ulster	Disadvantages.
					Secresy [sic] very uncertain & difficult as Italian rifles are carefully watched & only Ulster is buying.
			£26000 0 0		Time of delivery uncertain.
					Success more doubtful than with continental pattern.
Mauser or other Continental	Rifle & bayonet	20,000	50,000 0 0	6 weeks	advantages
					Greater secresy possible & therefore success much more likely. Sure of immediate delivery
	Ammunition	2 Million	11,000	Time required to be landed in Ulster	Disadvantages.
					Extra expense
	Incidental		2,000		Different ammunition, making this 3rd type in use, but IF distribution is carefully localized this is not of vital importance
			£63,000		

245

Rifles etc bought but not in Country

Italian V[etterlis] B'ham & enroute [sic]	5000 (about Rifles) 4751 Rifles (m.m)	9400 bayonets 2000 (here) .303	1,000,000 rounds of ammunition none

[Rifles etc bought, in country and distributed to volunteers]

	VETTERLIS		MARTINI-MET.		Remarks
	Rifles	Amm.	Rifles or Carbines	Amm.	
ARMAGH	320	24,000	—	—	
ANTRIM	150	—	150	52,000	
CAVAN			64	14,000	
DONEGAL			128	12,800	
DOWN			562	64,000	
Do, (1 Maxim Gun)			1	22,000	
FERMANAGH			132	14,500	
LONDONDERRY CITY	200	1,600			
LONDONDERRY CO.	145	—			
MONAGHAN	128	12,800			
TYRONE	—	—	352	35,200	
Do, (1 Maxim Gun)			1	20,000	
BELFAST—NORTH					
„ —SOUTH			500	325,000	
„ —EAST					

Ulster unionist organisation at the time of the third home rule bill

County	Stored	With	Issued	To
Antrim .	655	Greer	80	50 Reade, 30 Leslie (Lord Leitrims)
Armagh .	30	Allen	50	Crozier
Cavan .			25	Farnham
Down .	530	Waring 280 Black 125 Craig 100 Ross 25	50	Murland
Fermanagh .			50	Stack
Derry Co. .			25	Proctor
Monaghan .			20	Rogers
Tyrone .			75	Ricardo
Belfast .	420	Crawford		
Steamer	20	Crew		
	1655		375	Ammunition
	375			Black 16000
	2030			Scott 4800
				Crawford 29200
				50,000

137

Letter from W. Chaine, chairman of the Larne Harbour board, to J. T. Reade of J. T. Reade and Son, flax and yarn merchants, 4 Donegall Square North, Belfast, a member of the Ulster military committee, 31 December 1913, enclosing **(b)** information relating to the religion and politics of post office and railway employees and of policemen in and around Larne, as part of a thorough intelligence survey of the area (D 1327/3/21):

Dear Reade—I have been away for a few days and have not got all the information I would like. I send you all I have got and will send more later.

There is an A[ncient] O[rder] of H[ibernian] lodge here and in Carnlough the President here is J. Cunningham a railway clerk and the Secretary is a painter whose name I forget at the moment, will get this again.

I cannot find out yet about Carnlough. I wish I had never seen that district. Yours truly

W Chaine

(b)

I report as follows—

Larne post office.	Postmistress (Prot[estant]. Politics doubtful) 4 assistants (2 Pres[byterian]. 2 R[oman]. C[atholic].) 7 Postmen (2 Methodists 3 Presbyterian 2 R.C.).
Larne Burn-hill	Subpostmistress (Prot)
Cairncastle	Postmistress (Pres) 2 Postmen (1 Pres 1 R.C.)
Glynn	Postmistress (Pres) 1 Postman (Pres)
Magheramorne	Postmistress (Pres. Politics ?) 1 Postman (ditto)
Raloo	Postmistress (Pres)
Millbrook	Postmistress (Pres.) 1 Postman (Pres)
Kilwaughter	Postmaster (Unitarian Politics ?)
Glenarm	no information.
Carnlough	do.

It may be taken that Protestants are all Unionist except where so marked.

W Chaine.

Larne Harbour Post Office	(all Unionists)
Glenarm & Carnlough	(no information yet)

W.C.

I report as follows—

Larne R[ai]l[wa]y. station.	Station Master (Pres—Politics very doubtful) Clerks (all U[nionist] some in U.V.F.) Porters (mixed).
Larne Harbour station.	Station Master (Pres) Chief Clerk (President A.O.H) Signalmen (Epis. & U.V.F.) Clerks (Prot) Porters (Mixed).

Glynn Station	Station master (R.C bad).
Magheramorne station	Station master (Pres.) Porter (?)
Kilwaughter	Station mistress (?)
Headwood	Station mistress (?)

It is not worth reporting porters in detail as they are always changing.

W Chaine

I report as follows—

Larne Police	consist of 1 District Inspector. 1 Head Constable (R.C.) 3 Sergeants 2 (R.C. and one vacant) about 18 Constables (5 U 13 R.C.)
Glenarm Police	1 Sergeant (U) and 3 Constables (1 U & 2 R.C)
Carnlough Police.	1 Sergeant (U) and 2 Constables (?)
Glenarm Coastguards	1 Chief Officer (U) and 4 men (2 U and 2 R.C.)

W Chaine

138 Letter from General Sir William Adair, commander Co. Antrim U.V.F., 20 April 1914, summoning members of the motor corps to Larne on 24–25 April (D 1238/71):

SECRET

Sir—In accordance with your kind agreement to place a motor car at the disposal of the Provisional Government in a case of necessity it is absolutely necessary that your car should arrive at Larne in the night of Friday–Saturday 24th–25th instant at 1 a.m. punctually but not before that hour, for a very secret and important duty.

A reliable enrolled volunteer—an officer if possible—should accompany the chauffeur if you do not come yourself with him, two —but only two— persons should be on the car.

The car will probably be back in your own part of the country within a few hours, but a supply of petrol should be brought.

It is unfortunate that this unavoidable assembly must take place and Sir Edward Carson is particularly desirous that no trouble should arise. Arms are therefore not to be carried; a determined attitude will probably overcome any possible show of interference by the Police.

On approaching Larne no car is to attempt to overtake any other. Every car must be kept in file on the proper side of the road.

The strictest obedience must be paid to all instructions given by the Staff Officers and Marshalls [*sic*] until the car is finally dismissed to its destination.

Towns and villages should be avoided if possible, if passed through speed should be slow and as little horn blowing used as possible.

The enclosed card is to be brought and shown when asked for. Please reply by Thursday evening's post—not later—to Loughanmore—not on a postcard—simply saying "No. will be there" or giving a good reason to the contrary.

W. T. ADAIR
Commander, Co. Antrim Division U.V.F.

139

List of motor car owners in North Antrim who provided vehicles for the gun-running at Larne, 24 April 1914 (D 1238/74):

Car No	Owner		Bundles	Destination
1	Rev. Clarke	Connor	5	Rev. Clarke. Connor
2	Coyles	B'castle	4	Ballycastle
3	Dobbs.	Cushendall	4	J. K. Wilson Raceview
4	Greer	B'money	3	Leslie Hill B.money
5	O'Neill Capt			Shanes Cas[tle]
6	Hutchinson,	Stranocum	4	Dervock
7	Lyle.	B'castle	5	B'castle
8	Leslie	B'money	5	Leslie Hill, B.money
9	McConachie	B'castle	6	B'castle
10	Montgomery.	Benvardin	4	Benvardin Dervock
11	Matchette	Ballintoy		
12	Murray.	Portrush	5	Portrush
13	Patrick.	Glarryford	5	Dunminning, Glarryford
14	do	do	4	,, ,,
15	Ross	do		
16	Stuart.	Stranocum	5	Dervock
17⌉	Stewart.	Portrush⌉		Bushmills
18	do	do	38 or	Portrush &
19 ⎬	do	do ⎬	39	Ballintoy
20⌋	do	do ⌋		
21	Stott	Craigs		
22	Stuart.	Portrush	5	Portrush
23	Wilson	B'mena	5	R. P. Wilson Raceview
24	J. K. Wilson		5	Raceview Broughshane
25	Wise.	B'castle	5	Leslie Hill B.money
26	Young. Mrs.	B'mena	5	Galgorm
27	do	do	5	Crawford Moorfields
28	Col. Lyle		5	Leslie Hill. B.money
111				
112				
113				
114				
115				
116				
117				
118				
119				
120				
121	Mrs. Gibson [?]			Mr. Flynn Lisnafillon
122	Mrs. Casement		5	Galgorm
123	R. Morton Jr.		5	Oranmore, B.mena
124	Bruce Morton		5	,, ,,
125	N. C. Caruth		5	Drumard ,,

250

126	J. D. Caruth	5	Oranmore	,,
127	Sam. Kane	5	J. Crawford Collin the Moorfields	
128	Kane Bros.	45	,, ,,	,, ,,

140 Memorandum by Capt. F. Hall, military secretary to the U.V.F., c. 1 May 1914, describing the gun-running of 1914, particularly the dispute over where and in what manner the guns were to be landed (PRB 1559):

Prior to the passing of the second Reading (for the 3rd. time) of the H. R Bill it was decided that it wd. be necessary to fully arm the U.V.F. This decision had been in abeyance for a considerable time—although plans were formulated—but it was felt by many that it was inadvisable to bring in arms or to spend money on them if there was still a chance of a peaceful settlement or the resignation of the Cabinet.

Accordingly (1) [F. H. Crawford] was sent over to the Continent to buy a full cargo of arms & ammn. and to arrange shipment. This he did: the full detail of his movements are [*sic*] known only to a few but his plans were watched by the German authorities & he was searched by Danish Customs after loading out of barges which passed through the Kiel Canal, [word illegible] reports published in the papers on—?date. After clearing without his papers he cruised according to orders for some time in the Baltic & finally worked round to the N. Coast of Scotland. On some date between April 1st. & 15th. unknown to me he transhipped his whole cargo at sea from the "Fanny" to the S.S. Balmerino, which remained off the N. Coast of Scotland. (1) [Crawford] returned incog[nito] to Belfast.—I did not see him—just at the time of the "Army Crisis" & interviewed (2) [Carson] (3) [Craig] (4) [General Richardson] at Craigavon. In the meantime (5) [W. Spender] had been sent to the N. of Scotland to intercept the ship & had actually sold her & her cargo back to German dealers. (1) [Crawford] was not told this (I believe) as (5) [Spender] did not return until he had left. (1) [Crawford] & (3) [Craig] arranged that the whole cargo must be brought into Belfast and (2) [Carson] & (4) [Richardson] concurred. The whole matter was kept absolutely in the hands of a small committee consisting principally of (3) [Craig], (4) [Richardson], (5) [Spender], (6) [Lord Leitrim], (7) [S. Kelly] & no details were given out.

I personally was told of the scheme by 5 [Spender] at 6 p.m. on Friday 17th. April. A meeting was held that evening at the O[ld] T[own] H[all] at which (2) [Carson] told us that he desired that the job be done without conflict with the authorities & that a row at that time must be fatal to our interests. Prior to this meeting others had been told & the feeling quickly spread that any attempt to land the cargo in Belfast must lead to trouble. Orders had already been prepared for Belfast Divn. U.V.F. to man the streets, barricade bridges, wire entanglements, etc. The proceedings of the meeting were secret & everyone present was sworn not to divulge what took place at it: I therefore cannot say what took place then.

After the meeting I took strong exception to the way in which the arrangements had been made, without consulting any of those who really knew the local conditions & stated my views openly that such proceedings could only end in a furious riot. I also went dead against the proposed plan of handing out rifles & ammn. direct to the men in Belfast, or of storing them in bulk under armed guard in Belfast drill halls: also to a scheme whereby men were to be brought up from country towns & sent home by special trains with arms. (An earlier suggestion that a Great Protest Demonstration be held the same night in the Ulster Hall was dropped even before the above meeting.) In these views I found myself absolutely backed up by 8 [R. D. Bates], 9 [L. Campbell], 10 [E. Sclater], 11 [G. S. Clark], 12 [R. Cowzer?] and others.

A further meeting was held next morning and before it the plans as arranged were put before the "Commission" 3 [Craig], 4 [Richardson], 10 [E. Sclater], 11 [Clark], 12 [Cowzer?]. I was not present. It was then decided to abandon the "military" move & make it a purely "smuggling" move but still to adhere to the plan of bringing the ship into the Musgrave Channel. This relieved tension to a certain extent but the "moderate" element still held that it was unwise to attempt anything in Belfast. & the opinion was freely expressed that no attempts should be made to bring in arms in bulk in view of the then state of the political situation. (3) [Craig] left for London after the meeting on Friday evening 17th. April.

Considerable friction arose between the "Military" side & the "local political" with regard to the abandonment of the militant policy & on Monday 20th. relations were distinctly strained.

13 [G. H. H. Couchman], 14 [J. D. D. Scriven], 5 [Spender], (all strangers) were keen on the bold militant policy & 13 [Couchman] was distinctly annoyed at the orders given to him that force was not to be used.

Constant Committees were held on 20th. & 21st. mostly attended by men who had never taken any part in previous organisation work in Belfast. All arrangements were proceeded with in connection with the "smuggling" scheme—the vessel to berth in Musgrave Channel at 9 p.m. on Friday night 24th.

It appeared that (1) [Crawford] had left saying he wd. bring the vessel in at that hour: & that he wd. be stopped by nothing except a written order signed by (2) [Carson]. He had gone to sea in the S.S. Clyde Valley alias Mountjoy, which met the Balmerino somewhere off the Bristol Channel & transhipped her whole cargo at sea on the nights of 27th. & 28th [should be 19 and 20 April].

On Tuesday morning 21st. (4) [Richardson] & (15) [H. Paul] evidently realised that the scheme was not feasible & that local opinion was against it. An alternative scheme of landing at Larne & Bangor was proposed but not discussed—(it had been the intention all along that small ships should be loaded alongside the Clyde Valley while she was landing the bulk of her cargo in the Musgrave channel & that they shd. then proceed to Larne & Bangor & land their lots there.) I spoke very strongly to (4) [Richardson] & (15) [Paul]

& placed my objections before them. I stated openly that the scheme was forced upon us by (1) [Crawford] & (3) [Craig] & that I did not believe that (2) [Carson] realised the strength of feeling against it, the danger of not, or the difficulty of getting the men out for a "test mobilization" on a Friday night—(being pay night in the yards & mills.) I urged the advisability of laying the matter before (2) [Carson].

At 4.30 p.m. I was told that I was to go over to London & see (2) [Carson]. I left by Larne. (Incidentally: in the Stranraer-Euston Sleeping car, I got into conversation with a total stranger evidently an English visitor who did not know who I was & who told me that the Bangor Battn. U.V.F. were to be mobilized "for some big thing" on Friday night! so much for the secrecy of our plans!!!)

Wedy 22nd. I saw (2) [Carson] at 10.15 a.m. (in bed.) (3) [Craig] was staying with him & was sent for as soon as I arrived. I told them the state of feeling in Belfast. (3) [Craig] was much annoyed & was keen for the whole "military" scheme. We discussed matters for 2 hours. (2) [Carson] said little but was distinctly worried. I told them the suggested alternative scheme: i.e. the one which was eventually carried out. (2) [Carson] seemed to approve of it (3) [Craig] seemed to accept it 'faute de mieux'. I made one statement which I now regret. I said I did not expect that more than 5 or 10% of the men wd. turn out for a sudden "test mobilization" on a Friday night. (Subsequent events proved that—stimulated by all sorts of wild rumours which were about —nearly 50% turned out.) I left (2) [Carson] & (3) [Craig] at 12.15. with orders to meet them again at the House at 4 p.m.

At 4. I met (2) [Carson] alone at the House & went up with him to the Carlton: I told him exactly what I had told (4) [Richardson] & (15) [Paul] with regard to the hot-headed policy of (1) [Crawford] & (3) [Craig]. He said he knew it & knew the feelings on the subject but that he took responsibility himself. He gave me verbal orders to ask (4) [Richardson] to act entirely for him & to do what he considered advisable: he also gave me 3 letters in his own handwriting & signed to (1) [Crawford].

(A) Proceed to Sea again—report a rendezvous to G.O.C. & dont land anything.

(B) Plans altered. You will proceed to Larne Act under orders of G.O.C.

and C was also written at my suggestion. "In my absence act absolutely under the orders of G.O.C. & obey his directions explicitly. This is essential."

I returned via Greenore. (I mistook the time of the Larne mail, thinking it was 8.30, as on Sundays. It left at 8.)

Thursday. 23rd. I saw (4) [Richardson] & (15) [Paul] at the O.T.H. & gave (4) the verbal orders recd. from (2) [Carson] also the 3 letters. He then informed me that plans had been definitely changed & that the "Larne" scheme that actually [was] carried out was substituted.

Other details of the first wild scheme which I omitted above:—

1. A mass meeting to protest against the Army "Plot" was to have been held in the Ulster Hall on Friday night 24th. as an excuse for calling the men out. This was squashed by (2) [Carson].

2. A special train was to be loaded on the Dock Sidings & run through to Armagh & Monaghan with rifles. (5) [Spender] was mad on this & said it cd. easily be done!! I pointed out the impossibility of it: 20 heads of Departments wd. have had to be warned, 5 gates kept open. 2 changes of control. Dock to B[elfast] C[ounty] D[own] R[ailway] J[unction]—B.C.D.R.J. to G[reat] N[orthern] R[ailway]. Danger on the road from police and/or Nationalists. No possibility of blocking telephones or telegraphs as they wd. be required for working the train. It was given up at 4 p.m. on Thursday 23rd.!!

The actual details for the work which was carried out on the night of the 24th/25th were not taken in hand until midday on the 23rd. A fairly accurate account has now got into the papers.

Head Quarters U.V.F. moved from the O.T.H. to "Maryville". The O.T.H. being considered (rightly) untenable if a row started or if police interfered.

Orders were issued to mobilize Belfast, Down, Antrim, Derry & Armagh & such roads as were to be used in Tyrone to be picketted [*sic*] by local Battns.

All Motor Sections were mobilized & placed under orders of local Commanders. Cars for Larne assembled at Antrim. Those for Bangor at various places.

Arrangements were made to "short circuit" (not to cut or damage) all telegraph & 'phone wires to Larne at Magheramorne, at 9.15 p.m. after last train had gone down. All lines on Bangor Road & rail to be "shorted" at midnight except the Glasgow Trunk Lines.

The private telephone connecting H'wood [Holywood] Barracks to Exchange was tapped & a man sat at it from 10 p.m. till 3 a.m.

G.P.O. exchange was watched carefully—all operators being special men —also night telegraph staff!

The Staff were distributed: McCammon at Bangor, Spender at Larne, G.O.C. C.S.O. Davis & self at Head Qrs. also Lloyd Campbell.—Craig at Donaghadee. 10 Motor Cyclists at Larne—10 at Bangor 12 at Head Qrs. 5 @ Donaghadee.

I dined with the Ropers, having arranged a code message with Hd Qrs. in case R was called up to go to Barracks.

At 10 p.m. I went round all districts in the City. Battns. were mobilizing everywhere no excitement—no disturbance anywhere. I visited the Guard at O.T.H. & walked down to Musgrave Channel. Found about 1000 men E. Belfast Regt. U.V.F. fallen in on roadway about 20 yards from wharf. Steam up on two cranes ordered for the S.S. Balmerino. (Bates & X.X. [Cowzer?] had gone out in S.S. Milewater to intercept the Clyde Valley—alias Mountjoy —off the head.)

At 11. p.m. a vessel came dead slow up the Channel & took about 25 minutes to get alongside. By this time 15 Customs officers under Mr. Jones, Chief Customs Surveyor Belfast, had collected. As the vessel came alongside the Customs hailed her "Whats your cargo." Skipper replied "I am instructed to tell you its coal." Having made sure it was the Balmerino—(we were desperately afraid of the Clyde Valley refusing to obey orders & that she wd. come straight in)—I motored up to Maryville. The City was absolutely deserted, except for our pickets.

Communications between Larne, Bangor, Donaghadee & Head Qrs. was [*sic*] kept up by signallers & cyclists. Both worked without a hitch.

At 1 a.m. we recd. word by cyclist from Larne that the "Mountjoy" was short of coal water & engine room stores. She had only just enough coal to take her to Bangor. We secured a motor lorry & loaded it in an hour with the oil & other engine room stores she wanted. We told Bangor to have 30 tons of coal ready for her. They did so. When she arrived there all was put on board while she was unloading—the hose on the pier was not long enough so they called out the fire brigade & watered her with their hose!! When she had finished unloading 5 of her crew refused to go to sea so Volunteers were called for from the U.V.F. & they took her out!

At 3.30 a.m. I recd. orders from G.O.C. to allow the Customs to inspect the Balmerino & went down again to Musgrave Channel. I wouldn't have missed that job for £1000. 4 a.m. just day light, I got down to her, found 1500 U.V.F. fallen in, 15 Customs men, 2 Harbour Police, Commissioner Smith, D.I. Dunlop, (Detection Staff) probably 6 detectives & a few R.I.C. men not more than 4.

We fell in the U.V.F. ordered them to march home, telling them that their work had been eminently successful—just before they marched off I went up to the ship—with Smith on one side of me, Dunlop on the other & ordered the mate to remove hatches for the Customs. The 15 Customs men stood round like mutes round a grave [?]. Their faces when those hatches were taken off I shall never forget. After hold empty: forard [*sic*] Hold—40 tons of bunker coal!!

I returned to Head Quarters 4.30 a.m. found reports all correct from Larne. At Larne the "Mountjoy" burthed [*sic*] at 10.10 p.m. & immediately commenced unloading on to the quay. At the same time two small vessels were brought alongside her. "Roma" took 30 tons & was to steam straight round to Workman & Clarks Yard. "Innismurray" took 20 tons to Donaghadee. The Mountjoy herself took 80 tons to Bangor.

The only hitch in the whole proceedings was with the Roma. She had been chartered in a hurry that morning (Friday.) Her crew were "wrong" & we had to put men on her to bring her round: she made a very bad passage, took 3½ hours instead of 2½, and just as she was berthing at Workman & Clarks the Customs men whom I had released from the Balmerino came up the river in their motor boat & spotted her. They boarded her, took her papers but could not touch the cargo, which was landed in the yard. She was arrested next day in Ayr, but she had done her work.

At Bangor all worked well, ditto at Donaghadee although they did not start to unload there till 6. a.m. & finished at 8 a.m.!

Stories of queer incidents are still coming in:—

1. Dist. Inspector Dunlop sent his car to his brother—a parson on Friday 24th. Its number was taken by the police at Larne & reported to the Castle for gun-running!

2. At Lisburn the signal to mobilize was given on the factory hooters: when they sounded a Sergt R.I.C. (R.C.) & 4 Constables (Prot) were just having their tea. The 4 Constables dashed upstairs put on plain clothes & were off! They went to the local Battn. Com[mande]r. & asked if it was "business" or only a test mobilization. He assured them it was only a test. "Oh! Well, they said, then we needn't lose our jobs yet!!" & went back & got into uniform.

All the stuff as it was landed was immediately carted away. Larne stuff was sent straight away up country—some as far as Omagh. Bangor & Donaghadee stuff was dumped in depots. They shot some 1300 rifles on to Bob Maxwell at Finnebrogue much to his annoyance, but of course he played up. All this was practically distributed by Thursday 30th.

Throughout the whole proceedings there was not—so far as has been reported up to 7 p.m. Friday May 1st.—a single casualty of any sort. Nor have we been interfered with in any way whatsoever.

141 Extract from the diary of Lilian, wife of Captain W. Spender, April 1914, conveying some of the atmosphere, secrecy, tension, then relief, surrounding the Larne gun-running (D 1633/2/19):

Monday. Ap. 27th.

Olive's Birthday: Many Happy Returns to her!

I am going to send this particular chapter of diary over to England by hand, as my account of Friday night is confidential, & must not go beyond Wilfrid's & my families.

Last Wednesday [22 April] afternoon, I went over to Mrs. Surrey's [?]— she is our Commandant—for a practise [sic]. I found 5 or 6 others camped on a rug on the lawn, cutting out mustard plasters & there were tables close by containing linseed mustard, basins, water &c. It was such a funny sight, especially when we started making the plasters & poultices, as the wind blew everything away, but it was far better than being indoors, especially as Mrs. S. always has every window tight shut. Then we bandaged each other till rain drove us indoors—the first break-up of our marvellous fine weather. It was pelting when I went back.

Thursday [23 April] I paid a long-owed call on Mr. Torrens, Lord Shaftesbury's agent, who has a lovely home down by the sea, near Belfast, & was rewarded by being taken over the really beautiful gardens, & given tea, & an armful of Arum lilies & Cineraria to take home. I wish all the other 14 calls I owe would have similar results!

Friday [24 April] I went to the O[ld]. T[own]. H[all]. as usual, to help send off pamphlets, & Eva came too, & came back to lunch with us, & I eventually persuaded her to stop for the night, as W[ilfrid]. had told me he would have to be away that night with the General, seeing after the big Test Mobilisation which was to take place then, but which was being kept a profound secret until the last moment. He left soon after lunch, taking a latch key, as he said it was possible he might get back early Saturday morning. Eva & I had a busy afternoon, bandaging each other &c., & Miss Johnson & a Cousin turned up to tea. When they'd left, we flew off to the 'Drill' at the O[ld]. T[own]. H[all]. Jack was able to come, & gave us a splendid drilling, both Stretcher Drill, & ordinary. We really are improving. We were all wondering if we were to mobilise too, but had had no orders, so concluded we wer'nt [*sic*] wanted. Jack came away with Eva & me, & managed to tell me in a hurried aside, that "they" were to "get them in tonight". Of course I knew what that meant, & so will you, in the light of Saturday's evening papers. His post was to be at Musgrave Channel, assisting at the Hoax which took in all the Customs Officers, & kept them occupied all night, watching the 'Balmerino' which of course contained nothing but coal!

You can imagine my anxiety, realising what was afoot, and what the dangers were, & not in the least knowing what part W. was taking in the night proceedings. I could'nt [*sic*] tell Eva, but she knew I was anxious, & we occupied ourselves as best we could, by catechising one another in First Aid & Home Nursing. It was a comfort having her. Imagine my delight when, about 6 o'clock next morning my door opened, & in came a muddy, tousled, disreputable Wolf, whose shining eyes, however, told me that all was more than well. Then I learned that he had been sent to the danger-point, to Larne itself, & had been up all night, helping to unload the precious goods, & to carry them to the motors waiting by the wharf. The papers will describe it all to you better than I can, & how 'they' were all safely landed, and all reached their various destinations without mishap. The whole proceedings are almost incredible, and nothing but the most perfect organisation, combined with the most perfect and loyal co-operation on the part of all concerned, could have carried it through without a single case of bloodshed. Need I say that for the organisation W. himself was mainly responsible, the scheme having been originally drawn up by him?

Tuesday 28th. The plans had been maturing for two months or more, & it had of course been a source of great worry and anxiety to W. It made it worse that he could not talk to me about it, but so much trouble had been caused by others talking, that he felt he must be able to say that he, at any rate, had not even told his wife. Of course I knew about 'the Fanny' and all about W.'s adventures in Scotland, but not about the final scheme. Some day you shall hear the whole story. What a tale R[obert]. L[ouis]. S[tevenson]. would have made out of the adventures of 'the Fanny' alone! Can you imagine what it meant to W. (& therefore to me) to have this scheme, that he had toiled at for months, brought off without a single hitch? He had bicycled part way into Larne that night, & ridden the whole way back, getting a tow for some miles by a motor cycle—one of the Despatch riders—. He had a spill near the end, but luckily escaped with a bad graze on the leg, & some bruises. I was proud to bandage him up in my best hospital style! & then he came to bed to snatch a little sleep before having breakfast, & going off to report to the General [Saturday 25 April]. Eva and I went 'down town' to do some shopping, & buy our Ambulance Uniform hats. At the latter shop, the owner greeted me with "Hope Capt. Spender got back all right last night?", then began telling me his own experiences, he being one of the Belfast U.V.F., and having been up all night. There must have been a good many sleepy people in Ulster that morning! But everybody was too delighted over the success of the night's work, to mind the loss of sleep. After lunch, Eva having gone, and Jack too, who had turned up to bring W. a wire, we set off for our week end at Cushendall, and got there about 7 p.m. An absurd little narrow-guage railway (exactly like the Newfoundland railway, & just about as jolty) takes you on from Ballymena, & at Parkmore dumps you down in the middle of the moors, about 1,000 ft. up, whence there is a $6\frac{1}{2}$ mile drive in an outside car to Cushendall on the coast. It was a perfect evening, & the scenery simply lovely. The road winds down through larch woods into the wide vale of Glenarrif [*sic*], & the banks & fields & woods were gay with gorse and broom, primroses, violets, anemones, & rives [?], and the air was heavenly—sweet with the scent of them and of the fir trees. Across the sea the Scotch coast looked astonishingly near: the Mull of Cantire [*sic*], Ailsa Craig, & the low hills about Stranraer. Cushendall is a pretty little village, thickly-wooded, & with clustering hills all about it. The Inn we went to is very primitive, but quite all right for a short time.

Sunday [26 April] was grey all day, but quite fine. I went to church, but would'nt [*sic*] let W. come, as he was completely worn out from the reaction after the long strain of all these months, & needed absolute rest and 'lazing'. In the afternoon we found our way to a grassy slope just above the beach, and lazed there till tea-time. . . .

VII

The determination of Ulster unionism was never put to the final test. Although on 25 May 1914 the third home rule bill was passed once again and for the last time by the house of commons, it was never implemented. June and July were taken up with abortive attempts to make special provision for Ulster that would permit the measure to operate peacefully; and, just as an impasse had been reached, the outbreak of the first world war put the Irish question into cold storage. When it was taken out again Ireland was partitioned.

There can be little doubt that the U.V.F. would have fought anybody to prevent a Dublin parliament from ruling over the north. There can also be little doubt that most of the political leaders of Ulster unionism hoped and thought that the volunteers would not have to fight. They saw the U.V.F. as a factor in the propaganda war waged in Britain against home rule. Seeing that orderly demonstrations had little impact upon opinion in Britain, they turned to drilling and arming to convince British opinion of Ulster unionists' determination not to have home rule. This propaganda element accounts for the strict discipline maintained among the volunteers and the tight rein kept upon extremists. While the political leaders took precautions, especially at the time of the so-called Curragh mutiny, against arrests and the seizure of arms, they did not think that the government would move against Ulster unionists, unless presented with a convenient opportunity. The whole object of the orders issued to the volunteers from headquarters was to prevent them from becoming involved in skirmishes. In the main, the leaders were confident that if they were careful, the British people and parliament would respect their demand that Ulster, or at least part of it, should remain British.

142 Printed circular memorandum containing 'directions as to the protection of arms and ammunition' and as to the 'prevention of arrest of leaders', issued. 14 May 1914, from the U.V.F. headquarters (D 1238/139):

PRECAUTIONARY MEASURES.

All Arms and Ammunition should be concealed in small packets in various convenient centres, carefully selected, where the arms, &c., will be well hidden but easily accessible to the men who have to use them, and where there will be such custody and watchfulness as are likely to prevent surprise and ensure immediate warning to the local officers of U.V.F. of any attempt to seize or search.

PROTECTIVE MEASURES.

In the event of any attempt being made to seize arms, &c., or to search for the purpose of such seizure, the following procedure will be adopted:—

1. The general policy to be observed in acting on these directions is that—

   (*a*) It is of the utmost importance that the U.V.F. should not be responsible for any violence which can be avoided, and that there should not be on their part any firing or extreme measures, except so far as necessitated by the attacking force having commenced firing, or such extreme measures.

   (*b*) To this end, it should, so far as practicable, be arranged that at the particular time and place of any such attempt, the U.V.F. should be present in such strength as by sheer weight of numbers to overpower the attacking force, and to render its success manifestly hopeless.

259

2. In the event of information being received that an attempt at such seizure or search is to be made, or is proceeding in any particular locality, the Battalion in the area in which such attempt is to be, or is being made, will at once mobilize in full strength, a proportion only to be armed with rifles; they will proceed to the place of such attempt, and endeavour in the *first instance* by force of numbers quietly to prevent it. If the Constabulary use ordinary force, this will be met by superior force used in the same form as that employed by the Constabulary. If the Constabulary produce arms, a superior number of armed Volunteers will take the place of the unarmed men in opposing them, and intimation will be given to the officers in charge of the Constabulary that their armed attempt will be promptly and firmly resisted. Every means will be used to point out to the Constabulary officers in charge that responsibility for any action they may take and its consequences will rest with them. Only if and when the Constabulary commit the first act of aggression by firing will the Volunteers fire in reply.

3. The principle to be carefully borne in mind and acted on is that force is to be met by force, but in greatly superior numbers, and accordingly if the number of the Constabulary employed in any such attempt render inadequate upon this principle the force available in the Battalion area where the attempt is made, one or more, as circumstances may require, of the Battalions of neighbouring areas are likewise to be mobilized and concentrated to resist the attempt.

4. To render effective this system of protection, it is most essential that intelligence should be obtained at the earliest possible moment of any concentration or movement of Constabulary, and probably such information might be obtained from Police Constables in sympathy with the movement. Any information obtained at Headquarters will at once be forwarded to the particular locality affected.

PREVENTION OF ARREST OF LEADERS.

In the event of the Government attempting to paralyse or embarrass the Ulster Movement by the arrest of its leaders, the protective measures above directed will be employed to prevent such arrests.

So far as time permits these measures should, in reference to attempted arrests, be taken only by and under directions from Headquarters.

But in case of emergency not admitting of communication with Headquarters, and if, from the position of persons threatened with arrest and other circumstances, it is manifest to the local officers of the Volunteers that such attempt by the Government is in progress, they will take the measures above directed to prevent such arrests.

G. HACKET PAIN,

COLONEL,

CHIEF STAFF OFFICER.

143 Memorandum as to the behaviour of volunteers, issued 14 June 1914 by R. Hall, commanding 2nd battalion South Down regiment (D 1540/3/74B):

Ulster Volunteers are not to mix themselves up in riots or Street fights unless to protect themselves or other Protestants, who may be assaulted, or when called on by the Police to assist them.

The Police are there to deal with ordinary Rowdyism—Volunteers are not to interfere unless the Police find themselves unable to cope with the disturbance, and call for help.

Unless it is found necessary to mobilize the U.V.F., no party of Volunteers is to be paraded or marched to the scene of Action.

No Rifles or Revolvers are to be used until the last extremity.

Indiscriminate Revolver firing is strictly forbidden.

The use of firearms is always taken as putting the user in the wrong, unless it can be proved that someone on the other side fired the first shot, which is very difficult to prove.

Revolvers are not authorized in the U.V.F. Any Volunteer carrying one does so on his own responsibility, and must take the consequences if arrested.

Volunteers have already been advised to provide themselves with Batons or thick sticks.

(Signed)   Roger Hall

Commanding 2nd Bn. S. Down Regt.

144 Letter from Lord Dunleath, Ballywalter Park, Co. Down, to Sir Edward Carson, 9 March 1915, enclosing **(b)** a full statement of his views on the role of the U.V.F. (D 1507/1/1915/7):

My dear Sir Edward—Many thanks for your letter. I hope you will excuse me for informing you unreservedly as to my views about the Volunteers, which may be somewhat displeasing to you. The matter, however is of such vital importance that I have felt it to be my duty to keep nothing back, but to tell you exactly the conclusions I have arrived at. I have written 'Private' on the envelope, because I naturally wish to take every precaution to prevent the letter, or any part of it from becoming public property. With kind regards I remain Yours sincerely

Dunleath

(b)

As one of the Pioneers of the Volunteer Movement I should like to say something to you with regard to their present position, and their probable future actions.

The general idea in the minds of the men who promoted and organized this movement was to give as strong an expression as possible of their resolve

261

to resist the policy of Home Rule. Speeches in and out of Parliament, and Monster Demonstrations in Ulster had apparently failed to interest the English and Scotch electors, or to concentrate their attention on the passionate abhorrence of Home Rule, on the part of the Protestant population of Ireland and of the industrial inhabitants of Ulster.

We felt that it was the plain duty of those of us who were possessed of influence to take some step, which would convince the Government of the reality of our determination to resist this policy by every means in our power, and at the same time to attract to Ulster the attention of the masses in England and Scotland. We commenced by drilling our Orangemen, and our Unionist Clubs, wherever drill instructors could be obtained, and suitable halls and lodges were available. Later on we amalgamated these forces, organized them into Companies and Battalions, appointed officers and section leaders, and gradually equipped and trained them into a very fairly efficient force of Volunteer infantry. Finally we succeeded in providing them with a good supply of arms and ammunition.

We can certainly claim that we have succeeded in turning the attention of Englishmen and Scotchmen towards Ulster and its inhabitants; we can also claim that the existence of this large armed force of Volunteers has materially assisted our political leaders, and that it will continue to assist them in the future.

In conducting this movement, we advanced, from one step to another, in our desire to make our Force as efficient as we could, until a few months ago we found ourselves on the brink of a conflict with the armed forces of the Crown.

The European War has now given us a favorable opportunity to carefully estimate and consider our position and future policy.

Many of us are undoubtedly willing, if necessary to risk our lives in defence of what we believe to be our rights and liberties, but I venture to think that an encounter with the armed forces of the Crown would inflict a serious injury upon our cause, and that every possible effort should be made to avoid the possibility of any calamity of this character. Moreover I do not believe that our men are prepared to go into action against any part of His Majest'y [sic] Forces, and we (their leaders) should not consider ourselves justified in calling upon them to do so.

It must be remembered that we are a democratic force, and that our discipline is very different from that of a Regular army; consequently orders even from General Richardson would not necessarily be carried out, if the policy embodied in such orders failed to commend itself to the men and to their officers.

If any political action should be contemplated, which requires the co-operation of the Volunteers, it would be expedient to consult the Battalion Commanders, as well as the Head Quarters Staff.

I quite understand that Unionist Politicians would like very much to be able to assert in their speeches that the Volunteers will undoubtedly come out

262

and fight at the first attempt to administer the Home Rule Act, but I venture to express a strong hope that this assertion will not be made or encouraged by the leaders of the Unionist Party.

If Ulster is not to be excluded by an Amending Act, I submit with all deference to your superior wisdom and judgment, that our policy should be, in the first instance, one of passive resistance (especially against the payment of taxes imposed by a Home Rule Parliament). If the enforcement of these taxes is left to the Home Rule Government, our Volunteers would always be available to resist; our men would like nothing better than to go out against the Nationalists.

What I am asking for is briefly this—(1) that our men shall not be ordered to mobilise against the forces of the Crown and (2) that they shall not be placed in such a position that they may be branded as cowards if they should remain quiescent when the Home Rule Act commences to operate.

Our political position as Passive Resisters, supported by a large body of armed Volunteers, should be a strong one—whereas if even a single British soldier or sailor was killed or wounded in Ulster, I am afraid that our future prospects would be extremely gloomy.

As I said just now, many of us are prepared to risk a great deal for our cause, but even our Covenant does not compel us to run our heads against a wall; we want to do everything in our power to defeat Home Rule. In the words of the Covenant we are prepared to use "all means, which may be found necessary to defeat the present Conspiracy—and in the event of such a Parliament being forced upon us—we shall refuse to recognize its authority."

Chapter VIII

The Irish unionists in British politics: the anti-home rule campaign

Unable to contain the nationalist movement within Ireland, Irish unionists had to fight it within the whole field of British politics. Their aim was to persuade British electors and politicians to maintain the union. From 1886 until the outbreak of war in 1914 they carried on a reasonably effective anti-home rule campaign throughout British politics; and for a short while in 1916 the southern unionists resumed their agitation, although in a limited way. Often Ulster and southern unionists would cooperate in this campaign which, despite sources of friction, was carried on mainly through the conservative and liberal unionist parties of Great Britain. It was waged in two spheres: in the more restricted sphere of parliamentary and party politics, and at a constituency level. Whenever home rule seemed likely to be a dominant issue, the Irish unionists were ready to present their case in order to keep the unionist party firm on the union and to ensure that the electors did not return home rule candidates. The campaign reached its peak at the time of the crisis over the third home rule bill, 1912–14, when Irish unionists hoped that a dissolution on the home rule issue would result not only in the defeat of the liberal party but also in the defeat for the third and last time of the whole policy of home rule.

In the N.I.P.R.O. there is a wide range of material relating to this campaign, and the object of this chapter is to give an idea of the range and nature of this material.

II

In the main, this campaign in British politics was carried on in conjunction with the conservative and liberal unionist parties of Great Britain. Such cooperation was not without its difficulties. It was often endangered by the attitude taken up by British unionists on such sensitive issues as the land question, local government and a catholic university. These difficulties, some of which have been mentioned in chapters V and VI, were ever present; but in the early years special problems were presented by Joseph Chamberlain, co-leader with Lord Hartington of the liberal unionists.

At first Irish unionists were very wary of him. On the one hand, a lurking contempt for Irishmen and Irish politics occasionally showed through in his speeches. On the other hand, Chamberlain, who believed that coercion without reconstruction would be fatal to the union and to the parties standing for it, put forward very advanced views on local government and the land question. Among other things, he advocated a wide measure of local government, including not only the reform of county and municipal administration but also the establishment of representative provincial councils with powers to deal with local taxation, liquor and other licences, charities, public works, railways and tramways, matters affecting agriculture, fisheries and emigration, and perhaps education. He also advocated the settlement of the land question by a scheme of land purchase based (for obvious electoral reasons) not upon British credit but upon Irish credit. His proposed Irish county councils would act as middlemen between landlord and tenant and buy and administer estates using funds raised on Irish securities.

Such views disturbed Irish unionists, including those belonging to the Liberal Union of Ireland. His ideas about provincial councils smacked too much of home rule and were disliked by commercial men such as Frederick Pim junior and lawyer-politicians such as William Kenny, unionist M.P. for the St Stephen's Green division of Dublin (1892–7), and founder member of the Liberal Union of Ireland; while landlords, such as H. de F. Montgomery, objected to Chamberlain's ideas on land purchase. Montgomery objected to any scheme that had even the suggestion of compulsion, and, having no confidence in the stability of Irish credit, thought that the help of the British taxpayer was essential for the successful completion of land purchase begun by Ashbourne's act of 1885.

The best statement of Chamberlain's Irish views appeared in a series of articles, issued on his own initiative, in the *Birmingham Daily Post,* beginning 21 May 1888, and later published as *A unionist policy for Ireland.* Liberal unionists from Ireland thus looked forward with apprehension to the first annual assembly of liberal unionists at Birmingham in April 1889. Any danger of a rift was avoided, however, partly because of the tact and good sense of Lord Hartington and partly because of the attitude taken up by the conference. There was no attempt to push the *Birmingham Daily Post* scheme, and Montgomery, who attended to put the landlord's case, was agreeably suprised at the attitude to land purchase. There was little support for compulsory purchase; and, despite the fact that unionists had criticised Gladstone's 1886 land purchase bill as creating an enormous British liability, there was a general acceptance of the need for British credit in Irish land purchase. Most notably, the conference was willing to amend a resolution on the land question which otherwise would have relieved the British taxpayer from any share in the completion of land purchase. As a result of much talking behind the scenes, the word 'undue' was inserted; and a relieved Montgomery felt that the words 'undue burden' established the principle of a British contribution. The amended resolution ran: 'That this meeting, believing that the land question is at the root of Irish disaffection and discontent, respectfully urges her majesty's government to introduce into parliament without delay a measure under which the Irish agricultural tenants generally may become the proprietors of their holdings by methods which do not impose undue burden and responsibility upon the imperial exchequer'.

145 Letter from W. Kenny, Fitzwilliam Place, Dublin, to H. de F. Montgomery, 21 April 1889, discussing the attitude to be taken up by the Irish delegates at the forthcoming conference of liberal unionists at Birmingham (D 627/428/97):

Private

My Dear Montgomery—With regard to our "speaking" privileges at the Irish meeting of the conference our organisation stands thus. I was, myself, asked to speak in the first instance but had to decline owing to my engagements (professional) here. Our committee then selected Mr. Fredk. W. Pim as our spokesman. Subsequently I received a letter from Mr. Bagwell asking if I could secure him 10 minutes. This I did—but he will not speak in any representative capacity. I have made this clear with Baily

Pim & some others much fear—and I think rightly so—Chamberlains awful scheme of Provincial Councils & with a desire to counteract it were anxious to join in the demand for a local Gov. Bill as soon as possible. I objected to pressure and we all thought it well that I should communicate with Ld. Hartington—who replied very fully & frankly. He said he thought each delegate should on a question like this on which there was not complete unanimity of opinion in the body that he represented, give his own individual views & accompany them with a statement that difference of opinion on the subject existed.

It seems to me that the same rule ought to govern any observations upon the Land question.

I could not get Pim to speak from the point of view of opposition to compulsory purchase and I rather think our committee would be in favour of it: we have not discussed it at all and are somewhat in the dark as to the reasons to be given in opposition to it. If you had time to write in a few lines on the subject [?] from your point of view I would be obliged. It seems to me that once the Landlord is in the position of a mere rent-charger—which the fixing of a judicial rent places him in—it can make no difference to him to get the capitalized value of that rent—provided of course—he gets the full value & that none of it is tied up. The Landlords I fear must recognise that there is very little sympathy for them and, however much we may regret it, that there is small chance of altering that feeling in their favour

Please do not take it that I have given in my adhesion to compulsory purchase. My mind is quite open & to a very large extent so are those of our Committee here.

We have had some small friction with Birmingham & "Joe" as to Local gov., but I think it is smoothed over Very truly yours

W. Kenny

146 *Letter from H. de F. Montgomery, writing from 60 Harborne Road, Birmingham, to E. Willis of the Irish Landowners' Convention, Dublin, 26 April 1889, describing how at the conference of liberal unionists a resolution on the land question was amended to permit the use of British credit in future land purchase schemes (D 627/428/99):

Private

My dear Willis—I am sorry I could not get a minute to write before post time yesterday—but there was really nothing substantial to add to my telegram—except that, as far as I could see, Brights letter was not distributed after all—though Cornish's manager had distinctly undertaken on Wednesday to arrange to have it done.

I considered it on the whole wiser not to go & stir him up about it—and Bagwell confirmed me in this. I would not, of course, in face of your wire have taken upon me to countermand the distribution but as matters seem to me to stand now I am disposed to think the wide distribution of the letter among hasty readers might do more harm than good by setting many against any expansion of Ashbourne's act.

There is absolutely no attempt to push the B[irmingham]. D[aily]. P[ost]. scheme. It does not seem to be even on sale in the booksellers—

The drift of opinion is clearly going against compulsion and in favour of the necessity of bringing imperial credit to bear in the arrangement. The words added to the resolution put the thin edge of the wedge well in & as the matter comes to be worked out it will become more and more apparent to the workers that the more directly the British Treasury is brought into play— the cheaper the job will be done in the long run.

I now regret rather that we bothered with these arrangements with Cornish—I think we have only wasted our money—but we could not know that beforehand—There was not a single speaker that touched on the Irish Land question with the partial exception of the Ulster farmers representatives, that did not dwell strongly upon the necessity of treating the Landlords fairly however it was settled & on the fact that the tenants had now no grievance—had had more done for them than farmers in any other country in the world &c.

I [do] not know the full secret history of the altered resolution.

This much I know: My Belfast friends agreed with me that as it stood it was nonsense, would comit [*sic*] the party to a sort of contradiction in terms— amounting to addressing a request to the Government to do what most of us were convinced was impossible. I put this to Chamberlain himself at his own house on Wednesday night. He said "The government dont think so. There is a way. If you dont agree with the resolution you need not speak to it you know" I said I did not want to speak to any of the resolutions but I objected to joining in passing a resolution that I thought absurd: that I had not met with a single Irish man of business who could conceive a security on which the scheme could be founded. He said it was too large a subject to discuss there, but he thought I need not make myself uneasy—surely we were all agreed that if there was a way to do this thing it would be desirable, and therefore there could be no harm in asking the government to do it. I said I thought it a mistake to lead the public to believe a thing could be done when we could not see how—after which I said something civil & moved on.

I said the same thing to Kenrick and got the same sort of answer but in rather less confident tones—but both he & Chamberlain said it was impossible to get British credit, so some other way must be found. I then went a tour of the rooms and put the matter before the Duke of St. Albans, Lord Northbrook, Lord Camperdown & some others and finally spoke very strongly about it to Lord Hartington—who seemed entirely to agree with me,—but said there was the difficulty created by the way in which Gladstone's Land Bill had been attacked by unionists—to which I said: "Is it not the business of these men (meaning Chamberlain & Co.) to do all they can to extricate us from the mess this has got us into, instead of getting is [us] in deeper & deeper by going on assuring the British elector he is to contribute no share & take no responsibility in the settlement of the Irish Land Question? Is not the broad distinction between Gladstone's proposal and any Unionist proposal so plain that even the British elector can easily be made to understand it?" He said yes: and I again pointed out the mischief of the resolution & said it would be very desirable it should still be altered if possible. Meanwhile Richard Patterson had taken the wording of the resolution in hand and made the suggestion of the interpolation of the words "any undue" of which you know.

I found in conversation with various people that most people, including Lord Hartington, Bagwell, Sinclair, my host, (a leading local L[iberal]. U[nionist].) held distinctly that "generally" did not mean universally & that the resolution did not imply compulsion.

At the conference the Resolution (no. 2) was proposed by Mr. Cross of Glasgow in the absence of Professor Calderwood.

He said little or nothing any one of us could object to—and when he came to read the resolution as printed he said (as to the last part): "Well I dont quite agree with that. I think the British taxpayer is bound to bear his share in finding means to carry out a healing measure in a portion of the United Kingdom (or words to that effect) and said he wished to insert the word "undue". This was applauded by part of the meeting, and produced no expression of dissent whatever. Kenrick M.P. (Chamberlains brother-in-law) seconded the resolution & accepted the alteration & in explaining why used words almost identical with part of the last paragraph of my "notes" on the B.D.P. scheme.

One of our Belfast men (W. J. Hurst) made a very moderate little speech in favour of compulsory purchase—but stating very fairly & clearly some of the reasons against it, and strongly supported the necessity & justice of the direct help of British credit, without any dissent from any part of the meeting.

Mr. Black (whom we put forward as the representative of the out and out Presbyterian Radical compulsory purchase tenant farmer party) went for compulsory purchase as being absolutely necessary & inevitable & was met with very decided expressions of disapproval from a good part of the meeting & no applause. He spoke in a tiresome ridiculous preaching way & was called to time just as he invited the meeting to accompany him to Saxe-Coburg to see how well compulsory purchase worked there—having produced a bad impression. The motion was then put—distinct stress being laid on the added word by the chairman (Powell Williams—the reputed author of the B.D.P. scheme) and passed unanimously—one man protesting—not as I understood against the resolution, but because he had not been allowed to speak—the time allotted to the subject being up.

No allusion was made to any part of the B.D.P. scheme was made [sic] during any part of the discussion on either local Government or Land. Neither did I see it on sale in Cornish's. I opine it is dead.

I thanked Kenrick afterwards for accepting the alteration—He said he quite felt that it was both right & necessary—I then pointed out to him some of the chief objections to compulsion & gave him the answers to the arguments in its favour that seemed to have impressed him.

He appeared to me still undecided—but on the whole disposed to be rather against compulsion.

Mr. Baily—the Secretary of the National Liberal Union—Chamberlains organization, lunched with the Ulster delegates. I asked him whether he did not think there had been a very exaggerated fear of telling the British Tax-payer he must put his hand in his pocket to settle the Irish Land Question. He said he thought so: if the British Tax-payer was told plainly a thing had to be done & paid for, he would do his duty. I asked him whether he did not think the distinction between Gladstones bill & Ashbourne's Act or any similar measure was not clear enough to enable us to escape any trouble or difficulty arising out of Unionist attacks on Gladstones measure? He said: certainly.

I then had a chat with him about compulsory & voluntary methods & he seemed to me to admit that the latter were safer & better.

I have marked this letter private—but you may show it to safe members of our committee or others to whom you think it desirable to impart its contents.

I shall however be much obliged if you will either let me have this letter back—or a copy of it—as it is a record of my visit here which I should like to keep & I have not time to take a copy myself now. in haste yrs very truly

H de F Montgomery

147 Letter from W. Kenny, Fitzwilliam Place, Dublin, to H. de F. Montgomery, 26 October 1894, expressing dissatisfaction with a speech made by Joseph Chamberlain at Clapham (D 627/428/259):

My Dear Montgomery—I quite agree with you that we must subordinate any opinions of our own to those of Chamberlain. It is a matter of policy—in which he is entitled to obedience—

But it is really hard to keep ones temper. In his Clapham speech he rails against Catholics & shows me clearly what an intolerant man he is. We dont care to have our religious emblems spoken of as "so called" religious emblems. I am sorely tempted to give him the rough side of my tongue over this & I am not sure that I wont Sincerely Yours

W Kenny

III

As **147** suggests, Irish unionists could not afford to reject their conservative and liberal unionist allies lightly, in view of the overwhelming importance of maintaining the union. Owing to the liberal commitment to home rule, their range of manoeuvre, as far as constitutional agitation was concerned, was strictly limited. This was made abundantly clear when Gladstone introduced his second home rule bill in February 1893. Until then, though contemptuous of (what they regarded as) the unthinking attitude of liberal politicians such as John Morley, many Irish unionists especially in Ulster had been reluctant to condemn Gladstone out of hand. Though in 1886 Irish conservatives had hung up cartoons of Gladstone and Parnell in their lavatories, other Irish unionists, especially in Ulster, had been liberals, once bound to the liberal party by 'ties of old political association and a love and reverence for Mr Gladstone'. However, the liberal leader's refusal to accept the views of Irish unionists, such as those presented by a deputation of businessmen and liberal unionists from Belfast in March 1893, broke finally the spell of Gladstone's personality and underlined the futility of hoping for any favourable consideration from the liberal party.

148 Letter from J. Byrne, Ergenagh, Omagh, Co. Tyrone, to H. de F. Montgomery, 21 March 1890, criticising the unthinking attitude of the liberal party towards the Irish question (D 627/428/134):

My dear Sir—I thank you most sincerely for your admirable pamphlet "Gladstone and Burke" and the correspondence which followed. Burke was indeed a master of civil wisdom who proclaimed it to the world with the music of trumpets, Gladstone is an inscrutable mystery of whom it is impossible to say whether he is a saint perverted by vanity and ambition or a madman who honestly mistakes the suggestions of parliamentary advantage for inspirations of true wisdom. Mr. John Morley seems to me to be a superficial litterateur and doctrinaire, as deficient as his leader in the power or habit of thinking in a comprehensive manner of the conditions of political problems, which the great complexity of human affairs requires absolutely in a statesman. One of the conditions of the Irish question which seems to be overlooked too much on all sides, is the history of Ireland in the 17th. and 18th. centuries. Two hundred years of warfare and mutual vengeance, of rebellion and confiscation accumulated in the defeated party a bitter tradition of national hatred and fierce thirst for restitution, which is the essence of the Irish difficulty and the danger of an independent Ireland. This statesmen will not see. The source of the evil is with them, now the establishment of the church, now the oppression of the landlords or the inequality of educational arrangements, now the blackguardism of the Union, but never the great historical facts whose consequences can be removed only by patient justice and a union in which there will be the least friction between the two islands. Believe me with many thanks Yours truly

James Byrne

149 Letter from A. Duffin, writing from London, to his wife, 29 March 1893, and reporting on the progress of a liberal unionist deputation visiting political leaders in London, including Gladstone (Mic 127/10):

Dearest—As I expected we did not get much change out of Gladstone yesterday but he didn't have at all as good a time with us as he expected. His deliberate plan was not to hear us at all on the plea that our case was before him on paper and then to read us a lecture ex cathedra. However, we got in on him a little by straining the bounds of courtesy. I bowled him over the first shot on the customs figures. He gently insinuated that our zeal to magnify the importance of our City had led us into egregious error. Greenhill was not equal to the occasion so I had to get up and point out politely how he had been misled by his ignorance of the special facts & that we were absolutely right in our statement which I read & he had misquoted. He dropped that subject. Tom Sinclair had a hard time to get in even half of what he had to say, but the old man was jumping with impatience & we have at least got it clearly brought out that he closured us. I made the excuse of thanking him for giving us even such scant opportunity as we had had of stating our views in order to fire our parting shot on the ancient history branch of the argument. But none of us got a chance of fair play. However he has challenged us to reply on paper & we mean to. This will give us a grand chance of bringing the whole controversy before the Gladstonian word [?], which is all I ever expected to get by the interview

We had afterwards an interview with Balfour. Ewart made a capital speech. Musgrave made an abject fool of himself and I did very well on some main points. We dined with Harland, fearfully stupid, all our own gang, & Arnold Forster who lectured the Assembly in his worst style.

I am dining here tonight & shall meet some more interesting people Expect to leave for home tomorrow via Liverpool. Have just been to Devonshire House to look for John Dunville but find he is at Brighton. Tom (Sinclair) & I are off to the House now to seek further interviews. They say it is no use going to Morley but I mean to have a try for Asquith.

I had a long talk with David Plunket yesterday. He is a fine fellow but wants grip badly. I may be able to add a line later. Love & kisses to the chicks. We shall defeat this conspiracy. I am more sure than ever. Ever your own

Adam Duffin

Geo. Clark says the old man is mad & we ought to publish the fact & give no other answer! I say he is bad. He has the look of a bird of prey and the smile of a hyena. It was positively shocking to see the hideous mechanical grin with which he took leave of us.

IV

The exigencies of party politics thus forced the Irish unionists to work through and with the conservative and liberal unionist parties in Great Britain (hereafter referred to jointly, for convenience, as the unionist party). When the liberals were in office (1892–5, 1905–15), and whenever home rule was or looked like becoming an issue, Irish unionists were active, presenting their case to the opposition, the unionist leaders and politicians in Great Britain.

They were assisted by the fact that they were well represented in both houses of parliament and in the hierarchy of the unionist party. Among the leaders of the unionist party in Great Britain were prominent Irish unionists such as Lord Hartington (later 8th duke of Devonshire), the 5th marquis of Lansdowne, the 6th marquis of Londonderry, the 9th Viscount Midleton (St John Brodrick); and ardent sympathisers such as Walter Long and Andrew Bonar Law. In the house of lords, over 100 peers had landed or close family interests in Ireland, three-quarters of them in the southern provinces; and northern and southern unionists had representation in the house of commons. Ulster unionists usually returned at least 16 M.P.s; and though the southern provinces returned only two or three unionist M.P.s, a number of southern unionists sat for British constituencies. Irish unionists relied upon such representatives not only to present their case in parliament, but also to work behind the scenes, establishing intimate contacts with British unionists. Lord Templetown, president of the unionist clubs organisation, was active on their behalf, explaining on one occasion to members of parliament and their supporters in and around London the objects of the clubs.

Such individual efforts were supported by more formal and official deputations sent over to interview leading unionists in parliament. For instance, in March 1907 the U.U.C. and the I.U.A. cooperated and sent a joint deputation to interview unionist leaders in both houses of parliament and explain Irish unionist objections to the impending Irish councils bill. (This proposal by Campbell-Bannerman's liberal government to set up an Irish council, partly elected and partly nominated and with limited powers, was as objectionable to Irish unionists as full home rule. As the witty Professor Dowden said on one occasion, it was no consolation to Irish unionists to be told that their 'mangled limbs' would find a half-way ledge to rest on before plunging to their final descent.)

Nor did the Irish unionists neglect the annual party conferences. They attended regularly to ensure that anti-home rule resolutions were proposed and endorsed. Occasionally Ulster and southern unionists cooperated in sending delegations to the annual conference of conservative and unionist associations, as in 1909; but as the crisis over the third home rule bill developed Ulster preferred separate representation. It was at this time that the Ulster unionists began to rely heavily upon Sir Edward Carson to present their case in Great Britain, and it is interesting to see that some Ulster landlords who now developed an intense loyalty to him had formerly—in 1892—objected to his being backed for one of the Dublin University seats by Arthur Balfour, then Irish chief secretary. Balfour appreciated Carson's forensic talents, but some landlords would have preferred a solid champion of landlord rights, willing to attend regularly to such matters as the Morley committee, set up in 1894 to examine the working of the land acts.

150 Report by 4th Viscount Templetown of his visit to England, June 1893, to publicise the unionist clubs movement, presented to and approved by a meeting of the Unionist Clubs Council, Central Hall, Belfast, on 8 August 1893 (D 1327/1/1):

Gentlemen, in company with Mr. B. W. Montgomery, one of our hon. secretaries, I went to London on June 5th with the object of explaining the organisation of the Unionist clubs of Ireland, and obtaining for it the approval and support of the most influential political associations. On Tuesday, 6th, we were most hospitably entertained by the Committee of the City Carlton Club, afterwards, also by the invitation of the Committee, the constitution and object of the Unionist clubs in Ireland were explained. As a full report of what transpired was duly published I need only say that the enthusiasm and sympathy of the members with the Unionist cause in Ireland was highly gratifying. I would take this opportunity of bringing specially before your notice the very valuable assistance rendered to our organisation, as well as to the Unionist cause, by Mr. Henry Kimber, M.P. for Wandsworth, to whose kindness and energy we owe the invitations received to address not only the members of the City Carlton Club, but other political associations as well. On June the 7th, Mr. Montgomery and I addressed the members of the Balham and Upping Tooting Conservative Club, of which

275

Mr. A. J. Balfour is president, where a hearty vote of sympathy with us was unanimously passed, and in connection with this I may mention that the Committee have done me the honour to elect me to their Club, and to be one of their vice-presidents. The following Saturday I had the pleasure of accepting an invitation to luncheon at Mr. Henry Kimber's, Putney, to meet several well-known metropolitan and other members of Parliament; amongst them, Sir F. Dixon Hartland, Sir John Blundell, Mr. St. John Brodrick, Mr. Bartley, Mr. Wootton-Isaacson, Mr. Percy Thornton, and others; and after luncheon, at Mr. Kimber's request, I explained to them at some length the organisation and objects of the clubs. I would here remark that before we went to England Mr. Montgomery suggested to me the linking of Unionist clubs in Ireland with Unionist clubs or organisations in England and Scotland. Well, at the meeting at Mr. Kimber's, Mr. Arnold-Forster suggested the linking not only of one club in Ireland- to one organisation in England, but a triple linking—*i.e.,* linking a Unionist Club in Ulster and one in the South or West of Ireland with one in England. As his scheme has appeared in the newspapers I need not describe it again, but I may at once say that with our Executive Committee I entirely agree in thinking it an excellent scheme, and we shall be very happy to consider its application where practicable. Well, gentlemen, to return to the meeting at Mr. Kimber's, the immediate result was a meeting at Stepney, the constituency of Mr. F. Wootton-Isaacson, and now I have the honour and great pleasure of reporting to this meeting that the magnificent Union Jack you see before you was entrusted to me to bring over to you as a token of sympathy from the Unionists of Stepney, in public meeting assembled, as you will see by the streamer. The kind reference to the Irish Loyalists by Mr. Wootton-Isaacson when presenting the flag was received, gentlemen, by that magnificent meeting, with cheer after cheer, and bodes well to the Unionist cause in that East End constituency. I will ask you, gentlemen, to pass a vote of thanks presently to Mr. Wootton-Isaacson and the Unionists of Stepney; also, to decide in whose keeping that "Union Jack" shall remain. Then Mr. Bartley, M.P. for North Islington, introduced me to Mr. Crump, the chairman of his committee, who very kindly entertained me at dinner, and organised a meeting of the committee afterwards, at which a hearty vote of sympathy with our cause was passed, and promises of help to this organisation were numerous. They did me the honour at the Merchant Taylors' dinner to ask me to respond to the toast of "The Visitors," and my declaration that the Unionists of Ulster declined to be separated from the Queen and the Union, or our civil and religious liberties, was received in the only manner worthy of loyal Englishmen. As showing the interest awakened in England by the Unionist clubs in Ireland, I may mention that the Executive Committee of the Yorkshire Council of the National Union of Conservative and Constitutional Associations invited me to explain our system to them. I went to York to their meeting on the 22nd of June, when our late popular Viceroy, the Marquis of Zetland, was in the chair, and I explained our system to them, with the result that, as in other cases, most cordial promises were made to consider any means put before them for helping our organisation. To summarise the results of this visit to England, I would say that the deepest interest is taken in our organisation, and it is understood as representing the existence of the fixed determination of the Loyalists in Ireland never to submit to Home Rule. Universal desire is expressed by all I have met to consider any proposal for linking or other method of co-operation which we may advance for their consideration. I had numerous opportunities for consultation with men of political influence, and I was glad to find that the best thought in Ireland was quite in line with all that is more essential to the success of the Unionist cause in Great Britain, and I think I may fairly express the hope and belief that the work done by us in England will yield good results. In this connection I can only regret that Mr. Montgomery was unable to remain longer than he did to help me in the work in the same valuable way he did in our negotiations for obtaining the approval of the Executive Committee of the National Union of Conservative and Constitutional Associations, and that of Mr. Powell Williams, as representing the Liberal Unionists. As this will lead to the question of the nature of our scheme of future work, it is a matter for separate consideration. I will now only ask you to receive and adopt this report, and then I will proceed to put forward for your consideration modes of future work, after having asked you to pass a vote of thanks to Mr. Wootton-Isaacson and the Unionists of Stepney, and to Mr. Henry Kimber, M.P., for his valuable services, and to the Committee of the City Carlton Club. (Applause.)

151 Extracts from *Notes from Ireland,* April 1907, reporting and commenting on the deputations from the U.U.C. and I.U.A. that visited London, 19 March 1907, to lay before unionist leaders their views on the liberal government's impending Irish councils bill (D 989C/3/44A):

A valuable day's work for Unionism was done on the 19th ultimo by the distinguished deputation organised by the Irish Unionist Alliance and the Ulster Unionist Council. The spokesmen, one and all, on that date ably presented to Mr. Balfour and to the other Unionist leaders the case of Irish Unionists against the Government, and most sympathetically and vigorously did Mr. Balfour respond to their statements. Since its birth, the dishonest "instalment" policy has not got such a full and authoritative exposure. "A deliberate and intentional fraud upon the British electorate" was Mr. Balfour's description of that policy, and no honest politician can doubt the truth of it. Will the British electorate fully awake to a true conception of the case, while there is yet time? Mr. Balfour has no doubts on that head, and Irish Unionists are with him in believing that—as before on two occasions—Great Britain will become thoroughly aroused as to the danger and incalculable folly of legislation calculated to hand over the government of Ireland to Nationalist hands.

In the meantime, under the auspices of the Ministry of Devolution and Instalments, many parts of Ireland are fast lapsing into a state of disorder and lawlessness, as the following pages will testify. Mr. Redmond and his friends say no—Ireland is at peace. Crimes, says Mr. Redmond in effect, are unknown. We are at peace with ourselves, and at peace with our neighbours. Can you say, he asks, that the same thing prevails in England? This evasion of a real issue has become so common that Irish Unionists treat it with disdain and contempt. Crime in England, as everybody knows, is the crime of individuals against general society: in Ireland (not to make little of its exemption from ordinary offences) the supreme task of our judges is to deal with organised crime—the crime not of individuals but of whole associations embodied for the purpose of making constituted law impossible. Therefore there is no proper comparison to be instituted between lawlessness in England and lawlessness in Ireland. Compare, for instance, the most severe remarks of the English judges on English crime, with the observations of Irish judges placed in the same position. At Ennis the Lord Chief Justice of Ireland lately stated that many parts of Clare were in a demoralised and lawless condition, and asked what Englishmen would think if, in any English Shire, thirty persons had to live under police protection? Mr. Justice Kenny also noted in his address to the Grand Jury of Leitrim, that many people were "wholly boycotted, and were under police protection." What he called "the chain of terrorism," and which is simply the coercion of the League, rendered, he said, the law a nullity. As a matter of fact, juries often cannot be got to convict, in spite of the earnest exhortation of the judge to decide the case according to the evidence. In whole districts of Ireland the King's Writ is of no effect. Postmen proceeding in the course of their duties to deliver letters have been waylaid on the King's highway, and letters containing legal documents have been taken from their custody by force. The police have as yet been unable to make the offenders amenable.

A hundred quotations might be given of the utterly lawless condition of these League-blighted districts. Take the following as a specimen. It is from the *Sligo Champion* of March 2nd. Edward Layng, who occupies an evicted holding, resisted the pressure of the League, and the Mullinabreena Branch at a meeting passed the following resolution:—

"That our secretary be instructed to write to Messrs. Redmond, Dillon, M'Hugh, and O'Dowd, and ask them to fix the first convenient date for our monster demonstration; we feel we are compelled to adopt this course, as Edward Layng has not replied directly to our resolution of last week; a copy to be sent to Edward Layng."

This and many more evidences of the bold and untrammelled procedure of the League branches show that the law of the land is practically inoperative in those districts.

In the presence of this state of disorder it is alarming to think that Dublin Castle, charged as it is with the impartial administration of affairs, looks not only calmly on, but seems by its mien of indifference to incite the fomenters of this disorder to further efforts in the interests of their insane policy of "instalments" of Home Rule.

IRISH UNIONIST DEPUTATION TO MR. BALFOUR.

On the afternoon of March 19th, 1907, Mr. Balfour received at his residence in Carlton Gardens a large and influential deputation from the Irish Unionist Alliance and the Ulster Unionist Council, who laid before him their views with regard to the instalment of the "larger policy" promised in the King's Speech.

Mr. Balfour was accompanied by Lord Lansdowne and the Right Hon. Walter Long, M.P.

There were also present—The Right Hon. J. H. Campbell, K.C., M.P.; Mr. Lonsdale, M.P.; Mr. C. Craig, M.P.; Captain Craig, M.P.; and Mr. S. H. Butcher, M.P.

The members of the deputation were as follows:

IRISH UNIONIST ALLIANCE.

Sir John Arnott, Bart., D.L.; Lord Barrymore, Mr. Percy Bernard, D.L.; Mr. Robert Booth, J.P.; Mr. S. P. Boyd, J.P.; Mr. W. H. Boyd, D.L.; Major Courtney, Mr. R. G. Carden, D.L., Templemore; Sir Malbay Crofton, Bart., D.L., Ballisodare, Sligo; Sir R. U. Penrose Fitzgerald, Bart., D.L., Whitegate; Sir W. Goff, Bart., D.L., Waterford; Gerald S. Guinness, D.L., Raheny, Co. Dublin; Lord Inchiquin, Viscount Iveagh, K.P.; Mr. Andrew Jameson, D.L., Sutton; C. Brinsley Marlay, D.L., Mullingar; Mr. R. H. A. M'Comas, J.P., Dublin; Mr. L. Perrin-Hatchell, J.P., Dublin; Rev. S. Prenter, D.D.; Mr. G. F. Stewart, D.L., Killiney; Captain Wade Thompson, J.P., Clonskeagh Castle; Mr. Fane Vernon, D.L.; Sir Wm. Watson, D.L.; Mr. J. M. Wilson, J.P., Garvagh, Edgeworthstown.

ULSTER UNIONIST COUNCIL.

Mr. W. J. Allen, Lurgan; the Right Hon. Thos. Andrews, D.L., Comber; Sir A. Douglas Brooke, Bart., D.L., Brookeboro'; Mr. R. Dawson Bates, Belfast; Captain Crawford, Belfast; Colonel Doran, Brookeboro'; Mr. Edward Dougan, Belfast; Mr. Charles W. Dunbar-Buller, D.L., Donaghadee; Mr. Wilfred Haughton, Cullybackey; G. Herbert Ewart, J.P., Belfast; Sir Jas. Henderson, D.L.; Mr. R. M. Liddell, J.P., Donaghcloney; Mr. S. M. Macrory, J.P., Limavady; Major Madden, D.L., Clones; Mr. R. D. Perceval Maxwell, J.P., Downpatrick; Major-General Montgomery, D.L., Greyabbey; Mr. B. W. D. Montgomery, Belfast; Mr. James Moore, Belfast; Mr. R. G. MacCrum, D.L., Milford, Armagh; Right Hon. the Earl of Ranfurly, Dungannon; Right Hon. Thomas Sinclair, D.L., Belfast; Sir James H. Stronge, Bart., D.L., Tynan Abbey; Captain F. H. Watt, J.P., Portrush; Right Hon. John Young, D.L., Ballymena; Mr. W. R. Young, Belfast; Mr. Geo. S. Clarke, J.P., Belfast; Mr. Geo. J. Preston, D.L., Belfast; Mr. R. Armstrong, Belfast; Mr. James Johnston, Lurgan.

The deputations were introduced by the Duke of Abercorn.

The speakers appointed on behalf of the Irish Unionist Alliance were Mr. Percy Bernard, D.L., and Mr. Andrew Jameson, D.L.

For the Ulster Unionist Council the spokesmen were the Right Hon. Thomas Sinclair, D.L., and Sir James Stronge, Bart.

The speakers having addressed Mr. Balfour, the latter replied in a striking speech, in which he said that he and the Unionist party were as determined now as ever they had been in the past to resist Home Rule or any measure of Devolution that might lead up to that policy.

Lord Lansdowne also addressed the deputation, promising them his strong support.

A vote of thanks to Mr. Balfour was moved by the Duke of Abercorn, seconded by Lord Barrymore, and passed with acclamation. The deputations then adjourned to the House of Commons where they were entertained to luncheon by members of the Union Defence League.

Later on the deputation met in the large Committee Room off Westminster Hall, a considerable number of Unionist Members of Parliament being present. In the absence of Mr. Long, Colonel M'Calmont took the chair, and the deputations were introduced by the Right Hon. J. H. Campbell, K.C., M.P. The meeting was addressed on behalf of the Alliance by the Rev. Dr. Prenter, Sir Wm. Watson, and Sir Malbay Crofton, Bart., and for the Ulster Unionist Council by the Right Hon. J. Andrews, Mr. MacCrum, and Mr. Dougan. Mr. R. Clarke, D.L., the selected candidate for the vacancy in Belfast caused by the death of the Right Hon. Sir. D. Dixon, Bart., also spoke.

Colonel Kenyon Stanley, Mr. Meysey-Thompson, and Mr. Butcher replied on behalf of the English Members of Parliament, strongly urging that they should be supplied with the details of genuine cases of boycotting and intimidation, which they could place before the English electorate.

The meeting concluded with a vote of thanks to Colonel M'Calmont, proposed by the Right Hon. J. Young.

DEPUTATION TO THE DUKE OF DEVONSHIRE.

On Wednesday afternoon the Duke of Devonshire received at Devonshire House a number of gentlemen representing the Irish Unionist Alliance and the Ulster Unionist Council. The deputation consisted of the following:— Right Hon. Thos. Andrews, Sir Rowland Blennerhassett, Sir Douglas Brooke, Captain Crawford, Lord Inchiquin, Major Madden, Right Hon. T. Sinclair, Captain Wade Thompson, Right Hon. J. Young, Messrs. W. J. Allen, Percy Bernard, Robert Booth, R. Dawson Bates, Edward Dougan, R. G. Carden, Brinsley Marlay, James Moore, R. H. A. M'Comas, Macroy L. Perrin-Hatchell, G. F. Stewart, J. M. Wilson, W. R. Young, etc.

The deputation was again introduced by the Duke of Abercorn, and after speeches by the Right Hon. Thomas Sinclair, on behalf of the Ulster Unionist Council, and Mr. George Stewart, for the Irish Unionist Alliance,

The Duke of Devonshire assured the deputation that his objections and opposition to Home Rule, or any policy leading up to it, were in no way diminished, and that they might rely on his active assistance in the coming struggle.

152 Extracts from the *Annual reports* of the U.U.C., 1909, 1911, 1912, relating to the visit of delegations to annual conferences of the conservative and unionist party in those years (D 972/17/1909, 1912 and 1913):

(a)

The Annual Conference of the National Union of Conservative and Constitutional Associations was held at Manchester on the 16th, 17th, and

18th November. Twenty delegates appointed by the Unionist Associations of Ireland attended, the Ulster representatives being:—Sir James Henderson, D.L.; Major Madden, D.L.; Rev. Andrew Leitch; Messrs. Anketell Moutray, D.L.; John Carmichael-Ferrall, D.L.; William T. Miller, J.P.; W. J. Allen, J.P.; S. E. Smythe-Edwards, and R. Dawson Bates.

The following resolution was put forward on behalf of the Associations:—

"That this Conference desires to express its determined and unabated hostility to any legislative proposals which may tend to the eventual granting of Home Rule, or which are calculated to weaken the Imperial tie between Great Britain and Ireland. It does so with the more emphasis, in view of the fact that the leader of the Nationalist Party in Ireland has recently declared that, however different may be their methods, the principles of the Party are the same as those of the Fenian rebels of 1867."

This was ably moved by Mr. S. H. Butcher, M.P., representing the South of Ireland, and seconded by Mr. W. J. Allen, representing Ulster. The reception given to the proposer and seconder was of the most cordial nature, the speakers receiving the rare compliment of being asked to continue speaking beyond the allotted time. Mr. Balfour addressed a mass meeting in the Drill Hall on the evening of the 17th, and in a speech of great impressiveness put forward the principles on which the General Election would be fought. The reception accorded the leader of the Unionist Party in the city that led the rout of the Party four years ago, must have been particularly gratifying to him, and it is peculiarly fitting that the same city should be the scene of the call to arms.

(b)

The Annual Conference of the National Conservative Union was held at Leeds on the 15th, 16th, and 17th November. The Ulster Unionist Council, was represented by Mr. W. J. Allen, J.P.; Major Head, General Montgomery, D.L.; Mr. Anketell Moutray, D.L.; Mr. D. D. Reid, B.L.; Mr. Edward Sclater, J.P.; Mr. S. E. Smythe-Edwards, Sir James Stronge, Bart., D.L., and Mr. R. Dawson Bates.

The following resolution was proposed by the Right Hon. Walter H. Long, M.P.:—

"That this meeting protests against the attempt of the Government to force Home Rule upon the country at the dictation of the Irish Nationalist Party, desires to record its opinion that in the interests of Great Britain and of Ireland alike it will be disastrous to the present satisfactory development of Ireland to provoke a bitter and prolonged controversy, and declares its determination to resist any attempt to coerce the loyal minority in Ireland." Mr. W. J. Allen seconded.

The speeches were received with the greatest enthusiasm. Mr. Bonar Law addressed a mass meeting in the Coliseum on the night of the 16th. This being his first public appearance since his election as Leader of the Opposition, his speech was naturally awaited with the keenest interest by Irish Unionists. The masterly manner in which he presented the Unionist case showed that Irish Unionists have in Mr. Bonar Law an uncompromising supporter of their cause.

(c)

ANNUAL CONFERENCE OF THE NATIONAL UNIONIST ASSOCIATION OF CONSERVATIVE AND LIBERAL-UNIONIST ORGANISATIONS.

This Conference was held in London on the 13th, 14th, and 15th November. Your Committee were represented by Sir James H. Stronge, Bart., D.L.; Captain Somerset Saunderson, Messrs. J. J. Kirkpatrick, J.P.; J. R. Fisher, B.L.; Lloyd Campbell, and A. Newton Anderson. The Executive Committee of the Unionist Clubs of Ireland sent two representatives—Mr. Edward Sclater, J.P., and Captain Frank Hall.

The following resolution was moved by Sir Edward Carson, who received a most cordial reception from the delegates:—

"That this meeting is of opinion that the Home Rule policy of the Government is both disastrous to Ireland and a danger to the Empire, and emphatically condemns the action of the Government in attempting to force through Parliament without adequate discussion, in disregard and in deliberate defiance of the settled practice of Parliament, a Home Rule Bill which has never been, and is not, if the Government can prevent it, to be submitted to the electors."

Lord Lansdowne and Mr. Bonar Law addressed a crowded and enthusiastic audience in the Albert Hall on the night of the 14th. The Leader of the Opposition gave a masterly exposition of the Home Rule question.

153 *Letter from H. de F. Montgomery to A. J. Balfour, 19 April 1894, asking him to ensure Carson's attendance at the Morley committee (D 627/428/244):

My dear Balfour—The Irish Landlords seem likely to get a good deal less than fair play on Morley's Committee, owing to the electioneering exigencies of Irish Unionist members & other causes. I now hear that Carson is likely to be an irregular attendant & to absent himself altogether after a short time for a trip to Portugal on professional business. Now, as you prevented the Irish Landlords from capturing one of the Dublin University seats last election and sending a man to parliament who, though doubtless not so smart as Carson, would have stuck to his post both in the Committee & in the House, as a protector of Landlord interests like a leech and is quite capable of asking witnesses very pertinent questions; may I say that I think the least you can do for us Landlords & for Dublin University which, both as a Corporation and as a collection of individual Masters of Arts is largely dependent on the Landlords Landowner [sic] interest in Irish land, is to make Carson stick to his post on the Committee, when he can do work for us no one else able to serve on it can do, even at considerable sacrifice of professional business? He owes his position & his cheap seat to you & is bound to do what you bid him. Yrs very truly

H de F Montgomery

154 Letter from Balfour, 4 Carlton Gardens, London S.W., to Montgomery, 21 April 1894, expressing confience in Carson's effectiveness as a spokesman for Irish landlords (T 1089/260):

My dear Montgomery—You and I have never been able to agree on the subject of Carson's utility to the Irish Landlords. But experience has only confirmed my view: and, in fighting their battles, I would rather have 10% of Carson's time than 100% of that of the gentleman to whom you refer. This, of course, is only my private opinion, and I may be wrong; but I can most truly say that Carson's presence in the House since the last General Election, has been absolutely invaluable, and that his utility is not to be measured by the speeches he has made, admirable as those in many cases have been.

He is quite alive to the need of attending as far as possible to the work on the Committee, and I have spoken to him more than once on the subject, but, believe me it would be madness to attempt to find a substitute for him.

Why David Plunket does not throw himself more into the details of the work, I do not know. I gather that he has refused to go upon the Committee. Yours Ever,

Arth[ur] James Balfour.

V

Energetic letter writing also formed part of the Irish unionists' propaganda work in Great Britain. Sometimes, as in October 1913, letters to the press would be used as an instrument of policy to bring pressure to bear upon the unionist party. By the autumn of 1913, when conversations were in progress about the possibility of a compromise on the third home rule bill on the basis of the exclusion of Ulster, southern unionists tried to draw attention to their situation and opposition to home rule by a tactfully worded letter to the press. The letter, written by the chairman of the I.U.A., Lord Barrymore, epitomises the spirit of southern unionism. Persistent and determined, yet appealing and tactful, its protest succeeded in making an impact upon the unionist leadership. Lansdowne, leader of the unionist party in the house of lords, wrote to Carson that the letter 'will receive a good deal of backing', and reminded him that although southern unionists were helpless to organise resistance to home rule in Ireland, 'they are quite powerful enough to provoke a serious outcry against us if we throw them over'.

Official and published correspondence by the unionist organisations was supplemented by the efforts behind the scenes of private individuals, such as the indefatigable James

Mackay Wilson at the time of the 1916 home rule crisis. At the beginning of June, Lloyd George, minister of munitions, interviewed various southern unionist deputations and tried to persuade them on patriotic grounds to agree to a settlement of the Irish question on the basis of immediate home rule plus safeguards and the exclusion of six Ulster counties. Wilson, however, tactfully rejected such overtures, arguing that a 'settlement' would not assist the war effort.

This southern unionist tact in their dealings with British politicians contrasts with the lack of tact which was shown on occasion by Ulster unionists (such as Captain Frank Hall, military secretary to the Ulster Volunteer Force), and which was in danger of alienating the sympathy even of their staunch supporters in the British League for the Support of Ulster and the Union.

155 Letter from G. F. Stewart, vice-chairman of the I.U.A., to Sir Edward Carson, 8 October 1913, describing steps to be taken by southern unionists to bring their case more prominently to the British electorate (D 1507/1/1913/5):

Dear Sir Edward—In compliance with your suggestion we have asked some of the leading Unionist business men of Dublin to meet at this office on Tuesday to discuss the present situation from their point of view & we shall endeavour to get them to prepare a Protest against the Home Rule Bill from the financial stand point.

As you are aware there is a strong feeling amongst a number of the Unionists in Dublin, Cork & elsewhere in the South that their claims to the consideration of the Electorate in England & Scotland are in danger of being overlooked in the present crisis and some of them were desirous of having a resolution passed by the Executive of the Irish Unionist Alliance but we at Headquarters here are most anxious that nothing should be done at the present juncture which could in any way embarrass you & Mr. Bonar Law. We therefore thought it would meet the situation & satisfy our people if Lord Barrymore (our Chairman) were to write a letter to the Times & other leading newspapers reminding their readers of the position of the Unionists of the South and West without, as we think you will agree when you read the letter, in the least complicating the situation for either you or Mr Bonar Law.

We have written to Mr Cambray of the U[nion] D[efence] L[eague] asking him to bring you the letter, which Lord Barrymore has signed, tomorrow & unless you see some strong objection to its publication we will make immediate arrangements to have it published.

We propose to do nothing further in this direction pending the meeting on the 28th November without consulting you. We are confident that the meeting will be very large & representative & that it will do an immense amount of good

Hoping you are not over fatigued after all your hard work I am Yours very sincerely

Geo. F. Stewart

156 Letter from Baron Barrymore, chairman of the I.U.A., stating southern unionist determination not to have home rule, published in the press, 13 October 1913, and reprinted in *Notes from Ireland,* November 1913 (D 989C/3/66):

Sir—In the present crisis in the history of our country the position of the loyalists in the South and West of Ireland is, I fear, somewhat overlooked by the people of Great Britain. It seems to be largely assumed that in the Southern and Western provinces hostility to the Home Rule Bill is either non-existent or so insignificant as to be unworthy of consideration.

Probably the reason for this erroneous impression is to be found in the fact that the determination of Ulster to resist Home Rule by physical force has to a large extent overshadowed all other considerations.

But, in truth, the opposition of the loyal population outside of Ulster is absolutely undiminished.

In the City of Dublin, in the City of Cork, in the City of Limerick, in almost every county in the South and West of Ireland, large, enthusiastic meetings, attended by thousands of Unionists, have been held denouncing the Home Rule Bill as being destructive to the best interests of our country, and affirming our determination to remain citizens of the British Empire.

Ten thousand pounds has been subscribed by the Unionists of the Southern and Western Provinces, within the last few months, in support of the campaign of the Irish Unionist Alliance against Home Rule. This sum has been mainly subscribed in small sums, as shown in the Dublin and Cork daily Press.

It is quite true that the Unionists are in a minority in these provinces, and consequently are not in a position to take up the same attitude as their brethren in Ulster, but their position should none the less attract the sympathy and assistance of the loyal population of Great Britain.

They represent substantial business interests; they contribute in many cases the largest share in the rates and taxes of their districts; they have been faithful to the Empire, and, viewing, as they do, with the greatest alarm this measure of Home Rule, and believing it means financial ruin and social disorder, and that it will bring about the disruption of the Empire, they demand that before the disastrous step is taken, they should have an opportunity of laying the true facts before the British people and taking their verdict at a General Election. Yours, etc.,

BARRYMORE
Chairman, Executive Committee.

157 *Letter from J. M. Wilson of Currygrane, Co. Longford, writing from Brooks's, St James's Street, London, to D. Lloyd George, 6 June 1916, disagreeing with the latter's plans for a settlement of the Irish question (D 989A/8/10):

Dear Mr. Lloyd George—I should like to place on record my appreciation of your great courtesy and candour yesterday, but may I say a word or two of warning.

I feel confident that your appeal to us of patriotism would not have fallen on deaf ears had we been persauded [*sic*] that the fate of the war, conceivably if not probably depended on a "settlement" in Ireland, but sir we are absolutely convinced that no settlement at such a moment as this would have anything but the opposite effect which you surmise.

To place [power?] in the hands of the National Party which Mr. Gladstone described as the "plant of an armed revolution" is surely a dangerous step.

That body if once constituted in Dublin would very soon be under the control of the extremists, and resolutions would be soon carried, if not of open sympathy with Germany, yet of plain threats to England. The safeguards which you outlined and which I am sure you are genuinely persuaded [*sic*] would prove of use, are to my mind quite immaterial and would be utterly worthless. The ideals which people like ourselves and the 400,000 whom we repesent [*sic*], cherish, are so hopelessly different from those who glory in a sort of Tammany Hall regime that nothing would reconsile [*sic*] us.

At the moment however what we have to face is the problem as outlined by you, and with all the force I have—1st. in interest of the Empire, next in that of Ireland and lastly as it may effect [*sic*] the career of the Minister of Munitions, I beg of you to call a halt.

Do not, I pray allow the matter to be rushed, if you still think it must be pushed on. The crisis is too grave, the issues too appalling to warrant any thing like a hurry.

You will forgive my intrusion.

158 Letter from T. C. Platt, honorary secretary of the British League for the Support of Ulster and the Union, writing from the League's headquarters, 25 Ryder Street, St. James's, London S.W., to R. D. Bates, secretary of the U.U.C., 6 April 1914, complaining of the critical attitude of Captain Frank Hall (D 1327/4/2C):

Private

My dear Bates—I am a long-suffering person and particularly so where the "true and brave" are concerned. I am quite prepared to admit that this office exists to make blunders, and that we have, in the past, carried out our mission to the fullest extent on those lines. But to be perfectly frank, I am getting just a little bit sick of the constant charges that are being levelled against us by Hall. Hardly a week passes that we are not accused of indulging in some condemned stupidity! This, of course is to be explained, in a way, by the fact that Hall has never made a mistake in his life, and of course never will—that is the penalty of having to deal with brilliant soldiers! I wonder whether you could put a brake on him? I know perfectly well, and you know too, that whenever one has anything to do with a big Organisation—except there are angels on the committee—mistakes are bound to occur. But what I object to is that, according to Hall, all the idiots in the Universe are lodged at 25, Ryder Street! That is all I have to say, and I say it perfectly frankly to you, because if you will allow me to say so, and that quite privately, I have the greatest respect for your good self and I am nearing the greatest comtempt [*sic*] for Hall. As I say, we are doing our level best here to help you as much as we possible [*sic*] can; it may not be a great deal but you will do me the justice, my dear Bates, to admit that we are trying, and if we fail it is not because we wish to. Yours sincerely

T Comyn Platt

VI

The Irish unionists' propaganda campaign in the more restricted sphere of parliamentary and party politics was supplemented by a campaign in the constituencies. This had been Irish unionist policy since 1886. The campaign was four-fold: the production and distribution of literary propaganda; the organisation of anti-home rule demonstrations; canvassing; and the maintenance of what may be called a 'follow-up' service. The volume and intensity of such work depended upon the state of home rule politics and crystallised around elections. At times, especially in 1892–5 and 1907–14, the southern and Ulster unionists found it advantageous and economical to cooperate for propaganda purposes. There is much material relating to the campaign in the constituencies in the N.I.P.R.O., but the nature of the work can best be illustrated by looking at the joint committee of the Unionist Associations of Ireland, 1907–14.

In 1907, on the initiative of the I.U.A., the southern and Ulster unionists decided to cooperate once again for propaganda purposes. The impact of the anti-home rule agitations of the 1880s and 1890s could not last forever, and it was felt by 1907 that a new generation of electors had since grown up to whom the dangers of home rule and the (alleged) intolerance of the nationalist movement were not apparent. Therefore, the electorate had to be 'educated' and a joint committee was set up. Initially it consisted of six members of the I.U.A., five from the U.U.C., and one member of the Ulster Loyalist Union; but in 1911 the Ulster Loyalist Union was dissolved and the U.U.C.'s representation increased to six. The secretaries of the two major unionist organisations acted as joint secretaries to the committee which met alternately in Dublin and Belfast. It first met on 19 December 1907, and was announced to the public at a banquet in Belfast on 22 January 1908, following the annual meeting of the U.U.C. The sole function of the committee was to organise propaganda work on behalf of the Irish unionist organisations; it had no control over the respective policies of the I.U.A. and U.U.C. This fact enabled the southern and Ulster unionists to cooperate amicably for propaganda purposes, despite the growing rift between Ulster and southern unionist policies at the time of the third home rule bill. In 1918 there were allegations that the joint committee had been upset by differences over exclusion, but these allegations are not borne out by the minute book. In fact, smooth-running characterised the work of the committee. There were, of course, many administrative problems in the first year to be solved, particularly in respect of the distribution of work and funds as between the Belfast and Dublin offices. But these were overcome by discussion, and among the members of the committee a corporate sense seems to have developed.

159 Minutes of the first meeting of the joint committee of the Unionist Associations of Ireland at the I.U.A. offices in Dublin, 19 December 1907, recording the steps taken to open the propaganda campaign in Great Britain (D 1327/2/1):

The first meeting of the Joint Committee of the Unionist Associations of Ireland was held at 109 Grafton St. on the 19th December 1907. The Right Hon. Lord Ardilaun was on the motion of Professor E. Dowden LL.D. seconded by Mr. E. M. Archdale D.L. appointed permanent chairman of the Joint Committee. Other members present:—Professor E. Dowden LL.D., R. H. Reade D.L., E. M. Archdale, D.L., Sir Wm. G. D. Goff Bt. D.L., Sir Fredk. W. Shaw Bt. D.L., W. R. Young., F. Elrington Ball., G. F. Stewart. D.L., Gerald S. Guinness, D.L., R. Dawson Bates, Secretary Ulster Unionist Council, R. G. Carden D.L., Secretary Irish Unionist Alliance.

The following circular letter of appeal to be issued in connection with the raising of a special Guarantee Fund to be spread over the succeeding 3 years was adopted and was ordered to be issued after the signatures of the Presidents, Vice-Presidents, Chairmen, Vice-Chairmen, Hon. Secretaries, Hon. Treasurers, and Secretaries of the Associations, as well as the signatures of the Irish Unionist Members of Parliament had been appended thereto:—

Dear Sir,

The present position of the Unionist cause in Ireland calls for immediate and vigorous effort on the part of Irish Unionists. A generation has almost passed away since the case against Home Rule was laid before the entire Electorate of Great Britain, other political questions have arisen, and the danger that the cause of the Union may be forgotten is no less imminent than great. At the same time the reception, remarkable for its cordiality, which was accorded to the Irish deputation at the Conservative Conference at Birmingham, as well as the prominence given to the Irish Question at the annual meeting of the Liberal Unionist Associations at Edinburgh, assures us that platforms are open to the representatives of Irish Unionists, and that a desire exists for authorative [*sic*] information on Irish affairs.

The Irish Unionist Alliance conjointly with the Ulster Unionist Council, the Ulster Loyalist Union, and the Irish Unionist Members of Parliament have therefore resolved to make a combined appeal for financial assistance to enable them to undertake an adequate Campaign throughout the constituencies of Great Britain, and have decided to initiate a guarantee fund spread over three years, similar to that raised on the occasion of Mr. Gladstone's second Home Rule bill.

It is proposed to open the Campaign by making arrangements for meetings in selected British Constituencies during the coming months to be addressed by speakers with knowledge of the condition of Ireland under the rule of the present Government, and capable of exposing the inevitable result of their insidious Irish policy. In addition it is intended greatly to extend the present circulation of Irish Unionist literature in Great Britain, for which there has been an increasing demand since the General Election.

A movement emanating from purely Irish Unionist organisations representing the whole of Ireland, will it is felt carry the utmost weight in English and Scottish constituencies, and no exertion will be spared to make the arguments against Home Rule, and any policy leading thereto known in every part of Great Britain.

We earnestly hope that you will feel disposed to contribute towards the object of this urgent appeal, for which a very large sum will be required; the effectiveness of the proposed Campaign being practically dependent on a liberal response to this circular.

We trust you will kindly fill up the enclosed form and return it to the Secretaries, Joint Committee Unionist Associations of Ireland, 109, Grafton Street, Dublin, or 1 Lombard Street, Belfast.

Confidently relying upon your prompt and generous aid, We have the honour to be, Your faithful servants,

Presidents.
Vice-Presidents.
Chairmen,
Vice-Chairmen,
Irish Unionist Members of Parliament,
Hon. Secretaries, and Hon. Treasurers,
Secretaries.

The following circular letter to be issued to the Unionist Agents in Great Britain was also adopted and ordered to be issued:—

DRAFT CIRCULAR LETTER TO UNIONIST AGENTS IN GREAT BRITAIN.

As some 13 years have elapsed since Irish Unionist Associations have made any combined effort to instruct the people of Great Britain on the Irish question, a Joint Committee of these Associations have resolved to undertake a Campaign in certain selected British constituencies during the present Winter and the early Spring. The urgency of the present situation in Ireland, and the fact that a new generation of British Electors has arisen since Gladstonian days, are impelling reasons for this movement. The condition of disorder and lawlessness that exists in Ireland as a result of the incapable administration of the Government of the day, and the fact of the Government's legislative policy being designed to lead up to Home Rule and its attendant evils both for Ireland and the Empire, cannot be too forcibly explained and illustrated, and it will be the object of the Unionist Associations of Ireland to bring these matters fully and effectively before their audiences in Great Britain.

Will you kindly let me know at as early a date as possible if you would wish your constituency to be included in the programme to be considered by the Joint Committee.

It is proposed that a large meeting should be held in the chief town of each selected constituency to be addressed by prominent Irish Speakers—such meetings to be followed on the ensuing days by minor meetings in suitable parts of the constituency.

Of course it will be understood that all expenses in connection with the meetings will be defrayed by the Irish Unionist Associations; but if any help in the way of supplying rooms, or other local assistance can be given, such aid will be welcomed by the Joint Committee of the Unionist Associations of Ireland.

It was decided that the response to the special Appeal for a Guarantee Fund be lodged to the credit of the Unionist Associations of Ireland in a new Account to be opened in the Bank of Ireland, Dublin for that purpose.

On the proposition of Sir Frederick W. Shaw Bart D.S.O. seconded by Mr. E. M. Archdale D.L. it was unanimously resolved that Colonel Sharman Crawford D.L. and Mr. G. F. Stewart D.L. be appointed Hon. Treasurers of the Joint Committee of the Unionist Associations of Ireland and that all cheques be signed by either of above two gentlemen and the two Secretaries Mr. R. G. Carden and Mr R. Dawson Bates.

The following resolution of thanks to the Union Defence League was passed unanimously:—

That the Joint Committee of the Unionist Associations of Ireland at this their first meeting, desire on behalf of the Unionists of Ireland to express their grateful thanks and high appreciation of the services rendered by the Union Defence League during the last 18 months.

> Proposed by Wm. R. Young, Ulster Loyalist Union
> Seconded by R. H. Reade, Ulster Unionist Council

160 Minutes of a meeting of the joint committee of the U.A.I. held in Belfast, 27 May 1908, to discuss miscellaneous matters arising out of the campaign (D 1327/2/1):

A meeting of the Joint Committee of the Unionist—Associations of Ireland was held at Mayfair, Arthur Square, Belfast on the 27th May 1908. Lord Ardilaun in the chair. Other members present:—Mr. R. H. Reade: Mr. G. F. Stewart: Mr. W. R. Young: Col. R. G. Sharman Crawford: Mr. F. Elrington Ball: Mr. Gerald S. Guinness: Mr. R. Dawson Bates, and Mr. R. G. Carden, Secretaries.

The Minutes of the meeting held on the 30th of April 1908 were read and signed.

Apologies for non-attendance were received from:—Professor E. Dowden: Sir Wm. G. D. Goff Bt.: Sir F. W. Shaw Bt.: Rt Hon. Thos. Andrews: Mr. W. J. Allen: Sir James Stronge Bt.: Mr. E. M. Archdale.

The following report of the Sub-Committee appointed to consider the question of the remuneration of the officials of the Irish Unionist Alliance and the Ulster Unionist Council for the carrying out of the work of the Joint Committee of the Unionist Associations of Ireland was read:—

> "The Committee having considered the question referred to them at the last meeting of the Joint Committee of the Unionist Associations of Ireland recommend that for the year 1908 a sum of £200 be allocated to the Dublin Office, and a sum of £150 to the Belfast Office to remunerate the respective Staffs for the extra work imposed on them by the operations of the Joint Committee."

> SIGNED—ARDILAUN
> 19th May 1908.

The following resolution proposed by Mr. R. H. Reade and seconded by Mr. Gerald S. Guinness, was passed.

> "That the decision as to the payments to be made to the Dublin & Belfast Office Staffs of the Joint Committee, arrived at by the Sub-Committee, at a meeting held in Dublin on the 19th of May 1908, be approved.

> SIGNED—ARDILAUN.
> 27th May 1908.

The question as to what arrangements could be made with the Irish Unionist Alliance as to their supplying the Unionist Associations of Ireland with literature, was considered; and Lord Ardilaun having intimated that the Irish Unionist Alliance would be prepared to provide such literature as may be required from time to time by the Unionist Associations of Ireland; it was resolved that such publications, leaflets, etc. that might be required for the use of the Unionist Associations of Ireland, be procured from the Irish Unionist Alliance with the imprint of the Unionist Associations of Ireland on same. The cost of the production of such publications etc., to be paid for by the Joint Committee, it being understood that for the present the Irish Unionist Alliance continue to bear the cost of the newspaper articles, and the publication of Notes from Ireland.

The list of Constituencies in which it is suggested to undertake work during the Autumn Campaign was considered, and the following resolution proposed by Mr. W. R. Young, and seconded by Mr. G. F. Stewart was passed:—

"That the Secretaries be empowered to work 25 constituencies. The selection of these constituencies to be left to them."

SIGNED—ARDILAUN.

27th May 1908.

The Secretaries reported the completion of the Insurance of the 2nd and 3rd instalments of the Guarantee Fund to the amount of £12384–16. 0. with the Norwich Life Insurance Society, and same was approved.

Letters were read from Mr. Mark B. Cooper in regard to being allowed 15/– per day for Hotel expenses in place of 10/– as previously arranged, and it was decided in the present instance to pay him the amount of £3.10.0 the balance he asked for on account of his hotel expenses at the Montrose and Dundee Elections.

The following cheques were passed and ordered for payment:—

The Norwich Union Life Insurance Society.	£477.19.4.
„ „ „ „ „ „	37.14.11.
T. H. Packer—Cheltenham.	49.13.8.
Manager,—Irish Times.	27.13.0.
Messrs. W. G. Baird.	3.15.0.
W. Copeland Trimble.	39. 6.0.
R. G. Carden (Petty Cash).	87. 4.9.

The following letters were read:—

Mr. G. W. Wolfe—Mr Bates to write and explain.

Mr F. G. Houston—Mr. Bates to write and explain.

Secretary of the Union Jack Committee—Mr. Bates to reply, request cannot be complied with.

Ocean Accident Insurance Company—Counsel's opinion to be obtained as to the liability of the Joint Committee of the Unionist Associations of Ireland in regard to their officials and Speakers & Canvassers.

161

Letter from R. D. Bates, secretary of the U.U.C., to H. de F. Montgomery, 11 May 1918, denying allegations made by Sir James Stronge (of Tynan Abbey, Co. Armagh) that there had been friction between the northern and southern members of the joint committee (D 627/432):

Dear Mr. Montgomery—Many thanks for your letter of the 9th inst. What I fear—and, of course, this is only my personal opinion—is that there would be a danger that anything approaching an amalgamation between the Ulster Unionists and the "Call" Southern Unionists at the present time would do the whole cause of Unionism harm, insomuch as the English Radical Press would suggest that there was the same difference of opinion in Ulster among Unionists as exists in the South. What has saved the Ulster situation up to the present has been Ulster as such remaining a separate entity. If there had been only one Organisation for the whole of Ireland, one could easily imagine the harm that might have been done by the Midleton split. I am only thinking of how to save the Union, and the best method to accomplish this, and I do think that the South of Ireland Unionists should first of all put the Irish Unionist Alliance in order and then we would have an official body to deal with.

With regard to the Joint Committee, I quite agree with you that a great deal of good was done by the co-operation resulting from the Joint Committee in carrying on propaganda work, but I really do not think George Stewart was in any way responsible for the Joint Committee breaking up. I know only too well the heartburnings and the bitter disappointment which the Members of the Joint Committee met with when the war broke out, and we had to recall all our workers. The last Meeting was held on the 15th of January 1915 when the final accounts were dealt with, and, unfortunately, there was no occasion for it to meet again. .

There is one factor which caused a certain amount of feeling between the North and the South. Captain Bryan Cooper, (who, by the way, was a Member of the Joint Committee) shortly after the outbreak of the war practically repudiated the Irish Unionist Alliance and joined the National Volunteers. This was done at a time when Sir Edward Carson was doing his best to stave off the Home Rule Bill being put on the Statute Book. Captain Bryan Cooper's example was followed by several others, and although the action of these gentlemen may not have resulted in the Bill being put on the Statute Book, at the same time I know it handicapped Sir Edward very much in dealing with the Prime Minister who quoted the action of the South of Ireland Unionists in joining the National Volunteers, as showing how the war had altered entirely the question of Home Rule.

As regards the working in the Joint Committee, the only friction I ever knew that took place was between Mr. George Stewart and Mr. Carden, the late Secretary, but Mr. Carden resigned some time before the war broke out and matters got normal again. Sir James Stronge was abroad a good deal subsequent to the appointment of Captain Shaw, and probably what Sir James was thinking about is the friction above referred to between Mr. George Stewart and Mr. Carden. Personally, so far as I was concerned, and the Ulster

Members, the greatest friendliness existed between the Northern and the Southern Members, and although the respective organisations took independent action in every matter that cropped up, without reference to each other, no exception was taken to it.

I hope you will forgive me troubling you with this lengthy letter, but I hope you will not for one moment imagine that I had any other motive in my letter but to make suggestions which I thought would bring about the main object which we desire, and that is the defeating of Home Rule. I have always held the view, but in this I may be quite wrong, that the only way to successfully fight Home Rule is from the Ulster point of view. I know this fact is not appreciated by a large number of the South of Ireland Unionists, but I am glad to say a great many of them who have spoken to me on the subject appreciate the necessity of fighting Home Rule from the purely Ulster point of view as a means of saving the South.

I would like to have a talk with you if you are up in town.

You will be glad. to hear that the Deputation of Workingmen which I sent over to England are doing extremely good work. They have interviewed Mr. Bonar Law, Mr. Barnes, The Prime Minister, Sir Edward Carson, Mr. Hodge, Mr. Arthur Henderson, Mr. Walter Long, and in addition the Labour Members. I arranged several mass meetings down at the Shipyards of different branches of Trades Unionists, who passed resolutions approving of the Deputations' action. Yours very truly,

R Dawson Bates

VII

The campaign work of the U.A.I. was launched with a banquet in Dublin on 20 March 1908. The work was continued until the outbreak of the first world war, though the committee was not finally wound up until 15 January 1915. Its activities fell into three phases, each adapted to the state of British and home rule politics at the time: between 1908 and 1909 a limited anti-liberal and anti-nationalist campaign was mounted; during the general elections of 1910 the resources of the association were more widely diffused; and between 1911 and 1914 there was a continuous and highly flexible campaign against the third home rule bill.

The first phase consisted of two series of meetings. The first series comprised eight meetings beginning with 'artistic propriety' in North Bristol, the constituency of the liberal chief secretary for Ireland, Augustine Birrell. The second series comprised two groups, one of sixteen meetings beginning at Brixton on 23 November and ending at Tipton on 17 December; the other of nineteen meetings, concentrating upon

Scotland and beginning at Crieff, 5 January, and finishing at Lockerbie, 6 April 1909. Such meetings, supplemented by work at certain by-elections, were thoughtfully organised, with reporters, posters, handbills and admission tickets, and flattering attention was paid to local unionists. In this first phase the Irish unionists sought to create a revulsion of feeling from the liberals by emphasising the persecution suffered by loyal, decent, honest men in Ireland, the religious or 'racial' identity of the loyal minority being stressed to suit personal taste and audience. Speeches were reinforced by the distribution of such leaflets as *An Irish cattle-driving case,* and later were 'illustrated by powerful lime-light views showing instances of outrage, intimidation and boycotting in various parts of Ireland'—often with lively debates with hecklers as to their authenticity.

162

Extracts from the minutes of a meeting of the joint committee of the Unionist Associations of Ireland at the I.U.A. offices in Dublin, 30 April 1908, detailing work done in Great Britain in the first stage of the campaign (D 1327/2/1):

Mr R. G. Carden read the following report marked "A" in connection with the mass Meetings held in Great Britain during the months of March and April:—

REPORT OF MEETINGS HELD IN GREAT BRITAIN DURING THE MONTHS OF MARCH AND APRIL 1908.

Eight meetings were held in Great Britain during the months of March and April by the Unionist Associations of Ireland in the following Boroughs:-

Bristol—N.	—	24th March.
Cheltenham	—	30th ,,
Reading	—	1st. April
Colchester	—	3rd ,,
Lincoln	—	6th ,,
Scarborough	—	8th ,,
North Shields	—	9th ,,
Glasgow	—	13th ,,

The following speakers addressed the respective meetings:

Rt Hon. J. H. Campbell K.C.M.P.	—	North Bristol Meeting
Mr. H. T. Barrie M.P.	—	,, ,, ,,
Right Hon. Earl of Donoughmore	—	Cheltenham Meeting
Lt. Colonel Macartney Filgate	—	,, ,,
Mr. S. H. Butcher M.P.	—	Reading Meeting.
Mr. A. W. Samuels K.C.	—	,, ,,

Rt Hon. Lord Oranmore & Browne	—	Colchester Meeting
Capt. Bryan Cooper	—	„ „
Capt. J. Craig M.P.	—	Lincoln Meeting
Jas. Chambers K.C.	—	„ „
Mr. C. C. Craig M.P.	—	Scarborough Meeting
Mr. H. D. Conner K.C.	—	„ „
Mr. H. T. Barrie M.P.	—	North Shields Meeting
Hon. Cecil Atkinson	—	„ „ „
John Gordon K.C.M.P.	—	Glasgow Meeting
W. J. Allen J.P.	—	„ „

Audiences varying in number from 1,000 to 2,500 attentively listened to and enthusiastically received our Speakers, and it was a fully recognised fact that as all the meetings were open to the general public considerable numbers of Liberal Electors were present at each meeting.

So successful were these meetings that it has been placed beyond any shadow of doubt that the British Electors are ready and willing to have the Irish Question put before them.

Resolutions of thanks to the Speakers for their addresses, and expressions of appreciation of the Unionist Associations of Ireland for untertaking [*sic*] their Campaign in Great Britain to place the Irish Question fairly and clearly before the British Electorate were passed at each meeting.

The local Unionist Agents were most cordial in their co-operation and help in making arrangements for our meetings which resulted in a great saving of expense to the funds of the Association.

The total cost of the eight meetings amounts to the sum of £711. 19. 3., being a total average expenditure of £89. per meeting. . . .

Mr. Carden read the following report marked "B" as to where Speakers etc. had been sent by the Associations to the Constituencies and to By-Elections.

"B"

Oxford Central (Henley).	—	Mr. W. Copeland Trimble. 19th to 26th March inclusive.
Oxford Mid.	—	Dr. Tristram. 6th to 10th April inclusive. By-Elections.
Kincardine.	—	Canvassers—R. Young: E. Lunn: Literature.
MONTROSE BURGHS	—	Speaker, Mark B. Cooper. Canvassers, P. Young E. Lunn. Literature.
WOLVERHAMPTON	—	Speakers, Capt. B. Cooper, W. Copeland Trimble.
DUNDEE	—	Canvassers, Thos. Bryars, J. D. Sharkey. Literature. . . .

The Secretaries were directed to draw up a list of Constituencies to be embraced in the Autumn Campaign of the Associations, and submit same to next meeting.

It was decided that no meetings be held in the meantime in Great Britain unless direct application is made to the Joint Committee for same, with the exception of help that may be given at By-Elections. . . .

The Secretaries were instructed to take immediate steps to call up the first instalment of the Guarantee Fund.

163 Report by the secretaries, read at a meeting of the joint committee of the U.A.I., 31 December 1908, of the progress of the committee's campaign, resumed in the previous November (D 1327/2/1):

. . . The Secretaries' report of the progress of the Campaign in Great Britain was received and approved, and was as follows:—

The second series of meetings organised by the Unionist Associations of Ireland opened at Brixton on the 23rd of November and the following meetings have been since held:—

BRENTFORD—24th November
HOUNSLOW—25th November
HACKNEY N. 26th November
HAWES (Yorks) 30th November

NORTHALLERTON (Yorks) 1st. December
WORKSOP (Notts.) 2nd December
YORK CITY 3rd and 4th December
ACOMB (York) 5th December
SLEAFORD (Lincs.) 7th December
GRANTHAM (Lincs.) 9th December
OLDBURY (Worcester) 14th December
LYE (Worcester) 15th December
DARLASTON (Staffs) 16th December
TIPTON (Staffs) 17th December

The following gentlemen were the Speakers at the meetings:— Lord Ashbourne: Hon. Cecil Atkinson: John Gordon M.P: H. T. Barrie M.P.: Capt. Craig M.P: T. S. F. Battersby K.C.: R. G. Carden D.L: Mark B. Cooper Esq., W. Copeland Trimble Esq:

At the above meetings the local Agents gave the greatest assistance, and co-operated in the organising of the several meetings, and the Presidents of the Unionist Associations in the different constituencies, and in most cases the Unionist Candidates were present, and supported the Irish Speakers.

The lantern slides which had been prepared from actual photographs taken throughout the different Counties of men who were fired at, houses that had been fired into, maimed cattle, people that have been boycotted etc., were exhibited at most of the meetings after the Irish Speaker had delivered his address they brought home most forcibly to the minds of the audience the present condition of things in many parts of this Country.

A very large meeting has been arranged to be held at Preston on the 11th January, and Mr. J. H. Campbell, M.P. has kindly consented to speak.

Another mass meeting will be held in Oxford City on the 29th of January. Mr. S. H. Butcher to be principal Speaker.

Three meetings have also been arranged to be held in East Perth at Crieff on the 5th January, Blairgowrie on the 6th, and Perth on the 7th January.

In many places where we have already held meetings the Agents have written asking us to hold further meetings, and the applications from places which we have not yet visited, for our Speakers and lantern lecture, are more numerous than we are likely to be able to arrange for. . . .

VIII

During the dispute over the 'people's budget' in 1909 the U.A.I. was quiet but watchful, awaiting the threatened dissolution of parliament and aware of the implications for home rule of the debate over the powers of the second chamber. Irish unionists relied on the power, the veto, of the house of lords to block home rule, and the liberals' threat to curb or to abolish the veto was made all the more serious by their announcement that this would enable them to introduce home rule in the next parliament. The joint committee thus set itself to secure the defeat of the liberal and labour candidates and to place home rule squarely before the electorate in both the general elections of 1910. During these elections its former efforts were generalised. The total number of workers employed in the January election campaign was 324, of whom 155 were lay speakers, 45 clerical speakers, and 124 canvassers. Of this total the Ulster unionists provided 90 lay speakers, the 45 clerical speakers and 112 canvassers. For the second general election, 381 canvassers and speakers, including 83 clerical speakers, were able to work in over 202 constituencies in England, 75 in Scotland and 5 in Wales. In both campaigns a vast quantity of literature was circulated. In January 3,783,000 copies of eleven new or revised leaflets and large coloured posters were put into circulation; and in December posters were dropped as being too expensive, but over three million copies of 18 new and 27 revised publications were circulated.

Five points in particular are worth noting about these campaigns, which will be illustrated largely by the reports made by the two secretaries and their assistants of the work done in the December election. First, there is the fact of flexibility. The line taken in the campaign depended upon the state of British politics. In January, the U.A.I. took the line that the

164

Handbill announcing a meeting organised by the U.A.I. in conjunction with the York Conservative Association, 4 December 1908 (D 1327/7/6C):

UNIONIST ASSOCIATIONS OF IRELAND.

ST. HELEN'S CHAMBERS,

R. G CARDEN, D.L., ⎫ Joint Secretaries
R. DAWSON BATES, ⎬ Unionist Associations
of Ireland.

DAVYGATE,

YORK, *27th November*, 1908.

DEAR SIR (OR MADAM),

I enclose particulars of a **PUBLIC MEETING** to take place under the auspices of the UNIONIST ASSOCIATIONS OF IRELAND, with the co-operation of the YORK CONSERVATIVE ASSOCIATION, in the

CENTRAL HALL, EXHIBITION BUILDINGS, YORK,

ON *FRIDAY EVENING, 4TH DECEMBER, 1908,*

TO BE ADDRESSED BY

The Right Honble. LORD ASHBOURNE,

(Ex-LORD CHANCELLOR of IRELAND),

J. G. BUTCHER, Esq., K.C.,

H. H. RILEY-SMITH, Esq., J.P., and others.

Chair to be taken by CHAS. E. ELMHIRST, Esq.,

(President York Conservative Association,)

at 8 o'clock.

You are cordially invited to attend, and I herewith enclose Two Tickets for self and friend, and more tickets may be had on application.

Yours faithfully,

W. H. DUNLOP,

Secretary, York Conservative Association.

best way to impress upon the British electorate the twin dangers of the abolition of the lords' veto and of its consequence, home rule, was to appeal to their pockets. The U.A.I. therefore emphasised the economic and financial dangers to Britain of the liberal policy. It argued that home rule would mean the ruination of Ireland, would aggravate the employment situation in Great Britain, and would be detrimental to the interests of all British taxpayers, especially by depriving them of the security for money invested in Irish land purchase. Then in December 1910, in common with the rest of the opposition, they found the liberal dependence upon the nationalist vote in the commons a congenial issue on which to hammer the government and its supporters. John Redmond, the nationalist leader, had just returned from a successful fund-raising mission to the United States, and unionists were able to argue that here was a government which depended for its parliamentary existence upon a party financed by Irish-Americans, hostile to the British connection. These changes in nuance in the anti-home rule campaign can only really be appreciated by reading through the U.A.I.'s vast output of pamphlets and leaflets; but the election manifesto issued in December 1909 in preparation for the election in the following month does give an idea of the way propaganda was altered to suit changes in British politics.

The second interesting feature of the campaign was its organisation. In the allocation of workers the committee exercised 'discretion and choice in accordance with ascertained local circumstances': for instance, non-conformist ministers were concentrated upon Scotland and certain parts of Cornwall and Wales. Great care was also taken to ensure efficiency. Here the committee was hindered by the fact that it could not rely to any great extent upon British unionist, especially central, organisation, which Irish unionists regarded as inefficient, if not absolutely incompetent. The reports of the work done in the second election are particularly interesting in showing the difficulties encountered by Irish unionists when they relied overmuch on the unionist central offices in Britain. Generally speaking, the Ulster secretary supervised the work in Scotland

and the southern secretary the work in England and Wales, and speakers were placed at the disposal of the local unionist agent in Great Britain. In the December campaign, however, an experiment was tried. One R. J. Herbert Shaw of Dublin, future secretary of the I.U.A., took up residence in Bristol to organise and supervise a third body of speakers to act in Bristol and its neighbourhood. The success of this experiment in direct local control contrasts with the inadequacies of co-operation with the central offices: the method employed by F. E. Ball, the acting southern secretary. Ball opened an office in London from which he negotiated with the central offices of both sections of the English unionist party to obtain platforms for his leading speakers, but the inadequacies of the central offices served only to increase the inefficiency of the central pool idea. Speakers arrived in London from Ireland only to be immediately despatched to the north of England and often found themselves overlapping with other Irish speakers sent direct to the constituencies by the Irish offices. Evidence of such inefficiency appears in the secretaries' reports, which were based on the more detailed reports by individual speakers and canvassers on their respective constituencies. It is unfortunate that the more detailed reports appear not to have survived.

Thirdly, the December election illustrates how reluctant some constituencies with large Irish populations, such as North Bristol, were to take up the Irish question; and how the Irish unionists' contacts in British politics helped them to overcome such difficulties, which in 1908–9 had been serious.

Fourthly, it was in the second election that the religious and Ulster unionist cause received more prominence, as a comparison between **165** and **166** suggests.

Lastly, it is interesting to see that British unionists appreciated such aid, despite the fact that at both elections the liberals were returned to office.

In January the liberals won 275 seats; the conservatives 272; labour 40; and Irish nationalists 82; and in December though liberals and conservatives both won 272 seats, the liberals' nationalist and labour allies won 84 and 42 seats respectively.

165

Extracts from a 'Manifesto to the electors of Great Britain' issued in December 1909 by the U.A.I. and reprinted in *Notes from Ireland*, January 1910 (D 989C/3/44A):

One million five hundred thousand of your fellow subjects in Ireland, that is to say, about one-third of the whole population of the country, call for your help at the polls. They are loyally devoted to the Legislative Union between Great Britain and Ireland under which they have been born and lived. They include, beside many thousands of scattered loyalists in the West and South of Ireland, the overwhelming majority of the most progressive and prosperous parts of Ulster, including the great city of Belfast. They comprise Episcopalians, Presbyterians, Methodists, and other religious persuasions including a minority of loyal Roman Catholics. Be assured that they know from experience the danger under Home Rule of religious, social, and political tyranny from the men who have been the enemies of Great Britain. We are convinced that the injury caused by Home Rule to the great industries of the North and other parts of Ireland would send thousands of workmen to your shores competing with you for employment and adding to the existing mass of unemployed. . . . We are certain that a country within a few miles of you governed by those who have shown their hostility to Great Britain may constitute, especially at the present time, a standing menace to you from a naval and military point of view. . . .

Any form of Home Rule would pave the way towards complete "national independence." In America Mr. T. P. O'Connor, M.P., has been touring the country on behalf of the Redmondite party, and has received Separatist Irish-American money on his assurance that the suppression of the House of Lords will remove the last obstacle to Home Rule, which all Irish-American Nationalists understand to be the prelude to Separation. . . .

The British Tax-payer should carefully take note that the Legislative Union offers the only sound security for the immense sum of British money with which the Imperial Parliament is buying out the Irish landowners, estimated at some one hundred and fifty millions. That money will require to be repaid in instalments by the purchasing Irish tenants, over a long course of years. In this immense transaction the British Tax-payer is supremely concerned, and without the sure protection afforded by the Union the return of the capital would be gravely imperilled. Under an Irish Nationalist Parliament there would practically be no security.

The Irish policy of the Unionist Party is constructive and progressive, accompanied by a firm and impartial administration of justice. . . . Unionist Governments have given to Ireland great measures of popular legislation, . . . and have shorn from the Home Rule movement the plausibilities which were then urged in favour of an Irish Parliament.

The record of misrule in Ireland under Radical Government is notorious. . . .

In the present Radical conspiracy against the Veto of the House of Lords . . . every vote given for Radical and Labour candidates will be a vote for a form of Home Rule. . .

166

R. D. Bates's report of the work done by the Belfast office of the U.A.I. in the second election of 1910, and his comments on unionist organisation in Great Britain, submitted to the joint committee on 4 January 1911 (D 1327/2/1):

My Lord and Gentlemen,

I beg to submit a short report on the work done by the Belfast Office at the recent Election. The following were sent out:—

Lay Speakers	118
Clerical Speakers	83
Canvassers	77
Total	278

The number of Constituencies worked from this Office were as follows:—

England	202
Scotland	75
Wales	5
Making grand total of	282

Our men, in accordance with the previous decision of the Committee, were sent direct to those Constituencies in which help of this nature had been offered and accepted. A London Office was, however, established by the Irish Unionist Alliance with Mr Farquharson as representative. The latter requested me to send him a certain number of Speakers and Canvassers for allocation by him in England. This I did.

With regard to literature, this was dealt with mainly through the Dublin Office but was supplemented by this Office as the Home Rule Question became more acute, by several new pamphlets suitable especially for Non-Conformists Constituencies. In addition, selected leaflets were posted direct to every Non-Episcopal minister in England, Scotland and Wales, and to 15,000 representative Scotch lay men.

The demand for this kind of literature increased enormously as the Election proceeded, and I think special attention should be given to the preparation and circulation of pamphlets suitable to the Non-Conformists of Great Britain.

I have no doubt whatever that the result of the Elections in Birkenhead, Torquay, Bodmin, Montgomery Burghs. St. Andrews Burghs, etc. etc. was mainly due to the distribution of leaflets dealing with the attitude of the Church of Rome towards the Protestant religion in Ireland, and to the influential advocacy of our Cause by the Presbyterian and Methodist Ministers who represented us in these Constituencies.

I have prepared and here annexed a report as to the work done by our men. This is based on the reports received by me from the Agents. It shows that the men sent out by us were, with few exceptions, a great success, and did their work extremely well. Great tact was shown in not offending the susceptibilities of the English Roman Catholic. Every Speaker and Canvasser was requested by me to give his impression of the conditions existing in each constituency in which he was working. From this an analysis has been prepared which should prove of considerable value to this Committee in deciding what future steps should be taken regarding each constituency.

With reference to overlapping I found that this only took place when our men were delegated to the London Office. This was caused by the fact that having already complied with the demands of the Local Agents, one or two of the Head Agents, who apparently were not in close communication, with the Sub-Agents also applied to Mr Farquharson for help.

In my judgment, the existence of the London Office caused wastage of both men and money, as in some instances our men on reporting themselves in London were at once directed to proceed to the North of England.

I regret that our Speakers' reports show gross incompetence and indifference on the part of many of the English and Scottish Agents. This does not apply particularly to the Home Rule Question but to the general working of the Elections including the distribution of literature, and in my opinion unless the Central Office takes certain steps to reorganise the working of several of the Constituencies, it would simply be a waste of time and money to send our Speakers to these Constituencies again, if they had to work under the same conditions.

I am strongly of opinion that the decision of the Committee already referred to should be adhered to, namely that each Constituency should be dealt with direct from the Belfast and Dublin Offices. The Scotch Agents are accustomed to look to us in Belfast for assistance, and I submit that Scotland should be worked from here, the nearest centre.

The reports show extraordinary ignorance of the Home Rule Question on the part of the electorate, and to counteract this I would suggest that a limited number of Constituencies should be selected after careful consideration of the reports, and picked men suitable to the existing conditions in each Constituency should be sent there as soon as possible. They could be moved about from place to place and travelling expenses would thereby be saved.

In conclusion I would wish to draw the attention of the Committee to the good work done by Mr. A. Newton Anderson. Owing to the vast amount of work that had to be done by this Office, the selection and despatching of Speakers and Canvassers largely devolved on him.

Although the Election was sprung rather suddenly upon everyone, I am happy to be in a position to state that every request for help was acceded to without delay, and indeed I could have sent more workers had they been required.

R. Dawson Bates.

167 2/1): F. E. Ball's report and defence of the work done by the Dublin and London offices of the U.A.I. in the second election of 1910, submitted to the joint committee on 4 January 1911 (D 1327/

With respect to the Speakers and Missionaries sent directly from Dublin during the General Election of November–December 1910 I beg to report as follows—

Owing to the late period at which I was called upon to take charge of the office the only course that seemed open to me was the one which I had adopted in the General Election of 1906. My aim then and in the present elections was to obtain for our leading speakers opportunity of addressing important meetings, and to place the remainder of the speakers and missionaries under the direction of agents in England who appreciated Irish assistance and were likely to make the best use of those whom we put at their disposal. In order to carry out the first object an office was opened in London. It suffered from all the imperfections of a temporary and hurriedly planned expedient, and the methods pursued were not always those which I should have desired. The negotiations carried on by it were mainly with the Central Conservative Office and with the Office of the Liberal Unionist Council, through which suitable platforms for our leading speakers can alone be obtained. In the Conservative Office one official endeavoured to make the speaking arrangements for all the mass meetings held under its auspices in England and Wales, and it is needless to say that as he attempted a task beyond the power of any single individual, there was hopeless confusion. In the Liberal Unionist Office the arrangements were excellent, but as the constituencies with which it deals are comparatively few in number, the officials could only make use of a small proportion of our speakers. It is satisfactory, however, to be able to report that in spite of these difficulties our leading speakers addressed a large number of mass meetings in London and throughout the country.

Of the remainder of our speakers, the larger number were divided into three bodies acting under the direction of Mr. Croston, the district agent of the Conservative Office for Lancashire and Cheshire, Captain Kennedy, the district agent of Conservative Office for the Eastern Counties, and Mr. Herbert Shaw of the Irish Bar, who by arrangement with Mr. Long undertook the organisation of the Irish speakers and workers in Bristol and its neighbourhood. Two members of the Irish Bar remained in Cumberland throughout its contests, and rendered help in various constituencies, and a few speakers acted under the direction of Mr. Bury, the district agent of the Liberal Unionist Office for Yorkshire, and of Mr. Wyvill, the district Conservative agent for the same shire. Others were allocated to particular constituencies, and at the request of the candidates remained in several instances in them until the polling took place. To the great value of the assistance rendered by the speakers, various letters which have been received bear testimony. The concluding paragraph of the one from Captain Kennedy deserves special mention. In it he says, "Let me thank you and those with you for the immense help you have given us; my only sorrow being that the results appear perhaps to you to be meagre. But let me assure you that without your help the Conservative party at the present moment would not be nearly so strong as they are."

It is far from my desire to underrate what is being done at the present time, but to my mind there is no doubt that much more might be accomplished if the volunteer assistance that was given in the past was still available. During the present Elections I missed sadly the Committee which sat day after day in these offices during the General Election of 1906, and lightened the burden that falls upon the officials at such a time. The questions to be dealt with are so complex, the interests to be protected so diverse, that no wise solution can be expected until they have been debated by men of varied attainments and experiences. Perhaps one of the most successful schemes of political organisation ever known was that of the Irish Unionist Alliance for the purposes of the great struggle between 1892 and 1895, and its success was in the largest degree due to the work being divided amongst departmental committees on which men of every walk in life devoted themselves ungrudgingly to what is popularly called "spade work."

In conclusion I venture to suggest that during a General Election, and in times of stress, the first consideration should be the establishment of an office in London adequately manned and equipped. No one that has had experience of such an office can doubt its necessity; the facility and rapidity of communication from London with every part of the United Kingdom, and proximity to the chief offices of the party, combine to make it essential. It is impossible for one or two officials to interview the speakers who pour in during a General Election, and at such a time the presence in London of some members of the Committee would be most desirable. Further I would urge the advantage of a Speakers' Committee with the object of enlarging and classifying the list of speakers. With no clue to their abilities mistakes must occur.

I append lists of the speakers and missionaries in the various centres, of the speakers and missionaries arranged in alphabetical order, and of speakers and missionaries who were unable from one cause or another to act for us. In all 81 speakers, and 22 less experienced speakers and missionaries, visited England & Wales.

For great kindness and consideration, and loyal co-operation, I am indebted to all with whom I came in contact, and I desire to take this opportunity of expressing my gratitude.

F. Elrington Ball

168 R. J. H. Shaw's report of his work in Bristol and parts of the west country in the second election of 1910, submitted to the joint committee on 4 January 1911 (D 1327/2/1):

As organiser of an Irish Campaign on behalf of the Unionist Associations of Ireland in the four Bristol City Constituencies, Thornbury Division of Gloucestershire, and North Somersetshire, during the General Election of December, 1910, I beg to report as follows:—

On the 22nd of November I arrived at Bristol and immediately got into touch with the local agents and candidates from whom I discovered the needs of the various constituencies in my district for special and ordinary speakers, and literature, and the general lines which our policy should pursue.

I took a sitting-room at the principal and most central Hotel in Bristol which I used as an office, where I was able to meet all the men who were under my charge, where they were able to get all information, to refer to such books of reference as I had brought with me and to prepare their speeches. From this office I was able to keep in telephonic communication with all the central Committee Rooms in my district.

I was generously supplied by the Dublin, Belfast and London Offices of the Unionist Associations of Ireland with speakers and canvassers, a list of whom with observations on the work done by them, I append.

My general policy was to concentrate as far as possible on the four Bristol city constituencies until their polling on the 3rd of December, and then to move such men as I needed to the County Constituencies under my charge. Such men as I did not actually require after the 3rd I, in accordance with the directions of Mr. Ball, placed at the disposal of Mr. Maclachlan of the Liberal Unionist Council.

During the whole time I was in Bristol my object was to use each speaker according to his abilities to the best possible advantage.

I daily communicated with all the Central Committee Rooms, found out the meetings arranged for my speakers, saw that these were the best possible, and where advisable interchanged or moved the speakers.

I made all arrangements for the provision of such special speakers from London as were necessary, and oversaw the arrangements made for them.

I superintended or arranged for the preparation of special lists of such persons as I considered our canvassers could work among with the greatest advantage, so that these lists were ready for them on their arrival, and that no time was lost in getting them to work in the most valuable way. I found out the amount of literature necessary for each constituency, ordered it, oversaw its distribution, and prevented any waste by sending on the surplus from one constituency to another. With the permission of the Dublin Office I did special advertising in the press, a matter on which I have already reported, and advised them on the necessity for the preparation of special handbills, and arranged for their distribution.

I wrote articles on the Irish Question in the Bristol Times and Mirror, a very important provincial paper, and kept the Press supplied with all necessary information. I cannot speak too highly of the assistance I received from the local press.

In every instance I received the most ready assistance and sympathy from the Local Organisations, with the exception only of North Bristol, where there was a certain disinclination to press the Irish Question strongly. Acting on the advice of Mr. Walter Long with whom I discussed the matter, I was, however, able to arrange for an Irish Campaign of very considerable strength in that Constituency. I have already fully reported on this matter.

In addition to the work done in my own district, I supplied speakers for special meetings at Chippenham and Weston-super-Mare.

In every instance the speakers and workers under my direction were kept regularly and profitably employed, and the best arrangements possible were in every instance made for their convenience.

169

Report as to the literature distributed through the Dublin office in the second election of 1910, submitted to the joint committee on 4 January 1911 (D 1327/2/1):

The following report as to the distribution of literature in connection with the recent General Election, through the Dublin Office, was submitted:—

For distribution during the General Election leaflets Nos. 118 to 130 and 135 to 144 were revised. Nos. 131 to 134 inclusive were re-written. 18 new leaflets were prepared (Nos. 145–162). Of these No. 157 was a reprint of Sir Edward Carson's letter to Irish Unionists, and No. 160 (Home Rule—Means Bankruptcy) was written by Mr. Samuels.

The selected constituencies in Great Britain all received literature at the earliest moment. The leading Agents in Scotland asked for and received large supplies. Many applications were received from other constituencies by wire and letter, and were complied with.

Over 1200 clubs in Great Britain were supplied with bound sets of leaflets and pamphlets.

18,000 copies of Mr. Samuel's pamphlet have been circulated.

There were constant demands for the literature from individuals by letter, and numerous personal applications at the office.

There was a total of nearly 3,000,000 leaflets distributed.

IX

The unionist defeat in the second general election of 1910 and the passage of the parliament act forced Irish unionists to take further action. Now hoping for a dissolution of parliament on the home rule issue, they redoubled their efforts to create an anti-home rule opinion in Great Britain. The U.A.I.'s previous experience proved invaluable and the scheme of operation adopted in 1911 was a nice combination of central control and local initiative.

The U.A.I. now aimed at creating a politically effective anti-home rule opinion by directing its efforts at a selected number of marginal constituencies, some 200 in England and about 50 in Scotland. (Wales was left to the Union Defence League.) General policy was controlled by the joint committee, working through the joint secretaries and two standing committees, one for the northern members of the committee and another for the southern members. The responsibility for the day to day arrangement of affairs, however, rested with several sub-agents employed in Great Britain.

England was originally placed under the supervision of five agents: one for London and the home counties, one for the west, one for the east, one for Lancashire and Cheshire, and one for the north; while Scotland was divided into the eastern and western agencies. The agents set up offices in a convenient town in their respective areas. Their function was to organise the anti-home rule campaign, within the limits set by the joint committee, in their respective areas. They had to circularise the local unionist agents of the constituencies marked out by the committee, and on receiving a favourable response, to arrange for meetings, canvassing and the distribution of literature, as well as providing for other organisations to use the services of their workers.

To assist him each agent had a number of speakers and canvassers working under him, selected for their tact and ability. At first there were six workers attached to each agent, paid at the rate of ten shillings a day; though their numbers fluctuated according to the state of the committee's finances and the progress of the campaign. Initially, all these workers came from Ireland, the larger proportion from Belfast, but as the campaign expanded English and Scottish workers were used. (When the association suspended its activities in August 1914, of the 32 canvassers employed in the English groups, 20 came from Belfast, 11 from southern Ireland and 1 from Manchester.) This paid core was reinforced by other canvassers and speakers sent from Ireland as the need arose. The committee kept a register of speakers and had a considerable reservoir to draw upon. The larger number of these special workers came from Ulster (from the Ulster Unionist Women's Council and the Speakers' Club, an organisation consisting of Belfast businessmen and professional men whose object was to assist the joint committee by placing at its disposal free of all expense a number of its members as speakers); though the Irish Unionist Alliance, particularly the Ladies' committee, did provide workers from the southern provinces.

Economical to operate and capable of occasional modification, the scheme was responsive to local conditions and to changes in national politics. Constituencies that proved un-cooperative could be dropped and others worked instead, while the venue of meetings could be shifted, as in Scotland, to the seaside resorts during the holiday season. More importantly from time to time the emphasis or intensity of the scheme was altered to suit developments in home rule politics. This was particularly so during the autumn of 1913 and the spring of 1914, when talk of compromise was in the air. By the summer of 1913, at a time when compromise talks were about to begin between Asquith and Law, demonstrations of public hostility to home rule were considered essential. The joint committee therefore decided to concentrate on the crowd rather than on the individual by increasing the number of public meetings and cutting down on canvassing. A symptom of this change of emphasis was the introduction of anti-home rule vans, fitted with magic lanterns. The vans had the advantage of being easily mobile, able to reach outlying districts and able to attract and hold attention. When the committee decided to step up its campaign again in the following February, when the home rule bill was on its last parliamentary lap, these vans proved useful.

Altogether, in England from September 1911 to the middle of July 1914, over 5,000 meetings were organised with the aid of local unionist organisations; and 1,246,225 doubtful voters had been canvassed in over 200 constituencies. In Scotland over the same period, 3,843 meetings were held and 205,654 doubtful voters canvassed in 50 constituencies, some of which had been visited twice. For Great Britain as a whole, over six million booklets, leaflets and pamphlets were distributed. Finally, there were the tours of Ireland organised for British electors **(87)**.

170 The joint committee's comments on the satisfactory nature of the statement of accounts submitted to its meeting on 31 July 1913 and covering the period from September 1911 (D 1327/ 2/1):

The accounts submitted to the Joint Committee of the Unionist Associations of Ireland show a Total Expenditure of £33,239. Without going into fractions it should be most satisfactory to the Committee and the subscribers to know that a careful investigation of the accounts shows that of this sum—

$79\frac{1}{2}\%$ has been actually expended on the working of the 7 Groups—

13% on literature—i.e. leaflets, pamphlets etc., issued and distributed by the Joint Committee—

or $92\frac{1}{2}\%$ of the whole amount on the actual work for which the money was collected—

$2\frac{1}{4}\%$ was spent on an attempt to get better accounts of South of Ireland affairs in the English and Scotch Press—

$5\frac{1}{4}\%$ or £1747 being spent on working expenses

100%

Items of Expenses of working in Dublin and Belfast Offices etc.

Postage & Tel.	£175	
Travelling	170	
Stationary [*sic*]	105	
Advertising etc.	143	
Rent	76	£1747
Gen. Expenses	58	
Audit	10	
Bonus to Mr. Crowe	50	
Tours	69	
Salaries	891	

These returns are most satisfactory in showing that $92\frac{1}{2}\%$ of the money collected was actually expended on direct work, while $5\frac{1}{4}\%$ was spent on expenses of working—of which only £891 or $2\frac{3}{4}\%$ was spent on Salaries—

171

Report by the Belfast office of work done in Scotland between 21 May and 20 June 1913, submitted to a meeting of the joint committee on 20 June 1913 (D 1327/2/1):

Since I submitted my report on 21st May 62 meetings have been held and 5,214 "doubtful" electors have been canvassed. This makes a total to date of 1,710 meetings held and 138,665 electors personally interviewed.

MOTOR CAR TOUR.

The motor-car tour undertaken by the members of the Speakers' Club in Ayrshire proved most successful, and it is hoped shortly to undertake another series. We owe a debt of gratitude to the members of the Club for carrying out this work entirely at their own expense.

SEASIDE RESORTS.

Our campaign in the seaside resorts in the West of Scotland commences on 1st July. Arrangements have been made to hold meetings throughout the Summer at Dunoon, Rothesay, Millport, Gourock, Helensburgh, Largs, Ardrossan, Troon, Prestwick, Girvan, Saltcoats, Stevenston, Ayr, and Irvine.

It is hoped that the Speakers' Club, who work at their own expense, will not only assist at these but that they will undertake to address meetings in Dunoon, Tarbert, Ardrishaig, Lochgilphead, Campbeltown, Oban, and Inverary.

Mr Wood reports that he proposes to commence a canvass of South Lanarkshire on Monday next. This will leave only two constituencies, Buteshire (Unionist) and Govan (Radical) still to do. With reference to the latter, a considerable amount of work was done at the bye-election in December, 1911. In connection with this it is gratifying to know that Mr. George Balfour, who made such a splendid fight on that occasion, is again the Unionist candidate.

In the East and North Division, the re-canvass of Peebles and Selkirk has been finished, and Mr. Bamford has commenced a re-canvass of Roxburghshire. Both our agents report a decided increase of interest as a reulst [*sic*] of the great meetings in Glasgow and Edinburgh.

I would strongly recommend to the Committee the advisability of dropping Hawick Burghs and Dumfries Burghs from our list of selected constituencies in the East and North of Scotland. We have completely canvassed these constituencies, and our speakers have addressed a series of meetings in both. Our workers complain of bad local organisation and a decided want of sympathy, and a marked degree of apathy in the Unionist agents and electors. This is probably due to the fact that the records from 1885 show that neither constituency has ever returned a Unionist.

Mr Wood's staff at present consists of two speakers, five speaker-canvassers, and nine ordinary canvassers; while Mr. Bamford has two speakers and ten canvassers.

172 A report on the effectiveness of the anti-home rule vans by R. R. Smylie of 14 Lansdowne Road, Dublin, a member of the executive committee of the I.U.A., March 1914, submitted to the joint committee on 8 April 1914 (D 1327/2/1):

Gentlemen:

As requested by Mr. Shaw, I visited the Van working in the South and East of England, viz:—

No. 1 Van (Messrs. Bulmer and Mack in charge) at London Fields, South Hackney, on the 25th March. No. 2 Van (Mr. Branston in charge) at Rothwell, Northamptonshire, on the 27th March, and No. 3 Van (Mr. W. Young in charge) at Marston, South Somersetshire on the 31st March.

By Mr. Wilkins request I visited the Union Defence League Van (Messrs. Harman and Corporal Weir in charge) at Ilford on the 26th March, he being of opinion that it would help me in coming to an opinion on the matter.

When the weather permits, the meetings are held in the open air, the Van arrives at the pitch some time previous to the commencement of the meeting, the doors at the back are opened and a screen for the pictures is fixed up and a few pictures shown by a Magic Lantern worked from the front part of the car or Van, the pictures of the King, the Bank of Ireland and a few others having the effect of drawing together some persons. A rostrum is placed to one side of the pictures beside the Van. The lecture generally lasted over an hour and questions were then invited. At each of the meetings I attended, the lecture was listened to with much interest and attention by the crowd, the pictures were "put on" in much the same order, the lecture followed on precisely the same lines and indeed in each case the lecturer might well be complimented for delivering a connected address illustrated by these pictures and not merely explaining a series of pictures. Certainly I thought the lecturers most conscientious in the discharge of their duty, and save for the particular remarks below made I think it would be difficult to get better or more suitable men for the work.

It would be impossible to over estimate this quality in your men—from my experience of the professional open air politician, and I have met many of them, there is such an air of insincerity and an inclination to get their hours talking through, that I have often wondered why they are employed at all. In criticising these Van speakers a great injustice would be done them if in the course of reading the following remarks, the sincerity, ability, and general fitness and conscientious desire to win over persons to their view were forgotten or overlooked. I cannot too strongly emphasise this and it is with these qualities strongly impressed on me that I feel free to submit the criticisms I venture to make.

The general conclusions I came to were:—

First as regards the lecture:—I concluded that the speakers had been lectured before starting on the campaign or had been given a written lecture to study, whichever it was it occurred to me that that took place at a time when the Home Rule Question had not assumed its present prominent position, and many other topics were then introduced to sustain the interest of the audience, some of the lecturers (Messrs. Bulmer and Branston, I think) made occasional reference to the Insurance Act, South Africa, the strike in Dublin, the Budget, I felt that this was not now necessary, while in their reference to the recent strike in Dublin, what I would consider the chief point was omitted, i.e. having dealt with the Redmondite hostility to the strikers to go on to show that under Home Rule Redmond instead of having the leader imprisoned, as had happened, could have had him exiled. There were also too frequent assertions of honesty and truth on the part of the lecturers, this would give rise to doubt rather than remove it.

The Home Rule Question has that position now that all possible time should be devoted to the facts of the case and the arguments to be used, and much time might be saved for this purpose, that is now being needlessly wasted.

I could not compliment the lecturers upon their replies to questions or rather to be precise in reply to questions on the emigration from Ireland, the slums in Dublin, and the fact that the evil deeds of the Nationalists are being repeated today. The latter two questions were, I felt, especially weakly handled. It occurred to me that a picture of the diagram drawn up by Mr. Bryan Cooper, dealing with the emigration argument, and which I had reduced to scale, would be a useful addition, a similiar [sic] picture might be drawn showing the emigration from Scotland and England. Photographs of Dublin slums might be shewn and the lecturer better instructed on the subject.

The crowd gave great attention to the recount of the remedial measures passed for Ireland, but the strong impressions left on my mind was [sic], that, had I been one of the crowd and known no more than the lecturer told me, I would have thought that Ireland was an enormous expense to England, an expense which might well be got rid of and I would have little sympathy with that party that caused England to spend such sums. I think when these facts are being related care should be taken to implant in the minds of the audience the fact that by far the greater portion of this money was a loan, a loan that is being repaid by Ireland and by the granting of Home Rule, Great Britain parts with her security for this repayment. This was not done by any of the lecturers.

Before dealing with the meetings particularly there remain two points which I noted and which I should like to state. First, I thought that the disloyalty of the Nationalists might have been made more of, it was dealt with but not to such an extent as would itself suggest to an ordinary mind the terrible danger to Great Britain of those men having a parliament of their own in Ireland. In the next place practially [sic] no reference was made to the fact of their [sic] being a large number of Unionists in the three Southern Provinces—and I felt that the impression was that the exclusion of Ulster was the solution of the whole matter. Having said so much by way of remarks equally applicable to all the meetings, I think I should give a brief account of each meeting.

Wednesday, March 25th: Broadway, London Fields, a cold wet night—a crowd of from 100 to 150 listened attentively. Mr. Bulmer seemed to be ailing from a cold and I know was not at his best. I felt that he was a little stale, and might be improved by himself attending some good rousing meetings, which would act as a needful tonic. At one time he was speaking as a Unionist, and at another time as a trade Unionist, his "we" would at times refer to something the Unionist party had done, and at another time something that trade Unionists had done. This certainly confused his hearers, and he seemed at a loss to appreciate the misunderstanding, and confusion and trouble caused thereby. He would do well to keep to the points of Home Rule more. All he says is good, but his reference to extraneous subjects takes away his time. He seemed to think that the slums of London were quite as bad as the Dublin ones, and that was the way he answered the question put to him on that subject. He attributed the cause of Irish emigration to the repeal of the Corn Laws—very good in its way, but I always found (having fully dealt with the subject and the decrease in emigration) it well to ask will emigration cease under Home Rule, or will it be increased to an extent never before reached, and also by dealing with emigration from agricultural England to commercial England, and from England generally. I think his lecture might be freshened up a little. It suggested to me that it was the same lecture that he had been delivering for many months back.

Friday, March 27th. At Rothwell—I got to this village by about 6 o'clock in the evening. I saw no notice of any kind about a meeting, though I carefully examined all places where a notice might be exhibited. There was not one even on the outside of the Conservative Club.

I heard afterwards that the meeting would take place in the Oddfellows Hall at 8 o'clock.

The village would have a population of a couple of thousand or more, and is not near any place. Had the meeting been held out of doors I am sure there would have been at least 500 there, there being no attractions in that village. Most of the inhabitants, if not all, seemed to be the [be] Conservatives.

The Meeting commenced about 8.30 p.m. by which time some 30 persons had strolled in. Mr. Bramston was the lecturer. He has many good points as a speaker. He could, I think, be trained to be a first-rate speaker. His great fault is the rapidity of utterance. I could not follow him or know what he was saying at times. I am sure few present understood him. He dropps [sic] the final syllable of his words. He knew his subject well, and he delivered a lecture lasting an hour or longer, and I am certain I could not recite the same in less than two hours.

Tuesday, March 31st at Martock. Also a small village: A warm night, yet not more than 100 were present. The meeting was in the open air. The lecturer, Mr. Montgomery, was, I thought, one of the ablest speakers I have heard. He spoke slowly and quietly and never had to think for a word. But I thought him weak in dealing with the few questions asked him.

I thought the attendance at these village meetings might be worked up if some resident ladies were asked to visit the houses, and ask the people to come out. I could see no excuse for the poor attendance at both the village meetings.

The Union Defence League meeting at Ilford I might remark gave me great encouragement. Mr. Harmon and Corporal Weir, held a crowd of about 500 for well over an hour and a half. Mr. Harmon, an Englishman, and an attractive speaker; Corporal Weir, an Irishman with a pronounced non-Ulster accent.

I have tried to state everything that occurred to me, and should anything be omitted or questions wished to be put to me, I would gladly supplement this report if my attention were directed to the particular matter required.

I remain, Yours v. faithfully,

R. R. Smylie,

14 Lansdowne Rd.,
Dublin,
April, 1914.

X

As the two reports on work done in Scotland and by the anti-home rule vans suggest, the U.A.I. did meet with some difficulties. First, there was the problem of the training of workers, which was never adequately overcome. Secondly, there was the problem of developing satisfactory relations with local unionist organisations in Great Britain. In some constituencies, the local unionist associations were indifferent and apathetic; this was overcome, as in east Scotland, simply by dropping them from the list of constituencies to be worked. In some other constituencies the prospective unionist candidates proved 'difficult' and felt that the intervention of the U.A.I. was ill-timed or misplaced. Fortunately, on only one occasion did this problem reach serious proportions. The west country agent, R.F.H. White, upset certain candidates for the Bristol constituencies by appearing to ignore them when at first he devoted his energies to the other constituencies in his group. Their complaint was taken up by James Campbell, the junior member for Dublin University, who had recently addressed a meeting in Bristol—which White did not attend. Since, however, the grouse was confined to difficult or absentee candidates, like Major George Cockerill, the candidate for the Thornbury division and later M.P. for Reigate, the U.A.I.'s work was not seriously hindered.

Thirdly, there was the question of maintaining amicable relations with other anti-home rule groups, such as the Irish unionist M.P.s and the Union Defence League (formed in 1907 by Walter Long). Lastly, there was the problem of finance; for such massive propaganda work was expensive. These last two problems were largely overcome in what was known as the Londonderry House agreement of 6 April 1911. A meeting that took place on that date in Londonderry House, London, between representatives of the joint committee of the U.A.I., the Union Defence League and the Irish unionist parliamentary party, defined their respective areas of action. It is interesting as showing how much, despite the claims of Walter Long's Defence League, the anti-home rule campaign depended upon the joint committee who rightly regarded the Defence League and the Irish unionist M.P.s as auxiliaries.

173

*Letter from the joint committee to J. H. Campbell, 11 August 1911, rebutting Campbell's charge that R. F. H. White, the U.A.I.'s agent for the west country, had failed to cooperate with some of the unionist candidates in his area (D 1327/2/1):

Dear Sir,

We are directed by the Joint Committee of the Unionist Associations of Ireland to acknowledge the receipt of your letter of the 1st August, 1911. which has been received by them through the medium of the Parliamentary Sub-Committee of the Irish Unionist Alliance, and to inform you that the Committee having carefully investigated the facts as mentioned in your letter in connection with the work of the Joint Committee's Sub-Agent, Mr. White in the Western Group, are of opinion that Mr. White is doing all that is possible at the present time to carry out the instructions of the Joint Committee; and that in regard to the specific remarks in your letter they would wish to acquaint you.

1. That it was by the instructions of the Joint Committee Mr. White was exclusively devoting his energies to the Rural Constituencies in his group versus the Urban, during the summer and early autumn, leaving the latter Constituencies to be worked in the winter, hence his not offering to undertake work in the Bristol Constituencies up to the present. But it should be understood that though Mr. White had interviewed many of the Agents in the rural constituencies all the Agents in the Bristol Constituencies were circularized by him in the same way as were the Agents in all the other selected Constituencies in the Western Group, as to the various particulars in connection with their respective Divisions, with the view to having a programme of work arranged, when it would be possible for the Joint Committee to undertake same: This list of queries was sent to the Agent for North Bristol (Mr. Nash) who passed same to his Candidate Mr. Magnus, who for some unknown reason refused over the 'phone to give the information himself or instruct his Agent to do so, it should also be added that Mr. White wrote a tactful reply to this communication asking Mr. Magnus at his convenience to let him know of his return to Bristol so that Mr. White could arrange a call and have an interview with him.

2. That the reason Mr. White was unable to attend the meeting in Bristol at which you spoke was that he was temporily [*sic*] laid up by the excessive heat, and had gone away from Bristol for the week end from Friday evening to Monday to recuperate.

3. As regards Mr. White not having met Major Cockerill the Candidate for the Thornbury Division. This gentleman resides in London and in his periodical visits to his Constituency Mr. White did not happen to be in that particular Constituency at that time. The former Agent for that Constituency Mr. Lazenby and the present Agent Mr. Vernon are on the best of terms with Mr. White and have placed on record their high appreciation of the work Mr. White has carried out in that Division.

While being ever willing and anxious to give every consideration to any suggestion put forward by you, the Committee would further wish to mention that they trust, that, should you at any time wish to raise any point as regards their programme of work or in connection with that of any of the officials or workers employed by them, you will kindly address the Joint Committee directly on the subject. We are, Yours faithfully,

R. G. Carden
R Dawson Bates

174 The Londonderry House agreement, 6 April 1911: memorandum of the working agreement entered into between the Irish unionist parliamentary party, the joint committee of the U.A.I. and the Union Defence League (D 1327/7/6B):

All matters arising out of this working agreement requiring adjustment between the Associations to be forwarded, in writing, to the Hon. Secretary of the Irish Unionist Parliamentary Party, to be by him submitted to the next meeting of the Party; or, if that be impracticable, to the Chairman (or, in his absence, to the Vice-Chairman) of the Party, whose decision shall be binding.

NOTE.—

It is desirable, as far as possible, to concentrate the final authority in some one convenient body or responsible person in order to obviate the calling together of further round-table Conferences or Committee meetings, which, necessarily, entail delay and expense.

The Chairman, Vice-Chairman, and Hon. Secretary of the Irish Unionist Parliamentary Party are, naturally, in close touch with all the members of the Party, the Office-Bearers and Officials of the Associations, as well as with the leaders and rank and file of the Unionist Party.

THE JOINT COMMITTEE

(*a*) To have a free hand to deal with the whole of the campaign, including meetings in England (London included), Scotland and Wales, including General Elections and by-elections.

(*b*) To appeal for funds in Ireland only, but to be at liberty to accept unsolicited voluntary contributions from elsewhere.

THE UNION DEFENCE LEAGUE

(*a*) To undertake such special important Demonstrations and other necessary work throughout England (London included), Scotland and Wales, as may be approved of by the Chairman of the Irish Unionist Parliamentary Party, or, in his absence, by the Vice-Chairman; such to be advertised as being under the auspices of the Union Defence League and the Unionist Associations of Ireland, in order to emphasise their representative character.

(*b*) To act as a Bureau of Information, especially for the convenience of Unionist M.P.'s.

(*c*) To share such premises as may be suitable, with the Joint Committee and its Staff, who, while working London and the Home Counties under the

Joint Committee's scheme of allotted districts, would keep in close touch with the Union Defence League and with members of the Irish Unionist Parliamentary Party. Unionist M.P.'s generally may prefer to consult with the Union Defence League, which is better known to them.

For the convenience of Members of Parliament, and others requiring information, both Offices to be clearly identified by the necessary name plates and other notices.

The Joint Committee to pay a fair proportion of the rent for such accommodation.

(*d*) To appeal for funds in England, Scotland and Wales only, but to be at liberty to accept unsolicited voluntary contributions from elsewhere, and, having less costly work allocated to it, and a wider and more wealthy area in which to appeal, to make substantial contributions to the funds of the Joint Committee as and where necessity arises.

The Joint Committee to prepare and keep up to date a Register of at least 60 tried and dependable Speakers, pledged at short notice to undertake meetings in England, Scotland and Wales, to be at the disposal of the Union Defence League and the Joint Committee.

The number to be expanded as found necessary.

NOTE.—

These 60, together with the 20 Irish Unionist Members, would bring the number of readily available Irish Unionist Platform Speakers up to 80 approximating the Nationalist Party.

It is obvious that during the actual crisis of the Parliament and Home Rule Bills, Irish Unionist Members would require to be in close attendance in the House of Commons and, therefore, would not be available for Platform work.

If prominent Speakers of acknowledged platform ability are not prepared to make the necessary sacrifice by enrolling themselves for such a purpose, not only will the Irish Unionist Cause suffer in Great Britain, but apparent support will be given to the constantly repeated allegation of Nationalist Speakers that Irish Unionists are less opposed than they formerly were to Home Rule, or to the establishment of a Dublin Parliament for purely Irish affairs, and the chance of staving off Home Rule by constitutional methods will be gravely endangered.

So important is this subject that it is recommended that a letter above the signatures of the Duke of Abercorn, the Marquis of Londonderry, Lord Ardilaun, the Rt. Hon. Sir Edward Carson, the Rt. Hon. Walter Long, and Mr. John B. Lonsdale be addressed to those considered as tried and dependable by the Joint Committee as follows:—

Confidential.

DEAR SIR,

At a large and influential meeting of representatives of the Irish

Unionist Parliamentary Party, the Unionist Associations of Ireland Joint Committee and the Union Defence League, held at Londonderry House, on the 6th April, it was decided, in view of the approaching Home Rule crisis, to form a Register of prominent Irishmen willing to enrol themselves for Platform work in Great Britain.

It was felt that unless a sufficient number consents to undertake this all-important work, from now onwards, not only will the Irish Unionist campaign be weakened in Great Britain but the chance of staving off Home Rule by constitutional methods will be gravely endangered.

May we count on your assistance? Every consideration will, of course, be given to your convenience.

We sincerely hope to receive a favourable reply, which kindly address to the

Joint Secretaries,

Unionist Associations of Ireland

109 Grafton Street,

Dublin.

Yours faithfully,

Signed,

ABERCORN.

LONDONDERRY.

ARDILAUN.

EDWARD CARSON.

WALTER H. LONG.

JOHN B. LONSDALE.

To prevent overlapping, and needless expense, when either of the Associations desire to initiate or deal with correspondence in the Press, or to issue a pamphlet, leaflet, or poster, intimation, and, when convenient, an advance proof, to be forwarded to the other Association, not for approval, but for mutual information and benefit.

No restriction to be placed on Press correspondence or such issue of pamphlets, etc., independently by either Association through its own recognised channels.

A copy of the working agreements, when arrived at, to be sent to each member of the Irish Unionist Parliamentary Party and to each member of Committee of the Irish Unionist Alliance, Ulster Unionist Council, Ulster Loyalist Union and Union Defence League, so that as many as possible of those interested may understand the amicable arrangement concluded.

The Hon. Secretary of the Irish Unionist Parliamentary Party to immediately communicate with every English, Scotch, and Welsh Unionist M.P. and candidate, intimating that, as the question of Home Rule will be the principal factor in politics for probably the next three years, the Joint Committee is anxious and willing, as far as possible, to give assistance in the constituencies.

Any substantial suggestion, with a view to ensuring a continuity of smooth working in the future, occurring to anyone nearly concerned, to be forwarded, in writing, to the Hon. Secretary of the Irish Unionist Parliamentary Party, to be by him submitted to the Chairman (or, in his absence, to the Vice-Chairman) of the Party, who, if he deems it of sufficient importance, will forward it to the Association concerned for consideration and the necessary action.

XI

As before, the propaganda work of the I.U.A. crystallised around by-elections. Between 1911 and the outbreak of war in 1914 the joint committee was active at 33 of the contested by-elections that occurred. At first help was given only to unionists in marginal seats, such as Cheltenham, where the unionist candidate scraped home by a few votes, but when home rule came nearer to law on the 'oiled castors' of the parliament act, the Unionist Associations of Ireland intervened at all contested elections. Happily for Irish unionists, these occurred at times when government and opposition leaders were considering the possibilities of a compromise, particularly in February 1914; for they could hope that unionist victories would harden the unionist party's attitude and force a dissolution of parliament.

Throughout the period the U.A.I. suffered only three rebuffs when it offered to assist unionist candidates and on each occasion it tactfully withdrew its workers. Usually, as soon as a by-election seemed imminent, the U.A.I.'s agent would consult the local unionist agent about work on the home rule question, though sometimes the U.A.I. was approached first by the British unionists. If local agents were willing to allow the joint committee to work the Irish question, the Irish unionist agent would take offices in the constituency and concentrate there in support of the unionist candidate (without cost to the candidate or his organisation) speakers, canvassers, literature, and, later on, the vans. Often, too, he would telegraph the Dublin and Belfast offices for further help and receive it in the form of workers, especially women, and literature. Speakers addressed meetings daily in support of the unionist candidate, stressing the iniquities of the government. Frequently they were placed under the control of the English unionists, as in all the London by-elections, and in all British by-elections an Irish unionist speaker was always on the unionist candidate's platform. Canvassers, well armed with maps and literature, also worked among the electors, sometimes under difficult conditions. In some constituencies the local unionists had been slack in watching electoral registers, as at Grimsby. Despite *The Times's* praise of efficient local organisation there, the joint committee found in May 1914 that 'owing to the complete absence of any records of removals they all had to be traced by canvassers during the election'. In this work the joint committee's canvassers 'largely assisted, tracing over 600', and at the request of the local unionist agent 'kept the various committee rooms posted daily on the result of the canvass'. Often, though, they had the advantage of having previously worked in constituencies such as Leith Burghs as part of the general propaganda campaign since 1911. Occasionally, local agents seem to have taken unfair advantage of the generosity of the joint committee, setting the Irish workers, as at South Bucks., the more arduous areas to cover.

A useful basis for a study of the U.A.I.'s intervention in by-elections are the regular reports of the joint secretaries and those of the association's agents in Great Britain. Usually the latter were added as an appendix to the southern secretary's report while the Scottish reports formed an integral part of the northern secretary's reports.

Ten of the joint committee's by-election interventions occurred in Scotland. Such interventions were on the whole considered to be successful, especially in putting over the Ulster unionist case, for the religious objection to home rule was largely pressed in these Scottish campaigns.

On one occasion, however, the joint committee met a reverse. In December 1913 a by-election took place in Wick Burghs, where the sitting liberal member, Robert Munro, had to seek re-election after being appointed lord advocate. Despite reluctance on the part of some Scottish unionists to contest this seat, an exhaustive five-week campaign stressing the religious objection to home rule was carried out by the joint committee.

Before the official contest began, two canvassers worked in the area; and on the seat's being declared vacant extra canvassers, including one clergyman, were brought in. Four speakers held several open-air meetings and large quantities of literature were distributed, including an edition of the *Witness,* the organ of the presbyterian church in Ulster. Until a week before the poll the joint committee was optimistic, but then there was a reaction in favour of the liberal candidate. Apart from the help he received from Ulster liberals, three factors assisted Munro: local pride at his appointment to high office; local self-interest, stimulated by a hint from the principal Scottish liberal whip that a grant would be made for Wick harbour—for which he and the prime minister subsequently apologised in the house of commons; and local prudery, set off by the 'damaging allusions' made to the unionist candidate's connection with the Gaiety Theatre, London. A. G. Mackenzie was a director of the Gaiety Theatre Company, where the audience could be assured of 'catchy tunes, entrancing girls, and adroit comedians'. The home rule and Ulster questions were thus completely obscured and Munro was returned with a record majority.

These were, however, exceptional circumstances, and it would be unfair to judge the joint committee's work on the results of this by-election. Given 'normal' conditions, the joint committee was able to make a considerable impact upon Scottish by-elections. Perhaps the most notable contest in which it took part was that in Leith Burghs in February 1914.

There a unionist victory, the first since 1832, of 5,159 votes to the liberal's 5,143 and labour's 3,346 was regarded as of national significance, convincing unionists that the government had completely lost the sympathy of the electorate. The joint committee dominated this campaign. For fifteen months previously its canvassers had worked over a 'very incompletely marked register', and during the election campaign the committee had six speakers and nineteen canvassers at work. There was a fierce battle with the liberal Home Rule Council, but it was the joint committee that made the greater impact, as *The Times* and even the liberal press and workers admitted.

Perhaps, too, it was the size of the joint committee's contribution to his campaign that caused G. W. Currie, the unionist candidate, to play up the theme of his own and his wife's ancestry. Through his father, a protestant minister, his descent could be traced from Scottish covenanters, while his wife was descended from George Walker, the protestant parson who took so prominent a part in the siege of Derry. This is how Currie explained to one audience the basis of his hostility to the third home rule bill. Since there was a three-cornered contest, there is room for debate as to the cause of the unionist victory. However, most commentators attributed the result in part at least to the Ulster question and the work of the joint committee. On the day of the poll *The Times's* special correspondent reported that the labour candidate was not winning more support on account of his advocacy of home rule, for 'the electors of Leith Burghs . . . are deeply stirred by the Ulster question, and are determined to make it the leading question in the present contest'.

175 R. D. Bates's report on the work of the U.A.I. in the by-election at Wick Burghs, December 1913, submitted to the joint committee on 20 February 1914 (D 1327/2/1):

The Unionist Associations of Ireland carried out a most exhaustive Campaign in the above Constituency both before and during the progress of the fight. Two Canvassers had been working in the Constituency for a considerable time before the seat was declared vacant and the reports from them from time to time pointed clearly to a majority of the Electors being opposed to Home Rule.

As soon as Mr. Munro was appointed Lord Advocate, extra canvassers were sent up to the following towns comprising the Burghs:— Wick, Kirkwall, Dornoch, Cromarty, Tain and Dingwall. They were distributed as follows:— 2 in Kirkwall, 2 in Wick, 2 in Dingwall, and one each in Cromarty, Tain, and Dornoch. The total Electors in these three smaller Burghs was small, so one canvasser to each was thought sufficient. This opinion turned out correct as all the Electors were called upon before the day of the poll.

In addition to the canvassers, 4 speakers for open-air meetings held several meetings daily, weather permitting, for the 4 weeks of the Contest, almost 70 meetings being addressed.

Large quantities of literature were distributed and one pamphlet in particular by Sellar of Quebec was sent to every Elector in the Constituency.

Early in the campaign we arranged with the Editor of the "Witness" the weekly organ of the Presbyterian Church in Ulster, to prepare a special issue containing articles dealing with the Home Rule Question and to send a copy to every voter. Two weeks later our example was copied by the Ulster Liberal Association, who posted a copy of their weekly newspaper the "Ulster Guardian" to the Electors. This necessitated a further issue of the "Witness" which we arranged should be in the hands of each voter on Saturday morning, the Polling Day being Monday.

Everything went well until the week before the Poll when a decided reaction set in. This was said to be due principally to two causes. One, a report that was assiduously spread abroad about a grant for Wick Harbour. The other was allusions and innuendoes in relation to the Unionist Candidate's connection with the Gaiety Theatre in London.

I am absolutely convinced that the result of the Election was not due to any desire on the part of the Electors for Home Rule, but was solely due to the following factors:—

1st. The honour done to the Constituency by the promotion of a North of Scotland man to the important position of Lord Advocate.

2nd. Vague hints and promises that were made from time to time about grants for Wick Harbour.

3rd., and by no means the least important of the three. The damaging allusions made to the Unionist Candidate's connection with the Gaiety Theatre, London.

176

Report of the east and north of Scotland district agency of the U.A.I. on the work done before and during the Leith Burghs by-election, February 1914, submitted to the joint committee on 25 March 1914 (D 1327/2/1):

Summary of work—prior to Election.

CANVASSING.

Robert Collins spent from September 1911 to March 27th, 1912.
J. Benson   ,,   ,,   Sept. 20th ,,   ,, November 4th, 1911.
Wm. Orr   ,,   ,,   Novr. 15th ,,   ,, 27th March, 1912.

This work consisted of calling upon Radicals and Doubtfuls in a very incompletely marked register.

SPEAKERS.

Mr. Bamford	—	4 meetings.
Mr. Bryars, 1912	—	6 ,,
,, ,, 1913	—	14 ,,
,, Bell, 1913	—	9 ,,

SUMMARY OF WORK DURING BY-ELECTION.

8 Canvassers started on 10th February, and nine others started on the 12th February, three extra men being added on the 17th. One of the Canvassers (James Anderson) was transferred to the Speaking Staff, leaving nineteen canvassers in all.

These men made in Leith, Musselburgh and Portobello, 4,997 calls and had 3241 actual interviews with electors, care being taken that they should not be asked to call upon Irish and Nationalist electors, and so waste time. The high percentage of calls, where the elector was not in, was due to three causes:—

(1) absence from home of Electors at Sea.
(2) absence from home of Electors, attending multitude of political meetings.
(3) absence from home of electors, attending 'Chapman Alexander Mission'.

Both these latter circumstances caused many men to be out in the evenings.

MEETINGS.

Speaking Campaign started on the 10th February, by Messrs McIntyre and Arthur, who held nine meetings before the official campaign started on the 16th. On that date, Messrs Thompson and Corrigan; Buller and Anderson, also started speaking, as also did six speakers of the Scottish Unionist Association. In all our Speakers held:—

33 meal-hour meetings and
30 evening meetings.

The reception accorded and the numbers present, being in the opinion of the men, better than during any Bye-Election in their experience.

REMARKS.

There can be no doubt that the seed sown in 1911, 1912, and 1913, has borne fruit, as demonstrated by the result, or as the "Evening News" (Radical) leading article has put it:—the leakage in the Liberal Poll was due amongst other causes to "persistent Campaign against Home Rule, pushed on for months". In the same paper a "Liberal Worker" in a special article, has stated "It was discovered in the course of the Contest that for a long time past, large staffs of canvassers had been patiently working religious objections to Home Rule, for all they were worth, and more, with the result that over and over again Home Rule Canvassers, (i.e., Dick, Semple and Company) came across Liberals, strong Church people, who told them they had genuine scruples over the granting of Home Rule". This attitude told against Provost Smith.

Our experience in West Lothian has been strengthened here, that where the cause of Ulster is brought home to Scottish Radicals, a few will vote Unionist, but the majority will do the next best thing, viz., abstain from voting at all.

326

Beyond all question our Campaign was the deciding factor in the Contest. Superhuman efforts of the Home Rule Council, mostly Englishmen, were completely countered by our Workers, and certainly if we have a purely Home Rule Election, we ought to be able to more than hold our own in Radical Scotland.

Compared with the Polling in the last three-cornered fight, in January 1910, the Labour vote is increased by 622, the Radical vote decreased by 1987, and the Unionist vote increased by 619. There have been 700 abstentions. This change in the political atmosphere of a Constituency which has been persistently Radical since 1832, is in itself both a justification and a reward for the work put in by the staff of the Unionist Associations of Ireland.

XII

The U.A.I. made less of an impact on English than on Scottish by-elections, though useful work was nevertheless done. Between the second general election of 1910 and the outbreak of war in 1914, the association assisted at twenty-three contested elections in England. The first two months of 1914 were a hectic time for the U.A.I. Its help was sought in a rash of by-elections, and its response in three elections in London and the home counties illustrates its flexibility. There were almost simultaneous contests in South Buckinghamshire, Poplar and South-west Bethnal Green. By adroitly switching his resources between constituencies and by borrowing from other divisions, the London agent, Wilkins, managed to play a large role in South Bucks. and Bethnal Green, and to show a 'presence' in Poplar.

At South Bucks. the Irish unionists were responding to an appeal by the chief unionist agent, John Boraston, to help maintain the unionist majority. Accordingly, over thirty Irish workers, including nine intrepid women, assisted in the return of the unionist candidate with only a slightly reduced majority. Whereas in 1910 the unionist majority had been 2,556, in 1914 the unionist beat the liberal by 9,044 votes to 6,713, a majority of 2,331. The Bethnal Green contest was of great significance. C. F. G. Masterman, a rising young liberal minister, was presenting himself for re-election on his promotion to cabinet rank. Since his majority at his last re-election was only 184, the U.A.I. had been carefully nursing this constituency. When the contest was announced in February 1914 the association immediately drafted workers in, telegraphing for help from Belfast and using the Jewish canvasser specially employed by the U.A.I. to work among his co-religionists in England. Such efforts helped in the defeat of Masterman by 24 votes. In Poplar the association could make little headway against the combined liberal and Irish nationalist vote there.

Also illustrative of the association's determination and flexibility was the by-election in North-east Derbyshire in May 1914. As soon as a vacancy was declared in this constituency, following the death of the sitting member, the Lancashire and northern agents of the joint committee pooled their resources. It was a mining seat previously held, owing to a liberal-labour agreement, by a labour member with a majority of 1,750; but as in May 1914 liberal and labour put forward different candidates, there was a good chance of a unionist victory. Therefore, after consultation with the local unionist agent, Blackham, the U.A.I. moved in with eight speakers and many canvassers, 'including a body of Belfast workingmen . . . seeking quietly to convince their fellow trade unionists of the justice of Ulster's opposition to home rule'. In addition, a magic lantern van held five meetings with an average audience of 300. For such aid the unionist candidate, Major H. Bowden, and the local agent were duly grateful. Bowden was returned by 6,469 votes to the liberal's 6,155 and labour's 3,669.

177 Report submitted to the joint committee, 20 February 1914, by H. V. Wilkins, the London agent, of work done by the U.A.I. in the South Buckinghamshire, South-west Bethnal Green and Poplar by-elections, February 1914 (D 1327/2/1):

SOUTH BUCKS

Mr. John Boraston, the Chief Agent of the Unionist Party, made a special appeal to the Unionist Associations of Ireland and to the Union Defence League to give every possible assistance in this contest owing to the importance of maintaining the majority.

I was perfectly prepared to commence operations at an early period of the election, but owing to uncertainty as to the date of the poll I was unable to obtain the sanction of the Agent to start our campaign January 29th. In making my arrangements I decided that the men canvassers should work in the rougher parts of the Division and the ladies in Slough and District.

Committee Rooms were secured after considerable trouble at 101, Oxford Street, High Wycombe, and in addition I arranged for a room to be placed at the disposal of the lady canvassers at 106, High Street, Slough.

The London Group of Canvassers were drafted into the Division on January 29th. Mr. Shaw visited the constituency with me on February 4th, and after consultation with the local people it was decided to draft the Western Group into the Division as well.

Owing to the bye-elections in East London it was found necessary on February 12th to transfer the London men to Bethnal Green, and I made arrangements for the Eastern Group to take their places in South Bucks.

Seven Ulster ladies and two South of Ireland ladies took part in the contest, and I cannot speak too highly of the work these ladies performed. They have really rendered most valuable assistance. Miss Leatham, who took charge of the party, was a most efficient leader, and I cannot thank her sufficiently for the help she and her colleagues gave me. To quote only two instances:— It was found necessary to send out an extra person with one of the Vans in order to thoroughly advertise the Van meetings. Miss Kingsborough, the Ulster Lady Dispatch Rider, volunteered for the job, and although on many occasions the weather was simply deplorable she insisted upon carrying out her duties.

It was suggested that a distribution of literature should be made to those electors who left Slough by the early trains and who did not return until late at night. The ladies who were working in Slough, Miss Leatham, Mrs. ffrench Beytagh and Miss Kingsborough readily undertook this work although it necessitated their getting up at 4.30 a.m.

MEETINGS—At the express request of the election agent we did not hold any meetings in High Wycombe itself, but we have systematically held meetings in the other polling districts. Up to the present we have held 44 meetings in the constituency. The majority of these have been well attended, and although some of the speakers have been subjected to a considerable amount of heckling it is apparent that the majority of the audiences are opposed to Home Rule.

In view of the importance of the election two of the Motor Vans that were engaged in the London Campaign were drafted into the Division. Both these Vans are accompanied by two speakers who hold meetings nightly. The speakers were also instructed to arrive in the villages early to distribute literature and carry out missionary work.

I arranged for Mr. S. T. L. Maunder to speak on the Candidate's platform, and he has addressed some meetings.

LITERATURE—The Radicals issued a telling leaflet dealing with "bigotry in Ulster". A special reply was prepared and this, together with two other leaflets, has been sent by post to every elector in the constituency. About 110,000 leaflets will have been distributed during the contest.

PROSPECTS—During the election I have kept in close touch with the constituency, and have visited it practically every other day. My relationship with the Official Party Organisation has been a most happy one, and everything possible was done to prevent overlapping. The Election Agent has expressed himself as most pleased with the work performed by our people. When this report is read the result will be known, but I shall be disappointed unless we have a majority at the least of 3,000.

SOUTH-WEST BETHNAL GREEN

We were very fortunately placed with regard to this constituency as owing to rumours having been prevalent for some time past that Mr. Masterman would shortly receive Cabinet rank, we carefully nursed the constituency, holding meetings weekly, and in addition during the month of December last the London canvassers carried out a systematic canvass of the constituency. Their work was very much appreciated, and I had a very kind letter from the agent thanking us on behalf of the candidate for the work performed. When the men returned from South Bucks they were therefore well acquainted with the constituency and no time was lost in getting to work.

COMMITTEE ROOMS—I had considerable difficulty in securing suitable premises, but eventually a very good place was secured at 251, Bethnal Green Road and an excellent display of posters has been made on the walls of the building.

As soon as the news of the election was officially confirmed I telegraphed to Belfast for six additional missionaries, who were very promptly dispatched; so that we have 13 men working in the constituency. In addition, Travers, the Jewish canvasser, was sent from Manchester and he is working amongst his co-religionists.

I am very pleased to state that the reports of the missionaries are extremely satisfactory, and numerous instances have been brought to my notice of people who have turned over on the Irish question.

MEETINGS—As is usual in London bye-elections, in order to avoid overlapping the open-air meetings are arranged by the National Unionist Association. I have placed 8 speakers at their disposal for work in South-West Bethnal Green and Poplar, and in addition I withdrew the No. 4 Van from South Bucks on Sunday, and this Van will hold meetings in the constituency up to the eve of the poll and will also parade the constituency daily.

The No. 1 U.D.L. Van will return from Bucks on Wednesday and will hold a meeting in the constituency on Wednesday night.

PROSPECTS—I have kept in close touch with the constituency, and from what I have seen myself and from the reports received, I am sanguine that we shall succeed in defeating Mr. Masterman. The presence of a third candidate to a certain extent, complicates the situation, as I am convinced that he will take more votes from us than he will from Mr. Masterman. However, all things considered I believe that unless our opponents resort to wholesale bribery that we shall succeed in winning the seat.

POPLAR

With the limited time at our disposal I decided to primarily concentrate all our efforts as far as canvassing was concerned on South-West Bethnal Green. I am, however, arranging on Thursday next for the 14 canvassers to proceed to Poplar to carry out a canvass in No. 6 and 7 Wards which, I am informed, are the Wards requiring special attention. It is possible that we may also have the help of some of the ladies who have been working in South Bucks. I am arranging for the Vans to hold meetings on Thursday and to 'parade' the constituency that day.

PROSPECTS—The Unionist Agent—Mr. Johnson—is unfortunately seriously ill, but Mr. Smith, the Agent for Bow and Bromley, is taking his place. The presence of a third candidate here assists our prospects as he is certain to take more votes from the Radical than from our side. There is a large Nationalist vote in the constituency—at least one thousand—and although the Socialist candidate may take a few of these the majority will record their vote for the Liberal. Although the local Unionists are hopeful of winning the seat I am afraid that the majority against us is too large for us to expect a victory. Much. however, depends upon the poll of the Socialist candidate and should he succeed in securing the Labour vote it is quite possible that we shall win the seat.

H. VERNON WILKINS,
LONDON. 17–2–14.

178 Report submitted to the joint committee, 4 August 1914, by Major H. E. Tombe, the northern agent, and R. N. Thompson, the Lancashire agent, of work done by the U.A.I. in the North-east Derbyshire by-election, May 1914, including a letter of thanks from the local unionist agent (D 1327/2/1):

Our canvassers were moved into this Constituency on Monday, May 4th, and after consultation with the Agent, were allocated to various Polling Stations throughout the Division, where they had sufficient work till the end of the contest. The men did extremely good work, and not one single complaint of any sort reached us. We visited our canvassers daily, and kept them under strict supervision. The following are the number of calls:—

For Home Rule 1110, against 1783, doubtful 3064. Total 5957.

Seven Speakers were engaged in the Campaign, and the following is a list of their Meetings and approximate audiences:—

Captain Bryan Cooper.

May 12th	Ridgway.	80.
	Mossborough.	150.
May 13th	Dronfield.	450.
May 14th	Killamarsh.	300.
May 15th	Barlbro'.	200.
May 19th	Whittington Moor.	400.

Mr S. W. Maddock.

May 12th	Clown.	500.
May 13th	Whitwell.	400.
May 14th	Cresswell.	500.
May 15th	Eckington	300.
May 16th	Bolsover	200.
May 18th	Staveley.	500.
May 19th	Totley Rise.	350

Mr J. Porterfield Rynd.

May 8th	Dore	300.
May 11th	Shuttlewood	120.
May 12th	Elmton	300.
May 13th	Unstone	120.
May 14th	Mossborough	350.
May 15th	Woodseats	500.
May 16th	Staveley Town	350.
May 18th	Eckington	1100.
May 19th	do	450.

Mr W. F. Wallis.

May 8th	Whittington	40.
May 12th	Mossborough	150.
May 13th	Staveley Cross	300.
May 14th	Ridgway	150.
May 15th	Norton	60.
May 18th	Poolsbrook	180.
May 19th	Dore	200.

Mr A. W. Hildreth.

May 8th	Whittington	40.
May 9th	Woodseats	500.
May 11th	Linthwaite	130.
	Bolsover	250.
May 12th	Ridgway	80.
May 13th	Woodseats	800.
May 14th	Marsh Lane	90.
May 15th	Woodseats	500.
May 16th	do	1000.
May 18th	Eckington	1100.
May 19th	Meersbrook	700.

Mr R. B. Pargiter.

May 11th	Staveley Town	100.
May 12th	Marsh Lane	Not called on to speak.
May 13th	Woodseats	50
May 14th	Eckington	70

Mr H. Gauld.

May 11th	Staveley Town
May 12th	Mossborough.
May 13th	Eckington.
May 14th	Marsh Lane.
May 15th	Beighton.
May 18th	Poolsbrook.
May 19th	Staveley Cross.

Mr J. Bramston, with magic lantern motor van.

May 14th	Eckington	80.
May 15th	Dronfield	300.
May 16th	Meersbrook	200.
May 18th	Whittington Moor	200.
May 19th	Bolsover	500.

All these were good Meetings.

The Candidate and his Agent specially thanked us for our work, and we enclose copy of a letter from Mr Blackham written before the Poll.

We wish specially to mention the good work done by our two Head men, Mr Wilson Hildreth and Mr. H. Ross. The former was most successful as a Speaker, and was in great demand everywhere.

> H. E. Tombe.
> Robert N. Thompson.

To Major Tombe and R. Thompson, Esq.,

Gentlemen,

An opportunity presents itself of a few minutes quietness, owing to the splendid organisation which has enabled us to complete our arrangements somewhat in advance of our opponents, and I am taking the opportunity of writing to you to express my personal thanks for all the assistance you and your staff have voluntarily rendered during this hotly contested election.

Although I have not had much chance of seeing your men at work, I have had many congratulatory messages from wherever you have been—the quiet determination to present the case for Ulster, and the gentlemanly manner of your workers, have strengthened those who were already strong for the Union, and made converts of many who formerly were opposed to us on the Home Rule Question.

If we win this election, and I think we shall, no small portion of the credit will be due to you and your gallant band, and the least I can do is to tell you so.

I shall long remember this happy bye election, let the result be what it may.

We have done our work and the verdict remains in the "lap of the gods", but I feel that right will surely prevail.

> Yours faithfully,
> (signed) A. P. **BLACKHAM.**

333

179 2/1):

Captain B. Cooper's favourable comments on the work of the U.A.I. in the North-east Derbyshire by-election, May 1914, submitted to the joint committee on 4 August 1914 (D 1327/ 2/1):

I arrived in North East Derby on Tuesday May 12th 1914. and was there at intervals till the polling day on the 20th. The U.A. of I. were represented by Major Tombe and Mr. Thompson, who had been at work with the canvassers of their groups for a week previous to my arrival. I was pleased to find that they had established friendly relations with the Unionist candidate and his agent, and the footing they were on greatly facilitated our work. We had five speakers in the division (including Mr. Hildreth, head canvasser in Major Tomb's [*sic*] group, who spoke most admirably and did invaluable work), and these speakers were in request every night for indoor meetings, usually in conjunction with the candidate and a member of Parliament. These meetings were well organised and well attended in spite of the fine weather: they were a great improvement on those I have been to in other bye elections. In all our speakers must have addressed 50 meetings and at least 10,000. people nearly all being voters.

I visited all our canvassers generally finding them out at work. They all, seemed keen, and could give an intelligent description of the situation in the village they were working in. They seemed to find the industrial Map of Ireland extremely useful in giving extempore address[es]—as on Ulster. Some of the Miners thought that Ulster was a town.

A van was in the division for five nights but I did not see anything of its work.

I must pay a tribute to the way in which Major Tombe and Mr. Thompson co-operated both with one another, and with the Unionist agent for North East Derbyshire and the representatives of the Central Conservative Office. Their tact and good temper coupled with their enthusiasm and energy did much to secure the effective presentation of our case which enabled us to increase the Unionist poll by 600 votes and so secure a remarkable victory.

Bryan Cooper.

XIII

The vital question is how effective was the Irish unionist campaign in British politics? The documents quoted above give at least an indication of its successes and limitations. First, while the campaign did not turn Britain completely against home rule and kill that policy absolutely, it did help to isolate the Ulster question, emphasised after 1911 by the U.A.I. largely for tactical reasons. Ulster unionists could, therefore, be satisfied that the campaign did implant the seed of the partition of Ireland effected eventually by the government of Ireland act of 1920. Secondly, and by way of compensation to southern unionists, the campaign made British unionists aware of the existence of an Irish unionist viewpoint, southern as well as northern.

Moreover, it could be argued that this awareness, and the links forged between Irish and British unionists, helped to give the unionist party a politically impelling commitment on the union. Ever since 1886, and especially in the period 1908–14, the services of the Irish unionists had been in constant demand by local unionist associations in Britain. The efficiency and persistence of Irish unionist campaigning created a feeling among local unionists that their success was dependent in large part upon the Irish unionists. The result was that the unionist party became tied at grass roots level to the cause of the Irish unionists, northern and southern. Southern unionists, therefore, need not have regarded the campaign as a complete failure, especially since the campaign in the constituencies strengthened the hand of their contacts among the party leadership and in parliament. Since the unionist majority in the lords was used to delay the third home rule bill, southern unionists could at least find comfort in the fact that the repeal of the union was delayed by their activities.

There are in the N.I.P.R.O. a number of letters showing the demands made upon the I.L.P.U. and I.U.A. in the early 1890s by local conservative and unionist associations; but the bulk of the evidence relating to the impact of southern unionism upon the conservative and unionist parties is to be found in collections deposited outside the N.I.P.R.O. On the other hand, there are many further illustrations in the N.I.P.R.O. of the impact that Ulster unionism made in 1912–14 upon people of conservative temperament in Great Britain. Some, like Miss Constance Williams, private secretary to the wife of one of the liberal undersecretaries, contented themselves with passing on advice and information they picked up. Others, however, involved themselves more closely with Ulster's plans for armed resistance to the third home rule bill. Susan, wife of the 15th duke of Somerset, not only prayed for Ulster but also made arrangements to send over an ambulance team as soon as the first shot was fired in Ireland and to receive refugees from Ulster. Others hoped to go beyond the provision of auxiliary services. One of the most formal indications of support for Ulster was the formation in March 1913 of the British League for the Support of Ulster and the Union. The moving spirit was Lord Willoughby de Broke, supported by over 200 members of both houses of parliament, and the organisation did not bind itself to use merely constitutional modes of protest. Branches were established throughout Great Britain, as were 'Ulster Athletic Clubs'. Before long the league was said to have had more than 10,000 men prepared to fight for Ulster, organised by 400 agents of the calibre of the 'deadly earnest' honorary agent for Birmingham, William Nightingale, who set himself the task of raising '1,000 soldiers of civil and religious liberty'.

180 Letter from D. L. Sprake, agent for the conservative candidate for the Accrington division of Lancashire in the general election of 1892, to the secretary of the I.U.A., 21 June 1892, successfully asking for help in attempting (unsuccessfully) to maintain a small unionist majority (D 989A/8/2):

Dear Sir—Knowing how very much pressed your Union is for Speakers during the coming campaign I feel much compunction in writing but really our position here is very exceptional. The constituency has the reputation of being thoroughly Gladstonian but by great efforts on the part of local workers with the assistance of prominent public gentlemen who came here and spoke in support of our candidate we secured the return of Mr Hermon-Hodge by a majority of 220. We are very anxious to again return him, and I need hardly say that our opponents are just as anxious that we should not. Last night they had Mr John Morley here speaking in support of their candidate and this has given them considerable advantage which we trust you will assist us to overcome by requesting some one of your leading speakers to come over and help us.

There is such a large body of Wesleyan Voters in this Division that we are convinced that one of their own body making an appeal to them would exercise powerful influence. May we rely on your doing us this very great favour. I am yours respectfully

D. L. Sprake.

181 Letter from Miss C. Williams, 101 Stamford Street, Blackfriars, London S.E., to Sir Edward Carson, 14 January 1914, tipping him off about the attitudes of various liberal ministers to the Ulster question (D 1507/1/1914/1):

Dear Sir—Can you not organize police of your own to suppress any rioting which may take place in Belfast among the Hooligan population? Perhaps this has already been done, if so, it should be known. I should not venture to trouble you, had I not exceptional opportunities of knowing what the govt.— or some of them — are aiming at in Ireland.

I am private secretary to the wife of one of the under-secretaries; members of the govt meet at his house socially & informally at all hours & discuss matters with considerable freedom. Less than a week ago Mr. Asquith, Mr McKenna & Mr Pease were there about the same time.

The plan is to procrastinate until the patience of the Hooligan element in Belfast is exhausted & they begin to riot. This is the moment when troops (they have decided which regiments are to be sent) will step in and crush riot & incidentally you & the Loyalists. Mr Asquith still hankers after compromise & is not much in favour of this policy, but is being overruled.

They have agents in Belfast—some pretending to be friendly to your people—who send regular reports and are to say when is the right moment to stir up riot. I tried to get hold of one of these reports, but Mr McKenna never lets them out of his hand & reads them out to the others.

Mr Lloyd George is the only one who does not think things are serious. He said casually over the tea-table, "Put the Crimes act in force, & the whole thing will fizzle out in a week".

Perhaps my action in writing in this way is mean, but the morals of one insignificant woman are of little account, when such crimes are going forward.

Please do not think it necessary to reply, I keep in such close [touch] with the papers that I shall not miss any movement. With every belief in your ultimate triumph I am yours faithfully

Constance Williams

182 Letter from the duchess of Somerset, 35 Grosvenor Square, London W., to Carson, 13 January (1914?), explaining the steps she is taking in support of Ulster's resistance to the third home rule bill (D 1507/1/6/41):

Dear Sir Edward Carson—This is to assure you of our unfailing support and to implore you to take all care of yourself—so as to save Ireland.

I think it was so kind of you to write I am laid up in my room with a cold and chill—otherwise I should have continued my endeavours to see you before your next great meeting at Belfast—

The Day that the first shot is fired in Ireland—I shall have my complete ambulance started and ready—2 medical men 2 surgeons 6 trained nurses and 32 orderlies—I have also undertaken to house 100 women and children from Ulster—The Duke and I will both come over to give all the help we can—

It is not for want of sympathy on this side the fight is so uphill at this moment but from the fatigue of the people to comprehend more legislation— However at a Meeting at Warminster the other night (and as you know Warminster is but a small place) when I spoke to them about the necessity of helping Ulster I got £200—at once guaranteed and I have £1200 also guaranteed for the ambulance—

People say what has the Duchess of Somerset to do with Ireland—The Duchess is the Great Great granddaughter of the Count de Lally—who was executed in the French Revolution and the great grandaughter [*sic*] of a Murphy!! So I feel for Ireland and am sure with the help of God you will yet save the Union—This little letter is just a note of encouragement for I know how depressed you must be at times but in such a noble cause! it is worth while and its the weakness of our Rulers at the present time who have helped the Traitors and little Englishmen to bring their evil doings to this impasse.

One word more I quote from the Life of Lady Shelley Vol II that in the Manchester Riots in the time of the Duke of Wellington 12 persons were shot in the streets there and 600 injured—by unduly reading the riot act! So things have been bad and have mended and the country will follow you now and we shall all help you to see this thing through and this Vile government will go out and perhaps a reign of peace will come—I feel that the danger to the State is their trying the temper of the troops too far. I was told that a certain officer in the Blues was told he must resign if he continued to drill troops in Ulster his reply was the day I send in my papers 8 other officers will send in theirs. Please let us meet later. We come to stay in town Saty. [Saturday] till Easter Yrs most Sincerely

Susan Somerset—

183 Letter (forwarded to Carson) from W. Nightingale, 3 New Street, Birmingham (branch office of the British League for the Support of Ulster and the Union), to the 19th Baron Willoughby de Broke, 17 October 1913, describing the progress in Birmingham of the Ulster Athletic Club (D 1507/1/1913/6):

My Lord,

Do you think it advisable that some public reference should be made at the Meeting which Sir Edward Carson is to address in Birmingham on Friday, of the Ulster Athletic Club?

We only had our first public Meeting on Friday last at Cromwell Hall, Heath Green Road. I gave a short address on the objects and advantages of the Club, and convinced them that we are acting within our legal right. The Meeting adopted the articles with hearty unanimity and appointed a local Committee of six with power to add to their numbers. As many signed on and bought the U.A.C. badge, and the Committee promised 70 to 80 signatures we have arranged for drill to commence to-night. One or two members of our Central Committee who have had military training will be there, and as they have three reservists among them two of whom signed the British League enrollment [*sic*] they will make a good start. They have decided to call themselves Company A. West B'ham Division. My young friend Mr F. J. Pritchard (one of your young Imperialists) is giving me good help, and before Xmas we hope to start a company in each Parliamentary Division.

I have an appointment with another member of our Committee Mr Bruce Wheeler, Corp: Warwickshire Yeomanry, for this afternoon to arrange for a public Meeting at Aston, shortly. I have long been of opinion that nothing but a strong display of force in Great Britain will influence Mr Redmond in the least. We will show him that in this district we can raise in a few weeks 1,000 Soldiers of Civil and relegious [*sic*] liberty. The time for mere talk is about over, I am my lord, Your obedient Servant,

Wm. H. Nightingale.

Chapter IX

The decline of southern unionism 1914-22

Up until the outbreak of the first world war the unionists of the three southern provinces and their organisation, the I.U.A., had remained opposed to home rule. As the third home rule bill went through parliament they had become less optimistic of the chances of defeating it, but they had still been determined to try. After 1914, however, this determination weakened, as southern unionists became less suspicious of Irish nationalists and nationalism and increasingly disillusioned with the union and the British connection. The unionist position taken up in 1885 was gradually abandoned. An increasing number of southern unionists became prepared to work for or, more usually, to accept a wide measure of self-government that contained some safeguards, formal or otherwise, for minorities.

The trend was sure, but not without interruptions in 1916 and 1918–19, and it was resisted by die-hard unionists. The trend was revealed by the significant and conciliatory role played by the southern unionist delegates in the Irish convention of 1917–18. Their action was repudiated by a group organised as the Southern Unionist Committee and resulted in a split in the I.U.A. in 1919. The more forward-looking founded the Unionist Anti-Partition League. They played a significant role in the shaping of the government of Ireland act of 1920, but were less influential in the negotiations in 1921–22 that led to the signing of the Anglo-Irish treaty of 6 December 1921 and the shaping of the constitution of the Irish Free State. Their secession from the I.U.A. left that organisation in the hands of the uncompromising opponents of Irish self-government. Optimistic in 1919 and reinforced by the unionists of Cavan, Donegal and Monaghan, even they found it increasingly difficult to maintain an effective opposition to home rule. By 1922, with the establishment of the Irish Free State, the unionist movement had petered out in the south of Ireland.

Material for a study of the views and attitudes of the more progressive southern unionists is to be found in the Midleton and cabinet papers in the Public Record Office in London, and in the Bernard papers in the British Museum and Trinity College, Dublin; but there is in the N.I.P.R.O. material relating to those southern unionists whose views changed more slowly and who prevented the I.U.A. from adopting a more accommodating attitude towards the Irish question. The object of this chapter is, therefore, to show how material in the N.I.P.R.O. can be used to trace and explain the gradual decline and demise of unionism in the south of Ireland, as seen in the I.U.A. and its die-hard elements.

II

Southern unionists contributed spontaneously and wholeheartedly to the needs of the war that broke out in August 1914. They enlisted in the regular forces and called for cooperation with the national volunteers, lately founded in opposition to the U.V.F. This call for cooperation with the nationalists was made against the advice of unionist leaders in England, who thought that such action was undermining opposition to the (successful) attempt to put the third home rule bill on the statute book in September 1914. Southern unionist attitudes to the war, however, were not governed by political considerations, and those that could not go to the front readily cooperated with nationalists in recruiting in Ireland. In Cork unionists and nationalists cooperated in the City of Cork Volunteer Training Corps, and were prepared to use nationalist slogans or banners to attract recruits; much to the disgust of some unbending unionists, like D. Williams, a Cork coachbuilder.

The effect of this absorption in the war effort upon the unionist movement in the south of Ireland was twofold. In the first place, enthusiasm for the union and the desire to resist home rule were weakened. Concentration on the war effort enabled southern unionists to see the home rule question in a different perspective; and cooperation with nationalists diminished some unionists' suspicions of Irish nationalists and Irish nationalism. Secondly, unionist organisation was weakened. At the centre the I.U.A. was merely kept ticking over and local organisation was almost fading out of existence —as J. M. Wilson discovered when he made a tour of some of the Irish counties in 1915–16 and reported his findings on a wide range of political issues to Walter Long. Thus the early years of the war paved the way for a *rapprochement* between unionists and nationalists in the south, whose rivalries had been stereotyped since the 1880s.

184 *Letter from R. J. Shaw, secretary of the I.U.A., to Sir Edward Carson, 7 August 1914, acknowledging the latter's advice to postpone publication of a resolution urging cooperation between unionists and nationalists in the war effort (D 989A/8/4):

Dear Sir Edward—Wick's wire conveying your advice to the Committee reached me this morning, and I laid it before the Advisory Committee, who immediately decided to recommend to the Executive that the consideration of the resolution should be postponed. The Executive unanimously adopted this course. When the Advisory Committee sent out the circular which you received they were fully under the impression that a truce had been come to between the parties until after the crisis. We gather, however, from your wire that this is not the case, and naturally the whole situation is completely altered if it is not so. As I told you the Advisory Committee believed that it was essential that some resolution should be passed, because during the last two days a very large number of prominent members of our Committee have been in negotiation with the Nationalist Volunteer Force in their locality. A very large number of replies were received to the circular letter, and the great majority of them were strongly in favour of the resolution.

In the event of a satisfactory agreement being come to with the Government as to the adjournment of the Home Rule Bill, we think it probable that fresh pressure will be put on us to pass some such resolution. I may say that Mr. Sclater came to Dublin this morning and suggested to us certain alterations in the resolution itself, which the Advisory Committee agreed on, as he told us that in the form in which it was originally sent out it would tend to provoke great criticism in the North. The amended resolution agreed upon would read as follows:—

"That we the Executive Committee of the Irish Unionist Alliance hereby welcome the patriotic spirit which has actuated Sir Edward Carson and Mr. John Redmond in this crisis in our country's history, and we call on all Unionists in Ireland, in the Imperial spirit which they have always shown, to co-operate with their follow [*sic*] countrymen in the defence of Ireland and the Empire".

The Advisory Committee are most grateful to you for having wired to them, and you may rely upon them being guided by you in this matter as in all others. Yours sincerely,

185

Leaflet describing the City of Cork Volunteer Training Corps (D 989D/6):

CITY OF CORK

VOLUNTEER TRAINING CORPS

(Recognised by the War Office)

Patrons :

Rt. Hon. THE EARL OF BANDON, K.P., H.M.L.

The Rt. Hon. THE LORD MAYOR OF CORK.

His Honour MATHEW J. BOURKE, K.C., Recorder of Cork.

Military Adviser :

Capt. H. W. GAYE, Staff Captain, 12th. District.

General Committee :

Chairman .... •A. W. SANDFORD, M.D.
Vice-Chairman .... •R. F. STARKIE, R.M.

•C. W. L. ALEXANDER, M.Sc.   FRANK LYONS.
•S. D. BUDD.   A. R. McMULLEN.
J. M. BROWNE, M.B.   J. F. McMULLEN, K.C.S.G., J.P.
•A. F. SHARMAN-CRAWFORD, J.P.   W. MORROGH.
•HENRY CRONIN.   JONATHAN MAGRATH.
JOHN CROSBIE.   MARTIN F. MAHONY.
J. A. CUNNINGHAM.   •MICHAEL J. MAHONY.
J. COTTER, M.D.   •JAMES MURPHY. (Ringmahon)
SIR ALFRED G. DOBBIN, J.P.   •W. P. MUSGRAVE.
W. T. GREEN.   •VINCENT J. MURRAY.
BARRY C. GALVIN.   P. T. O'SULLIVAN, M.D.
JOSEPH GIUSANI, M.D.   J. J. O'CONNELL,(National Bank)
•SIR STANLEY HARRINGTON, J.P.   JOHN PICKERING.
ROBERT HALL, jun.   JOSEPH PIKE, D.L.‡
P. J. HARDING.   BRAHAM E. SUTTON.
JOHN P. HOWARD   S. SPIRO, J.P. ‡
•THOMAS JENNINGS, J.P.   NORMAN I. TOWNSEND, M.D.
    T. H. DENNY TOWNSEND M B.

•Members of Executive Committee.

Hon. Treasurer .... R. A. PELLY, Hibernian Bank, Cork.
Hon. Secretaries .... { D. T. BARRY, M.D., Tel. 681.
         { S. SEYMOUR,   " 116.

Headquarters :

The Drill Hall, Mardyke, Cork.

Guy & Co., Ltd., Printers, Cork.

Rules of the City of Cork Volunteer Training Corps.

1. That the force be called the "City of Cork Volunteer Training Corps" and that only such men be enrolled as those provided for by the Conditions laid down by the War Office.

2. All applications for enrolment to be considered by the Enrolment Committee. Should any case arise on which the Committee are unable to decide as to whether the applicant be eligible or not under Condition 1, the matter to be referred to the Recruiting Officer of the District, whose decision will be final.

3. SUBSCRIPTIONS.—Each Member shall pay an Entrance Fee of 2/6, and a Subscription of One Shilling per month, due the first drill night of each month. Members may pay their Subscriptions in advance if more convenient to them.

4. Each Member shall attend an average of at least two drills of one hour each per week, except when specially exempted by the Commandant on giving a good and sufficient reason, and when sufficiently advanced will be expected to attend one afternoon drill or parade in each fortnight, if necessary in lieu of one of the evening drills.

Members are expected to make it a point of honour to attend the full number of drills required.

5. HONORARY MEMBERS.—Honorary Members may be admitted and exempted from drill on payment of a Subscription of not less than One Guinea, provided that the Committee be satisfied that such Members are not in a position to drill.

Such Honorary Members may be Members of the General Committee.

6. Route marches of gradually increasing length to be undertaken at regular periods. All route marches to count as drills.

7. UNIFORM.—A. The "Brassard" must be always worn when on parade.

B. Should the Corps be required to take up local military duties it would be necessary then to adopt the uniform prescribed by the Central Association.

Under other circumstances all questions of uniform to be regulated by the Executive Committee.

8. Members on parade must strictly obey all instructions from the Officers of the Corps or the military instructors.

9. With the exception of the Commanding Officer and second in command, who may be appointed from outside, all appointments, such as platoon commanders or section leaders, etc., shall only be made from those who have gone through the ranks of the Corps, and none such shall be appointed until the Committee and the drill instructors be thoroughly satisfied that they are fully qualified for the posts. If thought advisable an independent officer or sergeant to be called in to examine them.

10. Should the Corps be called upon for local military duties, it shall be the duty of the Committee to arrange the order and time in which they then shall undertake the work, so as to interfere as little as possible with the Members' business or profession.

11. RIFLE PRACTICE.—It is desirable that this should be made a special feature, and Members will be required to fire a minimum number of rounds per week on an average.

The ammunition to be sold to the Members at the lowest rate which will provide for expenses being covered.

12. The Committee shall have power to suspend or expel any Member guilty of disobeying instructions on parade, or for irregular or bad attendance, or for non-payment of Subscriptions, or conduct unworthy of a Member.

———:o:———

It is not intended that drill shall be confined to ordinary squad drill, but that special subjects should be taken up later on, such as bayonet exercise, signalling, cycling, ambulance and stretcher work, etc., so that Members may be fitted to take up any duties which may be required of them.

186 Letter from D. Williams, Carriage and motor works, Union Quay, Cork, to J. M. Wilson, 15 February 1916, lamenting the weakening effect of the war effort on unionist sentiment in Cork, and deploring local recruiting methods, which involved on one occasion the use of a large, white home rule banner (D 989A/8/7):

Dear Sir—I apologise for delay in reply—rather unavoidable, & when it was necessary to see my friend (who took & typed your notes here) I wrote you fully Sunday except that I could not say I got corroboration re Printed matter on white banner you ask[ed] me about. I failed to catch him @ house, failed to get him at office, & on Sunday night went to city again specially, & as I had not caught him up to posting time @ G.P.O. I sent you p[ost] c[ard], & hoped next morning (Monday) to send that letter with the bit added he had offered to find out for me on Friday, when I asked him if he had seen what I saw, (& I mentioned to Mr Franks, as you say).

Having told me he did not see the large new white banner that I saw Saturday fortnight last, & if he had known he would have sent it to Dublin & Belfast papers, but he could not credit I was correct, & so he was to ascertain exact reading on it, & it was to see him on Sunday for this, I was looking him up, I got corroboration from one or two working men, but he advised me [to] wait a day or two & make absolutely certain, in case you wanted to make use of it in important directions. Hence it is, that only tonight I have been able to write you fully & hurriedly, & I destroyed letter I had written, having now seen my friend late Sunday night, but his details left me much where I was, except that it bears out I was right in the main words I quoted Mr Franks. As a result of our talk I had to see a certain gentleman, and caught him today, but as he could not give me the small lettering, but did give me certain details, I cannot tonight even give you the complete reading matter on it, but am in a position to say I was not wrong.

Now I will give you all I know, & though I could have sworn to what I saw, still I was anxious to know some other reliable person or persons saw it as well as myself, but this may be due to indifference on their part, whilst I have been on the alert all the time, & as I now have arranged to send Mr Franks any little cuttings or bits of news of use or interest, I mentioned this casually, & am astonished to find you seem suprised at even green flags with the military. Why, Sir, these have been going round here for weeks & months in recruiting marching & meetings. We are quite used to not seeing the pure Union Jack, but green flags. On one of these two very green flags carried by the fresh new recruits of each particular week, (who are marshalled around principal streets wearing green rosettes, & in their private clothes) is a small "Jack" in one corner only. I took special note on Saty. last. The rest of this flag all plain green. The 2nd one has nothing on the green but simply the "Harp" in yellow colour on the green flag, & no Jack at all on this. The new couple or few dozen new recruits for the particular week are accompanied by two military bands, (one taking up when other stops playing). The recruiting sergeants are present, drum major or other officer, the two bands, an officer leading the bands, & recruits in centre 4 to 6 deep—usual crowd gathers & follows around the city. They parade usually Wednesday (early closing day) & Saturday (half holiday for mechanics like my own). On last Saty., & evidently since the one Saturday, end of Jany. (I think 29th) this white sheet has not been round, & the cause I have heard & give you. The green flags are carried all the time for a long time, & on Saty. last, as usual, & as described, & the bands play Irish airs or tunes, including the novelty very frequently, & amusing for a military brass Band—"A Nation once again". Also—"For the wearing of the green." &c. To go back a bit—

I was rushing out to a meeting, Sat, Jany 29, (a very blustery day) when the bands, &c, were coming along South Mall, with a crowd. I saw with usual 2 green flags a big white banner or sheet. With the high wind there was difficulty in carrying it— two recruits with a large pole at each end, (& I think a few more holding strings to keep it open in wind). Still, with the weight, the marching & bobbing up & down, & the high wind, it was utterly impossible, unless they stopped, to read all on it that day, but my eye caught the word "Home", & I dashed into crowd to try and read it. Unfortunately my hat was blown off, but ere they passed I read undoubtedly first top line in large printed letters of black—words—"HOME RULE". Then next large lines "Ireland (freed or relieved, or released,) from CONSCRIPTION & COMPULSION." A number of lines of smaller matter printed after this, but once I saw—"Home Rule", I passed on.

Now my friend could scarcely believe it, & advised me, (as I already intended) not to state this top line unless I had corroboration. This I was anxious for, though I should be dreaming were I told "Home Rule" was not on it, in prominent printed letters. From one of his colleagues my friend learned this was a very large & heavy banner, & found awkward to carry, & it now lies at City Recruiting offices in Patrick St rolled up. It was printed in City on the white cloth by a painter, & that some of the Recruiting Com[mitt]ee objected to "Home rule" line. The Captain @ present leading the bands, &c, is a local gentleman, was wounded in Scotch Regt & with usual uniform wears glengarry cap (Scotch) with streamers. He, I'm informed, snapped his fingers at them & insisted he would use it. Still through awkwardness & weight I believe it was not since out. Am further informed War office have given authority for the marching Tunes referred to, as well as the green flags referred to. And now this is the full extent of information my friend could get for me, but suggested my seeing some prominent member of the Recruiting Com[mitt]ee who could tell me the whole reading matter, & which I am told included a quotation from John Redmond, &c.

After this I went yesterday to see a prominent & active member of Recruiting Com[mitt]ee, whom I knew to be a staunch Unionist, & I caught him today at his business place & had a word with him. Let me say he is one of the otherwise staunch Unionists who, like many big & small men, does or did not identify himself openly with our Unionist work & party here.

He is, I know, reliable, but was not on our platforms or active, tho' possibly he may, on the quiet, subscribe to our funds. It was through open identification I suffered in business myself, business that, to a great extent, never returned to me, & it galls me—a poor man— to see big rich business men so cautious & guarded, though I also growl at the smaller people. I suppose these are all the "wise acres", & we "hot-heads" have to pay the price, where, like in my case, we can be made suffer in way mentioned. However, I believe in availing of the liberty that is still there for all, & I believe in hot or cold, but not "lukewarmness". Hence I knew my man, but was sure he would think of this banner as I do. Well, he told me, he really did not bother to read this. It was now rolled up there—too cumbersome to carry. He was not aware of any objection made by Unionist Recruiting Com[mitt]ee members, & he knew War office gave permission for green flags & Tunes (like, "a nation once again", "For the wearing of the green", &c). I said—"Apart from that, is it not playing the game very low to put "Home Rule" out. You know it is unlikely, present Bill, & this practically says—'You are getting it.' " He replied—"I dont say we will get that Bill, but we will get some form of Home Rule. I believe matters will be much altered & politics much dead after the war." I said that was a question, & I was sick of people saying—"The soldiers playing "A nation once again", &c ! ! Why what a change in the times. We would be imprisoned for playing or singing that in public streets before." My friend answered—"And there is a great change, & I, personally, see nothing in playing these airs, in green flags, banner or anything else, for recruiting purposes. I thought it wonderful for me, differing both ways, to be on platforms in the county @ meetings with parish priest on one side & the biggest of nationalists on other side of me." I said—"What was wonderful in it? Surely you realize they all know their skins are in danger as well as yours & mine. It is to their interest as well as ours to save the country. What thanks is due. As to the hereafter, I disagree with you as to no politics, & present unanimity prevailing still. Wait & see." He said—"Oh, the Shin [sic] Fein men must be put down, & whatever you may think of Irish National Volunteers, you will find very soon now the Govt will recognise them; they will take the oath, be armed, put on Home defence, & then the Irish volunteers will be disarmed or put in jail if caught with arms, as, when we have the National Volunteers under war office recognized, there will be an order— "No arms allowed only [sic] to men having taken the oath of allegiance." I replied—"They will be useful (?) if they guard the bridges as they did before for few weeks they were recognized without the oath, & it would be better business on Govt part, & safer test, to get all these young men in National Volunteers to join army & go across from here. The Police can do the Home defence. Otherwise, the volunteers are armed for another war, "nearer home", after the German war is over." A person came in to him them [sic] & we broke off. What passed may be of some use to you, as to how the wind blows, & what is evidently to happen regarding volunteers. This gentleman, I forgot to say, also told me, whatever, flags, banners &c, are used, or tunes played, the military are doing all, the Recruiting Com[mitt]ee have nothing to say to it, & the military have War office sanction.

In Conclusion, to go back to my other "shorthand" friend who did the typeing [*sic*] for you, I should have said that he found I was quite correct re white banner & large printing I saw, but so far we both failed to get the small wording. Still, I think, I give you enough to suprise you even more than your letter conveys to me you have already been. I hope I have not worried you, & only hope, as I am very pushed, & write late every night (& day often) re honorary work & public Board duties, you will be able to read this scribbled epistle. I say, Sir, in conclusion, one word of request—"Keep our flag flying". Yrs faithfully—D. Williams.

P.S. Forgot to put this on plain notepaper. You will of course, keep this, & keep me, from publicity, or my ruin may be completed here—D.W.

187 Extracts from J. M. Wilson's notes of conversations with anonymous or semi-anonymous informants during a tour of the Irish counties in 1915–17, revealing the decline of unionist sentiment and organisation in the south of Ireland (D 989A/9/7):

(a) [Co. Clare, 23 January 1916]

Lord A. No meeting since War, if the problem arose again the same men would turn up again. Have not weakened in their faith. Before War, at every meeting here all enthusiastic about it, say 120 present.

Mr. B. We are very small, but agree with above. A bitter feeling engendered owing to little or no acknowledgment by anyone in the House that bulk of recruiting in South and West has been from the two classes, Landlord and the lowest. The former claims no special kudos, but surely the fact ought to be mentioned and rubbed in. I feel too disgusted for words at times.

Mr. C. Very weak in this County. Intimidation is awful, not a decent shopkeeper in Ennis but is a Unionist at heart.

[Parties interviewed:] Lord A. Large Landowner. Mr. B. A landowner in extreme West. Mr. C. Local resident gentleman.

(b) [Co. Sligo, 24 February 1916]

Mr. A.—We are saying nothingnat [*sic*] all since the month of July 1914.

Mr. B.—Absolutely dormant since the War started; doubt if it could ever be galvanized into life again.

Mr. C.—Politics not going on at all.

Mr. D.—Nothing doing, dropped into abeyance. The Unionists would again stand up—a feeling in favour of Federal settlement is talked about a good deal.

Mr. E.—Nothing doing, a dead letter, all parties here working in harmony with regard to War Work.

[Parties interviewed:] Mr. A. Local Solicitor. Knows County well. Mr. B. Jeweller. Mr. C. A Government Official. Mr. D. Railway Director. Big Merchant. Mr. E. H.M.L.

(c) [Co. Tipperary (South Riding) 16 and 18 January 1916]

Mr. A.   Nothing doing.

Mr. H.   Very weak here. They are lying low.

Colonel C.   Everything is quiet and everyone who used to support the cause has gone to the front. I know of a few very bigoted Protestants who are dead against the Government because of the betrayal by the late Government. Feelings are just as bitter as ever.

[Parties interviewed:] Mr. A. A large landowner. Col. C [recruiting officer.] Mr. H. A large land agent.

(d) [Co. Waterford, 14–16 January 1916]

Mr. A.   A negligible quantity. The Committee hardly exists. Every unionist has gone to the war.

Mr. B.   Dormant.

Mr. G.   Also says they are dormant but they have not thrown up the sponge. The attitude of some of them before the war was very unsatisfactory because they had to declare themselves.

Mr. H.   Things are fairly quiet. They are very few and very scattered and very halfhearted. Most of them do not wish to take any part and wish to let things slide.

Mr. I.   Says they would probably turn up again. They are the only independent people. They think that Redmond's position is insecure.

[Parties interviewed:] Mr. A. A local Solicitor and a man of wide knowledge of the County. Mr. B. A local Landowner who knows this county, but resides in Co. Kilkenny. At the same time in Waterford Union. Captain G. Royal Navy; doing Coastguard protection. Mr. H. A Comptroller of Recruiting. Mr. I. A Land agent.

(e) [Co. Wexford, 13 January 1916]

Miss B.   - - - Says nothing is doing and everything is dormant.

Mr. C.   Says the Unionists around this district are growing less and less and those that remain are not as staunch, in their opposition to Home Rule as they formerly were. Many of these would now fail to raise objections to Home Rule, apparently being complacent and they have not got the fear of it they used to have.

[Parties interviewed:] Miss B. [landowner.] Mr. C. Sergeant of Recruiting.

III

The *rapprochement* between southern unionists and nationalists was temporarily interrupted by the Easter rising, 24 April 1916. The rising caused a unionist reaction in the south leading a revived unionist movement to demand stern measures and the appointment of Walter Long as Irish chief secretary. In the longer term, however, the rising and the aftermath caused southern unionism to move to the left and consider the positive merits of Irish self-government. Before the rising southern unionist opinion, though changing, had been vague and negative; after 1916, once the immediate crisis was past, some southern unionists began to consider plans for a settlement of the Irish question on lines other than those laid down by the 1914 act.

There were two broad reasons for this change. In the first place, political developments after the rising convinced some southern unionists that there was no future in the British connection as it then stood. The liberal section of the coalition government, formed in May 1915, reckoned that the rising provided an opportunity to effect a settlement of the Irish question. Asquith, the prime minister, persuaded the cabinet to agree that Lloyd George, then minister of munitions, should attempt to bring the various Irish parties to agree upon a settlement that could be implemented after the war. Lloyd George soon discovered that Redmond, the nationalist leader, would not agree to any settlement that did not include immediate home rule. Therefore Lloyd George proceeded on that basis, without further reference to the cabinet. He tried to persuade the southern unionists to agree to a settlement on the basis of home rule and the exclusion of six Ulster counties by suggesting certain safeguards for the southern minority. The southern unionists reacted strongly against these proposals, and stirred up opposition in cabinet, parliament and press, by deputations, speeches and letters. Such pressure helped to ensure that the proposals were not implemented; but the episode brought home to them the fact that there was on the statute book an unsatisfactory home rule act, with few safeguards for southern unionists, which would come into operation at the end of the war; and the episode also made many feel that they could no longer count upon considerable support in British politics as they had done in the past. Moreover, they resented the U.U.C.'s decision to accept partition. Not only did this decision remove one of the biggest obstacles to the implementation of the 1914 act, but partition would make home rule even less tolerable to the southern minority by depriving it of the support of the compact unionist group in the north.

This pessimism was balanced by a sense of opportunity created by the growth of Sinn Fein, the second reason for adopting a new policy. It was felt that the nationalists of the Irish parliamentary party would now have to look for allies to maintain their position, and that they would need the co-operation of southern unionists. Unionists would not now be reduced to impotence in a Dublin parliament, for nationalists would be willing to make concessions to them in any home rule scheme to win their support. It was, therefore, a curious blend of pessimism and optimism that led southern unionists to take up a more positive attitude to home rule. Some concluded that their own and Ireland's best interests could be served by some form of self-government, which would supplant the act of 1914, prevent partition, and contain adequate safeguards for them.

The opportunity to act upon their changing views came in 1917 at the Irish convention. The Irish question had again been in danger of hindering the war effort, and in an attempt to solve the problem the government, now headed by Lloyd George, made two alternative proposals. It offered immediate home rule, plus the exclusion of six Ulster counties, plus a joint council which could be empowered to extend the legislation of the Irish parliament to Ulster; or it offered to set up a convention of representative Irishmen 'to endeavour to find a settlement for themselves'. The latter proposal was accepted. On 1 June 1917 the I.U.A. agreed to southern unionist participation in the convention, and their delegates (and others) interpreted this consent as authorising them to work if necessary for a scheme of self-government.

The convention, with Sir Horace Plunkett as chairman, first met on 25 July and among its 95 members were 10 southern unionists, led by Lord Midleton, chairman of the I.U.A. Five—Sir Henry Blake, an ex-colonial governor, Andrew Jameson, head of the distilling firm, Midleton, a former cabinet minister, John Blake Powell, later a judge, and George F. Stewart, a prominent land agent—were representatives of the I.U.A. John Bernard attended as the protestant archbishop of Dublin. Lords Mayo and Oranmore and Browne represented the Irish peers. Edward Andrews represented the Dublin chamber of commerce. Lord Desart, a distinguished lawyer, and Sir William Goulding, a man with a wide range of business interests, were government nominees. A small but distinguished minority they exercised considerable influence in the convention, trying to bring it to agreement on the basis of an all-Ireland parliament with substantial safeguards for unionists in the south and in Ulster. When, in the autumn of 1917, the convention was approaching deadlock owing to a disagreement between nationalists and Ulster unionists over fiscal autonomy, the southern unionists, with the approval of the executive committee of the I.U.A., suggested and canvassed among all parties and the British cabinet a compromise scheme. Their scheme was eventually superseded, but it paved the way by April 1918 for majority agreement (by 44 votes to 29) upon a scheme of Irish self-government containing a variety of safeguards for southern and Ulster unionists. In face of Sinn Fein and Ulster unionist opposition this scheme was not implemented, but the convention was a significant stage in the decline of southern unionism. It was the first time that a representative body of southern unionists had come out in favour of home rule.

188 Extant part of a letter from J. M. Wilson to Sir Edward Carson, 11 May 1916, calling for firm measures following the Easter rising (D 1507/1/1916/19):

Dear Sir Edward—There is no use in blinking the fact that the greatest apprehension is felt here that too much indulgence will be granted by the Cabinet to the pleas "ad misericordiam" of Redmond & Co.

No one asks for vengeance, but weakness now would be fatal. The following are outstanding points, viz:

1. Martial law to be kept in force for at least six months.
2. The fact brought home to the English people that this is far from being merely a Sinn Fein movement. I assert positively that amongst large sections of U[nited]. I[rish]. L[eague]. and A[ncient]. O[rder of]. H[ibernians], the utmost sympathy exists with the rebels.
3. The disarming of all. Not merely of Sinn Feiners, including shot guns & revolvers.
4. The absolute necessity of discounting the pretended concern of Redmond & Co. for the interests of the Empire.
5. The urgent necessity that you or somebody for you should employ at this great crisis someone thoroughly competent to piece together all the parts of evidence which may prove hereafter invaluable as showing how widespread the conspiracy may be.
6. No successor to Birrell yet having been appointed, there is a tremendous necessity for a strong man—Harcourt or Tennant would be disastrous. The man you & I talked about would be far the best I have urged him strongly, but, I fear it may be impossible for him, but, nothing at this moment would so re-assure public confidence as that he was coming to Dublin.
7. The weak-kneed action of the P[rime]. M[inister]. last night in refusing conscription because, forsooth, Redmond opposed it is disastrous. I learn on all sides that the feeling here amongst all except the farmers, is one of astonishment & disgust that the Cabinet has not had the strength of mind to apply it to Ireland.

189 Letter from G. F. Stewart, vice-chairman of the I.U.A., writing from the I.U.A. office, to H. de F. Montgomery, 18 June 1916, replying to his question as to whether or not Ulster members should attend committee meetings of the I.U.A. (D 627/429):

Dear Montgomery—In reply to your straight question. My opinion is that it would be pleasanter both for you & for us Southerners and also more conducive to future harmony between North & South if you did not attend the meetings of the I.U.A at present while our minds are—as they are—sore over our abandonment.

I myself felt that we were really abandoned long before the war & the preaching of the new larger Patriotism but when I said so I was told the movement for the exclusion of Ulster was pure strategy & could never be a real policy. Now we know otherwise.

We shall, I am sure, all try to make the best of whatever comes but meanwhile I have no doubt that you are better away from our Councils.

190 Extract from an undated, but c. mid-1914, I.U.A. memorandum entitled 'The position of the unionist minorities outside Ulster', discussing the importance of Ulster to the southern minority under the third home rule bill (D 989A/9/8):

1. The fundamental fact in the position of the minorities in the South and West of Ireland is that, by no system of election, could they expect to secure any independent voice, much less any influence, in an Irish Parliament. Making an estimate on the basis of the relative proportions of the Catholic and non-Catholic populations outside Ulster, as shown in the last Census (1911) they ought to return from 12 to 13 members out of a total of 103 to represent the three Southern provinces. So widely diffused is this non-Catholic population, however, that only in one, or at most two, of the areas is it probable that a non-Catholic will be returned. On the assumption, for example, that a proportional representation system were adopted—and from the point of view of the number of members which might be returned, this system of election offers the best promise of results—the non-Catholic members of the Irish Parliament would amount to from 5 to 6. Four of these might be returned in and around Dublin, and one or two around Cork.

2. By a similar calculation the non-Catholic members for Ulster divisions in an Irish Parliament would amount to from 32 to 38 out of a total of 59 allotted under the Home Rule Bill. Associated with the Ulster members the maximum size of the non-Catholic party in the Irish House of Commons would probably range between 37 and 44, or say one-fourth of the entire House of 162 members. Non-Catholics would of course be permanently overborne by the Catholic majority; but the minority would nevertheless be of dimensions sufficient to make itself heard on any matter in which they were interested. Non-Catholics in the South of Ireland feel that, with Ulster in, there might be some chance for their grievances to be taken up, exposed, and, in flagrant cases, remedied. This would apply especially to such matters (e.g.—religious, educational, etc.) in which the views and sympathies of the Ulster and other non-Catholics coincided. Where the interests of Ulster and other Non-Catholics were less close, the association would would [*sic*] probably be less effective in securing the permanent support of Ulster members for the grievances of Southerners. The Southerners could never hope to muster a sufficient number of members to make their influence felt in the Opposition or in the non-Catholic party.

3. Without this association the position of the Southern minorities is, of course, infinitely worse. With Ulster out, there would never be a party capable of commanding the attention of an Irish House of Commons for the redress of grievances which, by their nature in a country like Ireland, would not command any sympathy from a permanent, wholly-Catholic majority under clerical influence and secret society comination [*sic*].

4. Much would, of course, depend on the nature of the power which the Protestant minority would wield. It is sometimes asserted that a new division of parties would come into existence in an Irish Parliament. This division might be as between agrarian and industrial, rural and urban, conservative and radical. A solid non-Catholic party standing outside these divisions of

Catholic parties would probably exert the most weighty influence by holding the balance of power between such parties.

5. But such an equilibrium of forces would probably prove unstable. The agrarian or rural elements are likely to be in a large permanent majority. There would be a tendency to form a coalition of groups in opposition, such as a combination between the industrial and labour elements. The co-operation of the non-Catholic group with such an alliance would probably be short-lived. The economic interests of the Ulster Protestant members might make themselves evident, and in combating threatened Socialistic propaganda, the solidarity of this group would steadily diminish. . . .

191

Circular letter issued to members of the general council by the I.U.A., 15 April 1918, justifying and defending the attitude taken up by the southern unionist delegates to the Irish convention (D 989A/8/22):

For some weeks past appeals have been widely made for support to a "Call to Unionists," based on statements reflecting on the conduct of the Executive of the Irish Unionist Alliance and the Southern Unionist delegates to the Convention, the misleading nature of which we have been unable to expose owing to the secrecy attaching to the proceedings of the Convention. Now that the Report of the Convention has been published, we venture to put the true facts before you.

The "Call" proceeds on the assumption that Home Rule is still an open question, that the agreement of the Southern Unionists to enter the Convention in no way committed them to any separate Government for Ireland, and that the delegates instead of supporting Ulster in uncompromising resistance, have bargained away the Union behind the backs of those whom they represent.

These assertions have to our surprise been circulated, and signatures obtained to a protest with the concurrence of gentlemen who were cognisant of the facts which we now venture to set forth.

In September, 1914, the Home Rule Act was passed and received the Royal Assent. The Act did not provide any safeguards for the interests of the minority either as regards representation or otherwise, and its financial provisions were of the most unsatisfactory character.

In July, 1914, an Amending Bill was introduced and passed in the House of Lords by which it was provided that Ulster should be excluded from the provisions of the Act.

This Bill was introduced in the House of Commons and its consideration was postponed pending a Conference between the leaders of the Unionist and Liberal Parties in England, the Nationalist Party, and the Ulster Unionists. The Conference took place on the 21st July, 1914, and following days. No conclusion was come to, but it is well known (1) that the basis of the settlement discussed was the exclusion of Ulster or part of Ulster from the Home Rule Act, and the application of that Act to the rest of Ireland; (2) that failure to come to a solution on these lines was due to the impossibility of an agreement as to the particular counties in Ulster which were to be excluded.

The Southern Unionists were, it is well known, bitterly opposed to this scheme of Partition. They were, however, not represented at the Conference, nor, as far as we are aware, were they consulted in any way nor was any attempt made to safeguard their interests.

On the 18th September, 1914, the Home Rule Act was placed on the Statute Book, and thus became the law of the land though owing to the outbreak of war it was not put into immediate operation.

In June, 1916, proposals for partition were again started on the basis of excluding certain counties in Ulster, and of putting the Act into immediate operation for the rest of Ireland and an agreement was actually arrived at between the representatives of the Ulster Party and the Nationalist Party, respectively, upon these lines. This agreement was subsequently abrogated by reason of an acute difference between the parties to it as to whether the exclusion was to be temporary or permanent.

It will be remembered that a very large deputation of Southern Unionists went to London at the time to protest against this scheme. The deputation was received by the Prime Minister and also by the Unionist Members of the Cabinet, and it will be in the recollection of those who were present at these interviews that we were repeatedly reminded that the Home Rule Act was on the Statute Book. So far as we, the Southern Unionists, were concerned, no hope whatever was held out to us that the Act would not be put in force as against us, and we were invited to make suggestions as to safeguards. We did not, however consider that "paper safeguards" would be of any benefit to us as we should not have had a single representative in the Irish House of Commons to see that they were enforced.

Thus matters remained when the Prime Minister, on behalf of himself and his colleagues in the War Cabinet, approached the leaders of the different political sections in Ireland, addressing them in the interests of the Empire and of the better prosecution of the War, and suggesting that to secure these ends a conference of Irishmen of all sections should assemble with the view of arriving, if possible, at some agreement for the "future government of Ireland within the Empire."

It would be of course futile to suggest that the "settlement" for which the Cabinet thus appealed included the possibility of the repeal of the Home Rule Act and a return to the *status quo ante.*

The appeal of the Cabinet was considered at a meeting of the Executive Committee of the Alliance on the 23rd May, 1917, and the following resolution was carried unanimously:—

> "That we hereby express our approval of Viscount Midleton's letter to the Prime Minister and in accordance with it we shall take steps to lay the question of the proposed Convention before the Council of the Irish Unionist Alliance at an early date."

In pursuance of that Resolution, a meeting of the General Council was called for the 1st June, 1917, to consider the whole question.

On the 31st May, 1917, a further meeting of the Executive Committee of the Alliance was held, at which the following resolutions were passed:—

"That while deprecating the opening of this question during the War, the Irish Unionist Alliance is prepared to take part in a Convention of representative Irishmen in Ireland as proposed by the Prime Minister **"to submit to the British Government and the British Parliament a constitution for the future government of Ireland within the Empire"** provided that the Convention includes a fair representation of Unionists of the three Southern Provinces."

"That a Committee be appointed with power, subject to the above, to carry out all necessary arrangements on behalf of the Irish Unionist Alliance, including the selection of delegates to attend the Convention, and that the said Committee shall consist of seven Parliamentary members in London, and seven members in Dublin, together with the Chairman and Vice-Chairman."

Before these resolutions were put to the Executive Committee, it was made perfectly clear what the effect would be of agreeing to enter into the deliberations of the proposed Convention, and what would necessarily be the functions of any delegates who might be selected to represent the Alliance.

It was pointed out that while the delegates would naturally be bound to express in the Convention their belief that the maintenance of the Legislative Union was the best and safest solution of the "Irish question," they would be also bound to consider and discuss and possibly agree to such other solution as would safeguard imperial interests and the rights of the minority in the South and West.

On the 1st June, 1917, the General Council met in the Molesworth Hall.

The resolutions of the Executive Committee of the previous day were placed before them for their consideration, and for their rejection or approval. The matter was fully discussed, and the position which the delegates would occupy, their functions, and their duty, was placed clearly before the Meeting. The Meeting agreed in the view of the Executive Committee, and affirmed the resolutions of that body with one solitary dissentient. It was never suggested that the General Council should be consulted as to the attitude which the delegates should take up from time to time in the deliberations of the Convention. Indeed the impossibility of adopting such a course is shown by the statement issued by the authors of the "Call" that "the Convention commenced its meetings in July, and as you are doubtless aware, these are held in secret session and public discussion of the topics introduced is not permitted."

It must be obvious under these circumstances that it would be a flagrant violation of the honourable obligations of secrecy by which the delegates were bound to reveal to a General Council consisting of over 600 Members the proceedings of the Convention.

The delegates under these circumstances, and with this mandate, entered upon their onerous duties, not departing in the slightest degree from their convictions as life-long Unionists, determined to assert these convictions in the Convention but ready to consider, to discuss, and, if possible in the interests of the Empire at this terrible crisis, to arrive at some "agreement for the government of the country within the Empire," which would provide safeguards for that Empire and secure, as far as possible, the rights of minorities.

During the progress of the Convention, we have called together the Executive Committee of the Alliance four times, and on January 1st, 1918, before any vote was taken, the Committee was summoned by a notice marked "most urgent," to hear a "very important statement from the Chairman." The Committee was so largely attended, that it was necessary to adjourn to the Shelbourne Hotel. The Chairman stated explicitly what the delegates proposed to do, and the Committee after full discussion, expressed their entire confidence in them by 41 votes to 4. It is extraordinary that it should now be urged that the members of the Executive Committee were not aware of the critical nature of the occasion, and still more so that in a paper widely circulated the authors of the "Call" should assert "After Lord Midleton's statement had been made, another member of the Convention, who is not a member of the Executive Committee, or even of the Alliance, was called upon to address the meeting. We submit that the introduction of a stranger to, and the pressure of outside influence at, a meeting of the Executive Committee, is not only irregular but highly improper."

The facts are, that the Chairman asked the meeting if, before voting, they would wish to hear the views of a very distinguished member of the Convention, the Archbishop of Dublin (Rev. Dr. Bernard), and having left it to the Committee to decide, they unanimously requested him to invite the Archbishop to give them his counsel.

It is noteworthy that on the same day Lords Mayo and Oranmore, at a well-attended meeting of Peers, made a similar statement of policy and received a unanimous vote of confidence.

The "Call" makes certain practical suggestions all of which have been anticipated by the delegates. These are

(1) The firm administration of Law. The delegates have made their views on this subject known to the highest quarters with most beneficial results.

(2) The development of the resources of Ireland. The delegates, besides insisting on Customs and Treaties being left to the powerful Parliament of the United Kingdom, and ensuring the financial stability of the proposed measure, have assisted to secure the settlement of Land Purchase and of Housing.

(3) The Federation of the Empire. The delegates have throughout insisted that any proposals adopted should be such as would be a secure foundation for any future Federation of the Empire or the United Kingdom.

But beyond these important principles, the delegates have secured a drastic change in the inequitable provisions of the Act of 1914.

(1) The Act of 1914 left the Southern Unionists without a single representative in the Irish Parliament. The Convention have agreed to Unionists having an effective 40 per cent. of the Lower House

together with a Senate constituted on such a basis that the two Houses voting together, as under the Constitution they would be, in case of disagreement, would give Unionists an equal voice with other Irishmen in the future Government of the country.

The Southern Unionists, being scattered, are assigned 20 seats in the Irish Parliament for 15 years—after that time the Senate will be strengthened.

(2) Irish representation at Westminster will continue, and Southern Unionists will send representatives in proportion to their representation in the Irish Parliament to the British Parliament.

(3) There will be no "Partition" as proposed by the Amending Act in 1914, and as accepted by the Ulster representatives in 1916, and again proposed by them in the Convention.

Our case, therefore, is that while all Imperial services, including National Defence and the levying of Customs Duties have been left to the Parliament of the United Kingdom, and an adequate contribution will be made by Ireland to Imperial Services, we have secured that, if Home Rule is established, the Government of Ireland, in which Southern Unionists have had no participation for over 30 years, will be controlled not by one section of Irishmen as under the Act of 1914, but by leading Irishmen of all classes.

Under these circumstances we hold that the transfer of the Police after the war to a Government which controls the Judiciary and the Magistrates is a safer guarantee of good order than the entirely unsatisfactory methods of administration under which we have lived since 1906.

These conclusions were presented to a specially summoned meeting of the Executive Committee on March 23rd, 1918, when the Chairman stated the issues, and the authors of the "Call," after being fully heard were defeated by 43 to 17—a vote of confidence as follows being passed:—

"That this meeting desires to place on record its unbounded confidence in the delegates sent to the Convention by the Irish Unionist Alliance, and desires to thank Lord Midleton and the other delegates for their efforts on its behalf, and to express its hope they will continue those exertions."

In the face of this decision, many signatures have been obtained from persons, who holding the principles of Union no more firmly than the delegates, are unaware of the immense change which has been obtained by them in the provisions of the Act of 1914.

You will shortly have the opportunity of registering your opinion on our action. May we hope that in the interests of the Empire, which can only be secured at this unparalleled crisis by a majority in whatever Parliament exists, capable of overawing Republican and Separatist doctrines, you will suspend your judgment till you have the full details which will demonstrate the wisdom and patriotism of the course adopted by your delegates.

IV

As document **191** indicates, the delegates' (Midletonites') action was consistently opposed by a group of southern unionists. Whereas the Midletonites, with large interests and prominent on a national level either in Great Britain or Ireland, tried to take a long term view of the British and Irish situations, their opponents tended to have narrower horizons and refused to abandon the unionist position taken up in the 1880s. They were mainly country gentlemen, spurred on by two barristers, John E. Walsh of Dublin and William Jellett, M.P. for Dublin University (1919–22) and later 'father' of the Irish bar, and with some Ulster sympathisers, including H. de F. Montgomery. On 20 February 1918 they formed themselves into the Southern Unionist Committee, a pressure group with Walsh as honorary secretary; and on 4 March twenty-four of them issued the 'Call to unionists', a restatement of extreme unionism and a protest against developments in the convention.

Their grounds for opposing their delegates' action were twofold. On the one hand, they claimed that the delegates had betrayed southern unionists by violating the fundamental principle of the I.U.A. without the permission of the general council. The S.U.C. denied that the general council's decision of June 1917 had empowered the delegates to work for Irish self-government; and they argued that the approval of an unrepresentative and hastily summoned executive committee was irrelevant. On the other hand, and more importantly, they totally disagreed with the Midletonites' interpretation of how southern unionists' interests could best be protected. Where the delegates and their supporters were optimistic, the S.U.C. was pessimistic, and *vice versa*. The S.U.C. denied that the union was a losing cause and argued that the 1914 act could be disregarded. It did not begrudge Ulster separate treatment; for some southern unionists had long thought that exclusion was not necessarily a selfish policy and could work to the south's advantage. Lastly, it remained suspicious of Irish nationalism and refused to be optimistic about the Irish situation or to be satisfied with fancy safeguards. The Irish parliamentary party it had long regarded as a spent force, and it thought that an Irish parliament would be dominated by the even more intransigent nationalists of the Sinn Fein party.

The pro-German attitude of Sinn Fein was not the only thing that dismayed men like Harry Franks of Cork and Queen's Co. and James Mackay Wilson, and confirmed their objections to any form of home rule. The determined nature of Sinn Fein, as evidenced by the efficient victory by 3,022 votes to 1,708 over the Irish parliamentary party in the North Roscommon by-election, February 1917, made a deep and fearful impression upon them. They felt that southern unionists and their property could expect short shrift from such men under any system but the union. Moreover, in 1918 their fears were underlined by land grabbing which affected among others the Misses ffolliott of Hollybrook, Co. Sligo, who were in close touch via H. de F. Montgomery with the work of the S.U.C. Such men and women thus saw little virtue in the policy of the convention's recommendation of an Irish parliament in which they thought they would have little say, and under which they thought their lives would be uncomfortably circumscribed.

192 Letters from J. E. Walsh, honorary secretary of the S.U.C., 36 Molesworth Street, Dublin, to the *Irish Times,* 11 March, 6 April 1918, reprinted with other letters by the S.U.C., and **(a)** challenging the competence of the executive committee of the I.U.A. to speak on behalf of southern unionist opinion or even of the I.U.A., and **(b)** denying that the 1914 act was an obstacle to the maintenance of the union and that Irish nationalists had proved their loyalty to the empire during the war (D 989A/8/20B):

(a)

In your issue of the 9th inst. Lord Barrymore asks all Southern Irish Unionists to support the Irish Unionist Alliance, which, he says, "may be trusted to represent their interests at the present crisis, as in the past." He also informs your readers that "the whole situation was very recently laid before the Executive Committee of the Alliance, and full confidence was expressed in our leaders by an overwhelming majority."

It is difficult to believe that Lord Barrymore would have written in this strain had the real facts been present to his mind. The facts are as follows:—

By the constitution of the Alliance, the General Council is to meet annually for the purpose (inter alia) of electing twenty members on the Executive Committee, who, with the President, Vice-Presidents, and representatives elected by county branches, have power to co-opt a limited number of additional members on that Committee. No meeting of the General Council, for the purpose indicated, has been held since early in 1913, with the result that the Executive Committee does not, even under the constitution, represent the views of the Irish Unionist Alliance, much less of Southern Unionists.

The members of the Executive Committee, so constituted, were not even notified, in the summons convening the meeting referred to by Lord Barrymore, that they would be called upon to decide the momentous question of the abandonment of the one and only fundamental principle of the Alliance—viz.: the maintenance of the Legislative Union. Many members were consequently absent who would otherwise have attended. At the meeting in question powerful outside influence was introduced. The General Council was never consulted at all

Will Lord Barrymore maintain that this is the way to obtain the views of the Irish Unionist Alliance and of Southern Unionists, and can he be surprised that Southern Unionists, finding their cause abandoned by their "leaders," in the manner above indicated, are determined that the voice of true Unionists shall be heard, and that their country shall not be handed over to the enemies of our King and the friends of his foes?

All the signatories to "the Call to Unionists" are members of the Alliance, and their object is to place that body on a properly representative basis. Only then will it be in a position truly to reflect the views of Southern Unionists. When this has been achieved the Alliance can be "trusted to represent their interests at the present crisis."

(b)

Some former supporters of the Union, by way of emphasising their helplessness and weakness, are prepared to stultify their former convictions by repeating the formula: "The Home Rule Act is on the Statute Book." We all know this, but we also know that nobody wants it, that the electorate gave no mandate for it, and that it was placed there, in defiance of all pledges, by methods which were a fraud upon the Constitution. It is not thus that ancient constitutions are overthrown in a democratic country, or that any binding sanction can be claimed for the acts of those who were guilty of such machinations. The Union is not dead. It cannot be killed by means such as these.

There never was a time when all that Unionism stands for was of more vital importance to the safety of the United Kingdom and the Empire than the present. We see the forces of disruption, fostered by German intrigue, paralysing the arm and draining the life-blood of other countries. Ever since the war broke out we have seen the same intrigues and the same forces at work in Ireland, with the result that not only does Nationalist Ireland refuse to share in the burdens of the war, but also thousands of His Majesty's troops, sorely needed in the line of battle, are held back by the prevailing pro-Germanism, anarchy, and sedition. It is at a moment such as this that some would have us betray our cause, and agree to hand over our country to those who, with the help of the King's enemies, have made Ireland what it is to-day.

Much has been learned from recent events in Ireland which has only strengthened ten-fold the conviction that in the maintenance of the Legislative Union lies the only hope for the future of our country and the security of His Majesty's dominions. No one, by adhering to the Union, can "split the ranks of Southern Unionists." Those Unionists who abandon it will do so.

We rejoice to think that there are many thousands of Unionists in the South and West who refuse to play the part of traitors to their King and country, and "at the call of the malcontents to play into the hands of our country's foes."

193 Letter from W. Huggard, Estate Office, Tralee, Co. Kerry, to Sir Edward Carson, 30 March 1914, supporting the exclusion of Ulster from the operation of the third home rule bill (D 1507/1/1914/12):

Dear Sir—Kindly allow me to say that a very large proportion of the Unionists of the South and West of Ireland are heartily in favour of the exclusion of Ulster from the operation of the Home Rule Bill, if the Bill must go through, for three reasons,

(1) It will destroy the Bill from the Nationalists' point of view,

(2) It will if accepted and passed put the rest of Ireland on her best behaviour and be our best protection in the future,

(3) We do not envy Ulster but rejoice with her in her immunity from the treachery and power of those who were the Instigators of Moonlighting and Murder during the past thirty years.

We are under a lasting debt of gratitude to you for your courageous and self-sacrificing stand against the outrage and insult offered to the Unionists and Loyalists of the Empire, by the Government.

We would like to have a Covenant of our own to sign, pledging ourselves to support Ulster. Yours Faithfully.

Wm. Huggard.

194 Copy letter from M. H .('Harry') Franks of Westfield, Queen's Co. and Garrettstown, Co. Cork, to J. M. Wilson, 5 March 1917, commenting on Sinn Fein activities in Cork (D 989A/8/7):

Having enquired through reliable sources, the following are the results—Since the Sinn Feiners were released, they have been at work in the quietest way with what in view it is difficult to say. Meetings have been and are being held frequently in private houses in the city, and prior to the recent arrests a conference of Sinn Fieners [sic] was held—I think in Georges Street. Of this the police were perfectly aware—they saw the delegates from various parts of the country arrive and depart from the building. The police believe they were organising with some object in view. Something, they, said, might happen in Easter-week, but they did not get at the bottom of it. Hence the arrests of recent date. I have chatted with chaps who at one time were Redmondites, but they have now become ardent supporters of Sinn Feiner policy. Hundreds of these have altogether left the "Mollies" and are now as bitter against Redmond and his party as "agin" the English Government. They complain Ireland has been sold by Redmond & Co., and all denounce his action which they say favoured recruiting, and his silence in the House of Commons when the Rebels were being shot. The sympathy to Sinn Feiners is growing rapidly, and I believe thousands of "Mollies" would support a Sinn Fein candidate if an election took place in the morning. Indeed the enmity to the Irish party is nearly as great as the hatred of England. The change has been created in this way—Among all parties —the Redmondite and O'Brienite —there is and has been a terrible fear of being conscripted. For a time they lived in daily dread of it; and to prevent the Act applying to Ireland they would I believe sell body and soul. They believe the best means of preventing it is to give help to the rebels, as they think if conscription is moved to be applied the Sinn Feiners will give trouble, and that that trouble will not be worth the big force of soldiers who will be employed in rounding up the conscripts, whose dream it is to flee to the mountains. Such trouble they say will prevent conscription. If conscription was out of the way, it is doubtful if so many would extend sympathy to Sinn Fein, but hatred of John Redmond for Imperial feelings re the war sent many of his followers to the extreme side. The danger at present is this—The active Sinn Feiners are all young and intelligent men, generally teetotallers. Unlike the ordinary political fellows, they do not patronise public-houses and talk there over matters. They are silent and know how to keep their mouths closed, but they think and plot the more. Perhaps if they had a little latitude to let off steam at say a public meeting, it would act as a sefety [*sic*]-valve. But the fact is they are—a great many of them—"brainy" in well-to-do positions; they speak little in public, and as in all secret political gatherings—suffering as they think under great wrongs—there is a danger of an outburst. Of course you know in Cork we always talk and do not act—that may be the case, but this silence on a matter which is depp [*sic*] in the hearts of thousands of young fellows in the city is to say the least very ugly and portends something more than usual happening unless they [are] pulled up in time.

195 Memorandum by J. M. Wilson forwarded to W. Long, 27–8 March 1917, commenting on the recent Sinn Fein victory in the North Roscommon by-election (D 989A/9/7):

I have now had an opportunity of visiting this district and the advantage of consulting several people. Although there is some difference of opinion as to the strength of the Sinn Fein Movement at this moment, there is none regarding the point that the organization during the election, engineered chiefly from Dublin, was marvellously efficient. A person of great judgment who witnessed the incidents at close quarters put it in this way:– "I can only conceive that the type of person working the Sinn Fein Cause was exactly similar in appearance and manner with those who must have carried through the French Revolution." Even the best judges as to forecasting the election were hopelessly astray. Roman Catholic clergy of the younger class, notably one Father Flanagan, described to me as a fire-brand, were extremely active, and it is stated that some of the older priests who were undoubtedly opposed to the Revolutionary Cause were drawn into it. Fear was expressed that if John Redmond were put in control and had to face an election for a Legislative object in that country, he would be replaced at once by Sinn Feiners, and what then? In Local Government elections the whole tendency is to fall to a lower stratum on each occasion.

I am assured that the administration of justice through the Jury System has become a pitiable farce, and there is a general feeling in the atmosphere that all respect for law and property has disappeared. One of my informants seems to be of opinion that the Sinn Fein Cause was losing ground. But I think this is owing to the machined resolutions which are being passed by the Board of Guardians and published. And I was reminded by another friend that these very men when they left the Board-room practically represent nobody. There cannot be a doubt that the ordinary respectable farmer in North Roscommon is groaning under a system of intimidation and espionage which has never been severer in the History of Ireland. It is a sad comment on the administration of the country, that such a statement could be made with truth. A very prevalent feeling exists that if by any chance the present schemes for "settlement" were to fructify, unless absolute safeguards were included therein, to prevent the land of loyal people being seized by Sinn Feiners, disaster would overcome the loyal population. The idea is prevalent, that things which [sic] are much the same as they were in Parnell's day, only worse. A lady residing in an out of the way part of the county said, "they have tasted blood and they want more."

During the elections for Count Plunkett, seditious speeches were indulged in and seditious literature was everywhere to be seen. It is stated that one of the chief meeting places for Sinn Feiners is the office of the Buildings of the Co-operative creameries, but it should be mentioned that there was no trouble or rioting at the election. Bitter feeling of hostility towards England is shown. Manifested in a small way in a refusal in one part of the country to supply eggs for wounded soldiers in Hospital! If the U.S.A. comes into the war, on the side of the Allies, it would probably give a great shock to the extreme party in Ireland, because it would be looked upon as helping England. One of my informants gives his opinion that when opportunity affords, the Roman Catholic Church will come down like a steam-roller on Sinn Feiners, that time is not yet. A Bishop in this locality is credited with having said that the Sinn Fein Movement is like a submarine. I made some enquiries as to the ideas on a Federal settlement, but it was considered that this would never succeed because it would imply a partition of the country. What the extreme party would like to do, would be to coerce Ulster by military force. A Presbyterian Gentleman said to me that the feeling against the Protestant cause, but [among] extreme Nationalists is much similar to that which existed in the days of the Stuarts. In one of the chief towns of North Roscommon the ordinary shop-keeper and respectable commercial man are still on the side of John Redmond, and it is believed that large numbers of the farmers are also, but that the young members of the farmers' families used strigent [sic] intimidation on their elders to force them to the Poll on behalf of Count Plunkett. Some were of opinion that had Count Plunkett stated definitely before the election that he would not take his seat at Westminster, the result might have been different. Small bodies in country parts changed over to the Sinn Fein side in a twinkling of an eye, e.g. at Croghan bogus telegrams were sent early in the day and every means employed to turn the tables on the Redmond Party. At least 20 High power motors from Dublin worked during the election. It is not known of course where the money came from for this, but it is suspected that Germany was implicated in it. The bitterest feeling against recruiting is prevalent, at one time conscription would have been almost welcomed, but things are very different now. One of my friends dealt with the view already expressed above that the pendulum has swung a little back against Count Plunkett, but to show the pressure from Sinn Fein, he informs me that Mr. T. J. Devine, the Redmond candidate two months before the elections and no doubt on purpose, constantly wore a Sinn Fein Badge! In spite of all these signs of the time, I find the opinion dealt with, if Ireland could be polled to-morrow morning by an absolutely secret vote, that vote would be against Home Rule. The Sinn Fein Movement both in North Roscommon and also as reported to you in Cork illicits sympathy from the better educated class and is not at all confined to the corner-boy element. This feature makes it all the more dangerous. I have come away from that part of the country more convinced than ever that the only solution for keeping the country stable is to revert to the old policy of the Legislative Union, or failing in that to install a dictator, neither of these seem possible as things at present [are] tending but time alone can show what the future will bring forth.

196 Copy letter from Miss M. ffolliott of Hollybrook, Co. Sligo, to H. Duke, Irish chief secretary, Dublin Castle, 23 February 1918, asking for protection in face of the land-grabbing activities of local Sinn Feiners on her farm (D 627/432):

Dear Sir—Although no doubt you are already aware of the forcible appropriation of land by members of the Sinn Fein Association going on all over this part of the country, I venture to think it may nor [*sic*] be quite realised by the Government that an impression is abroad & spreading, that these proceedings are, in view of their ostencible [*sic*] object, i.e. the increase of tillage, not only condoned by it, but actually meet with its approval; & that owners of these lands will consequently receive no support from the Authorities in asserting their rights.

As the owner of a farm to which these methods are being applied, I should be extremely grateful if you could give me some idea of how we stand in the matter, & whether farmers attempting to check these Sinn Fein activities have any chance of backing from the Government in so doing?

It may help you to realise the state of the case if I give you as briefly as possible the facts concerning my own farm: They are as follows:

All the arable land, except that required for milch cows, has been tilled in rotation for the last ten years by a particularly capable & hard-working land steward. Last year the full amount of extra tillage was carried out, &, despite abnormally adverse weather conditions, fine crops were secured of grain, (including wheat) hay & roots. This year the increased proportion of tillage is being done, & lea broken in the best old pasture. A large number of pigs are bred & reared, (six litters in 1917) also calves and lambs. Some stall feeding done (14 head last year, 20 this.) & the usual dealing in store cattle carried on.

Besides this it has always been our habit to let a considerable amount of land in conacre for potatoes to labourers and tenants with small holdings, as well as grazing for their milch cows. Last year more conacre was asked for & given, 17 names being now on the list, (a large number for the size of the farm) & we were prepared to give the same or more this year.

On Monday Feb. 11. we received a letter from the Sinn Fein club in the village "demanding" an unspecified amount of land from us for two year conacre, at £2. below the usual rate. We answered that in view of all we were already doing for the neighbours we thought this an unreasonable demand, but were nevertheless prepared to meet it as far as might be possible, if applicants sent in their names & requirements.

This reply was ignored, & two days later a crowd of 200 men with 3 bands marched into a recently laid down pasture field of 19 statute acres which the leaders proceeded to divide "in the name of the Irish Republic" among about thirty of their number; several of these being sons of well-to-do farmers on the estate. This has since been followed up, & the field, containing a rick of Hay & a number of young cattle has been turned up in patches, all over, with nine ploughs & pairs of horses.

As this is the field on which we were cheifly [*sic*] depending for pasturing over 50 ewes with lambs this season, either these or 40 to 50 head of young cattle will have to be disposed of at considerable loss.

But what is, with, a view to future farming, of far more importance is the fact that the field in question is only now recovering from previous conacre tillage, & would, if made to produce a crop of potatoes this year, and one of corn the following season, under the usual conditions of conacre cultivation, inadequate manuring &c., be rendered useless for at lease [*sic*] 10 years to come.

If conduct of this sort is to be allowed to continue unchecked, you will I think admit that it will rapidly become impossible for any good, economic farming to be carried on in this country.

I feel obliged therefore to ask earnestly for protection in carrying on my farming operations. I request that you will give adequate police help to clear the land occupied by the Sinn Feiners, & to enable me to retake possession of the land, Also I request protection for my house which is occupied only by my sister and myself with out [*sic*] servants; & it would be vitally necessary also to have protection for my steward & his family & for my other labourers.

This matter is extremely urgent if we are to be able to do the cropping this year. believe me yours faithfully,

V

The opposition of the S.U.C. prevented the I.U.A. from adopting a more accommodating attitude to the question of Irish self-government and split the organisation by the beginning of 1919. This split had been desired by nobody and was largely the result of inadequate leadership by Midleton as chairman of the I.U.A. The S.U.C. wanted the I.U.A. to reaffirm its faith in the union; and, in order to prevent a recurrence of what had happened during the convention, started a move to put the I.U.A. on a more representative basis.

Despite having worked out a programme, the S.U.C. was largely on the defensive. It was never confident that it had wide support and was always anxious to avoid charges of intransigence or dishonourable conduct. For instance, before the general council of the I.U.A. met on 3 May 1918 to consider the convention report, the S.U.C. spent two long sessions discussing how, without incurring any odium, it could persuade the council to disassociate the I.U.A. from the delegates' action. It arranged that the Ulster members of the I.U.A. should attend the general council, that the proceedings should be reported in the *Dublin Daily Express*, and that members of the S.U.C. should avoid all reference to personalities in their speeches. In the event, a vote on the convention report was avoided, but the episode showed the reluctance of the S.U.C. to push things to extremes, and suggests that tactful handling on the part of Midleton and his friends might have prevented a split.

The Midletonites, however, proved incapable of conciliatory action. On 1 October the Midletonite executive committee did reaffirm its faith in the union and agreed to summon a meeting of the general council to amend the constitution of the I.U.A.; but suspicions were revived at the end of the year. At this point declarations by the prime minister and others in favour of a settlement of the Irish problem on the basis of six-counties partition led the Midletonites to insist that no members from the counties which it was proposed to exclude should be allowed to take part in the I.U.A. discussions of partition. This proposal raised the spectre of the convention in the minds of members of the S.U.C., who persisted in thinking that the closest cooperation between Ulster and southern unionists was essential for successful resistance to home rule. This disagreement finally split the I.U.A. The Midletonite proposal was put before a meeting of the general council on 24 January 1919 and defeated by a large majority. The Midletonites resigned and formed the Unionist Anti-Partition League, directed more against partition than home rule, and the S.U.C. found itself in control of an I.U.A. committed to resist home rule. In an optimistic mood the I.U.A. was reorganised and in March 1919 a committee was set up in London to mobilise right wing unionist energies in Great Britain and prepare for the next battle against home rule. Meantime, the Dublin and London committees, recognising the current British absorption in post-war reconstruction and the futility of negative opposition to home rule, interested themselves in the problems of Irish reconstruction and constantly discussed schemes of propaganda to be implemented when the home rule issue was resuscitated.

197 Rough notes on two meetings of the S.U.C. held in the Shelbourne Hotel, Dublin, **(a)** 24 April and **(b)** 2 May 1918, to discuss the tactics to be adopted when the general council of the I.U.A. met to consider the report of the Irish convention (D 989A/8/16):

(a)

Mr. Jellet [*sic*] said :– He wanted to point out that if we could win without the Ulster members, then we would have attained our object; but he [would] rather win with them than lose without them.

The position is that the Ulster members, so far as they are concerned don't propose to attend meeting on 3rd. May. They have not been summoned. We ought to let them know that the meeting will be held; so that they might make up their minds about it. Would it be advisable for us to write to Sir E. Carson, pointing out our position to him & ask him if he thought Ulster members of the Alliance ought to attend the meeting, & whether he would intimate his view to them.

Alternative. Do nothing than intimate to every member of the Alliance, that the meeting is to be held on the 3rd.

[It was said] The northern representatives are not going to attend; tho' they are sending a very strong statement to support the Southern Unionists; they won't attend meeting. We ought to use every means in our power to get as many votes as we can, write to Sir E. Carson . . .

Mr. Cusack. ? Suggested that Lord Middletons [*sic*] object [had been] to form a middle party between Ulster U. & Southern U. It is impossible to do so now, we must be either Sinn Feiners or Unionists.

[It was said we] must keep the personal element out of it.

Mr. Franks. Suggested that we disassociate ourselves entirely on the majority of the report. (Keep clear of mentioning delegates)

Capt Wade Thompson. Agreed that no personal element should be brought into the matter. It was the executive com[mittee]. that were to blame & not the delegates

[It was said] The delegates had worked very hard & done their best.

Limerick Co: A very strong feeling prevailed in the County against any personal attack on the delegates action.

General McCalmont? (at the [word illegible]) The delegates have gone wrong & ought to be repudiated . . . .

Mr. Franks proposed that:– Our working committee be authorized to consider these matters & appoint the speakers & the Press; & if Mr. Wynne could come to next meeting, we should know how matters stand as regards Press.

Mr. Shannon said. There ought to be some gentleman of the Unionist Alliance, who could report at the meeting & we should publish everything we thought right . . . .

Col. Guiness [*sic*]. Said:– We had received £25 from the D[ublin]. U[nionist]. A[ssociation]. toward S[?]. We have already got £306. We have about £10 in hand at present . . . .

(b)

Mr. Jellett said:– That a small subcommittee had discussed the question of reporting proceedings of meeting on May 3rd & had come to the conclusion that a report should be taken. Mr. Wynne had not been asked by the Alliance to take any report so we have asked him to have members of his staff present to report proceedings. We propose to inform Lord Midleton that meeting will be reported . . .

Mr. Wilson. It was only fair that a rough sketch of the resolution to be moved should be shown to Lord Midleton.

Mr. Jellett. Would there be any objection to seeing Lord M. alone before the meeting & telling him we propose to report the meeting; & give him the opportunity to fall in with our view. Our position is "stone wall", we won't move one inch; it is for him to move, not us.

[Mr] Bird. It is a very dangerous thing to have disunion, we should make it clear that we are meeting the delegates & Lord Midleton in brotherly love . . . .

[It was asked] If we are beaten we shall have to consider what our next steps will be. Could not see any objection to inform Lord Midleton as to the nature of the resolution . . . .

Mr. Jellett. It is possible that different policies may be adopted at the meeting. Lord M. may make a statement . . . or Somebody on Lord M's side may get up & say that the meeting will be asked to express approval with what the delegates have done. We want if we could to get in our resolution before them . . . . We should try to keep the discussion on a high level . . . . In the event of our resolution being defeated, we shall leave the Hall in a body & have nothing more to say to them.

Mr. Macnamara. I think their line of defence will be that they were forced to do the best they could. We want them to say they have made a mistake & they will do all in their power to maintain the Leg. Union. If they recant & admit they made a mistake & say that the Con[vention]. has been a failure, you give them a door of escape & they will work for us. Everyone must admit that the findings at the Con. are futile & inconclusive . . . .

[It was said that] Our action will be criticised afterwards, therefore we ought to realise the great importance of it.

An important matter is, what position will we be in if we leave in a body? . . .

Mr. Macnamara They will be loud in praise of delegates & will catch a number of weak votes. We ought to be prepared.

Col. G[uinness]. made a statement re our financial position We have very little in hand & ought to try & get in funds . . . .

198

Leaflet, *Unionists and the Anti-Partition League,* issued in March 1919 by the remodelled I.U.A. to explain the points of difference between the I.U.A. and the A.P.L. (D 989A/8/23):

The reason put forward by those who have formed an Anti-Partition League, for taking this step, was the rejection by the General Council of the Irish Unionist Alliance by an overwhelming majority of the Southern representatives alone of a proposal by Lord Midleton to exclude the Northern Members of the Alliance from all its deliberations should the question of Partition arise.

The points of difference have been summarised by a Western Unionist as follows:—

IRISH UNIONIST ALLIANCE.

1. The I.U.A., as its name implies, is an organisation embracing Unionists from every part of Ireland. It has at least one Branch in each County.

2. Its policy is strenuous and united opposition to Home Rule for the whole or any part of Ireland.

   Should the Government attempt to force a measure of Home Rule on Ireland involving partition, the I.U.A., while offering all possible opposition to such a policy, would certainly not join hands with Sinn Feiners and others in attempting to coerce Ulster. The one way to avoid partition is to maintain the Legislative Union.

ANTI-PARTITION LEAGUE.

1. The leaders of the A.P.L. were identified with the "compromise" and "Anti-Ulster" policy manifested at the Convention, and are supported only by a very small section of Southern Unionists.

2. Its policy is "the Union," or failing that, "Home Rule without partition," i.e., that under no circumstances shall Ulster be allowed to escape.

   While opposed to Home Rule, it approaches the question from the point of view that Home Rule is inevitable. This is a defeatist policy. Therefore if partition is to be avoided, Ulster must be coerced. This, too, is the demand of Sinn Feiner and Nationalist.

3. The above policy enlists the active sympathy and co-operation of Ulster Unionists with the Unionists of the South and West, to whom they have promised all the help and support in their power.

3. The above policy alienates the sympathy of Ulstermen, is a cause of rejoicing to Sinn Fein and other enemies of the Union, and weakens Unionist opposition to Home Rule by dividing Irish Unionists into different camps.

199 Extract from the minute book of the London committee of the I.U.A. recording the first meeting of that committee on 5 March 1919 at 25 Victoria Street, Westminster, London S.W. (D989A/1/11):

Correspondence with Mr. Walsh, Honorary Secretary, was read, arising out of which it was arranged that Sir John Butcher should see Sir Edward Carson regarding a public announcement that his Party was the Irish Unionist Party, and were prepared to work for the whole of Ireland, and not for Ulster alone, also to consider the desirability of calling together, in the near future, by Sir Edward Carson a full meeting of English and Irish Unionist M.P's to consider a joint parliamentary action on Irish questions in the House of Commons.

The announcement of the formation of Anti-Partition League was considered, and a view expressed that all Unionist activities in London should be concentrated in this one office, which is a joint office of the Union Defence League, Ulster [Unionist] Council and [Irish] Unionist Alliance. Sir Edward Carson also to be asked to nominate two or three Members of the Ulster Council to be Members of this Committee. The formation of the London Committee of the Irish Unionist Alliance was confirmed as follows:—

The Lord Farnham.
The Earl of Leitrim.
The Earl of Ancaster.
The Viscount Doneraile.
Colonel The Lord Ventry, D.S.O.,
Admiral The Lord Beresford, G.C.B., K.C.V.O.,
The Lord Bellew.
The Lord Dunalley, H.M.L.
Col. Sir Frederick Shaw, Bart, D.S.O.,
General Sir Hugh McCalmont, K.C.B.,
Sir J. G. Butcher, Bart, K.C., M.P.,
Major Pretyman Newman, M.P.,
Mr. G. Stewart, M.P.,
Mr. Lawrence Lyon, M.P.,
Colonel C. R. Burn, M.P.,
Colonel W. G. Nicholson, M.P.,
Mr John E. Walsh
Mr J. Mackay Wilson, D.L.

Mr Harry Franks, J.P.,
Mr Fane Vernon, DL.
Colonel Guinness.
Sir George Brooke, Bart. D.L.
Mr R. Sanders, D.L.

with power to add to their numbers.

Resolved to add Sir R. Cooper, Bart, M.P. to London Committee. Mr. Sanders undertook to act as Honorary Secretary pro tem and he was requested to communicate with Lord Salisbury and Lord Ancaster with a view of inviting them and other Peers interested in Ireland to join the London Committee. The forming of a Branch in London of the Irish Unionist Alliance was approved and it was also considered desirable, if possible, that an Irish Unionist Club where Irish Unionists resident in London could meet, and where discussions could take place, should be instituted. Further consideration of these matters was postponed to a future meeting.

Mr. Sanders reported that he had had several interviews with Sir Edward Carson who had impressed very strongly the importance of having a well organised press propaganda both at home and abroad. Also that information of the course of affairs in Ireland should be communicated frequently to this office, so as to keep Members of Parliament well informed on South of Ireland questions.

Mr. J. R. Fisher of the Ulster Unionist Council attended the meeting and gave his views on the question of propaganda, especially in America. It was pointed out that the American Press Agencies were unfavourable as a rule to our cause, also that the Government propaganda had been in the hands of Home Rulers, who were still exercising a very great influence. Mr. Lyon M.P., who is a Canadian, and has a good knowledge of American press methods, gave some valuable information and it was resolved to appoint a Propaganda Sub-Committee consisting of Mr. Lyon, M.P., Sir R. Cooper, Bart. M.P., together with three other Members to be nominated by the Ulster Council, and that this Committee should draw up a report and take such steps as might be desirable to start a joint scheme of propaganda both at home and abroad. Mr. Sanders reported that he expected to meet Sir Frederick Young, M.P., Sir Frederick Young being an Australian and one of the Leaders over here of the British Australian Party as opposed to Australian Sinn Feiners, he would consult Sir George on the best means of getting propaganda into Australia.

The Committee then considered the policy which should be adopted in Parliament as regards Southern Unionist affairs. It was agreed that no object would be gained at the present time by merely protesting against Home Rule. The English people are far too busy endeavouring to put their own "house in order" to think much of Irish Politics, and the best policy now to adopt is that of falling back upon the old Unionist policy of economic and social development in Ireland, supporting the present Chief Secretary in the Policy which he has outlined in this direction and keeping him up to that policy.

It was urged that to succeed in this policy it was necessary to have a strong group of Members in the House of Commons well informed on Irish Southern questions and instructed as to the wishes of the South of Ireland in regard to the Bills which are coming up.

It was resolved that the following be formed into the Irish Parliamentary Reconstruction Committee with power to add to their numbers, viz:—

All Peers and Members of the House of Commons who are Members of the London Committee and in addition Sir Hugh McCalmont, Mr. J. Mackay Wilson, Mr. Harry Franks, Mr. Robert Sanders.

The Committee adjourned to 4 o'clock on Wednesday, March 12th 1919.

VI

The home rule issue was revived in 1920 with a new government of Ireland bill. Outlined in the house of commons on 22 December 1919, it was formally introduced into the house on 25 February 1920. It proposed to establish two parliaments, one for the six north-east counties of Ulster, another for the remaining twenty-six, with power to create an Irish council with representatives of both Irish parliaments. Irish representation at Westminster was retained, for the powers of the Irish parliaments were restricted and the supremacy of the imperial parliament asserted. Nevertheless, apart from the principle involved, the bill was open to a number of criticisms from a southern unionist viewpoint. The financial powers were considered inadequate and unfair to Ireland; the bill would establish permanent partition; and there were few safeguards for the minority in the south and west—most notably the bill did not provide for a nominated second chamber.

These details concerned the unionists of the A.P.L. rather than those of the I.U.A. The latter wanted to oppose the bill outright, but they soon found that their earlier optimism had been misplaced. In the first place, anticipated support in British politics was not forthcoming, partly because Ulster unionists proved unreliable allies. On 10 March 1920, while undertaking to try and secure adequate safeguards for the southern minority, the U.U.C. decided not to oppose the bill. The I.U.A. had been able to accept Ulster unionists' refusal to revive the joint committee (70), but members were dismayed by the readiness with which some Ulster unionist M.P.s appeared to jump at the chance of having their own parliament. Moreover, the U.U.C.'s decision to accept the bill reacted upon the London committee of the I.U.A., which had been intended as the spearhead of resistance to home rule. The committee had been willing to oppose the bill, but the U.U.C.'s decision put them in a quandary as to whether or not to oppose the bill. Looking for allies and support, they consulted Midleton. He preferred amendment to attempted rejection and helped to convince the committee of the impossibility of killing home rule completely. The committee therefore decided not to oppose the bill outright or even to hold a meeting of unionist M.P.s, as the Dublin committee had requested them to do.

200 Letter from J. E. Walsh, honorary secretary of the remodelled I.U.A., to H. de F. Montgomery, 15 April 1920, expressing concern at the attitude of some Ulster unionist M.P.s towards the establishment of a northern parliament (D 627/435):

My dear Montgomery—I hope you will be able to be present at the meeting of the Executive on Wednesday next, as the Ulster situation is puzzling us not a little, and we would like very much to have your views, which are always statesmanlike.

I also write to ask a favour. We are anxious to have a short communique from some correspondent in Ulster for our May number of "Notes from Ireland." It is essential that it should be written by someone who understands the question in all its bearings. I wonder if you would be so kind as to help us by writing a short communique which would be headed "From our Ulster Correspondent."?

As I have said, we feel a little puzzled about Ulster's attitude. We gather that Ulster would only establish her parliament in the event of the southern parliament being established, but the speeches of some Northern Members lead one to believe that Ulster is inclined to jump at the idea of a parliament. If Ulster merely accepts her parliament in the event of the southern parliament being established, or demands to be omitted from the Bill altogether, the road back to the Union would remain open. Once, however, the Ulster Parliament is established, the road back to the Union would be closed. We would be glad to know your views on the situation.

Meanwhile I trust that you will be able to see your way to helping us by writing a short communique, as you so kindly did on a former occasion. Yours very truly,

John E. Walsh,
Hon. Secretary.

201 Report by R. Dawson, secretary of the London committee of the I.U.A., to J. E. Walsh, secretary of the Dublin committee, of a meeting of the London committee on 12 March 1920, which decided that it was impossible to oppose the government of Ireland bill as the Dublin committee had desired (D 989A/9/20):

[Dear Sir]—I write to report the result of last night's meeting of our Committee. There were present: Sir John Butcher, Lord Bellew, Lord Wolmer, L. Lyon, M.P., Pennefather, Turton, Capt. Foxcroft, Gershom Stewart and Marriott. Lord Midleton also attended by invitation of Sir. J. Butcher. Thus there were two peers and eight M.P's.

Lord Midleton made a long statement urging opposition to the Bill. He did not think it could be defeated, but a good showing on 2nd Reading would induce the Government to accept amendment on vital points. He especially emphasised the fact that the minority had no protection, that there was no 2nd Chamber and that, under Clause 23, loyalists could be taxed out of existence.

There was then a long discussion on the action to be taken on the 2nd Reading. And here it became apparent that the position is full of complexity. No Unionists would vote for Asquith's or Adamson's amendments which declare that the Bill gives too little; while the Labour men and Ind [ependent]-Liberals would not support a Unionist amendment based on the doctrine that the Bill gives too much.

Then arose this further point. An attempt to defeat the Bill by supporting Labour or Radical amendments would, if successful, bring the 1914 Act into operation, and might bring into power a Government which would pass an infinitely worse measure. It became clear that many members—and among them some of the very strongest opponents of Home Rule—would be deterred by these considerations from trying to beat the Bill on 2nd Reading. Their efforts, however, would be quite unfettered in Committee.

A proposal was then made that a Clause should be proposed suspending the operation of the new Act until law and order had been restored. Suspensory periods of 3 and 5 years were suggested, but the more indefinite period was preferred. All agreed to support that, and Lord Midleton and others thought it would have large support.

At this point I took up the running. I read the Resolution adopted by your Committee on Wednesday, and reminded the Committee that Lord Midleton advised making a good show on 2nd Reading as a step towards getting amendments carried, and urged the desirability of convening a meeting of Unionist members. I read your letter and Mr. Jellett's telegram. Lord Wolmer had left; but I had seen him and got his authority to put his name to a Whip.

The Committee then debated the idea of a General Meeting. The main objection taken to it was that it might reveal some serious divisions of opinion among Unionists. It was pointed out,—and there is a good deal in it—that there are several Coalition Unionists who are Unionists only in name. It might, therefore, happen that a meeting, called to get common action on the 2nd Reading, might in fact cause disputation which would tend to make the party less disposed to combine on amendments such as those mentioned above. On the other hand, a Party Meeting, called to consider some important amendments before the Committee stage, might be productive of good. Many men for instance, who would vote for 2nd Reading, would vote for a suspension of the Act until the restoration of order, or for changes which would not involve the existence of the Government, or the coming into force of the 1914 Act.

On these grounds the Committee turned down the idea of having a general meeting at the present time.

The decision, though it may seem disappointing, is not so injurious as it appears. There are several forces at work. First, there is to be a meeting of Unionists generally on the 24th, when the Provost and Lord Midleton will speak. It will doubtless be addressed from the Anti-Partition standpoint, but this does not matter from the point of view of opposition to the Bill, on which the A.Ps are not less strong than the I.U.A. Secondly, there is in the House a Unionist Reconstruction Committee, of which Mr. Gretton is Chairman. Mr. Pennefather and Mr. George Terrell, M.P. for Chippenham have been in consultation with me, and an Irish Sub-Committee is being formed to oppose the Bill. Both these gentlemen are determined enemies of Home Rule, as is Mr. Gretton. I think that this Sub-Committee can exercise good influence in quarters which we could hardly reach, for it will not be supposed to be biassed by self interest as Irish Unionists might be. The members of the Sub-Committee are being selected from the Unionists of the most stalwart views. The Reconstruction Committee numbers about 250, among whom, of course, will be many of the new men, whose unionism is less strong than that of the elder statesmen, and they may listen to their own, purely English Sub-Committee better than to us.

This decision brings me to your question as to a delegation coming over to do some lobbying on the Bill. I think it would be desirable that some delegates should be here in the week, March 22nd–March 29th. Sanders is over here, but just now is in bed with an attack of influenza. But I hope he will be fit by that time, as he does excellent work in the lobby. The presence of Lord Farnham would be very desirable, as would that of yourself. What the delegates would have to bear in mind is that the question has to be dealt with in a broad view, with full regard to the existence of the 1914 Act—which is a kind of strait waist-coat—and Ulster's decision. The latter tends to weaken opposition, the former makes the rejection of the Bill practically impossible.

The line to be taken, it seems to me is this. Those who dislike the Bill should be urged to free themselves from the responsibility for its results by voting against the 2nd Reading, or, in default, not voting for it. They should have the necessity of uniting upon certain amendments pressed upon them. For, even if they failed to carry a suspensory Clause in the Commons, a big vote in favour would enable the Lords to carry and insist upon such a Clause.

I am afraid you will not read this report with much satisfaction, nor do I have much in writing it. But the same may be said of practically the whole Unionist Party. Sir George Younger, whom I did not know, came up to me yesterday in the Lobby, and was kind enough to say some nice things of my speech at Southport. We then talked about Ireland, and he is clearly upset and depressed about the matter, and the same may be said of others.

The Committee evidently thought their decisions might disappoint you, for I was specially instructed to write a formal letter on their behalf with the terms of which, as you will receive it separately, I need not trouble you, but which says that they are heart and soul with you and adopt the line they take as tactically the best in the interests of the Southern Unionists.

I have only to add that I fought very hard to get our points carried, so much so that I had to express a hope that I was not transgressing beyond the duties of a Secretary. The Committee were most kind and patient and begged me to present every point. Their hatred of the Bill and anxiety to do their best is beyond doubt. But the conditions are such that they are like men walking in fetters. Yours very truly,

Richard Dawson

VII

Not only did the die-hards directing the I.U.A. find support for the union diminishing in Ulster and Great Britain, they also found it diminishing in the south and west of Ireland in face of the Anglo-Irish war. In view of their victory in the I.U.A. in January 1919, the die-hards expected widespread support for the union in the south and west and had re-organised the I.U.A. accordingly. In 1919 there had, perhaps, been some grounds for this optimism; for the unanimous refusal of nationalist Ireland to accept conscription in April 1918, and the supersession of the Irish parliamentary party by Sinn Fein in the general election of December 1918, had made futile and anachronistic the convention policy of fruitful cooperation between unionists and constitutional nationalists and had underlined the need to maintain the union. The trend away from unionism had thus again been interrupted, but only briefly.

It was resumed again by 1920. The development of terror and counter-terror, and the failure of the British government to dominate the situation in 1920–1, led to further questioning of the value and desirability of the union. There had been outrages in 1918 and 1919, but by 1920 the campaign of murder and intimidation seemed to have assumed a systematic form all over the country. From 1 January to 31 December

1919, 17 policemen had been killed; but from 1 January to 31 December 1920, 165 policemen were killed and 251 wounded. The state of the country may be judged from the following figures: between 1 January 1919 and 1 January 1921, 182 policemen were killed and 265 wounded; 50 military killed, 122 wounded; 39 civilians killed and 108 wounded; and from 1 January 1919 until 19 February 1921, 70 courthouses and 536 police barracks were destroyed; 212 police barracks were damaged and there were 3,052 raids for arms. Throughout the south and west there was a general sense of insecurity, felt most acutely by the southern unionist class because of their politics, religion and property. Despite the presence of considerable crown forces, southern unionists could expect little protection from such forces which were more concerned with waging war on Irish terrorists than with protecting life and property. Certain areas, such as Cos Clare and Cork, were particularly badly hit, but a report on the condition of the west of Ireland by a Clare unionist seems typical of what any member of the southern unionist class might have had to experience at any time.

This sense of insecurity further weakened support for the union. On the one hand, many southern unionists left Ireland from 1920 onwards never to return. A case in point was Edward John Beaumont-Nesbitt of Tubberdaly, near Edenderry, King's Co. Born in Suffolk in 1860, he had inherited Tubberdaly in 1886 and had been a consistent unionist and a prominent figure in King's Co. ever since; but he retreated to England and died there in 1944. On the other hand, those who remained had no desire to work for or support the union. A resigned acceptance of facts rather than panic was at the root of this attitude. The union had proved incapable of maintaining the peace and stability of Ireland, and its former supporters were now willing to accept a large measure of self-government to restore peace and save what remained to them. If they subscribed to any organisation, it was not to the I.U.A. but to the A.P.L., which took up where the Midletonites had left off at the convention.

202

Description of the extent of terrorism in the west of Ireland, sent to the I.U.A., 23 April 1920, by R. F. Hibbert of Woodpark, Scarriff, Co. Clare (D 989A/8/23):

The condition of affairs in my neighbourhood in Co. Clare is beyond description; there is no protection whatever for life and property.

Recently an attempt was made by some forty masked men, armed with rifles, revolvers, and axes, to raid my house. They got in by rushing the back premises of the house. They reduced the servants to a state of terror by threatening to shoot them, seized the Steward's gun, and tried to gag him with a rifle butt. I immediately armed myself with a repeating rifle, and fired on the raiders from the lobby, forcing them to retire, one of their number being wounded. I have since been warned repeatedly that my life is in danger.

The houses of most of the respectable people in the neighbourhood have been raided, but such is the terrorism that exists, that many who have suffered in this way are afraid to report what has occurred to the authorities, lest worse should befall them.

I reported the raid on my house to the authorities, who sent down a small detachment of infantry, but recalled them after about three weeks. The police were then withdrawn from Scarriff, and the barracks closed, leaving no police at all for a distance of over fifteen miles.

Two nights after the closing of the barracks the Petty Sessions Court, opposite the barracks, was broken into, and everything in it destroyed. A week afterwards about two hundred men pulled down the barracks with pickaxes and crowbars.

As far as personal property goes, last week my boathouse, and other outhouses, were raided, while timber is constantly stolen, fences and walls thrown down, etc. As there are no police and no Petty Sessions, there is no redress.

I hear their next move is to smash up all the post offices and post office equipment, and should they wish to do so, there is absolutely nothing to prevent them.

About a month ago one of my herds tried to join the Royal Irish Constabulary. Fifteen masked and armed men surrounded his house one night, and searched for him, but luckily did not find him, as he was hiding under the bed in a back room. Had they found him he would undoubtedly have been shot, as has happened in the case of other young men who expressed their intention of joining the police.

Every night gangs of armed men assemble in different houses, and walk the countryside, terrorising the respectable inhabitants. It is because they are so well armed, and so reckless in the use of their arms, that this terrorism exists. They collect subscriptions in this way, as everyone is afraid to refuse to subscribe. From dark to dawn law-abiding people scarcely dare to sleep.

Owing to the withdrawal of police all regulations are disregarded, and the public houses remain open night and day, consequently, as may be imagined, the state of drunkenness and robbery is appalling. Even the farmer's crops are stolen out of the ground to buy drink

Our tenants, having previously refused to purchase their holdings, decided to do so just before the war. So far as I can see, they will now adopt the attitude that if they wait a little longer, they will get their lands free.

The state of the country is such that I and my family have to leave and shut up the house. I have little doubt that when we are gone, and there is a care-taker [*sic*] in charge of the house, it will be broken into and destroyed. Others in the same position as myself agree with me that we will find great difficulty in procuring care-takers who will undertake to look after houses which have had to be abandoned in this way.

Personally I believe that the raids on houses were field days, and preparations for something bigger, for the Republican Army, and also the attacks on barracks.

I am making arrangements to remove my furniture, etc., as it is impossible to insure in Ireland against damages caused by civil disturbances.

203

Part of a letter from R. E. Longfield, Longueville, Mallow, Co. Cork, to H. de F. Montgomery, 16 March 1920, expressing apprehension at the state of the country (D 627/435):

. . . Is it not disgusting that our Herbert Shaw sh[oul]d be writing outrageous articles in The Times. I wrote to him & have a long letter in reply—rubbish about differentiating between ordinary & political crimes &c—that the S[inn] F[ein] leaders do not approve of the outrages but can not control their followers.—They have never condemned any outrage!

I dont think Lord French can be much good, I hear he does not realize the State of the Country & sees v[ery] few people, and many of them are fair ladies. I hear the work done round Timoleague as preparation for the attack on the Police Barracks must have required a very large number of men—all the roads blocked, Big trees felled across the road & telegraph posts. A trench 4 ft wide & 5 ft deep cut through a road &c &c During the attack an order was heard "Tell the ladies to get back from the firing line" This is supposed to refer to ladies of the "Green Cross" who attended as nurses.

At Ballybunion in Kerry walls & all sorts of obstructions were put across the roads.

There are now patrols of police & soldiers in motor cars but the chance of their being in the right place at the right time, is as a Police officer said to me "very remote". The small police barracks about this country ought to have been strengthened & not vacated.

Dr Cohalan RC Bishop of Cork has at last spoken out condemning crime, without the usual qualification "After all you got great provocation" He is said to have been appointed by German influence & is certainly a S.F. sympathiser . . . .

204 Letter from E. J. Beaumont-Nesbitt, writing from 56 Rutland Gate, London S.W.1, to his cousin, Mrs. M. Savage-Armstrong, Strangford House, Strangford, Co. Down, 19 January 1925, explaining why he did not want to return to his former home, Tubberdaly, King's Co., or invest more money in his property there (D 618/172):

My dear Marie—I didn't get time to answer your very kind letter of the 11th: before. It was good of you and Raymond to help to look after my interests and send the advice you did, but unfortunately there are difficulties in the way of doing anything in the way of reinstatement at Tubberdaly. I did know all that you tell me, and in many cases believe the policy has been adopted, but I do not think I can carry it out very well. To begin with I have raised difficulties myself by all the building of Labourers' Cottages that I undertook, as, now that I have left, there is no employment, and these people have joined the ranks of what is called the "landless men", who clamour for a division of any land, and would prevent anyone from outside coming to the place till they had received a block of land. Also on one farm of about 40 acres a man whom I befriended when he was down has proved a thorn in the flesh, and has stood in my way ever since I had to leave Ireland by claiming that this farm is in some way his. I bought the "tenant right" years ago from the last occupier of the farm and house, and the occupier went to America. But he had in his house a lodger, one Jones, who was then working for me as carpenter, and a jolly bad carpenter at that. This man in 1919 went out with my agricultural labourers on strike, and I never took him back, so he laid out to give me all the trouble he could. At first he could do nothing, but when the bad times came he put stock on my land, turned mine off, and later on when I was letting the grazing, he threatened to shoot anyone who disturbed him. I took him into Court, and he was bound over (after about two years of trouble) to keep the peace, but he still prevented anyone taking the farm till about a few months ago, and he, with a good many of my ex-labourers have decided that if any dividing up takes place no one is to come on till they are satisfied. You know the country and the impossibility at present of trying to do much, so I have offered the whole place to the Land Com[missio]n. and shall sell it to them, to do what they please with it, if they make me a reasonable offer. It is no use trying to fight out my corner, and isn't worth while, as I am too old to hope to see it finished. There are several of my old labourers whom I want to help as much as I can, and if I do sell I think I can arrange that these get helped first, and thereby I can put a spoke in the wheels of some that I do not want to help. I am quite philosophic about it all, I've had my innings, and am out now, and if I can help any decent men to get a living out of the wreck, that is all I care about. But in the face of all the opposition it isn't worth while to try to build any other houses, and I have nobody there to look after my interests in the least, and if I started to rebuild or build anything new, I should just be robbed. You can I know understand the position, and will, I think feel that I am right, though I agree it is a great pity.

I'm afraid it will be long before the rich Irish-American does very much in the way of buying up farms in the 26 counties, as till the country settles, and till taxes are reduced (and when can that be?) it will be hard to induce anybody to go to live in Ireland.

I don't often agree with John Dillon, but he made a speech the other day with which I cordially agree, and he realises, what everyone here does, that the so-called Free State is broke, and that for generations there will be poverty and want far greater than ever occurred in the remembrance of anyone now living. It is the price of "Freedom", but I dont think the country is very happy at paying the price. As I hear it, all over the country they are asking "when the English will come back?" The English will never come back, they have washed their hands of the whole business, and till it becomes a military or naval question, a return will never even be considered.

I was so glad to hear your news about Raymond, and am so glad he finds such a lot to do. He cannot be dull when he is always so occupied.

I do hope you will soon have better news of Gwen, it is bad luck on her.

All best wishes, and good luck to you all. Ever yr. affec. cousin

E.J.B-N.

205 Letter from J. W. Garvey of Tulley House, Louisburgh, Westport, Co. Mayo, writing from Woolwich, to F. H. Crawford, 21 August 1921, which voices southern unionist resignation to the ending of the union (D 1700/5/4):

My dear Crawford—I was indeed very pleased to receive your letter couched in such terms of friendship and I trust and believe there will never be any interruption in our good relations.

My only anxiety was to prevent a repetition of the calumnies but I am not sanguine that I have succeeded. Certainly there never could be seen a happier pair than Stuart & Sheelagh and it grieves me that they and their peace should be disturbed. I spent a week at Woolwich and they were very kind to me and my little wife. The latter remained on as Sheelagh has not been very well and at times she is very seedy. I am going to above address [Berner's Hotel, Berners Street, London] tomorrow and if I am fit I hope to see the finals for the county cricket championship.

I have suffered a good deal from gout and both my feet are swollen but I am hopeful the acute stage has passed.

I may not get back to Ireland till the first prox and the prospects are not very bright for us in the West. Personally I am anxious to see a peace much as I regret any severance from the Union. I w[oul]d have preferred to see the Union cemented rather than dismembered but the Union is now a thing of the past. We have "our all" in the West and our only chance of saving anything we have is by silence in the midst of this great revolutionary change. I well realize that you northern [sic] would have preferred the Union as it stood but as you have had to accept a charter of Home Rule, so we must, if our lives and properties are to be spared, make the best terms we can. Any aggressive word or act w[oul]d be fatal to us now and our chances of security and safety are not very hopeful. I had no idea the Government would have offered such large terms to Dail Eirann [*sic*] and I think Mr de Valera, from his own point of view, shews a great lack of statesmanship in not accepting the terms. The only one bright prospect is that he may lose American sympathy and American dollars if he holds out for a Republic. It is American money that is the strength of the movement. All Irish revolutionary movements in the past failed for want of funds and the present rebellion is the one exception —its success being primarily traceable to the influx of American money.

Your position in the north is a very difficult one chiefly on account of the religious atmosphere but with us there has been a very tolerant spirit evidenced at all times. Indeed were it not for this spirit we, a few people swiming [*sic*] in a great ocean, could not survive. Personally I w[oul]d have preferred to see one Ireland but I fully appreciate the northern objections from their standpoint.

At [the] same time I think you w[oul]d have been better off with one Parliament than under these partition schemes but my opinion is not worth much.

With all good wishes & assuring you of my friendship always Yours very truly,

John Garvey

VIII

Despite the loss of crucial support in British politics, and despite its increasing isolation in Ireland, the executive committee of the I.U.A. still clung to the union. Throughout 1920 and 1921 it refused to believe that the union would be superseded. Displaying considerable faith in the unionism of the unionist party, these die-hards tried to put the case for the union and firm government as best they could. (They painted pathetic pictures of life in Ireland and tried to point out to the British cabinet and parliament the dangers to loyalists and the empire of granting self-government to a revolutionary movement; which, the I.U.A. held, was in reality an unstable combination of bolsheviks, republicans and land-grabbers.)

These activities had no effect. Where the government wanted southern unionist views, it preferred to look to Midleton and the unionists of the A.P.L., who were anxious to achieve a broad settlement with safeguards. The I.U.A. had no influence on discussions over the government of Ireland bill of 1920 which was passed in December 1920, after being amended to meet some of the Midletonite objections. The act operated in the north but was still-born in the south. Nor could the I.U.A. (or, for that matter, the A.P.L.) decisively influence the course and outcome of the negotiations between Sinn Fein and the British government carried on intermittently between July and December 1921 but begun in earnest only on 11 October 1921. All that the die-hards of the I.U.A. did, in conjunction with those British M.P.s hoping to break up the coalition, was to make life a little uncomfortable for the government and for Sir Hamar Greenwood, the Irish chief secretary. On 31 October, for instance, some unionist M.P.s, including William Jellett M.P. for Dublin University, unsuccessfully moved by 43 votes to 439 a vote of censure on the government. It did rouse some sympathy for the plight of the southern minority, but it also caused the government to make special and successful efforts to secure a vote in favour of the Irish negotiations at the National Unionist Association conference which met at Liverpool on 17 November.

Thus the I.U.A. was unable to prevent the Anglo-Irish treaty being signed on 6 December 1921. The 1920 act had been regarded by the I.U.A. as the limit of British concessions, but the treaty superseded that act, and granted larger powers to the Irish parliament. Ireland was to become, not a republic as Sinn Feiners demanded, but a self-governing dominion within the empire, under the style of the Irish Free State. The treaty was to apply to all Ireland, but Northern Ireland quickly took up the choice left open to her of opting out and retaining her status under the 1920 act. Most of the reservations and many of the safeguards for minorities contained in previous home rule schemes were omitted: there was no provision for the completion of land purchase; no safeguard against double taxation; no provision for compensation for losses incurred in the recent unrest; and no indication as to the powers and composition of the second chamber of the proposed southern parliament—the 1920 act had provided for a strong senate with a large nominated or ex-officio element, on the lines of that proposed at the Irish convention.

206 Printed circular from the executive committee of the I.U.A., 2 February 1921, explaining to members of the general council the committee's unanimous decision to keep the maintenance of the union as the prime objective of the I.U.A., in spite of the government of Ireland act of 1920 (D 989A/8/23):

Dear Sir—Now that the Home Rule Act of 1920 is on the Statute Book, it has become necessary for members of the Irish Unionist Alliance to reconsider their position both with regard to their own action as individuals and as members of the Alliance.

Certain members, whose attachment to the cause of the Union is beyond question, have expressed the view that, while the necessity for maintaining the Alliance as a working and efficient organisation for the expression of loyalist views and the protection of the interests of the loyalist and law-abiding section of the community is as great as, and perhaps greater than, ever before, there is now something unreal in continuing to carry on the Alliance as an organisation for the "maintenance of the Legislative Union." They argue that a change of name, and to some extent of aims, might attract to its membership some at least of that section of the Irish public which has hitherto been known as Nationalist, and that by this means an organisation might be built up around the nucleus of the old Alliance, more likely under the changed circumstances to be of practical use in helping to counteract the lawless and irreconcilable anti-British sections which now as heretofore constitute the gravest danger to the country.

Your Executive Committee, after very careful consideration of the views above outlined, have come to the unanimous conclusion that unless and until existing political conditions undergo a very radical change, it would be a fatal mistake to alter either the name or the aims of the Alliance, and that only in the event of a Southern Irish Parliament being elected, and succeeding in carrying on the functions of a Parliament, would it be advisable to consider the question of doing so.

A Parliament is essentially a peaceful institution, and so long as the atmosphere in many parts of the country continues to resemble that of civil war, they consider that it is highly improbable that those parts of Ireland can achieve any satisfactory form of self-government; and further than this, that it is by no means certain that any satisfactory form of self-government can ever be established.

For these reasons, they think that, under existing conditions, it would be futile for Unionists to take part in the elections for any Parliament which could come into existence in Southern Ireland under the recent Act.

The Alliance has consistently maintained that there is no practicable half-way house between the Legislative Union and complete separation, and that it is only under the former that the country can truly prosper and good government be secured. The Unionist Party in Great Britain have in the recent Act gone as far as they can go in the direction of separation, and if, as is extremely probable, Southern Ireland refuses to work the Act, the restoration of the Legislative Union can only be a matter of time. Your Executive

Committee are of opinion that in the interests of the Empire, as well as of individual Unionists resident in Ireland, the right and proper course for the Alliance at present is to maintain unaltered its name, its principles, and its organisation.

That there is nothing unreal or academic in such a course, is evidenced by the recent history both of the English Liberal and the Irish Nationalist Parties. The latter have never compromised, although at various General Elections, extending over more than a generation, their cause was to all appearances irretrievably lost. At last they have succeeded in obtaining Home Rule, although in a form which they all detest. It may well be that it will take a very much shorter period than a generation to restore the Union. The best help towards this end which the Alliance can give is to adhere unfalteringly to its principles.

The situation therefore demands more than ever the maintenance of the Alliance as a working and efficient organisation, not only to voice the views of Irish Unionists, but actively to promote their interests.

Events will show, if they have not already done so, that the policy of the Alliance was not only right but the only possible one. In the meantime it is incumbent on Irish Unionists to stand firm by their principles and maintain their organisation, not only in their own interests but in the interests of their country and the Empire.

In the ordinary course the Executive Committee would have consulted the General Council of the Alliance before considering these important matters. Owing to the physical difficulties in the way of holding a special meeting of the General Council under present conditions, they regret that it has not been possible to do so. They have requested me to convey to you, as a member of the General Council, the unanimous conclusions at which they have arrived, before making any statement of their views.

Should you wish to offer any criticism, would you kindly communicate with the representative of your Branch on the Executive Committee, before the 10th February, requesting him to bring it before the Executive Committee at their next meeting.

In the meantime I would ask you to regard this communication as confidential. Yours faithfully,

Hon. Secretary.

207 Report by R. Dawson, an official of the Union Defence League and the London representative of the I.U.A., to the secretary of the I.U.A. in Dublin, 1 November 1921, describing reactions to the attempted unionist vote of censure on the coalition government on 31 October (D989A/9/20):

The division on the Vote of Censure on Monday last was as good as our friends in Parliament expected and they are satisfied with the result; but much more satisfactory was the debate itself. It was obvious that the Government were very uncomfortable while the indictment of their policy was being made and to those who have heard the Prime Minister on various occasions the defence which he put up showed that he was conscious of the difficulties of his position; and that he should have been compelled to represent Lord Midleton and his few friends as representative of Irish Unionism in the face of the representations which had been repeatedly made to him showed the weakness of his case. I should add that Mr. Jellett in his speech emphatically contradicted the Prime Minister on this point, and stated the real facts of the position

The feeling amongst Unionist Members is not to be measured by the votes they gave. Very many admitted that they were in complete sympathy with the minority though they had, for various reasons more or less convincing, to give their support to the Government.

It remains to be seen what effect the debate and division may have in the country and on the National Unionist Conference at Liverpool. Personally I am a little apprehensive that it may have the effect of stimulating the supporters of the coalition in the country who did not have the advantage of hearing the debate.

I believe that the Party wire pullers are using every means to secure an obedient following at the Conference; for which purpose they are, I believe, doing everything they can to get well known mug waps sent up as delegates.

The questions which are being asked daily cause the Government great embarrassment. The floundering of the Chief Secretary sometimes arouses mingled feelings of compassion and derision. So long as the session lasts it is all important to have every embarrassing fact sent over promptly. The information wired to me on Monday afternoon about Beggar's Bush Barracks had quite an effect when mentioned in debate. On the whole, our friends on this side are hopeful and confident.

Richard Dawson

IX

The dismantling of British rule in the twenty-six counties and the establishment of the Free State meant the end of unionism in the south. In 1922 the A.P.L. was wound up, and the die-hards of the I.U.A. finally abandoned their political activities on behalf of the union and British connection. In the first place, the legal establishment of a southern Irish government made the continuance of unionism and unionist organisation constitutionally impossible. Southern unionism had always been a constitutional movement and could never contemplate resistance to the established government. The conciliatory attitude adopted by Arthur Griffith, Michael Collins and, later, William Cosgrave, towards minority interests made this principle less irksome to act upon. Secondly, there was little will to carry on any fight for the re-imposition of British rule. The treaty was regarded as a betrayal and this feeling was enhanced as republican opposition to the Free State—and civil war—developed. Even the most persistent unionists felt that they had been thrown to the wolves by the British government and people. The consequent resentment snapped that emotional bond that had existed between Great Britain and Irish loyalists and had been one of the props of southern unionism.

By 1922, therefore, the old unionist position in the south existing since 1885 had been completely abandoned. There were suggestions for adapting the I.U.A. to form the basis of a conservative party in the new state, but, in face of the confused political situation in the south and civil war, these came to nothing. Instead, the standing committee of the I.U.A. devoted itself to relief work among distressed loyalists. It was, perhaps, an ignominious end for what had been the oldest unionist organisation in Ireland.

208 Letter from J. M. Wilson, writing from Brooks's, St James's Street, London, to Lord Carson, 14 December 1921, thanking him for his scathing attack in the house of lords that day on the government and the Irish treaty (D 1507/1/1921/284):

A thousand thanks, for your great speech, from a poor Irish refugee, who is nearly heart broken at the duplicity, mendacity, &, cowardice of our former friends. God help those of us belonging to the S or West.

J. Mackay Wilson

209 Memorandum on 'The Irish situation' by R. Dawson, London representative of the I.U.A., 24 January 1922, forwarded to the I.U.A. in Dublin, and reflecting upon the courses open to southern unionists after the establishment of the Irish Free State (D 989A/9/20):

No more difficult political and social problem has ever been propounded than that which lies for solution by the Unionists of the Irish Free State. Not the least of the difficulties lies at the threshold of the inquiry. For the first time in the long Irish controversy the political ideals and the material interests of Unionism are in opposition. A return to a closer connection with Great Britain can only come through the breakdown of the new Irish Constitution, but a breakdown of this Constitution must inevitably involve Irish Unionists in ruin more or less complete. To attain their political ideals therefore they must sacrifice their material interests, to retain their means of living they have to support a form of Government which they hate.

It is doubtless this consideration that has already induced some Unionists, of an invertebrate order, to come forward with effusive professions of loyalty and confidence in the Provisional Government, and offers of assistance. And it is not to be ignored that even Unionists of a more robust type may be driven in the same direction not only by motives of self interest, but by angry disgust at their shameless betrayal by Great Britain. Such motives are natural, but it is not by emotion or passion that the difficulties of Irish Unionists are to be met, but by a very calm and detached recognition of facts.

The facts, as we know them, do not seem to encourage any profuse advances to the Provisional Government. Apart from any consideration of political honour and consistency—which indeed are at present regarded as old-fashioned prejudices—the action taken by Lord Mayo's friends does not seem tactically wise. The Sinn Fein leaders are quite clever enough to appraise at its true value the support of men who so readily desert their former convitions. If Irish Unionists are ever driven to make a bargain with the new rulers of Ireland, they will get all the better terms by having been steadfast in their faith.

But the question suggests itself—is it not premature to make proffers of friendship and allegiance to the new Government? It would seem infinitely more prudent to await the turn of events. There is no surety that the Government of today will be the Government of this day six months. And even were the stability of the Government greater than it is, there has been no time or opportunity to judge of the trend of their policy. It is impossible to judge how much is reality and how much is camouflage. Still less is it possible to foretell what forces may be arrayed against Mr. Griffiths and Mr. Collins, which may profoundly modify their intentions, or, perhaps, make their task impossible.

From every point of view the attitude of silent expectancy adopted by the Irish Unionist Alliance seems the wisest. But abstinence from any public declaration of policy need not, and should not, connote complete passivity. Though the Alliance may have in the immediate future an altered objective, it can set before itself another aim, and subserve another purpose, of great importance. It may form the nucleus of a conservative Party, representing the stable interests of the country. Such a Party—at least in its early stages—would mainly concern itself with social and economic questions. Probably the less it concerned itself with pure politics at first the better, in order that it might enlist the sympathy of the property owning classes irrespective of politics.

Purity and efficiency of administration, protection for property and civil rights, the maintenance of personal freedom, these would be the main planks of the platform of such a Party. It would place any infringements of its policy before the Irish Government. This, of course, would not prohibit it from seeing that Great Britain was adequately acquainted with any such infringements, but it should be careful to avoid any appearance of appealing to the British people against the legally constituted Government of Southern Ireland.

It will be necessary for Irish Unionists to consider the action they should take at the Irish General Election. To me it appears that abstention from voting would be the wisest course. Should they vote, each of the rivals—the Moderates and the Republicans—would suspect them of voting for its opponents, and they would be subject to the buffets of both. So much for the attitude of the Alliance in the immediate future.

What may happen in, say, six months, must be a matter of speculation. There are two alternatives.

1. That when the British garrison is withdrawn, the entire Sinn Fein Party will move towards a Republic.
2. That there will be a fierce struggle between a genuine Moderate Party and the Republicans, reinforced by the Irish Labour Party.

It is extremely difficult to determine in advance which of these is the more probable development.

The Conservative Party in Great Britain would resolutely oppose any further concession to Ireland. The great majority, I believe, voted reluctantly for the concessions already made. Should the first alternative be the outcome, the Conservatives would probably make it clear that any attempt at meeting it by negotiation would involve their secession from Mr. Lloyd George's Government.

In the event of the second alternative, the position would be more difficult and obscure. The Moderates of Sinn Fein—Griffiths and Collins—would be reluctant to assert their authority by the aid of British troops, and in the absence of any such request the British Government might be unwilling to send troops to Ireland. The Conservative Party, I apprehend, would urge the taking of measures for the protection of the loyal inhabitants, and on this the Coalition might well break up.

I indulge in these speculations with diffidence, but I am absolutely confident that the Conservative Party would be sternly resolved to stand by the Unionists and other loyal citizens of Southern Ireland.

I have to apologise for the length of this Memorandum, which I trust may be ascribed to the very nebulous character of the political situation.

210 Letter from Rev. H. S. Verschoyle of Manor House, Dunkineely, Co. Donegal, writing from Kircubbin, Co. Down, to J. E. Walsh, the secretary of the I.U.A., 22 March 1922, resigning from the I.U.A. on the ground that maintenance of the union was no longer practical politics (D 989A/8/30A):

Dear Sir—I have just received yr letter of 21st.

I am much exercised what to do about continuing to be a member of the Alliance. In view of the fact that the Free State had been set up, & that so to work for the Union w[oul]d be to put myself in opposition to the established government of our country, I some time ago made up my mind to resign my membership. I was just on the point of writing to do so when I received the letter of the Hon. Secs saying a meeting of the Council w[oul]d be held some time to consider what c[oul]d be done with the Alliance. I therefore held back my resignation, hoping that, now that the Union was no longer practical politics, some means m[igh]t be found for turning the Alliance into a body w[hic]h w[oul]d work in the Free State for the good of our country.

I hope the meeting referred to may soon take place so that I may be able to decide whether or not to resign, for to continue a member of a Unionist Alliance while desiring to be loyal to the Free State w[oul]d place me in the invidious position of "running with the hare & hunting with the hounds". This consideration has for me been accentuated by the fact that I lately had to communicate with Mr Collins to make a suggestion about the Constitution ere it sh[oul]d be too late. I pointed out to him that I, as a Donegal man, am a citizen of the Free State, while reasons of ill health of a member of my family oblige me to live in a hired house in this, the driest part of Ireland, instead of in the damp climate of Co Donegal where our own house is. I asked him c[oul]d some way be found by w[hic]h taxes deducted from Dividends received by residents of the Free State who happened to be resident in N. Ireland sh[oul]d be paid to the Exchequer of the former & not to that of the latter. Yrs faithf[ull]y

H S Verschoyle.

I fear it may be too compromising to remain any longer a member of the Unionist Alliance, for the reasons mentioned above, & so I must now, with regret, offer my resignation of membership.

I think I owe a subs[cription] to "Notes from Ireland" for two years, so enclose a p[ostal]. order for 2/–.

H.S.V.

211

Letter from F. Vernon, honorary treasurer of the I.U.A., Erne Hill, Belturbet, Co. Cavan, and 1 Wilton Place, Dublin, to J. E. Walsh, the secretary of the I.U.A., 27 January 1922, commenting on and returning **(b)** a memorandum by the English economist, Professor H. Hewins, which sought the help of southern businessmen in regularising economic relations between Great Britain and the Free State, and pointing out that southern businessmen should now be putting their weight behind the Irish Free State (D 989A/9/30B):

Dear Mr. Walsh—I have discussed the Professor's memorandum with some of my Bank directors, who understand such matters better than I do.

They have offered no special criticsms [*sic*], as practically all the statements made appeared to be quite correct. As regards paragraph (5) however, it is not quite correct to say that the Irish Free State will have its own coinage. At present there are various schemes afoot, and it is possible that British coinage may continue to be used. As regards paragraph (6), it is doubtful whether the balance as between Irish capital invested in Great Britain, and British capital invested in Ireland is on the side of the latter.

I do not quite know whether the Professor desires to discuss the whole question from the point of view of Great Britain, or of Ireland. In any case it rests with the Free State to carry out the details of the new arrangement, and it is hard to say what they will do. All depends upon this. However this may be, the proposed change is a "fait accompli", as the British Government is pledged to carry the proposals into operation.

Great Britain has, through her responsible ministers, given the case away, and nothing is left but to make the best of a bad bargain. Can Irish business-men [*sic*] do more than look after their own interests, when the English Government has thrown them to the wolves in order to get out of the political difficulties which it has itself created. Irish business-men have been left to shift for themselves; and all that they can do is to endeavour to help the rulers of the new Free State to build up the economic fabric in the way that will be most beneficial to itself. So far as matters of finance are concerned, the bank experts will do all that they can to help Ireland, and English business-men must look to their own interests. I make no allusion to Northern Ireland, as it is, for the present, at any rate, in a different position.

I do not desire that you should quote me if you should pass any of these remarks on, for what they are worth, which is not much. Yours truly,

) Signed) Fane Vernon.

(b)

The Irish Agreement and Economic Questions.

There has been so much sentimental talk about the Irish Agreement that the business aspects of the agreement are almost entirely ignored. But Banks, Insurance Companies, Industrial Companies, Agricultural interests, Railway and Shipping Companies will be obliged to make arrangements to meet the new conditions. At present they do not seem to realise that the economic unity of the United Kingdom is about to be broken up, and the work of generations of statemanship [*sic*] undone.

(1) There will be a difference of practice over the whole economic field between Gt. Britain and Ireland, and between the North of Ireland and the South—the Free State. All the economic powers, legislative and administrative, reserved under the Government of Ireland Act (1920) are to be transferred to the Irish Free State.

(2) The Irish Free State will be able to make its own commercial treaties, irrespective of Gt. Britain, and to accede or refuse to do so, to treaties made on behalf of Gt. Britain.

(3) The Irish Free State will have complete control of its trade relations, internally with the North of Ireland, externally with Gt. Britain and all other countries, and of navigation, including merchant shipping.

(4) The Irish Free State will have complete control of direct or indirect taxation, and all matters relating thereto. There must therefore be customs barriers between Gt. Britain and Ireland, and between the North of Ireland and the Free State.

(5) The Irish Free State will have its own coinage, its own legal tenders, its own negotiable instruments (including Bank Notes) its own standards of weights and measures.

(6) The Irish Free State will have its own law as to Trade marks, designs, merchandise marks, copyright and patent rights.

Now an immense proportion of the capital of the Irish Banks, Insurance and Industrial Companies and Railways is not Irish at all, but English and Scottish, and it is time the effect of the changes proposed on these investments was considered by those responsible to the shareholders.

At present there is no such thing as Irish credit. Ireland is just part of the United Kingdom, and the credit both of Ireland and Gt. Britain depends to an extent we cannot imagine on the economic integrity and unity of the United Kingdom. The breaking up of that unity in the manner set forth above is certainly a leap in the dark.

At the best, if the new Constitution works as well as its most ardent advocates hope, there must still be uncertainty for an [*sic*] long time. What business arrangements are to be made for this period?

If the uncertainty is removed, the change will still involve inconvenience, expense and permanent differences in the prospect of all undertakings affected by the economic relations of Gt. Britain and Ireland. Therefore business men must consider the position.

There is also the hypothesis, to be considered in no political spirit, but with cold business acumen that the new arrangements will not work at all. What then?

[*Note by Vernon*] The foregoing is all true, but none of it is new

212 Circular letter from the standing committee of the I.U.A., March 1926, explaining the limited and changed role of the I.U.A. since the establishment of the Irish Free State (D 989A/9/32):

The Standing Committee desire to draw the attention of members to the following:—

Since the Free State came into existence, the political activities of the Alliance here in furtherance of its fundamental object have necessarily been suspended. Its Constitution can only be altered by the General Council. The difficulties that have existed in the way of holding a representative meeting will easily be appreciated

In the interval that has elapsed, the Standing Committee have applied themselves to trying to relieve cases of acute distress among members and other loyalists, suffered in consequence of loyalty to the Crown. With this object they formed themselves into an Advisory Committee, and in a large number of cases bordering on destitution have obtained and administered grants in money, food, and clothing. In other cases they have assisted claimants, who were unaware of the procedure, to obtain advances from the Irish Grants Committee in London on foot of their claims or decrees under the Compensation Act. Further, they have procured and administered relief in a very large number of cases of destitution amongst British ex-service men.

The Standing Committee feel that it is essential that an organisation such as this should be maintained so as to act in the interests of loyalists as occasion arises. The figures on the appended page indicate the extent of the relief work carried on during the last two years.

They suggest that it would be helpful to them if members were to keep in closer touch with the Alliance by calling more frequently at the offices or by writing.

Chapter X

Ulster unionists and partition 1914-23

Their organisation in Ulster and their campaigning in British politics had assured Ulster unionists of special provision in the event of a parliament being established in Dublin. This had been the theme of various compromise conversations in 1913–14 and at the Buckingham Palace conference of July 1914, which failed to reach agreement 'either in principle or detail'. That the liberal government recognised Ulster unionists' claims was indicated not only by attempts in July 1914 to pass a bill amending the home rule bill, but also by later declarations. When in September 1914, despite unionist opposition, the government put the third home rule bill on the statute book under the provisions of the parliament act, two reservations were made. The operation of the act was suspended until after the war and an amending bill was promised which would make special provision for Ulster.

After 1914, therefore, Ulster unionists were presented with two problems. First, the form of the special provision had to be determined. This had two aspects: the nature of the provision—whether safeguards within an all-Ireland parliament, exclusion with a northern parliament, or exclusion with direct rule from Westminster; and the area of Ulster to come under this special provision. As to the nature of special treatment Ulster unionists had little influence: they could refuse to accept safeguards in an all-Ireland parliament, but the type of exclusion depended upon the attitude of the British government and parliament. Over the area to be excluded they might have had more influence. It was a difficult problem, because the protestant population of Ulster was concentrated in certain counties. Apart from the borough of Belfast, only the counties of Antrim (79.5% protestant), Armagh (54.7%), Down (68.4%), and Londonderry—including the city (54.2%) had protestant majorities. In Fermanagh the protestants comprised 43.8% of the population; and in

Tyrone 44.6%. In the remaining three counties of Cavan, Donegal and Monaghan, the protestant percentage was 18.5, 21.1 and 25.3 respectively. These differences, reflected in parliamentary representation, had been the subject of fruitless discussion at the Buckingham Palace conference. They might, for instance, have justified a four-counties split; though when exclusion was discussed it was usually in terms of six or nine counties. The latter was emotionally satisfying, but the former was a viable area with a substantial unionist majority.

The second large problem facing Ulster unionists was to maintain their right to special provision and to defend the form of special provision which from their own point of view was reasonable. At one time it had seemed possible that the war would dissolve old party divisions in Ireland. But it did not, and Ulster unionists had to resist pressure, armed and otherwise, from the nationalists, who regarded Ireland as a seamless garment, and moral pressure from southern unionists and the British government. They also had to meet criticisms from within—from three-counties unionists and from 'labour democrats' and their sympathisers.

The object of this chapter is to show how the documents in the N.I.P.R.O. can be used to study some of these problems and Ulster unionism's responses to them. It was these problems and responses that resulted in the exclusion of six Ulster counties from the jurisdiction of any Dublin parliament and in the establishment in 1921 of the present government of Northern Ireland.

II

Despite an initial temptation to use the outbreak of the first world war and the need for recruits as a bargaining-counter to secure their position, Ulster unionists fully supported Great Britain in the war effort. They provided troops, most notably the 36th (Ulster) Division, formed from the U.V.F. In October 1915 the division crossed to France and later distinguished itself with heavy losses at the battle of the Somme, 1 July 1916. Those remaining at home helped in recruiting, like William Copeland Trimble, proprietor and editor of the Fermanagh *Impartial Reporter*. He however resigned his command of the volunteer Enniskillen Horse as a protest against not receiving a (promised) honorary commission for his part in raising the Inniskilling Dragoons and in recruiting infantrymen in the early days of the war. In Belfast they assisted in munitions work; and in general they avoided politics and controversy.

Despite the hopes of optimists who saw in a war effort supported by both Redmond and Carson the prospect of future harmony between nationalists and unionists, Ulster unionists' contribution to the war only enhanced their expectations of special provision. For instance, after the Easter rising, during which some of the U.V.F. had been mobilised to release crown forces for duty elsewhere in Ireland, the government wanted to disarm all civilians. It could hardly enforce the regulation in the south of Ireland while leaving the Ulstermen armed, but it was plainly told that an attempt to seize arms in Ulster would be resented and resisted. An amicable arrangement was therefore made: rifles were to be concentrated in stores under military protection, 'chiefly in Belfast and Londonderry, and receipts issued stating that they were being held in trust for their owners'.

213 Copy letter from Major H. Singleton, of the Ulster Division's field headquarters, to General C. H. Powell, The Lower House, Wickham, Hampshire, July 1916, describing the division's gallantry at the battle of the Somme—the words underlined were marked 'omit' either at the time by the censor or later by the U.U.C., who published the letter (D 1327/3/21):

Anniversary of the Battle of the Boyne—surely it should be a good omen for the boys of Ulster—this being the day for which we have been longing for the past two years nearly—

We were all astir early, as may be well imagined, having tried to get some sleep, which was difficult owing to the incessant cannonade all night, intermingled with the excitement at what was going to take place on the morrow.

All the fighting Troops were got up during the night into the Assembly Trenches, crowded & packed like Herrings in a Barrel.

The months of preparation—ration dumps; ordnance dumps; R[oyal]. E[ngineers']. stores; heavy Railways; Light Railways; Trench Tramways; water supply; Artillery—heavy & light; amm[uni]t[io]n &c; were all completed, & nothing more could be done but to await the fortune of war which was not in our hands. We knew that we had a difficult task ahead, as the French had already tried to take the German Lines opposite us, when they held this portion of our Line at a former period.

Our men were never fitter & were like Blood Hounds straining at the leash to be set free.

The day broke—a lovely day—but very hazy & misty. At 6.30 a.m. our guns opened an intense Bombardment which lasted for one hour. The "Barrage" then lifted, & the hour for the Ulstermen had arrived.

The task allotted to us was to take the German trenches A.B.C.D. Lines.

Feverishly we all waited at the Telephones to hear results. The roar of guns & machine guns was truly awful: how anything could live under it was to all of us a miracle.

Soon the Bell of the Telephone rang to say we had occupied A. Line; shortly afterwards B. Line; again a short period elapsed, & we heard C. Line was taken.

We then heard that some of our lads had got into D. line. A period of Telephonic silence then asserted itself. Presently cries of help came through the Telephone; we had been obliged to abandon D. Line, & information was rec[eive]d that our Boys in the C. Line were being severely punished from their left front from a Redoubt on high ground; and, from their right-rear, from a village, which apparently had not been taken from the enemy.

The Redoubt was the objective of the Division on our Left, & the above mentioned village was part of the Attack of the Division on our Right. We rang up these two Divisions, and found, to our horror, that the Division on our Left had not even got German Line A. trenches, while the Division on our Right had not taken the village in question.

There we were isolated, having performed our allotted task at tremendous loss & sacrifice, but unsupported on both Flanks. What was to be done? We made the best of our time: we took 540 German prisoners, & then tried to Consolidate what we had taken, praying that, sooner or later, the other Divisions would push through & so straighten the Line. However, it was a case of hoping against hope, &, as no help was forth coming, we had to fall back on B. Line, where we were still practically isolated.

The Germans put a very heavy Artillery Barrage on our Trenches, so that Communication with our men was hopeless. All telephone Lines were cut by shrapnel, and any Runners who tried to run across the open (and many brave lads attempted it) we instantly cut down by machine-gun fire. On our left two of our Companies got right through thinking they were being helped on their Left Flank, & have not been heard of since, BUT, we hear there was no surrender—it was the Anniversary of the Battle of the Boyne.

Night soon began to fall, & all we heard was that we still had some men hanging on to A. & B. Lines, but that they were more or less isolated, the trenches full of dead, dying, & wounded, & the fire on them was terrific They stuck to these Trenches all through the night; &, the following night of July 2, were relieved. Thank goodness we still hold A. Line, & so our effort was not for absolutely nothing. BUT, our casualties for so little appear indeed terrible.

To go into deeds of gallantry would be impossible: every man that went over the Parapet was a Hero, & as I heard one Brigadier remark: he looked upon them as Gods. The carnage was terrible, & some Companies that went over the Parapet 180 strong returned about 20.

I have served with Regulars, Volunteers, Colonials, but never in my life have I ever seen such deeds of heroism & gallantry as those displayed by Ulstermen. They may be equalled, but cannot be surpassed.

And now, the Ulster Division has practically ceased to exist; at any rate for the time being. We are withdrawn into Reserve to re-organise & recoup. Doubtless we shall fill up from Englishmen & others, but we still have a smattering to go on with, and, although most of the Ulstermen are now no more, still, the spirit of the Ulster Division must continue, and doubtless we have glorious times for us in the future—La Division est mort, vive la Division.

One mustn't imagine that, because we got badly knocked here that the whole offensive is being badly treated elsewhere. On the Contrary we hear good reports from the South. It was our luck & we must make the best of it.

(sd) H. Singleton
Major
H.L.I.

Casualties......Officers—222
Other ranks—5,300.

214 Letter from W. C. Trimble, Century House, Enniskillen, Co. Fermanagh, to Sir Edward Carson, 20 January 1915, complaining of lack of recognition for his work in recruiting (D 1507/1/ 1915/4):

Dear Sir Edward—It is extremely kind of you to go to so much trouble in a matter that belongs to the Ulster Division and not your own department, as conveyed by your kind letter.

The matter is simple. Major Craig telegraphed to me to call at head-quarters. I went, & then & there I was asked to raise a squadron of Horse for the Ulster Division, & Brig. General Hickman promised military rank. I said I would do it.

His Grace of Abercorn (whom we all admire) had been here twice or three times to obtain recruits for the North Irish Horse, & had not got one recruit: I raised the full squadron of the Inniskilling Dragoons, (6th service squadron,) which with the approval of head-quarters I so named.

I expected that the military rank would have come to me within a few days to ease my path & facilitate the work, but, as it did not come I was in a unique position, of being while a layman in sole command of the barracks, & administrator of & commander of the squadron. And while officers at head-quarters very properly had their rank & pay, I received neither one nor other for my weeks of work & energy.

I am satisfied that Brigadier-General Hickman would have conferred a lieutenant-colonelcy (honorary) on me if the power had remained with him. When General Powell came to inspect the Dragoons he told me that I was well known at head-quarters, & also at the War Office. I replied to these kind things by saying that I was too small a man for that: & the General replied—"The War Office know you well, for they spoke to me about you." He then asked me to assist recruiting for the infantry, which, of course, I promised to do,—saying that I had sent many men to the infantry & would continue to do so. I may mention that my newspaper gave me unusual influence in this direction, so that it extended far beyond the bounds of the Dragoon squadron.

Personally, I do not trouble about military rank, although since I wrote the Historical Records of the Inniskillings in 1874 I have been closely identified with military life & movements. But when a Nationalist is made a Captain for bringing 52 men to the Irish Brigade at Fermoy, my own men of the Volunteer Enniskillen Horse feel hurt at their commander being ignored, & as one of them said—"If you were the 33rd cousin of a lord, sir, you would have been appointed long ago." And another said—"If our own people treat you that way, what may we expect?"

I did not ask any compliment: but when it was promised it should have been carried out or let me know the reason why: & because there was a distinct reflection upon me—& that that reacted on my men of the Enniskillen Horse—I thought it well to take the step I mentioned to you in my letter—though not in any degree weakening my attachment to yourself or cause.

I now note what you are so good as to say, and we can wait to see if the slur be removed from me. Assuring you of my personal devotion, Vy sincerely yours,

W. Copeland Trimble.

215 Copy letter from Sir Crawford McCullagh, lord mayor of Belfast, writing from the City Hall, Belfast, to H. H. Asquith, prime minister, 8 May 1916, to protest against a suggested arms proclamation (D 1507/1/1916/17):

Sir—I have just learned that a suggestion has been made that a Proclamation should be issued directing that all Arms in Ireland should forthwith be delivered up to the Crown and as I am satisfied an attempt to enforce such a Proclamation would be fraught with great risk to the peace I have deemed it my duty as Lord Mayor of the City and responsible to a very large extent for its peace to intimate my views to you.

I have occupied the position of Lord Mayor for over 2 years. I have also occupied the position of Hon. Director for Recruiting in Ulster and in both capacities I have come into contact with not only Belfast but Ulster opinion.

Since the beginning of the war Belfast and Ulster have practically ceased their political and religious wrangles and their energies have been devoted to the production of Munitions and at the same time Belfast and the district have contributed towards the fighting forces of the Empire in round figures about 60,000 men.

There are undoubtedly Arms in this district but outside the Arms which would be covered by the Proclamation already in force with regard to the Sinn Feiners I am satisfied there are no Arms held by anyone with any disloyal motive. If an order is made now to have all Arms delivered up, I fear an attempt to enforce it would very possibly lead to disturbance as it would be looked upon by the population that they were being punished for the offence of the Sinn Feiners with whom they have had no connection and which movement has had their strongest disapproval.

Throughout the excitement of the past few weeks Ulster has retained its normal condition and has been able in many other ways to assist and relieve both Military and Police for the establishment of peace in the disaffected areas in other parts of the Country. Anything that would disturb the feeling of confidence and rest that now exists will be very dangerous not only so far as the peace of the district is concerned but also so far as the supply of munitions is concerned. To show the interest which the population here has taken in the latter work I may say that although the recent disturbances took place during the Easter holidays the return of labour after the holidays in the Belfast Shipyards and Engineering Works never was so good as at the present time. The people here are intensely loyal and I would deplore very much anything that would cause a revival of either religious or political animosity at the present time, as I am satisfied action such as suggested would do.

So far as the safety and peace of the country are concerned, there is no necessity for anything of the kind and I sincerely trust that in the steps taken to put down the rebellion nothing will be done which would interfere with or reflect in any way upon the loyalty of those who stand for the King and Constitution.

I have felt so uneasy since I heard the rumour referred to, as to what the effect of it would be, that I have deemed it my duty to confer with the principal people in this district dealing with the working-class population and the views which I have expressed above are their views also. They further express the view, in which I agree, that this is not a matter in which the people would be willing to follow the view of any political leader. I am not, however, writing from the political aspect at all; I am only writing from the point of view of the peace of the City and the district and I feel satisfied that that peace and willingness to serve the Empire which now exist will not be helped forward by any interference with the peaceable and law-abiding subjects such as is rumoured. I have the honour to remain, Your obedient servant,

(Signed) CRAWFORD McCULLAGH,

LORD MAYOR.

III

Their contribution to the war effort did nothing to diminish Ulster unionists' determination not to submit to a Dublin parliament. They, therefore, had to face the first problem—what form special provision for them should take. The answer to the problem—a six-counties parliament plus representation at Westminster—came in two stages.

In June 1916 the U.U.C. for the first time accepted the principle of the exclusion of six counties. In unusual circumstances the council decided that, if the union could not be maintained intact, then at least part of Ulster should be exempt from Dublin rule. Ulster unionists had expected firm action after the Easter rising; instead it caused the liberal section of the coalition government to take conciliatory action. Lloyd George, exceeding the brief the cabinet had given him, tried to effect a settlement of the Irish question on the basis of the immediate implementation of the 1914 act plus the exclusion of the six north-east counties of Ulster. Arguing that a settlement was necessary to further the war effort by conciliating opinion in America, he misled Carson into thinking that the cabinet, unionists and liberals alike, supported this offer. On 6 June Carson laid the proposals before the U.U.C. which on 12 June, acting on his advice, unanimously decided to accept them as a basis for discussion. While doubting the validity of some of Lloyd George's arguments, Ulster unionists felt that to refuse the six-counties offer would alienate British sympathy, and accordingly those in the three counties of Cavan, Donegal and Monaghan waived their claims under the covenant. 'Men not prone to emotion shed tears' on the occasion. Largely because of nationalist dissatisfaction these proposals were abandoned and the three counties were not called upon to make their sacrifice until 1920.

Then the second crucial decision was taken. By the government of Ireland bill, formally introduced into the house of commons on 25 February 1920, the government proposed to set up two Irish parliaments, one for the six counties of northeast Ulster, another for the other twenty-six, both elected by proportional representation. The decision of the British cabinet to exclude six counties rather than nine had been arrived at only at the last moment, after prolonged discussion and after consultation with Ulster unionist leaders who had advised a six-counties split. It was, therefore, possible for Ulster unionists to have the decision modified; at least there was room for discussion. On 10 March 1920 the U.U.C. met to decide its attitude towards the bill, but, egged on by Thomas Moles, M.P. for the Ormeau division of Belfast, it decided to accept the government's offer of a six-counties parliament. The six counties with 52 seats would contain a safe unionist majority of 10 or 12; whereas the situation in nine counties with 64 seats would be precarious. Estimates varied: proponents of the six counties thought that at best the nine counties would yield a unionist majority of two; though one estimate suggested that owing to the growth of the socialist vote in and around Belfast it was possible that unionists would be in a minority of two.

In 1916 and in 1920 the business community—concerned to get down to the details of a settlement—accepted the principle of partition on a six-counties basis more readily than the gentry. The Ulster solemn league and covenant posed a particular problem, but when it was considered it was neatly circumvented by the arguments that the pledge was anachronistic or that the six-counties decision kept the covenant. It was argued that a strong unionist area or government in the north with a catholic minority would be adequate guarantee for the just treatment of protestants in the south. It is perhaps ironic that in 1920 Ulster unionists had themselves to accept a form of home rule, but they felt they had no alternative. In view of changes in British opinion, absorbed first in the war and then in the problems of post-war reconstruction, they thought the six-counties solution was the most they would get by fighting the 1914 act due to come into operation as soon as the last peace treaty was signed. As Carson told the Ulster Unionist Labour Association, 'It is all very well to say "Why don't you go on fighting as you did before?" What were they to fight for? Could they fight for more than the freeing of Ulster from a home rule parliament in Dublin? If the bill passed they had won, and won without fighting'.

216 Letter from A. Duffin, 9 Waring Street, Belfast, to his daughter, Dorothy, in London, 25 April 1916, giving his first reactions to news of the outbreak of the Easter rising—some words have been erased or censored (Mic 127/17):

Dearest Dorothy—We are having a little rebellion here just by way of a change. You may have seen or perhaps heard in the Admiralty that we have sunk a German Auxiliary Cruiser off the West Irish coast carrying arms and Sir Roger Casement, but you probably have not heard as it is not published here yet that the Irish Volunteers (Sinn Fein) have risen in their might in Dublin [and] have taken the G.P.O. [*words erased*] are entrenched in Stephens Green. Rumour says they have sacked the Bank of Ireland but that is not confirmed. The L[or]d. L[ieutenan]t. was to have been here at 6 oc[lock] yesterday but did not arrive and it turned out [*words erased*] the wires all cut. A wireless got through via Larne and gave the news.

Troops went up from here last night and more are coming from [*word erased*].

I hear they have commandeered all the Motor Cars coming back from Fairyhouse races and detained the owners as hostages! I hope they have got hold of Birrell.

Isn't it all like a comic opera founded on the Wolf [*sic*] Tone fiasco a hundred years ago?

I am only afraid of [*words erased*] and isolated Protestants in out of the way places being murdered. Otherwise it is good business its having come to a head, & I hope we shall deal thoroughly with these pests. Yours

A. Duffin

217 Resolution passed unanimously by the U.U.C., 12 June 1916, accepting six-counties partition as the basis for discussion with the nationalists and the government (D 627/435):

"We, the delegates constituting the Ulster Unionist Council, representative of the Unionist population of the Province of Ulster, have considered the proposals laid before us for an adjustment of the Home Rule question on the basis of the definite exclusion from the Government of Ireland Act, 1914, of the six counties of Ulster, in view of the critical situation of the Empire arising out of the European war, declare as follows:

"That, as Unionists, proud of our citizenship in the United Kingdom, we reaffirm our unabated abhorrence of the policy of Home Rule, which we believe to be dangerous to the security of the Empire, subversive of the best interests alike of Ireland and of the United Kingdom; and we decline to take any responsibility for setting up such a form of Government in any part of Ireland.

"As, however, the Cabinet—which is responsible for the Government of the country—is of opinion that it will tend to strengthen the Empire and to win the war in which it is now engaged, if all questions connected with Home Rule are settled now, instead of—as originally agreed—at the termination of the war; and as these suggestions by the Government put before us by Sir Edward Carson have been made with that view; we feel, as loyal citizens, that, in this crisis of the Empire's history, it is our duty to make sacrifices, and we consequently authorise Sir Edward Carson to continue the negotiations on the basis of the suggestion explained to this meeting, and to complete them if the details are arranged to his satisfaction.

"We further desire to make it clear that if, from any cause the negotiations referred to prove abortive, we reserve to ourselves complete freedom of action in the future, in opposition to the policy of Home Rule for Ireland."

218

*H. de F. Montgomery's explanation and defence of the U.U.C.'s decision to accept partition, contained **(a)** in a letter to M. F. Headlam, treasury remembrancer and deputy paymaster for Ireland, 19 June 1916: and **(b)** in the postscript to a letter to his son, C. H. Montgomery of the foreign office, 22 June 1916 (D 627/429):

(a)

There is a good demand for houses in Fivemiletown, but I do not think George Armstrong could find a good tenant for the present police barracks who would pay him more than £31 a year. It is not a favourite part of the town.

On the face of it the present Government Policy about this country seems absolute lunacy; but statements were made in private to the Ulster Unionist Council which persuaded us that it was expedient to accept Lloyd George's proposals under protest. I do not like what we did a bit, but it still seems to me the only thing we could do under the very extraordinary circumstances. Bonar Law, Walter Long, etc. seem to be "Asquixiated." Carson seems to have kept his head better than any other of our leaders, so all we can do is to take his advice and hope for the best.

I am going to Dublin to-day for a couple of nights, and may perhaps see you. Yours very truly,

(b)

P.S. What puzzles me most about this Lloyd George Irish Settlement business is that <u>you</u> should apparently be quite ignorant of the alleged cause of the whole thing, which must be a F[oreign]. O[ffice]. matter, and though you are on a particular job, it seems to me that the nature of that job would require you to be informed of a critical matter of this kind, although the original despatch or whatever it was did not pass through your hands. I do not think either Carson or Craig or the other Irish Unionist members would have taken Lloyd George's word without corroboration for the exceedingly alarming nature of the complication which induced the Cabinet (as C[arson] & C[raig] were given to believe) unanimously to resolve to give Redmond Home Rule at once, and ask Lloyd George to arrange for it being done peaceably as regards Ulster From the way in which both Craig and Carson put the matter to us at Belfast I am convinced that they were convinced that the Cabinet were unanimously resolved to do this and that the American and Colonial complications were of a sufficiently serious nature to account for (though not to excuse or justify) such a very unfortunate decision. From what I have heard since, I think it is probable that they obtained their information in corroboration of what Lloyd George told them from Bonar Law, as I saw a man yesterday who saw Bonar Law last week, and said he appeared to be absolutely helpless.

Under these circumstances I do not find any difficulty in understanding why Carson came to the conclusion that it would be bad tactics to simply oppose the introduction of a measure of Home Rule at the present time.

I think I gave you in a letter I wrote to you on the 9th the main details of the situation as it was put before us in Belfast. It took Carson an hour and a half to explain the situation at the private meeting of the Unionist Council, and I cannot pretend to tell you all he told us; but the main point was this— The Cabinet having unanimously decided that under the pressure of difficulties with America, the Colonies and Parliament (but chiefly with America) they must offer Redmond Home Rule at once; and (not being prepared to coerce Ulster) having authorised Lloyd George to arrange a settlement, Carson, after what had happened at the Buckingham Palace Conference in 1914, could not well refuse to submit to his followers the exclusion of six counties as a basis of negotiation. Carson had satisfied himself apparently that he had lost all the ground he and his colleagues had gained in their anti-Home Rule campaign before the war, and that the majority of the Unionist members and voters took the same view as the majority of the unionist papers as to the necessity of a settlement. If Ulster Unionists refused to consider such a settlement the Nationalists and radicals would hold them up to odium as the people who were preventing a settlement of the Irish question, and they could not hope for any sympathy or support in Great Britain now or hereafter. The Home Rule Act was on the Statute Book and now that the Unionist leaders in the Coalition Government had become parties to a proposal to bring it into immediate operation in 26 counties there was no hope of removing it from the Statute Book at the end of the war. If we did not agree to a settlement we should have the Home Rule Act coming into operation without the exclusion of any part of Ulster, or subject only to some worthless Amending Act which Asquith might bring in in fulfilment of his pledge, and we should either have to submit to this or fight. To begin fighting here at the end of the great war would be hopeless and we could not hope for any support. If, in spite of our apparent weakness we succeeded in our fight we could not possibly hope to get more than we were now offered without fighting, viz. the exclusion of six counties, we should probably get less: We should be in a better position to hold our own and help our friends with only six counties excluded returning 16 Unionists and 9 Nationalists than we should be with 9 counties excluded returning 17 Nationalists and 16 Unionists. We should be in a better position to help Unionists in any part of Ireland if we are excluded than if we formed portion of a permanent minority in a Dublin Parliament: therefore on the whole Carson was justified in coming to us and recommending us to authorise him to enter upon negotiations on the bases [sic] of the exclusion of six counties, and the chief reasons for recommending us to agree to this were:—(1) that if we did not agree to do this we should lose any remaining sympathy we had in Great Britain as the people who had prevented Ireland being pacified. (2) That if we did not take this offer we should never get as good a one again. (3) that the Cabinet having unanimously made up their minds to give some form of Home Rule at once we could not prevent it; of course if the Home Rulers themselves refused the offer that is a different pair of shoes.

It appears now, however, that Lloyd George told a great many lies, and that some of the Unionist members of the Cabinet were not parties to the decision which was the basis of all this negotiating. I conjecture that Walter Long and Lansdown [sic] were both rather ill at the time and did not fully take the thing in, and that Bonar Law was, as my friend says he found him, last week, helpless in face of Colonial opinion in favour of Home Rule; but if Redmond's Convention refuses to accept the terms in spite of his having interpreted them in a different sense to that conveyed to Carson by Lloyd George, of course, the thing must fall to the ground, and then the Nationalists, and not the Unionists will bear the blame for preventing the settlement. The only danger is, that Lloyd George should come back to us and say the Nationalists wont accept the six county basis you must sacrifice something more for the sake of the Empire and agree to a four county basis or to no exclusion. Carson will, I am confident, refuse to put any such proposal before the Unionist Council. It was quite clearly understood that the six counties was the minimum. The Nationalists will then try after all to say that we were the people that prevented Ireland being pacified; but I do not think they would succeed, as all the papers have put on record their view of the reasonableness or [sic] our decision.

Carson holds a letter from Lloyd George stating that the proposed Amendment of the Government of Ireland Act is to be a definitive one and not an Emergency Measure for the duration of the war; but of course if the Nationalists refuse to approve of the whole thing to-morrow even as presented to them by Redmond that question will not arise. The Ulster Unionists will be more or less on velvet when the matter comes to be finally settled.

The machine is evidently being worked for all it is worth to secure a decision at today's Nationalist Convention in favour of agreeing to the Lloyd George Settlement; but it seems to me that if Redmond accomplishes this his difficulties will be only beginning. I was in Dublin for two or three days last week, and the Southerners I met are all convinced that there will be another Rebellion whether the Lloyd George terms are accepted or not. The fact that these terms were suggested has enormously strengthened the Sinn Feiners in the country. The mischief has been done by the suggestion. The acceptance of the suggestion by the Ulster Unionists has not had much effect on this part of the question. The Unionists acceptance under protest had only increased Redmond's difficulties, and as we are given to believe placed us in the position in the eyes of British public opinion of being very reasonable people. If Redmond actually forms a Government and tries to rule this country the Rebellion will be directed against him; if he does not the Rebellion will be directed against the existing Government: in any case the country will have to be more or less reconquered outside the six counties, and that may possibly be the best way out of all our troubles, which all have their root in a British Prime Minister having brought in a Home Rule Bill. The only actual serious harm done by the action taken by the Ulster Unionists on Carson's advice is the creation of bad feeling towards us among those who think we have abandoned them on [*sic*] order to secure the privileged position for ourselves. I don't think this charge is justified; but it is difficult to get it out of the heads of our Southern friends.

I have just seen the "Morning Post," and think the remark with which they begin their leader is not very far astray.

"To set our Government against the German Government is rather like putting a doe rabbit to fight a tom cat."

219 Letter from A. McDowell, solicitor, 51 Royal Avenue, Belfast, to Sir Edward Carson, 20 July 1916, describing the attitude of the business community to six-counties partition with particular reference to the question of control of railways (D 1507/1/8/1):

Dear Sir Edward—There has been a good deal of underhand dirty work going on here for a very considerable time past in the shape of attempts being made by "Unionists outside our district to create a feeling that would be prejudicial to the arrangement for the exclusion of the six Counties. I am glad to say, however, that the efforts have not been successful and I think the business people and our working people are more satisfied with the arrangement now after all the discussion that has taken place than they were when the matter was originally put before them. Amongst the Business community they have commenced to appreciate thoroughly the advantages to be gained from getting an arrangement now such as is proposed and they foresee pretty clearly the risks connected with a postponement to the termination of the war. Evidently what has happened vindicates thoroughly the course which you adopted and the advice which you gave and the underhand work which has been going on has to a very great extent removed the sympathy that formerly existed. Major Saunderson's action is reprobated, while that of the Monaghan people is adored and your treatment of the matter as appearing in the Press is as usual diplomatic and able.

There has been a good deal of talk recently emanating principally from the South of retaliation on the part of the Southerners against the North for consenting to the exclusion and this takes the shape of something in the nature of a boycott through the Great Northern Railway.

About two-fifths of that Co's line would be outside the excluded area, the three-fifths which is within the excluded district is the more important but the idea is that if the Dublin Parliament is to have the control of the Railways within their district they could by legislation so block and obstruct operations on the Great Northern Line as to bring about what would practically be tantamount to a blockade of the North.

There have been several private meetings of leading business men in relation to this matter and in the end I was asked to go across and see you with the view of putting the position before you to see if anything could be done in connection with the proposed Bill that would obviate any risk of the adoption of such a procedure. I do not know what is intended with regard to the Railways in Ireland generally. I have gathered from the Newspapers that so far as the Harbours are concerned they are to remain under Imperial control but the Harbours remaining under Imperial control will be of very little service if the Railways are not also kept under Imperial control for a Harbour without a Railway is practically of no service beyond shelter in bad weather. At the present all the Railways in Ireland are subject to the Board of Trade but the arrangement with regard to the Telegraph service is in Ireland different from what it is in England. In Ireland the Postmaster owns all the wires and posts along the railway and the Railway Coys. give him wayleave getting in exchange a free telegraph service and that would be one very good reason for the Imperial Government keeping the control at present of the railways as well as the Harbours. If an Irish Government got control of the railways and anything took place like what happened at Easter it is all very well to say under the Defence of the Realm Act the Government could take possession of the railways but the railways without those to work them would be of very little service and I think there can be no doubt if the Irish Government have control of the railways it will only be a question of time and that a very short one before all the servants on the railways would be practically nominees of one party. Of course if the Railways are excepted from the jurisdiction of the Irish Parliament and kept as they are subject to the Board of Trade the question of a boycott or retaliation from the south is out of the question.

I wired you this morning to know if you could have seen me to-morrow or Saturday and it was to talk this matter over with you I wanted to see you but I got your wire that you would be out of town. I will be in London on Tuesday and if it would be convenient for you to see me then I would arrange to call on you at any time you appointed. Yours truly,

Alex McDowell

220

Leaflet, *Why I voted for the six counties,* printed and circulated in April 1920 by Lt-colonel F. H. Crawford (D 1700/5/16):

WHAT WAS MY OBJECT IN SIGNING THE COVENANT?

To prevent Ulster by every means in my power from being placed under a Dublin Parliament, and to "stand by one another" for this purpose only.

Ulster's Solemn League and Covenant.

BEING convinced in our consciences that Home Rule would be disastrous to the material **well-being of Ulster, as well as of the whole of Ireland,**[1] subversive of our civil and religious freedom, destructive of our citizenship and perilous to the unity of the Empire,

WE, whose names are underwritten, men of Ulster, loyal subjects of His Gracious Majesty King George V., humbly relying on the God whom our fathers in days of stress and trial confidently trusted,

DO hereby pledge ourselves in solemn Covenant throughout **this our time of threatened calamity**[2] **to stand by one another in defending**[3] for ourselves and our children our cherished position of equal citizenship in the United Kingdom and in using all means which may be found necessary to defeat the **present conspiracy**[4] to set up a Home Rule Parliament in Ireland.

AND in the event of **such a Parliament**[5] being forced upon us we further solemnly and mutually pledge ourselves to refuse to recognise its authority. IN sure confidence that God will defend the right we hereto subscribe our names.

AND further, we individually declare that we have not already signed this Covenant.

1. **"Ulster and the whole of Ireland."** We had to recede from "whole of Ireland" and stick to Ulster only, sometime previous to this or we should have lost all.

2. **"This our time of threatened calamity."** Bill of 1912 and 1914 is referred to. Nothing to do with the present Bill before Parliament.

3. **"Stand by one another in defending"** Ulster from a Home Rule Parliament, by keeping a strong Protestant Ulster that will insure a lasting Protestant majority.

4. **"Present conspiracy"** meaning the Bill of 1912 and Act of 1914. At the time the wording of the Covenant was passed some of our friends had the word "never" in the body of it. At the request of some of those who were in the outlying districts of Ulster (three counties) as well as some local members the text was changed from "never" to "present conspiracy," as it was felt it would be a mistake to pledge ourselves indefinitely as times change and at some future date it might hamper free action. It was thought best to face each crisis as it occurred. On the Committee that passed the final wording of the Covenant, it was distinctly understood at the time that it was the 1912 Bill that the Covenant referred to.

5. **"Such a Parliament"** refers to the 1912 and 1914 Bill and Act in which Ulster was not recognised in any way, but it was proposed to put her under a Dublin Parliament. In the Bill at present before Parliament, Ulster for the first time is officially recognised as an entity and is offered different treatment.

A solid Protestant Ulster will be a prop in Ireland to the Empire without which the whole Naval strength of England would be jeopardized. A Protestant and Loyal Ulster would be an invaluable jumping-off point for the British Navy and Army if it were found necessary to use them in case of serious trouble in Ireland or elsewhere. This is sufficient justification for supporting the six county policy. The Empire should count for something.

It is Ulster's duty, on this score alone, to see that whatever is left of Ulster must be dominantly Protestant, for the safety of the Empire, even though one county only remained.

I consider that by voting for the six counties I have kept my Covenant both in spirit and in letter. My one object in signing the Covenant was to keep Ulster Protestant, and free from any possibility of becoming a part of a Home Rule Ireland with one Parliament in Dublin.

If I had voted for the nine counties I would have been going against both the spirit and letter of the Covenant.

Take for example, a ship that has struck a rock and is sinking. The last lifeboat is pushing off with men and women and children. It is so dangerously full that there is no more room. Several people on the wreck jump over-board, swim for the lifeboat and try to scramble into it, with the result that it begins to sink. If they get into the boat they will go down just as surely as if they had stayed on the wreck, and they will have drowned the lifeboat load of passengers who would otherwise have had their lives saved.

Surely this is not what our Unionist brethren in the three counties wish to do in Ulster. I do not believe that if they carefully consider the matter that they will wish to drag down the six counties.

Take another illustration. Three men are walking on a pier. None of them can swim. One falls into the sea and is being carried away. The remaining two can either jump in and drown with their friend or they can throw him a rope. Standing on the pier they can make a good effort to save their drowning friend. Jumping in all three will be drowned.

For the six counties to jump into an Irish Parliament in Dublin and drown in it with the other three may look heroic, but it would be disastrous to all nine of the counties.

If, however, six strong Unionist Protestant counties hold together on the firm pier of a Protestant Ulster Parliament they will be able to help their brother Unionists in the three counties when these need assistance far better than if all nine were in a hopeless minority in an Irish Parliament, as they undoubtedly would be.

There are 890,880 Protestants in the whole of the nine counties of Ulster. There are 70,510 Protestants and 260,655 Roman Catholics in the three counties. I cannot believe the Protestants in the three counties are willing to swamp 820,370 Protestants merely for the satisfaction of knowing they are all going down to disaster in the same boat.

IV

Having resolved one problem, Ulster unionists were faced with the second problem of maintaining their right to special provision and defending the six-counties decision in face of a number of pressures and influences. This involved a series of difficulties which required almost constant attention.

The first difficulty was defending the six-counties decision in Ulster itself. On both occasions, in 1916 and 1920, the decision, which could be regarded as a breach of the covenant, aroused criticism. In 1920 especially there was an organised and determined protest on the part of Ulster unionists who believed that if the union could not be maintained, at least the whole of Ulster should be excluded from the jurisdiction of the Dublin parliament. At the meeting on 10 March the 11th Baron Farnham put the case for maintaining the covenant and moved an amendment demanding a nine-counties parliament. It was rejected on a show of hands. Three-counties unionists and some six-counties men objected not only to this decision but also to the way it had been reached—without adequate discussion. They rejected all the arguments against the nine counties, especially the view that the parties would be too finely balanced; and they argued in favour of a nine-counties parliament not only on the grounds of the Ulster covenant, but also on the grounds that Ulster formed an economic, a geographical and a political entity and that too large a unionist majority in the north would be unwise.

Feeling betrayed and that the council had been rushed into a decision by a 'Belfast clique', three-counties unionists and some sympathisers resigned from the U.U.C.; but these resignations were not to become effective until after a determined effort had been made to have the 10 March decision reconsidered. They requisitioned a meeting of the U.U.C. Meantime some six-counties men such as H. de F. Montgomery and Sir James Stronge of Tynan Abbey, Tynan, Co. Armagh, grand master of the Orange Order, began to regret having voted with Farnham on the 10th. They therefore tried unsuccessfully to persuade the dissidents of the wisdom of the six-counties decision, by arguing that it was a tactical move to defeat the 1920 bill and not a breach of the covenant. The U.U.C. met as requisitioned on 27 May, but the resolution in favour of nine counties was heavily defeated.

221 Extracts from a pamphlet, *Ulster and home rule. No partition of Ulster,* being a statement issued in April 1920 by the U.U.C. delegates for Cavan, Donegal and Monaghan—the figures in square brackets indicate the differences between the three counties' estimate and the most pessimistic U.U.C. forecast of unionist representation in Ulster under proportional representation (D 627/435):

The FIRST occasion on which the value of the Covenant came to be tested was in 1916, when we were in the midst of the war, and when it was represented by the Government that for the sake of the Empire, and in order to ensure Victory it was necessary the Irish question should be settled and that the Nationalists were willing it should be settled on the basis of excluding six Counties. The Ulster Unionist Council considered the situation but no one then thought for a moment (serious as the crisis was) of violating the Covenant. All was made dependent on the attitude of the three Counties. We met in a room by ourselves and the Council sat awaiting our decision. Had we rejected the proposal that would have been an end of it. We decided, in view of the then alarming state of affairs when the existence of the Empire was at stake; that we would leave the decision in the hands of the representatives of the six Counties. Our determination was recognised as a patriotic act of self-sacrifice, and it was declared that should the matter not go through we should never again be called on to make such a sacrifice. The matter did not go through owing to the attitude of the Nationalists, and we returned to our former position. . . .

The facts about the three Counties were as clear when the Covenant was signed as they are to-day, and they have not altered. The position of Ulster as a whole remains the same. Why were we asked to come in and sign if, when the emergency comes, we are to be thrown over?

The SECOND occasion on which the test of the value of the Covenant arose was at the meeting of the Ulster Unionist Council on the 10th March, 1920, but what a change? Our consent was not considered then to be necessary. The delegates by a majority rejected a proposal that the Northern area should consist of nine Counties, and limited it to six as proposed in the Government Home Rule Bill regardless of our protests. This we bitterly resent, and yet there are excuses to be found.

1. The decision was rushed. Not only had the delegates insufficient time to consult their local associations, except in a few instances, but the meeting itself was hurried. Several delegates, both in the six and the three Counties, who desired to speak being refused a hearing.

2. The meeting was misled. It was represented that a Parliament for the nine Counties would have a Nationalist and Sinn Fein majority. Mr. Moles, M.P., had the hardihood to state that it would consist of 33 Nationalists and 31 Unionists. It was pointed out to him in vain that the population of Ulster was:—

Protestants 890,880
Roman Catholics 690,816

Leaving a Protestant Majority of 200,064

and that it was impossible a majority of 200,000 should not be able to return a majority of members.

It was further shown that at the last Election for the nine Counties, when the number of members to be elected was 38, the members returned were—

Unionists 23
Nationalists 15

Unionist Majority 8

and that Election was held on the PRESENT FRANCHISE.

413

It was further pointed out that the new Bill gives Ulster 64 Members and that if there had been 64 at last Election the numbers would have been—

Unionists	..	..	..	..	..	38
Nationalists	..	..	..	..	..	26

Giving a Unionist majority of	..	..	..	12

All was in vain. Mr. Moles persisted in his estimate but gave no reasons for it except that the result of the last Municipal Election in Belfast was not satisfactory to certain interests there. It was insinuated that the Unionist working men of Belfast could not be depended on as heretofore, and therefore we must be cast out. This is a libel on the Unionist Labour Voters in Belfast. To those who are acquainted with municipal affairs in Belfast it is not surprising that Labour should assert itself in Elections for the Corporation, but to infer from that fact that the sturdy working men of Belfast are not as staunch Unionists as ever they were is not only unjust but untrue. After all why should not Unionist labour be represented in the Belfast Corporation, and even in the Ulster Government, and why are we to be abandoned lest that should happen?

3. No poll of the Council was allowed to be taken, although a poll was claimed, but only a show of hands. If, as should have been done, the votes had been counted, it would have been seen that the majority was a comparatively small one, and we were thankful to see such a large number of the delegates from the Six Counties respect the Covenant they had signed, and are confident that they represent a large majority of the Unionists of Ulster.

4. One argument used was so childish that we hardly like to repeat it. It was said that the Covenant only applied "throughout this our time of threatened calamity" and was only to "defeat the present conspiracy to set up a Home Rule Parliament in Ireland" and that our present position is "a new calamity" and a "new conspiracy"! ! and yet the parties who used this argument pointed out that the Bill of 1914 (which the Covenant was entered into to oppose) was on the Statute Book and would come into force unless repealed.

We must, however, do the Council the justice to say that had they not been led to suppose that our inclusion would mean a Nationalist majority they would never have thrown us over, and we feel sure that had the members had time to reflect they would have felt that the decision they arrived at was the very thing the Covenant was intended to prevent. . . .

There is no reason why the historic Province of Ulster should be partitioned. The three Southern Provinces consist of 23 counties with a population of 2,808,523. The population of the nine counties is 1,581,696. If three counties are taken from Ulster the difference between the population of the two areas will still be more marked, viz.,

26 Counties	..	..	..	..	3,139,688
6 Counties	..	..	..	..	1,250,531

This latter is too small for a Parliament, and it is bound to become parochial with its 52 Members as compared with 128 for the Southern area. Are not nine counties a small enough area for a Northern Parliament? Anyone looking at the map will see what a ridiculous boundary six counties would present. Donegal cut off with its habours [*sic*] and rivers and no access to it except through the six counties. Cavan and Monaghan form a natural boundary to the South of Ulster, and Monaghan runs up to a point between Tyrone and Armagh into the very heart of the Province.

The Members returned at last Election on the present Franchise were as follows:—

For the Six Counties—

				Unionist	Nat. & Sinn Fein
Antrim County	..	..	..	4	0
Armagh	..	..	..	2	1
Down	..	..	..	4	1
Londonderry	..	..	..	2	0
Fermanagh	..	..	..	1	1
Tyrone	..	..	..	1	2
Belfast University	..	..	..	1	0
Belfast Borough	..	..	..	8	1
Londonderry do	..	..	..	0	1
				23	7

For the Three Counties—

Cavan	..	..	..	0	2
Donegal	..	..	..	0	4
Monaghan	..	..	..	0	2
				23	15

Under the new Bill there will be 52 Members for the six counties and 12 for the three.

If there had been this number at last Election and it had been conducted on P[roportional]. R[epresentational]. principles the numbers would have been as follows—

For the Six Counties—

			Unionist.	Nat. & Sinn Fein.
Antrim County	..	..	6 [5]	1 [2]
Armagh	..	..	2	2
Down	..	..	5	3
Londonderry, including City	..	3	2
Fermanagh & Tyrone united in Bill	..	4 [3]	4 [5]
Belfast Borough	..	..	12 [10]	4 [6]
do University	..	..	4 [2]	0 [2]
			36 [30]	16 [22]

Monaghan and Cavan, which we propose should be joined like				
Fermanagh and Tyrone	..	..	1 [0]	5 [6]
Donegal	..	..	1	5
			38 [31]	26 [33]

A majority of 12 in a Parliament of 64 is a good working majority and gives the minority a fair representation.

A majority of 20 in a Parliament of 52 is rather large. It would appear to be unwise that the Northern Parliament should have too great a Unionist majority, just as it is to be deplored that the Southern Parliament should have (and will have) too great a Nationalist majority, if it should contain any Unionists at all. The ideal position would be to have a fairly strong Nationalist minority in the North and a fairly strong Unionist minority in the South. If this ideal position cannot at present be effected in the South it can and should be in the North. . . .

An argument that has been used is that the three Counties contain a majority of Nationalists and Sinn Feiners. That is true. But so does Derry City, Fermanagh County, Tyrone County, South Armagh, South Down and the Falls Division of Belfast. Yet no one proposes to exclude them. The truth is that it is impossible to fix upon any exclusively Unionist area. There are more Unionists in the Southern area than there are Nationalists in the three Counties and no provision whatever is made for them. In their case we are told minorities must suffer, but that doctrine seems to be ignored where the minority is a Nationalist one.

The sacrifices already made by the Unionists of the three Counties during the War will surely be recognised.

Belfast is the commercial capital of Ulster. All our trade, business and railways are connected with it. The G[reat].N[orthern].R[ailway]. runs direct from the town of Cavan through the County Monaghan to Belfast. If a barrier is to be erected between our Counties and Belfast it will be injurious to all.

The County Donegal entirely surrounds Lough Swilly, and everyone knows how important it was during the war. The county also runs along one side of Lough Foyle and up to the City of Derry.

It has been said that the traders of Belfast are in favour of the Six County area, but that is not so. They want as large an area as possible to be connected with Belfast for business purposes. The smaller the area the worse for them. It narrows the limits for their travellers, who at present penetrate every town and village in Ulster. The large shipbuilding and linen firms who are not dependent on this do not care how small the Northern area may be if their works in Belfast are safe as their business is world-wide, but the general body of Belfast traders know how they would be hit and that the cost of maintaining a Parliament, Government and Law Courts in Belfast will fall more heavily on six Counties than on nine.

If the Province of Ulster as a whole is established and well governed under a settled Government in Belfast, it will be the greatest inducement to the three Southern Provinces to become settled and well governed also; and will appeal to them in a way that a portion of Ulster round Belfast would not do.

We appeal to our fellow-Unionists in the six Counties not to desert us and not to violate their Covenant when they can take us in with perfect safety to themselves.

222 Letter from Sir James Stronge, Tynan Abbey, Tynan, Co. Armagh, to H. de F. Montgomery, 12 March 1920, reviewing the decision of the U.U.C. on 10 March to accept six-counties partition (D 627/435):

My dear Montgomery—I will attend the IUA meeting tho' it will practically prevent me from taking part in the Emergency Fund Committee meeting at the RB House.

I must say that the more I think of the 3 Counties debate, the more unfortunate it appears to me. I can't be sorry that Farnham's resolution was defeated because to have carried it would possibly have killed the last chance of Unionism in Ireland

But I think the result should have been reached some other (and less objectionable) way—and I believe it would have been so reached if the matter had not been rushed.

The impression left is that the 3 Counties have been thrown to the wolves with very little compunction.

It would have been better for the 6 Counties to have unanimously asked them to stand aside, and dissolve the Covenant on the ground that it is no longer applicable to the state of politics. They, the 3 Counties could hardly have refused—and if they did refuse. we might have made a declaration to that effect by an overwhelming vote of the Council!

I think that my vote was probably wrong but that my speech was nearly all right, and I am glad I made it if it gave a crumb of comfort to the 3 County people.

I think that the Covenant is certainly well nigh out of date.

The Conspiracy against which we covenanted no longer is effectual, and as to equal conditions with England & Scotland—if this proposal to have local Parliaments in England & Scotland is carried out there will be no inequality.

It would have been more honest to abrogate the Covenant openly than to give it the "go by" without saying anything

But we had no time given us to consider the best way of dealing with the situation Yrs very truly

James H Stronge

223 Letter from Brig.-general A. Ricardo, Sion Mills, Co. Tyrone, to Montgomery, 8 April 1920, describing efforts to have the 10 March decision of the U.U.C. reconsidered (D 627/435):

Confidential

Dear Mr Montgomery—I will be brief—Directly after 10th March meeting, I resigned from [the Ulster Unionist] Council in anger & disgust—I am too stupid to appreciate the arguments which go to try & prove that the Covenant is but a pledge among friends.

I heard from a few casually & found a very strong body of feeling in 6 counties agin' the proceedings. From that some of us met for a weekend— & wrote to Farnham asking if he would not get delegates of 3 counties to ask for a special meeting of Council (which can be demanded by any 25 members) to reconsider. He was in London—& eventually said no—he was done with them for all time.

Our knot grew & some of us met in [the] Ulster club & drafted a circular which it was proposed should go to all members of Council over signatures of Lord Bangor, Lord Clanwilliam, F. Gardiner, Sir R. Kennedy, H. MacGeagh, Mrs. Greer, Lt-Col. P[erceval]. Maxwell, Stouppe McCance, Maj. R [?]. McLean, Lord Roden, Sir J. Stronge, & Mr. Waring & myself. It was to be sent out when Farnham & Co's resignation was in press. I was at a meeting at Clones yest[erday]. (as a guest) of the 3 counties delegates. Cavan resigned on 5th, Monaghan yesterday, & Donegal will follow suit—but meeting unanimous (Farnham not there) that a special meeting ought to be called before resignations become operative to try & save a split never to be healed.

Results of Clones meeting are to be in press tomorrow. Now Sir R. Kennedy & Maj McLean think we ought to tell Carson what we are doing.

We are having a meeting at [the] Ulster Club 2.30 p.m. Saturday 10th [April] to settle this point and to make absolutely sure all signatories agree with every word sent out—they are scattered & you know how easy it is to go wrong & let men in for what they dont approve.

I dont know what your views are:– but we propose to ask for Special meeting" "To consider the situation created by the impending resignations of Delegates from 3 Counties from U.U. council & to give further consideration to the question of the exclusion of these Counties from the Ulster Area as proposed in the present Bill, which proposal many in the six counties believe to be a violation of their solemn covenant, & one that will ultimately lead to an irrevocable schism in the Ulster Unionist party."

I value your judgment so much, that if you could join us on Sat: or give me your views, I believe it would be greatly appreciated.

You will understand that I am only by chance acting as convener for Sat: so as to avoid any possible misunderstandings.

It is a miserable situation & Carson on 10th fell from the pedestal that many had placed him on. Yours very sincerely

A Ricardo

224 Copy letter from Lord Farnham, writing from the Grand Hotel, Pau, France, to Montgomery, 13 April 1920, disagreeing with the latter's interpretation of the six-counties decision and asserting that both in policy and honour the U.U.C. should not have accepted six-counties partition (D 627/435):

My dear Montgomery—Your letter has been forwarded on to me, for which many thanks. I fear I disagree with very much that is in it. But in the first place I entirely disagree that Carson and his political satellites are out to kill Home Rule either by flank direct or other attack. On the contrary they are going to make it a certainty and have given Lloyd George a definite pledge that they will bring it in to the 6 counties and see that it is put into operation and worked. I myself heard Carson make this definite pledge to L.G., and I know also L.G. intends this to happen whatever else happens to rest of Ireland.

There is only one way to prevent this happening, and that is to put the 3 counties back into the Bill again before it is passed. Carson would then say he couldn't work it, as [and] so the bill would be hung up, the 1914 Bill having been got rid of. I got this from one of the Ulster party, as the best thing that could happen, but of course he had to give it privately as his own view and didn't bind the party to it.

Also I am afraid we must differ about the Covenant. The County people who signed that Covenant do not understand that way of looking at it. Our people look upon themselves as betrayed and deserted, and the people of 6 counties looked upon themselves as shamed and dishonoured. It has gone far further and far deeper than you imagine. Any movement that comes must come from the 6 counties themselves. We only protest and resign from Council. How can we remain members of a body that have plainly told us they don't want us and that we are an incumbrance to them and have, "you may say what you will, but you can't get away from the fact," have broken a solemn Covenant, in order to get rid of us. No self-respecting man ought to remain a member unless the people themselves repudiate the action of their leaders, and ask us to come back again.

Believe me, I appreciate very much your writing and for so clearly putting your viwes [*sic*] before me. But I can't accept them. I know I am right about point No. 1. and I can't look at any breaking of Covenant for tactical reason[s]. Again many thanks. Yours. sincerely,

Farnham.

225 *Letter from Montgomery to Sir James Stronge, 28 May 1920, describing a special meeting of the U.U.C. called on 27 May to reconsider the 10 March decision (D 627/435):

My dear Stronge—The actual vote being over by half-past two, I was tempted to bolt home without waiting for the conclusion of the U.U.C. meeting yesterday, which I have been rather repenting since, as the temper of the meeting after the result of the poll was declared is a very important feature in the situation. Shaftesbury, who spoke in favour of Ricardo's motion, and strongly, concluded by saying that he would, (though he besought the meeting to pass the resolution) support whatever conclusion the Council came to. I hope others may have followed his example, but there are one or two out-and-out fanatics who will, I suppose, retire from the Council, but in view of the majority supporting the decision of March 10th., I do not think they can do very much harm. I am rather sorry they turned Coote on to second the Carsonite amendment, as I fear he rubbed the other side the wrong way rather more than was necessary. He spoke with his back to where I was sitting, so I did not catch all he said. He made a most impassioned harangue, and elicited much cheering from the majority of the meeting, culminating [in] an appeal to support our leader. Farnham got up after Carson had summed up the discussion before taking the vote, ostensibly to repudiate the suggestion made I suppose by Coote, that their resolution was a vote of want of confidence in Carson, but he wound up his little speech by saying that he considered that he (Carson) had betrayed him, but did this without much heat or emotion, so I suppose it is a move in some game he is playing. Carson was evidently in pain and depressed by the neuritis he is suffering from; nevertheless, he put his case extraordinarily well, and told us things about the history of the matter and his dealings with it which made it more clear that the line taken is the only one possible. I came away from the Hall before the poll was declared, but Best just caught the train after hearing it, and told me the numbers were 301 for the amendment and 80 for Ricardo's resolution. This, I think, reduces the cave to insignificance. I hope you are on the mend. Yours very truly,

V

Besides pressure from three-counties unionists, Ulster unionists had to face moral pressure from the British government and from southern unionists. Some southern unionists thought that, if home rule was inevitable, Ulster's presence was essential for the well-being of minorities; and the government thought that nationalists would more readily accept a limited form of home rule compatible with imperial supremacy if Ireland was not partitioned. Ulster unionists were thus on occasion under pressure to abandon the principle of partition established in 1916 and to accept an all-Ireland parliament with safeguards.

This pressure was very evident during the Irish convention, 1917–18, which, on 8 June 1917, the U.U.C. reluctantly decided to enter. Among the 95 members were originally 20 Ulster unionists (though one died while the convention was in progress), representing the U.U.C and other interests. These Ulster unionists acted together as a group, with Hugh T. Barrie, M.P. for North Londonderry and later vice-president of the department of agriculture and technical instruction for Ireland, as chairman, and the 7th marquis of Londonderry, future Northern Ireland and British cabinet minister, and a man more prone to compromise than some of his colleagues, as honorary secretary. They adopted a negative attitude to the proceedings. They contributed little to the early and general discussions on possible constitutions for Ireland, and, by insisting on the fiscal unity of the United Kingdom, they brought the convention to deadlock by November 1917.

This attitude was severely criticised. The southern unionists, attempting to bring the convention to agreement on the basis of an all-Ireland parliament, tried to persuade Ulster unionists to accept a compromise on the fiscal question and invoked the aid of the prime minister and cabinet. Stressing the need for a settlement 'now during the war', Lloyd George, in a letter to Barrie on 21 February 1918, appealed to Ulster unionists to make concessions and to accept an all-Ireland parliament with safeguards and with limited powers. He urged that a settlement was necessary for the sake of Ireland, the empire and relations with the United States; and that the unsettled state of Ireland involving possible coercion was not only weakening the war effort but would also undermine Britain's position at any peace conference. On the other hand, he listed possible safeguards for Ulster unionists, including leaving customs and excise under imperial control, additional unionist representation and an Ulster committee within the Irish parliament 'to modify or if necessary to exclude the application of certain measures. . . inconsistent with the interests of Ulster'. 'Inspired' pressure on Ulster was also maintained by the Northcliffe press which, emphasising the need to conciliate opinion in America and the dominions, attacked Ulster unionists' negative attitude as weakening the allied cause.

These pressures put the Ulster unionist group in a difficult position, but it was sustained by frequent consultations with advisers such as Adam Duffin, who was often in Dublin and always used his influence against agreement, and with a representative advisory committee set up by the U.U.C. This committee (which included H. de F. Montgomery) had been promised that 'nothing in any way binding would be done without consultation with the Ulster people', and it used its influence to tie down the delegates. For instance, the committee was not impressed by Lloyd George's arguments in favour of an immediate settlement and would not give the delegates a free hand to deal with the letter of 21 February.

This solidarity not only prevented the delegates from succumbing to the compromise atmosphere of the convention; it also enabled Ulster unionists confidently to refuse undemocratic safeguards, to demand exclusion and vigorously to defend themselves against criticism. In 1918, acting through an agent in London, Joseph R. Fisher, an experienced publicist, they tried to counter Northcliffe's campaign against them. Such adamant insistence on partition did much to render the convention a failure. The Ulster group voted against all proposals involving recognition of the principle of establishing an Irish parliament; unsuccessfully moved (by 19 votes to 52) an amendment providing for the exclusion of Ulster from the jurisdiction of the Irish parliament; and issued a separate report dissenting from the majority report of southern unionists and certain nationalists.

226 Draft letter from A. Duffin to Lord Londonderry, 16 November 1917, arguing that Ulster unionists should not propose a federal alternative in the convention (Mic 127/24):

Dear Lord Londonderry—I was sorry to leave Dublin without having another opportunity of speaking to you.

I am fully impressed by the view held by you and Mr. Barrie on the desirability of the Ulster Unionists on the convention showing readiness to consider if not to initiate some alternative constructive policy while breaking with the Nationalists on the demand for fiscal autonomy. I gather that you think this should take the shape of a federal scheme which would fit it with a wider one likely to be adopted before long for the United Kingdom.

I think such a plan would be better described as devolution rather than federation; which is centripetal, the bringing together of existing separate units under a controlling Government keeping what might be called Imperial Interests in its hands, while devolution implies an existing central Parliament remitting some of its work, especially administration to local representative Authorities—that by the way—

I am sure you will see the necessity of confining any such suggestions to the most general terms. I feel that you may be launched upon a sea of fresh controversy if they are even tentatively accepted as a basis for discussion by the other side, especially as you would have to make large reservations for Ulster, including probably education and judiciary.

I am more than ever convinced that it should be frankly confessed that the Convention cannot come to any agreed settlement at the present time and that its deliberations should be suspended until such times as they may be renewed at the request of the Government.

This is no time to succeed in framing a constitution for Ireland. That time may come when all our energies are not absorbed, as they ought to be, in the prosecution of the war, and when, as the Nationalists contend, Sinn Fein has proved to be a passing phase, as it well may, as it has no basis of reality or sense.

I do not say that this suggestion should come from us; it might be interpreted as an indication of weakening in our position, but I think it might be privately put before Sir Horace

227

Letter from A. Duffin, writing from the Shelbourne Hotel, Dublin, to his wife, 28 November 1917, describing a meeting with the southern unionist delegates (Mic 127/26):

Dearest—I sent you a wire not to expect me tonight. The[y] want me to stay till tomorrow & I think I am of use if only in supporting Pollock & keeping some check on L[ondonderry].

We had a very interesting pow-wow with the Southern Unionist lot last ev[enin]g. They want to capitulate & make terms with the enemy lest a worse thing befall them. They are a cowardly crew & stupid to boot. We shall do all we can to stiffen them & keep them in our ranks & they may be driven to reconsider their position. Anyhow nothing they can propose can be accepted but the scene is constantly shifting like a kaleidoscope.

I slept till after nine this morning fully making up for arrears, feel first rate & am glad to be here. Yours

A. Duffin

Expect to be home some time tomorrow. Quite a nice lot of people here. Different stamp from Belfast general[ly].

228

Extract from the minute book of the Ulster unionist delegates to the Irish convention, relating to their meeting on 16 January 1918 in the committee rooms, Trinity College, Dublin, which discussed partition and the need for propaganda in Great Britain (D 1327/3/10):

. . . The Chairman, on behalf of the Ulster Group, expressed their appreciation of the speeches made by Mr. Pollock and The Moderator.

A discussion took place as to handing in the Partition Scheme. It was decided that Mr. Barrie should hand it in at what he considered the proper time and in the name of Sir George Clark.

The question was raised as to the desire expressed by the Lord Mayor of Belfast and the Mayor of Derry, that they should be permitted to be present at the Election proceedings in their respective cities. It was decided that the question should be raised in the Convention so as to permit them so attending.

It was decided to raise an objection to having a sitting on Friday.

A discussion took place as to the attitude to be taken on the forthcoming Divisions.

On the motion of Sir George Clark, seconded by Sir Crawford McCullagh, the following circular was approved of, and the names of those to whom it should be sent left in the hands of the Chairman.

16th Jan., 1918.

Private & Confidential.

Dear Sir,

To off-set the pernicious Press Campaign, which has been launched against Ulster in a section of the English Press, we are of opinion that immediate steps should be taken to get Ulster's position brought prominently before the British public. We shall be glad therefore if you will kindly attend a meeting, to be held on Friday, 18th January, 1918, in the Old Town Hall, Belfast, at 3.30 p.m. Apologizing for short notice. Yours faithfully,

H. T. Barrie. Chairman, Ulster Delegates
Londonderry. Hon Secretary
R. Dawson Bates. Secretary.

Mr. Barrie intimated, in connection with this matter, that Col Wallace and he were prepared to subscribe the sum of one hundred pounds (£100) each.

A further meeting will be held at the Shelbourne Hotel at 9 p.m.

Hugh T. Barrie

23 Jany. 1918

229 Letter from J. R. Fisher, 25 Victoria Street, Westminster, London S.W., to H. de F. Montgomery, 25 January 1918, acknowledging the latter's suggestions for propaganda work (D 627/433):

My dear Mr Montgomery—Your letters of 22d & 23d duly received with copy of Memorandum enclosed.

I am in entire agreement about the lines on which our propaganda should be run. Seeing that the Northcliffe suggestion was & is that Home Rule should be forced on us to "please" the United States & our own Dominions, the Imperial side of it is that which first arose in my mind. Indeed I had dealt with this aspect pretty fully while in U.S.A. last year & on my return. I found that Americans took up quite quickly the "Secession" argument:– every possible reform within the lines of the Constitution, but sheer treason & secession to be put down with the strong hand. Also the Virginian analogy of the two tendencies in the same State, resulting in partition. This is well handled in a letter by Professor Alison Phillips in today's Times. So important did I regard the American public that I at the very outset opened up relations with the "Associated Press" which goes into every Newspaper Office in U.S.A., and with whose managers both in New York & in London

I am on friendly terms of old standing. The <u>Times</u> Washington correspondent is a well-meaning but colourless young man who sends just what Northcliffe tells him to send. It is a great pity: but I hope to get something prominently into the <u>Times</u> shortly that will tend to counteract it.

Generally, with regard to the situation in the Convention & in the Government, there is nothing but confusion & uncertainty. The Church, the Murphyite wreckers, the Sinn Feiners of the mild George Russell type, & the Redmondites are all pulling in different directions: not to speak of the Southern "Unionists" who are selfish & ill guided as usual. Some weeks ago there was a possibility of the Ulstermen finding themselves isolated with all these other elements united against them. That danger is, I believe, averted—Middleton [sic] & the Bishops are not working together & the question of finance is less near a settlement than ever.

Ever since 1886 I have been clear on the point that "artificial" safeguards are utterly useless & dangerous as well as being—as you say—unworkable in these democratic days.

(I learn that both Lloyd George & the other old Home Rulers in the Cabinet are becoming more & more alive to the Imperial & Naval danger of a separate Ireland) I am always glad to get your suggestions: so please write me whenever you feel inclined. Here among a multitude of counsellors one's mind sometimes gets clogged with details, whereas at your distance you can concentrate on the essentials. Yours very sincerely

J. R. Fisher.

230 *Letter from Montgomery to Lord Londonderry, Mount Stewart, Newtownards, Co. Down, 26 February 1918, explaining his attitude to the Lloyd George letter as expressed at a meeting of the advisory committee (D 627/433):

My Dear Londonderry—It is difficult when one is quite out of practice of anything like debate, to say the right thing on a difficult subject when one has had no time to consider the matter.

This was my position yesterday, as I could not risk missing what everybody at the meeting said while considering what I was going to say.

It may have appeared unnecessary and perhaps offensive to insist so strongly on your bringing L[loyd].G[eorge]'s proposal before us again before giving any sort of consent to it, but what I felt was that your statement was to the effect that Lloyd George had asked you to bring the suggestion before us, and that you had done so, therefore, merely to give you a free hand, would have implied that you were at liberty to consent to this proposal if you liked, which I was sure the Advisory Committee or the majority of them were not prepared to do. L.G's reasons for urging you virtually to come to some agreement, with the majority of the Convention seemed to me absolute bunkum What is really meant is that Lloyd George has involved himself in promises to the Home Rulers and possibly to the Americans and other sentimental sympathisers and finds he cannot deliver goods, and wants us to enable him to do so, he gives absolutely no reason for the statement that a settlement would make it easier to get on with the war. Would handing over the administration of a great part of this country to the friends of the enemy or to persons either in sympathy with the friends of the enemy or in dread of the friends of the enemy help to win the war. Does anybody with any knowledge of this country imagine that the setting up of an Irish Parliament would bring in any recruits to the army or enable any British Troops to be withdrawn from Ireland, and if not how is it going to help the war. As to the position of H.M's Government at the Peace Conference Is any country belligerent or neutral going to insist on the principles of self-determination, being applied in a case where their application would mean the placing of a part of the Bulwarks of the Country in question in the hands of the friends of the enemy?

Carson in his speech at Belfast dealt sufficiently with the theory that it was necessary in order to enable the Americans to help to win the war to yield to the Home Rulers and rebels in this country.

Having said this much I may add that I think at the present stage of the Convention it would be quite useful to represent the upshot of our meeting as a refusal to consider the suggestions in Lloyd George's letter, till they are put in a clearer and more detailed form. The more we get other peoples cards on the table the better.

I was never able to see the force of the argument that in the present troubled state of Ireland and in the war going on we ought to join the Redmondites. It appeared to me that the proper conclusion to draw from the state of things was that the moderate Redmondites ought to join us. It appears to me that one advantage may be snatched from the present deplorable state of the Country, namely, that everybody who has anything to lose may get sufficiently alarmed, to think that as we will not join the Redmondites they had better join us in insisting on the Restoration and maintenance of Law and Order.

The argument that if we do not agree to some form of Home Rule with safeguards now the next Parliament with 200 or 300 Labour Members will enact something worse makes very little impression on my mind, because if the coming Parliament would do anything of this kind it would be equally ready to sweep away any safeguards that might be agreed upon now, and it would be far easier for a Parliament to do that than to pass an elaborate amending Bill to the existing Home Rule Act. We should have given away our principles and our chance of [sic] and ultimately get this credit for saving the Empire by our obstinacy from great danger, for nothing or less than nothing. Yours very truly,

VI

Besides pressure from three-counties unionists, southern unionists and the British government, Ulster unionism was faced with the growth of what may be described as a democratic, labour consciousness which threatened the unity of Ulster unionism.

First, there was growing discontent with the unrepresentative nature of some local unionist associations, said to be dominated by aristocratic cliques. How far this feeling was in danger of undermining local unionist unity was underlined at the East Antrim by-election in 1919. Following the retirement of the sitting unionist member, the local unionist association was presented with two names and chose Major W. Agnew Moore of Ballygally Castle, Larne, Co. Antrim; but his rival, George Hanna of 15 Rosetta Gardens, Belfast, a vice-president of the association, solicitor and orangeman, refused to accept the decision. Several unsuccessful attempts were made by the U.U.C. and Carson to mediate, but in the end two unionists and a liberal went to the polls after a bitter and rowdy contest. Hanna, taking as one of his main planks the unrepresentative nature of the East Antrim Unionist Association, stood as an independent unionist and won by 1,165 votes. He polled 8,714 votes to Moore's 7,549, and the liberal's 1,778.

Secondly, there was the possibility that the growth of a socialist vote would, if worked on by nationalists, deprive unionism of working class support, particularly in a key area such as Belfast (whose parliamentary representation was increased from four to nine in 1918). The problem was highlighted in the Belfast strike of January–February 1919, part of a general movement to secure a forty-four hour week in the engineering and shipbuilding industries. The main centre of discontent in Belfast was the two shipyards of Workman, Clark and Co. and Harland and Wolff, where men were working a fifty-four hour week. They came out on strike on 25 January, and soon sympathetic strikes on the part of the municipal gas and electricity supply workers dislocated the whole life of the city. Not until 19 February did the ship-builders return to work on a forty-seven hour week, pending a national settlement of working hours. Though the strike had nothing to do with politics, watchful Ulster unionists were able to see the hand of Sinn Fein at work, hoping to 'let matters drift on in Belfast until a condition arises in which the men would be embittered with the authorities that they would join hands in a universal strike for the whole of Ireland'.

427

231 Letter from R. D. Bates, secretary of the U.U.C., to Sir Edward Carson, 15 April 1919, describing efforts to reconcile unionist differences in East Antrim (D 1507/1/1919/21):

Dear Sir Edward—You will have gathered from my previous correspondence that we were doing everything possible to try and put an end to the unfortunate friction which exists among Unionists in East Antrim. You will recollect that both Hanna and Moore's names were submitted to the East Antrim Association; Hanna refusing to give a pledge that he would abide by the decision of that body. Moore was selected, whereupon Hanna decided to go forward as an independent Unionist Candidate; one of the chief planks on Hanna's platform being that the Association was not representative of the democracy of East Antrim. This contention gained many powerful adherents among the Unionists of that Constituency. Hanna is an Orangeman while Moore is not.

As regards the unrepresentative character of the East Antrim Association, there is a good deal to be said for Hanna's contention. The Association was originally formed by the late Colonel McCalmont, Blackburne being his Agent and Secretary to the Association. During the whole of Colonel McCalmont's Membership in the House of Commons he had only to practically fight one contested Election, which he won handsomely. Subsequently his son, Colonel R.C.A. McCalmont, was returned as Member without a Contest, but no steps were taken to bring the Association into modern lines; one of the principal defects of the Association being the existence of Vice-Presidents who could be selected from Constituencies outside that of East Antrim. Following the last General Election Colonel McCalmont who, owing to his absence at the Front, was unable to give much attention to local affairs, decided to re-form the Association, and this was in process when he received his present appointment and retired.

What was felt by Unionist Headquarters (an opinion which was also shared by yourself) was that it was absolutely necessary that the Official Candidate should be backed and aided by the party machinery; that to do otherwise would admit the principle of individuals posing as Unionists, contesting seats, many of them with the sole object of splitting the Unionist vote. In addition it was felt that many of the Electors looked upon the dispute as purely a personal matter, and as between the merits of Moore and Hanna, and did not realise the far-reaching results the success of the Independent Candidate would have.

Under these circumstances efforts have been made for some considerable time past to see if anything could be done to bring about a re-approachment[*sic*]. As a result, mainly of Captain Dixon's efforts, a meeting was held of Mr. Hanna's chief supporters, which was attended by Captain Dixon. The situation was put before them, when the following suggestions were unanimously agreed to:—

That the Election should be put off.

That in the meantime the East Antrim Unionist Association should be re-formed, new Members being brought in, on the lines laid down in a letter sent by Captain Dixon in connection with his own Constituency (Pottinger).

That new Delegates should be elected to the parent Body, and that both Candidates should re-submit their names to the Delegates; the Candidate not chosen to support the selected one.

These, however, are details that could be worked out later if the principle is adopted.

That you should be asked to receive both the rival Candidates with, say, two of their chief supporters, who would have an opportunity of putting the facts before you.

These suggested arrangements to be carried out if they have your concurrence and approval.

We subsequently had a Conference with Captain Dixon, Mr. Chaine, and Mr. Johnston Kirkpatrick (Members of the East Antrim association), and these gentlemen approved of the suggestions.

To put the matter in a nutshell, if you can see your way to do so, you are asked to write a letter to Hanna and Moore asking them to attend with, say, two of their supporters with a view to avoiding a continuance of the existing friction, (and in this connection I might point out that the third (Candidate, a Home Ruler—Mr. Legg—has some idea that he (might possibly slide in between Hanna and Moore). If this invitation is sent out it will be gratefully accepted by both Mr. Hanna and Major Moore. That you should hear their respective statements, after which you will be asked to decide as to the course to be adopted.

I have no doubt that following on the statements which you will have placed before you, if you could see your way to write to Major Moore and Mr. Chaine, the Chairman of the East Antrim Unionist Association, and on similar lines to Mr. Hanna, pointing out the advisability of re-forming the Association, and the election of new Delegates; that the two rival Candidates should put their names before such new Delegates, the matter will be accepted on both sides, and an armistice will then be called. What I would suggest is that Mr. Chaine, when he brings your letter giving your decision before the East Antrim Association, should appoint a sub-committee to confer with Mr. Hanna's supporters with a view to carrying out the election of Delegates.

It is, of course, clearly to be understood that the proposal that you in the first instance should ask both Mr. Hanna and Major Moore to a Conference, is entirely unknown except to Mr. Hanna and his immediate supporters, Major Moore, Mr. Chaine, Mr. Kirkpatrick, Captain Dixon, and myself.

I feel very sorry to trouble you at the present time when I know you are having a rest, but I am sure if it is at all possible you will acquiesce in the above suggestions.

In conclusion, I think it only fair to Mr. Hanna and his supporters to tell you that at the Conference which Captain Dixon had with them, nothing but expressions of the deepest loyalty to yourself were heard. Many of them could not realise that you could not & would not tolerate disunion in our ranks and as to the consequences that might possibly follow if it continued. These gentlemen looked upon the matter as purely a personal one, and not largely a question of policy. They all realise what they and Ulster owe you. Some of the papers may have given you wrong reports as to some of the Meetings that were held, but you will quite appreciate that these were attended by Nationalists who sought to drive a wedge in between the parties. If you will send the letters of invitation under cover to me I will see them delivered. Yours very truly,

R. Dawson Bates

232 Letter from the Rev. J. L. Donaghy, The Manse, Larne, Co. Antrim, to Sir Edward Carson, 17 May 1919, asking him to address a meeting in support of Major Moore's candidature in East Antrim (D 1507/1/1919/32):

Dear Sir Edward—I hope you will excuse this letter. My only apology for troubling you is that I am thoroughly in earnest regarding the matter. The other M.Ps are doing exceedingly well, but I know the feeling in the community is that if you would only come to Larne for one meeting next week, you would get a magnificent reception, & secure Major Moores return.

Hanna, to put it plainly is a liar & a trickster, & he has so gulled a large number of the lower class voters that they actually do not believe that you wrote the letter in favour of Moore. One man, & he is typical of hundreds said last night, I'm for Hanna, but if Sir Edward Carson would come here & tell us with his own lips that he wants Moore, I and hundreds of others would vote as he desires, but as matters are at present, we don't believe all thats in the papers, & unless Sir Edward comes we will continue to support Hanna.

Now Sir Edward, I know it's asking a great deal, but at the same time, I do honestly feel that unless you come the position is in danger.

I have been persecuted by a number[?], but I don't mind, if only we put Moore in.

It is Hanna's Orangeism that is doing all the harm, & the fellow doesn't care for Orangeism any more that [*sic*] I care for Mohammedanism.

Hoping you are keeping well, & with Kindest Regards, I am, Dear Sir Edward, Yours with sincerity,

John Lyle Donaghy

233 Typed extract headed 'West Down and Mr. Hanna, M.P.' from the *Irish News*, 16 June 1919, showing the repercussions on West Down of Hanna's victory in East Antrim, forwarded by R. D. Bates to Sir Edward Carson, 18 June 1918 (D 1507/1/1919/35):

Significant Unionist Resolution on the East Antrim Result.

At a special meeting of the delegates to the West Down Unionist Association from the Annaclone polling district, held at Annaclone, Banbridge, on the evening of the 9th. inst., the following resolution was proposed, seconded, and passed unanimously:—

"That we, the delegates to the West Down Unionist Association of the

Annaclone polling district, hereby tender to Bro. G. B. Hanna, M.P., our heartiest congratulations on his magnificent victory in East Antrim over the aristocratic clique, a clique which we regret to say had been in evidence in the West Down Unionist Association on the last occasion when selecting a candidate for Parliamentary honours.

Signed—Robert H. Gibney, Chairman.

John W. Marshaw, John Mills, Andrew Kennedy, Delegates.

David Mills, Secretary."

The sitting Unionist member for West Down is Mr. D. M. Wilson K.C. He was elected by a large majority over a Sinn Fein Candidate, but only a comparatively small proportion of the electorate voted.

234 Copy letter from R. D. Bates to Sir James Craig, Westminster House, Millbank, London S.W., 31 January 1919, describing the strike situation in Belfast (D 1507/1/3/34):

PRIVATE

Dear Sir James—I duly received your letter on the 30th inst., and I agree with you in the view which you take. I had several talks with Hacket-Pain who, notwithstanding a certain amount of pressure from scare-mongers, declined to bring out troops, or do anything to make the workers think they were being intimidated. What one wants to try and get the workers to see is that really no one is against them, except themselves; that the question is not a local one, but is a national one. The Leaders are practically Sinn Feiners, who have taken advantage of some of the rank and file, and as time goes on their action is being found out. Two of the prime movers are Waugh and Freeland. You will see from the "[Northern] Whig" of to-day, which I send you, that already resentment is being shown at men like the Russian Jew being brought from Dublin to teach the Belfast men their business. I am firmly convinced that at the present time it would be most injudicious to drag Carson or any of the other Leaders into it. In the first place they were not consulted as to going out on Strike, and, in the second place, if the men went back unsatisfied they would subsequently say that they were "let down" by their Unionist political leaders. I was speaking to Fleming, who was one of the Organisers of the original meeting, and he tells me that he believes the men would be glad to go back at the 47 hours on the understanding that the matter was to be considered, but having taken to the streets it is difficult for them to do so. His only fear is that Devlin, who you will see is bucking up, will take credit for any settlement that may be arrived at, and that our party will be "let down", so what I would like you to do is to keep in touch with Sir Robert Horne and not let him do anything without the approval of the Belfast Unionist Members and yourself. Sir George Clark takes the view that he is rather in favour of 44 hours, but he cannot give 44 hours if the Clyde say 40; otherwise all his men go to the Clyde, and in the same way he doesn't know what Harland & Wolff will do. I have heard on very good authority that, contrary to the expectations of some of the ringleaders and the men, that Lord Pirrie does not intend to climb down, and this is brought about by the fact (a) that the Executives of the Trade Unions don't want to climb down; (b) the Government apparently don't; and (c) the Shipping Federation, whom Pirrie is interested in, don't want to do so either.

Circulars were issued by about 44 out of 47 firms, excluding the Ship-building Firms, to the men whom [when] they were down for their lying-by money, to the effect that the whole matter in dispute must be dealt with on a national basis, and that if it is so considered they are willing to fall into line. Saxon Payne of Harland & Wolff practically told the same to the men, and this was followed by Workman & Clark.

To show the "ram-stam" way in which the Strike was undertaken, the men never considered the question of piece-work. The Shipwright's Society— which consists of some of the most level-headed men—have had this under consideration, and McWhirter is in London negotiating to ascertain if they can get a 20% increase on piece-work or "leu" work. If they can get this the nett effect will be that the piece-workers will be in as good a position working on the 47 hours' basis as they were on the old 54.

As regards the Strikers, you may take it that less than $\frac{1}{4}$ are out-and-out Socialists and "extremists"; one-fourth are quite satisfied with 47 hours; and the half are prepared to agitate on Constitutional lines.

At one time the Strike[r]s had decidedd[sic] to call out the Crane men, but they were warned by the local Coal Controller that if they did so coal would be deflected from Belfast, which they would never get again. The result was they stopped that. They have also refrained from calling out the Linen Factories and the Spinning Mills.

To sum up it would be a mistake for any of the Leaders to interfere at the present time, but if the workers indicate a desire to going back, pending a national arrangement being carried out, the question of getting the political leaders over to mediate is a question that could subsequently be raised.

I am glad to say that looting has ceased.

I will keep you informed. Yours ever,

VII

To counter these disruptive, democratic influences, Ulster unionist political leaders reorganised the U.U.C., encouraged the reform of local unionist associations and made sympathetic utterances on labour and social questions. In particular they took two decisions which are well documented in the N.I.P.R.O.

In the first place, to maintain party discipline and to sustain local organisations, they refused to admit Hanna, the successful independent unionist candidate in the East Antrim by-election, to the Ulster unionist parliamentary party.

Pressure and threats from Hanna and his supporters were resisted; to do otherwise, it was felt, would have encouraged other independent unionists to come forward and undermined party discipline and solidarity.

In the second place, there were attempts to associate trade unionists and labour in general with the work of the U.U.C. The aim was to mobilise and canalise the working class vote and to counteract the impression, spread by nationalists and their allies, that unionism in Ulster was dominated by conservative property owners. Unionist labour had emerged at the time of the Irish convention, but the significant steps came thereafter. In June 1918 was formed the Ulster Unionist Labour Association. Its membership included only two non-trade unionists—Carson as president, and John Miller Andrews, businessman and future prime minister of Northern Ireland (1940–3), and it was intended to be the 'medium of expression of the views of labour unionists'.

This development was carried further by Carson's insistence in 1918 that three of Belfast's nine seats should be contested by trade unionists. Accordingly, in the general election of December 1918 a labour unionist member was returned in each of the old non-nationalist Belfast divisions—Shankill (one of the North Belfast constituencies), St Anne's (South Belfast) and Victoria (East Belfast). This elevation of trade unionists and labour was not without its critics. There was some difficulty in persuading constituencies to accept unionist labour candidates; and the allocation of seats was carried out only on Carson's insistence and after some hard work by Wilson Hungerford, the secretary of the Ulster Unionist Labour Association, and several consultations between the labour sub-committee of the U.U.C. and representatives of the Belfast unionist parliamentary associations. Reservations were also expressed by some employers about proposals to extend the association's activities in 1919; but the association did not in fact lead to increased working class influence in the party, either in respect of personalities or issues. Neither, however, according to Hungerford, did it provide the key to mobilising and canalising working class support for the Ulster unionist party.

235 Copy letter from R. D. Bates to Captain C. C. Craig, unionist M.P. for South Antrim, 29 Brompton Square, London S.W., 18 June 1919, urging that, at least for the present, G. Hanna should not be admitted to the Ulster unionist party (D1507/1/1919/35):

Dear Captain Craig—The position in regard to what action should be taken in regard to the future status of Mr. Hanna as an Official Ulster Unionist Member is one, in my opinion, of considerable difficulty. It seems to me that the question can only be looked upon as to what is best for the party, and what action is likely to cause least damage to the Ulster Party in the future. I fear that in the near future we are going to have attacks made on all the Associations. No Association is perfect, and it is absolutely impossible, as you are well aware, to get people to take an active part in the routine of the management of an Association in normal times. The result is that the management of such Associations get into the hands of a few, and it is only the good judgment of these few in nominating a Candidate, and in nominating a man who is generally popular in the neighbourhood, that saves the Association from defeat.

The Labour question is becoming acute in Belfast & the North of Ireland and egged on by Nationalists, many of the Electors are finding fault with the respective Associations in the various Districts. It is a well-known fact that the class of people who are the most active in finding fault with the Association's selection of a Candidate, are people who will not take anything to do, or share in the work which falls upon the Association during the Registration period. There is a general desire to kick against all authority and all discipline all over the three Kingdoms, and this found vent in the East Antrim Election. We have got to face this sooner or later, and face the prospect of having Independent Unionist Candidates standing against the Official Candidates, and the only thing that will save the Official Unionist Candidate will be the latter's personality and influence in the Constituency. It should be borne in mind that practically all the Roman Catholic vote was given to Hanna. The jubilation of the Roman Catholics at Hanna's victory, and the various paragraphs in Nationalist papers, are rather remarkable, and have done a good deal to embitter Major Moore's supporters, and in addition, caused many of Mr. Hanna's supporters to reflect as to the real meaning of Hanna's victory. I enclose you copy resolution which was passed at one of the Polling Districts in West Down. West Down Association is in my opinion very representative, and no one can accuse Mr. Wilson of being anything but a thoroughly representative Candidate, and yet you find an attack being engineered against him.

As you know we got a good deal of outside support and assistance for Major Moore, but this was given with a tacit understanding that Hanna, if returned, would not be admitted to the party. One of the strong arguments used by Hanna's supporters was that if he was returned he would be admitted to the party.

The East Antrim Unionist Association have already held two Meetings, and they are taking steps to re-organise their Association with the object of defeating Mr. Hanna at the next Election, and I think it is most probable that if they do this they will win the Seat at the next Election. I was not present at any of the Meetings, but I understand they were most enthusiastic, and money is being put up by the Official people in the Constituency to provide for the re-organisation. Some of the people at this meeting stated that if Mr. Hanna was admitted into the party, they themselves would ask Major Moore, or someone else, to stand as an Independent Unionist. If Hanna is admitted into the Party at the present stage, I very much fear that the people who supported the Official Candidate—especially the outsiders who were brought in by Headquarters—will consider that they have been "let down" badly, and the result will be that many people will refrain from supporting the Official Candidate if they think that if an Independent wins he will be admitted into the party. At the present time one of the greatest safeguards we have against the Official Candidate being opposed is if he is not a follower of Sir Edward Carson he will not be admitted to the party, even though successful. As a result, the only Seat that was strongly contested at the General Election was Ormeau where Mr. Stewart, who has unlimited means, went forward. If Hanna is admitted into the party I fear that several Seats will be contested by people calling themselves Unionists, who will adopt the same tactics as Hanna did so successfully in East Antrim. For example, in Victoria we would probably have Duff contesting the Seat against Donald; Twaddell against Lynn in Woodvale; Stewart against Moles in Ormeau; North Antrim is almost certain to be fought; Clark is talked about as fighting Hugh O'Neill in Mid Antrim; and North Down will probably be again fought. These Seats will probably be contested by people either representing Labour interests, or Farmers' interests.

I can quite see the difficulties of refusing Hanna, and if I thought that this would put an end to Independent Unionists going forward, I would strongly advocate it, but I very much fear that his admission would only encourage the break-up of all Officialdom. People always chafe against discipline and Organisation, and as you remember, in the old days, when there were comparatively few Constitutional Associations, Unionist fought against Unionist. You and Judge Moore were instrumental in encouraging the growth of Associations in all the Constituencies, and banding them together under the Ulster Unionist Council, and I fear that if this goes on it means a break-up of all Official control. The result will be that no man, no matter how good a Member he may be, will be safe from attack if an adventurer comes along. What is adding to our difficulties at the present time is that the rank and file do not realise that Home Rule is not as far off as some of them think. When another Home Rule attack is made you will find that people will tighten up, but at the present time they are only too ready to back up any "wind-bag". I know Hanna's supporters are most anxious to get him admitted to the party, first of all to justify their statement that if Hanna was returned he would be admitted to the party, and, secondly, to "whitewash" themselves. The Ulster Protestant Home Ruler still exists, though in small numbers, but they can make a lot of mischief.

If the matter could be shelved for say six months it would give Hanna an opportunity of making good, and then on application by him, the matter might be considered. In the meantime the Association might be re-formed, and local steps might be taken to bring about a re-approachment[*sic*]. Of course, if Hanna is not immediately admitted into the party he may fly into the Radical ranks, but he is not likely to do this, as that would damn his chances of again winning the Seat, and this both he and his supporters fully realise.

I understand that a Deputation is going to see Sir Edward from Hanna and his supporters, urging that he should be admitted into the party, and pointing out the painful penalties that will fall upon the party if they don't admit him. On the other hand, I understand from Mr. Chaine that a Deputation is going from East Antrim Unionist Association to lay their case before Sir Edward, and tell him what steps they are taking to re-organise their Association, and to point out the complications that will ensue if Hanna is admitted to the party.

I have endeavoured, so far as possible, to put the facts of the case before you. I have no personal feeling in the matter, and nothing would give me greater pleasure than to be able to express the opinion that Hanna should be admitted into the Party, if by doing so I thought that it would prevent future trouble, but I cannot but feel that the admitting of Hanna at the present time to the party would have very serious results in other Constituencies, and result in the future break-up of Unionist Organisation.

In short, I feel that as Hanna was never a Member of the Party, it is, therefore, not for the party to admit him into their ranks. At the same time I would not close the door to his admission at a future date. This might possibly be arranged after the re-organisation of East Antrim, but nothing should be done to hold Hanna up, or to prevent a re-approachment at a future date. Yours sincerely,

(Signed)   R. DAWSON BATES.

236 Letter from Bates to Sir Edward Carson, 30 June 1919, describing the origins and possible future development of the Ulster Unionist Labour Association, and enclosing **(b)** a resolution passed by the association regarding the formation of branches and clubs (D 1507/1/3/41):

(a)

Dear Sir Edward—The question of extending the area of the work of this Association has given Andrews and myself a great deal of concern. You know the circumstances which led to the formation of this Association (of which you are President), and which ultimately led to three Labour Members being selected for the City of Belfast.

The two principal Unionist Organisations which exist at the present time in Ulster are the Parliamentary Associations and the Orange Institution. Having regard to the fact that Members of both these Organisations compose all classes, it is obvious that it is a practical impossibility that matters outside the question of the Union should be the subject of discussion and action. Therefore, no subjects, except those directly affecting the Union, are discussed. The working people in Belfast have felt for a very considerable time past that means should be placed at their disposal whereby domestic matters could be discussed by them under Unionist auspices. As you are aware the Trade Unions are practically precluded from discussing political matters other than those affecting Labour Questions, but while this is strictly accurate, at the same time many of the Unions are controlled by Officials who hold Home Rule views. The result has been that frequently the opinions of the working classes in Belfast on the question of the Union are misrepresented in England and elsewhere. The absence of such means as I have indicated above frequently leads to the younger members of the working classes joining Socialist and Extreme Organisations run by the Independent Labour Party, where they are educated in views very different to those held by our Body. The defect has to a very large extent been made good by the Ulster Unionist Labour Association, but at the same time it is felt that having ordinary meetings, such as they have about once a month, is not sufficient. In other words, the Association will have to extend its sphere of operations.

The matter has been discussed at several of the Meetings of the Association, and finally on Saturday last a Resolution was passed, of which I enclose a copy, which puts the matter in a nutshell. If the Resolution is given effect to, it means the formation of four working-men's Clubs in Belfast, on the lines of the Working-men's Conservative and Liberal Clubs in England. These Clubs will be kept linked with the Ulster Unionist Labour Association, and, consequently, with the Ulster Unionist Party.

I have had many talks with Andrews on this subject, and I think if this arrangement could be carried out it would do an incalculable amount of good. On the other hand, if nothing is done the Association will die, because its Members will feel that it is not sufficiently progressive to meet an admittedly felt want.

Andrews you will naturally understand feels in his position, as Chairman of the Association and one of the Honorary Secretaries of the Ulster Unionist Council—in addition to being an Employer of Labour himself—a good deal of responsibility, and he would not be a party to extending the sphere of the existing Association without your approval.

As you are aware, there are many Employers in Belfast who take the view that Andrews goes too far on Labour Questions, but, on the other hand, the vast bulk of thinking Employers, and those who have the interests of the Empire at heart, realise that Andrews' actions have been most beneficial. Andrews suggested to me that the whole matter should be laid before you, and, if you approve of it, at a Meeting of the Standing Committee, and in this connection I propose, with your approval, to have a Standing Committee during the time when you are over for the 12th, on say Friday or Monday, whichever is most convenient to you.

At the Meeting of the Labour Association, held on Saturday evening last, a strong wish was expressed that if you had time when you are over, you should be asked to say a few words to them. This would give you an opportunity, if you wished, of dealing with domestic matters, particularly those affecting the working classes.

I should be grateful for a line at your leisure. Yours very truly,

R Dawson Bates

(b)

That having regard to the fact that the Orange Institution and the Parliamentary Associations are precluded to a large extent from dealing with domestic matters affecting the working classes, it is felt that it is desirable that this Association should extend its operations so as to afford a greater opportunity to the working classes to belong to it, and so prevent them from joining political Labour Associations whose primary object may be the advancement of Home Rule.

That four Unionist Labour Clubs should be formed forthwith, namely, one in each of the old Parliamentary Divisions of this City, and that later Branches should be formed in such Country Towns as may be deemed advisable.

That during the Winter Lectures should be arranged by prominent speakers on the various topics of the day, and open discussions held, and that Debates should take place between the Members of the different Clubs and branches.

That only those eligible for Membership of the Ulster Unionist Labour Association can become Members of a Club.

All the Members of Clubs and Branches shall by virtue of such Membership be Members of the Ulster Unionist Labour Association.

That the Executive Committee be appointed a Special committee, with power to add to their numbers, to carry out the necessary details.

237 Extracts from the minutes of the labour sub-committee of the U.U.C. relating to a conference with representatives from the Belfast unionist parliamentary associations, 13 September 1918, which discussed labour unionist representation at the next general election, and which heard **(b)** a memorandum of a conference held between the Pottinger, Victoria and Ormeau divisions to consider Mr Scott's statistics relating to the labour vote in Belfast (D 1327/3/11):

(a)

A Conference was held between the above Committee and representatives of the nine Belfast Unionist Parliamentary Associations in the Old Town Hall, Belfast, at 8 o'clock on Friday, 13th September, 1918.

The following were present:—

Mr. H. T. Barrie, D.L., M.P., (in the Chair);   )
Mr. J. M. Andrews, D.L.; Sir George S. Clark, Bart., D.L.;) U.U.C.
Dr. Wm. Gibson; and Mr. R. Dawson Bates.   )

Mr. Geo. S. Massingham, 384 Woodstock Road.   )
Mr. J. W. T. Watters, 32 Ava Street.   ) Ormeau.
Mr. W. H. Snoddy, 66 Ardenlee Avenue.   )

Mr. John S. Shaw, J.P.,; Mr. John McCormick;   ) Pottinger
Mrs. J. Harding.   )

Mr. D. E. Lowry, Oakley, Belmont Church Road.   )
Mr. Robt. Cnambers [*sic*], 123 Antrim Road.   ) Victoria.
Mr. W. H. Scott, 69 Victoria Road.   )

Mr. A. Shaw; Mr. James McGaughey; and Mr. Thos. Mitchell;) Shankill.
and Mr. S. Waring.   )

Mr. John McClatchey; and Mr. S. Cunningham.   ) Woodvale.

Mr. Robt. Tougher; and Mr. E. J. Elliott.   ) Duncairn.

Mr. Hugh McLaurin; Mr. J. S. Reade.   ) St. Anne's

Mr. F. Wheeler;   ) Cromac.

Dr. Gibson made a report as annexed as the result of the Conference between Pottinger, Victoria, and Ormeau Divisions, and read the following resolution which has been passed:—

"That in the opinion of this Meeting it is desirous that each of the old Parliamentary Constituencies of North, South and East Belfast should adopt one Labour Candidate."

After discussion the following resolution was passed:—

"That as North and East Belfast Divisions have each offered a Seat to Labour Candidates. It is requested that the South Division (St. Anne's and Cromac) Executives meet and offer a seat for the third Labour Candidate.

In the event of their doing so, the Labour Unionist Association preferring the third Seat in some other Division, the latter are requested to suggest a suitable third Seat."

Mr. Wheeler stated that he would hold a Meeting of the Executives of St. Anne's and Cromac Divisions.

Mr. Andrews was requested to hold a Meeting of the Ulster Unionist Labour Association on next Saturday subsequent to the Meeting of St. Anne's and Cromac Division.

The Meeting stood adjourned, it being left in Mr. Barrie and Mr. Bates hands to summon the Meeting.

(b)

Resolved that it is advisable that Labour Unionist Candidates should be nominated in three Constituencies containing the largest Labour vote.

That Labour Unionist Members should if possible be returned for each of the old Party Divisions, so that Labour may be represented in North, South and East Divisions.

That on the statistics placed before the Conference by Mr. Scott the Divisions in which there is a preponderating Labour vote are Court and Woodvale, Shankill, Victoria, and St. Anne's.

That the joint Conference of Pottinger, Victoria, and Ormeau Divisions agree to meet in friendly Conference at a subsequent date and with full information before them to allocate one of the East Belfast Seats to a nominee of Unionist Labour.

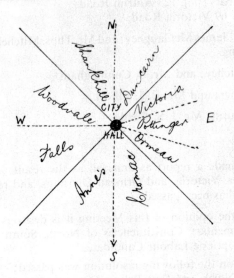

OLD AND NEW PARLIAMENTARY DIVISIONS.

The heavy lines indicate the OLD DIVISIONS, which have been split into 9 New Divisions, viz:—

		Population	The authorities estimate average of five persons to each residence or a total of:—	No. of houses at £8. valuation and under:—	Total percentage of working men's houses in each Division:—
WEST	(Woodvale	43994	8798 Houses	7599	90%
	(Falls	Nationalist	—	—	—
EAST	(Victoria	47260	9452 ,,	6009	69%
	(Pottinger	39173	7834 ,,	5411	80%
	(Ormeau	35257	7051 ,,	4151	60%
NORTH	(Shankill	50467	10093 ,,	6067	60%
	(Duncairn	44080	8816 ,,	6292	80%
SOUTH	(Annes [sic]	40430	8086 ,,	5470	67%
	(Cromac	48537	9707 ,,	3600	40%

238

Extract relating to the Ulster Unionist Labour Association, taken from the report of the interview between Sir Wilson Hungerford and members of staff of the N.I.P.R.O., November 1965 (PRB 987):

Sir Wilson was secretary of this association from its foundation, c. 1917. Sir Edward Carson was increasingly conscious of the need to have card-carrying Trade Union members associated with the Unionist movement to disarm the obvious criticism that it was a movement largely dominated by Conservative landowners. Unionist Labour representatives were invited for the first time to participate in the Irish Convention, 1917, and the Ulster Unionist Labour Association was established shortly afterwards: some English Labour M.P.s had "sent a letter to America concerning the Irish situation" and the Unionist Labour Association was hurriedly established to send a counterblast. In the 1918 election when the representation of Belfast was increased to 9 seats, Carson refused to return with representatives exclusively from the landed gentry (e.g. Gustave Wolff, Dunbar Buller, one of the Downshire family, etc.); he insisted that at least three of the nine M.P.s for Belfast should be Trade Union representatives. Sir Wilson, as secretary of the Unionist Labour Association, went round the various constituency associations in Belfast to try to persuade them to accept Trade Unionists as prospective candidates, but he failed, and it was only when Carson insisted, that Thompson Donald, a shipwright, was accepted for the Victoria division, part of the old East Belfast division, Sam McGuffin, a tenter, for Shankill and Henry Burn, lithographic printer, for St. Anne's. These three members were in fact elected but the experience at Westminster "went to their heads". Entertained by the Duke of Abercorn, Marquis of Dufferin and Ava, etc., they got "swelled heads" and were largely failures in their political careers. These men were obviously unable to live in London on the £400 a year salary which was paid to M.P.s at this time, so the Ulster Unionist Council had to subsidise them considerably. After the establishment of the state in 1921 Donald wanted to continue as member for Victoria in East Belfast but he was pushed out because Herbert Dixon wanted the seat; Donald was never afterwards prominent in politics and ended up as caretaker of the Police Courts. McGuffin and Burn both took seats in the Northern Ireland Parliament for a short time. Herbert Dixon disliked this experiment with Trade Unionists as Unionist M.P.s and the scheme was not pursued. Sir Wilson was critical of Herbert Dixon in this respect and thought that the present weakness of the Unionist vote in working class Belfast may thus be largely explained.

The chairman of the Unionist Labour Association at this time was "Johnnie" Andrews and other prominent members were John F. Gordon and William Grant, both of whom later became Ministers.

Both Grant and Gordon had stood as Unionist candidates at the 1918 election, without success. Another unsuccessful Unionist Trade Union candidate at this election was Robert McBride who was put up to attract the farm labourer's vote. Another prominent member of the group was John Hanna who was selected to represent the Unionist Trade Union element at the Irish Convention, 1917.

Sir Wilson described the usually monthly meetings of the Unionist Labour Association, with "Johnnie" Andrews suprisingly masterful in the chair, and Grant and Gordon dodging away before the end of the meeting to avoid being pestered by members with grievances. The implication was that the whole proceedings became increasingly futile since the movement had not the support of the Chief Whip, Dixon. Sir Wilson mentioned incidentally that it was very striking how uncontrollable the meeting became when someone like Grant or Gordon, of working class background, had to take the chair as deputy for Andrews. In general he thought the great weakness of Trade Unionists in politics was their bitter jealousy of each other.

VIII

The six counties did not escape the Anglo-Irish war, so Ulster unionists in addition to their other difficulties had to concern themselves with the maintenance of law and order and the defence of the border. As distressing as the actual number of outrages which were perpetrated was the general sense of uncertainty, especially in Belfast with its clearly defined but contiguous Roman Catholic and protestant areas such as the catholic Falls and the protestant Shankill. In this atmosphere of uncertainty one incident could easily spark off a chain of events. In Lisburn on 22 August 1920 Inspector Swanzy of the R.I.C., recently transferred from Cork where the I.R.A. held him responsible for the death of lord mayor MacCurtain, was murdered. This murder led to the burning of catholic houses not only in Lisburn, but also in Banbridge, Bangor and Belfast, where troops had to open fire on 25 August.

To assist in the protection of life and property, the U.V.F. was revived in July 1920 under the command of Lt-colonel Wilfrid Spender and with the tacit approval of the government. The experiment was not wholly successful, partly because of the attitude of Neville Macready, commander-in-chief in Ireland, and partly because the work was too arduous for a volunteer force. Therefore Spender suggested the reorganisation of the force into a special constabulary. This force, financed by the British government, was enrolled from November 1920 onwards. It comprised three classes, 'A' a full-time and paid force, 'B' an occasional force with an allowance, and 'C' an unpaid reserve. Working in conjunction with the police, the special constabulary provided the government with a formidable armed force with which to keep law and order and to maintain the border against I.R.A. attacks. By March 1922 it was said that the government of Northern Ireland controlled an armed force of 20,000 men over and above the police force. As soon as the state seemed secure the 'As' and 'Cs' were disbanded, but the controversial 'Bs' remained until 1970. Initially these 'Bs' were not equipped with full uniform; and it is, perhaps, interesting to note that, much to the disgust of some orangemen, care was taken lest the force be identified with orangeism.

239

Extracts, 21, 22, 23, 25 July, 26,27 August, 6, 11 September 1920, from a diary of riots and disturbances in Belfast (July 1920–April 1923) kept by F. H. Crawford (D 640/11):

(a)

While out today at Speech Day at Campbell College we heard there had been some trouble on the Queen's Island ship-building yard between Sinn Feiners & Unionists. . . .

While I was cutting tennis lawn I heard a machine gun playing for quite a while. Last night my works were invaded & some stuff destroyed by what I consider must have been mischevous [*sic*] boys. About 10 p.m. I went down to see that all was right in the works & then [went] up the Shankhill [*sic*] Rd. and down the side streets to where the soldiers & Police were holding the Falls Rd. entrances

In one street as I arrived where the piquet was stationed The police who were nearer the Falls end of street drove back five or six young fellows thro[ugh] the piquets & told latter not to allow them back again. One was the worse of liquor & had lost his cap, he insisted on going back again to get his cap & was so persistant [*sic*] that at last the soldiers lost patience & pressed several bayonets against his chest. I tried to persuade the youngster to go back but he was very obstinant [*sic*], at last an elderly man (we were all well within the Unionist bound[a]ry & the youngster himself was a Unionist) caught him by the shoulder & another took him by the other shoulder and walked him off. I followed, but when about 20 y[ar]ds from the piquet he shook himself free of those who held him & said he was going back to "bate" the police, and it looked as if the young fool would insist in getting into trouble, two of the piquet had followed him up about 10 yds off & when he stopped & talked about "bating" the police they came along & there probably would have been trouble only an idea struck me, so turning round to some young men I said (So that the young fool would hear) this fellow must be a Sinn Feiner then I turned to him & said he was no protestant or Orangeman but a mean low sinn Feiner or he would not interfere with the soldiers doing his [*sic*] duty. Others

round [him] then took it up & said he must be a sinn Feiner. When the youngster saw he was likely to be taken for a Sinn Feiner & realising that this would
mean a good hammering once it was believed, he disappeared about as quickly
as it was possible to do so . . . .

(b)

Three of my men not in today one came in for his money wounded in the
hand & knee . . .

(c)

. . . The Unionists were running down the street apparently with a view of
engaging the two boys & the Sinn Feiners at the other end & a holy? row
there would have been but I got in front of our lot and ordered them back . . . .
The two brothers (for such it turned out they were) stayed half way between
the two hostile crowds (tho their own lot gave them no encouragement)
shouting & jeering at the Unionists. At last the tall one came up to me, . . .
struck me a blow on each ear & made off followed by the other, I drew my
automatic pistol & am thankful I did not fire as I was very angry. But soon
my hands were full trying to keep back the crowd of Unionist[s] who on seeing
the treacherous was [way] I had been attacked they were neither to be bound
nor tied. However I appealed to them for the credit of the district & also for
the sake of our Great Leader Sir Edward & with the exception of throwing
back the bricks the two brothers were throwing at them nothing happened.
The nuicence [nuisance] of the thing is that the women & children instead of
staying indoors fill up the street so that they hamper their own side and offer
excellent targets to the enemy. I came down thro the Sinn Fein district as
usual on my way home. I was stopped by several of these people who
apologised for what had happened and explained that one of the two brothers
had been twice in the Lunatic Asylum . . . .

(d)

When Marjorie Bea & I were going out to church Robt. Johnston &
another man came in at the gate and reported that they had got notices to
leave the district & that several houses had been attacked & the windows
smashed. They wanted some protection. I have some hand grenades that I
have had made for the protection of the City Hall & which are not required
just at present so I went with the two of them & filled two grenades with
dynamite fuze & detonator.

. . . I am using these hand grenades & lending some of them to reliable
men who reside in danger zones & where they may be murdered any night.
Three of unionist workmen were shot dead on last Wednesday or Thursday as
they were coming from their work, by Sinn Feiners in a house opposite where
they were walking . . . .

(e)

. . . The burni[n]g has started badly after D[istrict]. I[nspector]. Menzcy
[Swanzy?] was murdered in such a brutal way. Lisburn is like a bombarded town
in France. There were 14 or 15 fires in Belfast. All this is done by [protestants-
erased] Unionists as a protest against these cold blooded murders & the
victims are Rebels or their Sympathisers . . . .

(f)

. . . On my arrival up this afternoon I had a walk round & saw that all the pains [*sic*] of our works & office . . . were smashed & in protestant houses in Hastings St & adjoining streets . . . . On the way home I saw big fires in Sandy Row. It is so senseless this destruction of property, but we can't get the responsible better class working men to interfere with the result they will have to pay for all this destruction of property . . . .

(g)

. . . We have been the only firm who have kept their works open in the district. They have raided several in the vicinity. They threatened to burn down our works because just now we happen to have no R.C. employees & they want to stop our men & women earning their wages when the R.Cs cant get into the Mills & other places owing to their being closed. . . .

(h)

. . . I took Adair up to Lisburn to see the state it was It reminded me of a french town after it had been bombarded by the Germans as I saw in France 1916. We visited the ruins of the Priests' house on chapel hill it was burnt or gutted & the furniture all destroyed. When coming down the avenue I found a small pair of manicure scissors that had been thro the fire. I kept them as a souvenir of the event. We called at Mr. Stephensons & had tea there Mrs. Thompson his sister was also with him They told me of some very hard cases of where Unionists had lost practically all they had by the fire of the house of a catholic spreading to theirs, and also of some very decent respectable families of long standing loosing [*sic*] everything also. But when one thinks of the brutal cold blooded murder of Inspector Swanzie [*sic*] one does not wonder at the mob loosing [*sic*] its head with fury . . . . It has been stated that there are only four or five R.C. families left in Lisburn others say this is wrong that there are far more. Be that as it may there certainly are practically no shops or places of business left to the R.Cs . . . .

240 Extract relating to the formation of the Ulster special constabulary, taken from Lt-colonel W. Spender's account of the U.V.F. and the Larne gun-running, written c. 1959 (D 1295/2):

I will now deal with the events in 1920.

At this time the Government under Lloyd George was trying to find some compromise of a Council in Irlenad [Ireland] which would deal with local affairs, but retain in Westminster the conduct of Foreign affairs, Customs, Postal services &c. There would still be M.P.s from all Ireland, but in reduced numbers. Those old Irish Liberals who were still loyal to the British Empire were favourably disposed to some such solution, but the majority of the Southern Irish were filled with hatred of any British control, and caused violent disturbances to prevent any such solution. The Black & Tans under General Tudor were raised to assist the R.I.C. in restoring order. There was a sub-committee of the Cabinet dealing with Irish affairs, of which Craig was a member. At Carson's suggestion he proposed that the U.V.F., which by then had more or less ceased to function, should be re-raised, and I was asked to come over from England to take over the command, giving up my post as Officers' Friend at the Ministry of Pensions. Hamar Greenwood, Secretary of State for Ireland, told me that this proposal had Lloyd George's tacit approval, but that it would be politically unwise to announce this publicly, and Hamar Greenwood apparently did not take the trouble to inform Macready, then C. in C. of the Army in Ireland. Macready continued his fatuous policy of transferring loyalist constabulary and other officials to the South, and replacing them in the North by extreme Nationalists. Luckily I knew General Tudor, and was a warm friend of General Carter-Campbell in Belfast. He had invited me to go as Chief Staff Officer to him when he got command of the Highland Division. I did not however know the other General in Ulster who was stationed in Londonderry. Of course at this time there was a very large number of officers and men in Ulster who had returned from War service, as well as those members of the old U.V.F. who, as I have mentioned, did not join up. Many of them were war weary, but most of them responded to the request for their support in getting the U.V.F. on to a proper footing. I decided to concentrate my attention on Belfast and Londonderry, leaving it to County Commandants—Perceval-Maxwell, Ricardo, Lord Massarene [*sic*], Sir Basil Brooke and others—to run their own areas. I persuaded Colonel Moore-Irvine to go to Londonderry as my representative where he established friendly relations with the local general.

On the whole we were getting on fairly successfully until Macready determined that if he could disarm everyone in Ireland he would secure peace. This was to apply not only to the murderers and rebels, who could of course hide away their arms until they intended to commit an outrage, but also to those who merely wanted to protect their homes, and to the U.V.F. who were helping the loyal R.I.C. commissioners and the Army to keep things quiet. Matters came to a head when the U.V.F. learned that Sinn Fein was going to attack the G.P.O. in Londonderry, and turned up just in time. When the troops, who would have been too late, came on the scene, they had orders to take away the rifles from the Volunteers. I crossed to London that night, and told Sir Hamar Greenwood that the situation was now impossible, and that I could not carry on unless the Army and R.I.C. authorities were told officially that the Government recognised the U.V.F., and wished them to cooperate in keeping order. At first Hamar Greenwood tried to make light of the affair, saying that when he was in Canada he was always ready to defend his own home. I asked him whether he could have done so if the R[oyal]. Can[a]dian Mounted Police had orders to take away any weapons he might have. This shook him, and he undertook to let Macready know that the Army and the R.I.C. were to cooperate not only with the Black & Tans but equally with the U.V.F. in Ulster. After this there was an improvement in the situation, and I was able to allow the U.V.F. to resume their patrols with the Military forces, although even then Macready wished them to store their arms with the constabulary, and to return to their homes unarmed. I then gave an order to the U.V.F. that no Volunteer was to take his weapon outside his house exceot [except] on some authorised mission, and that if he were asked to give up his rifle at home he would be fully supported if he refused to do so. I sent a copy of this instruction to

446

Macready, and both General Carter-Campbell and the Londonderry General gave orders to their troops to work with the U.V.F., and to use our intelligence services.

All these duties, mainly at night, were unpaid, and were putting a severe strain on our men, and I then put forward the proposal that the U.V.F. should be changed into three types of Special Constabulary, Class A, Class B, and Class C, and should be paid as such. Sir John Anderson, later Lord Waverley, then one of three Under Secretaries for Ireland, sent his Assistant Secretary to meet me and the County Commandants in, I think, Belfast City Hall, and it was due to Sir John that the British Government accepted our proposals.

You will appreciate that the situation in 1920 was quite different from the one in 1914. Everything was decentralised as far as possible, not only to counties but also to districts. There was no big central Headquarters in Belfast, no central post-office &c. The U.V.F. Despatch Riders were no longer required in sections, but still worked with the U.V.F. and sometimes even with the Army units. I can however remember one occasion when they acted for the Northern Government, and that was to keep in touch with the Boundary Commission under Mr Justice Feetham.

241

Memorandum describing the purpose and nature of the special constabulary, issued by Spender to all officers commanding battalions of the Belfast U.V.F., 29 October 1920 (D 1700/5/16):

The Government has decided to raise a Force of Special Constabulary in the Six Counties of Ulster, and it seems advisable to let you know the views of the Ulster Volunteer Force Headquarters in regard to this Force.

Sir Edward Carson and our Leaders are anxious to help the Government in restoring and maintaining order in the Province, and they consider that the Government's scheme of Special Constabulary will do much in carrying this into effect. In these circumstances, I confidently rely on the Members of the Ulster Volunteer Force to do all they can to make the Special Constabulary Forces a success. Moreover, by restoring order in their own district they are making it possible for the Government to do more in the other parts of Ireland where the rebel forces predominate, and where our comrades are now being subjected to measures of terrorism.

The Government plans are a great advance on all previous proposals. The Government has definitely recognised that there are two distinct elements among the population:—Those who are loyal to the British Crown and Empire, and those who are not. The Government is asking the help of all Loyalists in Ulster, and proposes to arm with Firearms all those called on for duty, to confer certain privileges, to recognise them, and to indemnify them for injuries incurred by the performance of their duties.

I know that our Great Leader can feel certain that all members of the U.V.F. who join the Special Constabulary will recollect that the good name of Ulster will depend upon their performing their duties conscientiously and impartially, under discipline, and with that restraint towards those who disagree with us which has always marked the attitude of our Organisation.

The new Ulster Parliament will depend for its initial success in a large measure on the efficient way in which the Special Constables perform their duties, and Ulstermen will, I am confident, again show to the world that their country's difficulty is their opportunity to prove their loyalty and their worth.

The system of enrolment is that, as soon as the Proclamation is issued, Forms of Enrolment will be available at each Police Station, and these forms can either be filled in individually or collected in at any suitable centre, *e.g.*, Battalion Headquarters, and sent in in bulk.

The names will be considered by a Selection Committee consisting of Magistrates specially appointed, and other assistants.

I have no doubt that the U.V.F. will give to these Magistrates all the help in their power, so as to ensure that its members who join this Force are reliable and can be trusted with Firearms.

No Medical Inspection is required for Classes "B" and "C," but is of course required for Class "A." It is, however, the duty of U.V.F. Commanders to see that no names are sent forward of men who would be obviously physically unfit for performing their duties.

The Arms for the "B" and "C" Forces will probably be kept in the Local Police Barracks, at which the men will consequently have to parade.

The terms of service have been outlined in the papers, but the following explanatory notes may be useful though not official:—

CLASS "A."

This is a paid Force, and though it is very desirable that the best type of men should join this Force, we can only make clear the conditions and let the men judge it for themselves from a business point of view.

The Weekly Cash Pay will be £3 17s 6d, in addition to Uniform and quarters, and an extra sum of nearly 10s. a week will be given as a Bounty at the end of approved service in lieu of pension. Married men will receive additional allowances.

This Force will only be employed in the Six Counties.

The Contract for Service will be for six months, but it is confidently expected that those who do good service and who wish to remain on will have a chance of making it a career. Should the Ulster Government be established, the Ulster Unionist Council will watch the interests of this Force.

It must be made clear to the men who join this Force that except for the fact that their service is restricted to the Six Counties, they will be, to all intents and purposes, part of the Royal Irish Constabulary, serving under R.I.C. Officers and Sergeants of all religious creeds.

It is true that a portion of this Force will probably be formed into "Black and Tan" Companies, serving under Military Officers and their own N.C.O's, but no guarantee can be given to any individual joining this Force that he will be selected for one of these Companies, and therefore any man who is not prepared to serve loyally with the R.I.C. should not be urged to join.

Certain numbers of Class "A" have been ear-marked for each County, but should any County not reach its quota additional vacancies will be available for other Counties.

The numbers of Class "A" allotted to Belfast is believed to be approximately 400, and there is no doubt they will be forthcoming. Ex-service men will have a prior claim.

CLASS "B."

This is really a Volunteer Force, and the men who join will be under their own elected Officers and N.C.O's, subject in each case to the approval of the "next Senior."

In the case of Belfast, they will probably be asked to give one half-night's duty per week, or one night's duty per fortnight.

The number required in Belfast for this Force will be 4,000, and if the system of Night Duty is adopted, 500 men will be on duty each night in two reliefs of 250 each.

The probable tour of half-night duty will be about four hours, or more probably nearly five hours, in the longer winter nights.

I have said that this Force is really a Volunteer Force, but the Government propose to make the members an allowance, which will work out at nearly 4s for each tour of duty if the system of half-nights a week is adopted, or at nearly 8s if a whole night's duty is given once a fortnight. This is intended to cover wear and tear of clothes, and, if necessary, to pay for hot meals and also tram expenses.

These men will serve in the City of Belfast, as far as possible in the vicinity of their homes. They will always be armed with Firearms when on duty. The class of Firearm may vary. They will be given their own Caps and Armlets. Capes will be available for those who require them, but will not be the personal property of the Special Constable.

They will be indemnified in the same way as the R.I.C., against any injury which may be due to their undertaking these duties and it is believed that this indemnification will cover any malicious injuries that they may receive off-duty, if due to the fact that they have joined this Force.

Although no guarantee will be given that these men may not be called upon for duty more than one night a week, it is exceedingly unlikely that they will be required to do so as there is a large Reserve Force, Class "C," that would be called upon before any men of class "B" are asked to undertake further duty. It is exceedingly unlikely that day duty will be required for these same reasons.

It is not the intention of the Authorities to employ U.V.F. members who may join this Force on duty in Nationalist areas.

Although the men of this Force will act under their own Officers and N.C.O's and will have their own City Commandant, they must be prepared to co-operate with the R.I.C.

It is probable that Patrols will consist of three or more members of the Special Constabulary with one R.I. Constable. There are great advantages in this system of co-operation with the R.I.C., and any man who joins this Force must be prepared to work with them.

The 4,000 required for the City of Belfast means roughly 200 or 300 from each U.V.F. Battalion, and I feel that I can confidently rely that these numbers will be forthcoming.

It is understood that owners of bicycles who may use their bicycles on patrol duty will receive a bicycle allowance of 1s for each night's duty.

CLASS "C."

This is a General Reserve Force.

The members receive no allowances, but will be fully indemnified like the members of Class "B."

The number required in Belfast is 6,000.

The men who join this Force will not be called up for duty except in emergency, *e.g.*, if a situation in Belfast arises so that more than 250 men are required for the tour of duty any night the men of this Force will be asked to come out and help so that the men of Class "B" might not have to do more than one tour of duty per week. In normal cases the men of this Force will not be called up at all except for occasional drills.

The total number of Special Constabulary for Belfast (in addition to the 400 Class "A") will be therefore 10,000, consisting of 4,000 Class "B" and 6,000 Class "C." There is no reason why the U.V.F. should not furnish all the numbers required, and I confidently hope that this will prove to be the case, and that they will elect, as far as possible, those Leaders who have voluntarily helped in the past to perform the duty which the State is now prepared to take over.

242 *Letter from F. H. Crawford to Colonel R. H. Wallace, grand master of the Belfast orangemen, Myra Castle, Downpatrick, Co. Down, 16 December 1920, protesting against the Belfast grand lodge's lack of enthusiasm for the special constabulary (D 1700/5 /16B):

My dear Bob—I knew nothing of the meeting of the Belfast Grand Lodge till a number of Old Orangemen (I mean long time in the order) told me of it & were very indignant about it

As you know I have only joined the order a short time, but I have for many years held it in the highest esteem.

The two points to be considered are, Sir Edward put himself to infinite trouble to get the U.V.F recognised & by his enormous influence & weight, he has got it recognised in [the] B. & C. Class of the Special Constables. When over last, he said he would do what he could for the men who were crying out to be armed & organised by the Gov[ern]m[en]t. to protect their homes & persons. Sir Edward has got this force with all the privileges offered to the police if they are killed or wounded in the performance of their duty. When he got the sanction of the Gov[ern]m[en]t. to the present scheme he made an appeal to the people (loyal) of Ulster to come forward & join this force as either A. B. or C. Surely the "people of Ulster" includes orangemen. He made no special appeal to either Unionist Clubs or U.V.F. as such, but to all Ulster Unionists. How has the orange body met this appeal? Simply by telling their members to join or leave it alone, if this is not letting our chief down it certainly is not giving him a leg up. A district master was asked by a number of influential orangemen to call a meeting to keep forward the B recruiting, his answer was, "I cant call a meeting for this purpose tho I should like to, after the action of the Grand Lodge" There is a strong feeling amongst all the orangemen who have come to me of their own accord, that the action of the Grand Lodge was done hastily or without due consideration.

They all say Sir Edward wants them to join up & their leaders (orange) have turned the scheme down & no meetings can be held officially Orange to help the recruiting.

The next point to be considered is who will be responsible for the safety of life & property when the new Government of Ulster is established & the troops are withdrawn, which they shall be?

It will be the R.I.C. regular forces & A. B. & C. of Special Constables. Surely if this is a fact, the more orangemen we have in that force, the better it will be for Protestant interests & the success of the Orange body itself. This seems perfectly patent.

We must remember the old adage "He who is not with me is against me"

Orangemen must come out now or be very sorry later that they have been neutrals, when they see Nationalists filling the ranks of an armed force where they might have been.

Think over this Bob and dont let us have any regrets for what might have been. Yours very sincerely

Fred. H. Crawford

243 Letter from C. E. Duffin, 9 Waring Street, Belfast, to his mother, Broad Walk Hotel, De Vere Gardens, London W., 6 April 1921, describing incidents in Belfast and his first police duty with the 'Bs' (Mic 127/27):

Dear Mother—I was glad to hear that the Doctor is hopeful about your case & do hope he will put you right & not turn out a second Miss Knowles. Two fellows threw a couple of Mills bombs into the back entrance to the Ulster Club where we have a military guard but nobody was hurt as they were behind sand bags. It was at eleven o'clock just as I was going up to the Stock Exchange. I saw the crowd running but as usual nobody was caught. Yesterday a Corporation official was held up at revolver point on the Falls Road & a bag with money for wages seized but two detectives happened to be on the spot at the time & captured three of the robbers after a chase over the bog meadows. I did my first police duty on Monday night & found it dull work. I went on patrol with a policeman round Cavehill Rd district & except for "moving on" a crowd of youths who congregate at Fortwilliam Park in the evenings & among women, we had no excitement. I then did sentry go for two hours outside the barracks & Dermot Campbell & Smiles arrived triumphantly with a curfew prisoner. We got a cup of tea at 11 & then started off with a Sergt & policeman all round the Fortwilliam area & I got home rather weary at 2.30 AM Fortunately it was a fine night & we are allowed to smoke after curfew. We have a belt, baton, revolver, cap & armlet & look rather like Salvation army men.

We go off to a dance to-night at Holywood which I am not looking forward to much. It looks as if you will be stuck in London for some time but the change will do you good. Please sign & return the enclosed dividend warrant & I can then send Miss Hannay her cheque. Your loving son,

Edmund

IX

In 1921 the unionists of the six counties reaped their reward for their determined opposition to a Dublin parliament, when the government of Ireland act of 1920 came into operation in the north. Carson stepped down from the Ulster unionist leadership in favour of Sir James Craig who became the first prime minister of Northern Ireland.

On 24 May, empire day, elections to the Northern Ireland parliament were held—the first general election in the British Isles to be held under the system of proportional representation. 40 unionist candidates (including 6 unionist labour men), 12 nationalists, 5 labour men and 20 Sinn Feiners were nominated for 52 seats. The result was an overwhelming victory for the unionists who had expected to win 32 seats. All 40 unionists were returned, the other 12 seats being equally divided between nationalists and Sinn Feiners. The first Northern Ireland parliament assembled in the council chamber of the Belfast City Hall on 7 June 1921, and was formally opened on 22 June, when, despite the advice of his entourage, who were concerned about the violence in Ireland, George V and Queen Mary visited Belfast to perform the ceremony.

The opening was considered a brilliant success, but the northern state was not completely secure. On the one hand, British politicians tried to persuade Ulster unionists to cooperate in an all-Ireland parliament by threatening an unfavourable revision of the boundary between north and south. The Anglo-Irish treaty of December 1921, which ended the 'war of independence' and set up the Irish Free State, applied to the whole of Ireland; but Northern Ireland was given the choice, quickly taken up, of opting out of the agreement and retaining her former status. On the other hand, the existence of the state was threatened in 1922 by a campaign of violence and sectarian strife. In 1922, 232 people, including two unionist M.P.s, were killed, nearly 1,000 were wounded, and more than £3,000,000 worth of property destroyed. Belfast was particularly badly hit and it needed not only the British troops but also the special constabulary to prevent the state from dissolving into anarchy. It was not, therefore, until 1923 that Northern Ireland could feel reasonably secure. There remained the threat of the ultimately ineffective boundary commission, but by 1923, with the north in comparative peace and the south still convulsed by civil war, even 'Fred.' Crawford could turn his attention to his own personal problems. His chemical manufacturing business had run down over the past few years, and he now applied to Sir James Craig for a job in the new northern state to solve his financial difficulties. Appropriately enough, he was put in charge of an arms depot.

244 Extract relating to the first elections to the Northern Ireland parliament, from the *Annual report* of the U.U.C. for 1921 (D 972/17/1921):

On the 24th May, 1921, the Elections for the Northern Parliament took place. The Unionist Party put forward 40 candidates for the 52 seats. During the previous month meetings had been held in every town and village in the Northern area and stirring speeches delivered. Sir Edward Carson and Sir James Craig issued Manifestoes to the Loyalists of Ulster. Scenes of the greatest enthusiasm prevailed, and everywhere the most exhaustive poll was recorded, as the returns from the various constituencies showed. The Loyalists won a great and memorable victory.

The following are the names of the successful candidates:—

BELFAST, NORTH—
    Lloyd Campbell.
    S. M'Guffin.
    Wm. Grant.
    R. J. M'Keown.

BELFAST, SOUTH—
T. Moles.
Right Hon. H. M. Pollock.
Sir Crawford M'Cullagh.
Mrs. M'Mordie.

BELFAST, EAST—
Right Hon. Sir R. Dawson Bates.
Captain Herbert Dixon.
Thompson Donald.
James A. Duff.

BELFAST, WEST—
T. H. Burn.
R. J. Lynn.
W. J. Twaddell.

COUNTY ANTRIM—
J. Milne Barbour.
Major the Hon. Hugh O'Neill.
G. B. Hanna, B.L.
Robert Crawford.
R. D. Megaw.
John F. Gordon.

COUNTY DOWN—
Right Hon. Sir James Craig, Bart.
Right Hon. J. M. Andrews, D.L.
Hon. H. Mulholland.
T. R. Lavery.
R. M'Bride.
T. W. M'Mullan.

COUNTIES TYRONE AND FERMANAGH—
Right Hon. E. M. Archdale, D.L.
William Coote.
W. T. Miller.
James Cooper.

COUNTY ARMAGH—
R. Best, K.C.
Major D. G. Shillington.

COUNTY AND CITY OF LONDONDERRY—
Sir Robert N. Anderson, D.L.
Mrs. R. S. Chichester.
John M. Mark.

QUEEN'S UNIVERSITY OF BELFAST—
John Campbell, F.R.C.S., M.D.
John H. Robb, B.L.
Professor R. J. Johnstone, B.A., M.B.
H. S. Morrison, M.D., D.L.

The first Cabinet of the Northern Parliament contain[s] the names of those who have given freely of their services to Ulster, and they are all members of the Council. The Prime Minister is one of the original members, the Marquis of Londonderry is one of the Vice-Presidents; the Right Hon. J. M. Andrews is one of the Honorary Secretaries; the Right Hon. E. M. Archdale is Chairman of the Standing Committee; the Right Hon. Sir R. Dawson Bates was Secretary since the formation of the Council; and the Right Hon. H. M. Pollock is a member of the Standing Committee. To all these gentlemen we offer our heartiest congratulations.

245 Extracts relating to the opening of the first Northern Ireland parliament on 22 June 1921, from a 422-page typescript copy of part of Lady Craig's diary (D 1415/B/38):

Jun. 17. J[ames]. sends a wire to the Queen, asking if she would honour Ulster by coming over with His Majesty. We hear from the Palace authorities later, that many letters have been received there begging that Their Majesties should not go over to Ulster

Jun. 18. The twins arrive from Eton in a great state of thrill. Jimmy Hamilton has also been allowed to come over, a wire comes to J. "The Queen will have much pleasure in accompanying the King to Belfast, in accordance with the kind invitation contained in your message of yesterday. Stamfordham." This causes great delight, and excitement all over. We go to a Methodist garden party, where J. gets a great ovation, and has to make a speech.

Jun. 19. The Duke [Duchess] of Abercorn comes to stay, I arrange with her in London by telephone, about an address being presented to the Queen, now that she is coming too, from the Loyalist Women of Ulster. A very nice article about J. in the Sunday Express by Percival Phillips. "Ulster is safe in James Craig's hands, said an old Covenanter, when I asked him what the six Counties thought of their new Prime Minister; we trust him absolutely, and an Ulsterman cannot say more . . . His is the outstanding personality in the new Government . . . he is a tower of strength for Ulster, and he faces with serene confidence a task which might well stagger any statesman."

Jun. 20 The table plan for our luncheon finally settled, after endless work; and goes to be printed. The children and I GO IN TO see the Royal horses that have arrived for the procession, the straw edging their stalls is all plaited with red white and blue ribbons, and the Head Coachman assures us that it is an 'ome from 'ome.'

Jun. 21. Lord Fitzalan, and two A.D.Cs. to breakfast, also the Hamar Greenwoods, Dolly Abercorn, and Ruby Carson who are all stopping with us. The Senate of Northern Ireland meet for the first time, People in and out all day long. J. has his first Government dinner on the eve of Parliament opening, and I take all my other guests down to Crawfordsburn to dine, where we find a large party of people staying.

Jun. 22. The great day, (22, again!) The King and Queen have the most wonderful reception, the decorations everywhere are extremely well done

455

and even the little side streets that they will never be within miles of are draped with bunting and flags, and the pavement and lampposts painted red white and blue, really most touching, as a sign of their loyalty. Imagine Radicals in England thinking they would ever succeed in driving people like that out of the British Empire, or wanting to! J. goes to the Docks of course to meet them and gets a great welcome from the enormous crowds everywhere along the route. They drive up High Street, and Donegall Place, to the City Hall. Luckily it was not very far, and precautions had been taken of every description, trusted men stationed in each house, and on every roof top, and the closest scrutiny of all in the houses, and of course in the streets too. Every alternate policeman faced the crowd, but as there were troops in front, this was not specially apparent. The actual Opening was the first of the functions, after which the boys and I were taken along to the Parlour, and I went in to be received by the Queen, who told me they were quite astounded by their welcome, Pi had previously presented her with a bouquet. The boys and Jimmy Hamilton went in to be presented to the King, who said he had heard from the Head Master at Eton, that he had given them leave to come over. He also said to our Jimmy, that it was very unfair of him to be so much taller than his brother when they were twins. Then followed our big luncheon, J. sitting between Their Majesties. It proves to be a great success. We then all went across to the Ulster Hall, where addresses were presented, Dolly Abercorn and I handing one to the Queen from the loyalist women of Ulster. After that there was an investiture, the scenes in the Hall were unforgettable, as the people could not contain themselves, and cheered for several minutes, and broke into singing the National Anthem at a moment when it was not on the official programme. They finally left again for the Docks, J. and all the official people going with them, after a visit that was nothing but one huge success from first to last. When J. rejoined me at home again, he heaved the biggest sigh of relief imaginable, at having got them safely on to the Royal Yacht again, after such a marvellous day without any contretemps to either of them. The King said to J. when he was saying goodbye in the yacht, "I can't tell you how glad I am I came, but you know my entourage were very much against it". J. replied, "Sir, you are surrounded by pessimists, we are all optimists over here". The Press was of course full of it all for days, amongst the best accounts being that in the Morning Post . . .

J. receives messages from all over the world of good wishes to him, the people, and the new Parliament. the decorations had portraits of their Majesties and J. prominently displayed, the Tatler says "I wonder how he (J.) will like his new job. Not an altogether unmixed joy I should imagine, and life must be rather too full of excitements and alarms to make things very comfortable. Imagine always having to go about with guards and detectives, I hear Sir James' small daughter simply revels in the life, so somebody's pleased at any rate." The Daily Chronicle says "Sir James Craig had a fine reception when he drove up. He has been an outstanding figure of course in today's ceremonies, and this sketch of him flung at me in a few vivid words by one of his friends, is pertinent. He is a man of character rather than subtlety. He is ready with a plan and goes straight to his object, disregarding cross currents and side issues. A man of great common sense, he has much of the nature of General Botha. It may be added that he has as difficult a part to play as General Botha, but his friends believe he will succeed". All parties were represented at the day's events bar the Roman Catholic Church and Nationalists, Cardinal Logue in his letter . . . pleading an engagement elsewhere. . . .

Jun. 25. Letter from Dolly A[bercorn]. thanking us for their visit to us, in the course of which she says, "Everybody is rejoiced at the success of the visit, and the K. and Q. simply overcome by their reception, it has opened the eyes of a good many over here. Well you must be worn out, but if you will forgive my saying it, I never saw anyone carry out all your somewhat difficult duties with more dignity and poise; and you were a credit to that wonderful man, your husband." . . .

246

Extracts from F. H. Crawford's diary of disorder, relating to the changing condition of Northern Ireland and to his personal financial position, 22, 23 June 1922, 29 January, 17 April 1923 (D 640/11):

(a)

. . . When I got into the house my wife told me Sam Cosley had phoned up that the works had been set on fire but that he had got it out

Forbes & I had some cocoa & I started & walked down about 11.40 p.m. On the way I called at Donegall Pass B[arrac]ks and asked the Dover st H[ea]d Constable to send a man to have a look round at the back while I went into the works thro the front . . . . Parafin [*sic*] had been scattered about beside some empty barrels & three incendiary bombs had been left one had exploded or gone off as it was a simple tin canister & the head had been blown out the head was a peculiar shape, the others one on a tin roof & one on the floor had not gone off, but may do so yet. I lifted the one off the floor & put it in an open space where it had an earthen floor & could do no harm, if it does go off. I left the one on the roof & intend to visit it every hour . . . .

I have just come in to the office where I am writing this after my hourly inspection of the works, it is now 2.15 a.m. real time about 12.45 a.m. the darkest time of a summer night. Walking in the dark on my tip toes & rubber soles thro the works not knowing what the next step has in store for me, or if there is an intruder, for him [?] reminds me of the time in S[outh]. A[frica]. during the war 1900, when I went out on the veldt to lay & explode a dummy mine at the suggestion of the commandant . . . .

(b)

Nothing happened the night before last after I had written last para[graph]. I stayed till about 6.40 am then went home, after going round each hour, the incendiary bombs were machine made with alliminum [*sic*] fittings & of an exact pattern. Probably made in some South Irish munition factory, they had a triger [*sic*] leaver [*sic*] to set them of[f] on the same pattern as the "Mills" bombs used during the war, this struck a cap which ignited a short fuse with a primer at the end which caused the contents of [the] cylinder to ignite, the substance used was a mixture of aliminum [sic] powder & something else this burned for some time at a great heat the cylinders made of tin are $6\frac{5}{8}''$ long by 3″ diameter, a leaver [sic] & striker same as "Mills" bombs with a primer about $\frac{1}{2}''$ diameter & 4″ long runs [sic] down the centre filled with a much finer similar powder easier ignited . . . .

(c)

Since I last wrote about passing events in Ulster things have been quiet in Belfast & rest of Ulster . . . .

Tho things have been comparatively quiet it unfortunately has not been so in the S. & W. of Ireland but on the contrary an intensified war of pillage arson murder & outrage had been going on in all the southern & western Districts. When we were having outrages of all descriptions in Ulster & especially in Belfast, the people of Dublin twitted us with the condition of our city. The Authorities gradually got the situation better in hand in Belfast & rest of the six Counties with the result that now we are practically free from political crime. No doubt the Authorities have been assisted by the gun men practically all clearing down to the South . . . .

(d)

Lately my business has been going from bad to worse, since the war, In The commircial [sic] year before last, the business lost about £2500; Last year the business only made £150. I have an overdraft of £7,000, I have come to the end of my tether, If I sold all my property I would come out square with the Bank, & thank God I owe nothing to anyone else, but then I would only possess what I stood in so to speak, This is a very serious position with a wife & four children to provide for & see them educated for the struggle in life . . . . I felt that I could not conscientiously go on increasing my over draft at the Northern Bank any more, they had been very decent to me all along & it would not be honourable of me to do so, I had no alternative but to try and get a job. A lot of houses are to be built for ex-service men about £1,200,000 is alloted [sic] to Ireland for this purpose with five Commissioners to see that it is properly spent. The Imperial Gov[ern]m[en]t. will appoint three of these the Free state govmt (Ireland) one & the Ulster Govmt. one . . . .

I met Sir James Craig at Stormount [sic] by appointment today at 11.30 a.m.

He received me as he always does, as an old & trusted friend

I told him what I wanted, He informed me that these Commissioners will be honary [sic] & unpaid, I then told him frankly the position I was in, That during the war the gomt stopped me for 6 months & put my customers in a hole & my firm also in the same position. Now foreign starch was being dumped in from Hung[a]ry Switzerland & Japan at a price that I paid for my raw material, & the slump in the cotton trade had simply made the bottom fall out of my business which had been going in the family for over 100 years, I told him of my overdraft & that if I sold all my property I could meet my liabilities but this wd. leve [sic] me without anything, I could see that he thought perhaps some more security would pull me thro, but I pointed out that I could not live on the profits of my business, even if it improved a bit more, & that there was a limited sale for my starch, that I had a good man (Ernest Knowles) who could carry on if I got something else to supplement my income. & unless this were done I was down & out, He said "Fred Ill not let you down no matter who else is let down you will never be let down". I said I did not care what I did or where I went so long as it was strait [*sic*] & honourable, I would do it for my children's sake even should I be sent to Timbucktoo . . . . I would take the governorship of a prison or anything else & go anywhere he replied "Oh that is not nice or congenial work we will try & get you something better than that" I replied that people thought I was a rich man & on the whole preferred leaving Belfast as too much was consequently expected off [*sic*] me. He replied "I am in exactly the same boat peple [*sic*] think there is no end to my means. You must not leave & go away you really must stop don't worry old chap give me a fortnight to think over it & in the mean time don't you worry I'll not let you down".

I then bade him good bye with a lighter heart than I have had for two years . . . .

All I can do now is to wait & ask God to give Sir James the power (I know he has the heart) to get me a position . . . .

Chronological table

1169	Anglo-Norman invasion of Ireland.
1171	Henry II comes to Ireland.
1297	The first representative Irish parliament meets in Dublin.
1494–5	Poynings's parliament.
1541	Henry VIII declared 'king of Ireland' by Irish parliament.
1549–57	Plantation in Leix and Offaly.
1586–92	Plantation in Munster.
1592	Foundation of Trinity College, Dublin.
1608–10	Beginnings of Ulster plantation.
1649–50	Cromwell's campaigns in Ireland.
1652–3	Cromwellian land confiscation.
1660–5	Restoration land settlement.
1689	Arrival of James II in Ireland (March). Siege of Derry (April–July).
1690	Arrival of William III in Ireland (June). William III's victory at the Boyne (1 July); departure of James II to France.
1691	Treaty of Limerick (October).
1691–1703	Williamite land confiscation.
1692	Catholics excluded from Irish parliament.
1761	Beginning of Whiteboy movement.
1778	Institution of the volunteers.
1782	Volunteer convention at Dungannon (February). Parliamentary independence conceded by British parliament (April–May).
1791	Societies of United Irishmen formed.
1795	'Battle of the Diamond' (21 September); orange society formed.
1798	Abortive United Irish (Wolfe Tone) rebellion.
1800	Act abolishing the Irish parliament and establishing the legislative union of Ireland with Great Britain passed by Irish and British parliaments.

1801   Union of Great Britain and Ireland begins (1 January).

1829   Catholic emancipation act.

1831   Primary education system instituted.

1840   Loyal National Repeal Association founded by Daniel O'Connell.

1843   Proclaimed 'repeal year' by O'Connell.

1845–52 Famine years.

1848   Abortive Young Ireland rising in Munster.

1850   Tenant League formed.
        The Queen's University in Ireland founded.

1854   Catholic University of Ireland founded.

1858   Foundation of Fenian movement.

1867   Fenian outbreaks in Great Britain and Ireland.

1869   Church of Ireland disestablished and disendowed by Gladstone's
        first ministry.

1870   Gladstone's first land act.
        Home rule movement launched by Isaac Butt.

1873   Home Rule Confederation of Great Britain founded.
        Gladstone's university bill defeated.

1877   Parnell elected president of Home Rule Confederation of Great
        Britain in place of Butt.

1878   Intermediate education act.

1879   Land agitation opened with meeting at Irishtown, Mayo (20 April).
        Land League of Mayo founded (16 August).
        Irish National Land League founded at Dublin (21 October).

1879–82 The 'land war'.

1880   General election (March–April); liberals returned in Great Britain;
        in Ireland 60 home rulers, 23 conservatives, and 20 liberals elected.
        Charter founding Royal University of Ireland.
        Parnell elected chairman of Irish parliamentary party.
        'Boycotting' of Captain Charles Boycott (September–November).

1881   Gladstone's second land act.

1883   Nationalist victory at Monaghan (July) stimulates orange activity in
        Ulster.

1884   Third reform act.

1885   Redistribution act.
        Irish Loyal and Patriotic Union founded (1 May).

Defeat of Gladstone's second administration (8 June); Lord Salisbury forms conservative administration with earl of Carnarvon as lord lieutenant of Ireland and Sir W. Hart-Dyke as chief secretary.

Loyal Irish Union founded in Belfast (8 August).

Ashbourne's land purchase act (11 August).

General election (November–December); Parnell holds balance between British parties in house of commons; 18 Irish unionists returned, 16 for Ulster.

Gladstone's conversion to home rule prematurely announced by his son (17 December).

1886   Ulster Loyalist Anti-Repeal Union founded (8 January).

North-west Loyal Registration and Electoral Association formed (9 January).

Irish unionist party formed in house of commons (25 January); Edward Saunderson becomes leader.

Salisbury's government defeated (26 January); Gladstone forms third ministry with J. Morley as Irish chief secretary.

Lord Randolph Churchill visits Belfast to stimulate unionism (22 February).

Gladstone introduces home rule bill in house of commons (8 April).

Liberals and conservatives meet in Ulster Hall, Belfast, to protest against home rule bill (13 April).

Ulster liberal unionist committee emerges (30 April–8 June).

Liberal unionist party forming in Great Britain (May–July).

Orange plans for armed resistance to home rule announced (6 May).

Home rule bill defeated in house of commons (8 June).

General election (June–July); Gladstone defeated; 19 Irish unionists returned, 17 for Ulster.

Salisbury's second administration formed; Sir Michael Hicks Beach Irish chief secretary.

'Plan of campaign' announced in *United Ireland* (23 October).

1887   A. J. Balfour appointed Irish chief secretary (5 March).

'Parnellism and crime' articles published in *The Times*.

1888   *Birmingham Daily Post* scheme for Irish reform.

Special commission appointed to investigate charges against Parnell and others (8 August).

1889   Pigott forgeries exposed before special commission (February).

1890   Report of the special commission (13 February).

Divorce court verdict against Mrs O'Shea and Parnell (17 November).

Irish parliamentary party split, as majority reject Parnell's leadership (6 December).

1891   Irish Loyal and Patriotic Union becomes Irish Unionist Alliance (April).

Congested districts board established (July).

Death of Parnell (6 October); John Redmond becomes leader of Parnellites.

1892   'Monster' unionist convention in Belfast (17 June).

Convention of southern unionists in Dublin (23 June).

General election (July); unionists defeated; 23 Irish unionists returned, 19 for Ulster.

Fourth Gladstone administration formed; John Morley becomes Irish chief secretary.

1893   Unionist clubs movement founded (January).

Gladstone introduces second home rule bill (13 February).

Ulster Defence Union formed (February–March).

Foundation of Gaelic League (31 July).

Home rule bill passes house of commons (1 September).

Home rule bill defeated in house of lords (8 September).

1894   Resignation of Gladstone (3 March); Lord Rosebery becomes prime minister.

1895   General election (July); liberals defeated; 21 Irish unionists returned, 18 for Ulster.

Salisbury forms third administration; G. W. Balfour becomes Irish chief secretary.

1898   County councils established.

1899   First elections to reformed local councils, urban (January), county (April).

Department of agriculture and technical instruction established (August); Horace Plunkett as head.

1900   Redmond elected leader of reunited Irish parliamentary party (February).

General election (September–October); unionists retain office; 21 Irish unionists returned, 18 for Ulster.

G. Wyndham becomes Irish chief secretary (7 November).

1902   Salisbury resigns (11 July); A. J. Balfour becomes prime minister.

Sir Antony MacDonnell appointed under-secretary of state in Ireland with unusual powers of discretion (October).

1902–3   Dunraven land conference.

1903   Wyndham's land purchase act introduced (25 March); receives royal assent (14 August).

1904   Dispute begins over the Dunraven scheme of devolution (September).

Ulster Unionist Council established (2 December).

1905   Wyndham resigns; Walter Long becomes Irish chief secretary (12 March).

Sinn Fein movement organised as political party.

Balfour resigns (4 December); liberal administration formed by H. Campbell-Bannerman; J. Bryce becomes Irish chief secretary.

1906   General election (January–February); large liberal majority; 21 Irish unionists returned, 18 for Ulster.

Saunderson dies (21 October); Long becomes leader of Irish unionist party.

1907   Union Defence League formed by Long (January).

A. Birrell becomes Irish chief secretary (23 January).

Irish councils bill introduced (7 May) but dropped (3 June).

Joint committee of Unionist Associations of Ireland formed (December).

1908   C. J. Dolan defeated as Sinn Fein candidate for North Leitrim (February).

H. H. Asquith becomes prime minister (5 April).

Irish universities act, establishing National University of Ireland and Queen's University of Belfast.

1909   Irish Transport and General Workers' Union formed (January).

House of lords rejects 'People's budget' (30 November).

1910   General election (January–February); Irish parliamentary party holds balance between British parties; 21 Irish unionists returned, 18 for Ulster.

Carson becomes chairman of Irish unionist party (21 February).

Edward VII dies (6 May).

Constitutional conference fails to solve house of lords question (June–November).

General election (December); Irish parliamentary party again holds balance; 19 Irish unionists returned, 17 for Ulster.

1911   Unionist clubs movement revived in Ireland (January).

Parliament act (August).

Ulster unionist demonstration at Craigavon (23 September).

Ulster Unionist Council appoints commission of five to frame constitution for provisional government of Ulster (25 September).

Southern unionist demonstration against home rule in Dublin (10 October).

Bonar Law becomes leader of the unionist party in the house of commons (13 November).

1912   Balmoral (Belfast) demonstration against home rule (9 April).

Third home rule bill introduced (11 April).

Southern unionists hold county demonstrations against the bill (April–October).

Liberal amendment to exclude four Ulster counties defeated (18 June).

Ulster day; signing of solemn league and covenant (28 September).

1913   Carson's amendment to exclude Ulster defeated (1 January).
        Home rule bill passes house of commons (16 January) but defeated
            in house of lords (30 January).
        Ulster unionists lose Londonderry to nationalists (30 January).
        Ulster Volunteer Force formally established (31 January).
        British League for the Support of Ulster and the Union announced
            (27 March).
        Home rule bill again passes house of commons (7 July) and is again
            defeated in house of lords (15 July).
        Provisional government of Ulster set up (23 September).
        Compromise talks (October–December).
        Irish Citizen Army founded (October).
        Irish Volunteers founded (25 November).
        Unionist demonstration in Dublin addressed by Bonar Law and
            Carson (29 November).

1914   British covenant launched (4 March).
        Asquith's offer (9 March) of temporary exclusion for parts of Ulster
            to be determined by county plebiscite rejected.
        Ulster volunteers' gun-running (24–5 April).
        Home rule bill passes house of commons for last time (25 May).
        Amending bill introduced into house of lords (23 June); and peers
            substitute for county option and the six-year limit the permanent
            exclusion of whole of Ulster (8 July).
        Murder of Archduke Franz Ferdinand (28 June).
        Ulster provisional government meets (10 July).
        Buckingham Palace conference (21–4 July).
        Howth gun-running (26 July).
        Britain declares war on Germany (4 August); and Redmond pledges
            Irish support for the war effort.
        Supreme council of Irish Republican Brotherhood decides on
            insurrection before end of war (9 September).
        Third home rule bill receives royal assent (18 September), but its
            operation is suspended.
        Redmond at Woodenbridge calls on Irishmen to fight for Britain
            (20 September); resulting in split in Irish volunteers.

1915   Coalition ministry, including Bonar Law and Carson, formed under
            Asquith; Lloyd George becomes minister of munitions (25 May).

1916   Easter rising begins (24 April).
        Pearse orders surrender (29 April).
        Execution of leaders of rising (3–12 May).
        Birrell announces his resignation as Irish chief secretary (1 May).
        Cabinet authorises Lloyd George to investigate basis for a future
            settlement with Irish leaders (23 May).
        Lloyd George attempts immediate settlement (May–July); shows
            draft proposals to Carson and to Midleton (29 May).
        Ulster Unionist Council accepts permanent six-counties partition
            (12 June).

Nationalist convention in Belfast agrees to temporary exclusion (23 June).

Irish Unionist Alliance deputation over 50 strong waits on unionist cabinet ministers and then Asquith and Lloyd George to protest against proposed settlement (26–7 June).

Beginning of battle of Somme (1 July).

Midleton confirms Redmond's impression that the Lloyd George scheme was only provisional (13 July).

Lloyd George proposals dropped (22 July).

H. Duke becomes Irish chief secretary (31 July).

Lloyd George succeeds Asquith as prime minister (6 December).

1917 Count Plunkett elected as Sinn Fein candidate for North Roscommon (3 February).

America enters war on allied side (6 April).

Lloyd George offers Redmond partition or a convention; he chooses latter (16 May).

Sinn Fein refuses to take part (18 May).

Irish Unionist Alliance decides to participate (1 June).

Ulster Unionist Council decides to participate (8 June).

De Valera elected as Sinn Fein candidate for East Clare (10 July).

Irish convention meets (25 July).

General discussions (July–October).

Grand committee discussing a detailed scheme reaches deadlock (21 November).

Southern unionists produce compromise scheme (25 November).

1918 Irish Unionist Alliance executive committee approves delegates' action (1 January).

Lloyd George intervenes increasingly in convention (January–February); writes to Ulster unionists (21 February).

Southern Unionist Committee formed (20 February).

'Call to unionists' published (4 March).

Redmond dies (6 March); J. Dillon becomes leader of Irish parliamentary party.

Voting in convention (March–April); proposal to exclude Ulster defeated by 52 votes to 19 (15 March); report carried by 44 votes to 29 (5 April).

Report of convention published in *The Times* (13 April).

Nationalist Ireland protests against proposal to extend conscription to Ireland (April onwards).

Viscount French becomes lord lieutenant of Ireland and E. Shortt Irish chief secretary (5 May).

Conscription and home rule plans dropped (20 June).

Ulster Unionist Labour Association elects officers (3 July).

Lloyd George claims right to solve Irish problem by six-counties partition (2 November).

War ends (11 November).

General election (14 December); large majorities for Sinn Fein in Ireland and the coalition in Great Britain; 26 Irish unionists returned, 23 for the six N.E. counties.

1919   I. Macpherson becomes Irish chief secretary (10 January).

Sinn Fein representatives meet in Dublin as Dail Eireann which adopts provisional constitution and declaration of independence (21 January).

Irish Unionist Alliance splits (24 January); formation of (Unionist) Anti-Partition League.

Belfast strike (January–February).

London committee of Irish Unionist Alliance established (March).

De Valera elected president of Dail Eireann (1 April).

East Antrim by-election (April–June).

Lloyd George outlines principles behind a new home rule bill (22 December).

1919–21   Anglo-Irish war.

1920   Government of Ireland bill, providing for separate parliaments and governments in Northern and Southern Ireland, introduced into house of commons (25 February).

Ulster Unionist Council accepts bill (10 March).

London committee of Irish Unionist Alliance impressed by difficulties of opposing bill (12 March).

Sir Hamar Greenwood becomes Irish chief secretary (2 April).

Irish Unionist Alliance general council protests against the new bill (19 May).

Ulster Unionist Council refuses to revise six-counties decision (27 May).

Decision to revive Ulster Volunteer Force (24 June).

Anti-Partition League demands settlement on dominion lines (13 August).

Ulster special constabulary enrolled (November onwards).

Anti-Partition League unionists in lords insert safeguards in government of Ireland bill (December).

Bill receives royal assent (23 December).

1921   Irish Unionist Alliance decides to maintain its present form (February).

Anti-Partition League unionists try to bring British government and Sinn Fein together to discuss a broader settlement; Irish Business Men's Conciliation Committee formed (7 March).

Carson resigns Ulster unionist leadership (4 February); succeeded by Craig.

A. Chamberlain succeeds Law as leader of unionist party in house of commons (21 March).

Viscount Fitzalan becomes lord lieutenant of Ireland (1 April).

Nomination day for elections under 1920 act (10 May); Sinn Fein unopposed in south, refuses to work act.

General election in Northern Ireland (24 May); 40 unionists, 6 moderate nationalists and 6 Sinn Feiners returned.

Northern Ireland parliament opened by George V (22 June).

Conference between De Valera and Anti-Partition League unionists in Dublin (2–8 July).

Anglo-Irish truce (11 July).

Negotiations between British government and Sinn Fein begin in earnest (11 October).

Craig rejects suggestions for an all-Ireland parliament (November).

Anti-Partition League unionists consulted by British government (15 November) and Griffith (16 November).

National Unionist Association conference at Liverpool (17–18 November) approves negotiations.

Anglo-Irish treaty (6 December).

Irish Unionist Alliance protests against treaty (7, 21 December).

Anti-Partition League Dublin committee accepts treaty (12 December).

Carson makes scathing attack on treaty in house of lords (14 December).

1922   Treaty approved by Dail Eireann by 64 votes to 57 (7 January).

Powers formally handed over by British government to Free State (16 January).

Meeting of former southern unionists declares loyalty to Free State (19 January).

Midleton talks over minority problems with Irish ministers (13–14 March).

Irish Republican Army split over treaty (March).

Pact between Collins and Craig (30 March); southern campaign against border to be abandoned; Roman Catholics to be included in northern constabulary.

Midleton discusses proposed Free State constitution with Irish ministers (28 April).

Negotiations between British government and Irish ministers over proposed constitution; Anti-Partition League unionists consulted (12–14 June).

Anti-Partition League unionists protest against composition and powers of the proposed senate published (16 June).

General election in south (16 June); 58 pro-treaty, 36 anti-treaty, 17 labour, 7 farmers, 6 independents, 4 Dublin University.

Action against republicans occupying Four Courts (28 June) marks beginning of civil war in south.

Desart talks over minority problems with Cosgrave (18 October).

Midleton fails to persuade Irish ministers to modify the senate (9 November).

Irish peers decide not to attempt to amend Irish Free State (constitution) bill in house of lords (16 November).

Constitution of Irish Free State adopted (6 December).

Northern Ireland opts out of Free State constitution (7 December).
Anti-Partition League wound up.
Irish Unionist Alliance abandons political activity.

1923 End of civil war (24 May).

1925 Report of boundary commission submitted but not published; 1920 boundaries remain.

Further and background reading

A. GENERAL STUDIES:

Beckett J. C. — *The making of modern Ireland, 1603–1923,* London 1966.

Moody T. W. & Martin F. X. — *The course of Irish history,* Cork 1967.

Strauss E. — *Irish nationalism and British democracy,* London 1951.

B. SPECIAL STUDIES:

Bolton G. C. — *The passing of the Irish act of union,* London 1966.

Good J. W. — *Irish unionism,* London 1920.

Holt E. — *Protest in arms,* London 1960.

Macardle D. — *The Irish republic,* Corgi ed., London 1968.

McDowell R. B. — *The Irish convention,* London 1970.

Mansergh N. — *The Irish question, 1840–1921: a commentary on Anglo-Irish relations and on social and political forces in Ireland in the age of reform and revolution,* London 1965.

Pakenham F. — *Peace by ordeal,* London 1955.

Palmer N. D. — *The Irish land league crisis,* New Haven 1948.

Phillips W. A. — *The revolution in Ireland, 1906–23,* 2nd ed. 1926.

Pomfret J. E. — *The struggle for land in Ireland, 1800–1923,* Princeton 1930.

Ryan D. — *The rising: the complete story of Easter week,* 3rd ed. Dublin 1957.

Sheehy M. — *Divided we stand,* London 1955.

C. SOUTHERN UNIONISTS:

Buckland P. J. — 'The southern Irish unionists, the Irish question and British politics, 1906–14', in *Irish Historical Studies,* XV (1967), pp. 228–55.

Calwell C. E. — *Field marshal Sir Henry Wilson . . . His life and diaries,* 2 vols, London 1927.

Cooper B. — *The tenth (Irish) division in Gallipoli,* London 1918.

Desart earl of & Lubbock Lady Sybil — *A page from the past. Memories of the earl of Desart,* London 1936.

Digby M. — *Horace Plunkett. An Anglo-American Irishman,* Oxford 1949.

Dowden E. D. & H. M. (eds) — *Letters of Edward Dowden and his correspondents,* London 1914.

471

Dowden E. D. (ed.) — *Fragments of old letters: E.D. to E.D.W.*, 2 series, London 1914.

Lecky E. — *A memoir of W. E. H. Lecky*, London 1909.

McCartney D. — 'Lecky's *Leaders of public opinion in Ireland*', in *Irish Historical Studies*, XIV (1964–5), pp. 119–41.

Midleton Lord — *Ireland—dupe or heroine?*, London 1932.

„ „ — *Records and reactions*, London 1939.

Robinson Lennox — *Bryan Cooper*, London 1931.

Steele S. L. — *Arthur MacMurrough Kavanagh*, London 1890.

Thornley D. — 'The Irish conservative party and home rule, 1869–73', in *Irish Historical Studies*, XI (1959), pp. 200–22.

Whyte J. H. — 'Landlord influence at elections in Ireland, 1762–1885', in *English Historical Review*, LXXX (1965), pp. 740–60.

D. ULSTER UNIONISTS:

Beckett J. C. — 'Carson—unionist and rebel', in *Leaders and men of the Easter rising: Dublin 1916*, pp. 81–94, ed. F. X. Martin, London 1967.

Boyce D. G. — 'British conservative opinion, the Ulster question, and the partition of Ireland, 1912–21', in *Irish Historical Studies*, XVII (1970), pp. 89–112.

Crawford Lt-col. F. H. — *Guns for Ulster*, Belfast 1947.

Edwards O. Dudley — *The sins of our fathers: roots of conflict in Northern Ireland*, Dublin 1970.

Ervine St John — *Craigavon, Ulsterman*, London 1949.

Falls C. B. — *The history of the 36th (Ulster) Division*, Belfast and London 1922.

Hyde H. M. — *Carson*, London 1953.

Livingstone P. — *The Fermanagh story*, Enniskillen 1968.

Lucas R. — *Colonel Saunderson M.P., A memoir*, London 1908.

Lyons F. S. L. — 'The Irish unionist party and the devolution crisis of 1904–5', in *Irish Historical Studies*, VI (1948), pp. 1–22.

Macknight T. — *Ulster as it is, or twenty-eight years experience as an Irish editor*, 2 vols, London 1896.

McNeill R. — *Ulster's stand for union*, London 1922.

Marjoribanks E. & Colvin I. — *The life of Lord Carson*, 3 vols, London 1932–6.

Morrison H. S. — *Modern Ulster*, Belfast 1920.

Savage D. C. — 'The origins of the Ulster unionist party, 1885–6', in *Irish Historical Studies*, XII (1961), pp. 185–208.

Stewart A. T. Q. *The Ulster crisis*, London 1967.

Ulster Liberal Unionist *The Ulster Liberal Unionist Association. A*
  Association *sketch of its history*, Belfast 1914.

E. BRITISH POLITICS AND POLITICIANS:

Blake R. *The unknown prime minister* (a biography of Andrew Bonar Law), London 1955.

Curtis L. P. *Coercion and conciliation in Ireland, 1880–1892. A study in conservative unionism*, Princeton 1963.

Fergusson Sir James *The Curragh incident*, London 1961.

Gollin A. M. *Proconsul in politics: a study of Lord Milner in opposition and power*, London 1964.

Hammond J. L. *Gladstone and the Irish nation*, new impression with introduction by M. D. R. Foot, London 1964.

Hurst M. *Joseph Chamberlain and liberal reunion*, London 1967.

Jenkins R. *Asquith*, London 1964.

Long W. *Memories*, London 1923.

Magnus P. *Gladstone*, London 1954.

O'Brien T. H. 'Lord Milner's Irish journal, 1886', in *History Today*, XIV (February 1966), pp. 43–51.

Ryan A. P. *Mutiny at the Curragh*, London 1956.

Salvidge S. *Salvidge of Liverpool*, London 1956.

Young K. *Arthur James Balfour*, London 1963.

F. ANTI-UNIONISTS:

Armour W. S. *Armour of Ballymoney*, London 1934.

Colum P. *Arthur Griffith*, Dublin 1959.

Fox R. M. *James Connolly*, Tralee 1946.

Gwynn D. *Life of John Redmond*, London 1932.

Gwynn S. *John Redmond's last years*, London 1919.

Henry R. M. *The evolution of Sinn Fein*, Dublin 1920.

Larkin E. *James Larkin, Irish labour leader*, London 1967.

Lyons F. S. L. *The Irish parliamentary party, 1890–1910*, London 1951.
  John Dillon, London 1968.

O'Brien C. C. *Parnell and his party*, corrected impression, Oxford 1964.

O'Brien R. B. *The life of Charles Stewart Parnell*, 2 vols, London 1898.

Thornley D. *Isaac Butt and home rule*, London 1964.

Younger Calton *Ireland's civil war*, London 1968.

List of collections consulted

A. ORIGINALS:

D618 Presented by Major R. Savage-Armstrong, J.P., Strangford House, Strangford, Co. Down. The collection contains c.280 documents and includes very varied material ranging from Spanish maps of 1767 and 1798 to letters referring to the Easter rising and the position of the Anglo-Irish after the establishment of the Irish Free State.

D627 Presented by Captain Peter Montgomery, Blessingbourne, Fivemile-town, Co. Tyrone. The collection consists of family and estate papers of the Montgomery family of Blessingbourne, Co. Tyrone, and contains much of the correspondence of H. de F. Montgomery, including: his political correspondence for the period 1880–94 (D627/428/1–270); and files of letters dealing with unionist politics in 1916 (D627/429), with Ulster and southern unionist attitudes to the Irish convention (D627/432 and 433), and with the protests of unionists of Cavan, Donegal and Monaghan in 1920 at 'the treatment which has been given to us by the Ulster unionist party' (D627/435).

D640 Presented by District Inspector M. Crawford, R.U.C. Barracks, Donegal Pass, Belfast. This collection of c.100 documents, 1881–1937, comprises some of the private papers of Lt-colonel F. H. Crawford relating to unionism, resistance to the Sinn Fein forces, and the formation of a civilian defence force in Northern Ireland. There is also his diary of riots and disturbances in Northern Ireland, July 1920–April 1923 (D640/11).

D950 Presented by H. A. Torney, Esq., 88 Church Road, Holywood, Co. Down. This collection contains, apart from genealogical tables, estate correspondence and church lads' brigade minute books, the minute book of the Kingstown and District Unionist Club, Co. Dublin, 1911–14 (D950/1/147).

D972 Presented by S. W. Smyth, Esq., 40 Belfast Road, Lisburn, Co. Antrim. This collection contains, apart from reports of linen manufacturing associations, 1892–1927, the year books and annual reports of the U.U.C., 1907–21 (D972/17).

D989 Presented by the U.U.C., Glengall Street, Belfast. This large collection of manuscript and printed material comes from the incomplete archives of the I.L.P.U. and I.U.A. Among the more important items are several minute books, including those of the executive council, 1886–9 (D989A/1/3); the organising sub-committee, 1886 (D989A/1/2); the executive committee, 1893–4 (D989A/1/5); the speakers' committee, 1893–4 (D989A/1/6); the parliamentary consultative committee, 1894–1900 (D989A/1/7); the finance committee, 1907–12 (D989A/1/9)—including the minutes of all other committees of the I.U.A.; the London committee, 1919–39 (D989A/1/11). N.B. The executive council minute book, 1889–1920 (D989A/1/4 and Mic 110), refers after 1890 to the newly established general council.

Among the correspondence are the following items: file of in-letters (P–S), 1891–3 (D989A/8/2); correspondence with Sir Edward Carson, 1912–14 (D989A/8/4); manuscript material relating to the split in the I.U.A., 1918–19, minutes of meetings of the S.U.C. (D989A/8/16 and 1/10) and assorted correspondence (D989A/9/16A, 8/17, 9/11C and 11/10); reports by Richard Dawson of the London committee of the I.U.A. on movements of English opinion on home rule, 1919–22 (D989A/9/20); and memoranda, circular letters etc., relating to incidents affecting loyalists in the Anglo-Irish and civil wars (D989A/8/23).

Also in this collection are miscellaneous writings by J. M. Wilson of Currygrane, Co. Longford, including: letters and memoranda relating to his activity in the Irish crisis, June–July 1916 (D989A/8/10 and 9/5); letters and vouchers relating to his tour of the Irish counties, 1916–17, with draft manuscript and typescript notes reporting, on a county by county basis, local feeling with regard to current issues—the war, conscription, Redmond, Sinn Fein, unionism etc. (D989A/9/7); 'reflections' on the Irish situation, c. 1915–16 (D989A/11/9).

There is also a wide range of printed material, most notably bound volumes of the annual reports (D989A/7/1–4 and D989C/3/38) and of the propaganda publications of the I.L.P.U. and I.U.A., (e.g. D989C/3/3–6, 10–25, 28–32, 34, 36–8,43–4, 62, 66, 68).

D1096   Presented by Messrs Cooper and Cooper, Solicitors, Enniskillen. This collection of papers of S. C. Clarke, later Clarke and Gordon, Solicitors, Enniskillen, 1896–1936, contains, apart from 45 letter books and c.15,000 legal papers relating to families and property in the Enniskillen area, some election and revision list correspondence, 1902–12, some correspondence involving the U.V.F. patriotic fund, and papers relating to the action arising out of the riot at Tempo on 28 August 1896 (D1096/9/2).

D1238   Presented by Lord O'Neill, Shane's Castle, Antrim, Co. Antrim. This is a collection of c.200 documents—correspondence and circulars relating to the organisation of the North Antrim regiment of the U.V.F., 1914.

D1252   Presented by Messrs Carleton, Atkinson and Sloan, Solicitors, 14 Church Place, Portadown, Co. Armagh. These solicitors' records consist of some 30,000 documents including 155 volumes of out-letters, 1838–1944, with in-letters from 1839. Apart from miscellaneous legal papers, the collection includes accounts and correspondence relating to the Armagh borough election of 1868 and the Co. Tyrone by-election of 1873, and some 60 letters and papers concerning the dispute over the unionist nomination for North Armagh in 1885 (D1252/42/3).

D1295   Presented by Lady Spender, Petersfield, Hampshire. The collection contains the correspondence etc. of Sir Wilfrid Spender relating to his part in the organisation of the U.V.F., his service with the Ulster Division in France, and his position as a senior civil servant in the newly formed government of Northern Ireland.

D1327 Presented by the U.U.C., Glengall Street, Belfast. This is a large collection of c.100 volumes relating to the unionist movement especially in Ulster, 1893–1923. There are the minutes etc. of the U.C.C., 1893–1919 (D1327/1) and the records of the U.A.I., 1907–15, including minute books (D1327/2/1, 2) and a register of speakers and canvassers (D1327/2/4).

The records of the U.U.C. include: the minute book of the 'Ulster Day' (demonstration joint) sub-committee, 5 September 1911–4 October 1912 (D1327/3/1); the minute book of the businessmen's executive committee, 19 May 1913–17 April 1914 (D1327/3/7); the minute book of the Ulster unionist delegates to the Irish convention, 21 July 1917–5 April 1918 (D1327/3/10); the minutes of the labour sub-committee of the U.U.C., 2 August–8 October 1918 (D1327/3/11); and a file of letters and papers relating to the setting up of the provisional government and the U.V.F., 1913–14 (D1327/3/21).

The material relating to the U.V.F. includes: the minute book of the Down county committee of the U.V.F., December 1912–January 1915 (D1327/4/1); the minute book of and some letters to the headquarters council of the U.V.F., December 1912–January 1915 (D1327/4/2); files of U.V.F. confidential circulars, 1913–15 (D1327/4/8–10); and files relating to the scheme of organisation and to the county returns of membership, 1913–14 (D1327/4/18, 19, 21).

There are also volumes of press cuttings, political cartoons and publications relating to the Liberal Unionist Council, the I.U.A. and the U.U.C., with photographs of a number of U.V.F. meetings.

D1390 Presented by Messrs Falls and Hanna, Solicitors, 29 Townhall Street, Enniskillen, Co. Fermanagh. This solicitors' collection comprises c.50,000 documents, including out-letter books, 1900–27, with in-letters, 1875–1937, and Irish land commission and other papers relating to various estates in Cos Fermanagh and Tyrone. There is also a considerable quantity of important and detailed unionist agents' correspondence and accounts particularly for the 1885 and 1903 Co. Fermanagh elections (D1390/26).

D1415 Presented by Hon. Denis Craig, M.B.E., Brook House, Preston, near Bath, Somerset. The Craigavon papers consist of 102 volumes and 77 documents, including 59 volumes of press cuttings covering all aspects of the life of 1st Viscount Craigavon, 1903–41; the diary and letters of Lt James Craig during the Boer war, 1900–2; descriptions of the U.V.F. gun-running at Larne, 1914; and visitors' books and official programmes. There are also typescript copies of portions of Lady Craigavon's diaries, the originals having been destroyed, 1883–1900 and 1905–40 (D1415/B/38–9).

D1507 The Carson papers purchased by the N.I.P.R.O. These c.3,000 documents, the surviving papers of Lord Carson of Duncairn, are an incomplete archive and consist of the material not destroyed in his London house in the Blitz. No records have survived of Carson's distinguished legal career and large gaps exist in what does remain. The collection divides into five main sections: correspondence; Irish material; cabinet papers; admiralty papers; and a miscellaneous section.

The correspondence section (D1507/1) runs from 1896 to 1937. Much of it is political, but there is no real sequence of letters in any field, except for those from Dawson Bates, secretary to the U.U.C. (D1507/1/3), and from Alexander McDowell, the Belfast solicitor (D1507/1/8). There are some interesting letters dealing with Irish affairs.

Much of the Irish material (D1507/3/1–11) is composed of memoranda by various people on possible variations of home rule or alternatives to it. Several documents relate to the position of unionist minorities in the south of Ireland under a home rule parliament and to the safeguarding of their position (D1507/3/9).

Cabinet papers (D1507/2/1–50) are extant on a variety of topics from 25 September 1915 to 20 November 1917, but there is no proper series of documents except for the imperial war cabinet papers which deal with the inauguration of a definite peace policy.

The Admiralty papers (D1507/5/1–217) run from November 1916 to July 1917. There are c.200 small groups of documents, each dealing with a specific topic, such as the inefficiency of the Dover command in 1916 and guns in merchant ships.

The miscellaneous section of the papers (D1507/5/1–84) includes a series of Blood cartoons and various memoranda attached to letters from F. S. Oliver on topics such as the October revolution, an assessment of the war situation in November 1917, and an analysis of the basis of war finance in 1915.

D1540 Presented by R. Hall, Esq., Rosetta, Warrenpoint, Co. Down. This collection of c.200 documents, 1613–1949, relates to the Hall family and property in Cos Down and Armagh, and contains papers relating to the U.V.F. (D1540/3). The latter papers comprise correspondence, orders and circulars in connection with the organisation and running of the U.V.F. in South Down, and are mainly between the U.V.F. headquarters in Belfast and Captain Roger Hall, Narrow Water, Co. Down, who commanded the South Down volunteers.

D1633 Presented by Lady Spender, Petersfield, Hampshire. The collection includes Lady Spender's personal diaries, 1914–41.

D1700 Presented by Mrs. J. H. Penson, 15 Bladon Drive, Belfast 9, and Mrs Nina M. Crawford, 33 Cranmore Avenue, Belfast 9. The collection contains the correspondence and testamentary papers of the Crawford family, c.1820–1910, and letters to and from Lt-colonel F. H. Crawford relating to gun-running and unionist politics, c. 1906–23.

D2073 Presented by Messrs J. Jordan Ltd, General Merchants, 20 High Street, Enniskillen, Co. Fermanagh. This collection of c.200 documents, c.1900–c.1940, contains the trading accounts, correspondence etc. of Messrs J. Jordan and some of the papers of Jeremiah Jordan, c.1885–c.1909, the protestant home rule M.P. (D2073/2).

D2223 Presented by Messrs Martin and Henderson, Solicitors, English Street, Downpatrick, Co. Down. This solicitors' collection of c.30,000 documents includes political correspondence relating to Co. Down in the nineteenth century and to the first county council elections in the Downpatrick division in 1899 (D2223/21).

B. COPIES OF DOCUMENTS IN PRIVATE HANDS:

T1089 Copies obtained from Captain Peter Montgomery, Blessingbourne, Fivemiletown, Co. Tyrone. These are photostat and typescript copies of family and other papers, including political correspondence to and from H. de F. Montgomery after 1885.

Mic127 Copies obtained from the Misses Duffin, Summer Hill, Bryansford Avenue, Newcastle, Co. Down. These are microfilm copies of 36 letters and other documents of Adam Duffin and his family of Belfast, relating to unionist politics and containing comments on political personalities, 1886–1921.

C. REPORTS OF INTERVIEWS BETWEEN ULSTER UNIONISTS AND MEMBERS OF THE STAFF OF N.I.P.R.O.:

PRB 1559 Correspondence and memoranda relating to an interview between Captain Frank Hall, a leading Ulster unionist before the first world war, and members of the staff of N.I.P.R.O., 14 April 1964.

PRB 987 Correspondence and memoranda relating to an interview between Sir Wilson Hungerford, U.U.C. official and later chief unionist agent in Northern Ireland, and members of the staff of N.I.P.R.O.

Personal names index

A

Abercorn, 2nd and 3rd dukes of, see under Hamilton
Abercorn, duchess of, see under Hamilton, Rosalind Cecilia
Acheson, Joseph, 113
Adair, Gen. Sir William, 239, 243, 249
Adams, Capt. Benjamin Samuel, 132
Adams, C., 131, 132
Adrian IV, 84
Agnew, Mr, 234
Aiken, H. H., 199–200
Alexander, Mr, 41
Allen, W. J., 279, 280, 281, 291, 296
Ancaster, 2nd earl of, see under Willoughby, Gilbert Heathcote-Drummond-
Anderson, A. Newton, 282, 304
Anderson, George, 153
Anderson, James, 326
Anderson, Sir John, 1st Viscount Waverley, 447
Anderson, Sir Robert Newton, 423, 454
Andrews, Edward, 352
Andrews, John Miller, 212, 280, 433, 436, 437, 438, 439, 441, 442, 454
Andrews, Thomas, 279, 280, 291
Annaly, 3rd Baron, see under White, Luke
Archdale, Sir Edward Mervyn, 109, 186, 187, 188, 189, 195, 200–1, 288, 290, 291, 454
Archdale, William Humphreys Mervyn, 40, 109
Ardilaun, 1st Baron, see under Guinness, Arthur Edward
Armagh, R. C. archbishop of, see under Logue, Cardinal Michael
Armaghdale, 1st Baron, see under Lonsdale, Sir John Brownlee
Armstrong, George, 405
Armstrong, Mrs Marie Savage-, 382–3
Armstrong, R., 279
Arnold, George, 184, 185–92
Arnott, Sir John, 279
Arthur, James, 326
Ashbourne, 1st Baron, see under Gibson, Edward
Asquith, Herbert Henry, 1st earl of Oxford and Asquith, XIII, 152, 172, 173, 273, 310, 337, 350, 353, 376, 400–1, 406, 408
Atkinson, Hon. Cecil, 296, 297
Atkinson, J., 114–5
Atkinson, J. Buckby, 112, 114–15, 116, 117–20

B

Babington, Mrs T. I., 132
Bagenal, B. F., 172
Bagwell, R., 123, 171, 268–9, 270
Bainbridge, Capt. John Hugh, 43
Balfour, Arthur James, 1st earl of Balfour, 25, 71, 157, 196, 197, 199, 202–3, 204–5, 273, 275–7, 278–9, 281, 282–3
Balfour, George, 312
Balfour, Gerald, 157, 195, 198
Ball, Frederick Elrington, 156, 160, 288, 291, 304–6, 307
Bamford, J. M., 312, 325
Bandon, 4th earl of, see under Bernard, James Francis
Bangor, 6th Viscount, see under Ward, Maxwell Richard Crosbie
Bannerman, Sir Henry Campbell-, 274
Barbour, John Milne, 60, 71–2, 454
Baring, Thomas George, 1st earl of Northbrook, 269
Barnes, George, 294
Barnhill, W. W., 204–5
Barr, C. J., 180
Barrie, Hugh T., 295–6, 297, 420, 422, 423, 424, 438
Barrington, Sir Charles, 170
Barry, Arthur Hugh Smith-, Baron Barrymore, 43–4, 279–80, 283, 284, 285, 361–2
Barry, J. Greene, 170
Barrymore, Baron, see under Barry, Arthur Hugh Smith-
Bartley, Sir George Christopher Trout, 276
Barton, Capt. Charles R., 199–200
Bates, Sir Richard Dawson, as part-time secretary of U.U.C., 205; and Balmoral demonstration, 219, 220; and Larne gun-running, 252, 254; and U.U.C. deputations, 279, 280, 281; and British League for the Support of Ulster and the Union, 286–7; joint secretary of U.A.I., 288, 290, 291, 292, 317–18; reports on work in December 1910 election, 303–4; reports on work in Scottish by-elections, 324–7; on allegations of friction in U.A.I., 293–4; wants to avoid Ulster unionist involvement in southern unionist split, 293–4; helps organise Ulster unionist defence of role in convention, 424; and East Antrim by-election, 428–30, 434–6; on unionist tactics in Belfast strike, 431–2; on labour challenge in Belfast, 434, 437; and Ulster Unionist

D

E

F

Place names index

A

Accrington, Lancashire, 336
Acomb, Yorkshire, 297
Ailsa Craig, Scotland, 258
Altnaveigh, Co. Armagh, 231, 235, 237
Annaclone, Co. Down, 430, 431, 434
Annahunshigo, Co. Down, 235
Annalong, Co. Down, 235
Annsborough, Co. Down, 231
Antrim, County, 240; protestant population of, 395; evictions in, 30, 32; political complexion of county council, 50; county council cooperates with U.U.C., 209; U.V.F. in, 226, 229, 238, 239, 243; gun-running in, 246–7, 250–1, 254; unionists divided in, 432–3, 434–6; possible representation under home rule schemes, 415; representation in Northern Ireland parliament, 454. Parliamentary divisions: (East and 1919 by-election), 427, 428–31, 432, 434–6; (Mid), 435; (North), 435; (South), 137, 434
Antrim Town, Co. Antrim, 254
Ardara, Co. Donegal, 74
Ardee, Co. Louth, 130, 131
Ardelea, 42
Ardglass, Co. Down, 236
Ardrishaig, Argyllshire, 312
Ardrossan, Ayrshire, 312
Ards, Upper, Co. Down, 235
Arklow, Co. Wicklow, 148
Armagh City, Co. Armagh, 114
Armagh, County, protestant population of, 395; evictions in, 27, 30, 32; political complexion of county council, 50; difficulties of early unionist organisation in, 110–20; U.V.F. in, 229, 254; arms in, 246, 247; possible representation under home rule schemes, 415; representation in Northern Ireland parliament, 454. Parliamentary divisions: (Mid), 111, 115, 134; (North), 93, 106, 110–20; (South), 209, 416
Arnos Vale, Co. Down, 238
Ashantee [Ashanti], Gold Coast, 82, 84
Ashton, Gorey, Co. Wexford, 215
Athboy, Co. Meath, 147
Athenry, Co. Galway, 25
Athy, Co. Kildare, 72, 73–4
Aughentaine estate, Co. Tyrone, 42
Aghlisnafin, Co. Down, 235
Australia, 373
Ayrshire, Scotland, 33, 255, 311, 312

B

Ballinamallard, Co. Fermanagh, 108, 109, 195
Ballinran, Co. Down, 235
Ballintoy, Co. Antrim, 250
Ballisodare, Co. Sligo, 279
Ballybrick, Co. Down, 235
Ballybunnion, Co. Kerry, 381
Ballycastle, Co. Antrim, 250
Ballyclander, Co. Down, 236
Ballyculter, Co. Down, 236
Ballyhay, Co. Down, 235
Ballyholme, Co. Down, 235
Ballykeel, Co. Down, 235
Ballymacanallen, Co. Down, 236
Ballymacshaneboy, Co. Cork, 46
Ballymagough, Co. Down, 235
Ballymartin, Co. Down, 235
Ballymena, Co. Antrim, 16, 250–1, 258
Ballymoney, Co. Antrim, 250
Ballynagarrick, Co. Down, 236
Ballynahinch, Co. Down, 236
Ballyreagh, Co. Fermanagh, 191
Ballyroney, Co. Down, 235
Ballyshannon, Co. Donegal, 74
Ballyskeagh, Co. Down, 236
Ballyvaddan, Co. Tyrone, 179
Ballywalter, Co. Down, 231, 235, 261–3
Ballywillwill, Co. Down, 235
Banbridge, Co. Down, 231, 236, 442
Bangor, Co. Down, 235, 252–3, 254–5, 442
Bantry, Co. Cork, 45
Barlborough, Derbyshire, 331
Barrow, Lancashire, 144
Beighton, Derbyshire, 333
Belleek Parish, Co. Fermanagh, 109
Belfast, 48, 56, 60, 99, 125, 180, 194, 199, 217, 230, 238, 240, 248, 256, 258, 279, 288, 302, 337, 345, 404, 406, 408, 426; impresses British electors, 174–5; parliamentary representation of, 427, 438–40; possible representation under home rule schemes, 415; sectarian rivalry in, 16, 84, 442; application of *Ne Temere* decree in, 72–3; disturbances in, 213–15, 442, 443–5, 453, 457–8; quiet in first world war, 400–1; growth of labour and socialist consciousness threatens unionism in, 202–3, 414, 426–7, 434; strike in (1919), 427, 431–2

Early unionist organisation in, 100; corporation cooperates with U.U.C., 209, 218,

495

Portadown, Co. Armagh, 16, 84–5, 92–4, 110, 112, 114, 116, 117, 118
Portaferry, Co. Down, 235
Portobello, Midlothian, 326
Portrush, Co. Antrim, 250, 279
Portugal, 282
Portumna Demesne, Co. Galway, 24, 26
Prestwick, Ayrshire, 312
Princetown, Co. Down, 235
Purdysburn, Co. Down, 236
Putney, London, 276

Q

Queen's County, 361; evictions in, 30, 32; political complexion of county council, 50; unionist registration work in, 125, 133; I.U.A. branches in, 146

R

Raheny, Co. Dublin, 279
Raloo, Co. Antrim, 248
Randalstown, Co. Antrim, 209
Rathfriland, Co. Down, 231, 235
Reading, Berkshire, 295
Reigate, Surrey, 316
Ridgway, Derbyshire, 331, 332
Roscommon, County, evictions in, 30, 32; political complexion of county council, 50; I.U.A. branches in, 146; unionists impressed by Sinn Fein activity in North Roscommon by-election, 361, 364–6
Roscommon, Co. Roscommon, 146
Rossfad, Ballinamallard, Co. Fermanagh, 108
Rostrevor, Co. Down, 235, 237–8
Rothesay, Isle of Bute, 312
Rothwell, Northamptonshire, 312–15
Roxburghshire, 312

S

St Andrew's Burghs, Fifeshire, 303
Saltcoats, Ayrshire, 312
Scarborough, Yorkshire, 295, 296
Scarriff, Co. Clare, 380
Schull, Co. Cork, 45
Scotland, 5, 6, 9, 15, 51, 143, 144, 147, 173, 179, 257, 262, 295, 308, 309–10, 311–12, 316, 322, 324–5, 327–8, 417
Seaforde, Co. Down, 236
Selkirk, Selkirkshire, 312
Shannon, River, 24
Sheepbridge, Co. Down, 232, 237
Shercock, Co. Cavan, 131
Shinan, Co. Cavan, 132
Shrigley Mills, Killyleagh, Co. Down, 60
Shuttlewood, Derbyshire, 332
Sion Mills, Co. Tyrone, 417

Skibbereen, Co. Cork, 129
Sleaford, Lincolnshire, 297
Sligo, County, evictions in, 30, 32; political complexion of county council, 50; I.U.A. branches in, 146; unionists weakening in first world war, 348–9; land-grabbing by Sinn Fein in, 366–7
Sligo, Co. Sligo, 172, 174, 183
Slough, Buckinghamshire, 328–9
Snowhill, Co. Fermanagh, 186
Somersetshire, North, 306
Southern Ireland, 386
Southport, Lancashire, 378
Springhill, Co. Down, 236
Stafford, Staffordshire, 144
Staveley, Derbyshire, 332, 333
Stepney, London, 276–7
Stevenston, Ayrshire, 312
Strangford, Co. Down, 236, 382
Stranocum, Co. Antrim, 250
Stranraer, Wigtownshire, 258
Suffolk, 379
Sutton, Co. Dublin, 279
Swanlinbar, Co. Cavan, 191
Swilly, Lough, 416
Switzerland, 34–5, 458

T

Tain, Ross and Cromarty, 324
Tarbert, Argyllshire, 312
Templemore, Co. Tipperary, 279
Tempo, Co. Fermanagh, 108; sectarian disturbances in, 84–92, 108
Thornbury Division, Gloucestershire, 306, 316, 317
Timoleague, Co. Cork, 381
Tinkerhill, Co. Down, 231
Tipperary, County, evictions in, 30, 32; political complexion of county councils, 50; I.U.A. branches in, 146; unionism in, during first world war, 349
Tipton, Staffordshire, 294, 297
Torquay, Devon, 303
Totley Rise, Staffordshire, 332
Tralee, Co. Kerry, 138–40, 145, 172, 363
Trim, Co. Meath, 147
Trory Glebe, Co. Fermanagh, 41
Tubberdaly, King's County, 379, 382
Tullyherron, Co. Down, 236
Tullylish, Co. Down, 236
Tullymurry, Co. Down, 236
Tullynacross, Co. Down, 236
Tynan Abbey, Co. Armagh, 279, 293, 412, 417
Tyrella, Co. Down, 235
Tyrone, County, 33; protestant population of, 396; evictions in, 30, 32; political complexion of county council, 50, 135–7;

Subject index

A

Act of union, nationalist criticism of, 1; Irish unionists' view of benefits of, 1–12, 13, 15–16, 17, 51, 52–3, 61–7, 362. See under southern unionists for loss of confidence in union

Adullamites, 25

Agriculture, 366–7; improved under union, 8–11

Amending bill, see under Home rule bills (third)

Ancient Order of Hibernians, 13, 16, 85, 248, 355

Anglo-Irish, xi, 1, 96; see also under Southern unionists

Anglo-Irish treaty, xiv, xv, 56, 341, 385, 453–4; few minority safeguards in, 385; condemned by southern unionists, 389; and Northern Ireland, 385, 453–4

Anglo-Irish war, 378–9, 380–1, 442

Anti-Partition League, see under Unionist Anti-Partition League

Ashbourne act, see under Land acts

B

Baird, W. and G., Ltd, 292

Ballot act, 60

Balmerino, 251, 252, 254, 255

Bank of Ireland, 69, 290, 404

Battles: Aughrim, 103; Boyne, 103, 397; Somme, 396, 397–9; Waterloo, 103

Belfast Banking Co., 208, 211

Belfast corporation, 16, 209

Belfast News-Letter, 218

Belfast strikes, see under Labour movement (Ireland)

Black and tans, 445, 446, 448

Board of intermediate education, 83

Board of works, 40, 63

Boundary commission, 447, 453

Boycotting, see under Cork Defence Union

Bristol Times, 307

British army in Ireland, 345–8, 379, 381, 397, 401, 446, 453

British governments and Ireland: (unionist governments, 1886–92, 1895–1905), 16, 17, 155–9, 201–5; (liberal government, 1892–3), 272, 274, 277–8; (liberal governments, 1905–15), xiii, xiv, 54, 65, 66, 299–300; (Asquith's coalition, 1915–16), 350–1, 356, 397, 402, 404–8; (Lloyd George's coalition,

British governments and Ireland *(contd)* 1916–22), 351, 356, 378, 385, 387–8, 389, 391, 392–3, 395, 396, 400, 402–3, 420, 421, 425–6, 442, 445

British League for the Support of Ulster and the Union, 244, 284, 286–7, 336, 338

'B Specials', see under Ulster Special Constabulary

Buckingham Palace conference, 355, 395, 396, 406

Businessmen, economic and financial objections to home rule, 59–60, 67–71; and home rule, 59, 60, 61–71, 71–2; and I.U.A., 59, 61; and U.U.C., 59–60, 71–2, 403, 408–9, 416, 433; and Free State, 392–4

C

Call to unionists, 293, 355, 358–9, 360

Catholic emancipation, 12

Cavan, Leitrim, and Roscommon Light Railway and Tramway Company, Ltd, 68

Census commissioners, 10, 26

Church of Ireland, 12, 37, 73, 74, 80–1, 84, 93, 302

City of Cork Volunteer Training Corps, 342, 344

Clyde shipyards, 431

Clydevalley (also named *Mountjoy II*), 252, 254, 255

Congested districts board, 61

Conscription, 48, 55, 378

Conservative associations and clubs: Central, 144; Co. Armagh, 115; North Armagh, 113; City and County of Dublin, 134, 149; City and County of Dublin Workingmen's, 149; Portadown, 111

Conservative Central Office, 334

Conservatives: (Southern provinces), xi, 95, 96, 97. (Ulster), xi, 95, 99, 100, 101, 106–7, 108, 109, 111, 113–14, 114–15, 117–18, 119–20; rivalry with liberals, 99, 100, 101, 110–11, 112–13. For British conservatives, see under Unionist party of Great Britain

Constitutional associations: Armagh, 114; Co. Armagh, 114–15; Charlemont, 114; Loughgall, 114, 117; Lurgan, 114; Portadown, 112, 113–15; council of constitutional associations in Ulster, 203, 205

Cork Defence Union, 42–6, 95

Cork Hundred, 125

Cornish's bookshops, 268–70

Council of Ireland, 445

503

County councils, 50; Antrim, 209; Cavan, 136; Down, 209; Fermanagh, 136, 184–93; Londonderry, 16, 209; Tyrone, 135–7, 209; elections to, see under Elections (local government)

Covenant, see under Ulster solemn league and covenant

Curragh incident, 251, 253

D

Dail Eireann, 384
Daily Chronicle, 456
Daily Express (Dublin), 73, 157, 164–5, 368
Daily Mirror, 154
Defence of the realm act, 409
Department of agriculture and technical instruction, 16, 61, 156, 157, 420
Devolution, 274–5, 277–80; 'devolution crisis', 201–5
District councils: Enniskillen, 185, 193–4; in Tyrone, 135–7
Dublin Castle, 118, 366
Dublin Review, 81, 82, 84

E

Easter rising, 350, 397, 401, 402, 404
Economist, The, 67
Education, 12, 77, 81, 82–4
Elections (local government), 135–7, 183–5, 189–92, 364; consequences of proportional representation in, 135–7
Elections (parliamentary): By-elections, (East Antrim), 427, 428–31, 432–3, 434–6; (North Fermanagh), 195, 200–1; (North Roscommon), 361, 364–6; General elections, (1885), 95–6, 97–9, 99–100, 106–10, 110–23; (1892), 72, 74–5, 195; (1895), 195; (1900), 156; (1910, January and December), 301; (1918), 48, 54–7, 378, 428; (1921, Northern Ireland), 452, 453–5
Erin Rifle Clubs, 153
Evening News, 325, 326
Evictions, 24, 26–33
Exclusion, see under Partition

F

Fairyhouse races, 404
Famine, 5, 12
Fanny, 239, 251
Farmers, and 1881 land act, 100; suspicious of Ulster landlords, 100–1, 108–9, 195; landlords attempt to win support of, for union, 106, 107, 108
Farnhamites, 136
Federalism, 422
Fenianism and fenians, 13, 18, 215

First world war, xiii, xiv, 55, 341, 342, 396, 397–8, 401, 402, 404–5, 412, 425–6
Freeman's Journal, 73, 171

G

Gaelic League, 161
Government of Ireland act (1920), xiv, 334, 341, 384–5, 386, 393, 452; minority safeguards in, 385
Government of Ireland bill (1920): terms of, 374, 402–3; southern unionists and, 374–5, 376–8, 384–5; Ulster unionists and, 375, 402–3, 411–12, 413, 418
Grand juries, 47, 147
Great Northern Railway Co., 70, 408, 416
Great Southern and Western Railway Co., 70
Gun-running: amount and location of arms purchased by Ulster unionists by Jan. 1914, 238, 244, 246–7; ban on importation of arms, 238, 242; dissatisfaction of U.V.F. with available arms, 238, 241, 243. Larne gun-running, April 1914: F. H. Crawford's plans for, 239, 243–4, 251; Crawford's adventures, 239, 251, 252; W. Spender's role in, 239, 251, 252, 254, 257–8; F. Hall's role in and account of, 239, 251–8; secrecy surrounding, 239, 252, 253, 257; disagreement over landing place, 239, 251–4; thorough intelligence work, 248; U.V.F. mobilised and takes over communications in Ulster, 254, 255; diversion staged in Belfast, 239, 254–5, 257; the landing at Larne, 239–40, 255; difficulties at Larne, 255; landings at Bangor and Donaghadee, 255; efficient distribution by motor car corps, 240, 249, 250, 256; some 'queer incidents', 256; unionist jubilation at, 240, 257–8; steps to protect arms, 240, 259–60

H

Harland and Wolff, Ltd, 427, 431, 432
Home rule act (1914), 410, 426; provisions of, xiii; regarded as dead letter by some southern unionists, 360, 361, 362; Lloyd George's attempt to implement (1916), 350–1, 402, 404–8; threat of operation affects Irish unionist thinking, 350–1, 355–6, 358–9, 376, 377–8, 403, 406, 414, 419
Home rule bills: (First), xiii, 101; financial consequences of, 59, 67–71. (Second), xiii, 143, 144–5, 148. (Third) introduced, xiii, 207; provisions, xiii; financial proposals criticised, 61–7; protestant churches and, 78–81; southern unionist opposition to, xiii, xiv, xv, 61–7, 134–5, 163–4, 170–4, 283, 284–5, 341, 342, 343, 363; Ulster unionist opposition to,

Dd. 471967. K16. 4/73. Gp. 3100

SBN 337 23082 X